RADICAL

RADICAL

WHY YOU SHOULDN'T DISMISS A *RADICAL*

THE COMMONER

PALMETTO
PUBLISHING
Charleston, SC
www.PalmettoPublishing.com

Copyright © 2024 by The Commoner

All rights reserved.

This book or any portion thereof may not be reproduced or used in any manner whatsoever without the express written permission of the publisher except for the use of brief quotations in a book review.

Hardcover ISBN: 9798822956940
Paperback ISBN: 9798822956957
eBook ISBN: 9798822956964

CONTENTS

	Introduction: Aristocracy	7
1	The Early Radicals	11
2	Power at The Top	19
3	Racists State Laws Prior to Civil War	33
4	Slave Trade	45
5	⅗ Compromise	59
6	Abolition	70
7	Confederate statues	155
8	Discrimination After the Civil War	157
9	Religious Bigotry	185
10	Hatred of Mexicans	240
11	Deportations	259
12	Women	361
13	Wealth Inequality	405
14	LGBTQ community	466
15	Healthcare	495
16	Tuition	541
17	Climate Change	558
	Conclusion	629

INTRODUCTION ARISTOCRACY

What is a Radical?

What does it mean to be a radical? Some would say crazy. Others would say intense. Many would say wild and wide-eyed. Some West-coasters might even think gnarly bro. Well it just is that radical can often mean different things to different people, however, often used in political contexts, radicalism is frequently described as a negative connotation to someone or some idea that is just absolutely crazy and is out of mainstream thinking. Radical is someone who is extreme, someone who doesn't understand. Or is it? Aren't those radicals behaving and believing what is just and right to them? And who is it that calls someone a radical? Maybe the radical isn't really a radical at all. Maybe they are a force of moral good.

Many politicians use the term radical to describe their opponents in elections, just like Senator Kelly Loeffler, in her dreadful debate performance against Raphael Warnock, used one time too many the phrase "radical liberal Raphael Warnock." Obviously she used this phrase to point out that Warnock's ideas were crazy to ordinary Americans and would never gain traction in American politics. The ironic story is that Warnock would go on to defeat Loeffler in a fairly comfortable margin of victory, proving the exact opposite that even Loeffler herself was proven more radical than Warnock. Funny how that works. It's often the politicians that label their opponents as radical who are the ones who are desperately clinging to the belief that they represent the views of ordinary Americans when, in fact, they couldn't be wronger. Why do politicians, leaders, and powerful people do this? Well it's quite obvious. They try to cling to power. They try to suppress the will of the people. They are tied up by big-money contributors. Their only response to the people is anything else is radical.

When Bernie Sanders ran for president in 2016 and 2020 he was consistently labeled as a radical not just by Republicans, with their deep affection, bordering even on gross get a room like stuff with corporations and big money, but even by some conservative democrats who know that their time in politics is ending rapidly. To Bernie's supporters none of them would say that his proposals were radical, none would say that his ideas are crazy. Indeed, most of his main goals and proposals received wide support from public polls, not just from democrats but from republicans too. Ideas like a single payer health care system were supported by democratic as well as republican presidents dating all the way back to the days of Harry Truman. Even Richard Nixon, perhaps the most racist and clinically disturbed president we ever had, supported a single payer system. So why is it radical? Perhaps it's radical to the establishment whose fortunes would turn upside down if there were some sort of disturbment in the system. Perhaps it's because health care industries spend hundreds of millions of dollars a year in contributions to policymakers from the local to the federal level. Perhaps it's because all we hear are the rich and powerful voices on the radio, tv, social media, and not the voices of everyday people who struggle and toil under the weight of our backward health care system.

In so many ways what's termed as radical isn't really radical at all, but a movement by average people everywhere voicing their concerns. Some have to protest, some have to yell, and some even have to go to prison to finally be heard above the voices of affluence and privilege. This book is a book that is radical in the views of corporate America, to the healthcare industry, the drug industries, the fossil fuel companies, and most importantly the establishment. This book is for common sense proposals that main street supports, not wall street. This book calls not for a revolution of military matters, but one of revolutionary ideas that will fundamentally transform the way of life as we know it today.

This book is for the future. And one way that we can predict the future, or understand the present, quite frankly, is by looking at the past. Through this scope we will see how radicals came to promote some pretty important and needed things in our country. If it weren't for the radicals, slavery would still be the law of the land, women would not have the right to vote, and children would still be working in our factories and mills.

And what exactly is it that left these institutions going strong and even, in many cases elevated? It is GREED. It is POWER. It is LUST. And simply, it is IGNORANCE. Together, these powerful forces have kept minorities struggling for the simple natural rights of God. They have kept the poor in a state of destitution and want. And they have left disastrous effects on our environment, for the sole purpose of fattening their wallets. This has to end, and with the help of the people it will.

This book does not even come close to exploring all of the ways that Americans were considered radical at some point or another. There is only so much that one person can write in such a short amount of time. My goal here was to paint an outline as to how many times our heroes were portrayed as radical to gear us towards the upcoming elections and help us have a greater idea of what path we want to choose for ourselves. Therefore, I regret that I was unable to include the Mass Removals of the First Americans, we could really consider this the first great deportation, although they still were forced somewhere onto American lands. I also left out details, stories, and events that we are probably more familiar with, given the history lessons that we learn through schools, to save time.

Lastly, I want to say that I am an ordinary guy. I am an average middle class/working class American who is fed up with the state of our affairs today. I felt it my patriotic duty to share with the world how we can make not only this country better but the world better as well. I know that this book gives off strong partisan bias, however, it is one group of Americans overwhelmingly playing the radical card game over the other group and it's time that we put an end to this fear-mongering once and for all.

1   THE EARLY RADICALS

Americans take great pride with anything to do with the American revolution. We have a whole day devoted to those great men who signed the Declaration of Independence. We sing songs, we write poems, and we light off dazzling fireworks that every year result in fines and mutilated limbs. (I was once at a fourth of July party where people screamed for the heavens at the fireworks and danced in crazy trances, and the worst part is they weren't even drunk.)

Why do we do those things?

The answer might have to do with a number of reasons after all. We love to sing, we love fireworks and massive explosions, but in a much deeper sense we love being free. We love that we have rights that are inherent and inalienable, which is a fancy way of saying that these rights can't be taken away by any force or authority. That these rights that we have were given to us by a just and fair God. No person, no king, no president, and no businessman can take them away.

We have an abundant amount of patriotism in our country, our culture, and our traditions. But this might never have been. If it wasn't for men like Samuel Adams, Richard Henry Lee, Patrick Henry, and so many other rabble rousers and women such as Abigail Adams, Mercy Otis Warren, and Martha Washington, our land might still just be another territory of Great Britain, without the "city on a hill", and "American dream". Yet, so many, not just in the European theater but also in America itself, thought that these wide eyed dreamers, who longed for change and a better world for posterity, were simply lunatics and quite frankly radicals. I mean, come on, who would have thought it was a good idea to raise hell against the most destructive, powerful military the world has ever seen? We didn't have anything. No standing army. No navy. And hardly any supplies and resources to wage a long drawn-out conflict. And yet, that didn't stop these brave men and women. Many of whom would rather die than live in an abject state of slavery, though of different means, as obviously they were slaves of tyranny.

It is a case of extreme irony that the many figures that we revere today, like George Washington and Thomas Jefferson, were slandered with all sorts of horrible language because of their desire for freedom and hope from a vicious tyranny under King George the third of Great Britain, who took away the basic rights of his subjects.

Many people thought, and still think to this day, that the issue was simply over taxes. Though that had a role to do with it, it hardly captures everything that was going on at the time. The colonists were even more ticked off that they had to quarter British troops and obey a parliament a thousand miles away. So, the colonists did what they thought was honorable and just, not just for themselves but for future generations. They did what Patrick Henry was clanging for. They took up arms to defend their rights. Many of whom would rather die than watch their liberty die a slow, painful death.

Nobody took them seriously, even the hopeful of the hopefuls thought that they were in for a grueling tough challenge up against the strongest military in the world. But even up against enormous odds, these brave men and women never threw in the towel. They fought for a better life and nothing was going to stop them. So, after the disastrous Summer of 1776, when Washington and the Continental forces were beaten continuously to the point of desperation, Washington ordered his men to cross the Delaware and strike a deadly blow to the British, at the battle of Trenton. The same spirit was evident when all hope was lost after the battle of Camden, when the American forces were being annihilated in the Southern theater. Then came the famous battles of Cowpens and Yorktown that effectively ended the conflict giving the Americans the much desired taste of freedom.

The Americans were called radicals, beggars, and dirty scum for believing that they too should experience freedom and live under a government that gave them equal rights under the law. The British were the oppressors, never wanting to give up control and forcing a bloody battle, never giving in until it looked so dark that they couldn't see. And yet, the Americans never gave up.

It is sometimes called the first American civil war. Truly, it was brother against brother and father against son. Some Americans were patriots and some were tories, or loyalists, those who supported the crown and thought the patriots were unloyal and traitors all because they wanted freedom. With all the hostility, hate, and even violence being hurled at them, the patriots are who we praise today. It is for their "radicalism" that we have the fourth of July, firework celebrations, and picnics. It is for these Americans that we owe so much, for they gave us the right to "life, liberty, and the pursuit of happiness".

A lesson should be learned here. That lesson is there will always be those who fight for what is right. Those who stand up against the heinous acts of a few and demand justness and rightness in the face of adversity. Those who are brave enough to withstand the rainstorm of insults, violence, and character assassinations. Those who fight not for themselves but for all those that will follow. Those who will take on the toughest odds, like the Americans who fought against the strongest, most fearsome, army in all the land.

Likewise, there will always be those like Great Britain, in the

American revolution story, who care so much about retaining power and influence that they will topple anyone who comes their way. Those who are drunk with power that they only act in ways that serve their own self interests at the cost of everyone else. Those who work for special interests that will only advance their own selfish imaginations.

The question is what side will you be on?

The Articles of Confederation, the form of government the newly formed United States put together after the war for Independence, had proven too weak and futile to provide governance for a rapidly growing populace after Shays' Rebellion.

Daniel Shays was a former revolutionary war veteran who after the war took up farming in Massachusetts. Due to the inability of the Articles to provide any sense of stability and order in the new country, inflation was soaring since the government couldn't raise revenues or do much, for that matter, in economic policies. The many farmers all throughout the country were now burdened with increasing amounts of debt due to the miserable economic conditions they were forced under because of the incompetence of early governmental leaders. Shays, like many farmers, were summoned to the courthouse to pay for all his debt. Shays, however, could not pay this debt, he still hadn't been paid in full for his service in the war, a shameful and embarrassing way for a new government to start its business. Indeed, George Washington had to beg the congress not just for supplies throughout the war, but to actually pay the soldiers their promised wages. Shays soon discovered he was not alone in his financial plight.

Many former soldiers and farmers tried desperately to petition to the various state legislatures. These so-called beacons of liberty, who were supposed to represent the will of the people, turned their backs on these poor individuals who served their country well. Instead these petitions fell on deaf ears and nothing came from the desperate cries of Daniel Shays and his followers. What Shays and so many others wanted was more printing of paper currency, therefore the currency would lose value, making it easier for debt ridden farmers and common laborers to pay off vast amounts of debt. Not surprisingly, the big-money interests won out. Led by wealthy merchant James Bowdoin, any proposals to depreciate the currency failed, mostly because the incredibly wealthy would lose some "hard earned money" and debt collectors would see their enormous vaults shrink in real value.

Bowdoin, who became governor of Massachusetts, another example of how the wealthy obtained power, made the situation worse when he stepped up the collection of back taxes and decided to raise property taxes to pay off foreign debt. Even John Adams, who was himself decidedly conservative called these measures "heavier than the people could bear."[1] The people clearly had had enough. The growing protestors prevented the court from hearing important cases, virtually shutting down a key portion of the government. The rioters had other plans as well, however, such as a planned attack on the Springfield arsenal. The attack was squandered when militia and regular forces were able to muster the force to drive them back.

The reactions from leading figures of the day are troubling and, quite frankly, miss the mark. Samuel Adams, a man whose great guidance and heroism helped pave the way for America's revolution from Great Britain called on the rioters to be executed.[2] To make matters worse a bill was passed, after the rebellion was successfully

---

1 Richards, Leonard L (2002). Shays's Rebellion: The American Revolution's Final Battle. Philadelphia: University of Pennsylvania Press. ISBN 978-0-8122-1870-1. OCLC 56029217.
2 History.com Editors. 2023. "Shays' Rebellion." History. A&E Television Networks. June 20, 2023. https://www.history.com/topics/early-us/shays-rebellion.

defeated, in Massachusetts excusing sheriffs of any wrongdoing if they killed or seriously maimed any rebels. One bill even went so far as to propose the death penalty on anyone associated with the rebellion. Now was the rebellion wrong? No. These rioters had every right to protest against any wrongdoing by the government. They weren't paid their promised salaries, they were pushed against strong special interests that protected the wealthy at the expense of the poor yeomans, when they easily could have defused the situation and made the wealthy pay a little more to erase the foreign debt. To Shays and his followers they were standing up for their rights and against wealthy aristocratic tyranny that perverted their chance at raising up in the world and keeping the wealthy in a state of continued command over the poor and destitute. To the rich and mighty opponents, who shook in their boots fearing a disturbance in their profitable ways, Shays and his rebels were radicals.

Shays' Rebellion left a lasting mark on the country and concerned the wealthy enough to propose sending delegates to fix what was wrong with the Articles. Their concern was that the Articles didn't give the federal government any ability to effectively run a country, levy taxes, create treaties with foreign governments, protect commerce, and raise a proper army.

Hence the colonies sent delegates (all but Rhode Island, who feared a strong central power) in May of 1787 to the Constitutional Convention. Here, the delegates were tasked to reform the Articles and quickly decided on abandoning the Articles all together. Their aim was to make a better, stronger, more efficient form of government that was going to prevent instability, rioting, and rebellions like Shays'. It's worth mentioning that almost every single delegate that was chosen to represent their state and work towards drafting the constitution was incredibly wealthy. Some estimates have the

THE EARLY RADICALS   17

signers five to ten times more wealthy than their average constituents.[3] Not exactly what you would call an assembly of the people. It's quite telling that the Constitution's signers were immensely rich individuals who argued vociferously for their interests, sometimes over the interests of the greater good.

Over the many months of haggling over the fine details, a framework was set up to be what we know the Constitution is today. This set up three different branches of government with totally unique and independent functions. Alexander Hamiliton, a brilliant, if not genius man, and James Madison, often dubbed the "Father of the Constitution," worked as a carefully coordinated team to showcase to the people that the new constitution just hashed out was, indeed, in their best interest. It just happens to be that the constitution was ratified by state legislatures and not the actual democratic vote of the people. We give much credit to Hamilton, Madison, and John Jay, who wrote the Federalist papers, a carefully organized and brilliantly designed set of essays that tipped the balance in favor of ratification, a cozy spot in the heart of history. However, we must not forget that these essays, though beautifully written as they were, were designed not to influence the people but to influence those with power: the landed and the elite who consisted of the various state legislators who were debating the ratification of the new Constitution. Most state legislators were lawyers, merchants, or wealthy planters, not individuals who worked on small farms and common laborers. Again, impoverished individuals were thought to be ignorant and unwise.

And so one by one each state began its ratification conventions starting with Delaware, which passed the constitution very easily

---

[3] Shachtman, Tom. 2020. "The One Percenters Always Helped Rule America. They Weren't Always so Self-Serving." *The Daily Beast*, January 20, 2020, sec. politics. https://www.thedailybeast.com/the-one-percenters-always-helped-rule-america-they-werent-always-so-self-serving.

thus becoming the first American state. All of the succeeding conventions passed the Constitution, over some opposition that the original Constitution lacked a bill of rights, that the three branches of government weren't fully separated, and that the government would be ruled by an aristocracy. An aristocracy occurred in most, if not all, governments up to this time, where wealthy elitists would control the functions of the government. This was a massive fear early in American history, especially when Great Britain's government had a branch formed of the aristocracy called the House of Lords. Somewhat surprisingly, early American leaders believed the government of Great Britain was the best form of government known to man, which is interesting considering they went at great lengths to separate from them. The belief was that a perfect government would derive from three criteria: an executive, an aristocratic, and a democratic branch.

The democratic form would be the House of Representatives, who the people chose to represent them. Some strengths would be they were responsible to the people, would represent their interests, and be a check on the other powers.

The aristocratic form of government would be the Senate, where state legislatures would most likely elect men of the highest standing, from well-born and respected families. In this way senators would be wise and intelligent when dealing with national affairs, and although they were not elected directly by the people, they would check the more dangerous and hasty decisions from the democracy.

2 POWER AT THE TOP

It is quite telling from the constitution and the framers that the government was intended to be controlled by the wealthy, and heaven forbid if the government would be controlled by the yeomen peasants, there would be no laws at all, no order, no tranquility. Why were the wealthy who created the constitution so fearful of the ordinary people? Perhaps they were afraid of losing their power to the interests of the majority.

After New Hamphsire ratified the Constitution on June 21, 1788, the framework was now legal across all the United States. Alexander Hamilton, the leader of the Federalist party and Washington's secretary of the treasury, naturally believed that the only way the country would succeed is if it had leaders who were quite wealthy, as they would protect their interests and the interests of the United States. It wasn't just Hamilton but the many who attended the constitutional convention. That idea made sense back then, since the nation was young and we needed leaders that would set us down a right course that would eventually make us a superpower. However, perhaps it never occurred to him that if a poor man would run the country he would naturally care for his interests and the interests of the United States just as much as a rich man would.

As I mentioned, Hamilton was by no means the only influential American who believed that the wealthy should be running things. George Washington had famously declined a salary and instead asked congress to cover his presidential expenses. The congress declined and instead awarded him an annual salary of just about $25,000 a year or approximately $798,715.91 today counting inflation, far and away more than any of his predecessors.[4] His belief, and the belief of many, was that public servants should not be paid to serve. Instead they should serve American interests from the goodness of their hearts. Well, as nice as that sounds that would mean that if congress had never set aside a salary for government workers our country would always be run by wealthy elitists (unfortunately it did anyway) who have no idea of the struggles of ordinary folk who toil and stress with pressures totally unfamiliar to the aristocratic class. It would mean that an average person like you and me would never be able to run for congress or play a pivotal role in our country's policies. We would never be able to work full time and serve in congress without a salary to support our families, like those who sit upon fortunes of wealth. Who would be watching out for us? Who would stand as a check upon the powerful interests who would always get their way? Who would be a voice for the voiceless and eyes for the blind?

It is a good thing that the constitution granted salaries to members of congress, the judiciary, and the executive for the sole purpose that ordinary people can serve. It turns out, anyway, that our country has always been run by elitists who have dominated politics and decision-making at most all levels of our daily lives. Most of our chief executives have come from wildly successful backgrounds. I could go down the list from Washington to prove my point, however, to shorten things up: We had Washington, a wealthy plantation owner who had hundreds of slaves, followed by Adams, a successful lawyer and prominent diplomat. After Adams comes

---

[4] Schmidt, Ann. 2019. "Presidential Salaries, from George Washington to Donald Trump." FOXBusiness. June 28, 2019. https://www.foxbusiness.com/features/presidential-salaries-from-washington-to-trump.

the Virginia-Jeffersonian dynasty consisting of Jefferson, Madison, and Monroe, each owning an extensive plantation with hundreds of slaves to boot. Not what you would call an ordinary citizen by any means. Most of these early presidents lived with enormous debts because of the extravagant lives they lived while at the same time engaging in an exercise where they received free labor every day for their whole lives. In other words, these men and their families lived in giant, gorgeous mansions filled with all sorts of delicacies and furniture of the highest standard, while hundreds of yards away lived their "property" with barely enough insulation to keep them warm at night and scant amount of food to keep them nourished. These men of fortune were having extravagant balls, where hundreds, if not thousands of dollars were spent for each one, while down the road the farmer toils in the soil, the laborer breaks his back, and the children are malnourished. And yet these men were tasked with running our country with a special emphasis on the "democratic republic" and "liberty" that they would continually tout.

Many presidents, past and present, held fancy dinners at least every week for the congressmen, cabinet officials, and other official dignitaries. Some of these meals are designed to impress foreign dignitaries. In 2011, Barack Obama served dishes like "D 'Anjou pear salad with fresh goat cheese, poached Maine lobster, and dry-aged rib-eye with buttermilk-crisped onions served on gold-rimmed plates" and for dessert apple pie a la mode.[5] I don't know about you but I don't even know what most of that stuff is. And according to the Washington Examiner, president Obama, spent nearly $1.25

---

5 8 Most Lavish White House State Dinners." 2011. TODAY. com. October 13, 2011. https://www.today.com/food/8-most-lavish-white-house-state-dinners-flna1c9005029.

million on his first two official state dinners.[6] If you're wondering who pays for all of this incredibly expensive food, given to wealthy governmental leaders, it is us, the American taxpayer. This is not anything particularly against President Obama, both republican and democratic presidents alike have had a tendency to live above the means of the ordinary masses.

Even Mary Todd Lincoln was criticized for her exorbitant, lavish dinner parties in the midst of the civil war. Benjamin Wade, a prominent Senator from Ohio remarked "Are the president and Mrs. Lincoln aware there is a war?"[7] Apparently even in the midst of great suffering and turmoil the White House still needed parties and extravagance. One of my favorite remarks made regarding the White House actually came from a surprisingly effective president, Chester Arthur. Ol' Chet made his living on patronage, that old dirty privilege of to the victor belongs the spoils, where Arthur landed himself in some pretty generous gigs due to loyalty given to the right people. He corrupted his way to make bank, while royally screwing over the government which he would eventually be head of. He was thrusted to the presidency after president James Garfield was unfortunately shot and more unfortunately died to the cause of physicians using unsterilized medical equipment to treat the wounds. Pretty much the entire medical community and historians mutually agree Garfield would have survived if it wasn't for the nasty medical equipment that was used on the president. Nevertheless, we ended up with Chet Arthur as president, and if you couldn't tell already, he was a bit of a dandy. Upon his inauguration with almost no time for mourning for the fallen president he promptly stated

---

6 "White House Invoices Show Excessive State Dinner Costs." 2012. Washington Examiner. December 6, 2012. https://www.washingtonexaminer.com/white-house-invoices-show-excessive-state-dinner-costs.
7 Presidential Families: Smithsonian

of the White House "I will not live in a house like this."[8] He didn't say it because the house was overwhelming or because he wanted to be modest leading a nation of modest people. No, he was referring to the white house as being too shabby to live in, not fit for a man as used to comfortable living as he. Can you imagine that? He was unwilling to live in the White House until all the furniture and decorations were thrown out, as they were too "department store" style and more renovations were completed. The Red Room, wrote a reporter from the Century Magazine, "was painted a deep, purplish Pompeiian red, the wainscotting in a darker red... a delicate frieze an abstraction of stars and stripes. The ceiling... was covered with stars of shiny bronze and copper so that they caught every flash of light... The State Dining Room was painted in glowing yellows, an elaborate painted and stenciled frieze around the ceiling."[9] Apparently before Arthur would belittle himself by living in such a dump as the White House, huge renovations had to be completed to his liking.

The original cost of construction of the White House dating all the way back to 1792 was approximately $232,000. Taking into account the changes and maintenance that takes place in today's dollars the cost of building the white house would be $100 million.[10] That seems good enough to me. Again, taxpayers had to cough up the bill. This comes to my next point on how wealthy buildings were designed for wealthy people.

Most of our "leaders" have come from an aristocratic background, many born to it. Is wealth made or born into? Apparently for many of our leaders wealth was born into. Why is it that those of us who

---

8 Ibid
9 Ibid
10 Talati, Sonia. n.d. "How Much Is the White House Worth?" Www.barrons.com. https://www.barrons.com/articles/how-much-is-the-white-house-worth-1471060823.

were born into poverty shall not be in the same contention as those who were born elitist? Is it because they were born with more intelligence? Were they born with more work ethic? Were they born with celebrated fanfare as was the case with Christ? No! They were born rich, born with immediate favor and privilege that the working class would have to work their whole lives for just a taste, if a taste at all. Who should say that just because someone is born rich they should rule countries and rule men? Why do we entrust our hopes and aspirations on those who know nothing of what it's like to walk in our shoes? Why elect people like Ronald Raegan, who lived behind the glamor and prestige of show business? Why elect people like Donald Trump, who received hundreds of millions of dollars from his rich daddy?[11] Clearly, an actor doesn't understand what it's like to struggle to pay for groceries one week to the next. And clearly, a real-estate mogul whose net worth is in the three billion dollar range doesn't understand what it's like to have to decide between getting prescription drugs that saves lives or paying the energy bill.

It's not just presidents that are out of touch with Americans, it's the congress as well. According to *Open Secrets,* as of 2018 and 2019, the net worth of members in congress is just flat out astonishing. Rick Scott, a Republican senator from Florida leads the pack with well over 250 million dollars, followed by Mark Warner, a Democratic senator from Virginia. I make the point here to say that it's not just one party who runs the gauntlet with wealthy candidates, it's a fault of both parties that they can't seem to elect anyone else but the aristocratic privileged to serve the needs of the poor and vulnerable. As of 2020 more than half of all our elected officials, indeed a vast majority, in Washington are millionaires and the average net- worth

---

11 NY Times: Trump Got $413M from His Dad, Much from Tax Dodges." 2018. AP News. October 3, 2018. https://apnews.com/article/0452d29cd2564eaf97605ab90acc3a67.

of people in congress is over a million dollars[12]. Compare that to the average median net-worth of Americans as a whole of just over $120,000[13], and that includes billionaires like Jeff Bezos and Elon Musk in that calculation. That roughly equates to members of congress on average having almost a ten times higher net-worth. That doesn't quite seem like any ordinary Joe Smoe can have a place in the congressional halls does it? And yet America prides itself on liberty and justice. Capital Hill bequeathed itself as the "people's house". How is that so? Maybe it should be called the "the rich house", the "gallery of affluence". Again I implore, tell me how it is that someone who owns $250 million can understand my plight as a middle class or working class voter? How is it that with members who are overwhelmingly millionaires can have the wherewithal to get people like me, who has to make decisions day in and day out about what I can purchase and what I have to sacrifice to make ends meet so that my family isn't hungry, that the lights stay on at home, and that we all stay healthy? They don't understand. That is why our politics is so dysfunctional. We are asked every election cycle to throw our support behind someone who has an absurd amount of riches, hoping, praying, dreaming that things will get better for us at the bottom, knowing full well that nothing will change. Nothing ever will change. It's always been this way. If the wealthy, special interest groups, and the establishment has their way it will always stay the same.

---

12 Evers-Hillstrom, Karl. 2020. "Majority of Lawmakers in 116th Congress Are Millionaires." OpenSecrets News. April 23, 2020. https://www.opensecrets.org/news/2020/04/majority-of-lawmakers-millionaires/.

13 Houston, Liz Knueven, Rickie. n.d. "The Average Net Worth in America by Age, Race, Education, and Location." Business Insider. Accessed January 7, 2024. https://www.businessinsider.com/personal-finance/average-american-net-worth#:~:text=The%20average%20American%20family%20has

So much for what John Admas had very brilliantly laid out to the fellow founders at the inception of the new country that our representatives should be a clone of our constituents. In other words, America's representatives should look like and act like and conduct themselves like the average farmer, mail carrier, and millworker. Can you honestly say that these top notch lawyers, CEOs, or career politicians who run things in this country today reflect this statement? No, they absolutely don't. They go parading in their fancy cars and throwing large gala parties in one of their many mansions. They are courting special interests, receiving huge sums of cash to do the biddings of the fossil fuel industries, insurance companies, and the privileged few, having extravagant meetings on million dollar yachts. They pay more attention to those that can give them millions of dollars in campaign contributions, so they can be reelected term after everlasting term than to listen to the ordinary voice of the so-called "constituent" that they are supposedly representing. Maybe we should have a special election so that the citizens can elect a candidate and the special interests can elect their own instead of stealing ours.

Of course, it's always been this way. Our representatives are so used to advancing their own motives that they don't care what we are going through. They have no awareness of the suffering and monotony, the paycheck to paycheck living that our majority are subjected to week after week, day after day.

And why shouldn't it stay the same? For the well off this is certainly the government and the politics that they want to see. This is exactly how they dreamed it to be. This is what it was all about, since the very beginning. Suppress the people and we will be rich and powerful. Oppress the poor and we shall stay at the top. Support racism and we shall be superior for all time. Banish immigrants and

God's needy and we shall have all the resources and privileges of being God's chosen. In a sense, suppress the radicals, who stand up for just causes, who bring change to a desperately needing environments, who look the devil in his face and say you are the devil, who stand with Tubman, Douglass, Lincoln, Susan B Anthony, and Martin Luther King who challenge wrongs and glorify in right. Who stand with the poor and dispossessed. Who put everything on the line to uphold the values of humanity and justice.

To be fair, not every representative and government official is corrupt and unworthy to be in Washington. Indeed some have stood up for the causes of the ordinary American and have taken up the fight for the common laborer and working man among us. To those who have the bravery and guts to stand up for the defenseless and vulnerable I thoroughly commend you. It shouldn't be hard to do what's right, however, in Washington today it's much more relevant and safe to support the current institutions and change little. In other words, it's safe.

We have had so many who came before us promising change. We have had so many who have pleaded for votes who have touted their record of helping the poor, or cleaning the environment, and busting the hierarchy of power and wealth… and yet nothing happens. Everything stays the same. Nobody does anything. We as taxpayers have to spend enormous amounts to pay the salaries of these governmental workers and representatives and yet everything remains the same. How long can we sit by and let this happen? There is so much that needs to be done and the American people are clamoring for relief. If our elected officials won't do their jobs then we must replace them and fill those positions will people like us. The mail carriers, millworkers, firefighters, and countless other middle class or working class laborers should be the ones we elect to represent us. Surely, they understand the struggle. They know because they are living it in their daily lives. They are working with coworkers, who just like them struggle to put food on the table for their families, keep the lights on at home, and afford quality health care. Why not make this change and start electing the American normalcy? Until we do this we have only ourselves to blame for continuing to entrust our needs to the wealthy few. If we elect the aristocratic class we show severe signs of ignorance and stupidity.

This sad reality has been the rule for the entirety of this nation. Yes, the early founders wanted the wealthy and the elite to have control over the lives of the ordinary folk like you and me. We need to accept the blame as well. Even though some of these candidates and lawmakers are exceptionally wealthy and spend millions of dollars, (Michael Bloomburg happily said he would spend one billion dollars for his presidential run), on tv ads and large events, that doesn't mean we need to vote for them.

Elections are getting more and more expensive with every new cycle. It doesn't matter if it's local, state, or federal, these elections are getting way out of hand, making it almost impossible for you and me to run for office.

In Wisconsin's race for governor a whopping $164.3 million dollars was spent just on three candidates alone[14]. Maybe not a problem for those at the top who can afford it, but it certainly would not be an affordable option for me and 99.9% of Americans.

Is this the way we are to proceed? We must make certain that going forward we elect people like us to lead the way and wrest the power away from the hungry rich. The constitution has never demanded that only wealthy people should be elected, even though the framers might have hinted at it, for the sole purpose of creating

---

14 Milwaukee Journal Sentinel, USA Today Network-Wisconsin, Corrinne Hess

a strong republic. Now the republic is strong, it has endured for generations as the strongest country on earth. In other words, it is established as a world power. Now we can elect average working class people to lead, they know our struggles and understand our way of life.

    I'm not just saying elect just anybody. Obviously, we need to elect smart, good natured people who know what they're doing. But we must stop fooling ourselves and elect those most likely to advance the interests of the common folk, not the wealthy few. And is this a radical view? Is this so crazy? And yet when progressive candidates launch an election campaign focused on the needs of the people, conservatives call them radicals. I don't get it.

Part One

THE UNITED STATES AND ITS RADICAL PAST

3 RACISTS STATE LAWS PRIOR TO CIVIL WAR

The United States Constitution is often looked at as the greatest parchment in the history of the world, or at least the greatest set of governmental principles the world has ever seen. Many countries look to the US Constitution as the hallmark of freedom, the gold standard of liberty. It wasn't an easy process, by any means, in order to ratify the Constitution. After many months of grueling debate, the cards were finally put in place for a complete overhaul of the Articles of Confederation. The Constitution very carefully tried to separate the three branches of government as much as possible, although the judicial branch was very attached to the executive in early years. Congress was supposed to be the branch of the people, the branch serving American interests from tyranny and oppression. Hence the Constitution worked hard to ensure that the executive and judicial branches were relatively weak when in comparison to the legislative branch.

Despite its many achievements the Constitution has some very glaring flaws to it and has been used by powerful people with lots of money to advance their own interests at the expense of everyone else. One of the greatest flaws that the constitution has is one that's quite difficult to judge in hindsight. No doubt the framers had a very interesting dilemma at hand. If they created a strong executive they would be chastised by the people for creating a government that parallels monarchical governments, which the people vehemently detested. And if they created too weak of a central government then what exactly were they in Philadelphia for? They instead decided to find that middle ground with the federal government powers: not too weak and not too strong. However, because of this pickle the framers made one BIG mistake. That mistake was that it gave the state governments too much power to suppress the people and trample on their rights.

The Constitution gives the states vast amounts of power to facilitate elections and set election rules. These election rules would prove to be a nuisance to America time and time again. Some states made it infinitely harder to vote than other states, while some states altogether barred whole groups of people from not even exercising their right to vote but also denied them the chance to be citizens! You would think that if you were a citizen of the United States then the state that you reside in would make you a citizen of that state as well. This was, very sadly, not the case in many states towards the Southern region that sought to suppress black people and submit them to their predesignated role of being "not human". And it wasn't all in the South either. Many Northwestern states had laws on the books that prevented blacks from voting, owning property, and even filling in for the occasional jury duty. Illinois was particularly notorious for some deeply held racist laws targeting black folk. Not only were free blacks not citizens in the state of Illinois but they were even expelled from the state totally.

Passed in 1853, the bill, after being approved of by the voters, outlawed any free blacks from being allowed to emigrate to Illinois. That's not all. If a free African American was found guilty of entering Illinois they had ten days to leave or else face severe fines. These fines were astronomical in most cases, especially since many free blacks were struggling financially anyway with the racist institutions of the day. If a violator of this law could not pay the fine the county sheriff could sell the FREE violator to the lowest bidder. This essentially turned a free African American to a slave just for entering Illinois territory that supposedly was free territory[15]. It's surprising that the "Great Emancipator," Abraham Lincoln, would hail from this state. It's a bit ironic, however, if you ever read some of Lincoln's letters or speeches you'll realize he wasn't the most racially impartial person by any stretch. Indeed, even the tall and sprightly president said some pretty horrible things about black people while he was running against an even more racist senator named Stephan Douglass. After being put on the defensive for quite some time about his views on race, Lincoln made it perfectly clear where he stood proudly stating he had "no purpose to introduce political and social equality between the white and the Black races" and that "a physical difference between the two" would likely prevent them from ever living in "perfect equality."[16] He even believed that it would be better if free blacks moved to another continent, espousing the beliefs of the American Colonization Society, who believed that whites and blacks could not live harmoniously together because of deep seated prejudices. Perhaps someone could have pointed out that hatred and bigotry is learned and not innate behavior. But nobody really thought of that at the time. In fact some of our biggest historical names were members of the infamous ACS including Henry Clay, James Monroe, Daniel Webster, Bushrod Washington, and Frances Scott Key to name a few.[17] (I still think Lincoln was the nation's best president regardless.)

A part of Illinois' racist law prevented free blacks from testifying in court. This might not seem like that big of a deal to some people.

---

15 Office of the Illinois Secretary of State, 100 Most Valuable Documents at the Illinois State Archives

16 History.com Editors. 2018. "Lincoln-Douglas Debates." History. A&E Television Networks. August 21, 2018. https://www.history.com/topics/19th-century/lincoln-douglas-debates.

17 The American Colonization Society." n.d. WHHA (En-US). https://www.whitehousehistory.org/the-american-colonization-society#:~:text=Originally%20 known%20as%20the%20American

Most people try to get out of jury duty as often as they can right? So why was it a big deal then? Oh yeah, because it completely screwed over an entire race from having justice. What is justice exactly? Justice is when people are treated fairly, or equitably, under the law. With no influence in court proceedings racists whites could set unfair and unjust sentencing just because of a dark color of skin.

Suppose that a black farmer is brutally beaten for the crime of being black by white perpetrators, which often happened before and after the civil war. With an all-white jury and a system that gives whites the benefit of the doubt and portrays blacks to be liars and deceivers, what do you think is going to happen? Of course, as it often did, whites quite literally could get away with murder, while free blacks had to live in fear, forced to come to the unpleasant reality that justice is not on their side.

Ohio, in many ways, led the pack of Northwestern states with its racist laws. Similar to Illinois, Ohio adopted a series of black laws that were imposed upon free blacks dating all the way to its original constitution of 1802. Despite the fact that slavery was prohibited in Ohio that didn't stop some insecure whites from trampling on free African-American freedoms. Blacks were barred from voting, testifying in court, holding political offices, or even serving in state militias[18]. And also like Illinois, free blacks were not entirely welcome in Ohio, however, with more leniency. They were allowed to reside in Ohio if they posted a $500 bond and registered with the state. Could you imagine if you wanted to move to a different state and had to raise $500 to do it? You probably wouldn't think it very fair and equal would you? Oh and by the way, just to point something out, I would have a really hard time finding $500 just so I can reside

---

18 "BLACK LAWS." 2018. Encyclopedia of Cleveland History | Case Western Reserve University. May 11, 2018. https://case.edu/ech/articles/b/black-laws.

in a state, but this wasn't the actual cost, as we would think today. According to CPI inflation calculator $500 in 1840 is equivalent to over $17,000 today.[19] Yeah, look in your savings, do you have that kind of money?

The law worked as it was intended in Ohio. Many Ohioans wanted to keep blacks out. Well, this law did exactly that, there weren't many who could afford to live in Ohio, unless they were Thurston Howell. Let's also not forget that schools were completely segregated to keep the races from co-mingling. It would be considered taboo for white kids to talk to black kids.

The reason why so many free states created laws to keep blacks out was partly due to pressure. Southern states such as Virginia, South Carolina, and Missouri, just to name a few, all had laws on the books prohibiting the entry of free blacks, mostly in fear of an insurrection. Insurrections among slaves were fairly uncommon, most attempts were caught in its infancy before any material plan was even set in motion. Some of the more famous insurrections in American history were Gabriel's Rebellion in 1800 and Nat Turner's in 1831, also called the Southampton Insurrection. In the former case, the plot was foiled before any serious harm was inflicted. In the latter case, many lives were lost as Nat Turner, an enslaved preacher, rounded up a gang of fellow slaves to fight for their freedom, while at the same time showing the world the evils of holding men, women, and children in bondage.

The rebels eventually killed somewhere around 60 to 65 white people, invoking frightening terror among the oppressive white folks, who now suddenly may be next. The revolt was neutralized a few

---

19 $500 in 1840 → 2024 | Inflation Calculator." n.d. Www.officialdata.org. Accessed January 7, 2024. https://www.officialdata.org/us/inflation/1840?amount=500#:~:text=Value%20of%20%24500%20from%201840.

days later, however, Nat Turner successfully hid for over six weeks as revengeful white people searched high and low for his capture. As would be suspected, the fallout of this event was especially severe. Militia groups from the region were sent in and immediately made its impact shown by beheading any slaves that were a part of the insurrection. What made the matter all the worse was that, in many cases, many that were beheaded had no role or part in the plans. These militias no doubt did this as vindication for the lives lost and as to post a sign. "Their severed heads were mounted on poles at crossroads as a grisly form of intimidation"[20].

Turner was eventually found after white militia groups caught his wife and tortured her to give up various details about Turner. He was sentenced to hang and before his death he was asked if he wanted to admit any transgressions for what he had done. His exact response "Was Christ not crucified?"[21] After the execution Turner's body was flayed and parts of his skin was used to make purses.[22] You read that right, they used his dead skin to make purses.

After all the commotion and hysteria, white folks just didn't feel comfortable with blacks, either free or enslaved. This is why numerous state legislatures banned free blacks from entering into their states, for fear of educated free blacks that would hatch up such a scheme. This in turn, put immense pressure on many Northwestern free states who now had to deal with the influx of free blacks who

---

20 Parramore, Thomas C. (1998). *Trial Separation: Murfreesboro, North Carolina, and the Civil War*. Murfreesboro, North Carolina: Murfreesboro Historical Association, Inc. p. 10.
21 Foner, Eric (2014). An American History: Give Me Liberty. New York: W.W. Norton & Company. p. 336.
22 Gibson, Christine (November 11, 2005). "Nat Turner, Lightning Rod". American Heritage Magazine. Archived from the original on April 6, 2009. Retrieved April 6, 2009.

had nowhere else to go. Hence the reason why Illinois and Ohio put together some very racist laws.

Life was beyond difficult for black people in general, free or slave. Many states had grotesque laws that were extraordinarily unconstitutional and racist in its intent for free blacks. For example, South Carolina passed a notorious measure called the Negro Seaman Act. This law, which was passed after Denmark Vesey's insurrection attempt, arrested free black sailors when their ship ports in any area under South Carolina jurisdiction. Imagine that. Seriously. Imagine you are employed as a sailor and literally just want to work, but instead because of where you land you end up in prison for no other crime than the color of your skin. If the captain of the ship somehow forgot and left without him the authorities of South Carolina could sell him off to a long life of involuntary servitude, slavery[23].

South Carolina was not the only state that did black sailors wrong. Alabama, Florida, and North Carolina all passed laws that targeted free black sailors. Proscribing to the principle of prima facie, which permitted the authorities to treat all black people as supposed runaways. In 1844, an attorney named Samuel Hoar traveled to the Palmetto State to rescue incarcerated black sailors through the court system. The South Carolina legislature responded by warmly denouncing Hoar and overwhelmingly passed a resolution that was meant to expel Hoar from the state. In December, of that year, local residents warned Hoar to leave or risk being attacked by a violent mob. Hoar, wishing not to put his or his family's safety at risk, promptly left the state never to return.[24] Thus, the threat of violence was used yet again by Southern slave interests.

South Carolina also denied black sailors, who were disgracefully

---

23 "Negro Seaman Acts." n.d. South Carolina Encyclopedia. https://www.scencyclopedia.org/sce/entries/negro-seaman-acts/.
24 Kate Masur- Book

treated and arrested, the right of habeas corpus and the right to appear before a court. This move essentially made South Carolina a government for whites and whites only, giving them the legal ability to suppress and oppress the rights of blacks.

Sadly, many states shielded bad acting whites from facing any legal repercussions time and time again. One of the truly understated stories of this era is the tragic lynching of Francis McIntosh and the gross miscarriage of justice that took place. After researching events like this one it makes me wonder why more Americans don't know about Francis McIntosh, it isn't taught in schools or even mentioned in our textbooks.

Francis McIntosh, was a free black man from Pittsburg whose age was 26. He worked on a boat as a porter and cook which arrived in St. Louis Missouri on April 28th 1836. While in St. Louis, the police stopped McIntosh looking for another black sailor who was involved in a fight, which McIntosh had not part in whatsoever. McIntosh was then arrested by some drunk cops who continued to berate him and insult him for his color. When McIntosh asked why he was arrested and how long he'd have to stay in jail, the officer who arrested him proudly stated he would be there for a long time. Naturally, not wanting to go to prison for a long extended period of time for a crime he wouldn't have been charged with if he wasn't black, McIntosh stabbed both officers who arrested him, killing one instantly and seriously wounding the other. When Mcintosh was making a mad dash out of there a crowd had begun to emerge and forcibly took McIntosh to jail, where he would have to await his fate. By this time the family of the slain officer came and wailed at the sight of their loved one's lifeless body lying in the street. The crowd became incensed when they heard his wife and children crying. The angry crowd marched to the prison and forcibly took

McIntosh without a trial or show of justice. They then tied him to a locust tree and proceeded to pile wood up to around his knees. When the crowd lit the wood on fire with a hot brand, McIntosh begged for onlookers to shoot him to put him out of his misery. When nobody acted upon his wishes he began to sing hymnals. And so the flames slowly but surely started to ascend up the tree, while McIntosh's body, inevitably burned starting at the feet, moving leisurely toward the knees and up his torso.

After a long prolonged period people began to think that McIntosh had finally died. When they began to murmur amongst themselves that he had died, McIntosh responded saying "No, no — I feel as much as any of you. Shoot me! Shoot me!"[25] So here you have it. This poor man who was literally in excruciating pain suffering a long drawn-out death begging for any humane individual among them to just shoot him and end the misery. There wasn't anyone among them that had any decency to do the right thing. Instead they were more than content to watch the suffering, like some ancient Romans watching the lions rip apart prisoners limb from limb. Francis McIntosh finally died after about twenty minutes of the worst kind of pain imaginable, after being arrested originally for doing absolutely nothing wrong. Where is the justice?

They kept the body burning all night long and a group of diluted children, who were obviously taught to hate, threw rocks at his long deceased body with the hopes that they would give McIntosh one more indignity and break his skull.[26]

When the grand jury gathered on May 16th to investigate the killing of McIntosh, the general feeling from the newspapers and from the judge himself would be that the accused would be given

---

[25] Freedom's Champion: Elijah Lovejoy. Carbondale, Illinois: Southern Illinois University Press

[26] Freedom's Champion: Elijah Lovejoy. Carbondale, Illinois: Southern Illinois University Press

an innocent verdict. The newspapers had been defending the mob ever since the killing of McIntosh took place. The judge, Luke Lawless, his name was not an indication of where he would rule in this case, though it could have been, actually believed that McIntosh deserved what happened to him and that his actions of attacking the officers was the definition of lawlessness and that this was a trend among the black race "atrocities committed in this and other states by individuals of negro blood against their white brethren."[27] And worse he claimed that abolitionist were the problem, not the broken rules of the South, saying "the free negro has been converted into a deadly enemy." Not surprisingly the accused got off with nothing, no crime for burning a free man to death.

It's sad to think that so many Americans don't know his story or any stories like it, as there have been many, many of which were not reported or witnessed. Stories of blacks being, whipped, burned, hanged, or raped. What we should be doing is telling their stories, remembering their lives and what happened and how we as a society, as a country, can do better and make certain that they will never be forgotten. Unfortunately, we are going in the wrong direction. Too many conservative public figures are railing against the so-called "critical race theory". Critical race theory is the belief that racism is embedded within our institutions. Critical race theory is not taught in public school districts. I know, I have been a teacher for many years, teaching a variety of subjects and seeing a wide range of curriculum. I know throughout my years of public education that critical race theory was never taught and much of what I know now about racial inequities were from my own personal research. Arkansas, Florida, Idaho, Iowa, New Hampshire,

---

27 Graff, Daniel A. (2004). "Race, Citizenship, and the Origins of Organized Labor in Antebellum St. Louis". In Spencer, Thomas Morris (ed.). The Other Missouri History: Populists, Prostitutes, and Regular Folk. Columbia, Missouri: University of Missouri Press. pp. 71–73

Oklahoma, and Tennessee have all banned the teaching of critical race theory.[28] Georgia, Alabama, Kentucky, Louisiana, Michigan, Missouri, Montana, Ohio, Pennsylvania, Rhode Island, South Carolina, Texas, Utah, Washington, West Virginia, and Wisconsin have similar bills moving through their legislators.[29] Only Delaware has passed a law to affirm the role that critical race theory has on our education and is only taught in higher learning institutions, not public schools.

One thing that is to note is the geography and political make-up of the states that have enforced a ban. Many of the Dixie states have enforced a ban, in fact, Misssissppi is the only state of the deep state that has neither banned or has a bill going through the legislature to ban critical race theory. Another aspect of note, though not surprising, is that of the states that have a ban or likely to have a ban the vast majority are heavy republican states.

It's interesting that politicians would make this an issue. Why would they? Clearly, they are playing to a script. A script that they think the people want to hear. When I travel around and ask people some simple questions on race and equality most people tell me that things are equal today. We will get into it more, however, the sad reality is things are absolutely NOT equal today. White families have on average a net worth that is nearly ten times that of black families. How is that considered equal? And yet many people believe we are exactly equal with exactly the same opportunities in life. When we have these conversations about race, inequality and racism of our past and present supporters of critical race theory call us radicals and "liberals" who want to push an ideology on all of us. They don't want to change the status quo. They don't want things to be equal and for everyone to have the same opportunity of success. They

---

28 "Critical Race Theory Ban States 2023." n.d. Worldpopulationreview.com. https://worldpopulationreview.com/state-rankings/critical-race-theory-ban-states.
29 ibid

view that their hold on our society, government, and culture could be in jeopardy if things are equal. In other words, they cling to the power that they have and at the same time they are depriving us of history, of the real story of what actually happened in the United States. This isn't something we should shun but something we should embrace. Perhaps if critical race theory were taught in schools we would remember the name of Francis McIntosh, and the millions of others whose lives have been suppressed out of existence.

4   SLAVE TRADE

"Article 1, Section 9 of the Constitution stated that Congress could not prohibit the "importation" of persons prior to 1808"[30]. In essence, the constitution set up for a law to be passed, which was in 1808, banning the practice of slave trading,

Slave trading was always despicable and heartless. Millions of Africans, some estimates are over 15 million, over the course of around 400 years, were taken forcibly from their homes, stripped from their families and crowded onto disgusting, filthy, disease-ridden ships.[31] They were chained and had no room to move an arm or a leg. The Africans were forced to live in their own excrement. Yes, live in it.

These voyages would last anywhere from two weeks to 2 months. The unfortunate "cargo" would be lucky if they survived the trip, others might've felt they'd be lucky if they didn't. In fact, some slaves did get loose and jumped off the ships in shark-infested waters as a way to avoid the uncertainty of a life filled with slavery. Around 10-15% of slaves perished on route. A sizable number, especially considering how many people would be cramped in the ship below deck.[32] Once the slaves set foot in the United States, the slaves would then be sold, auction style to the highest bidder, or just simply claimed, in a mad dash.

---

30 "The Slave Trade." 2016. National Archives. August 15, 2016. https://www.archives.gov/education/lessons/slave-trade.html#:~:text=Article%201%2C%20Section%209%20of..
31 Nations, United. 2015. "Slave Trade." United Nations. 2015. https://www.un.org/en/observances/decade-people-african-descent/slave-trade.
32 Digital History. 2021. "Digital History." Www.digitalhistory.uh.edu. 2021. https://www.digitalhistory.uh.edu/disp_textbook.cfm?smtid=2&psid=446.

For many, slave trading was a profitable business. With profitable business, comes wealthy men, and with wealthy men comes special interests. You can bet your top dollar that many men desired that nothing could come between them and their valuable slaves. (I say valuable here because slave traders would make a sound living selling healthy slaves that owners would pay more for, hence they considered them valuable for monetary purposes not sentimental purposes.)

The sad truth is, many feared the Constitutional Convention would grant a federal government that would have the powers to exterminate the institution of slavery, hence why there was even a strong debate growing over its ratification. Some historians have claimed that for the most part our founding fathers were against the perpetuation of slavery, however, nearly all of our most celebrated ones have at one point or another owned a slave.

Some, such as George Washington and Thomas Jefferson were actually very cruel masters. As a matter of fact, Richard Parkinson, who lived near Washington's beloved Mount Vernon once wrote "it was the sense of all his (Washington's) neighbors that he treated (his slaves) with more severity than any other man."[33] He regularly ordered his slaves to be punished, writing his overseers to lash his slaves. He was so harsh that many of the slaves that he was closest to, and dare I say had actual personal relationships with, had run away, some never to come back. After Pennsylvania passed the Gradual Abolition Act of 1780, Washington even instructed his private secretary, when he was in Philadelphia, to rotate his slaves every six months so that his slaves he brought with him could not become legally free, trying to conceal it from the public writing his secretary "I request that these Sentiments and this advise may be

---

33 Richard Parkinson, *A Tour in America, in 1798, 1799, and 1800* (London: Printed for J. Harding and J. Murray, 1805), 420.

known to none but yourself and Mrs. Washington."³⁴ It is ironic that for all of this Washington would later go on and free his slaves in his will. The interesting thing about this, however, is that he declared them free after his wife Martha kicked the bucket. Martha outlived George and was terrified the slaves would rise up, kill her, and ride off into the sunset as freemen and women. So, she ended up listening to some advice from family and friends and released them before she died.

Thomas Jefferson on the other hand I have a bit of a hard time with. He wrote the beautiful words in the Declaration of Independence that all men are created equal, yet he himself was the owner of hundreds of slaves. And although in many letters and writings he denounced slavery as an evil institution and accused King George the third of waging a "cruel war against human nature itself, violating it's most sacred rights of life & liberty in the persons of a distant people who never offended him, captivating & carrying them into slavery in another hemisphere, or to incur miserable death in their transportation thither."³⁵ This he wrote in his original rough draft of the declaration, before some "interested" men looking it over took it out with the belief it would upset the southern part of our colonies.

Clearly, he thought slavery was a pressing issue, mostly because of what it could do to the newly independent colonies, not because of the morality of the point. Yet, he didn't have the courage to free his slaves at the end of his life, like Washington, and surprisingly wasn't a huge fan of dogs. As a punishment to his slaves who weren't

---

34 George Washington to Tobias Lear, 12 April 1791, *Founders Online,* National Archives, accessed September 29, 2019,
35 Boyd, Julian. 2019. "Jefferson's 'Original Rough Draught' of the Declaration of Independence - Declaring Independence: Drafting the Documents | Exhibitions - Library of Congress." Loc.gov. 2019. https://www.loc.gov/exhibits/declara/ruffdrft.html.

working to the level he expected he demanded the "negroes dogs must all be killed. do not spare a single one" to his overseer,[36] the dogs would eventually be hung, for no other crime than being a slave's dog. Kind of sad isn't it. We don't really hear that one too often from the textbooks.

With that said, many of the Constitution's architects didn't really have that strong of a drive to limit slavery's growth. Clearly, they could have done what would have to be done 78 years later with a clear statement abolishing slavery. If they had done this however, the constitution certainly would not have been ratified, mostly from the opposition of the very wealthy slave owners.

And so the Constitution left open the slave trade until the year 1808, giving it a healthy 20 more years. It's worth noting that congress did, in fact, pass a law in 1808 that prohibited the continuance of the slave trade. This, though, was mostly a symbolic gesture, as slave trading was practiced, extensively, long after this was passed. Plus, delegates could not then know what a future congress would do. It was no guarantee that congress would ban the international slave trade or not. What's shocking about this is that the Constitution allowed, if not endorsed, the slave trade to go unimpeded for 20 more years, despite some prominent members decrying the clause. As a matter of fact, for some the slave trade clause was enough to reject the Constitution outright. Luther Martin, in his refutation of the Constitution, valiantly voiced "slavery is inconsistent with the genius of republicanism."[37] He feared that if allowed to continue, the slave trade would never be abolished, that it would grow and fester. In a way he was correct.

Even though Congress passed a bill outlawing the slave trade,

---

36 Jefferson to Edmund Bacon, December 26, 1808, Thomas Jefferson Papers, Huntington Library.
37 Luther Martin, The Genuine Information VIII, Maryland Gazette

this did little to stop the ever expanding and ever prosperous practice of slave trading. Many did this as a side hustle, to earn more cash. As the National Archives pointed out "Not only did it drive trade underground, but ships caught illegally trading were often brought into the United States and its passengers sold into slavery"[38]. Essentially, if slave traders were caught they would go to prison, or be fined, but their "cargo" would still be sold as slaves in America.

The law specifically outlawed international slave trading, meaning that slave traders couldn't go into Africa or any other country and import slaves into the United States. It said nothing, however, about the domestic slave trade. We've all heard those brutal stories about families being ripped apart. It's sad that slave owners would be so cruel as to actually rip a mother away from her kids and family. This, actually, was often used as a threat to indigent slaves. Even Washington himself threatened to sell his slaves to the Caribbean, a notorious place for any outsiders to go because of the disease and squalor conditions. Being shipped there not only separated them from everything they knew and held so dear but almost meant certain death.

Long after the "ban" on the international slave trade was on the books, the Amistad case came along. The Amistad case gets its name from *La Amistad,* the boat that was being used to traffic 49 innocent Africans from Sierra Leone. The official destination of *La Amistad* was Cuba, Spanish territory, where slavery was still legal based on Spanish law. It didn't take long, however, for the Africans to bust free from their shackles and take control of the ship. The enslaved Africans killed the captain of the ship and the cook, who had been subtly harassing the Africans the whole trip. Two other

---

[38] "The Slave Trade." 2016. National Archives. August 15, 2016. https://www.archives.gov/education/lessons/slave-trade.html#:~:text=The%201808%20Act%20imposed%20heavy.

members of the crew happened to escape the melee, after which the Africans forced two Spaniards to return the ship back to their native country. The two Spaniards had no intention of doing this, so they hatched a clever plan: by day they would sail toward the African coast, however, during the night they would slide closer and closer to the American shore.

The ship finally arrived off the coast of Long Island, New York, of all places, where a vessel named the *USRC Washington* discovered them. Lieutenant Gedney, who was the commander of the *Washington*, immediately claimed the vessel and cargo as his property. He chose to settle the claim in Connecticut as slavery was still legal there, though they hailed a gradual abolition law, whereas slavery was totally abolished in New York. It's clear from this, that Lietenent Gedney looked to make some extra cash by selling the Africans, even though the international slave trade was banned in the United States. Clearly, this had to be a mistake right? The law is the law and right would be on the side of the Africans.

What would soon take place is a somewhat mystifying, though not entirely shocking, display of judicial back and forth. Meanwhile, while the legal challenges were being brought forth the Africans officially were transferred to the care of the US government, where they suffered in prison. Not only did Lieutenant Gedney want the Africans, but so too did the two Spaniards, who filed a claim that the Africans were still Spanish property and should be returned. The Africans meanwhile, damned if they do and damned if they don't, because at least initially it looked like they were going to be slaves either way, regardless of whose possession they would be in, claimed that they were not property and couldn't be returned to the Spaniards. [39]

---

39 *US v. The Amistad*, p. 589

What makes the whole court case even more troubling, at least from an international sense, is the fact that Spain and England had signed a treaty prohibiting the internation slave trade north of the equator. In case you don't know, Cuba is well above the equator. Thus Spain was caught red-handed clearly in violation of their own treaty obligations. This fact alone should have put the Spaniards' claim to rest, even though the court cases were being processed in the US.

Thus the British began to call for the release of the Africans and even called upon the Treaty of Ghent to help enforce their pleas, as the Treaty specifically banned the international slave trade between the two countries. It's certainly an honorable thing that Great Britain decided to get its feet dirty in an international dispute of this sort, however, it would've been nice if the British got their feet dirty earlier and called out the Spanish for continuing to export slaves to Cuba like they were exporting rice and indigo. Even Dr. Richard Robert Madden, who testified in this case supporting the British claims cried out "that some twenty-five thousand slaves were brought into Cuba every year – with the wrongful compliance of, and personal profit by, Spanish officials."[40] If this is the case why didn't Great Britain go after the Spanish earlier? Perhaps this was an early sign of appeasement, that they were so fond of, that would come to haunt the rest of the world in a little over a century.

There is little doubt that the British got involved in this fight because of the instantaneous publicity surrounding the case. Therefore the British wanted to show off a little muscle on the international stage. Nevertheless, the British acted honorably by trying to force the hands of the American government. It just so happens that the Americans didn't give a crap about the arguments brought about

---

40 Iyunolu Folayan Osagie (2010). *The Amistad Revolt: Memory, Slavery, and the Politics of Identity in the United States and Sierra Leone.* University of Georgia Press. p. 11. ISBN 978-0820327259.

by the British. But it was a nice try. As it turns out, the British desperately wanted the US president, Martin Van Buren, to intercede on the Africans behalf. In fact, British minster Henry Fox, wrote a long, heartfelt plea, that honestly pulls at the heart strings a little, to save time I include just the final paragraph from the letter, in which Fox states, "her Majesty's Government anxiously hope that the President of the United States will find himself empowered to take such measures, in behalf of the aforesaid Africans, as shall secure to them the possession of their liberty, to which, without doubt they are by law entitled."[41]

Fox actually did a great job, not only using language to promote an emotional effect, but also correctly stating international statutes that the Spanish and the Americans are bound by, therefore building an awfully solid case. Martin Van Buren, on the other hand, was a tough nut to crack. Very much structured on the strict constitutional adherence, holding firm to the Jeffersonian principles of small government, translating to no interference at all whatsoever, Van Buren calmly stated that under the Constitution he needed to respect the separation of powers, and thus could not influence the case in one way or another from the power of the judiciary. Even more damning, the State department didn't necessarily see the case from the same light as the British, still pondering whether or not the enslaved Africans constituted a breach of international law. [42] If the Americans found that the Spaniards didn't break international

---

41 United States Congress (January 20, 1841). "Deposition of Richard R. Madden". Public Documents Printed by order of The Senate of the United States, during the second session of the 26th Congress. Vol. IV, containing documents from No 151 to No 235. Washington, D.C.
42 United States Congress (January 20, 1841). "Deposition of Richard R. Madden". Public Documents Printed by order of The Senate of the United States, during the second session of the 26th Congress. Vol. IV, containing documents from No 151 to No 235. Washington, D.C.

law they would give the Africans back to them to do with what they pleased.

Throughout all the haggling and turmoil surrounding this case there was some good that came out of it. The case made some serious headway with rising political and emotional aggravations seen from both sides. Southerners were looking hesitantly on the outcome of the case, obviously preferring the court to rule against the Africans' basic rights, therefore perpetuating the already deeply unfair judiciary. On the other hand, this court stirred up the rage of the abolitionists throughout the country who unwaveringly supported the captives.

As a matter of fact, the abolitionists even created the Amistad committee which helped to organize the legal proceedings and helped raise funds so that the imprisoned Mende Africans had the necessary resources while they were shackled under primitive conditions. [43]

Unbelievably, and quite bravely, the abolitionists did the unthinkable. They counterattacked and filed charges of assault, kidnapping, and false imprisonment against Ruiz and Montes, the two Spaniards. Just think of the significance of this case. It's quite risky that the abolitionists, under the leadership of Lewis Tappan, that a band of 40 plus Africans would file a suit in the American judicial system, a system that at this time catered to white interests, mostly wealthy white interests.

In the end the district court ruled that the Spanish claims were rejected and that they would not gain possession of the ship or the cargo. It also ordered the Africans to be returned to Africa, since they were, in fact, illegally seized in a treaty busting, international law breaking trafficking ring, and were free individuals to be returned to Sierra Leone. If you're wondering what happened to Lieutenant

---

43 "The Amistad Committee (U.S. National Park Service)." n.d. Www.nps.gov. Accessed January 7, 2024. https://www.nps.gov/people/the-amistad-committee.htm#:~:text=The%20Amistad%20Committee%20.

Gedney, he was awarded one-third of the property onboard *La Amistad,* though not the enslaved Mende Africans. Finally it feels like justice was, indeed, carried out fairly and properly. But not so fast.

Martin Van Buren, was still highly skeptical. He personally believed the greatest threat to the continuation was abolitionism, not the pro-slavery zealots. How can this even be comprehended? Van Buren was a northern Dutchman with pro-southern sympathies just, sadly, for political reasons. It was Van Buren, after all, who skillfully orchestrated the brilliant rise of the democratic party, which proudly supported Andrew Jackson to the presidency. In order to build a vast coalition of southern, northern, western, and eastern interests to blend together harmoniously they needed an answer over the slavery question. That answer was not to mention the s word at all to avoid any possible trouble that could arise because of it. And so the incredibly popular war hero, in Jackson, ascended to the president and Van Buren was able to ride his coattails.

In a completely hypocritical stance, remember when Van Buren stated that he had no say over the case and would let the judicial system play out due to the constitutional separation of powers? Van Buren instead insisted that the federal court made a mistake and called for the Supreme Court to hear the case in an appeal. Van Buren actually was hoping the courts would rule in favor of the Spaniards, believing that the Africans should be given back to Spain.

In the end even the Supreme Court ruled against the president and insisted that the Africans were free and should be returned to Africa, which they eventually would be. Finally, this saga would eventually come to an end. The controversy began lots of heated debate, back and forth, that prompted prominent national leaders to join the national stage. This included John Quincy Adams, who defended the Mende Africans in front of the Supreme Court.

The abolitionists won a great victory in the time being and there were plenty of individuals that stood up for what was right by returning the Africans to their rightful home. There were others, however, some in high places, that held significant influence and power, who tried to hold these innocent Africans under the most gruesome, egregious, violations of human rights.

The law passed by congress that banned Atlantic slave trading in 1808, was poorly enforced and many smugglers still practiced this activity to make large sums of money. According to the *Washington Post* "After the ban, American ships smuggled around 8,000 enslaved Africans to U.S. shores, usually through the Gulf of Mexico, and sold them illicitly to cotton planters in the Deep South."[44] It's also important to note that just because the US officially outlawed the international slave trade that meant little to nothing to some other countries, like Spain, which would ship literally boat loads of enslaved Africans to Cuba and Brazil, just to name a few.[45] The slaves would help to bring agricultural products to the market that would be consumed by countries around the world, including the United States, so in a way the United States was unofficially and explicitly supporting institutions that led to the perpetuation of the slave trade, even though the Unites States wasn'tt officially practicing in the trade. There is no doubt that many of these slaves were then illegally shipped to the US to begin producing in the American economy.

It is quite clear that the slave trade continued on thoughout the post-ban years all the way through until the enactment of the 13th amendment, which formally prohibited slavery. There, of course,

---

44 *Washington Post*. 2020. "Perspective | the Slave Trade Continued Long after It Was Illegal — with Lessons for Today," December 6, 2020. https://www.google.com/url?q=https://www.washingtonpost.com/outlook/2020/12/06/slave-trade-continued-long-after-it-was-illegal-with-lessons-today/&sa=D&source=docs&ust=1704667882808296&usg=AOvVaw2mtAgGxpmXNgJukMLwZce2.
45 ibid

were those like William Seward, Frederick Douglass, William Lloyd Garrison, and countless others who derided this practice as inhumane and unjust, however, their powerful opponents called them "great menaces to the continuation of the country". Even Martin Van Buren, who ironically, would go on to become the free soil presidential candidate, on a platform of outlawing slavery in the territories, was on the wrong side of history with the Amistad case, when he supported the Africans to be sold into neverending bondage.

To all those who were in the mainstream, I mean conservative, white, wealthy, slave owners, it was pretty easy to hold onto your "property" and alienate and belittle those that challenged you. They would say of course we should count them as ⅗ths, of course we should expand the international slave trade for an extra 20 years, of course slavery is moral, just, and humane. Of course, it's the best thing for them, the poor negroes wouldn't last without some "extra help." They actually convinced many people that they were doing the Africans a favor, they were taking care of them. Without the institution of slavery black people would just live like a bunch of barbarians, like animals. When anyone was brave enough to step up and take them on they were ridiculed, told that they would destroy the young nation with that rhetoric. Today we look at those who stood up against the slave trade as heroes and those who were in the right even despite those horrible slanders that were espoused on them. What's more jolting is that our constitution would ever have submitted to the horrible ⅗ths compromise, and the slave trade. Instead the drafters listened to the oppressors and the ones that would hold a tyranny over the many.

The fear was that the Constitution wouldn't pass without some pretty severe giveaways to slave owners. Originally, the founding fathers wanted to keep the slave trade proposal out of the document.

However, the Southern delegates were appalled at the injustice the Constitution was producing on the plantations by not protecting that "peculiar institution." The Northern delegates wanted a simple majority vote to determine trade policies in congress whereas the Southern delegates wanted a 2/3rds vote, fearing that because the Northerners held a population advantage they would have more congressional strength, therefore, they would shove unfair trade policies down Southern throats. As a compromise, the Northern delegates were willing to concede the point on the international slave trade clause to appease the wealthy southern interests.[46] I say wealthy Southern interests because only the wealthiest families could actually afford to keep slaves.

According to the census of 1860, all slaveholding states had more families that did not own slaves than those that did. In Maryland and Missouri, respectively, only 12% and 13% of their white population owned slaves. Even in the heavy plantations of Virginia, only 26% of white families owned slaves. Mississippi and South Carolina were the highest at 49% and 46%.[47] In Virginia, almost half of their total population were slaves, this means that the average slaveholding family owned multiple slaves, which of course meant that the family had some serious cash, as owning and maintaining slaves wasn't cheap.

It's so easy to forget about all the craziness that involved the slave trade, some even advocate for us to gloss over the story or whitewash history, however, this would be a serious crime to history and to ourselves. You have to ask yourself what reason do politicians and other "leaders" want to deprive us of our past, to rid us of our history? It is by educating and the continuance of learning that we

---

46 A biography of the constitution
47 "Selected Statistics on Slavery in the United States." n.d. Faculty.weber.edu. https://faculty.weber.edu/kmackay/selected_statistics_on_slavery_i.htm.

can put the pieces back together. Instead of suppressing the racist history of our past and of our constitution, it is important to keep teaching it so that as a country and community we can learn where our founders went wrong and where we can do better: to include everyone the way in which we want to be included, to love others the way we want to be loved, and to bring justice and fairness to all who reside in this country.

5   ⅗ COMPROMISE

In the very first section of the glorious Constitution of the United States, right behind the memorable preamble, we get a taste of just exactly one of the most despicable, inhuman statements that ever graced parchment. In the very first section of the Constitution, patriotic founding fathers should have been making a role model for other nations, and to make them envious and jealous of the right and justness of the American cause. Instead they made it abundantly clear who was accepted and who wasn't. Who was valued and who wasn't. Who had rights and who didn't. It's sad that the early Americans, who fought so fiercely and boldly against the tyranny and oppression of a distant king, would resort to being a tyrant and oppressor to many others who were born with darker skin pigments. Shortly before, these same Americans were called radicals by the British crown and by loyalists at home for the simple want of liberty and equality that they had so praised and expounded and craved. Now they had clearly stated to the world that the cause of freedom and equality was a very narrow one, that befitting of only the white man. Even generations later, the very popular senator, who would later debate Abraham Lincoln and defeat him in the US senate election of Illinois, proclaimed "I hold that a Negro is not and never ought to be a citizen of the United States. I hold that this government was made on the white basis; made by the white men, for the benefit of white men and their posterity forever, and should be administered by white men and none others."[48] Unfortunately, this was a view that certainly more leading men shared from the very beginning.

---

48 Lincoln- Douglass debates

The Constitution also gave, when discussing the appropriation of congressional seats, the slaveholders the right to count their slaves as being ⅗ths of a person.

Wow. Isn't that just a slap in the face. Not only do slaves live in deplorable conditions, under the most brutal form of human oppression, where they sweat and toil and suffer day in and out, but now they aren't even fully human. They are just a measly ⅗ths of a human. What then does that make them? Were they considered animals? Were they considered brutes who are totally inferior both mentally, physically, and morally to the white man? The simple answer to the early American founders was yes to all these questions. What's ironic about the whole thing is that clearly the early Americans were inferior to that of the African American race. For believing that one race is truly superior to that of another shows the extensive amount of ignorance in the minds of these people. To believe that African Americans are morally inferior is another blatant lie. Truly slaveholders were vastly inferior morally when in comparison to slaves, they obviously were subjecting innocent people to the most dreadful form of life in the history of mankind. To these slaveholders belongs the title of inferiority, for they were the lowest forms of human life and an insult to Almighty God, whom they claimed to revere and worship and faithfully went to church every Sunday, like a good Christian would.

Perhaps slaveholders thought that they were on to something. By baselessly spewing these lies they were more fond of believing them. Let me ask you this question. Since the vast majority of slave owners refused to allow their slaves any formal schooling, is it surprising that slaves would not have the education to prove these lies untrue about being intellectually inferior to a white man when the rich slave owners received top-rate educations? And let me ask you this. If so many slave owners thought that slaves were intellectually inferior to them, then why not allow them a decent education? Perhaps it was because they were scared of being wrong. Perhaps these dastardly slave drivers were worried about being outsmarted by the same group of people they accuse of being stupid and simple minded.

Some will say that there were those who tried to limit slavery. That there were abolitionists, like Alexander Hamilton and Benjamin Franklin, who detested slavery. Though this may be true, the pro-slavery faction still won out by guaranteeing that they could count their "property" as ⅗ths of a human being. I shouldn't have to say this but this put the slave owners in a remarkably powerful position. On top of having the Constitution say nothing condemning slavery, it also felt obliged at giving the slave states even more representation by being able to count their property in the apportionment of congressional seats. What a gift. Now the Northern states, that may find slavery as a moral stain on the character of the union, had an incredible disadvantage.

Another striking blow is that slave owners repeatedly thought of their slaves as their property. Nothing more than a pair of shoes, or an article of clothing, or an ass or pig. Given this line of reasoning it should be suggested that the Southern slaveholding states should have no right or ability to count their slaves in the apportionment of congressional seats, if all they consider them is property. This would mean that the Northern states should've been able to count their cattle, their sheep, their pigs as ⅗ths as well, considering it is their property. The fact that the Constitution granted the slave holding states so much power and influence really shows what the early revolutionary thinkers thought of minorities and those that were different from the Anglo-Saxon whites.

To the whites who were opposed to the ⅗ths compromise they

were shouted down by the Southern hotheads, who were more interested in their own self-aggrandizement than over the benefit of the country both politically and morally. Even though most Northerners knew that this whole slavery charade was rather sad and a "moral stain" on America, they were quick to give way to the Southern interests. So what does this mean? Were the opponents of slavery just a pushover? DId they give up too easily? Or were they just chastised for being a radical in their pursuit of the gradual extermination of slavery?

In all likelihood, the framers of the constitution were convinced of the fragility of the newly formed nation. Therefore, they were quick to acquiesce to the wishes of the more powerful, elite plantation owners, who viewed slavery as a necessary evil that would promote the economic satisfaction of the South. However, in so doing they quickly laid the foundational belief of all Southerners that they could control the spineless influences of the North since they were willing to back down to the pressure of the early special interest of slavery. And so, a valuable lesson can be learned here. The late eighteenth century Americans were willing to sacrifice morals, principles, and justness in the face of special interest pressures. The question is will we? And will we back down in the face of severe opposition from those who talk loudly but don't have morality on their side?

The very real consequence of the ⅗ths compromise had devastating effects on the future of slavery until its final eradication. The very basis of the ⅗ths compromise was another effort to appease the Southerners who were afraid of the newly founded representation based on population that the new constitution espoused. Prior to the constitution's enactment, the states all sent delegates to the confederation congress, however, each state had equal say in the voting. It did not matter if Virginia or Pennsylvania were vastly more numerous than Delaware or Rhode Island, each state had an equal voice. With the new legislative chambers consisting of the house of representatives, each state would be represented based on overall population. This was troublesome for many Southern states who were drastically more rural and thinly populated due to the massive plantation and agricultural way of life.

Of course, there was steady opposition to this proposal, again the Southern slave-interests were threatening to sink the very essence of a new constitution. The Southern states needed to include their slaves in the total apportionment of their congressional seats, therefore they would have more power. There is no denying that the Northern states did have a significant advantage over Southern states when it came to population. The extra advantage to many states was that they were able to count their free population, while the slave states couldn't or refused to acknowledge that slaves were, indeed, humans. So the idea of a ⅗ths compromise was resurrected, thereby a slave could be counted as ⅗ths of a whole free person.

I say resurrected here because the Constitution is not the first place where we see a ⅗ths clause in American history. It actually originated in the very first form of American government that ever existed, the Articles of Confederation. The idea behind this was not for any congressional apportionment, but instead to measure how much to tax individual states based on population and land values. Under the original clause which stated taxes "shall be supplied by the several colonies in proportion to the number of inhabitants of every age, sex, and quality, except Indians not paying taxes."[49] The South however, rejected this clause since it would include slaves in their original tax assessments, and to slaveholders slaves were not humans but property.

---

49 Wills, Garry (2003). "Negro President": Jefferson and the Slave Power. Houghton Mifflin. ISBN 978-0-618-34398-0.

It's quite interesting to see the back and forth and haggling over how the slaves should be represented in population measures. Benjamin Harrison, signer of the Declaration of Independence, insisted on a ½ clause, while other northerners insisted that ⅘ths should be the official number. All of these measures failed, however, due to steep opposition from slave states. Finally, a proposal, from none other than the father of the constitution himself, James Madison was accepted by both sides to set the official number at ⅗ths.[50] This too would eventually fail the Confederation congress, as all states would unanimously have had to agree on any proposal for it to be adopted and two states, New Hampshire and New York, stood firm against it. Nonetheless, the number was chosen as being acceptable to the majority of the congress and states, so ⅗ths it was.

During the Constitutional Convention the number was naturally brought up again this time not for taxing purposes, but for apportionment purposes. Obviously, this caused another round of vicious debate as Northerners wanted only free populations counted, while the southerners wanted slaves to count on an equal basis with free populations. Seeing that the only way to avoid the quagmire of unending debate and realizing that the slaves should not be counted on an equal basis the clause passed the convention by a vote of 8 states to 2 states.[51]

At first, from a founders perspective, it can be viewed that the ⅗ths clause was, at least initially, necessary. The Northern population was so much greater than the Southern population that the Northerners would have dominated politics in the house of representatives, which was based on population as a whole. To offset the

---

50 ibid
51 Madison, James (1787). Hunt, Gaillard (ed.). *1787: The Journal of the Constitutional Convention, Part I. oll.libertyfund.org*. The Writings of James Madison. Vol. 3. G. P. Putnam's Sons (published 1902).

imbalance of northern and southern states the ⅗th clause was figured to help bring some inkling of equality in terms of congressional apportionment. The clause provided for additional representation in the House so much so that in 1793 Southern slave states held 47 of 105 seats, almost half. Without the ⅗ths clause they would have had just 33 seats.[52] Fast forward to 1812 and the Southern slave states had a majority of the congressional seats. As the years moved on and western expansion grew exponentially, the need for the ⅗ths clause seemed to be null as it would come to be a severe disadvantage to Northern free states.

This advantage to the slaves interests not only influenced congressional elections but presidential contests as well, due to the fact that with increased congressional seats Southern slave states would have more clout in terms of electoral votes. Because electoral votes depended on seats in the house and senate combined, these slave states had quite an advantage due to the ⅗ths clause. As a matter of fact, 13 of the first 15 presidents were either southerners themselves who owned slaves or northerners with southern sympathies. (The 2 out of the 15 who were not of this sort were both Adamses who both despised slavery as abhorrent and immoral, both were only one term presidents who both barely squeaked by to win election in the first place.) It wasn't until after Lincoln and the civil war, with the abolition of slavery and the ⅗ths clause, that Northerners gained dominance in presidential elections.

As was said, it is quite clear that the sole purpose as to why the ⅗ths clause was even included in the Constitution was because of the population difference between the Northern and Southern regions of the country. However, even though the populations were quite different during the drafting of the Constitution, it was evident

---

52 Richards, Leonard L. (2000). *The Slave Power*. Louisiana State University Press. ISBN 978-0-8071-2600-4.

that the South would grow much faster than the North due the vast abundance of land available for population growth and the great push westward that would one day be called Manifest Destiny. As brilliant constitutional writer Akhil Reed Amar stated, the founding fathers made a major flub up. With the belief that the Southern region would grow exponentially, the founding fathers should have been aware of the advantages that the South would one day have at the expense of the North. With this in mind, it would have been genius and ideal if the founders took up what Amar calls the sliding scale. Under this plan slaves would count for ⅘ths of a whole free inhabitant during the decade of 1790, thereby giving the South some much needed immediate votes to equalize the initial imbalance. In return each decade that follows would see the proportion falling by ⅕th. For example, in 1800 slaves would count for ⅗ths, 1810 ⅖ths, 1820 ⅕th, and finally by 1830 slaves would not count at all for congressional apportionment. [53]

Using this scale would actually increase the likelihood of slavery's demise, as more slave owners would be compelled to free their slaves, therefore these newly freed slaves would count as one whole free person. In this scenario more slaves would become free. Instead, with the continuity of the ⅗ths clause, the opposite actually happened. More slave owners would be compelled to keep slaves and buy slaves, yes, some through the international slave trade, to increase their congressional apportionment. Therefore, the ⅗ths clause perpetuated slavery simply by throwing an extra bone for the wealthy slave owners.

The Constitution's ⅗ths clause actually did more than that, it inspired some states to follow in its footsteps. South Carolina and Georgia were some of them. These states allowed districts to

---

53 America's constitution, a biography

count their slaves as ⅗ths of a freeman. This proved to be really nice for those plantation districts who owned many slaves, as they gained an unfair advantage over the states' other poor citizens who either couldn't afford slaves or for those that thought slavery was evil, giving slave districts more state legislatures. These legislatures would elect the governor and the presidential electors, who select the president, refusing to let the principle of direct elections interfere with the plantation elite. It's no wonder why South Carolina had so many pro-plantation governors and elected so many pro-southern presidents.[54]

In an interesting twist on history, the revered historian Gary Wills concluded, that without the ⅗ths clause and the additional leverage that Southern states held as a result Thomas Jefferson may not have won the presidential election of 1800. He also believed that without the ⅗ths clause "slavery would have been excluded from Missouri ... Jackson's Indian removal policy would have failed ... the Wilmot Proviso would have banned slavery in territories won from Mexico ... the Kansas-Nebraska bill would have failed."[55] That's a lot of history that could have been re-written, all for the better, with the simple exclusion of the ⅗ths clause.

Of course, there were heroes who took on quite different stances over the issue of ⅗ths representation. Whereas William Lloyd Garrison believed that the Union should split over the gross miscarriage of representation, even going so far as to state that he would wish the Union to "crumble into dust" rather than let slavery continue.[56] Frederick Douglass believed in a much brighter future,

---

54 ibid
55 Wills, Garry (2003). *"Negro President": Jefferson and the Slave Power.* Houghton Mifflin. ISBN 978-0-618-34398-0.
56 Abolitionists and the Constitution https://www.crf-usa.org/images/pdf/Abolitionists-and-the-Constitution.pdf

"giving the provisions the very worse construction, what does it amount to? I answer—It is a downright disability laid upon the slaveholding States; one which deprives those States of two-fifths of their natural basis of representation. A black man in a free State is worth just two-fifths more than a black man in a slave State, as a basis of political power under the Constitution. Therefore, instead of encouraging slavery, the Constitution encourages freedom by giving an increase of "two-fifths" of political power to free over slave States. So much for the three-fifths clause; taking it at is worst, it still leans to freedom, not slavery; for, be it remembered that the Constitution nowhere forbids a coloured man to vote."[57] It is inspirational, to say the least, that Douglass beautifully laid out the hope for the black race, for the constitution never specifically said that a black man can't vote, and that the Constitution encouraged freedom by giving slave states an extra ⅖ths of representation for freeing their slaves.

Some of these prominent abolitionists, which we will discuss more at length later, truly were radicals. Some of them, like William Lloyd Garrison, even encouraged the breaking up of the Union over the issue of slavery. Others, like Frederick Douglass, who would become a source of inspiration for many black Americans, believed that the Constitution supported freedom and gave hope to the oppressed, an enlightening vision for hundreds of thousands of bondaged men and women that the end might soon come.

It is quite ironic that the Southern leaders who initially rejected slaves being worth ⅘ths of a freeperson, when the Articles of Confederation were discussing tax purposes, would settle for ⅗ths later on for apportionment purposes. Just imagine what could have happened if the Constitution accepted slaves as counting as ⅘ths

---

[57] The Cambridge Companion to the United States Constitution, Cambridge University Press, p. 458

of a free person. The whole history of our country would have been drastically altered with the Southern slave states occupying the power and authority to shove slavery down the throats of the territories and states that had banned it. Even the civil war might not have taken place and slavery would have had an even more profound hold on the American way of life.

The ⅗ths compromise was finally eradicated after the civil war and stated in section two of the 14th amendment "representatives shall be apportioned ... counting the whole number of persons in each State, excluding Indians not taxed."[58] Finally all blacks were considered a person, not ⅗ths of a person, but one whole person. To reach this point the bloodiest war in American history had to take place. Around 620,000 men lost their lives.[59] And it didn't need to be this way. Abolitionists, those that advocated for the immediate abolition of slavery, were called lunatics, they were heckled, ran out of business, and beaten, sometimes killed, like in the case of Elijah Lovejoy of Illinois. But it took them to put an end to the shackles, and an end to the infamous ⅗ths clause, written by our founding fathers in the most precious document, we, Americans, hold so dear.

---

58 Friedman, Walter (January 1, 2006). "Fourteenth Amendment". *Encyclopedia of African-American Culture and History*. HighBeam Research. Archived from the original on July 14, 2014. Retrieved June 12, 2013.
59 Faust, Drew. n.d. "Death and Dying--Civil War Era National Cemeteries: Discover Our Shared Heritage Travel Itinerary." Www.nps.gov. National Park Service. https://www.nps.gov/nr/travel/national_cemeteries/death.html#:~:text=The%20number%20of%20

6 ABOLITION

Yes, early American leaders, as we already discussed, gave way too much power and influence to the states that would eventually promulgate the civil war. In granting the slaveholding states the right to count their slaves as ⅗ths of a person they were able to greatly expand their power in politics due to the number of congressional seats they could obtain. For example, on a modest family farm to the North who had a family of seven that had no slaves to do their work counted only seven in proportion to their congressional district. Meanwhile, a modest family plantation that consisted of seven family members who owned ten slaves would count thirteen for apportionment purposes. In other words, this Southern plantation could count six people in their slave population to have greater representation in congress, even though the slaves in this region of the US were treated as subhuman and subjected to the labor of a mule, and dare I mention, couldn't actually vote themselves, which defeats the whole purpose of counting them as freepersons. This was the first sign of appeasement to the Southern slave owners, who held the country hostage on the brink of collapse.

Those who were opposed to slavery, mostly because of moral and religious reasons, although many slave owners used the Bible as justification for slavery as well, (the belief was that Ham, all the way back to the time of Noah, was dark skinned when Noah made him his servant) just flatly let the Southern slavocracy get their way. The ⅗ths compromise was just the start of a long ugly past of appeasement.

After the country developed an economic structure that rivaled those of the European standard, where they were able to compete, prospere, and have adequate security, more and more anti-slavery voices began to emerge. This happened mostly through influential writers like Willaim Lloyd Garrison, who was eventually attacked because of his anti-slavery writings when a Boston mob attacked him before an address, tied a rope around his waist, and dragged him in the street before the police rescued him, finding Garrison unconscious.[60] Garrison's work for the *Liberator*, his newspaper that he created solely for the abolition of slavery, greatly changed the framework for anti-slavery momentum.

At first believing that slavery should be gradually abolished, Garrison soon came to the belief that his prior opinion was morally wrong before God. Since he and many fellow abolitionists, who fervently denounced slavery, believed it to be a sin, then allowing sinful behavior, even for a short time while the country figured out how to live without it, was a sin as well.

With the rising of abolitionist fervor and anti-slavery groups came anti-slavery petitions. A petition was a request or specific action that constituents can make of their representatives during a legislative session. Oftentimes the reading of these petitions from congressional representatives would take place at the beginning of the session, as the representative would have time to gather them all and prepare them before the floor of the House.

Petitions could cover any ground and relate to anything that the public may think necessary. Indeed, the constitution granted this right to citizens by sending these petitions to their lawmakers. Afterall, the people should have some voice either directly or

---

60 MADEO. n.d. "Oct. 21, 1835 | White Mob Attacks Abolitionist William Lloyd Garrison in Boston." Calendar.eji.org. https://calendar.eji.org/racial-injustice/oct/21.

indirectly in the country's affairs. This is what democracy is all about. This is the foundation of what our country stands for and what other nations are desirous of. Yes, this is what America could boast of to enemies and friends alike about the level of inclusivity in the halls of government.

Some of these petitions, however, didn't quite sit well with the powerful elite. Of course, some petitions regarded the long controversial topic of slavery. When a petition was read regarding the institution of slavery, most of them came from Northern abolitionists, the South squirmed with discomfort. Even the word slavery caused them to panic to the mallow of their bones that their self-serving interests could perhaps be challenged.

This, of course, did not happen. Most slavery petitions were read and quickly tabled, which means nobody took any action on it and it died a slow painful death, most likely in the House garbage can. Though the mere thought that the glorious House of Representatives should be tainted by the idea of slavery being discussed within its chambers caused great disgust and alarm among the slavocracy.

In 1835, South Carolina representative James Hammond suggested the idea of a gag rule. The gag rule was, in effect, a rule that forbade any conversations about slavery to be held in the House. This rule then also forbade any petitions regarding slavery to be brought to the House. This was, quite obviously, in direct contradiction to the US constitution, not allowing the sacred right of freedom of speech from entering into the halls of the "beacon of liberty." However, who could stop this? Of course, some would stand up against the infamous decision. Those who had the guts to take on the hate from these rich and powerful planters, who counted on their slaves to make them an even greater fortune, soon found out how futile any effort at fighting back could be.

One of the greatest heroes of the time, who actually had the guts to stand up to wealth and power, was John Quincy Adams.

John Quincy Adams, the son of the former president John Adams, and a fellow president himself, was born of high standing and influence, befitting a president and forgotten founding father. As can be expected someone with this social standing had considerable admiration with members of congress and the people at large. Surely, when he spoke people would listen and show respect and gratitude to a man who had sacrificed his life for the benefit of the young nation.

Not the case.

As a matter of fact, when Adams, who by now largely ignored the abhorrent gag rule, announced yet more petitions begging for an end to slavery he was met by arousing fury. Not only did the House speaker, future president James Polk, rule him out of order and publicly slam him in the halls, but more and more powerful Southerners began to ostracize him in public. Indeed, a motion was presented to censure him, a form publicly ridiculing a member by showing disapproval. Shockingly, many members of the slavocracy voted to censure him even though the measure would fail.

And so, here we have it. Not even a former president of the United States, whose family had a high esteem for generations, was safe from being brandished as a radical abolitionist, who had disgraced the chamber. And all of this for what? For publicly announcing a petition, which the Constitution grants each and every single American the right to do, in the House. Clearly the Constitution could be thrown away or tossed aside to advance the interests of the few over the interests of the yeoman or average day laborer.

Honestly, we need to ask ourselves why this happened? Obviously, congress was willing to throw away Americans' God given rights at the behest of the privileged slave owners, who continued to dwell in a hated institution that no powerful person had the guts to take on.

It gets worse too. Adams, after receiving a petition from a few "slaves" asking him to retain the institution of slavery because they wanted to serve their masters, thought he had a brilliant scheme. The petition, though a hoax created by slave masters trying to cool the abolitionist fervor, could be the means that proves the wrong-headedness of the Southern slaveholders. Before he even began his announcement of the petition, just knowing that it was written by slaves was enough to throw the congress into an uproar. Southern congressmen hurled insults at Adams and demanded a strengthening of the gag rule. All this, while not even knowing that the petition would actually be a gift to the Southerners. Nevertheless, congress would go ahead and overwhelmingly vote that any petition from a slave was dishonorable to the House by a vote of 160-35. And, moreover, slaves have zero rights to write a petition to a congressman, with only 18 congressmen voting against the resolution.[61] Based on the votes, congressmen cared more about their political power and remaining in congress than standing up for what's morally right. And so the big question at the time is are African-Americans truly inferior to the white man? Even though some philosophical intellectuals might believe that there is no difference and they deserve the same rights that belong to a white man, the vast majority of Americans still believed that African-Americans were inferior, thus they had little rights and no rights as a US citizen.

Even the highly esteemed John Quincy Adams couldn't bring himself to the truth. Even insisting that he was not an abolitionist and didn't support the abolition of slavery in Washington D.C, nor did he support immediate emancipation. Adams was morally

---

61 John Quincy Adams book

opposed to slavery and believed that war would eventually tear this country apart because of the dreaded issue of slavery, an amazing show of prophecy, though many probably expected it, yet he was unwilling to fight the monster to its death. Sadly, like many politicians and leaders of the time, Adams was content letting the special interests of the South continue to bleed this country and force a future generation to deal with the ugliness.

In the midst of the petition imbroglio, mob action became much more frequent and attacks on abolitionists, especially abolitionists writers were becoming more common. Elijah Lovejoy is an example of the violence that erupted at this shaky time.

Lovejoy was born in Maine the son of a preacher and farmer who taught the young boy values and hard-work. After he graduated college Lovejoy moved out west to start a healthy career and support his family. In 1829 Lovejoy eventually settled into St. Louis Missouri, a slave state, co-editing a newspaper, the *St. Louis Times,* where he earnestly advocated for the election of Henry Clay for president. It is here where Lovejoy learned the ways of the American Colonization Society and local abolitionists. In 1833, Lovejoy started his own paper called the *St. Louis Observer,* which quickly began to publish more and more on slavery issues.[62]

Over the years, he grew more vehement in his attacks against slavery, eventually pushing for the Missouri Constitutional Convention to gradually emancipate their slaves. With growing boldness came growing resentment among those who disagreed with his principles. He would go on and call out Christians who supported slavery as being hypocritical. Among one of his most best-known quotes he stated "Slavery, as it exists among us . . . is demonstrably an evil.

---

62 Van Ravenswaay, Charles (1991). *St. Louis: An Informal History of the City and Its People, 1764–1865.* Missouri History Museum. pp. 276–277, 279–280.

In every community where it exists, it presses like a nightmare on the body politic. Or, like the vampire, it slowly and imperceptibly sucks away the life-blood of society, leaving it faint and disheartened to stagger along the road of improvement."[63] These were extraordinarily brave words for a man who was constantly being threatened with violence. Local pro-slavery bands were threatening to tar and feather Lovejoy if he kept up his attacks against the institution of slavery. Rumors spread, prompting his nearest friends to fear for his life. When he was away publishers tried to ease the storm, promising that when Lovejoy returned he would write no more about slavery, which Lovejoy rejected wholeheartedly. After the lynching of Francis McIntosh, pro-slavery proponents linked McIntosh with Lovejoy, claiming that Lovejoy helped to incite the violence not just of McIntosh but of other blacks, free and slave alike, against the white race. Even the judge who oversaw the case of the white mob who viciously murdered McIntosh, after announcing the mob innocent, went on a full attack on Lovejoy and other abolitionists editors for stirring the pot and called them responsible for what had happened.[64]

After the lynching of McIntosh, Lovejoy moved to Illinois with his family, where he started another newspaper called the *Alton Observer*. It was in Alton that Lovejoy advocated for an Illinois state chapter of the Anti-Slavery Society based on the Philadelphia version erected four years earlier. However, many local residents began questioning Lovejoy's presence in town, based on a fear that businesses would not conduct business where there's open hostility to slavery, therefore Illinois would lose Southern businesses.

---

63 Elijah P. Lovejoy: Anti-Catholic Abolitionist". *Journal of the Illinois State Historical Society*. **108** (2): 103–121. doi:10.5406/jillistathistsoc.108.2.0103. JSTOR 10.5406/jillistathistsoc.108.2.0103 – via JSTOR.
64 ibid

Throughout all the threats and mudslinging, Lovejoy never lost the hope that eventually all slaves would one day become free. "As long as I am an American citizen", he would write, "and as long as American blood runs in these veins, I shall hold myself at liberty to speak, to write and to publish whatever I please, being amenable to the laws of my country for the same."[65] One of the reasons why I personally have so much respect and adulation for Elijah Lovejoy was he never gave up. It would have been easy to see the threats and constant bickering and decide to give up but Lovejoy had principles and values that he wouldn't sacrifice even if it meant his life.

After being repeatedly harassed by pro-slavery crowds and having his press destroyed on three different occasions, Lovejoy eventually hid another printing press in a local warehouse were nobody would spot it and continued to write of the evils of slavery. Though it didn't take long for outsiders to find the press and Lovejoy.

On November 6, 1837 a pro-slavery mob began its attack on the warehouse, first by firing bullets where Lovejoy and his printing press were hiding. Lovejoy, and those with him, didn't give up the fight that easily, returning fire that killed a member of the vicious mob. After a while the shelling finally quieted down to the point where you could hear a rat crawling on the basement floor. Lovejoy waited another five minutes before opening the door to make sure the coast was clear. The moment he opened the door he was quickly berated by five bullets and died instantly, thus immediately becoming a martyr for the sake of human compassion and justice.[66] Again, to make it worse, the rioters, who viciously attacked Lovejoy,

---

[65] "Love and Devotion Marked Home Life of Elijah Lovejoy". *Alton Evening Telegraph*. July 22, 1937. p. 7. Archived from the original on June 7, 2021. Retrieved June 7, 2021.
[66] Wilson, J. G.; Fiske, J., eds. (1900). "Lovejoy, Elijah Parish" . Appletons' Cyclopædia of American Biography

were declared not guilty in another example of a gross miscarriage of justice. However, after the killing, abolitionists throughout the country gathered to denounce the merciless murder, where abolitionism grew by thousands, as men and women joined the cause and pledged that Elijah Lovejoy would not die in vain.[67]

With the murder of Elijah Lovejoy, came deep resentments and regional divides, the likes of which the United States never seen before. Of course, the abolitionist movement gained steadily as the years went by. Most abolitionists propaganda was spread through anti-slavery editors and mass meetings, where speakers showed off their oratorical flourish, or even church gatherings where pastors would speak out about the sinfulness of holding others in captivity. Among the earliest abolitionist church movements was the society of friends, or, commonly known as, Quakers.

Beginning all the way back to 1688, Quakers in Germantown, Pennsylvania began sending anti-slavery petitions and monthly meetings.[68] Elsewhere, throughout the country, some anti-slavery Christians were laughed at and harassed, with conservatives calling them "church-and-state" zealots, a bit ironic for conservatives to call Christians church and state zealots, especially in today's America.[69] Even some anti-slavery mailings, sent by church groups, to the South, faced severe opposition when New York's postmaster general, Samuel Governeur, tried to prevent the AA-SS, the American Anti-Slavery Society, from mailing the abolitionist literature to slaveholders. A pretty gutsy move by the AA-SS to directly confront the pro-slavery faction would come to naught, however, when Governeur, with the consent of the US postmaster general, Amos Kendall, a yes man

---

[67] "Elijah Lovejoy." n.d. The Free Speech Center. https://firstamendment.mtsu.edu/article/elijah-lovejoy/.
[68] London Yearly Meeting minutes, Vol. 6, 457–458
[69] Wyatt-Brown, Bertram. "American Abolitionism and Religion". *Teacher Serve*. National Humanities Center. Retrieved 14 November 2019.

to racist president Andrew Jackson, personally refused to send the mailings to the southern states.[70] Why would a New York postmaster general try to pamper the wishes of the slavocracy? Power.

Despite the setbacks, many members of church organizations voluntarily freed their slaves believing that keeping them was a sin in the eyes of Almighty God. This argument held special sway in America because Christianity had such strong roots in every community. Such work as *A Condensed Anti-Slavery Bible Argument,* written in 1845 by George Bourne, a Presbyterian minister, fundamentally changed the hearts of many churchgoing Christians who believed in morality. Bourne, in his work, disputes the argument that slavery is sanctioned in the holy scripture, proves that Africans are not under the "curse of Cannan", the son of Ham, praises Moses for freeing God's people in the Old Testament, and shows Jesus' disdain for slavery in the New Testament.[71] Another book, *God Against Slavery,* by George Cheever, another presbyterian minister, contradicted the arguments used by some southern ministers and preachers that the Bible did ordain slavery.

So what exactly were the thoughts of Christians who tried to use the Bible to their advantage of holding slaves? What kinds of sick and twisted arguments did they use? Well to name just a few, slaveholding Christians claimed that Abraham had owned slaves, with all of his patriarchs, but God didn't say anything against it. Even Abraham had sexual intercourse with his servant to have a son, Ishmeal. (Again, as we've already discussed they pushed the fact that Ham's son Canaan was made a slave to his brothers, with the asterisk that Ham was of a darker pigmentation.) That the Ten Commandments listed slavery multiple times, never in rebuke of

---

70 Schlesinger *Age of Jackson*, p. 190
71 "Summary of a Condensed Anti-Slavery Bible Argument, by a Citizen of Virginia." n.d. Docsouth.unc.edu. Accessed January 7, 2024. https://docsouth.unc.edu/church/bourne/summary.html#:~:text=In%20A%20Condensed%20

it was a huge rallying cry for slave masters. Indeed, slavery was widespread in Jesus' time, though he never spoke against it. And even St. Paul had written for slaves to obey their masters.[72] At first, these arguments look pretty solid. All of these are true and were mentioned in the Bible. However, throughout all of these arguments, the slavery that was conducted in America was based purely and simply on race. In Biblical times, in most cases, slavery was not race based, even poor families could sell their sons and daughters to servanthood, to pay debts. That wasn't the case in American slavery. Rarely, if ever, were slaves freed voluntarily, and this mostly comes from public men, who would look good in future generations if they freed their slaves. In fact, when slavery was race based in the Bible, as is the case with the Hebrews being subjected to slavery at the hands of the Egyptians, God sent Moses to free them and sent horrible plagues to the Egyptians while doing it. To actually make the argument that God created the African race to be inferior and liable to servanthood is quite laughable, however, this idea was perpetuated throughout our existence as a nation, even by some very holy and moral men of the cloth.

Some other, quite inexcusable, reasons why some "religious" folk in America supported the institution of slavery was based on a form of charitable kindness on the part of the slave owners. For example, it was widely circulated that the Africans practiced heathen religions back home where they worshiped the devil and performed witchcraft and voodoo with all their shamans and witchdoctors. (I don't need to mention that witchcraft and black magic happens

---

72 The Editors. 1992. "Why Did so Many Christians Support Slavery?" Christian History | Learn the History of Christianity & the Church. Christian History. 1992. https://www.christianitytoday.com/history/issues/issue-33/why-christians-supported-slavery.html.

everywhere, even in America, especially today.) However, this was one of the evangelical reasons why slaves were being continually repressed into servitude, to "Christianize" them.

It is quite true that the overwhelming majority of newly imported slaves followed religious practices that were formed by west African culture. Most believed in a supernatural being with inferior gods, thus believing in some sort of paganism where spirits both past and present mingled into everyday life.[73] It seems like "Christianizing" the Africans may make some religious congregations feel better even though early in American slavery's existence many plantation owners were very afraid of evangelizing their slaves for a number of reasons including that it would empower the slaves to seek freedom. Such views were in direct contradiction to the arguments that Christians used to perpetuate slavery, viewing that the Bible, somehow, ordained and encouraged slavery. By their own beliefs they had to know that this reasoning was not solid.

Most slave owners, however, simply didn't want their slaves to worship for fear of them learning to read and write. It is a much known fact that American colonists were some of the most literate people of the world and would continue to be for generations into the antebellum years of the country. This was due largely from the Puritanical ancestry that the very first immigrants brought over to this sparsely populated wilderness. Most every household would own multiple Bibles, which was read widely, much more than any other book known to man at the time. Even poor illiterate farmers, who couldn't read anything else, knew how to read the Bible.

---

[73] Mohamed, Besheer, Kiana Cox, Jeff Diamant, and Claire Gecewicz. 2021. "A Brief Overview of Black Religious History in the U.S." Pew Research Center's Religion & Public Life Project. February 16, 2021. https://www.pewresearch.org/religion/2021/02/16/a-brief-overview-of-black-religious-history-in-the-u-s/.

As I mentioned earlier, blacks were often thought of as being vastly inferior to whites when it came to intellectual capabilities and imaginative capacity. Thomas Jefferson once thought that blacks were brave in battle because they were unable to comprehend what dangers might arise just in front of them, therefore clearly hinting that blacks were too stupid to understand danger.[74] This one-sided view is deeply unfair to a whole race of people that have been numerously exploited to fatten the pockets of the oppressors. Most slave owners would never let their slaves near a book for the sole purpose of keeping them away from the chance to read. Once slaves would read they would never be so ignorant to keep staying in their current situation. There would be riots and slave rebellions, like those seen in Haiti and elsewhere. For these reasons, slave owners often let their slaves worship in their own way, not intending to evangelize any of their property for fear of rebellions and chaos. In some extreme cases, colonies would pass legislation in the early 1700s officially declaring that baptizing slaves does not grant them freedom, thus slaves and abolitionists could not even think about making that argument.[75]

Once slave-owners got past the initial hesitation to allow slaves to worship, they proceeded with the utmost caution, many not allowing for slaves to meet together in a congregation or even pray together for fear of, you guessed it, plans of rebellion against the masters. Many slaves met in secret anyways, forming prayer groups in cabins, thickets, and any other place where they could hide their activities, as though they were hiding witchcraft.[76]

Many slave-owners went to great lengths to instill in their Gospel teachings that slaves should be obedient to their masters, as to no

---

[74] What would jefferson say
[75] ibid
[76] ibid

any other would be to sin, while at the same time totally neglecting the teaching of the Golden Rule, to do to others what you would want them to do to you. It makes you wonder what other pieces of the Bible slave-owners purposely kept away from their bondaged property? One might think that slave-owners were especially nervous over the story of Moses. In Washington's museum of the Bible, one of their most prized possessions is the slave Bible, where the story of Moses and the Israelites Exodus is conspicuously missing.[77] Masters must have failed to fully suppress this practice of Bible fixing, as the story of Moses proved to be of great inspiration and importance to enslaved black men and women. Stories of slaves singing in the field sweet hymns about freedom were not fictional but, indeed, reality. Frederick Douglass recalled this, before he escaped to freedom and was a child, "a keen observer might have detected in our repeated singing of 'O Canaan, sweet Canaan, I am bound for the land of Canaan,' something more than a hope of reaching heaven. We meant to reach the north, and the north was our Canaan."[78]

Indeed, the growth of black church-goers both free and enslaved grew exponentially, and was the source of inspiration and encouragement to some millions of slaves, who both would and would not experience freedom. There are many reasons as to why black Americans would find comfort within the Bible. One of the most famous passages in the Bible speaks of those who are lowly now will have a high place in the future, as well as those who are sad now will be happy because God will comfort them.[79] This had to have

---

77 Zauzmer Weil, Julie. 2019. "The Bible Was Used to Justify Slavery. Then Africans Made It Their Path to Freedom." *The Washington Post*, April 30, 2019. https://www.washingtonpost.com/local/the-bible-was-used-to-justify-slavery-then-africans-made-it-their-path-to-freedom/2019/04/29/34699e8e-6512-11e9-82ba-fcfef-f232e8f_story.html.
78 Douglass, Frederick. 1855. "My Bondage and My Freedom.
79 Matthew 5:4-14

major implications to faith, as millions of slaves now found a God who cared and would redeem their toil and sadness.

To say the least, some Chrisitans could say that they successfully evangelized some slaves, though they didn't need to be slaves to be evangelized. If they were so worried about evangelizing the Africans they could have taken mission trips not resorting to the ever increasing institution of human bondage. So this argument doesn't pass the test, and is rather a far reach for southern appeasers to resort to sugarcoating human's greatest evil.

Many Chrisitans throughout history have been told to obey authorities such as governments and institutions. This is why so many Quakers had supported the King and remained loyal during the American revolution, even though they would be excoriated by Thomas Paine and others in doing it. But what about obeying institutions or governments that are evil or morally unjust? Some Ministers and church-goers found this deeply complexing and had mixed emotions regarding the peculiar institution. Some, like Bishop William Meade, even found punishments as a common good rather than a dastardly act. Suppose, he said, that you were even punished for supposed things that you didn't even do, "is it not possible you may have done some other bad thing which was never discovered and that Almighty God, who saw you doing it, would not let you escape without punishment one time or another? And ought you not in such a case to give glory to Him, and be thankful that He would rather punish you in this life for your wickedness than destroy your souls for it in the next life? But suppose that even this was not the case—a case hardly to be imagined—and that you have by no means, known or unknown, deserved the correction you suffered; there is this great comfort in it, that if you bear it patiently, and leave your cause in the hands of God, He will reward you for it in heaven, and the punishment you suffer unjustly here shall turn to your exceeding great glory hereafter.[80] This coming from a man of the cloth apparently totally fine with individuals being punished for no fault of their own.

His arguments are similar to what modern day Christians say today, that when we bear our punishments or afflictions God will redeem us. This, however, gives us no ground for being complacent when we see someone wrongfully abusing their fellow neighbors. Suppose that at our place of work we see our boss brutally assaulting one of our coworkers, according to Meade's advice we should just sit there and do nothing, believing that God will one day redeem that poor co worker for the wrongs committed against them. Instead, doesn't it make more sense to help your coworker and fight for justice?

Again, it is extremely ironic, and hypocritical, for these "religious" communities to teach the Golden Rule, to treat everyone the way we want to be treated and then turn around and watch a whole race of men, women, and children getting abused each and every single day without one remonstrance of helping, but instead encouraging it. Some of the Pastors and Ministers persuaded their congregants that it was the course of Divine Providence that white settlers would carry African slaves with them to this new land so that they could learn Christianity and morals. The underlying belief here being that Africans were immoral, many called them "barbarians" and, as a matter of fact, would be better off in slavery as opposed to being free, living like "ruffians".

There were some who believed that Africans couldn't make it on their own and that slavery was actually good for them "The physical condition of the American Negro", wrote Robert Walsh, "is on

---

80 Rae, Noel. 2018. "How Christian Slaveholders Used the Bible to Justify Slavery." Time. February 23, 2018. https://time.com/5171819/christianity-slavery-book-excerpt/.

the whole, not comparatively alone, but positively good, and he is exempt from those racking anxieties—the exacerbates of despair, to which the English manufacturer and peasant are subject to in the pursuit of their pittance."[81] Thereby, Southerners would use this reasoning to advance beliefs that they were actually right in God's eyes because they are saving the African race.

John Calhoun, who would become slavery's most ardent advocate in congress and act as an unofficial figurehead for the slavocracy went on, cheerfully, in a speech that "Never before has the black race of Central Africa, from the dawn of history to the present day, attained a condition so civilized and so improved, not only physically, but morally and intellectually... It came to us in a low, degraded, and savage condition, and in the course of a few generations it has grown up under the fostering care of our institutions."[82] Essentially, he was saying southerners should give themselves a pat on the back, they done good, they propped up a whole race that now, finally, is civilized and, maybe even someday, can be productive. Thus Calhoun believed that he was morally right before God, he brought up a "degraded" and "savage" race.

Frederick Douglass was one of the many who had a difficult time with southerners of the Bible-belt using Christianity to advance the bondage of what should be perfectly free men, women, and children. "Between the Christianity of this land" he said, "and the Christianity of Christ, I recognize the widest possible difference—so wide that to receive the one as good, pure, and holy, is of necessity to reject the other as bad, corrupt, and wicked. To be the friend of

---

81 Tise, Larry Edward (1974). "The "Positive Good" Thesis and Proslavery Arguments in Britain and America, 1701—1861". *Proslavery: A History of the Defense of Slavery in America* (Thesis) (1987 ed.). Athens, Georgia: University Press of Georgia. p. 97. ISBN 9780820309279. LCCN 86014671. OCLC 5897726.
82 John C. Calhoun, "A Positive Good – Teaching American History, 'Slavery a Positive Good'" (February 6, 1837).

the one is of necessity to be the enemy of the other. I love the pure, peaceable, and impartial Christianity of Christ; I therefore hate the corrupt, slave-holding, women-whipping, cradle-plundering, partial and hypocritical Christianity of this land. Indeed, I can see no reason but the most deceitful one for calling the religion of this land Christianity."[83] Harsh words, but accurate ones.

Many leading abolitionists pleaded with southern slave-owners not to use the Bible as a justification for slavery, but as Mark Noll, historian of American Christianity, points out, they were in the minority. "They were considered to be radical," and oftentimes described as infidels by masters.[84] There you have it, many Christian southerners used the Bible to justify what they were doing, though in direct contradiction to what the Bible actually teaches us about love and morality. All the way up until the end of the Civil War, many Southerners would use religion and believe that God was on their side. Clearly, to them, the abolitionists were doing the work of the devil. They wanted to set the blacks free and then who knows what will happen to them. They'll commit crimes, plunder our resources, live off of the generosity of others, and become heathens and barbarians, like the kind they were before they were rescued into bondage.

So how could both sides believe that God was on their sides and use the Bible to justify their positions? I'm no preacher but I do know quite a bit of religion and the history of its usages. Clever folk will try to use the Bible to justify anything that has to do with their own preconceived ideas, without becoming fully versed in the realities. For example, I once heard a college student make an argument that the Bible justified and supported the second amendment because some disciples, before Jesus' passion, grabbed two swords

---

83 ibid
84 ibid

to protect the disciples and Jesus. Therefore this event did not discourage Christians from using weapons and guns. This clever kid used this to mean that if Jesus doesn't say anything exactly opposed to his reasoning then his reasoning must be correct, thus the second amendment is supported by God. Perhaps he never read the verse where Jesus said to Peter, "Put your sword back into its place. For all who take the sword will perish by the sword."

In this way, many, from both sides, used the Bible to make them feel better about their positions. In reality the Bible does mention slavery, it mentions that the Israelites themselves owned slaves, and commanded that slaves should obey their masters. Masters took this and ran with it. On the other hand, the Bible talks about the Golden Rule, to love as we want to be loved, and to hold one another as precious children of God, not like chattel, this the abolitionists ran with. Not to mention the fact that American slavery was purely based on race and sported inhumane treatment on their "property". Of course, when looked at now we think these Southerners who twisted and morphed the Bible to excuse what they did as horrible and despicable. History has been harsh on them, but let us remember they thought they were right. They had called those religious abolitionists "infidels" and "radicals" who were going to destroy this country. Today we look at those brave Churches and Christian anti-slavery voices as heroes. It is the Christian organizations that got the abolition ball rolling.

It is a sad reality that many leading figures of the day, including prominent politicians and presidents, would come to view abolition as a scourge upon the country and likely to cause disaster to the Union. Henry Clay is just one example of this. Henry Clay was one of the most popular politicians of his time. Deeply influential, he seemed to cast a spell on all those he conversed with. Having an immeasurable hold on the Whig party, many of his programs came to dominate leading political thought of the time. And even though he owned many slaves throughout his lifetime, he generally viewed slavery as an evil that was bringing moral indecency to the republic. Yet, even he would come to draw the ire of the abolitionists. In a speech made in Congress he asserted that he was not an abolitionist and deemed abolitionists to be dangerous and likely to drive a wedge between the North and South. "If I had been a citizen of Pennsylvania when Franklin's plan (of gradual emancipation) was adopted, I should have voted for it, because, by no possibility could the black race ever gain ascendancy in that state. But if I had been then or even now a citizen of any of the planting states, I should of opposed or continue to oppose any scheme, whatever of emancipation, gradual or immediate, because of the danger of an immediate ascendancy of the black race."[85]

Martin Van Buren, who personally abhorred slavery, calling it, "Morally and politically speaking slavery is a moral evil," would come to embrace the idea of slave-wielding masters that slavery cannot be touched.[86] And in the infamous case of Dred Scott, Van Buren, who initially thought the Taney ruling, which declared that blacks had no rights that whites enjoyed, including basic citizenship, as absurd, came around to the prejudiced way of thinking "I am now convinced" he said "that the sense in which the word "citizen" was used by those who framed and ratified the Federal Constitution was

---

85 "Henry Clay on Slavery: Extract from a Speech by Henry Clay O... | Ann Arbor District Library." n.d. Aadl.org. https://aadl.org/signalofliberty/SL_18431030-p1-06.
86 Kinderhook, Mailing Address: Martin Van Buren NHS 1013 Old Post Road, and NY 12106-3605 Phone: 518 758-9689 x2040 Contact Us. n.d. "Martin van Buren and the Politics of Slavery - Martin van Buren National Historic Site (U.S. National Park Service)." Www.nps.gov. https://www.nps.gov/mava/learn/historyculture/martin-van-buren-and-the-politics-of-slavery.htm#:~:text=%22Morally%20and%20politically%20speaking%2

not intended to embrace the African race."[87] How could a public figure like this be so conflicted with what he knows to be the truth in his heart and what he eventually chose to endorse? Perhaps it has to do with the political pressure being mounted to portray the abolitionists as dirty, violent thugs, who were out to destroy the Union.

Lonnie Bunch, the founding director of the Smithsonian's National Museum of African American History and Culture, pointed out that it wasn't just the South, but many people of the North who thought "abolitionists were extremists whose views were far outside of the mainstream of American life."[88] Sound familiar? Bunch, even goes so far as to say that abolitionism generated the most influence in the South, "Many Southerners believed that most Northerners were influenced by the actions and rhetoric of those involved in the anti-slavery movement. Despite the relatively modest numbers of people who identified themselves as abolitionists, the South's fear of abolitionism was a central tenet of antebellum Southern political life."[89] This in turn, inspired the Southern slave-holding bloc to organize together and pass outrageously grotesque laws that only made matters worse and further inflamed the acidity of the abolitionists. They began to block free speech, in a direct contradiction to the Constitution, in fear of what the "anti" voices might say, by supporting the gag rule. Numerous slave-holding states passed laws outlawing the discussion of slavery in all cases whatsoever. In addition to this many southern states passed laws outlawing any presses where abolition is mentioned. For example, Missouri's general

---

87 ibid
88 Bunch, Lonnie. 2011. "Lonnie Bunch: How Pervasive Was the Abolitionist Movement and Did It Influence Any of the Southern States to Secede?" Washington Post. March 21, 2011. https://www.google.com/url?q=https://www.washingtonpost.com/blogs/house-divided/post/lonnie-bunch-how-pervasive-was-the-abolitionist-movement-and-did-it-influence-any-of-the-southern-states-to-secede/2011/03/14/ABoCfI7_blog.html&sa=D&source=docs&ust=170
89 ibid

assembly passed a bill to, "prohibit the publication, circulation, and promulgation of the abolition doctrines. A conviction subjected the offending person to a maximum fine of $1000 and two years in the state penitentiary. A second offense brought twenty years in prison; and a third offense translated to a life sentence."[90] If that weren't enough, a decade later the state assembly passed another which stated, "No person shall keep or teach any school for the instruction of negroes or mulattos, in reading or writing, in this State," in an effort to keep blacks uneducated, again for fear, this time of insurrections and rebellions.[91]

It's a sad reality today that many minority school districts lack some serious funding to stay up to speed academically to their white peer school districts, a fact that more often than not gets swept under the rug.

These laws, made on an individual state by state basis, just made the situation worse. In all likelihood, if the southern states had kept their calm, abolitionism may even have died a slow painful death, but as history has shown it only gained momentum with each atrocity.

It is precisely the fear factor that southerners came to detest the abolitionists in the North and South. Slave masters feared that the abolitionists were directly feeding their property with rebellious propaganda. This belief accelerated at a quick pace as more planned insurrections were foiled by local militia gangs. With each insurrection plot, news began to leak out, more plans were fostered, and life began to fundamentally change.

When many people think about the underground railroad they often associate it with Harriet Tubman and brave leaders who risked everything to experience freedom. What most people don't know is that more slaves fled for freedom during the Revolutionary war

---

90 "Laws Concerning Slavery in Missouri." n.d. Www.sos.mo.gov. https://www.sos.mo.gov/archives/education/aahi/earlyslavelaws/slavelaws.asp.
91 ibid

than the underground railroad. This mostly is due to a handful of reasons. In most cases, freedom seeking slaves traversed hundreds of miles, and still weren't totally safe, due to the Fugitive Slave Act of 1850, until they reached Canada. Another obvious reason is that the United States was not at war at the time and experienced an extended time of peace with foreign countries, this allowed authorities to spend more time and energy tracking down fugitive slaves. This makes the success and courage of the underground railroad movement even more breathtaking.

Under the first Fugitive Slave Act of 1793, Congress insisted that it was an obligation of the states to help masters recover their fugitive runaways, though some states repudiated this. With some friendly state legislatures that refused to assist slave-masters, runaways began to pick up steam. Of course, the underground movement was a path that hundreds of thousands of slaves would attempt throughout the 1800s, stopping at friendly homes or plantations to spend the night while continuing again the following day. The journey could take anything from a few days to a few months depending on the distance that it took to travel to freedom. Free blacks and white abolitionists were the blood, sweat, and tears, literally, of the underground movement.

Prior to 1850, estimates have predicted that as many as 100,000 slaves made the long, perilous, journey.[92] Some 30,000 to 40,000 slaves successfully escaped and resettled to Canada, where slavery was illegal since 1834, thanks to the Slavery Abolition Act passed by the British parliament making Canada safe territory.[93] The orig-

---

92 Vox, Lisa, "How Did Slaves Resist Slavery?" Archived July 11, 2011, at the Wayback Machine, *African-American History*, About.com, Retrieved July 17, 2011.
93 Henry, Natasha; McIntosh, Andrew (January 31, 2020). "Underground Railroad". *The Canadian Encyclopedia*. Archived from the original on May 9, 2021. Retrieved March 2, 2022.

inal act was brought about due to a controversy surrounding a free black man named John Davis who was forcefully kidnapped from Pennsylvania and transported to the Virginian plantations. The overall effects of the Fugitive Slave law did little to alter the confusion of the case. The kidnappers were never convicted of any crime and to the dismay of many modern historians, Davis remained a slave the rest of his life.[94] The effects of the law benefited the white man from the start. It did nothing for the free blacks who could be forcefully taken into bondage while failing to provide them justice and allowing white profiteers to continue kidnapping and making bank while doing it. And thus, this is just one small glimpse of the repugnancy of early American law and injustice.

The Fugitive Slave Act of 1793 wasn't quite strong enough for southern slave-owners though. True, some northern states actually required masters, or agents doing the master's bidding, to bring some sort of proof that the accused runaway was indeed a runaway and not a free man, as what happened with the famous story of Solomon Northup. Northup, who made fame writing *Twelve Years a Slave*, was born a free man in modern day Minerva, New York. Northup's father was born into slavery but was granted freedom when his master passed away, eventually starting up his own family farm, which Northup worked on growing up while receiving a quality education.

Northup would go on to get married and start a family, and interestingly enough he gained quite a reputation as a fiddler. However, fiddling and farming wasn't enough to support a growing family. He soon after, in 1841, was recruited by two white men to join the circus, to show off his fiddling skills, in Washington D.C. Soon

---

94 Finkelman, Paul. "The Kidnapping of John Davis and the Adoption of the Fugitive Slave Law of 1793", *The Journal of Southern History*, Vol. 56, (Aug., 1990), pp. 397, 422.

after he arrived in D.C. he was drugged, drifting in and out of consciousness, until he finally lost all consciousness. When he awoke he found himself in a dingy cell with shackles around his feet. He was shipped to New Orleans and sold to a plantation owner, where he would go on as a slave for twelve years being sold to numerous plantations along the way. Sadly, Northup wound up on several plantations with brutal masters who were known to exercise the lash. He attempted to escape numerous times, but never found himself successful.[95]

Northup was finally set free when Samuel Bass, an abolitionist carpenter from Canada, came to visit Northup's master, Edwin Epps. After hearing from Bass, noting his abolitionists views, Northup gained the courage to tell Bass his painful story. It is through Bass that Northup was able to send letters advocating on his behalf, working to achieve his long-sought after freedom.[96]

Bass is an interesting character, and a brave one at that. It should be stated that Bass helping an enslaved man in that region was something unthinkable and, quite frankly, dangerous, as he was depriving a master of his property and angering the community.[97] The letters eventually ended all the way at the top seat in New York, the governor, Washington Hunt. Northup had all the documentation revealing that he was a free man after all and had been illegally captured, where shortly after he gained his freedom.

Northup's reality was all too well known for many free blacks and those who had escaped the terror of slavery. Clearly, the first

---

95 Cole, Rachel. 2019. "Solomon Northup | Biography & Facts." In *Encyclopædia Britannica*. https://www.britannica.com/biography/Solomon-Northup.
96 Northrup, Solomon (1968). Eakin, Sue & Logsdon, Joseph (eds.). *Twelve Years a Slave*. Baton Rouge: Louisiana State University Press. pp. 211–212. ISBN 0807101508.
97 Szklarski, Cassandra (November 15, 2013). "Canadian connection to 12 Years a Slave has descendants buzzing". *The Globe and Mail*. Retrieved January 9, 2014.

Fugitive Slave Act made the situation for blacks so much worse in America, where, oftentimes, any black man, woman, or child could be kidnapped off the street with no sense of justice. In Northup's case the kidnappers were never charged, or found for that matter. He did, however, press charges against James Birch, the first who enslaved him, though he was unable to testify in court due to a D.C law forbidding blacks from testifying.[98] And so with the keeping Northup from being able to testify, no one was able to testify against Birch, so he got off without any charges for enslaving a free man. That was the reality for many blacks that were captured and taken hundreds of miles from where they call home. Rarely, if ever, would justice be on their side, they couldn't even testify in a court of law, thereby meaning that if someone captured a free black women, for example, the only way she would be able to become free again is in situations like Northup's where he was able to smuggle letters to sympathetic abolitionists, who had connections, or simply runaway. Both options were few and far between. Even if you were to consider running away, the risks associated with such an act would likely outweigh freedom itself.

Some of the brutal techniques that slave masters used to intimate and suppress their slaves as a deterrent to escaping were just mind blowing. Some of them deserve a mention here just so that we recognize the dangers associated with an attempt to run away. If they were caught, they were sure to get trouble. First, and worst, in my opinion, is family separation, or the threat of family separation. Can you imagine the day to day mental anguish associated with just the thought of being separated from your family forever? Many harsh owners routinely threatened to sell their slaves from their family if they misbehaved. Some, like even Washington, would threaten to

---

98 "Narrative of the Seizure and Recovery of Solomon Northrup". *New York Times*. Documenting the American South. January 20, 1853.

sell them to plantations where they knew it would be difficult for them. Washington even threatened to sell his slaves to the Caribbean, which at the time meant almost certain death due to diseases.[99]

Branding was another common usage among slave owners with disobedient slaves. The practice of branding involved taking an extremely hot iron, which needed to reach at least 500 degrees fahrenheit for the desired results. Once the iron got that hot, the monster, or overseer, would press the iron into the skin where it would go through the first two layers of the skin and damage the third layer, to receive life-long results.[100] Often, the owner would brand the runaway with their initials or with the letter R for runaway seared into their cheek, buttock, or shoulder. When an owner in Kentucky was looking for his runaway, he described her as having "a brand mark on the breast something like L blotched."[101] Apparently she ran away at least once before. Some states, such as South Carolina even endorsed these policies. If a slave ran away twice the correct punishment is branding with the letter R.[102]

Perhaps less well known is the practice of using iron bits. According to the Gilder Lehrman Institute of American History, these iron masks looked more like medieval torture devices. The masks had a piece of iron which would weigh down the tongue

---

99 Wood, Samuel. n.d. "The Horrors of Slavery, 1805 | Gilder Lehrman Institute of American History." Www.gilderlehrman.org. https://www.gilderlehrman.org/history-resources/spotlight-primary-source/horrors-slavery-1805.
100 https://people.howstuffworks.com/-body-branding2.htm#:~:text=While%20exact%20procedures%20vary%20by,%2C%20and%20finally%2C%20the%20subcutaneous.
101 Howe, S. W. (Winter 2009). "Slavery As Punishment: Original Public Meaning, Cruel and Unusual Punishments and the Neglected Clause in the Thirteenth Amendment". *Arizona Law Review*. 51 Ariz. L. Rev. 983. Retrieved Sep 20, 2013.
102 Higginbotham Jr., A. Leon (1978). *In The Matter of Color Race and the American Legal Process: The Colonial Period*. New York: Oxford University. pp. 176–184.

making it impossible to swallow, which would be dangerously uncomfortable.[103]

Obviously, the most common way that masters punished their runaway slaves was the practice of flogging. This was a practice that would be used for a number of reasons, anything from running away to reading a book could garner the use of the lash.[104] The most iconic picture of all time regarding the brutality of slavery is the picture of the slave Peter, with the lash marks wealted into his skin. Peter himself was a runaway who was whipped so badly that it almost took his life. When he escaped to find refuge in the Union army the soldiers were quite shocked at the horrible marks all up and down Peter's shoulders down to his buttucks.[105] The soldiers quickly took a picture of his scarred back, which soon propelled the anti-slavery movement further and extended the abolitionist crusade. As you would imagine, many moderates on the slavery issue decisively entered the anti-slavery camp after the pictures of Peter's distorted back made the rounds.

It wasn't an easy decision by any means for those who were bondaged to escape from their masters and learn freedom. The historian Carol Wilson mentioned at least 300 cases of free blacks who were kidnapped with the likelihood that even thousands more were captured who were not documented.[106] Of these it is impossible to know how many either were legally freed or experienced freedom through another avenue, that of running through the woods as runaways. After Northup's freedom he wrote the iconic memoir *Twelve Years a Slave*, where he mentions the cruelty and horrors of

---

103 ibid
104 ibid
105 https://www.history.com/news/whipped-peter-slavery-photo-scourged-back-real-story-civil-war
106 *Freedom at Risk: The Kidnapping of Free Blacks in America, 1780–1865*, University of Kentucky Press, 1994.

slavery and describes his story through the lens of a slave, something that American literature had been lacking.

Most runaway slaves were either young men or men with some sort of education, due to the grueling process of escaping using the underground railroad.[107] One study has estimated that approximately 76% of runaways were under the age of 35, while nearly 96% of them were male.[108] If this doesn't give you a glimpse of how difficult this journey was I don't know what will. As if it could get any harder, a new law passed as part of the Great Compromise of 1850 called the Fugitive Slave Act of 1850 made it increasingly difficult for runaways to become free or remain free for that matter.

The Compromise of 1850 did a number of things actually, however, the whole piece together was a bit of a disaster for the North, and even the South would come to hate it, even with the massive concessions given them by the North. The Compromise dedicated California as a free state, while allowing the territories of New Mexico and Utah to decide for themselves the question of slavery, which was a total undercut to the Missouri Compromise outlawing slavery below the 36/30 degree latitude line. If any of these territories would accept slavery, then slavery would fall above the Missouri Compromise line. But the real kicker is the next two acts filling in the Great Compromise.

Outlawing slavery in the District of Columbia was always on the agenda for most abolitionists. In fact, constitutionally speaking, Congress has sole authority and responsibility for the area. It was mutually understood that Congress could abolish slavery at any time in the district. Dating all the way back to 1805, Congressman Slaon of New Jersey offered a resolution emancipating slaves in DC

---

107 https://www.britannica.com/topic/fugitive-slave
108 ibid

once slaves reached a certain age. Of course, it was struck down, but only by less than 20 votes.[109] Struggles would come and go as congressmen would debate and shut down any mention of slavery in DC. However, the opportunity was ripe in 1849-50 for a big move to be made by the abolitionists to put pressure on the slave interest. But even in this the slave interests were able to achieve much more than what the North was able to. When it was all said and done the South could smile proudly at only giving up the *slave trade* in DC, and not slavery itself. (Slavery would officially be abolished in DC twelve years later in the middle of the Civil War).

The worst appeasement that the northerners gifted to the South, in exchange for the mild language banning the slave trade in DC, was the second coming of the Fugitve Slave Act. Much like the first bill, its main goal was to return captured runaways to their masters. One big difference, though, was it required the states to comply and enforce the law. In the past states could skirt around the fugitive slave act, where states made counterlaws to help shield runaways and citizens who were threatened to be kidnapped. Abolitionists became so incensed over this that they named it the "bloodhound bill" from the dogs that were used to chase runaways.[110] Now nobody was safe. Runaways that had escaped ten years ago and had been living free for all those years could not be viciously seized with nothing the states or authorities could do to stop it. In many cases free blacks were terrorized again, as this act sparked even more incentives for kidnapping and illegal seizures.

For someone to capture a "suspected" runaway, they had to bring

---

109 Tremain, Mary (1892). *Slavery in the District of Columbia; the policy of Congress and the struggle for abolition.* University of Nebraska Department of History and Economics, Seminary Papers 2. New York: G. P. Putnam's Sons.
110 Nevins, Allan (1947). *Ordeal of the Union: Fruits of Manifest Destiny, 1847–1852.* Vol. 1. Collier Books.

them to court where a judge would oversee the case and make a decision that would effectively make someone permanently free or permanently enslaved. The courts were again, no shocker here, incredibly biased. If judges ruled in favor of the slave-catcher, or "supposed slave-cather" the judge would receive $10, if they ruled in favor of the alleged runaway they would only receive $5. Who made these laws? Do you call that justice? Not surprisingly, 90% of cases were ruled in favor of the supposed "slave-catchers."[111] Let's put this in perspective, with adjustments for inflation, if you were a judge would you rather have $175 standing up for a "wretched" black runaway and be ridiculed by the community and potentially threatened, or would you rather have $390 and be a hero?[112]

No matter where runaways or even free blacks, for that matter, went in America they simply weren't safe. That's why so many went to Canada, and a few even heeded to the wishes of the ACS and decided to travel to Liberia, the colony for free blacks. John Brown, who we will talk about later, being a prominent, and perhaps most violent, abolitionist, once remarked that blacks all the way up in "supposedly" safe Massuchessetts were afraid, "some of them are so alarmed that they tell me that they cannot sleep on account of either them or their wives and children. I can only say I think I have been enabled to do something to revive their broken spirits. I want all my family to imagine themselves in the same dreadful condition."[113]

In 1855, Wisconsin seemed to be the only state to actually have the guts to stand up against the vicious slavocracy, and was the first and only state to declare the Fugitive Slave Act as unconstitutional.[114]

---

111 Bio of constitution
112 https://www.officialdata.org/us/inflation/1850?amount=10
113 Fried, Albert (1978). *John Brown's journey : notes and reflections on his America and mine.* Garden City, New York: Anchor Press. p. 41
114 "Booth, Sherman Miller 1812 – 1904". *Dictionary of Wisconsin biography.* wisconsinhistory.org. 2011. Retrieved June 28, 2011.

In 1855, abolitionist editor Sherman Booth was arrested when he blatantly ignored the act and helped incite what would become a mob, whose goal was to rescue a runaway slave named Joshua Glover.

Joshua Glover ran away from his master and the state of Missouri in 1852 to search for freedom. At first, he didn't know where to go, or quite frankly, where his journey would lead him. All he knew was that he wanted, no, needed freedom. Eventually, Glover would settle down in Racine, Wisconsin, a nice little town full of abolitionists and sympathetic officials, but here's where the story takes an interesting plot twist. After living in Racine for nearly two years working on a local saw mill in town, a mob of men who looked like trouble surrounded him and without much of a fight Glover acquiesced and gave himself up. The gang who captured Glover were slave-catchers, just now grabbing Glover after he settled his life in a free state where he developed relations with the community and had a respectable job. This was often a sad reality for fugitives, after the Fugitive Slave Act of 1850, that they were never safe, even years, in some cases, a decade after the fact.

The large group who captured Glover took him to a jail in Milwaukee where he would await the trial that would determine if he had to live the rest of his life as someone else's property. After the local citizenry of Racine heard about the tragic kidnapping of their neighbor, they sprang into action, determined to do something, even at the moment that very something was illegal. Here the citizens of Racine were willing to sacrifice it all for their values and morals. All those that were concerned gathered at Haymarket Square (presently Monument Square) where they quickly determined three things. First, that a delegation would be sent to Milwaukee to guarantee that Glover received a fair trial, something that took courage to do and that was desperately needed given the injustices of the court system. Secondly, they made sure that the newspapers received all the available documents so that they could publish the discussed issues as quickly as possible so that the community knew what was happening. Lastly, they set up a finance committee to handle funds to cover Glover's trial. It is very clear that this community was ready and willing to fight against injustice. In other parts of the country politicians and prominent members of society were calling them "dangerous" and "fools," "destined to bring about disaster on this country", but the people of Racine didn't care, they simply followed their heart, and their heart led them to Milwaukee.

The large delegation arrived in Milwaukee late in the evening where they ran into a crowd slowly gathering outside the courthouse. Sherman Booth, the Milwaukee abolitionist editor, was in the crowd. Soon, the delegation grew restless, and took matters into their own hands. Using anything that they could get their hands on, lumber, hatchets, and stones, the crowd broke into the jail and freed Glover, where he was quickly sped off on the underground railroad. "Imagine a crowd of four to six thousand persons smashing in the jail, releasing the negro and then running as they could the distance of a mile, and every man in town running too—windows open, handkerchiefs waving."[115] According to the Racine historical museum "Glover's next three to four weeks were spent in and around Racine County—being helped by men such as John Messenger, C.C. Olin, Alfred Payne, Richard Ela, Joel Cooper, Moses Tichenor and more. Glover traveled through Prairieville (now Waukesha), Rochester, Racine, Burlington, Spring Prairie and other areas, all the while being chased by Garland (his ex-master) and his posse."[116] The

---

115 *Racine Daily Morning Advocate, March 12, 1854*
116 The Joshua Glover Story · Racine County and the Underground Railroad · Racine Heritage Museum." n.d. Racineheritagemuseum.omeka.net. https://racine-heritagemuseum.omeka.net/exhibits/show/underground-railroad/joshua-glover.

beautiful thing about the underground railroad was that he could successfully evade the captors while living in a local abolitionist home or farmstead.

Glover would, in the meantime, come to the realization that life in Wisconsin, though, itself one of the safest Union states for runaways, was still too risky and dangerous, so he made his way to Canada, where most fugitives would find themselves. His life in Canada would seem somewhat mild and relatively problem free, but isn't that what every slave or runaway desired? "Joshua Glover's life in Canada was much like that of any other uneducated, laboring, tax-paying citizen. It was, to other average people, not all that interesting. To Glover himself, on the other hand, what may have been the most marvelous thing about it was its lack of drama and its predictability. There was no worry about being sold away to a cotton or sugar plantation in the Lower South because he had not been enthusiastic in his response to an order. There was no threat of physical punishment. He had ample food, a table to eat it from, and a bed to sleep in. He could indulge in a drink when he wished. He sometimes had money in his pocket and could choose how to spend it. Most of all, he knew that the body that laid itself to rest at night would awaken the next morning still free. He had no guarantee against personal tragedy or death, but he had freedom."[117]

Even after Glover successfully fled to Canada, debate in the States didn't die down that easily. First, there was the question of what to do with the crowd that broke into the jail? Who should be held responsible? And should they be arrested? From prior court cases dealing with white justice, one could assume that a mob is too big to be able to arrest anyone, so using this logic nobody would be arrested and incriminated. However, would this still apply to

---

117 *Finding Freedom, Ruby West Jackson and Walter T. McDonald*

abolitionists, a group of "radicals" that most people thought were crazy and deranged?

Amazingly enough, the court had decided that abolitionists were indeed liable for what happened. So, naturally the court sent out arrest warrants to leading abolitionists, among them Charles Clement, Thomas Mason, John Ryecraft, and Sherman Booth.[118] Booth's case was different. His was actually a criminal case, separating him from the rest of his abolitionists friends. His attorneys argued in court that Booth had just done his part as a good constitutional steward protecting everyone's right to a fair and just trial. Under the Fugitive Slave Act, accused runaways were not given this right and treated unfairly, thus Booth wasn't the one in the wrong, the Fugitive Slave Act was, it was unconstitutional.[119]

You can only imagine the slave power looking on nervously at this ruling. Depending on which way the state court decided it would either enforce the slavocracy's power, by declaring that each state needs to abide by these laws, even though it greatly disagrees with them, or the court could decide that the law is unconstitutional, which would open the floodgates to Southern hysteria. As so, here come the floodgates. Wisconsin Supreme Court Justice, Andrew Smith, issued an opinion agreeing with Booth and his attorneys, setting Booth free and declaring the Fugitive Slave Act unconstitutional. Finally, someone did something right for once right? But it wasn't over yet.

Soon after the ruling was made, US marshal VR Ableman, turned to the federal court system to appeal, surely the federal court system would be more sympathetic to the whole enslavement institution. It is little doubted that the federal courts would have ruled in Ableman's favor, therefore overturning the Wisconsin Supreme Court. But

---

118 ibid
119 ibid

the Wisconsin Supreme Court refused to recognize the power of the federal courts. Ableman didn't stop there though, the next, and final stop was the US Supreme Court. The Wisconsin courts even refused to give the official documentation to the Supreme Court, making it so that the court had to issue a decision without the proper materials to do so.[120]

Nevertheless, the Supreme Court decided, as you think it should under Chief Justice Roger Taney, the most pro-slavery justice and white supremacist that ever wore the justice robe. It declared that the Wisconsin courts had prioritized state courts over federal ones, thus making the Wisconsin courts superior to the federal court system, which itself is unconstitutional. If Wisconsin had the power to negate or ignore a federal law then any state could do this, making a similar situation as the nullification crisis in the early 1830s. For example, if the federal government passed a law freeing slaves after they turn thirty years old, all the states are subjected to that law. If Alabama decided that it wouldn't follow the rules that basically makes the purpose of the federal government null and void and would lead to chaos. This was the official reasoning of the Supreme Court.

The Supreme Court's over-ruling of the Wisconsin courts again made Sherman Booth a criminal, though Glover was able to successfully flee to a Fugitive Slave law free, Canada, while all of these proceedings were going on. If it was meant as a stalling tactic then it absolutely worked, for the Wisconsin abolitionists helped realize Joshua Glover's dream of freedom, while at the same time sacrificing themselves to do it. For even though Sherman was imprisoned and the Supreme Court sided with the pro-slavery force, Wisconsin was able to make a name for themselves as a strong, independent

---

120 Baker, H. Robert (2006). "Ableman v. Booth (Sherman Booth Case)". *Encyclopedia of African American history, 1619-1895 : from the colonial period to the age of Frederick Douglass*. Vol. 1. Oxford University Press. pp. 1–2

minded, state that fought against the powerful slave interests. In the end, the Supreme Court still validated the Fugitive Slave Act. However, Joshua Glover became truly free, and wasn't that the purpose of these abolitionists?

If you're wondering what happened to Sherman Booth, he had to sell his newspaper business to cover his increasing legal battles. And, while still in prison, Booth still maintained a steady following, to the point where he planned to give speeches from his second floor jail cell, which the guards would not allow. However, he and his supporters were undeterred. As many as eight attempts were made to rescue Booth from the jail, you would think that the guards would amp up security to prevent a prison riot, with a very popular convict inside? Wrong. On the ninth attempt Booth was successfully rescued from the jail, where, shortly afterwards, his most ardent supporters transported him back to his home in Wisconsin.[121]

During the Civil War, Booth kept up the fight of standing up for black liberties, founding *The Daily Life,* a pro-union and anti-slavery publication. He would go on to help lead the effort to provide enfranchisement to Wisconsin black men, and among other things, help create the Republican party, organizing an anti-slavery convention.[122]

This was just the tip of the ice-berg. Ableman vs. Booth was a major calling card for both northern and southern factions of the country. While the northerners were busy trying to undermine the institution of slavery, or at best, keep slavery where it already was but prevent it from spreading into the territories, southerners were too busy labeling northerners as being out of touch and being the agents that were going to destroy all of our liberties.

---

121 Diane S. Butler. "The Public Life and Private Affairs of Sherman M. Booth". *Wisconsin Magazine of History,* Spring 1999
122 ibid

The folks in Wisconsin weren't the only ones who openly resisted the new law. As a matter of fact, many now famous abolitionists put their lives on the line to save others affected by the law. The Reverend Luther Lee, who had a congregation in Syracuse, New York, proudly declared of the law that "I never would obey it. I had assisted thirty slaves to escape to Canada during the last month. If the authorities wanted anything of me, my residence was at 39 Onondaga Street. I would admit that and they could take me and lock me up in the Penitentiary on the hill; but if they did such a foolish thing as that I had friends enough in Onondaga County to level it to the ground before the next morning."[123]

There were numerous occasions where northern communities banded together to send fugitive slaves off to Canada, as well as freeing fugitives in an apparent prison break. The famous abolitionist Harriet Tubman saw the law as a potential setback to her plans rescuing slaves through the underground railroad, though the law certainly wasn't going to stop her or other abolitionists bent on doing the right thing. Even if abolitionists were caught and imprisoned, they likely had enough friends that would do anything to rescue them, as was shown in Glover's, Booth's, and Lee's cases.

Once the Civil War broke out the Fugitive Slave Act began to see its downfall. Many slaves escaped to join the Union's lines, however, some Union generals returned the escaped slaves to their previous masters. This practice stopped when General Benjamin Butler refused to return the runaways, strictly as a war measure.[124] Finally Congress backed up Butler's decision by making it law that runaways cannot be returned to their previous masters.

---

[123] Lee, Luther (1882). *Autobiography of the Rev. Luther Lee*. New York: Phillips & Hunt. p. 336.
[124] Goodheart, Adam (April 1, 2011). "How Slavery Really Ended in America"

Another straw slowly breaking the camel's back was the infamous Kansas-Nebraska Act. Popular Sovereignty is what it was called, when Stpehan Douglass proposed an effectual overturn of the Missouri Compromise, that was supposedly going to bring peace and harmony to the slavery question once and for all. The idea behind the Kansas-Nebraska Act was that it would allow the territories, as Kansas and Nebraska were not yet states, to determine for themselves if slavery should be allowed in their respective territories or outlawed.

Even bringing the possibility of Kansas and Nebraska to choose for themselves would bring an extension of slavery. At the time the Missouri Compromise was still the law of the land. Under the Compromise Kansas and Nebraska would not even be allowed to consider the question of slavery. It would have been excluded regardless of what the people wanted. With the Kansas and Nebraska Act the floodgates had officially opened. For if Kansas and Nebraska could choose for themselves, why couldn't the rest of the territories or future territories have the same right?

Not surprisingly, the debate over this new bill grew increasingly intense and even hostile at points. Thomas Hart Benton, a democrat whose allegiance and philosophy were in the Jacksonian ranks, was nevertheless unimpressed with the new act. Wanting slavery to be kept out of the territories he was a big roadblock for pro-slavery men hellbent on shoving slavery down the throats of the Union. "What is the excuse", he perfectly pointed out, "for all this turmoil and mischief? We are told it is to keep the question of slavery out of Congress! Great God! It was out of Congress, completely, entirely, and forever out of Congress, unless Congress dragged it in by breaking down the sacred laws which settled it!"[125] In this argument Benton clearly defines the key unequivocal hypocrisy and

---

125 Nevins, Allan. *Ordeal of the Union: A House Dividing 1852–1857* (1947)

contradiction of the pro-slavery faction. For so long the pro-slavery Southerners were playing hardball, declaring that congress had no right to interfere with slavery and passing laws restricted members not to even mention the word slavery. Now, however, because it suited their interests, slave owners chomped at the bit to get Congress to pass a bill potentially expanding slavery. If Kansas and Nebraska would vote for the inclusion of slavery in their territories it would make the disestablishing of slavery that much more difficult.

The bill ultimately passed in the end, now these territories held the power. They could decide for themselves the status of their territories, whether it should be forever free or tainted with that peculiar institution that many founding fathers prayed would gradually come to a halt. Now with the likelihood of people choosing, slavery just got more embedded with the country's institutions. What happened next was quite predictable. Free soilers would swarm into Kansas to swing the state into the free category, while pro-slavery men would pour in to do the same. Many of the pro-slavery faction came from neighboring Missouri, where slavery was alive and well. The unfairness of the elections, when deciding the ultimate question in the territorial constitution, was apparent when Missourians would move into Kansas to vote for a pro-slavery constitution then quickly slide back into Missouri like nothing even happened. Of course, the Jayhawks, as the abolitionists in Kansas were called, often did the same thing with Easterners moving out of Kansas once the elections were over.[126] It was obvious to everyone that violence would eventually erupt, especially when there was no compromising, or middle ground to be had.

The situation was not in any way calmed when Franklin Pierce, a weak president who did the southerners' bidding, appointed

---

126 Nicole Etcheson, *Bleeding Kansas: Contested Liberty in the Civil War Era*

territorial governors who were extremely sympathetic to slavery's cause. As a result, many of the early elections tilted to the pro-slavery men's favor, often because of massive fraud and intimidation.[127]

So much fraud occurred during the first legislature election that the pro-slavery wing received 37 of the 39 available seats, an unthinkable number especially considering that Kansas prior had no slaves, hence little baseline to vote this way.[128] The territorial governor disputed the seats of eleven to be incensed with fraud, thus a new election for these eleven seats was scheduled. When the returns came in a drastic shift had occurred, eight of the eleven went to free soil candidates, thus putting direct evidence that perhaps many more seats were fraudulent as well.[129]

Unhappy with the obvious fraud that had hampered Kansas state elections the free soilers convened their own legislature while the original pro-slavery legislature was still in session, creating a unique scenario where the territory had two legislatures both claiming to be the official one, with deeply different partisan divides nationwide. Pierce, for his part, would not recognize the free soil legislature, calling it an insurrectionist bunch who are stirring up trouble.[130] That didn't matter to the free soilists, they crafted their own constitution, called the Topeka constitution, while the pro-slavery, fraudulent legislature set up its own constitution called the Lecompton constitution. Pierce was so hostile to the free-soil legislature that he even called in the military to upset the free-soilers, in a desperate attempt to appease the southerners, maybe to win favor for a re-election bid.

Unable to settle the dispute peacefully, the Congress set up a

---

127 Territorial Politics and Government". Territorial Kansas Online. Archived from the original on July 14, 2014. Retrieved June 18, 2014
128 Olson, Kevin (2012). *Frontier Manhattan*. University Press of Kansas
129 ibid
130 Richardson, James D. "A Compilation of the Messages and Papers of the Presidents". Project Gutenberg. Archived from the original on September 30, 2007

committee to determine which legislature was the official. The special committee reported that if the land hadn't been ransacked with out-of-staters trying to push their own political will on the state, then Kansas' original settlers would have chosen a free soil legislature. It also stated that the Lecompton legislature "was an illegally constituted body, and had no power to pass valid laws".[131] So there you have it, it's settled, the United States congress officially agreed that the Lecompton constitution was a fraud, quite literally, and the Topeka constitution is the actual will of the Kansas people. That settles that right? Wrong.

Even though the Congressional special committee had declared the Lecompton legislature, and with it the Lecompton constitution, fraudulent, that didn't guarantee that the whole Congress would agree with that special committee. Sure enough, the pro-slavery territorial governor of Kansas, who Franklin Pierce had appointed, declared the exact opposite, that the anti-slavery Topeka legislature was extralegal and invalid. The Congress went along with the governor and rejected the Topeka constitution, which forbade slavery.

Franklin Pierce's time ran out too soon for any final answer on the whole Kansas slavery question. The next president was almost a spitting image of ole handsome Frank, just without the curly hair and dashing looks. His name, James Buchanan. Just like Pierce, Buchanan was a northern democrat, who was personally opposed to slavery. He would sometimes even go to slave auctions just to buy slaves, preferably families, and then set them free in his native state of Pennsylvania. Seems like a pretty nice guy right? Well that depends who you ask. He actually had one of the most corrupt administrations in American history, though this for some reason is left out of most history books, and he also was a southerner at heart. Or, at least he pampered the southern slave interests just to

---

[131] ibid

gain political fame. Actually, most party conventions elected this type of politician, someone who was from one particular region while at the same time being tolerable in another region.

At the time of Buchanan's inauguration the Kansas question was in its full prime. In 1857, the Lecompton constitution was ready and on its way to the people of Kansas to vote on a slavery section of the constitution. At least the Lecompton legislature gave the people a choice of if they wanted any extension of slavery in the new constitutions. There was one caveat though. Regardless of how the good folks of Kansas voted, slavery would still be allowed in the territory for those who already owned slaves. You can bet this ticked off a lot of anti-slavery voices, who, either way, were stuck with the evils of slavery. And what would happen to those slaves already in the territory? Could they be sold to other masters? Could they be passed down from generation to generation? Think about if a patriarch would split his slaves to his numerous sons, would slavery grow and expand because of it? We don't really know the legal controversies that could have arisen due to this interesting section, however, but it does make for entertaining conversation. Nevertheless, because of the lose-lose situation for anti-slavery Jayhawkers, many of them boycotted the election to show their displeasure. The pro-slavery article and constitution as a whole passed by a margin of 6,226 to 569.[132] So there you have it. The pro-slavery wing bullied and cajoled the opposition through fraud and intimidation to get what they wanted, in the process subjecting who knows how many slaves to the damnation.

But it didn't end there. Of course, it would have if brave, strong, courageous individuals would have kept quiet and let this thing pass. But yet again some had courage. Some wouldn't let others force an

---

132 Cutler, William G. "Territorial History, Part 55

evil way of living down the throats of mankind. They forced the US Congress to allow another election, free from intimidation and fraud, on the Lecompton constitution. The numbers in the follow up election, the ACTUAL election are really staggering and paints a pretty clear sign on where the Kansans stood on the issue of slavery. They overwhelmingly voted 11,812 to 1,926 to strike down the Lecompton constitution and write one again, this time the right way without massive lying and cheating.[133]

Throughout all the political wrangling and back and forths, massive violence was taking place all throughout the territory of Kansas. It started slowly at the end of 1855 but began to pick up more steadily by the beginning of 1856. On May 21, 1856, a pro-slavery group ransacked the unabashedly free town of Lawrence destroying or looting virtually everything they laid eyes on from homes, printing presses, stores, and even hotels.[134] The sacking of Lawrence drew the ire of the now famous abolitionist, John Brown. With a gang of several men, including his four sons, Brown approached the Pottawatomie Valley, in the Kansas territory, with eyes to see to it that the pro-slavery "settlers" would get what was coming to them. The gang dragged five men, some of them boys, and viciously murdered them believing that they were slavery sympathizers.[135]

Brown, as it turns out, had quite a bit of a wild streak in him. The type of guy you wouldn't want to mess with, Brown had grown up in a family that detested slavery. Hearing strong denunciations from his father, beginning at a young age, on the institution of slavery persuaded Brown to follow in his father's footsteps with

---

133 ibid
134 History.com Editors. 2018. "Bleeding Kansas." HISTORY. A&E Television Networks. October 19, 2018. https://www.history.com/topics/19th-century/bleeding-kansas.
135 American Battlefield Trust. 2019. "John Brown." American Battlefield Trust. March 25, 2019. https://www.battlefields.org/learn/biographies/john-brown.

the gnawing sensation that slavery was a moral evil. Brown would claim that Almighty God had told him to destroy the institution of slavery, a belief that he sincerely took to heart.

It seems a little odd that he was never seriously tracked down after the murder of five men, however, he didn't just stop here, I mean after all he didn't free any slaves yet. The only thing as of now was to kill some guys that may have been slavery proponents, probably not what God had in mind for him. So, soon afterwards he mounted a trip to Missouri where he freed some eleven slaves and to top it all off massacred the owner.[136] And yet the murderous rage would continue. Not content to just free eleven slaves and thus far murder six white men, Brown continued to plot bigger and better things.

He began by traveling to New England, a region overflowing with anti-slavery sentiments and brimming with abolitionist fervor, a great place to start raising money for an upcoming anti-slavery crusade in the South. New Englanders were eager to help Brown, as by this time he was a major celebrity within the abolitionists circles. Even though Brown had gone on to kill some six people at this point, his message was simple and heartwarming to many, simply the eradication of slavery. In some cases it is quite obvious to say that Brown was a lunatic, however, he was a lunatic for the right reasons, someone who had a conviction to do what is right and honorable to mankind and God Himself. There's no way in John Brown's mind that he could have done less, if he didn't do what is right and defeat a long lasting country-wide sin he would never learn to live with himself. And so his final campaign was on.

At around the time of Brown's first raids, another important, and dramatic event unfolded, that fired up the abolitionists and the

---

[136] ibid

slave-drivers. That was the caning of the venerable Charles Sumner. In the words of the United States senate itself, "On May 22, 1856, the world's greatest deliberative body became a combat zone."[137] In one of the more remarkable stories that you'll ever hear, Charles Sumner, a well-respected senator from abolitionist stronghold, Massachusetts, was brutally beaten with a cane by fellow congressmen, representative Preston Brooks.

It all began three days earlier, actually, when Charles Sumner boldly spoke out about the question of whether Kansas will become a free state or a slave state in his speech called "Crime Against Kansas", believing, quite literally, that it was illegal and criminal to push slavery down the backs of a people wholly unwanting of it. In a gesture of finger pointing, Sumner placed the majority of the blame on two democratic senators that had a great deal to do with the Kansas and Nebraska Act, paving the way for vicious quarrels and bloodshed. Sumner named Stephan Douglas of Illinois, the author of the bill, so it makes sense, and Andrew Butler of South Carolina, an ardent advocate for slavery and also a co-author of the bill. Altogether, if you want to place blame on somebody who you think is responsible for a horrible law that's causing much trouble all around the country, it makes sense to start with the people who actually wrote the law in effect.

It didn't make a lot of sense to Preston Brooks, Andrew Butler's cousin, though. To be fair, Sumner said some pretty nasty things. Today if these remarks were made in the US senate, he might actually be removed from the senate, or at the least censored. Sumner called Douglas, among other things, a "noise-some, squat, and nameless

---

137 United States Senate. n.d. "U.S. Senate: The Caning of Senator Charles Sumner." Www.senate.gov. United States Senate. Sumner." Www.senate.gov. United States Senate. https://www.senate.gov/artandhistory/history/minute/The_Caning_of_Senator_Charles_Sumner.ht

animal . . . not a proper model for an American senator."[138] He actually treated Andrew Butler much better, only resorting to making fun of his lover, "a mistress . . . who, though ugly to others, is always lovely to him; though polluted in the sight of the world, is chaste in his sight—I mean, the harlot, Slavery."[139] He didn't mean an actual lover, of course it was a figure of speech, but it still hurt.

In the good ole' days when two gentlemen were peeved at each other, they would most likely conduct a duel, where rules could vary, but mostly follow the lines of men distanced about 20-30 paces from one another and shooting to either maim or kill his opponent. Two of our most well known men of history, Alexander Hamilton and Andrew Jackson had a very different past with dueling. Hamilton threatened duels often but only took part in one, which killed him in Weehaken New Jersey, while Jackson took part in many, one in which a bullet was permanently lodged in his chest, inches away from his heart.

Preston Brooks was no gentleman, however. Instead of honorably notifying Sumner of a proposed duel, he decided to surprise us all, and Sumner most of all in a vicious kind of suckerpunch. Quietly moving through the senate chamber he finally found Sumner working at his desk. From behind he lifted his heavy metal cane, of all things, and crashed a blow upon Sumner's head. Brooks proceeded to hit Sumner over and over and over again while Sumner did his best to protect himself from the blows. The force of the attack struck Sumner so unexpectedly that after the first blow he lost his sight and struggled to remain conscious throughout the ordeal.[140] Sumner managed to escape from his desk and made a mad dash for

---

138 ibid
139 ibid
140 Green, Michael S. (2010). *Politics and America in Crisis: The Coming of the Civil War*. Santa Barbara, California: ABC-CLIO. p. 94.

the senate door. No one was available to help Sumner because the senate's day was over with most senators gone and heading home. While Sumner was running blindly, due to the blood skewing his vision, Brooks chased him the entire way, still beating Sumner as he tried to escape. Sumner eventually fell, losing consciousness, while Brooks still attacked, showing no mercy, even with a broken cane now.

The attack must've been pre-meditated, as Brooks was helped by a couple of his pro-slavery cronies, who's job it was to make sure that Brooks finished the job. These men were Laurence Keitt, a representative from South Carolina, slavery capital of the US, and Henry A. Edmundson, representative from Virginia. Together, they worked hard to keep onlookers away, who were now beginning to notice the chaos. Keitt was reported as saying, "Let them be! and Let them alone, God damn you, let them alone", as Keitt begged the onlookers to let the two men sort it out themselves.[141]

Representatives Ambrose S. Murray and Edwin B. Morgan, both from New York, finally got past Keitt and Edmundson to intervene and save Sumner's life. It's a sad piece of truth when you look closer at the details. The men that tried to save Sumner's life were New Yorkers, northern men who detested slavery and, in the process, the only ones humane enough to save a life. The men, like Brooks, who actually did the beating, or were trying to prevent any interference in the likely death were all southerners, those who were in love with slavery, defending it at all costs, even if that meant killing a United States senator. To make matters worse, this was the sentiment throughout the country.

Brooks immediately became a hero in the South, with many

---

141 Green, Michael S. (2010). *Politics and America in Crisis: The Coming of the Civil War*. Santa Barbara, CA: ABC-CLIO. p. 99

southern congressmen and senators embracing Brooks, congratulating him on a job well done. The pro-slavery newpaper *The Richmond Enquirer*, had quite a bit to say about the whole matter. It editorialized that Sumner should be caned more often, like every day, and denounced Sumner and his friends, "these vulgar abolitionists in the Senate" who "have been suffered to run too long without collars. They must be lashed into submission." Southern slavery sympathizers were so giddy and proud of Brooks that thousands of them even made a joke about it by sending Brooks more canes.[142] Could you imagine if that happened today? It would be unspeakable. Certainly, I would hope no one in Congress would ever condone such acts today, though I can't be sure. So many Americans are ready to hurl insults and hate our politicians when at the end of the day they don't realize there is a person beneath the politician. Somebody with a family and kids. Somebody who loves and gives to charities and belongs to a church and loves to be with friends.

As you might imagine, northerners were irate. "The South cannot tolerate free speech anywhere, and would stifle it in Washington with the bludgeon and the bowie-knife, as they are now trying to stifle it in Kansas by massacre, rapine, and murder", was the editorial of the *Cincinnati Gazette*.[143] "Are we to be chastised", harked William Cullen Bryant, "as they chastise their slaves? Are we too, slaves, slaves for life, a target for their brutal blows, when we do not comport ourselves to please them."[144] Sumner's speech was reprinted and distributed more than a million copies.

It's a bit ironic, Brooks who apparently thought himself a man

---

142 "The Caning Affair". *The Charlotte Democrat*. Charlotte, North Carolina. June 3, 1856
143 McPherson, James M. (2003). *Battle Cry of Freedom: The Civil War Era*. Oxford University Press. p. 150
144 Gienapp, William E. (1988). *The Origins of the Republican Party, 1852–1856*. Oxford University Press. p. 359

to beat a senator, who had no means of self defense, with the sole intent on killing him, showed how cowardly he really was in the aftermath of the beating. Once more northerners heard about the news more and more northern congressmen began berating Brooks. Brooks even challenged Anson Burlingame to a duel where they agreed to travel to Canada to be immune from anti-dueling laws in the States. Once Brooks heard of this he chickened out fearing for his safety by having to travel northward, to what might be a hostile crowd.[145] In other words, Brooks was perfectly happy boasting about his so called bravery taking on an abolitionist senator, and even accepting thousands of canes as gifts, loving his newfound popularity in his comfort zone of the South, but when push came to shove he was bitterly afraid to travel to what may be enemy territory that he totally made a fool of himself.

This wasn't the only duel that was contemplated in the cane beating followup. Another senator, Henry Wilson, future Vice President of the United States, called Brooks' attack "brutal, murderous, and cowardly," a slander that got Brooks' attention enough to challenge Wilson to a duel.[146] Wilson wisely declined by not giving Brooks any more attention, though Brooks still threatened to harm him or other abolitionist sympathizers within congress.

Many southerners mocked Sumner and laughed off his injuries. It was an unfortunate event which made the South look like bullies and unsympathetic to basic human decency. The caning of Sumner caused lifelong brain injuries, with some historians and experts calling it what we now consider as a traumatic brain injury, where it would take him three years to recover before returning to the senate.

As for Brooks, he was never imprisoned for the vicious attack on

---

145 Hollister, Ovando James (1886). *Life of Schuyler Colfax*. New York: Funk & Wagnalls. p. 98 – via Archive.org
146 *The National Cyclopaedia of American Biography*. Vol. IV. New York: James T. White & Company. 1895. p. 14

Sumner's life, and soon afterwards returned to the House to continue with business. When the House brought up a motion to expel Brooks from the chamber, it failed, though Brooks would later resign his seat after the public embarrassment. That embarrassment didn't last long, however, as he was overwhelmingly re-elected to the same House seat he had just given up. Clearly, his southern constitutions were quite happy with his performance, and maybe even wanting to see more vicious attacks against abolitionists.

This is where the story picks back up to John Brown, who was increasingly agitated by the southerners' contempt for those that disagreed with them about their peculiar institution. It was the abhorrent Kansas and Nebraksa Act, followed by swarms of pro-slavery settlers moving into Kansas, made worse by the caning of Senator Sumner, who was a major ally to the abolitionists, that prompted John Brown to act. Brown at this point had made some minor raids, which included the deaths of a few pro-slavery southerners, but up to this point he hadn't made a major dent in the slavocracy's armor. That would change very suddenly, however, with Brown's plan to attack Harpers Ferry.

According to his wife, Brown had been waiting for this opportunity for twenty years, and now it finally came. In 1859, John Brown, under the alias generic name of Isaac Smith, stayed at a farmhouse just North of Harpers Ferry, where he and a gang of twenty-one others, whom he had personally trained, planned a capture of the federal arsenal.[147] Part of his innovative plan was to free local slaves, whom he encountered in the area, and supply them with weapons, anything from rifles to pikes. The assumption

---

147 American Battlefield Trust. 2019. "John Brown." American Battlefield Trust. March 25, 2019. https://www.battlefields.org/learn/biographies/john-brown.

was that as the movement picked up more and more steam, slaves would be more likely to join the cause and free more slaves, thereby the raid would have a kind of snowball effect, which Brown had hoped would lead to a great insurrection, the likes of which might totally eradicate slavery.

The plan, though, didn't go as planned. The importance that Brown placed on local slaves to join the riot proved to be a serious miscalculation as few, if any, local slaves actually joined his rebellion. The rebellion did have significant force behind it though, as the local militia groups as well as the US army were called out to put an end to the threat. Brown did eventually seize the arsenal, but by then it was too late. A gathering of forces were heading his way, bent on putting down the rebellion, however moral its causes.

Fighting commenced for three days until finally Robert E Lee, the future Confederate general, was able to subdue Brown and his men. All told, seventeen men died in the epic battle, while Brown was indicted for treason and sentenced to hang.[148] Upon hearing his sentence Brown was reported to have said, "if it is deemed necessary that I should forfeit my life for the furtherance of the ends of justice, and mingle my blood further with the blood of my children and with the blood of millions in this slave country whose rights are disregarded by wicked, cruel, and unjust enactments--I submit; so let it be done!"[149] And so, even though Brown's truly heroic and brave act would end with his own demise, Brown was so bent on doing the right thing that he was willing to sacrifice it all to the good cause of ending slavery. After Brown's death, the poet Henry David Thoreau wrote, "I heard, to be sure, that he had been hanged, but I did not know what that meant—and not after any number of days shall I

---

148 The Editors of Encyclopaedia Britannica. 2019. "Harpers Ferry Raid | Definition, Date, History, & Facts | Britannica." In *Encyclopædia Britannica*. https://www.britannica.com/event/Harpers-Ferry-Raid.
149 ibid

believe it. Of all the men who are said to be my contemporaries, it seems to me that John Brown is the only one who has not died."[150] By this, the legendary writer hinted that John Brown will never die, he would go on in eternity as well as his movement.

Much has been said of Brown, and to this day he still remains a kind of controversial figure in America, but to many he is the epitome of a hero, someone who at the time was accused of being a criminal, with an extraordinary bounty on his head. (president Buchanan offered a $250 reward for Brown, a bounty of almost $10,000 today). Even Abraham Lincoln, the great emancipator had some misgivings about Brown and wasn't afraid to show it. "John Brown was no Republican," said Lincoln, the party's leader. He was a deluded madman who convinced himself that he was "commissioned by Heaven" to liberate the enslaved.[151]

How is it that so many people hated John Brown then, said some very ugly things and wanted to distance themselves from him, while now people embrace John Brown as the good terrorist and think of him as being a great American? Just like today, when people with moral opinions, though at the time may be deemed radical, are called "radical," "lunatic," and "madman," by those who are afraid of losing their preeminence and stature politically and socially. Lincoln may well have thought Brown to be a madman personally, but he no doubt was eager politically to distance himself from Brown, because he himself was being charged as a radical abolitionist by his political opponents who were trying to slander Lincoln any way they could.

---

150 ibid
151 Seagrave, Adam. n.d. "John Brown Was a Violent Crusader, but He Blazed a Moral Path That the Cautious Lincoln Followed to End Slavery." The Conversation. https://theconversation.com/john-brown-was-a-violent-crusader-but-he-blazed-a-moral-path-that-the-cautious-lincoln-followed-to-end-slavery-151805.

Another piece of irony is that today John Brown is hailed as a hero, while those of the age called him a "deluded madman."

While this violence was ongoing, the political world in Kansas was still spinning. In 1859, the state legislature proposed yet another constitution, again with a free state vision, called the Wyandotte constitution, which passed a referendum by a vote of 10,421 to 5,530.[152] This final constitution was pending before the Congress for years, however, the senate, which still had at least an even number of Slave state senators as free state ones, refused to recognize the new constitution, although the people of Kansas, through the newly found idea of popular sovereignty, had now twice voted to keep slavery outside its borders. The very idea that the southerners had loved and praised, popular sovereignty, was now being derided as being "fake" and not what the people wanted.

Skirmishes both big and small took place all throughout the Kansas territory, where many attacks were made at the border by pro-slavery and free state ruffians. When it was all said and done, approximately fifty-five individuals died during bleeding Kansas, no small number, that could have been avoided without the disastrous Kansas-Nebraska Act, permitting popular sovereignty.[153] It is just as sad when we think about the actual intentions of the people. In both Kansas and Nebraska genuine anti-slavery views prevailed. These were a people who were thoroughly disgusted with the institution. Anyone who had even the slightest idea of the region and the people would have come to this conclusion. But yet again, just

---

152 "***Wyandotte Constitution* Approved**". Archived from the original on November 5, 2014. Retrieved November 5, 2014.
153 "Bleeding Kansas." n.d. Www.pbs.org. https://www.pbs.org/wgbh/aia/part4/4p2952.html#:~:text=In%20September%20of%201856%2C%20

like today, politicians often think they know best, that they are all powerful and almighty, just as Douglas thought of himself when he introduced the act.

Little thought of, certainly without the scope of what we learn in our history books, is the detrimental effect that this act had on Native American tribes. Throughout this period Native American tribes have been pushed time and time again further and further West, often settling somewhere for years or even deceased to be roughed up again and driven out of their territory. The same effect happened in Kansas and Nebraska regions. The act made it much more likely that squatters, white settlers who would live and even work on land that wasn't their own, would move into Native territory. The devastating effects of diseases that the white settlers would bring in with them, like smallpox, measles, and cholera, the likes of which Natives had never experienced, led many Native people to drink excessive amounts of alcohol, even becoming a leading reason for death for many tribes.[154] To this day Native peoples still struggle with what's termed as intergenerational trauma due to many factors, most prominently white settlers taking over their land, assimilating them into American white culture, and trampling on Native treaty rights.

James Buchanan was undaunted with the new Wyandotte constitution, for he fundamentally supported the Lecompton constitution and was eager to get the mess behind him, even though the Lecompton constitution was rejected by Congress. Congress allowed the measure to go back to the state, where the voters again overwhelmingly defeated it. It's worth noting that Buchanan was

---

154 "History Collection - Collection - UWDC - UW-Madison Libraries." n.d. Search. library.wisc.edu. https://search.library.wisc.edu/digital/AHistory.

recommending the admission of Kansas as a slave state to the union. What would have happened if Kansas was a slave state? Since most of the people of Kansas were thoroughly opposed to slavery, only a few wealthy elitists would have had slaves, and they would have large slave farmsteads, consisting of hundreds of slaves each. What would this look like in terms of congressional actions? It's fair to assume that Kansas congressmen would be antt-slavery even though the state would be a slave state, a situation the country never experienced before, we can also assume that Kansas would be loyal to the union during the civil war, just like fellow slave states Missouri, Kentucky, and Maryland.

Kansas was eventually admitted to the union in 1861, roughly five years after bleeding Kansas and the turmoil that followed. Kansas would never have been admitted had it not been for the election of anti-slavery president Abraham Lincoln, which cascaded to the secession of eleven states. Had it not been for the secession of these states from the union, Kansas admittance might not have been a reality for years to come. Southern senators would never consent to another free state, therefore it wasn't until they were officially out of the union that Congress could admit Kansas as a free state, with mostly free state senators present.

The formation of the republican party was initiated based upon these events. First, starting with the Fugitive Slave Act; which united abolitionists throughout the country, the Kansas-Nebraska Act; where even anti-Nebraska democrats joined the republican cause, the caning of senator Sumner, and the John Brown Harpers Ferry raid; where Brown became a martyr for angry abolitionists' desire to finally see the land that Jefferson had long ago written about. A land where all men are created equal with certain inalienable rights, among them life, liberty, and the pursuit of happiness, that for so long had been denied to those enslaved and even those free blacks who found themselves unfairly targeted by various state black codes.

It's historically ironic that the southern slavocrats had thoroughly done the most damage to themselves. Had the southerners just kept to themselves, had not freaked out over the course of new territories, and had not overreacted to the threat posed by abolitionists, they would have been able to keep the slaves where they already had them. It is quite true that the fear of abolitionists was so strong that southern politicians overstepped, through immense pressure from their wealthy constituents, in rhetoric and congressional action. One of the big fears was the threat of an abolitionist insurrection, something to the likes of John Brown and his gang. Southerners greatest fear was an insurrection so big it would totally destroy their way of life and their hold of slavery. Part of this fear was based on the slave rebellion in Haiti, which fundamentally shook the inner core of slave circles. If it could happen there it could happen anywhere, even here, especially with anti-slavery activists running everywhere.

Ever since the Haitian uprisings, then called Saint-Domingue, in which slaves banded together to defeat the French regime, which controlled it, much like how the British controlled the colonies that became the United States. One of the reasons which led to the Saint-Domingue uprising was the treatment of slaves. Notorious for their poor treatment in Saint Domingue, slaves were often beaten to submission, much like the case in the States, just without the subtropical diseases that Haitian slaves had to contend with as well. Indeed, some "rebellious" or "lazy" slaves were threatened to be deported to the Caribbean Islands or Haiti, where death by disease or poor treatment was much more likely. Obviously, this in itself was a reason why any slave would want to rebel. However, soon the situation got much much worse. When a mulatto man named Vincent Oge furiously petitioned the National Assembly to allow local representation and assemblies with a special interest of letting all free people of the colony be a part of the local government all hell broke loose. Sadly for Oge, the petition was never fully enforced, despite the French giving it lip-service.[155]

This didn't sit well with Oge, who even wrote a letter to the legislature that if the petitions were to remain unenforced he would have to take up arms and defend basic human rights. Nobody in the assembly seemed to care enough even to respond to Oge's radicalism, nobody but the governor of the colony who instructed Oge and Jean-Baptiste Chavanne, another activist, to quit the dangerous rhetoric and activism on behalf of free persons of color. Oge, Chavanne, and other followers, refused to be subdued by higher authorities whose main objective was the status quo of suppression and tyranny. They were eventually caught in 1790 and executed in 1791, by the gruesome means of the wheel. Death by the wheel is one of the worst ways to die, without a doubt. In most instances the poor fellow is strapped to the spokes of a large wheel, while the executioner slowly breaks the legs of the accused and moves further up until it reaches the chest or head, where normally the victim dies, if not then the victim is left for scavengers and birds to eat until the accused finally perishes. All told pretty gruesome stuff, it's a good thing they outlawed this in most countries by the mid 1800s.

Oge's execution caused a frenzy all throughout the colony of Saint-Domingue. His brutal death awakened both free persons of

---

155 Tsakanias, Caroline. 2018. "Vincent Ogé (Ca. 1755-1791)." Blackpast. January 28, 2018. https://www.blackpast.org/global-african-history/oge-vincent-1755-1791/.

color and slaves of the brutality and oppression they were without end exposed to by the white leaders, and was one of the major events that led to the slave uprisings.[156] In 1791 the French national assembly granted extremely wealthy colored freemen the right to vote, however, the European whites living on the island didn't think it was a good law, so they ignored it, which really grew the flames. Thousands of slaves would revolt and join a now heated rebellion with rival factions springing up, further complicating the mess that Saint-Domingue was increasingly becoming. Under the leadership of Toussaint Louverture, followed by Jean-Jacques Dessalines and Henry Christophe, Haiti had now become an independent country, defeating the French, who tried desperately to hold on until Napoleon, the French dictator couldn't hold it any longer, mainly due to escalating conflicts with other European countries, primarily England. As well as enjoying the right to freedom and independence, the Haitians also became the first country that practiced slavery to permanently ban slavery in 1793, a prospect that totally freaked out the slavocracy in the deep South.[157] Many paranoid congressmen openly disavowed the rebellion, even Thomas Jefferson, who seemed at time to be hot and cold over slavery and the status of blacks, refused to send ministers to Haiti because the government was overwhelmingly black, he didn't want to have prominent white Americans disgrace themselves by negotiating with blacks, something at the time that was unthinkable.

It is easy to see what led to the Haitian uprising and independence movement based upon what we know. It is clear, and had been clear,

---

156 ibid

157 Gaffield, Julia. 2020. "Perspective | Haiti Was the First Nation to Permanently Ban Slavery." *Washington Post*, July 12, 2020. https://www.washingtonpost.com/outlook/2020/07/12/haiti-was-first-nation-permanently-ban-slavery/.

that the colony of Saint-Domingue was notorious for how it treated both their slaves and even free blacks, who they consistently treated as second rate citizens through and through. The barbarism and punishments that predominated in Saint-Domingue were gruesome and disturbing, hence the reason why so many masters in America threatened to boot their own slaves for misbehavior. It is little doubt that these conditions, added on top of the despicable and horrifying death of Vincent Oge, an activist just trying to bring equal rights to all members of God's given earth, lead to the dismay and dissatisfaction among those who were used to being oppressed that led to the rebellion. But oddly enough, southern slave masters were still fooling themselves with rose colored glasses, believing that slavery wasn't the cause of the rebellion, instead, they said, it was all the anti-slavery sentiment spread about by the abolitionists. They also used it to degrade and further explain why slavery was a necessity as for all blacks "violence was an inherent part (their) character."[158]

With increasinging vehemence the southerners were bringing the institution of slavery to a crashing halt by their own prejudiced views and hysteria. For one, right always beats might. It is inevitable for moral supremacy to overcome steep obstacles and rise victorious, as we will see more instances of with the continuance of this book. Slavery was certainly on that list. A moral wrong from the very beginning, America's system of slavery was bound to break loose from the chains, after all, Washington had predicted it, Jefferson had predicted it, Madison had predicted it, and most other enlightenment thinkers of our founding genuinely believed slavery was a temporary necessity, just here long enough for the beginning nation to get its legs strengthened and compete with other

---

158 Matthewson, *Jefferson and the Nonrecognition of Haïti*, p. 37

European economies. But the longer slavery persisted, the harder it was increasingly becoming to get rid of it. It spread throughout the new territories, it raised fear among the hearts of northerners, who now were concerned over a slave conspiracy that would dominate politics and social life in America. Indeed, even a purchase, or a military annexation, of Cuba was contemplated for quite some time prior to the civil war, just to fizz out of energy due to the concern of abolitionists that Cuba would just be another slavocracy satellite, a realization that was altogether true as many southerners actively pushed for another slave territory.

It is ultimately true that southerners were beginning to get crazy over protecting their true love of slavery. It became an obsession. An obsession that made masters look utterly foolish, looking for others to blame and chastise. Of course, ever since the foundation of the Constitution, many slave states were beginning to fear the authority of the central government. The Constitution allowed for the slave trade to be abolished in the year 1808, which drew criticism from northerners and southerners alike, but ultimately left open the question of if Congress can abolish the slave trade can they abolish slavery outright? Can the national or federal government interfere with state's rights? And these questions haunted the slave masters until the time of secession. Also, of significance, directly after, indeed in some cases before, the ratification of the Constitution, many northern states began to abolish slavery outright or provide for gradual emancipation. In this event, the slave states began to feel as if it were us against them and fought to expand slavery into the new territories, so that they wouldn't be outnumbered by free states, who might be willing to use the federal government to deprive them of their property. For the next fifty or so years, Congress had to meticulously admit a free state simultaneously with a slave state so as not to upset that balance.

I must admit, at the time, this fear of the southern slave owners might have been understanding, however, what we know now is that if they would have just acted normal, not pushed for slavery to expand like a bad rash, and had not blamed abolitionists for everything that went wrong, they would've held on to slavery a lot longer than they actually did. The slavocracy's obsession with expanding slavery, especially in territories or areas that didn't want it, caused a massive build-up of abolitionists activities, writing power, and membership. Had the slave interests not have pushed for slavery to be admitted to Kansas and Nebraska, and the repeal of the Missouri Compromise, that would have limited slavery to some extent, abolitionist agitation would have been much less intense. If slave interests would have not treated their slaves so cruelly the abolitionists could never use that argument to free slaves, an argument that they were able to make after the publication of Harriet Beecher Stowe's *Uncle Tom's Cabin*, which depicted the evils of slavery on an easily empathetic family. Of course, then-newly released photographs of slaves with gnarly marks on their backs and what looks like mideval torture devices around their heads didn't help masters' cases.

Even driving matters much worse were southerners' insistence that they were right and the northern abolitionists were wrong, apparently following the philosophy of always finding a scapegoat. For instance, whenever a massive plot was unearthed about a slave insurrection, it was commonplace for slave masters to place the blame on northern agitators, who somehow got through to the shackled "property." It never once occurred to the masters that there was a reason why they would plan an insurrection, or even simply to leave the plantation and flee northward. Perhaps it was because the masters treated them pitifully, with discord and discontent. Maybe the wretched souls were tired of the threat of beatings if they didn't haul in enough cotton from day to day or month to month. Maybe they were constantly afraid that their husbands or wives, daughters of sons, or fathers and mothers would be sold off some hundred miles away never to hear or speak to them ever again. Maybe their bodies were broken and scarred from all the days laboring under the hot son with only a few hours to rest every day before they had to submit their bodies to that cruel torture one more time and one more day. Or, even more obviously, maybe they just wanted what they heard so often about coming from the mouths of supposed patriots, that idea of liberty that all men are entitled to.

Of course, southerners couldn't believe that. They hardly thought that their slaves could think for themselves at all. Somebody had to put them up to this. Somebody, a northerner, a radical abolitionist had to lay the groundwork and cause a frenzy among the slaves. They thought, genuinely, slaves were too dumb to flee their plantation and their way of life, they had it too good. They were clothed and fed, at least that's what they would call it when they were given the scraps and wore clothing that was torn to shreds, showing almost every body part. Masters blamed abolitionists for circulating anti-slavery propaganda and distributing hate of the institution through the mail. How dare the abolitionists speak of liberty to the blacks, liberty was only a white word and for a white citizenry, not in the vocabulary of the blacks.

As we have seen with the insurrection in Saint-Domingue, the rebellion of Nat Turner, and even Bleeding Kansas, the slave interests always referred right away to black sympathizers for stirring up trouble. This kind of finger pointing turned back on themselves by making the northern free states increasingly embittered with the tactics of the southern states, which eventually morphed into a new rising party with deep appeal.

This new party grew its roots dating back to earlier parties that didn't have a whole lot of nationwide appeal. Beginning with the Liberty party, which was the first abolitionist political party created within the United States in 1839. Different from the American Anti-Slavery Society, which believed that the Constitution was a thoroughly slave-loving document and advocated for working outside the system of government to achieve its ends, the Liberty party believed that the Constitution was an anti-slavery document and worked to discredit slavery by working within its systems. It even included this statement, "*Resolved*, That the Liberty Party ... will demand the absolute and unqualified divorce of the general [*i.e.*, federal] government from slavery, and also the restoration of equality of rights among men, in every State where the party exists, or may exist", long before the sectional divides would grow even worse, in its party's official platform.[159] As you might have guessed this party was a little ahead of its time and didn't gather a whole lot of momentum at any point in its existence. Even though the Liberty party was abolitionist in its nature, it very well knew it couldn't affect slavery where it was, therefore it set out to draw a movement to slow the expansion of slavery where it didn't already stand. So this new party didn't really affect the slave interests who were bent on protecting their own slaves. Nonetheless, the Liberty party never accumulated any more than 2.5% of the vote in any presidential election, making the party effectively null and void.

---

159 *The National Conventions and Platforms of All Political Parties 1789-1905* by Thomas Hudson McKee

Even though the Liberty party was a dead flop it did influence the rise of another political party with a little more influence and stature, though not by much. This was the rise of the Free-Soil party. The Free-Soil party began immediately after the Mexican-American war, with the threat of a huge portion of new territory up for grabs and no clear plan as to what to do with it or if they should be slave or free. Many northern politicians, Whigs as well as Democrats, wanted the new territory to remain out of the hands of the slave-drivers. This event prompted the Wilmot Proviso, named after Pennsylvania representative David Wilmot, which stated "that, as an express and fundamental condition to the acquisition of any territory from the Republic of Mexico…neither slavery nor involuntary servitude shall ever exist in any part of said territory, except for crime, whereof the party shall first be duly convicted."[160] The Wilmot Proviso passed in the House twice, although strictly on party lines, before dying a slow and painful death in the senate, where getting enough support among southern senators, who had an equal vote total as the northerners, became impossible.

Nonetheless, the Wilmot Proviso and the growing agitation among northerners at the South's growing insistence of expanding slavery created the momentum of the Free Soil Party to gain strength. Former president Martin Van Buren, who ran for the 1844 democratic nomination for president was the Free Soil Party's standard bearer, mostly because northern democrats were incensed at the nomination of James Polk, a southern pro-expansionist candidate, in the 1844 convention. It is without a doubt that had Van Buren been the nominee in 1844 for the democrats, the Mexican-American

---

160 "The Wilmot Proviso." 2019. American Battlefield Trust. January 15, 2019. https://www.battlefields.org/learn/articles/wilmot-proviso#:~:text=neither%20slavery%20nor%20involuntary%20servitude.

war would not have been fought (Henry Clay, the Whig nominee, had spoken against expansionism as well.)

Because northern democrats felt abandoned by their party, and with growing sectionalism between the North and the South over slavery, many northerners felt inclined to support the Free Soil Party. To make things better the Free-Soilers also nominated Charles Francis Adams, grandson of the venerable John Adams and son of able John Quincy Adams, both former presidents, as the vice-presidential nominee. With an impressive party ticket and notable politicians following suit, the Free Soilers looked like they had a chance, at least a chance to play spoiler. Both of the two major parties, the Whigs and the Democrats, stood for the status quo in regard to slavery, almost like no one wanted to talk about it, though the Democrats consistently pushed for expansionist policies, which could be related to the expansion of slavery in the South.

Besides the party's standard bearers of Van Buren and Adams, top leaders also included, John Hale, who ran for president numerous times on the Liberty party ticket, Salmon Chase, who would later become Lincoln's treasury secretary and chief justice of the Supreme Court, and Charles Sumner, who later would become viciously caned on the Senate floor. The party gained former northern Whigs and democrats, as well as the former Liberty party voters, to form a pretty nice size voting electorate. The party called for an immediate abolition of slavery within federally owned territories and districts, while its motto "Free Soil, Free Speech, Free Labor, and Free Men," became an emblem of what many believed America was supposed to be.[161]

When it was all said and done the Whigs won the election, electing slave-owner Zachary Taylor president, further extending

---

161 Wilentz, Sean (2005). *The Rise of American Democracy: Jefferson to Lincoln*. W. W. Norton & Company

the lineage of presidents who owned slaves, becoming the tenth of twelve presidents to enslave others. The Free Soliers, however, garnered ten percent of the vote, a healthy amount for a third party ticket, in fact, the most ever up to that point by a third party. What's even more impressive is the Free Soilers managed to receive ten percent of the vote without any backing among the southern states. Van Buren received no votes South of the Maryland border. It is often said that Van Buren caused New York to shift towards Taylor taking votes away from democratic candidate Lewis Cass. This, however, is purely conjecture and most likely not the case, in any event many voters who voted for Van Buren would not have supported Cass as the alternative, especially when the democratic party nationally was doing more to protect slavery and housing dangerous heretics like John C Calhoun, who repeatedly left open the door of secession for trivial subjects, like a tariff, not to mention more important ones like the slave issue.

The Free Soil Party ran again in the 1852 presidential election, though receiving only half of what they were able to achieve in 1848, that is mostly because the slave issue was thought to have been settled. All of this changed when Stephan Douglas threw away the Missouri Compromise with the Kansas-Nebraska Act. No other act in history did more to thoroughly unwind a whole section of people and lead more to the establishment of a political party than the Kansas-Nebraska Act.

The Republican party political make-up of the 1850s and 60s formed a somewhat tight culmination of free soilers, northern democrats opposed to slavery, and, for the most part, the entire Northern section of ex-Whigs, a party that consistently declined in political power, mostly due to sectional rifts regarding slavery. The

Republican party grew exponentially and very quickly to become the leading opposition party to the still strong Democratic party. The Republican party thoroughly denounced slavery, though one important caveat remained, even though they opposed the institution and spoke of it as a great evil they genuinely believed they didn't have the constitutional power to eradicate it in places and states where it already existed. Remember the latter part because it is significant.

The first party meeting was held in Ripon, Wisconsin, on March 20, 1854, largely due to Wisconsin's impressive track record opposing slavery, helping runaway slaves find refuges, and defying unconstitutional and inhumane laws such as the Fugitive Slave Act of 1850. The name was given to pay due respects to the late great statesman Thomas Jefferson, who helped found the first republican party against the federalist.[162] Perhaps the 1850s republicans forgot that Jefferson himself was one of the largest slaveholders in the country and that many in his party, especially in the South, supported republican causes because they wanted to protect slavery from the nationalistic ideologies of the Federalist party. It is of great irony that a political party whose main goal was to excoriate slavery chose its name from an originally pro-slavery political party, even more so when we consider that the democratic party at the time proudly supported the policies of Thomas Jefferson rather than the newly minted republican party.

Nonetheless, the Republican party conducted its first official convention on July 6th, 1854 in Jackson, Michigan, no doubt trying to gather support and momentum to run a presidential contest, a feat they were able to succeed upon when they met to nominate a republican presidential candidate during the republican national

---

162 History of the GOP". GOP. Archived from the original on January 29, 2018. Retrieved May 9, 2017.

convention of 1856. The convention chose John C Fremont, former explorer, military officer, and senator of California to be its crowning jewel. When the 1856 presidential election came they lost handily, only taking the northern region of the United States, while losing every state below Ohio. Though the republicans fully got their butts kicked in this election, it did prove to be a menacing force in future elections, considering they gathered all this momentum in just two years and if they had taken just two more modestly popular states they would have carried the election. Never before was the political maps any more sectional than what they were now. The ground work had been thoroughly set for northern and southern divisions. Indeed, the southern states had been lambasting political opponents as abolitionists every time they wanted to stir up their political base, as a form of derogatory, politically harmful rhetoric. Now, however, the North had fully accepted abolitionism, and voting for abolitionist candidates under an abolitionist party.

Some historians will say that the republican party never stood for abolition, this, however, is a narrow minded approach. Though the party did allow slavery to stand in its original states, it did want to abolish slavery in federally owned properties, as well as take it out of the running in regard to future expansion.

The stage was set for the upcoming 1860 presidential election that would fundamentally change the United States forever. With the growing threat of the northern republican party, southerners began to lash out. They often referred to the republican party as the "black party", and "radical party." Many believed that if the republicans received nationwide success then the white man's way of life would be altered forever with blacks trying to receive equality with the whites. Stephan Douglas and Abraham Lincoln underwent a series of debates, that are now the most well known debates of all time, where Douglas, a democrat, railed against the republicans and their supposed equality "If you desire negro citizenship," Douglas said at the first debate, "then support Mr. Lincoln and the Black Republican Party." Such was the routine rhetoric used to scare the average white male voter into submitting to the will of the democratic party that was now becoming the party of white men. These types of scare tactics are used all the time to get the voters to vote for a certain cause and to label opponents as radicals and dangerous men. Pay attention, these tactics are used every election cycle, mostly by politicians and political groups who are hell-bent on retaining the status quo. This prompted Lincoln to make a statement, that was purely politically motivated by responding "The "white and black races" will never live "together on terms of social and political equality…and I as much as any other man am in favor of having the superior positions assigned to the white race," hardly what the terrified southern slave-owners were trying to get across to their voters.[163]

The senate debates and consequent election was one of the most highly viewed elections around the country. Abraham Lincoln won the popular vote in the Illinois senate race, but this didn't mean a whole lot because the seventeenth amendment wasn't in effect yet, so the Illinois legislature chose between Lincoln and Douglas. Because the legislature was democratic controlled Douglas was selected and Lincoln lost, in reply Lincoln gave one of his most iconic quotes of all time, "Somewhat like that boy in Kentucky, who stubbed his toe while running to see his sweetheart. The boy said he was too big to cry, and far too badly hurt to laugh," yet all the attention that Lincoln received propelled him to the national spotlight, where soon he would take the country by storm.

Among the other candidates seeking the republican nomination

---

163 ibid

for president in 1860 were anti-slavery hardliners, chief among them William Seward, former governor of New York, who gave a speech in the senate excoriating slavery and and bringing the wrath of the southern states. If Seward were nominated, at the beginning he was highly favored, it would have been interesting to see what other states would have left the union, or if states would have left the union even before the voting. States like Missouri, Kentucky, and Maryland, that ultimately remained in the union with Lincoln at its helm, could have easily left under the leadership of Seward, who was considered much more radical than Lincoln. Yes, it's hard to believe that for all the venom that was constantly being hurled at Lincoln, by southern whites scared about a northern takeover, Lincoln was a mere moderate in comparison to other republican leaders looking for the White House. Lincoln would say time and time again his problem was not with slavery in the states where it existed, just in the territories. But that wasn't enough for the southern slave-drivers, they viewed everything that disagreed with their opinions or ideologies of life to be radical, undemocratic, and unconstitutional.

When Lincoln was inaugurated, eleven states seceded from the union, many before he even became president. If these states would have just remained the likelihood is that slavery would have continued much longer than what it actually was, in other words, the southerners shot themselves in the foot, badly. Without the drama and casualties of the civil war, Lincoln would have had no reason to issue the emancipation proclamation, it was signed only as a military exercise, and purposely left out freeing the slaves of the states and territories that remained loyal to the union. Just to play around, this means that had Mississippi decided to stay in the union, when all of its neighbors decided to quit, Mississippi would have been able to keep its slaves. However, this didn't happen of course and as the union troops moved into "enemy territory" they freed the "property" from the plantations and fields. (Lincoln himself prior to the civil war believed that slavery would mostly be eradicated in 100 years. He believed that the United States would still have slavery in the 1950s.)

Last, but not least, of course, was the thirteenth amendment, which forbade slavery anywhere in the United States, unless it were punishment for a crime. Lincoln had been working on this for many months, knowing all too well that when the civil war was over the emancipation proclamation would lose its effect and slaves would be no longer free. Unwilling to let that cruelty to become a reality he tried everything in his power to pass and implement the thirteenth amendment into effect. In order for an amendment to pass, two-thirds of both houses of congress have to vote in the affirmative as well as three-fourths of the states. If the whole southern slave-holding block had been part of the union during this time, the amendment would never have passed. However, because they were out of the union that meant that only the northern states, as well as slave-holding Missouri, Kentucky, and Maryland had representatives in congress to vote. Through intimidation and, no doubt, various forms of corruption the amendment finally passed the House by the narrowest of margins on January 31, 1865, having been previously passed the previous year in the senate, it then was onto the states, where it officially became ratified when the twenty-seventh state ratified it on December 6th, 1865. Lincoln's dream was not fully realized, at least for him. He was assassinated months earlier by a deranged actor named John Wilkes Booth.

Booth was, in every sense of the word, the embodiment of southern ideology at the time. Booth, who was living in the North while attaching himself to the southern Confederate cause, was determined to do something to hamstring Lincoln, but he didn't really know what. His first plan was to kidnap Lincoln and take him to the Confederate capital of Richmond, Virginia, where he would be a sort of political prisoner and would be forced to surrender to the Confederates. This plan didn't work out, however. Lincoln didn't appear at the spot he was supposed to. So, a new plan was needed. Booth was so devious he figured the only way for the Confederates to win would be to assassinate all the political leaders, the Union would be so distraught and disorganized they would have to surrender to the Confederates. The plan was to kill Lincoln, the vice-president Andrew Johnson, and secretary of state William Seward, Lincoln's former republican rival. It didn't matter to Booth that the Confederate general, Robert E Lee, had already surrendered his forces to Union general, Ulysses Grant, all but officially ending the war. And it didn't matter to Booth that the thirteenth amendment had already passed the House and was being ratified by the states, he still held out hope that Lincoln's demise would be the Union's demise.[164]

People started seeing trouble in Booth years before, in 1861, when he began applauding the southern secession movement, calling it "heroic."[165] It's safe to say that Booth hated abolitionists with a deep, harrowing, passion, even going so far as to attend the hanging of the abolitionist leader, who many consider a hero today, John Brown. To do this he had to pretend to be a soldier, using equipment and costumes from his theater performances, since the United States had a little over 1500 militia troops to guard against a rescue attempt

---

164 History.com Editors. 2018. "John Wilkes Booth Shoots Abraham Lincoln." HISTORY. August 21, 2018. https://www.history.com/this-day-in-history/john-wilkes-booth-shoots-abraham-lincoln.
165 Kimmel, Stanley (1969). *The Mad Booths of Maryland.* New York City: Dover Books.

made by Brown's adherents.¹⁶⁶ Perhaps Booth was just trying to be loyal to his native state of Maryland, who was still harboring slaves, yet remained in the Union, though it is no doubt that Booth had strong resentments about black equality. He even went so far as to wish "the President and the whole damned government would go to hell" over its desire to see slaves emancipated in the "militant" southern states.¹⁶⁷ The prospects of Lincoln's re-election deeply worried Booth and he became paranoid at the thought of it.

You might ask if Booth was so concerned with the path of the Union and his obvious desire to see to its destruction, couldn't he have just enlisted in the Confederate ranks? That would make more sense than plotting an attack against the government, where he would certainly be killed as a traitor, a most inglorious way to go. Booth himself hit it right on the head "I have begun to deem myself a coward," he wrote his mother, "and to despise my own existence."¹⁶⁸ How much better would it have been for us had he just found the courage to join the Confederate army rather than to live in infamy, known as the killer of our greatest president? And yet, Booth found it more practical for him to dance around and parade in military garb, without actually doing the duty of a soldier. For someone that held his beliefs, it doesn't get much lower than that.

Unfortunately for Lincoln, he gave a speech which Booth attended, on April 11, 1865, after the civil war had officially ended, in which he called for suffrage for "certain negroes," a reference for the black men who had served in the union. Booth was heard to have said "That means nigger citizenship. Now, by God, I'll put

---

166 Allen, Thomas B. (1992). *The Blue and the Gray*. Washington, D.C.: National Geographic Society. p. 41
167 Smith, Gene (1992). *American Gothic: the story of America's legendary theatrical family, Junius, Edwin, and John Wilkes Booth*. New York: Simon & Schuster.
168 Ward, Geoffrey C. (1990). *The Civil War – an illustrated history*. New York City: Alfred A. Knopf.

him through. That is the last speech he will ever make."[169] And so the plan was set for him and his fellow conspirators. Booth was to kill Lincoln himself, David Herold was to kill Seward, and George Atzerodt was to kill Johnson. Booth, as historians have claimed, meant to decapitate the leadership of the government, however, his knowledge of the Constitution was obviously not great as Seward would not have been next in line for succession being the secretary of state. Instead, if Johnson had been killed too, the new president would have been Lafayette Foster, at the time the president pro tempore of the senate.

Nevertheless, the only assassination that turned out as planned was Lincoln's, Atzerodt chickened out and didn't even bother to attack Johnson, instead Johnson was awakened in the middle of the night out of a deep sleep to receive the news of Lincoln's death. And Herold managed to break into the Seward home, but was unable to finish the deal and only was able to slash Seward's face with his knife. Still a pretty disturbing night for Seward and his family no doubt.

Booth thought that he was doing God's work, like somehow God had wanted Lincoln dead, if God had actually wanted this wouldn't he have killed Lincoln long before the Confederacy was breaking up? Booth didn't think so, even calling himself the instrument of God to make his point. Booth had long called Lincoln and the republicans radical for freeing the slaves and suggesting racial equality, those beliefs caused him to lose everything. Had he stayed loyal to the Union, or at least just kept his mouth shut, he could have had an amazing career as an actor, making big money. He wouldn't have lost his family, who increasingly became disturbed at Booth's concerning rhetoric. Last, but not least, he wouldn't have

---

169 Reynolds, David S. 2015. "Abraham Lincoln's Assassination, John Wilkes Booth, and John Brown." The Atlantic. The Atlantic. April 12, 2015. https://www.theatlantic.com/politics/archive/2015/04/john-wilkes-booth-and-the-higher-law/385461/.

been scorned from every future generation of Americans, as the man who killed our hero. In the end Herold and Atzerodt were hanged, and four other conspirators received life-time prison terms. Booth ended up hiding in a warehouse, where he was eventually found and shot by a trigger-happy sargeant who had the honor of saying that he killed Linclon's killer.

It's clear that Booth was not the only one who should be blamed for Lincoln's death. All of the southern slave-owners are just as much to blame. They consistently berated the politicians and people of the North for believing that slavery was immoral and a sin against humanity. They consistently called abolitionists dangerous, radicals, insane, and the like. They called Abraham Lincoln, who was no radical abolitionist by any means, a deranged monkey, and the "black candidate" hardly what anyone would prefer to be called back then. Contrast that to the unity and sincerity that Lincoln consistently employed. "I am loath to close," at the end of his second inaugural "we are not enemies, but friends. We must not be enemies. Though passion may have strained, it must not break our bonds of affection. The mystic chords of memory, stretching from every battle-field, and patriot grave, to every living heart and hearthstone, all over this broad land, will yet swell the chorus of the Union, when again touched, as surely they will be, by the better angels of our nature."[170] Does that sound like a radical to you? Does that sound like someone bent on destroying the Union? Do words like that warrant an assassination attempt? No, of course not. Yet the extreme slave interests were perpetuating a false narrative about a man, movement, and region that were pursuing morality.

Just what was so radical about abolishing slavery? In 1792, Denmark banned imported slaves to its colonies. In 1807, Britain outlawed the Atlantic slave trade, a year before America did. In

---

170 Second inauguration of Abraham Lincoln

1811, Spain outlawed slavery in all of her colonies and on the mainland, 54 years before America did. In 1813 and 1814, Sweden and the Netherlands banned slave trading. In 1833, Britain abolished slavery, 32 years before America. In 1846, the Danish outlawed slavery. In 1848, France outlawed slavery.[171] In fact, by the 1850s almost every other industrialized country abolished slavery except the United States. The only other two countries still allowing slavery were Brazil and Cuba, who at the time could hardly be considered successful economies. So, what was so radical about the United States abolishing slavery? Indeed, it seems more likely, in this case, that the ones calling abolitionists radicals, were the actual radicals. It was more radical to keep slaves in bondage when all the other advanced economies outlawed enslavement, in most cases, long before the United States.

This chapter would not be complete without mentioning a few abolitionists, out of many, who made a huge impact on bringing individuals closer to freedom and bringing our nation closer to normalcy. We've already discussed John Brown, Frederick Douglass, and William Lyold Garrison, but there are many others who played a pivotal role as well. Among them are Harriett Beecher Stowe, author of the classic *Uncle Tom's Cabin*, which became an instant best-seller. Stowe was born into a prominent family and didn't need to make the deep splash that would eventually propel her to become one of the faces tied to the abolitionist movement. In 1851, Stowe, unfortunately, lost her 18 month old baby, which made her think about the horrors that enslaved mothers went through when they actively watched their children being stolen away from them during a

---

171 Reuters Editorial. 2007. "CHRONOLOGY-Who Banned Slavery When?" U.S. Reuters. March 22, 2007. https://www.reuters.com/article/uk-slavery/chronology-who-banned-slavery-when-idUSL1561464920070322.

slave trade or auction. After the Fugitive Slave Act was passed, Stowe was determined to write about slavery and its evils, hence the birth of *Uncle Tom's Cabin*. The book awakened many northerners about the horrors of slavery, as slaves are routinely moved from plantation to plantation with some kind masters and some cruel and prone to violence. Stowe, who was deeply religious, wanted her readers to see the stark contradiction between slavery and the Christian doctrine, laid out in the story when Tom, an obedient and honorable slave is beaten to death by his masters while all the while holding steadfast to his religious conviction in Christ.

The book sold over 10,000 copies in its first week and over 300,000 over the first year of its publication, quite an amazing feat back then without the marketing skills we have today. Her sex had limitations, however, so she couldn't speak about her book publicly due to her inferior role as a woman in a men's day and age. Instead one of her brothers, Calvin spoke on her behalf, and the message would soon spread. The message being sent among the northern states was that slaves had feelings just like the average white, they had hopes, they had dreams. According to *The New York Times Sunday Book Review*, Frederick Douglass praised that Stowe had "baptized with holy fire myriads who before cared nothing for the bleeding slave," as many northern whites didn't realize or care about the plight among the blacks.[172] The book was one of the first to be banned in some areas where intimidation and fear ruled over justness and compassion. According to the *First Amendment Museum*, "Booksellers were intimidated into not distributing the book. A bookseller in Mobile, Alabama was forced to leave town for selling the novel, for example. Stowe herself received many threatening letters from

---

172 History.com Editors. 2019. "Harriet Beecher Stowe." HISTORY. A&E Television Networks. February 7, 2019. https://www.history.com/topics/american-civil-war/harriet-beecher-stowe.

southern critics – one included the severed ear of a slave." So much for freedom of the press.

The book did so much to ripen abolitionist sentiment, which might have just carried Lincoln to the White House and led to the civil war, leading Lincoln, who met Stowe in 1862 to remark to her "So you're the little woman who wrote the book that made this great war." Quite a feat for a middle aged woman in the 1850s.

Stowe wrote other anti-slavery books, much less known than the block-busting *Uncle Tom's Cabin*. Among them are *The Key to Uncle Tom's Cabin,* which included letters and direct testimony authenticating the first book, and *Dred: A Tale of the Great Dismal Swamp*, which advocated for abolitionism and demeaned slavery in a society. Stowe passed away on July 2nd, 1896, at the ripe old age of 85, seeing her dream become a reality and slavery abolished once and for all in America.

Another woman who made fame writing for women's causes both black and white was Susan B Anthony. She was born in an abolitionist family in Massachusetts, which instilled in her at a young age the values and morals of equality. This meant not just black and white equality but man and woman equality, which Anthony would take up later in life. Growing up Anthony made herself very close to New York abolitionist leader Frederick Douglass, who would later join her in her crusade for women's rights and suffrage. Anthony even became involved in the Underground Railroad Movement where she wrote in her diary "Fitted out a fugitive slave for Canada with the help of Harriet Tubman."[173] She joined the New York Anti-Slavery Society and presided over a meeting in Rochester, New York, just after John Brown's execution for a time of mourning. Above all Anthony truly did believe that blacks and whites were equal and could live in

---

173 Judith E. Harper. "Biography". *Not for Ourselves Alone: The Story of Elizabeth Cady Stanton and Susan B. Anthony.* Public Broadcasting System. Retrieved January 21, 2014.

society hand and hand, a belief that even some abolitionists didn't even have, which made Anthony a hero in many circles and among many black families.

Anthony certainly wasn't afraid to stand up for the principles she believed in, even though her life was threatened numerous times throughout her life. During the civil war she had to be escorted by police from a mob attack at a home she was living in. She certainly upset many people by her equality speeches, at a time when even many northern states didn't allow black men to vote. "Let us open to the colored man all our schools," she said in one of those speeches, "let us admit him into all our mechanic shops, stores, offices, and lucrative business avocations ... let him rent such pew in the church, and occupy such seat in the theatre ... Extend to him all the rights of Citizenship."[174] Such language as this certainly added to the belief among many southerners that she was nothing more than a bright eyed liberal "radical" who wanted to mix cultures. No doubt they were kicking and screaming over interracial marriages, even though many slave-owners were holding enslaved concubines in a total show of hypocrisy. When Martha Jefferson, Thomas' wife, had passed away she made him promise to her never to marry again, a promise he would hold up for the rest of his life. She hadn't said anything, however, of a concubine, which Jefferson would take up in the form of a slave named Sally Hemings.

Anthony would later become one of the main leaders of the womens' suffrage movement, teaming up with Elizabeth Cady Stanton and becoming a role model to many children. She managed to make such a name for herself, never letting her unequal status as a woman of the time slow her down. She will always go down in history as a hero for girls all over the world, though at the time she

---

[174] Manuscript of speech in the Susan B. Anthony Papers collection at the Library of Congress. Quoted in McPherson (1964

was not liked, to say the least, in some areas of the country because of her "radicalism".

Last, but not least, although there are so many more noteworthy abolitionists that made an enormous impact on our country and freedom around the world, is a woman by the name of Sojourner Truth. Actually her real name was Isabella Baumfree, and she was born to enslaved parents, in 1797 New York, a fine way for us to realize that slavery wasn't always situated just in the South. Truth knew the heart ache of the slave trade in a deep and personal way, being separated from her parents when she was nine years old, getting sold with a flock of sheep for $100.[175] Her new owner, John Neely, was quite notorious for his open hostility and cruelty. He would beat young Truth regularly, and without mercy at times. Throughout her growing years, from the time she was ten to her teens, she was sold repeatedly to different masters with different expectations. One master would routinely rape her, she was only around thirteen years old.[176] Imagine the terrifying trauma that existed within this young girl. Yet she persevered through it all.

In 1799, New York began the process of gradual emancipation of slaves within the state, a process that would not be complete until 1827, yet the wheels were in motion. Truth was given assurances from her master that she would be freed prior to the emancipation deadline, a promise that time and again, was broken to better suit the needs of her master. Truth couldn't wait any longer, so she decided to free herself. She refused to run, thinking that shameful, so instead, she decided to walk to freedom, eventually finding good graces in the home of a man named Isaac Van Wagenen, who not

---

175 https://www.history.com/topics/black-history/sojourner-truth
176 Washington, Margaret (2009). *Sojourner Truth's America*. Urbana, Illinois: University of Illinois Press.

only took her in, but paid for her freedom, $20 which was a big sum at the time.[177]

Slave-masters always tried to rig the system, whether that be to illegally sell free men into slavery, lie about the status of their "property", or sell slaves from a state that was now completely free territory into a slave-wielding one. This is the case with Truth's son, who when the New York manumission act was officially enforced, freeing all slaves in New York, was sold to a slave-owner in Alabama. Truth felt helpless, what was she going to do? Well she certainly didn't just sit on her hands, she mustered up the strength to file a lawsuit in court against her former master to get her son back. She couldn't do this herself, of course, for the laws still heavily discriminated against blacks free or enslaved and women of all races. Not being able to file the lawsuit herself, she gained the help of the Van Wagenens, whom the court took seriously. They after all were white, and had money, exactly the type of people who the court systems paid attention to. After some months haggling in court, Truth won the lawsuit and thus became the first black woman to successfully challenge a white man in court. Why don't we hear more of this? The outright courage of this woman!

During her time living with the Van Wagenens, Truth developed a strong spiritual faith in God and became seriously devoted to the doctrines of Christianity. She would go on to work for a couple of different preachers, doing menial tasks like cleaning up the church or being a maid. Around her spiritual conversion she changed her name to Sojourner Truth, Sojourner means to reside someplace, thus her name meant to reside in the truth, a pretty clever and well-thought out name change. In the year 1844, she officially joined abolitionists movements, first joining the Northampton

---

[177] Andrew Pasquale. "Sojourner Truth". *David Ruggles Center for History and Education*. Retrieved February 14, 2020.

Association of Education and Industry, an organization that called for the immediate abolition of slavery and social equality.[178] It is here where Truth met leading abolitionists, like Frederick Douglass, who believed in her abilities as a speaker, since she had gained experience public speaking preaching the Gospel of the Lord.

In 1851, Truth gave her most famous speech on behalf of abolition and women's rights at the Ohio Women's Rights Convention in Akron, Ohio. Here is the speech in its entirety, it's too good to leave any out:

"Well, children, where there is so much racket there must be something out of kilter. I think that 'twixt the Negroes of the South and the women at the North, all talking about rights, the white men will be in a fix pretty soon. But what's all this here talking about? That man over there says that women need to be helped into carriages, and lifted over ditches, and to have the best place everywhere. Nobody ever helps me into carriages, or over mud-puddles, or gives me any best place! And ain't I a woman? Look at me! Look at my arm! I have ploughed and planted, and gathered into barns, and no man could head me! And ain't I a woman? I could work as much and eat as much as a man – when I could get it – and bear the lash as well! And ain't I a woman? I have borne thirteen children, and seen most all sold off to slavery, and when I cried out with my mother's grief, none but Jesus heard me! And ain't I a woman? Then they talk about this thing in the head; what's this they call it? [member of audience whispers, "intellect"] That's it, honey. What's that got to do with women's rights or Negroes' rights? If my cup won't hold but a pint, and yours holds a quart, wouldn't you be mean

---

178 "The Northampton Association of Education and Industry." David Ruggles Center for History and Education. https://davidrugglescenter.org/northampton-association-education-industry/#:~:text=Northampton%20Association%20of%20Education%20and%20Industry%20(NAEI)%20was%20an%20abolit

not to let me have my little half measure full? Then that little man in black there, he says women can't have as much rights as men, 'cause Christ wasn't a woman! Where did your Christ come from? Where did your Christ come from? From God and a woman! Man had nothing to do with Him. If the first woman God ever made was strong enough to turn the world upside down all alone, these women together ought to be able to turn it back, and get it right side up again! And now they is asking to do it. The men better let them. Obliged to you for hearing me, and now old Sojourner ain't got nothing more to say."[179]

She was a radical in the South for saying such things. It's one thing to talk about black equality, and abolishment of slavery. It's a whole 'nother problem to talk about women being the equal of men. Women couldn't vote and in many cases couldn't take out loans or own property, being totally subservient to their husbands. Yes, she was a total radical.

During the civil war, Truth helped with black soldier enlistment into the union ranks. She was a natural leader, encouraging people to donate clothing, food, and other materials desperately needed for the nation's union soldiers. Somewhat of an inspiration for Herbert Hoover, who did similar work during world war one, for some reason though, he gets talked about more. What's more, she openly defied segregation laws, riding on whites' only streetcars, to the growing frustration of even white northerners who were becoming annoyed.[180]

After the war, she focused her attention on helping newly freed black men get good paying jobs to support their families and help

---

179 Sojourner Truth's "Ain't I a women" speech in Akron, Ohio, 1851
180 "Sojourner Truth." 2009. HISTORY.com. A&E Television Networks. October 29, 2009. https://www.history.com/topics/black-history/sojourner-truth.

reduce black poverty. She even tried, exhaustively, to have the government resettle freed slaves to land out West, where good agricultural land abounded, with great opportunities for former slaves to find success and happiness working on their own lands. Like usual, the government refused this request, instead choosing to give the land to whites, who could get more from the land.

Truth died on November 26, 1883, at the age of 85. She lived her life full of doing what was right. Giving everything she had to see the success of her brothers and sisters both free and enslaved. She knew the horrors of slavery, she lived it. She knew what it was like to become separated from her family, to receive the brutal beatings from the whip, and to know the indignity of rape every day. She took on wealthy white slave-owners who tried to rig the system against those like Truth. She had an undying faith that went with her wherever she went.

7 CONFEDERATE STATUES

Believe it or not, there are more statues and memorials for Confederate generals and soldiers than there are for these brave men and women who stood up on the right side of history. Currently, at the time of this publication, there are nine United States forts named after former Confederate generals, think about Lee, Stonewall Jackson, and Bragg. Why are we supporting these Confederate generals by celebrating them with memorials, statues, and forts? Shouldn't we do the exact opposite? Shouldn't we really be celebrating those that brought about an end of slavery, fought to protect the union, and stood up for human rights? Apparently not so. Over 110,100 Union men lost their lives. Think about their families, their wives who lost a husband to support her and the kids and to love, their children who would live the rest of their lives not knowing what it's like to have a loving father, or their parents who would live to see every parent's worst nightmare come true, that of a child dying before them. Yet, America still hasn't taken down those statues, those memorials, those forts, named after the very men who had a hand in murdering loyal union men. And I still see people all over the South, proudly waving Confederate flags. I get it, it's in the Dukes of Hazzard, who cares? It's still a hurtful sign to so many, who either are direct descendants of slaves, or those who lost great-great-great-great grandparents fighting for this country.

The Confederate army was an enemy to the United States, pure and simple. We don't see us waving flags of other countries or armies that opposed us in times of war. We don't see people waving Nazi flags, and if you do they are neo-nazis who are anti-semitic bigots.

You don't see memorials praising the Japanese generals of world war two. You don't see statues of German generals in either world war. So why do we do it with the Confederates? Time for that to end. Time for us to be radical again, just like Sojourner Truth, Frederick Douglass, and Susan B Anthony, time for us to put people first.

And so, slavery was officially abolished in the United States in December of 1865, now freedom was offered to everyone, not just the privileged few who were born white. Abolitionists' jobs were done, slavery was gone, freedom rang loud, people didn't have to hide, times were good right? Not everyone thought so, Frederick Douglass told abolitionists that their work was just beginning. Inequality was still ripe everywhere, they weren't done until everyone was treated equally and had the means to be a productive member of society.

8 DISCRIMINATION AFTER THE CIVIL WAR

Today I hear many people, typically white people, tell me that things are pretty much equal today, that for the most part our laws are equal towards all races, genders, religions, ect. I generally hate to disagree with folks at public gatherings but something is a little off when so many people think that things are totally equal. Some white people get irked when they hear things like reparations for black families, believing that they should not be held responsible for something that happened so long ago. Why should whites have to pay for something that happened 200 years ago? And yet the people who make these statements and believe this to be the truth are wholly ignorant of the role the government, and people throughout history, have played to keep certain groups down. This couldn't be more of the case than with the black population in the aftermath of the civil war.

You would think that everything is fine and dandy now right? After the civil war and the 13th, 14th, and 15th amendments slavery was abolished, discrimination was outlawed, and black men finally had the right to vote, just like the white men who held this right since the beginning. Yet, nobody, at least not most white leaders, seem to think about how newly freed slaves would make it now that they were free. How would they get a job? Would they be paid enough to support a family? As you will see in this chapter things were definitely not peachy for the newly freed slaves and for the black population in general.

Immediately after the civil war ended, many southerners were in a state of denial, still believing that they were in the right, that they were totally justified to secede from the union, and totally justified for holding a whole race in bondage. Yet to gain re-admittance into the Union, the formerly seceded southern states needed to agree to the terms of surrender and that meant that they would have to give up slavery. This did not mean, however, that they would easily give it up. Right from the beginning the Southerners tried to keep the newly freed blacks as close to their previous condition as possible. In the brief time that Benjamin Perry was governor of South Carolina in 1865 he said and did much to revert to the old way of thinking. Prior to the civil war, Perry was a Unionist, just for the reason that a war would bring about an emancipation of the slaves, a prophecy that would later ring true. In the year 1865 with the civil war over, Perry did all he could to keep the freedmen down.

Well before the end of the civil war, Lincoln and his cabinet had discussed the general rules of the reconstructed country. Lincoln believed that only ten percent of each southern state had to swear a loyalty oath and that each state had to recognize the end of slavery. Just ten percent had to swear a loyalty oath? That's a little lenient isn't it? Many congressmen believed that it was too lenient as well, so they passed a law called the Wade-Davis Bill of 1864, that would make at least 50% of each state's white population swear a loyalty oath to the United States and declare that they had not taken part in any Confederate plots. Now this seemed too harsh, Lincoln pocket vetoed it shortly after it passed congress, preferring instead on leniency, believing the nation would heal quicker.

This leniency made it quite easy for states to be readmitted to the union at a fast rate. What makes it even worse is that originally congress had not barred former confederates to serve public offices.

This made it easy for states to fill their offices with the same men who waged war against the United States. That is exactly what Benjamin Perry did. In his first official act as governor he issued a proclamation reappointing former Confederate officials to their old posts.[181] Perry also added, with an icy chill, that just because the state was forced to free the "negroes," that doesn't mean that the "negroes" were citizens. Those radicals in the North, who were moving quickly to spread black suffrage "forget that this is a white man's government, intended for white men only." Even worse, Perry further demeaned the black race, "God created him", Perry sputtered, "inferior to the white man in form, color, and intellect, and no legislation or culture can make him equal… his color is black, his head is covered with wool instead of hair, his form and features will not compare with the caucasian race, and it is in vain to think of elevating him to the dignity of a white man."[182] This hardly seems like the language of a people who were sorry for what they had done. Instead it seems like language from a people who wanted the status quo, who would do anything to keep the black race down, even though other parts of the country were doing the right thing and increasing black suffrage and rights.

A letter written by a wealthy South Carolina landowner is a tell-tale sign that southerners weren't going to change their ways anytime soon. It reads:

"The general interest both of the white man and the negro requires that he should be kept as near to his former condition as law can keep him and that should be kept as near to the condition of slavery as possible and as far from the condition of the white man as is practicable…

---

181 Budiansky, Stephen. 2008. *The Bloody Shirt : Terror after Appomattox*. New York: Viking.
182 ibid

"I know that there are those who look to getting rid of the negroe entirely, and of resorting to white labor... for all of the cotton states all of the good lands are so malarious in the fall of the year as to render it impracticable for white men to labor under our suns. Negroes must be made to work, or else cotton and rice must cease to be raised for export."[183]

Enclosed in the letter were four pieces of legislation that were intentionally designed to keep the blacks as close to the institution of slavery as possible. Among them was "an act prohibiting all freemen, or persons of African descent made free... from ever holding real estate in South Carolina, or their posterity after them." This is a fancy way of saying that blacks in South Carolina would never be able to own any piece of property, neither those immediately freed or those who were the great-great-great-great descendants of those who were of African descent. This was due to direct fear among the southern whites that the newly freed slaves would receive 40 acres of land for them and their family, "Let the idea of their ever owning land pervade amongst them, and they will never work for a white man, or upon any land but their own." Clearly, southern whites still wanted and needed black labor for their vast plantations. Working all hours under the hot, malarious, sun would put whites in extreme danger, the whites knew that blacks would be suitable to work in the cotton or rice fields, they were less valuable than whites, indeed, they were inferior. If you let them ever have land to themselves they will become independent, they will never want to work for the white man again, the white man would be ruined. For, "the black man must then forever labor upon the capital of the white man... I regard it as the most vital law that can be made for our future prosperity."[184]

---

183 ibid
184 ibid

Obviously, this wealthy South Carolinian plantation owner didn't care about humanity, didn't care about justice or fairness, he only cared about his own needs, he was perfectly willing to let the entire African race in South Carolina toil under the yoke of the white man, for the white man's gain. His reasoning is a little curious, however. If blacks were prevented in South Carolina from owning land, they would have a greater interest to leave South Carolina and plantation owners there would lose vital workers. Nevertheless, many southern, former Confederate, states passed what would come to be known as the black codes, designed to discriminate against the African race.

One of the most disturbing laws, and longlasting, was the barring of interracial marriages. In all, twenty-one states banned interracial marriage between whites and blacks, all such laws coming after the commencement of the civil war, both in northern and souhtern states. West Virginia passed a law in 1863 that banned interracial marriage. This particular law was in effect until 1967, more than a hundred years later, when it was overturned in Loving vs. Virginia. Even decades after the civil war, Wyoming, in 1913, banned white interracial marriage with blacks, Asians, and Filipinos. These laws had more of a significance than you would think. Not only did they ban people who genuinely loved members of other races from enjoying a life together, but it also forbade, in those states that passed these discriminatory laws prior to emancipation, whites from being able to free enslaved blacks through marriage. Also, of important significance, blacks would not be allowed to receive any form of inheritance from whites whom they loved. It's important to note that at the time, and still to this day, whites had significant higher net worths than blacks, for those states banning interracial marriages, blacks would miss out on their rightful inheritance that any other lovers or families would have received.[185]

Banning interracial marriages was just the tip of the ice-berg, in regard to the racism and discriminatory measures that many states would enact in the coming years. South Carolina would pass their own state black codes, among them, according to the Constitutional Rights Foundation, it consisted of six pillars. Newly freed blacks did have more rights, as you would expect, following their emancipation. However, no laws were on the books to prevent anyone from discriminating against blacks in regards to property, social, or political rights. "The South Carolina code included a contract form for black "servants" who agreed to work for white "masters." The form required that the wages and the term of service be in writing. The contract had to be witnessed and then approved by a judge. Other provisions of the code listed the rights and obligations of the servant and master. Black servants had to reside on the employer's property, remain quiet and orderly, work from sunup to sunset except on Sundays, and not leave the premises or receive visitors without the master's permission. Masters could "moderately" whip servants under 18 to discipline them. Whipping older servants required a judge's order. Time lost due to illness would be deducted from the servant's wages. Servants who quit before the end date of their labor contract forfeited their wages and could be arrested and returned to their masters by a judge's order. On the other hand, the law protected black servants from being forced to do "unreasonable" tasks."[186] In the vast majority of cases, blacks that worked for their new "masters",

---

185 Palmer, Vernon Valentine (April 2006). "The Customs of Slavery: The War without Arms". *The American Journal of Legal History*
186 Costly, Andrew. 2019. "Southern Black Codes - Constitutional Rights Foundation." Crf-Usa.org. Constitutional Rights Foundation. 2019. https://www.crf-usa.org/brown-v-board-50th-anniversary/southern-black-codes.html.

were the newly freedmen working on their old masters plantation, as getting jobs proved quite a difficult task.

Vagrancy, the state of living homeless, was punishable as well, which forced many former slaves into signing contracts to work for their former master's plantation. The law stated that vagrants could be imprisoned and sentenced to work hard labor, or sent to work on a white man's plantation. What makes this law particularly damnable is that obviously not many, if any, former slaves had housing. These were people who lived their whole lives on a plantation living in shacks, while their masters lived in mansions. They had little to no connections and certainly didn't have the capital to be able to afford a home. What's worse is that even if blacks had a home there was no guarantee that they would receive work, which is why so many blacks try to acquire landed property so that they could farm the land and provide for their families, a task that would not be cheap and scarcely any could afford. The other option was to work for their previous masters. The vagrancy laws made it where only affluent freedmen could be able to work on their own independently.

In South Carolina, the racist legislature prohibited blacks from owning firearms, afraid of what the newly freed blacks would do to their former masters. They couldn't make or sell alcohol, received the death penalty for crimes that received much lesser punishments for whites, and had to continuously apply each year for a license to practice anything else except being a servant or a farmer, working on a white plantation.[187]

It turns out that Mississippi had pretty similar laws, almost identical to South Carolina's vagrancy laws, and also for forbidding freemen to own firearms. If any newly freed person should defy the Mississippi penal code:

---

187 ibid

"Be it further enacted, that if any freedman, free Negro, or mulatto convicted of any of the misdemeanors provided against in this act shall fail-or refuse, for the space of five days after conviction, to pay the fine and costs imposed, such person shall be hired out by the sheriff or other officer, at public outcry, to any white person who will pay said fine and all costs and take such convict for the shortest time."[188]

These laws again were made with the expectation that freedmen would return to their previous institution, that of de facto slavery. Exactly the way that southerners wanted to keep it, believing that freemen would never voluntarily work for themselves and had to be coerced into working, a belief that slaveholders maintained even though they never gave blacks a chance.

Mississippi was the first state to pass the black codes, followed by South Carolina, Louisiana, and Alabama in 1865, these states had the highest concentration of new freemen, the term being used to describe newly freed slaves. In 1866, Florida, Arkansas, Texas, North Carolina, Virginia, Tennessee, and Georgia all imitated previous black laws, taking Mississippi's and South Carolina's as inspiration.[189] In most of these states, the new black laws forbade blacks from testifying against whites in court, symbolizing that just because slavery was over and the Union army was victorious, just because the United States set up the Freedmen's Bureau, helping freedmen with various things like housing, employment ect, didn't mean things would be different in the South, where wide-spread hate still lingered.

---

188 McPherson, Edward. 1865. "Mississippi Black Code, 1865 | the American Yawp Reader." AmericanYawp.com. 1865. https://www.americanyawp.com/reader/reconstruction/mississippi-black-code-1865/.
189 Stewart, *Black Codes and Broken Windows* (1998), pp. 2259–2260.

Of course, the black codes preceded the much more famous Jim Crow laws that became dominant in the South at the end of the 19th century lasting all the way until the middle of the 20th century. As soon as the democrats gained control of the state legislatures in the South trouble loomed large for the newly freed slaves. (The democrats at the time were more likely to suppress the blacks). Due to the negligence of the democratic states the KKK was able to rise and strengthen, with its birthplace in Pulaski, Tennessee. Outright intimidation in the south contributed to the problems. If you ever are curious I encourage you to look at how lopsided the elections in the South were after the 1870s. You will find that the elections, in many state, county, and even federal elections were heavily skewed towards the democratic nominee or the nominee most likely to suppress the rights of the blacks. Because, in most cases, the ballots were colored, it made it very likely for southerners to see who their neighbors voted for, thereby making it much more likely that scared voters would just vote for the preferred candidate. Thus, under these conditions, the political landscape proved unfavorable to the blacks, and beautiful for those racists who wanted to control the blacks above all things.

In the next decades after the civil war, from 1880-1910, ten of the eleven former Confederate states passed state constitutions or made changes to their already existing constitutions, essentially disenfranchised black people, and poor whites as well, through the instruments of poll taxes and literacy tests.[190] The Constitution, at the time, banned states from barring citizens from voting, whether they be white or black. The problem was that the Constitution said nothing about the kinds of restrictions that states could erroneously

---

190 Perman, Michael. *Struggle for Mastery: Disfranchisement in the South, 1888–1908.* Chapel Hill: University of North Carolina Press, 2001

pass, like these literacy tests. The poll taxes that were required for citizens to vote blocked blacks who had virtually no money coming right out of bondage and poor whites who couldn't afford to vote. It also made for incredibly low voter turnout, as nobody would want to have to pay to vote. Literacy tests also directly targeted the black population, who were much more likely to not be able to read because of the laws passed by state governments banning the education of slaves. How can anybody control their futures if they can't even vote? In 1910, only 0.5% of blacks in Louisiana were registered to vote. Is that a democracy? Or is that authoritarian rule? You can decide for yourself. (Poor whites, in some states that enacted a literacy test, could vote due to a grandfather clause in which anyone who could vote before the year 1866 could vote now. Again, this totally left out the blacks who could not vote.)

Even public schools and libraries were drastically underfunded compared to those of the white schools and libraries. In fact, many of the black schools used textbooks and other resources that were second hand, with black kids often receiving heavily chewed up textbooks that were no good anymore, yet, that's all they had.

One of the most infamous court cases, one that compares to the equally infamous Dred Scott decision, at the time was the Plessy vs. Ferguson case that determined that segregation was legal as long as the segregation was equal. But how can anyone through metrics and data prove that certain practices are unequal? And even if anyone could prove this, nobody making the laws would listen, equating it to falsehoods and castigating progressive reformers who were pushing for civil rights.

In spite of what the states had done by discriminating so strongly against the black population, the federal government, thanks to Northern politicians, drafted laws to prohibit the states from acting in this way. Charles Sumner, the same senator that was viciously beaten on the senate floor before the civil war, orchestrated the Civil Rights Act of 1875, which guaranteed the rights of everyone, regardless of race, color, or history of servitude to have the same treatment in public. It was signed by president Ulysses Grant, who believed strongly in equal rights and tried to crush the KKK. This law was declared unconstitutional by the Supreme Court in 1883. I can't totally say why the supreme court declared this unconstitutional. Apparently treating everybody the same and equally is unconstitutional.

Of course, one of the ways that white southerners practiced white supremacy was through segregation. The whites received all of the most luxurious places to gather, eat, and travel, while the blacks were subjected to unequal facilities, schools, railroad cars, ect. Whenever any reformer would try to push back against the discrimination and unfair conditions racist whites would call them out as being "soft" and "communistic." Even worse, they tried to justify the unfair treatment and discrimination with bogus scientific reasoning that was conducted by racist scientists trying to be a race hero for the whites. Eugenics, which is still believed by a number of people today, is a scientific theory that paints non-whites in a very negative light. Eugenics was thoroughly embraced by the Nazis in the 1930s and 40s, as they determined to create the perfect race.

According to the National Human Genome Research Institute "Scientific racism (eugenics) is an ideology that appropriates the methods and legitimacy of science to argue for the superiority of white Europeans and the inferiority of non-white people whose social and economic status have been historically marginalized."[191]

---

191 National Human Genome Research Institute. 2022. "Eugenics and Scientific Racism." Genome.gov. National Human Genome Research Institute. May 18, 2022. https://www.genome.gov/about-genomics/fact-sheets/Eugenics-and-Scientific-Racism.

In other words, this form of science that was popularized in the late 19th and early 20th centuries, conveniently for the racist Jim Crow laws to exploit, gave racists another tool in their arsenal to keep minorities down. This time they could use science to back up their claims. Essentially, eugenics claims that minorities, particularly blacks, Hispanics, and Native Americans lack the mental capabilities of whites and that they were scientifically proven to be inferior to the intellectual prowess of the whites. It's incredibly ironic that these people claimed that just because of skin color blacks were mentally inferior to themselves. History would prove that these racists were wrong, they were dumber than the people that they castigated.

Nevertheless, these beliefs led to the further domination among the whites, especially in the South. Segregation was justified to prevent any racial mixing between whites and blacks, it would be horrible for any whites to have sex with blacks and cause their children to have mental disabilities. (Apparently, they conveniently forget the fact that many slave owners had children with their own black slave women. They didn't seem to care about all of that nonsense. At least not back then.) Even the famed 18th century American physician Benjamin Rush believed that having black skin was a form of leprosy and that everyone, regardless of color, actually had white skin beneath them. He advocated, since he believed blacks had leprosy, to prevent mixed marriages to prevent an increase in leprosy. Hence, the segregationists tried desperately to prevent the mixed marriages of their nightmares.

Widecale discrimination continued all the way through the 1960s and 70s. In the 1950s greater awareness was presenting itself about the need to ban discrimination and give everyone equal rights. Thanks to the likes of Martin Luther King Jr. and many others, both known and unknown to history, a national movement was once again being ushered in to deal with the gross injustice. The historic decision of Brown vs. The Board of Education overturned the disastrous Plessy decisions a half a century earlier. Though the decision only affected schools, declaring it unconstitutional for schools to be segregated, it was a powerfully important decision that paved the way for more equitable policies to follow.

In the 1950s Rosa Parks refused to give up her seat to a white man and was arrested. Martin Luther King developed a strategy to boycott the buses and even president Eisenhower sent in the national guard to ensure that the Little Rock nine would be safely integrated into Little Rock high school that once was an all white school. Clearly, our society was moving in the right direction, yet, there was, as is always, a massive resistance movement that wanted to squash all forms of progress. This was evident in the form of national, state, and local politicians, who showed zero interest in treating black Americans like real human beings, and even the public, in certain areas at least, who feared integration largely because of all the nonsense that their segregationist lawmakers were uttering.

Governors and local school boards were actively planning on resisting integration at all costs. Harry Byrd, Virginia senator, led the effort to what is now considered the "Massive Resistance" movement. "If we can organize the Southern States for massive resistance to this order," he declared "I think that in time the rest of the country will realize that racial integration is not going to be accepted in the South."[192] Of course, they were hell-bent on denying the "liberals" from getting their way in the South. The South was not their domain and they had no business trying to change things in their localities they believed. Thus, the radicals of the North were

---

192 *Brown v. Board of Education: Virginia Responds"*. State Library of Virginia. 2003

trying to tell the folks in Alabama what they could and could not do with their schools.

A Supreme Court ruling in 1969 further enhanced the case for desegregation following Brown vs. Board of Education. Instead of schools desegregating with all deliberate speed they had to desegregate immediately. Yet, even though this ruling went into effect the South still clung to the hope of the new administration of Richard Nixon, who was the main orchestrator of the republican party pandering to the wishes of white supremacists with the democratic party increasingly supporting civil rights movements and laws.

John F Kennedy is often credited with fully transforming the political landscape, in regards to race. Yes, it is true that black voters increasingly voted democratic thanks to the efforts of Franklin Roosevelt and Harry Truman. However, in the election of 1960, black voters were largely split on whether to support the republican party, the party of Lincoln, or the democratic party which was increasingly moving further to the left on civil rights issues. It helped that when Martin Luther King was again arrested due to his activities defying segregation in Georgia and Kennedy called to check in on him and his family, while Nixon was afraid to alienate white supremacists who were celebrating King's incarceration. This short, powerful, phone call eased the fears of many black voters who decided to support the Northern yankee over the republican nominee.

Initially, Kennedy didn't spend too much time and efforts on civil rights early in his administration. However, after the heroic activities of the Freedom Riders, boycotters, and sit-inners, national attention was shifting towards action on civil rights. In 1963, just a few months before he was assassinated, Kennedy gave an iconic address to the nation regarding civil rights. He urged Congress to pass laws confronting discrimination, segregation, and other unfair practices just because of skin color. When Kennedy was assassinated Lyndon Johnson, though being a Southern democrat, promised to fulfill Kennedy's promises to the nation, including civil rights. (As a side note, in 1956, Southern members of the senate signed what is considered as the Southern Manifesto, promising to oppose any efforts to integrate the races in public settings. Only three members of the senate consisting of the former Confederate states, Estes Kefauver, Al Gore Sr., and Lyndon Johnson refused to sign the manifesto. Kefauver was the democratic nominee for vice president in 1956, and Al Gore Sr. lost his job due to his liberal position on civil rights. The people of Tennessee decided not to send him back to the senate.) This might have offered some comfort to African Americans that the president was somewhat sympathetic to their causes.

The work of so many progressive reformers, the entire African American community, JFK and his brother RFK, Lyndon Johnson, and sympathetic Congressmen turned into the Civil Rights Act of 1964. The main provisions of the act banned discrimination on the basis of gender, race, ethnicity, religion, color.

The legislation was initially proposed by John F Kennedy in June of 1963. Kennedy was deeply involved with the wording of the proposal and personally called members of the Congress to lobby for its advancement. In October of 1963 the bill was reported out of the Judiciary committee and moved to the Rules committee where the chairman was Howard Smith an ardent segregationist and follower of the Massive Resistance movement. Not surprisingly, he was hell-bent on holding the bill up in committee, meaning that he intended to let the bill die a silent, still, death. Unfortunately, by the time that Kennedy died he hadn't realized his civil rights goal.

When Lyndon Johnson occupied the helm of power he used his magnificent legislative skills to shepard through the proposal. In fact, a few days after Kennedy's death he stated his resolve to keep pushing civil rights "No memorial oration or eulogy could more eloquently honor President Kennedy's memory than the earliest possible passage of the civil rights bill for which he fought so long."[193]

Eventually, members of the House were able to muster up enough votes to get the bill out of the Rules committee where segregationists were holding it up. The rules in Congress are pretty messy. Bills have to go through numerous different committees who then either vote to recommend the bill, dramatically alter the bill, or vote against passage of the bill. In order for a bill to be considered by the full senate it needs to pass all of these different committees. As a result, the next step for the bill would end up in the senate Judiciary committee, which at the time was chaired by senator James Eastland of Mississippi. Eastland, again, was a staunch segregationist who fought against integration of the races. In this state the bill had no chance of succeeding. To prevent Eastland from getting an opportunity to destroy the bill, the senate majority leader, Mike Mansfield, took the unusual approach of waiving a second reading of the bill, therefore the bill would be open to debate in the senate chamber.

The bill came up for debate at the end of March, 1964. 18 southern democrats and one southern republican followed the great filibusterer Richard Russel to filibuster this bill too. Russel proclaimed "We will resist to the bitter end any measure or any movement which would tend to bring about social equality and intermingling and amalgamation of the races in our states."[194] Strom Thurmond, another southern segregationist senator also railed against the bill,

---

193 "1963 Year In Review: Transition to Johnson". *UPI*. Archived from the original on April 29, 2020
194 Napolitano, Andrew P. (2009). *Dred Scott's Revenge: A Legal History of Race and Freedom in America*. Thomas Nelson

"This so-called Civil Rights Proposals, which the President has sent to Capitol Hill for enactment into law, are unconstitutional, unnecessary, unwise and extend beyond the realm of reason. This is the worst civil-rights package ever presented to the Congress and is reminiscent of the Reconstruction proposals and actions of the radical Republican Congress."[195]

The filibuster essentially meant that the senate would need at least a 2/3rds majority to bring the bill up for debate. For 54 days the senate could not overcome the filibuster mustered up by the segregationists and other sympathizing senators. Back in the day, to perform a filibuster congressmen needed to talk a long, long time to prevent any action on the bill from happening. It would take a supermajority to break a filibuster.

Robert Byrd, segregationist senator from Virginia, talked for 14 hours and 13 minutes, just talking about anything that occupied his mind at the time. When he finally finished, senate democrats concluded that they had the necessary 67 votes to break the filibuster. They actually defeated the filibuster in the summer of 1964 by the vote of 71-29. Finally a vote could be made on the historic legislation. (This was the first time that the senate was able to overcome a civil rights filibuster.) The final vote on the bill came on June 19th and was passed 73-27.

The reason why I bring this up is that it is ridiculous that there was such a resistance to giving all people in this country, regardless of color of their skin, where they were born, or what their ethnicity is, total equal rights. 27 senators, and 130 representatives in the House voted against giving equal rights, with some taking extraordinary measures to filibuster and speak for over ten hours to prevent this from becoming law. Richard Russel had warned Johnson that this

---

195 963 Year In Review – Part 1 – Civil Rights Bill Archived May 2, 2010, at the Wayback Machine United Press International, 1963

would come back to bite him, this "will not only cost you the South, it will cost you the election."[196] Even Johnson acknowledged that this would dramatically alter politics for years and years to come. After signing the Civil Rights Act of 1964 he remarked, "We've just lost the South for a generation." Of course when he said we he meant the democratic party. Some of these predictions came true while others did not. Johnson was not defeated in 1964, winning easily against conservative bomb-thrower Barry Goldwater, thereby defying Russel's warnings. However, with the emergence of Richard Nixon in 1968, the southern voters began to vote republican in larger and larger quantities, especially as the democratic moved further to the left on civil rights issues. To this day, the South is dominated by the republican party. This is a big reminder that racial bigotry is still lurking and alive. It should say something when because a democrat signed the Civil Rights Act the entire south would switch allegiance to the republican party and still be die-hard republicans to this day, considering that the democratic party is overwhelmingly supported by black voters due to openness and diversity.

The law by no means totally ended the race question once and for all. As a matter of fact, many southerners and northerners alike publicly opposed the bill, especially white business owners who protested that they had a right to serve whoever they wanted to, while having a right to deny someone service because of the color of their skin. Violence frequently was the answer in many communities who disagreed with the federal government and believed in the idea of segregation. When students in 1968 tried to desegregate a bowling alley in rural South Carolina they were violently attacked in what became known as the "Orangeburg Massacre."

Importantly , the Act did not eliminate literacy tests, poll taxes, and voter registration qualifications. Many black voters were still

---

196 Branch, Taylor (1998), *Pillar of Fire*, p. 187

intimidated at the polls by white supremacists as a result. The next year Congress passed the Voting Rights Act of 1965. The law banned states from discriminating on black voters and outlawed the use of literacy tests to vote. 74 House representatives and 18 senators voted against giving all citizens equal voting rights. A huge win was the 24th amendment which was ratified in 1964 eliminating the use of poll taxes. All northern states, with the exception of Wyoming ratified the amendment right away. Florida was the only state in the deep south that ratified the amendment within the period of 1962-1964. Virginia ratified the amendment in 1977, North Carolina in 1989, Alabama in 2002, and Texas in 2009. It took these states an unfortunate amount of time to do the right thing. Arizona, Arkansas, Georgia, Louisiana, Oklahoma, South Carolina, and Wyoming all have not ratified the amendment yet. Mississippi flat out rejected the amendment, the only state to do so. Again, one has to acknowledge the fact that the only states that have failed to ratify an amendment to further advance civil rights was the southern bloc who for so long failed to give equal rights to its people. Yet, many lawmakers from these states call liberals radicals for trying to push voting rights legislation. I think they are the real radicals.

Today, republicans in statewide and national office want to make it harder for people to vote. Shouldn't we be making it easier for people to vote? I mean after all we are a democracy, aren't we? Maybe because of political reasons republicans have decided to throw an all out war on voters. I mean, after all, republicans have lost the popular vote in 7 of the last 8 presidential elections. And, it is a scientific fact that when more people vote, democrats tend to win. (Republicans tend to win when there is a lower voter turnout.) Republicans know this and are trying to exploit this fact. And, again, minority voters overwhelmingly support the democratic party. Republicans know this and want desperately to lower the voter turnout among minority voters.

The 2020 election provides them ample ammunition to use based on Donald Trump's election lies. It's easy to convince republican voters, who have a cult-like following of Trump, to believe that their hero had the election stolen from him, especially when he keeps over and over again telling his followers this vicious lie. (All election experts and bipartisan officials claim that the election was legitimate. Sorry Trump voters.) It makes sense then that republicans would want to target voting laws to change what they don't like. For instance, in many states republicans have passed laws that drastically reduce mail-in-voting. They have closed voting stations, and have cut the amount of early voting days in minority districts. This is flat-out crap.

According to Democracy Docket, "House Republicans unveiled the American Confidence in Elections Act, an omnibus voter suppression bill, which includes a whole host of provisions designed to make it harder to vote. From banning private funding of election administration to implementing stricter voter ID and mail-in voting laws, the bill not only summarizes the GOP's playbook heading into 2024, but also mirrors what many states have already signed into law."[197] In 2023, Ohio passed a law "that shortens the period to apply for, and return, mail-in ballots. It removes a day for early voting and severely restricts the use of drop boxes. Another portion makes it illegal for election officials to provide prepaid return postage for mail-in ballot applications or completed ballots. None of these provisions prevent cheating. All of them make it harder to vote."[198]

---

197 "Republicans Want to Make It Harder to Vote and Easier to Cheat." 2023. Democracy Docket. July 18, 2023. https://www.democracydocket.com/opinion/republicans-want-to-make-it-harder-to-vote-and-easier-to-cheat/.
198 Ibid

Florida republicans passed a law that prohibits non-profit, non-partisan, organizations from registering voters. What's the problem with non-political organizations just trying to get people to vote in a democracy? Nebraska passed a restrictive voter ID law, forgetting, conveniently, that many college kids and minorities tend to be the ones most likely not to have a voter ID. Idaho passed a law that prohibits voters from using college IDs to register to vote, despite the fact that they have previously, throughout its history, accepted college IDs as a valid form of ID without hiccups. Georgia passed a law that made it virtually impossible for poor counties to be able to accept donations from organizations, making it so that these counties lack election workers, resources, ect., to run an election smoothly and effectively.[199] Other states are trying to outlaw ballot harvesting, and outlaw poll workers from going into nursing homes so that these residents can vote. What is the purpose for all of these restrictive laws? It's clearly for political reasons, as more and more republicans are trying to suppress the vote at all costs.

"In Arizona," according to Democracy Docket, "the Republican Party asked a court to eliminate early mail voting for most voters in Arizona. Over 80% of Arizona voters used an early ballot in the 2022 election. Its current mail voting system has been in place for over thirty years."[200] Even republicans are using the judiciary to support voter restriction. Republicans are targeting black and other minority voters in their efforts to take away voting rights from former criminals, as minorities are tragically way over represented in prisons. The key word here is FORMER. These are not criminals anymore, they served their time and they are American citizens that deserve a say in their country's future. In Virginia, the new and upcoming republican governor, Glenn Youngkin, reversed a rule that allowed

---

199 Ibid
200 Ibid

former criminals to have their voting rights back. As a result almost 315,000 eligible Virginians cannot vote, half of them are black, a group much more likely to vote democratic.[201]

Of course, if republicans don't do something to perpetuate the lies of Donald Trump and his MAGA crowd they would be termed traitors. So it's easy for them to target election laws as the reason why Donald Trump lost the election. It doesn't even occur to them that maybe Trump lost the election because he's crazy and dangerous to our democracy. Yet, scapegoating our election laws and making it harder for poor people and minorities to vote seems to be the solution for these republicans.

Conversely, efforts that democrats make, like trying to pass the John Lewis Voting Rights Act, and others that make it easier for people to vote have been lambasted by republicans. They call these proposals efforts to let criminals, illegals, and fraud rule the day during elections. Of course, all of these narratives are totally false. Every year fraud occurs, though on incredibly small levels, like 0.0005 percent of all votes turn out to be fraudulent. I personally don't think that there's any reason that in a democracy one group of people should be trying to suppress the voter turnout. That seems like tyranny not democracy. But, unfortunately, it's happened all throughout our history and is happening again.

The democratic bills that were designed to make it easier for citizens to be able to vote were unsuccessful because the republicans decided to filibuster the bill. As was already discussed, a filibuster essentially allows senators to prevent a bill from being debated and voted on, despite the popularity of the bill itself. In order to get passed the filibuster stage the senate would have to have a supermajority

---

201 Ibid

that moves for a vote. This can become impossible in this day and age when so many issues are highly partisan and the two sides don't want to agree with each other on anything. Most of the time, the senate is evenly divided, or close to this, between republicans and democrats. For important bills like healthcare, college tuition, COVID relief, minimum wage increases, they all need to get passed the supermajority phase. And for what? Why does the senate do this? There is nothing in the Constitution that says anything about a filibuster, and the use of the filibuster itself is very undemocratic, something that the leading democracy in the world should gut. It's only a rule. A rule made up in the early period following the drafting of the Constitution and really wasn't used until 1837 when the Whigs tried to prevent an expulsion of the censure of Andrew Jackson. Way back then senators, if they wanted to filibuster, had to talk and talk and talk in order to prevent a vote.

Since that time the filibuster has specifically been used to delay the advancement of civil rights. In 1946 it was used in opposition to a law that would have prevented discrimination in the workplace. In 1957, senator Strom Thurmond of South Carolina set a record by filibustering the Civil Rights Act of 1957, a law that was designed to prevent voter intimidation. Thurmond talked for more than 24 hours straight. That means he didn't leave to eat. He didn't leave to drink. He didn't leave to go to the bathroom. He just stood in the senate chamber talking for more than 24 hours straight.[202] All of this to prevent the federal government from making sure that everyone could feel safe voting in their own districts and to decide what they want the future of America to look like. In this way the filibuster was used to prevent democracy, not expand it.

---

202 Kelly, Jon (December 12, 2012). "The art of the filibuster: How do you talk for 24 hours straight?". *BBC News Magazine*

In the end, The Civil Rights Act of 1957 was passed, despite the efforts of racist senators. The law itself was really a dud, it didn't change much in the overall landscape, though it at least sent a message that the United States was serious about combating discrimination. During the passage of The Civil Rights Act of 1964, southern senators filibustered the bill for 70 continuous hours. Although in both of these cases the senate was able to muster enough votes to overcome the filibuster, in today's political climate a filibuster is almost impossible to overcome. The only way to overcome it today is if one party has significantly more members than the other, something that seems unlikely to happen anytime soon.

Shortly after president Joe Biden assumed the presidency, the democrats, in a bid to override all of the republicans efforts to suppress the vote, tried to pass the Freedom To Vote Act , which would have done some amazing things to fix our federal elections. Included in the bill is an expansion of voting rights, a change in our campaign finance laws to prevent the influence of money in federal elections, and a ban of the practice of highly partisan gerrymandering. All of these provisions were desperately needed. We needed to expand voting access and rights, making it easier for people to vote, especially those who may lack a photo ID, those that are disabled, and those who live in nursing homes. We need to stop the flow of money in elections. Every election year breaks its own record for the amount of money spent by each side. You've heard me say this over and over again, but there are way too many special interests spending way too much money trying to influence the outcome of elections. Fossil fuel companies are spending up the wazoo trying to keep big-oil politicians in Congress. Pharmaceutical companies are spending an arm and a leg to try to influence voters that liberal politicians will kill the healthcare system. Maybe this is the reason why we spend so much more for prescription drugs than every other major country on earth. I mean, the whole thing is a joke. And, of course, gerrymandering is a big issue. This is a problem from both parties that totally destroys the democratic process. There is nothing theoretically wrong with the Freedom To Vote Act. It would have increased voter turnout and led to more public confidence in elections.

Nevertheless, the republicans decided that the Freedom To Vote Act would have led to an increase in the number of voters who actually vote. They couldn't have that. So, of course, their first instinct was to prevent the bill from even having a chance at passage. They immediately decided to filibuster the bill. (Just another attempt at the filibuster being used to reverse democracy, not enhance it. And once again the filibuster is used to prevent people from voting, again targeting black voters in particular, who tend to live in areas where voting normally takes longer and casts more absentee votes than other demographic groups.) The bill most likely would have passed because the vote would have ended in a 50-50 tie vote with democratic vice-president Kamala Harris voting for the bill. The American people overwhelmingly supported the provisions of the bill, yet because republicans were adamantly opposed to it it didn't become law. Tell me, is that how democracy is supposed to work?

This is why democrats want to finally eradicate the use of the filibuster. It doesn't make sense. It isn't practical. It's undemocratic. And it has been used over and over and over again to suppress the rights of black Americans and other minorities. It isn't radical to eliminate a relic of segregation, racism, and discrimination. It is smart and we should do this now. Maybe then we can get some common sense things done in Washington.

Long story short, we still see the republican party going backwards and perpetuating the legacies of Jim Crow and other discriminations by doing these things. Obviously, it looks a little different today than what it did back then, but the same principles apply. We can and should do better, it is not that hard to expand voting rights, provide fair and free electoral maps, and help establish trust and security in elections. We do this not by being sore losers and questioning the system everytime our candidate loses but by guaranteeing everyone that is eligible the right to vote and that we are expanding democracy, not eroding it.

My point in this chapter is that common sense ideas, like human freedoms and rights were at all times in this country pushed back upon by various sects and groups that fought back against the radicals, and their big liberal plan to change America. There were still people who joyed in lynching blacks. There were still business owners who asserted their rights to deny equal service to all people. There were still people who actually believed that whites were superior to blacks, and they even had disillusioned science to back it up. To these people they considered the liberal reformers to be "radical," "socialists," and "meatheads." Yet, when we consider these events today we see things totally different than what was commonplace back then. See, back then demagogic leaders and politicians used the "radical" term to advance their own causes. They knew that enough white racists would support them if they lied about civil rights. They knew that they would get support if they pandered to the wishes of the racists. It was a very shrewd move on their part, but it totally screwed up America for a long time. Richard Nixon was a good one for this. He, like most shrewd politicians, will go where the public sentiment is. Nixon knew that the democratic party was increasingly becoming supported by blacks and other minority groups. To stem the tide of this, he led the republican party to offer the American south hope against the civil rights movement. He was a disaster for black Americans and he even tried to overturn the 1969 court decision that ordered all public schools to integrate immediately.

Because of these racist leaders and politicians we got the Jim Crow laws. Some historians will claim that the Jim Crow laws are still being used, just not the same tactics. Republicans are still making it as hard as possible for minorities to vote. The disastrous 1990s Crime Bill was a prison sentence for many black Americans who were caught up in the drug problem. As a result, more black Americans ended up in prisons, families were broken up, and children grew up without a father or mother. This is undoubtedly another reason why black Americans make so much less than white Americans.

Perhaps even more glaring, historians point to evidence that the Jim Crow laws were looked at with admiration by Nazi Germany. It is a known fact that Adolph Hitler long admired the American system, not the American system of statesman Henry Clay, but the American system of racism. He implemented many of the same ideas in regards to the Jews. "America in the early 20th century was the leading racist jurisdiction in the world," says James Q Whitman, who is a professor at Yale Law School. "Nazi lawyers, as a result, were interested in, looked very closely at, [and] were ultimately influenced by American race law."[203] You know that we are doing something wrong when the most suppressive genocidal regime in the history of the world looks at the United States for pointers. That's not right and we shouldn't be okay with this fact.

---

203 Little, Becky. 2017. "How the Nazis Were Inspired by Jim Crow." HISTORY. August 16, 2017. https://www.history.com/news/how-the-nazis-were-inspired-by-jim-crow.

So, here is another example of how Americans used the radical term to decry ideas that they were fighting against, just because they didn't believe that everybody deserves equal rights. When we look back at these events, whose side do we end up on? Who gets celebrated and who gets shunned? Martin Luther King, Rosa Parks, WEB DuBois, the Southern Christian Leadership Conference, and other organizations that paved the way for the expansion of rights get praised for their causes. Strom Thrumond, Bull Connor, George Wallace and the like are scorned for refusing to stand up and do what was right. Instead they did the opposite and fought against progress. How will history view our leaders of today?

9 RELIGIOUS BIGOTRY

Some people have this misconception that life back in early American history wasn't all that bad for white folks, since we hear so much about black tragedies. But this misses the mark as well. In numerous states there was a property threshold that individuals had to meet in order to exercise their right to vote. Most states had some serious property requirements to overcome in order to have suffrage. These state legislatures might have justified these decisions because they believed that if men were wealthy they would have more interests in the course of the country. To put it simply many people were left out of the voting process: blacks, women, Catholics and Jews, the poor who couldn't afford or own land, and those less than 21 years of age. Add all this together and approximately 10 to 20 percent of the overall population could vote[204]. Not exactly what you would call a thriving democracy, you know, considering a democracy is a system of government where the whole population have the ability to decide legislation or elect officials that will.

Isn't that a little shocking? Here are our leaders who just fought a long-drawn out conflict with a much superior military foe for the taste of freedom, freedom to choose our own destiny and our own path forward. And yet here are the same people who are shutting the majority out of this highly fought over right. How could they not let the poor and vulnerable have a say in this country's future? Isn't this country their country too? Shouldn't they receive the same

---

204 Constitutional Rights Foundation. n.d. "Constitutional Rights Foundation." Www.crf-Usa.org. https://www.crf-usa.org/bill-of-rights-in-action/bria-8-1-b-who-voted-in-early-america.

rights as the rich to make the decisions of the future? Why should they be shut out of democracy? Or is this just a democracy for the rich? According to some virtuous men, as in accordance with the early Maryland constitution, "high property qualifications stipulated in many states that someone of wisdom, experience, and virtue" would be elected.[205] So, according to these liberty craving republican zealots poor men didn't have wisdom. Poor men didn't have virtue. And poor men didn't have experience. Perhaps maybe poor men didn't have experience because the rich kept it that way. Of course, how can anyone have experience or gain knowledge of anything if the same established few have held the reins for so long?

Thankfully, due to the hard work and dedication of some "radicals," now there are no property requirements in order to vote, but it took many many years in order to accomplish this. It didn't occur until large numbers of Americans began to move west and the political world was beginning to look spicy again with the reemergence of the two-party system following a long spell of Jeffersonian Republican rule that saw the downfall of the Federalist party, a party largely drawn by the interests of the wealthy elite. And yes I say radicals were the reason why this changed. This change was not brought about by the wealthy few who could vote. Indeed, if anything they fought vociferously against it. If you have an amazing amount of limited power, would you want to share it willingly? Probably not. That's why these radicals had to pry it from the hands of power to receive their aims. These poor white men, without property were called radicals by these powerful rich white men, when in reality they were just asking for their rights that the constitution should have given them in the first place. Many religious clicks were left out of not just voting but basic human rights.

---

205 The Creation of the American Republic

The hate against Catholics would culminate in many ways throughout the decades in the United States. As was mentioned some states in early American history despised Catholics so much that they even banned Catholics from holding public offices and from voting altogether. Pretty serious stuff, considering that one of the main tenets to American liberty is freedom of religion. As you'll see some religions weren't entitled to that right, at least not right away. Anti-Catholicism in Europe, which eventually spread throughout the European colonies, began with the great Reformation, where many dissenting groups of Catholics formed their own religions, which would be called protestantism today. Many of the dissenting voices of the Catholic religion obviously had strong reasons for leaving the Catholic church which is why they grew to resent the Catholic way of doing things. Everything from church hierarchy, the Papal system, where the pope rules over the church, as well as extravagant buildings, which, no doubt, cost a fortune, persuaded many to leave the church in growing numbers, especially when considering that the Catholic church at times offered forgiveness of sins for church contributions. Forgiveness of sins is something only God can do, not a church or priest. Rumors of Church corruption fanned the flames of the rupture. Soon enough, Protestantism spread like a raging wild-fire, with the newly found religions taking shape everywhere throughout Europe. The English would fall victim to the roots of Protestantism next, providing for the profound anti-Catholicism among the English colonists.

In the Medieval period, Catholicism was the major religion in England, life revolved around it. With a devotion to Catholic doctrines, the English were under the guidance of the pope, which resided in Rome, as they always have. That religious connection to

Rome would soon evaporate as soon as English king Henry Vlll, in a selfish and self-possessing act, desperately sought to annul his marriage and take up another woman so that he would have a son. If anyone is at all versed in Catholic doctrine, he or she knows that the Catholic church does not condone separation of marriage, no matter if you're a peasant or a king, it is one of the most sentimental sacraments. But Henry Vlll didn't care about sacraments, he knew what he wanted and what he wanted was a woman.

When the pope wouldn't consent to this annulment, Henry Vlll went into a full on rampage against papal authority. He wouldn't let anyone stop him, so with the help of a totally subordinate parliament they threw off the rule of papal authority in England, naming Henry Vlll Supreme Head of the Church of England, the English clergy went along with the move, in fear of their lives.[206] Henry Vlll, for his part, would go on to have not one or two marriages, but six. That worked out quite well for him huh? If he didn't throw down the rule of the Catholics in England he would have been stuck with his first wife that whole time, poor guy. And, maybe most importantly to him, he did have a son, who would go on to become his successor and make the Church of England formally a Protestant church. The Church banned the English clergy from using anything Catholic in their sermons. Rosaries, holy water, images of Christ, and other "papistical superstitions," were thrown away.[207]

Over the next decades and generations, the Church of England would go on to have many confusing disputes revolving around religion, however, when William of Orange overthrew James ll in

---

206 Shagan, Ethan H. (2017). "The Emergence of the Church of England, c. 1520–1553". In Milton, Anthony (ed.). *The Oxford History of Anglicanism*. Vol. 1: Reformation and Identity, c. 1520–1662. Oxford University Press
207 Haigh, Christopher (1993). *English Reformations: Religion, Politics, and Society Under the Tudors*. Oxford University Press

1688. He tried vehemently to reduce religious tensions throughout the kingdom. The Act of Toleration passed by parliament in 1689, allowed nonconformists, those that followed a religion different from that of the Church of England, the right to worship in buildings and have their own preachers or priests. This opened the way for Baptists, Congregationalists and Quakers to grow, those left out and banned from this toleration were the Catholics. In the 1700s the Church of England became Anglican, thus many, especially, Southern colonies mainly consisted of Anglicans with plenty of Anglican churches and clergymen. The vast majority of immigrants coming from England were either Anglicans, hoping for opportunities to get rich, or nonconformists who left for greater freedom they were hoping to find in the American colonies. The majority of Catholics lived in other areas of Europe, such as France and Spain, which didn't have the numbers that the English had in inhabiting the new land.

Virginia, which became the first English colony, which quickly adhered to the Church of England, showed little tolerance for other churches, especially the Catholics, who generally weren't welcome there. Beginning at Jamestown, its charter, from king James l showed particular animosity towards the Catholics, "We should be loath that any person should be permitted to pass, that we suspected to affect the superstitions of the Church of Rome."[208] After Maryland received a charter as a haven for Catholics, Virginians brewed more anger, especially with Catholicism so near their border. They soon passed laws that prevented Catholic priests in Virginia from practicing their religion, where multiple priests were arrested. Later

---

208 "Virginia, Catholic Church in | Encyclopedia.com." n.d. Www.encyclopedia.com. Accessed May 16, 2024. https://www.encyclopedia.com/religion/encyclopedias-almanacs-transcripts-and-maps/virginia-catholic-church.

in 1699, Catholics were banned from voting for state legislatures and prevented from being a witness in court, believing Catholics were too ignorant to be valuable members of court.[209] Catholics in Virginia were so suppressed that by the 1780s a priest made a comment stating the depressing state of affairs among them "there are not more than 200 [Catholics] in Virginia who are visited four or five times a year by a priest."[210]

Because of the gross mistreatment by the Virginian authorities, Catholicism was a slow progressing religion, at least in Virginia. By 1820, approximately 1% of the Virginian population were Catholics, with priests finally getting permission to conduct mass.[211] State laws began to relax and show more toleration for the Catholic church in the 1830s-1840s, mainly due to the flow of high ranking and important families that accepted the Catholic doctrines. It also helped that more Irish immigrants began arriving, expanding the population of those who practice Catholicism.

In Massachusetts, the famous Puritans were the first to reach Plymouth rock, and became the first to set the ground rules for who was allowed and who wasn't. One of the most sadly ironic facts of history was that the Puritans left their native lands to settle into a new land for the pursuit of freedom, to be able to pray, teach, and worship as they say fit, yet these same people were bitterly intolerant of other religions. The Puritans received their name from their goal of purifying the Church of England, who they viewed as corrupt and not the right way to worship. Rebuffed by the king of England, nearly 20,000 Puritans settled in the Massachusetts

---

209 CATHOLIC ENCYCLOPEDIA: of the w Virginia". *www.newadvent.org*
210 ibid
211 "Virginia, Catholic Church in | Encyclopedia.com." n.d. Www.encyclopedia.com. Accessed May 16, 2024. https://www.encyclopedia.com/religion/encyclopedias-almanacs-transcripts-and-maps/virginia-catholic-church.

bay colony. (Massachusetts would eventually drop the whole Bay thing.) It quickly became obvious, to most unbiased observers, that Puritans wanted freedom only for themselves, not for others. They couldn't stand the Pequot Indians, describing them as "heathens." When the Puritans just kept on showing up and taking over land that belonged to the Pequot, not surprisingly the Pequot resisted, leading the Puritans to massacre around 600 of the Pequots, burning most of them alive. This doesn't sound very Puritan does it? But heck, the Puritans didn't care, they massacred some "heathens," not the end of the world, they were pure right? William Bradford, governor of the colony, witnessed the whole event. His statement best sums up how the majority of the Puritans took this massacre. "It was a fearful sight", he wrote "to see them frying in the fire but the victory seemed sweet over so proud an enemy."[212] That gives me chills, not in a good way.

Of course, Puritan ministers didn't really help much with the whole toleration thing. Reverend John Cotton, grandad of Cotton Mather, essentially told his congregation that it was wrong for Puritans to accept anything other than Puritanism, supporting any other religions was like helping the devil himself. No wonder why Puritans didn't show kindness to other beliefs. Put yourselves in their shoes. If you had a trusted minister, priest, or pastor who told you allowing other religions would be like helping Satan, wouldn't you oppose different religions too? Apparently that kind of belief led to the massacre of the Pequots. And it makes sense why, at least originally, Quakers, Jews, and Catholics were excluded from the Massachusetts Bay colony. Smart Catholics avoided the colony from the 1630s up to 1700, as laws there forbade Catholics priests from being in the colony, not just leading a service, but actually

---

212 ibid

stepping foot within the colony would risk imprisonment or even death. As professor James O'Toole stated "If a priest came in he'd be ordered out of the colony. If he came back, he'd be put in jail for a while and thrown out of the colony again and if he came back a third time he'd be hanged." Massachusetts was a dangerous place to be for Catholics.[213] Of course, Massachusetts was a mainly Puritan colony for many generations, which didn't help the Catholic cause all that much.

One prominent Puritan minister by the name of Roger Williams disagreed that Puritans had to be so intolerant of others, believing that "forced worship stinks in God's nostrils," something that most religions believe today. Williams was definitely ahead of his time. He respected other people's beliefs and ideas. He believed that only churchgoers should finance the church, not tax-payers in general. He even thought it unjust and inhumane to take land from the Indians, or as the Puritans would call them "heathens." But back then this thinking was taboo. He was soon arrested and banished from the colony. A short time later he would buy land, not steal, from the Natives to create the colony of Providence, which became Rhode Island.[214] More on Williams in just a bit.

It wasn't until the beginning of the American revolution when that bitter resentment began to fade. Catholics, with some few exceptions, generally supported the revolution and gained some respect among the American protestants for that reason. And when France signed a treaty of alliance with America in 1777, (France being a majority Catholic country), brought some form of toleration amongst most Americans. That loosening of resentment finally showed up in law, as movements throughout the United States and Massachusetts

---

213 Sanna, Emily. 2018. "Holy Votes: A History of Catholic Voting." U.S. Catholic. November 6, 2018. https://uscatholic.org/articles/201811/holy-votes-a-history-of-catholic-voting/.
214 ibid

finally made practicing Catholicism legal, even though people still practiced the religion when it was illegal, finding all sorts of methods to still worship freely.

The story of Massachusetts is a crazy one indeed. At the beginning of the colony's existence, Catholics were shunned, treated as outsiders, and considered ignorant and radical for their beliefs. Now over half of the total population in Massachusetts is Catholic, making the codfish state one of the most heavily Catholic states in the United States, how things can change.[215]

New Hampshire, the Granite state, originally was a part of the Massachusetts bay colony, because of this Catholics weren't welcomed here either. When New Hampshire broke off from Massachusetts in 1680 it developed a strong protestant majority with many Puritans to boot. After the revolution, when New Hampshire became an actual sovereign state, the state constitution banned Catholics from holding public office. Does that sound like freedom of religion? The state laws made it so uncomfortable that by 1835 there were only around 387 Catholics, two churches, and two priests in the entire state.[216] Things started changing quite rapidly though as Irish immigrants began to start pouring in the state, causing a massive explosion of the Catholics population. Even though there were many Catholics now in the state, the majority were still Protestants, and these Protestants didn't like them. They elected a Know-Nothing governor, (more about the Know Nothings later), who gave chilling anti-Catholic speeches within the state legislature. He must have made quite a fool out of himself, his name doesn't even deserve to be mentioned, that the voters chose a different path. Due to in-

---

215 ibid
216 "New Hampshire, Catholic Church in | Encyclopedia.com." 2014. Encyclopedia.com. 2014. https://www.encyclopedia.com/religion/encyclopedias-almanacs-transcripts-and-maps/new-hampshire-catholic-church#:~:text=Abenaki%20natives%2C%20converted%20by%20Jesuit.

creased agitation among the voters, the New Hampshire legislature passed substantial constitutional changes that virtually did away with religious qualifications for office.[217] Today, nearly 30% of New Hampshire's population are Catholics, a remarkable turnaround for a state that discriminated heavily against the Catholics.

In North Carolina, as well, there was initially little toleration for Catholics dating all the way through the revolutionary war. In the war's aftermath, the North Carolina constitution contained a test oath, which again banned officials who don't believe in a supreme being and "the truth of the Protestant Religion." This clause stood until 1836, although Dr. Thomas Burke, a known Catholic, served as governor in between that period, a tell-tale sign that people didn't really care about that clause. Nonetheless, the atmosphere of North Carolina was not a very accepting one for many Catholics or religious dissenters, so much so that by the year 1821 only 150 Catholics were open about their faith in a state of well over 600,000.[218]

New York wasn't much better, actually it was worse. Way before New York was a colony, let alone state, it was a vast wilderness made up of a powerful Native confederacy consisting of the Mohawks, Oneidas, Onondagas, Cayugas, and Senecas. Many Europeans would visit the area in search of trading opportunities and valuables, though Henry Hudson, employed by the Dutch, officially set up the first successful settlement. The colony's initial name was New Netherlands, a nod to the Dutch city. Under control of the Dutch, the only religion that would be tolerant would be the reformed Dutch church. It turns out that the English wanted a piece of the land as

---

217 ibid
218 "North Carolina, Catholic Church in | Encyclopedia.com." n.d. Www.encyclopedia.com. Accessed May 16, 2024. https://www.encyclopedia.com/religion/encyclopedias-almanacs-transcripts-and-maps/north-carolina-catholic-church.

well. They sent the Duke of York as lord proprietor in additional land. All of this would later be called New York, when the Dutch governor surrendered to the English, without a loss or casualty.

The transition from New Amsterdam to New York was a major plus for the Catholic community who couldn't worship freely under the Dutch, the proprietor of New York, the future James ll, converted to Catholicism in 1672, which soon was felt throughout the colony. In 1682 he appointed a Catholic to be the new governor of the colony, a first in the young land's history. It turns out James ll was pretty nice for the folks in New York, he also let New Yorkers have a representative assembly, another unique feature at the time. When the new governor, Thomas Dongan, arrived he brought with him an English Jesuit and two other priests. Dongan wasted no time in persuading the New York legislature to pass a bill of rights which called for the guarantee of freedom of religion, though there were still a dainty number of Catholics within the colony.[219]

After the English revolution of 1688, which saw the accession of William and Mary, at James ll's expense, threw the colonies into a serious uproar of excitement and energy, the revolution caused such a stir that Jacob Leisler, a Calvinist, led a rebellion against the sitting governor Francis Nicholson. This rebellion ushered in a sort of reign of terror as religious toleration in New York was gone in a blink of an eye and replaced with a series of restrictive measures against the Catholics. The Jesuits were forced to abandon the colony as the Church of England became the established church of New York. This was exactly what Jacob Leisler wanted, as he himself was a die-hard Protestant and detested everything to do with Catholicism.

---

219 "New York, Catholic Church in | Encyclopedia.com." n.d. Www.encyclopedia.com. Accessed May 16, 2024. https://www.encyclopedia.com/religion/encyclopedias-almanacs-transcripts-and-maps/new-york-catholic-church.

Even after the Leisler rebellion was crushed and Leisler executed for his insurrection, the anti-Catholic tirade kept strengthening. A New York law in the year 1700 made it illegal for a priest to be found. Worse, anyone found harboring a priest would be found subject to a fine of 200 pounds, a very huge amount at the time.

Perhaps the most serious religious discrimination of the time, at least in regards to a Christian religion, was the "Great Deportation." The "Great Deportation" was a forced removal by the British of inhabitants in the Canadian- American region during the French and Indian war. The deportations amounted to the deaths of thousands of innocent people, all because the British used it as a war measure to attack New France, a version of imperialism that the British were doing all over America. The inhabitants were forced to leave the land that they had farmed for centuries. Their houses were destroyed and their land was given to settlers who remained loyal to Great Britain. To put this in perspective, imagine the Russians coming in and taking your homes that you've lived in your entire lives, giving it to loyal Russians and deporting you from your country, while in the process you or your family would be constantly threatened with starvation and disease. Estimates have the number of those who succumbed to disease, shipwrecks, and starvation as greater than 5,000 people.[220]

Many of the inhabitants were distributed throughout the American colonies from Massachusetts to Georgia, and because these inhabitants had been part of New France, and with France being a Catholic country, most of the inhabitants deported were Catholics. This made a bad situation worse for these poor Catholics who now found themselves far from home in colonies that were

---

220 Plank, Geoffrey (2001). *An Unsettled Conquest: The British Campaign Against the Peoples of Acadia*. University of Pennsylvania Press. ISBN 978-0-8122-0710-1. Archived from the original on April 3, 2023. Retrieved November 6, 2018

not accepting of their faithful beliefs. In New York, the quota of inhabitants that were shipped there were sold as indentured servants. Worse, families were broken up so that Catholic children could be sent to Protestant families, in an earlier account of family separation. This state of conditions would remain until after the revolutionary war, and mass itself was not celebrated in the state until the French chaplains offered mass to the French soldiers who were sent to bail the Americans out.[221]

As a matter of fact, things got pretty rough for many Catholics on the eve of the revolution. When the British, in an effort to appease the Canadians, who were still mostly Catholic, passed the Quebec Act, which vested the government of Quebec with a governor and council, preserved the French civil code, since France had owned the territory for a century before the British, and protected the Catholic church in Canada.[222] The law simply would allow the inhabitants to practice Catholicsim and since most were Catholics, it outlawed the test act, which would require the lawmakers of the colony to be protestants instead of Catholics, something that the colony simply couldn't do. Because of the vast majority of Catholics within the colony, if the test act had been in place, there would be an insufficient number of men governing Canada. So, put simply, the British created the act to please the colony of Canada, who were mostly Catholics, doing little else than allowing the residents to continue practicing their religion. There shouldn't be much harm in that right? Well the colonies weren't too happy about it. They

---

221 "New York, Catholic Church in | Encyclopedia.com." n.d. Www.encyclopedia.com. Accessed May 16, 2024. https://www.encyclopedia.com/religion/encyclopedias-almanacs-transcripts-and-maps/new-york-catholic-church.
222 The Editors of Encyclopedia Britannica. 2016. "Quebec Act | Great Britain [1774]." In *Encyclopædia Britannica*. https://www.britannica.com/event/Quebec-Act.

believed that the British crown had greatly expanded its authority and taken away lands that they believed should be theirs. The worst thing about it however, was how the act was promoting "popery", or Catholicism.[223]

The "popery act" was a direct threat to colonial Protestantism and many colonists feared the worst, which is another reason why the Americans came to the conclusion that independence must come soon. It is rather interesting when the Catholics had to make a decision as to what side to support during the American revolution. The British had for many centuries been quite repressive to the Catholics within their domain, many were persecuted, banished, and executed. While at the same time, the British did open a new safe haven for Catholics in Canada, while the American colonists long harbored deep resentments against the Catholics and were in the process of making discriminatory laws, or already had discriminatory laws on the books towards Catholics. What most Catholics were thinking was the same thing that most Native Americans were thinking, who would grant me the best opportunity to be free. In the end the majority of the Catholics would go on and support the revolutionaries, a move that garnered some newly found respect for the Catholics as those who stood up for the republican cause. The massive aid, which without the Americans may well have lost the campaign, from France and Spain, both of whom were Catholic countries, helped soothe the colonists' resentments.[224]

Nevertheless, that didn't stop New York from discriminating against the Catholics still. During the 1777 state constitution, the New Yorkers put in a naturalization clause, which essentially barred

---

[223] Joseph J. Casino, "Anti-Popery in Colonial Pennsylvania", *Pennsylvania Magazine of History and Biography* Vol. 105, No. 3 (Jul., 1981
[224] "New York, Catholic Church in | Encyclopedia.com." n.d. Www.encyclopedia.com. Accessed May 16, 2024. https://www.encyclopedia.com/religion/encyclopedias-almanacs-transcripts-and-maps/new-york-catholic-church.

Catholics from becoming citizens. This clause lasted until 1806. As time went on, new advancements in industry and innovation, such as the Erie canal created a melting pot as immigration, and particularly Catholic immigrants from Ireland came swarming in. With the rise in Catholics immigrating into all the colonies and New York, the discriminatory laws were annulled and Catholics were free to practice their religion again free from governmental influence.[225] (North Carolina would be the exception as the state still held a test oath that banned Catholics from public office until it was abolished in 1868.)

Just because the government no longer discriminated against Catholics in state and local laws, doesn't mean that anti-Catholic sentiment died down too. Many Americans abhorred the use of publicly funding parochial schools, and many states passed the "Blaine amendments" that prohibited public funding for parochial schools. Even though the amendments failed, they are still being debated today and are a big issue in most elections, especially when tied to charter school funding. It's safe to say that the reason why these amendments passed in some states is because of the anti-Catholic sentiments of the people of those states, it wasn't because the people were opposed to publicly funded schools. It's also safe to say that had Protestant schools sprung up around the country like the Catholic schools did, many states would have supported them, as the country was overwhelmingly a faith based Christian nation.

As more Catholics began to immigrate to the new country searching for better opportunities, they tended to support political parties that mostly fit with their perception of what the better course was.

---

225 "New York, Catholic Church in | Encyclopedia.com." n.d. Www.encyclopedia.com. Accessed May 16, 2024. https://www.encyclopedia.com/religion/encyclopedias-almanacs-transcripts-and-maps/new-york-catholic-church.

In the late 1700s and early 1800s the small Catholic population may have found itself in another tough decision as to what political party to support. On one hand the Federalists had passed a naturalization act that required immigrants to live in the country 14 years, as opposed to only 5 years before, to become legal United States citizens, a move that many immigrants took to heart and that's why more immigrants tended to support the opposition party, the republicans. The republicans were led by Thomas Jefferson, and although immigrants might not have been able to vote, they certainly weren't banned from speaking their mind, which they did by far outpacing the federalists in terms of the press. The republicans, however, supported full throated democracy, which didn't bode well for the Catholics at the time. Catholics constituted just about 1% of the total population at the time, with widespread anti-Catholic sentiment, a greater democracy would have hurt the Catholics' cause and set them back to discriminatory measures. Charles Caroll, the only Catholic to sign the Declaration of Independence, was a die-hard federalist for this reason, as the federalists were opposed to democratic rule, comparing it to mob rule.

The decision for the Catholics as years went on became easier as the new parties formed were the Democratic and Whigs in the 1830s-50s. Most Catholics, who were immigrants, supported the democrats because the democrats were more accepting of immigrants and Catholics as a whole. Meanwhile, in the 1850s another, rather strong, party sprang up bent on bringing the country back to its first principles. This party was called the Nativist American party, better known as the Know-nothing party. The Know-nothing party got its name by party leaders telling reporters, who were curious about the strange meetings, that they knew nothing. The Know-nothings became sort of a laughing stock, as Lincoln's secretary of

State, William Seward would later remark "I know nothing of the Know-nothings," though some didn't take them so seriously, even though they should have.²²⁶

The Know-nothings were created because of the immense anti-Catholicism still strong in America in the 1830s and 40s. Although anti-Catholicism was high among traditional protestants, it really didn't play a huge role politically speaking. Actually, as we've seen, many states began loosening restrictions on Catholics, allowing them to participate politically; to vote, and hold office, as well as reducing discriminatory measures that had been haunting Catholics for so long. While some states were allowing Catholics to run for office, other states were allowing Catholics to actually practice mass in the state. Clearly things were moving in a positive direction and America was becoming more gentle and kinder towards its inhabitants, well, at least religiously speaking. Obviously, the reason why states and localities began to loosen the discriminatory measures against Catholics was because of the influx in immigration that really culminated in the 1840s.

Just like today, when the government begins to accept and acknowledge those who are different, people begin to push back, fearing that, in this case, Catholics would steal their culture from them. Allowing the Catholics to be equal was just too much for some who quite literally believed the country was doomed for hell. Those who pushed back were mainly white male Protestants, who believed that Catholics were "papists", those who bowed down to the pope and worshiped symbols as idolatry. As Irish Catholics began swelling the country, these angry Protestants felt attacked, they had to do something, or their whole way of life would come crashing down. The ensuing political movement that would take

---

226 Stahr, Walter. 2013. *Seward : Lincoln's Indispensable Man*. New York: Simon & Schuster Paperbacks.

place is one that often gets missed in our history textbooks. It was certainly a dark time when anti-Catholicism mingled with hatred towards millions of people who were different gained some serious momentum. It wasn't just anti-Catholicism, since most Catholics were immigrants, it was anti-immigrants, or what is considered nativism, the want to protect native-born interests, a curious belief, considering that Nativism, theoretically, would not be the immigrant Puritans whose interests they would be preserving but the Native Americans. Of course they didn't view the Native Americans like this, English immigrants who emigrated to this land centuries before believed they were the natives, a belief that some still have today, it was a belief that certainly was commonplace in the 1840s at least.

Anti-Catholic, nativist politics originated in the 1840s in New York, a bastion of anti-Catholicism for centuries. The majority of Irish immigrants coming to America settled in New York, particularly New York City, as we've seen as more and more people come into a region with different cultures the more and more traditional population pushes back, which is what happened in New York in 1843 with the emergence of the American Republican party. The American Republican party was exactly the kind of anti-Catholic, anti-immigrant party that the Know-nothings would gain inspiration from. The party was mainly a regional third party, with not much support outside the Middle states of New York and Pennsylvania. It pushed typical measures, not much different from normal party platforms, such as local, direct election to school boards, anti-fraud measures, and a few other normal things. However, it got very shaky when the platform directly attacked immigrants calling for the amount of time immigrants needed to wait to become citizens to twenty-one years for new immigrants, a jab at Irish-Catholics in particular as they were increasingly becoming the majority of new arrivals.[227] Waiting twenty-one years to become a citizen is a big deal, you miss out on voting, citizenship for children, ability to get jobs, and the ability to travel. Voting, for obvious reasons, was one of the deeply political purposes of waiting twenty-one years to become a citizen. Most of the members of the American Republican Party were nativist Whigs who feared that an increase in immigration would lead to more votes for democratic candidates across the country. Another somewhat subtle provision of the party platform was the calling for mandating the use of the protestant version of the King James Bible, undercutting the use of Catholic Bibles.

Not surprisingly the party didn't receive much success, although surprisingly some groups of voters came out in favor of the party, showing the inner hatred and resentment for religious toleration and immigrant toleration. Some victories in 1844 resulted in the election of a mayor, city commissioners, a city auditor, and two congressmen, all in either New York and Pennsylvania.[228] The party was actually growing so furiously that they called a national convention in 1845 and changed their name to the Native American party, what would be known as the Know-nothings. The party was never able to formulate a national political backing in the 1840s, partly due to a few major changes in the United States at the time. At the end of the 1840s the Mexican-American war took too much attention away from rival three party groups that otherwise needed more coverage to make a substantial run. Directly preceding this was the Philadelphia nativist riots in 1844, which severely weakened the party.

Again, the same story of new arrivals causing chaos among those "nativist" settlers is the theme of this crisis. In Philadelphia,

---

227 "American Republican Party | Encyclopedia.com." n.d. Www.
encyclopedia.com. https://www.encyclopedia.com/history/
dictionaries-thesauruses-pictures-and-press-releases/american-republican-party.
228 ibid

immigrants were coming left and right, these were mostly German and Irish born immigrants. The cultural and economic differences that arose between the different groups was too much for the native population to handle. Angry, and confused, over the increase of Irish Catholics flooding their land, the native population began forming anti-Catholic, nativist groups in Philadelphia. The groups distributed letters and newspapers with a strong anti-Catholic bias. In a move that further inflamed situations, Catholic priest, Francis Kenrick, asked the Board of Controllers of the Philadelphia schools to allow students to use whichever Bible their parents want them to use, as opposed to the longstanding tradition of just using the Protestant King James version. The Board of Controllers agreed with the Catholic priest and immediately the Protestants in Philadelphia were enraged. Now, heaven forbid, their children would be forced to sit and watch Catholic kids read their version of the Bible, a little over-reaction considering Catholics were Christians too.[229] Protestants, meanwhile, took to the false belief that Catholics were trying to get rid of the use of Bibles in schools, even though this clearly was not the case. "The school controversy, writes historian David Montgomery, "had united 94 leading clergymen of the city in a common pledge to strengthen Protestant education and "awaken the attention of the community to the dangers which ... threaten these United States from the assaults of Romanism." The American Tract Society took up the battle cry and launched a national crusade to save the nation from the "spiritual despotism" of Rome."[230]

When the American Republican Party held a mass meeting in a predominantly Irish neighborhood, something that may have been

---

229 Peixotto, Ernest C.; Agnes Repplier (1898). *Philadelphia: The Place and the People*. The Macmillan Company
230 David Montgomery, "The Shuttle and the Cross: Weavers and Artisans in the Kensington Riots of 1844," *Journal of Social History*, (1972) 5#4 pp. 411–446, quoting

done to provoke outrages, a group of Irishmen attacked the meeting where the nativists went scrambling for cover. They didn't run off with the intention of staying quiet, however. Soon after, the nativists came back, this time with a great number destined to quash anything the Irish minority could muster up. Holding another rally, again designed to provoke and excite anger among the Irishmen in the neighborhood, the nativists increased their rhetoric, calling the Irish "papists" who would destroy the Protestant religion, taking Bibles away and forcing innocent inhabitants to bow down and worship the pope. It is not surprising that with all of the hateful rhetoric fighting would follow, it seems that this is what the nativists really wanted. Shots rang out from behind the windows of the market where the rally was taking place, two nativists in the crowd were reportedly killed. To make matters worse, in a particularly heinous act, a nativist gang banded together to destroy and ransack the Sisters of Charity, a religious community of women determined on helping the poorest of the poor.[231] They also destroyed a number of Catholic homes, trying to make a statement that Catholics weren't welcomed there. When it was all said and done many people were injured and a few even dead, all because the nativists went on a spree attacking the very way of life that Catholics knew their whole lives.

The next day, nativists made yet another verbal attack against Catholics, admonishing fellow Americans to beware of "the bloody hand of the Pope."[232] When a vicious mob arrived at Kensington, gun fighting ensued. Nativists destroyed more than thirty homes, the market where the rally took place the day before, and the Hibernia fire station. It's impossible to know how many Catholics lost their lives during this brutal confrontation, but at least one Catholic is known to have been shot in the head, while many others were

---

231 Fitzgerald, Margaret E. (1992). "The Philadelphia Nativists Riots". Irish Cultural Society of the Garden City Area. Archived from the original
232 ibid

severely wounded. The fighting only ended when the local militia was called out, a little too late to stop the hatred. The next day "On May 8, (nativist) mobs gutted several private dwellings, a Catholic seminary, and two Catholic churches: St. Michael's at Second Street and Master and St. Augustine's at Fourth and Vine", according to the encyclopedia of greater Philadelphia.[233] "Only a flood of new forces—including citizen posses, city police, militia companies arriving from other cities, and U.S. army and navy troops—ended the violence by May 10." During the attacks at least fourteen died and as many as fifty mortally wounded, the total amount of damage consisted of around $150,000, today that value would be near $5 million.[234]

In the aftermath the city mayor set up a small force to protect the Catholics from the nativist violence, churches closed until the violence subdued, and valuables were placed in safe facilities so the gangs couldn't destroy the priceless pieces of art and statues from the churches. Catholic priests urged their followers to not engage in any act of physical violence and to trust the law enforcement in suppressing the nativist gangs, a somewhat hard pill for many Philadelphia Catholics to swallow considering the law enforcement did relatively little to suppress the violence up to that point. Many people, however, blamed the riots on the Catholics, the grand jury accused the Catholics of starting the violence. The outbreak of violence was due to "The efforts of a portion of the community to exclude the Bible from the public schools."[235]

---

233 Schrag, Zachary. n.d. "Nativist Riots of 1844." Encyclopedia of Greater Philadelphia. https://philadelphiaencyclopedia.org/essays/nativist-riots-of-1844/.
234 1634–1699: McCusker, J. J. (1997). *How Much Is That in Real Money? A Historical Price Index for Use as a Deflator of Money Values in the Economy of the United States: Addenda et Corrigenda* (PDF).
235 "The Nativist Riots: Southwark 1844" (PDF). *The Church of St. Philip Neri Parish History*. Church of St. Philip Neri. Archived from the original (PDF) on August 22, 2007

In all fairness, the Catholics in and around Philadelphia were mortally afraid of another outbreak in violence, especially with the upcoming July 4th parade, where the nativists were to have another massive rally. In preparation for the parade the Catholic church appealed to the Pennsylvania governor for assistance, which he granted by calling out the Pennsylvania militia to be ready just in case.[236] The church also gathered weapons and stored them in the church, just in case of the worst. When the parade went by on July 4th without any violence, many in the city were relieved. Although the relief was short lived when a nativist bystander happened to witness five defective muskets being brought back to the church. Soon the next day, July 5th, thousands gathered outside the church demanding the weapons. The mob refused to leave the situation, they returned the next day in greater numbers, causing the sheriff to call out the militia. When the mob refused the militia's orders to disperse, the militia presence grew, in which they were finally able to remove the mob, despite being physically attacked themselves, being pelted with rocks. In response to seeing his own men being pelted by rocks, a scene from biblical times, general Cadwalader ordered cannons fired into the crowds. If you think tear gas is bad, imagine a canon.

Starting at around 9PM the vicious crowd counterattacked, this time with a cannon of their own, threatening to knock down the church. For the next four or so hours the two sides fought back and forth demanding the ammunition and, by this time, prisoners out of the church. By morning four militiamen were dead, as well as dozens of rioters.[237] At this point the fighting seemed to have fizzled out. The governor kept state troops in Philadelphia for weeks to

---

236 ibid
237 Schrag, Zachary. n.d. "Nativist Riots of 1844." Encyclopedia of Greater Philadelphia. https://philadelphiaencyclopedia.org/essays/nativist-riots-of-1844/.

make sure no more attacks took place, and none did after the July 4th debacle. Again grand juries would blame the Catholics for the violence, even when nativists were initiating violence by planning massive rallies, and denouncing Catholicism and immigrants in a majority Irish district, hoping for a reaction they could use to help their cause.[238]

The aftermath of the violence didn't bode well for the American Republican Party. In 1844, the democrats were able to pin most of the blame on the party along with the Whig party, for not thoroughly renouncing the attacks. As a result the democrats won the White House, by appealing to immigrant voters and to religious toleration compared to the Whigs, which were still mainly a Protestant political party. The democrats also held a huge lead in the congressional elections of that year, winning 142 seats to 79 for the whigs. The American republican party won no major offices, much of it out of fear from their fellow Americans that more violence would ensue. In Philadelphia, for example, laws were passed calling for a permanent police force to help quell potential violence and protect the churches.[239] Bishop Kenrick, who had played a major role in the riots trying to make the public school system tolerant of Catholic children, ended up creating a separate school system, the Catholic schools of Philadelphia, which by 1860 had 17 schools, so that Catholic children could practice their religion without fear.[240]

Even though the American Republican Party was mainly a flop, it did succeed by influencing other states to pick up on some of

---

238 "The Nativist Riots: Southwark 1844" (PDF). *The Church of St. Philip Neri Parish History*. Church of St. Philip Neri. Archived from the original (PDF) on August 22, 2007

239 *Philadelphia: A 300-Year History,*

240 The Nativist Riots: Southwark 1844" (PDF). *The Church of St. Philip Neri Parish History*. Church of St. Philip Neri. Archived from the original (PDF) on August 22, 2007.

their ideas. For instance, shortly after the culmination of the party, Lewis Charles Levin, who was a strong anti-Catholic, was elected to the US House of Representatives from Pennsylvania. Levin was the first Jewish congressman ever elected to either house, making his verbal attacks against immigrants and Catholics all the worse. The year he won his seat, 1844, he had been drumming up claims that Catholic immigration would ruin the United States, and that since Catholics were always running to the pope to make decisions they were basically useless in a republican society.[241] In actuality, his inflammatory remarks can be blamed as the major escalator to the violence. As we have seen in recent years when a candidate running for office has a strong following, they can have a severe influence over their followers' thoughts and actions, even resulting in violence, as a result of believing lies that the candidate spews to promote their own political interests. It happened when Trump's followers ransacked the Capital, believing, falsely, that the election was stolen, and it happened in 1844 when Levin's followers believed that the Catholics would destroy America. Three months later Levin won the House seat, with the help from the same people who destroyed multiple churches and spread chaos all throughout Philadelphia.

Some enlightened individuals knew what Levin was all about. Writer Zachary Schrag had this to say about Levin, he "was a rabble-rouser, conspiracy theorist, bigot."[242]

Levin had a sense for violence, long before his infamous rioting, he engaged in a duel in the 1830s after quarreling about a fourth of July speech. His mere second, should give anybody a serious pause about the character of Levin, when he chose Jefferson Davis, the future Confederate president, to be his number two man in the

---

241 "19th-C. Jewish Rep. Lewis Charles Levin: The Original Nativist Troll." 2018. Tablet Magazine. October 23, 2018. https://www.tabletmag.com/sections/news/articles/lewis-levin-wasnt-nice.
242 ibid

duel. According to US senator Henry Foote, who was always helping Levins when he got into some serious beef, Levins's "very impulsive nature got him into several serious personal quarrels, from which I had much trouble in rescuing him."[243] He was even indicted for murder in 1834, though nothing seemed to have come of it, as proving a murder was much harder back in the 1800s. There's even much speculation that he stabbed lawyer Henry Stump with a bowie knife, when he disagreed with him. And we know he drank a lot, a lot, a lot. One observer was known to have said "His form, bloated with drink, was covered with tattered habiliments, every rag of which spoke eloquently to the passenger of want and constant inebriety. His swollen cheeks and sunken eyes were voiceful of dissipation. The night wind shuddered as it bore his maudlin song upon its wings, trilled from a handcart upon which some good Samaritan was conveying him home from a debauch, to keep him from being devoured by the swine while reposing in the filth-conduits of the streets of our city."[244] Seems like a pretty nice guy huh? Does that sound like someone you would support and vote for to represent you in Congress?

The fact that he was a common drunkard didn't necessarily hurt Levins. Back then the vast majority of people drank a lot. It makes sense that they would idolize someone who is like them, someone who can get down with the boys and have a good time at the local tavern. (Remember women still couldn't vote and women were also a major force in the temperance movement.) Secondly, Levins was able to make a recovery and use it politically to attract more voters. It's a feel good story to hear when somebody had some major struggles in the past to rise up and defeat his inner demons. As a

---

243 ibid
244 ibid

matter of fact, Levins would later be a major advocate for temperance movements, warning about the dangers of alcohol, becoming an editor of a temperance newspaper. So Levins's major political positions were anti-alcoholism and anti-Catholicism, the latter growing more intense after the British in 1829 allowed Catholics to serve in Parliament, a major step for that Protestant country to accept.

It's obvious to note that not all Catholics were Irish, similarly not all Irish were Catholic, but as the Irish began to move to America in increasing numbers they quickly became the face of the Catholic wave in the country. So Levins had a particular ethnicity to attack. When Daniel O'Connel, who was the leader of the Irish emancipation movement from the United Kingdom, called for the Irish to have their own parliament as opposed to being a part of a parliament controlled by England, he called for the repeal of the Act of Union. To most Americans, this reminded them of their own struggle to have representation and freedom from the English, and so began to sympathize with the Irish cause, even forming Repeal associations to help fundraise for the Irish effort. Not Levin, however, who grew increasingly agitated over what he called an Irish lead effort to corrupt the United States, it was used "as an engine by which to reach the United States, pollute our ballot boxes, disrupt our Union, light the flame of civil war in the States and combine the Irish Catholic vote," he warned, "for the purpose of extending the Romish denomination of his Holiness the Pope. This now appears to us, to be the genuine character of Irish Repeal; a torch of discord flung among the American people, to subjugate our Independence; to establish the supremacy of the Papal Church, in our Government; to control our elections contaminate our people, subvert free principles, and by tyrannous coercion force Heresy to bow the knee to Idols."[245]

---

245 ibid

Levins soon grew hostile to the Irish living in the states believing them to be part of a vast conspiracy to stuff the ballots with "papist conspirators." So he began the movement to expand the waiting period to become a United States citizen to twenty-one years, thereby saving this country from a "foreign dictator," meaning the pope. Eager to embrace this golden opportunity to represent the American republicans, Levins began to speak out against Catholics, energizing his base and sparking rioting throughout the city. When the rioting finally ended, he went on to blame the military, that responsibly stepped in to stop the bloodshed, instead of giving even the slightest blame to the vicious mobs that he himself helped to erect, "The dreadful slaughter of human life," he wrote defending himself, "was not the work of a mob of citizens, but of the military."[246]

Nativists loved Levins, not surprisingly, because of his fearlessness and defiance of the authorities. In a three way race for a seat to the US house of representatives, running against a whig and democratic challenger, Levins blissfully wrote, "Roman Catholics or Americans must rule the land. There is no other question before the people," an early form of fear-mongering, which happens during every election cycle.[247] Democrats resorted to a form of anti-semitism, trying to separate themselves as much as possible from the Levins faction, despite the fact that the democrats were the most welcoming party.

Despite the fact that Levins was still facing charges regarding his role in the Philadelphia riots, in which he would be eventually charged, Levins won his seat, thanks to the prejudices of the citizens of Pennsylvania's first district. Levins would go on to serve not just one, but three terms in the House, accomplishing nothing, and seeing his dream of expanding the waiting period for new immigrants come to nothing and dying an embarrassing death.

---

246 ibid
247 ibid

After he was defeated in 1850, by a democratic opponent, Levins lived out his final years in relative isolation, even spending a brief period of time in an insane asylum. And when the Know-nothing party came to fruition, expanding some of the nativist views of the original American Republican party, Levins supported it, though he disagreed with compromising to make it a reality. Although the American republican party fizzled, and Levins, the most successful American republican politician, would be ungraciously defeated, the movement regarding anti-Catholicism and anti-immigration in general would mutate into another political party called the Know-nothings. The election of Levins to Congress, even though long ago, should be a wake up call to all of us today. The fact that a bigoted, self-possessing, politician should win the hearts of so many by speaking demagoguery and using slurs in a politically advancing way to win, shows how fragile our democracy is and how quickly Americans can be fooled into believing lies and smears against those who are different.

Anti-Catholicism kicked up a gear with the failed revolutions of 1848, which many Protestants thought the pope was behind. Even Protestant ministers threw themselves into a fray. One Boston minister attacked Catholics describing them as "the ally of tyranny, the opponent of material prosperity, the foe of thrift, the enemy of the railroad, the caucus, and the school."[248] In an interesting twist, many Jews became leaders of the anti-Catholic vote, mainly because Americans weren't scared of the political power of Jews, at least not yet, as they were less willing to use their religion when making political decisions. Soon anti-Catholics societies like the Star Spangled Banner arose, pledging only to support the candidates that would advance their anti-Catholic viewpoints. By 1854, these

---

248 McGreevey, John T. (2003). *Catholicism and American Freedom: A History*. New York, New York: W.W. Norton & Company

societies would ban together to form what became known as the Know-nothing party.

In the beginning the Know-nothings won some pretty stirring victories, showing strong support in Boston and Salem, Massachusetts, as well as carrying most of the rest of the state in the fall 1854 elections. The Know-nothing's main goal; to prevent a "foreign invasion."[249] To be sure, in this book so far we have hit the immigration card to death already, but some extra caveats have to be examined to gain full appreciation of what the Know-nothings were all about. Historian James McPherson has written "Immigration during the first five years of the 1850s reached a level five times greater than a decade earlier. Most of the new arrivals were poor Catholic peasants or laborers from Ireland and Germany who crowded into the tenements of large cities. Crime and welfare costs soared. Cincinnati's crime rate, for example, tripled between 1846 and 1853, and its murder rate increased sevenfold. Boston's expenditures for poor relief rose threefold during the same period."[250] Given this, it's fair to say that most Protestants, of the middle class, looked at the Irish Catholics coming in as the reason for the increasing crime, and growing poorness surrounding the cities. WIth the increase of welfare being doled out on the new immigrants coming in it would be the middle class Protestants that would bear the brunt of this unfair treatment. It was not just purely bigotry that played a role here, it was also economic and social issues at play as well.

The party succeeded in industrial communities where deep fear that the Irish would come in and steal jobs won over common

---

249 "Anti-Outsider Platforms." n.d. Digital Public Library of America. https://dp.la/exhibitions/outsiders-president-elections/anti-outsider-platforms/know-nothing-party-1856.
250 "Know Nothings." n.d. Www.libertymagazine.org. https://www.libertymagazine.org/article/know-nothings.

sense and compassion. A newspaper editor, running as a whig, was elected mayor of Philadelphia after vowing that the American government would never be governed by anyone other than native born Americans. All the way from Washington D.C. to San Francisco, know-nothing sympathizers won elections, proving that the movement wasn't purely regional as was the case with the American Republican Party before it. As a result of these victories Know-nothing membership rose dramatically from just under 50,000 people to over one million members.[251]

The Know-nothing movement in California, particularly in San Francisco wasn't so anti-Irish as had been the case farther out east. The primary reason for the nativism in California was Asian immigration, again a deep rooted fear that Asian, especially Chinese immigrants, would steal jobs. Hence in California many Know-nothing candidates won landslide victories, as a result Chinese immigrants were treated very similar to free blacks in many states, where Chinese immigrants were banned from testifying against whites in court.[252]

Democrats in the South were able to stem the growing tide of nativism by tying the know-nothings to the radical abolitionists, thereby horrifying the southern citizenry to deny Know-nothingism, as a vote for them would be a vote for the freeing of blacks. Abraham Lincoln got it right when he declared that northerners who, in some cases, like the famous firebrand Thaddeus Stevens, would bemoan slavery for all its evils, treating humans as animals, while at the same time holding such resentment against poor white immigrants don't make much sense. In an 1855 letter to Joshua Speed, he wrote: "I am not a Know-Nothing. That is certain. How could I be? How

---

251 ibid
252 LeMay, Michael C. (2012). *Transforming America: Perspectives on U.S. Immigration. Volume 1, The Making of a Nation of Nations: The Founding to 1865.* Santa Barbara, California: Praeger Publishers

can anyone who abhors the oppression of negroes be in favor of degrading classes of white people?"[253]

Know-nothingism was so popular in the Northern industrial cities that Know-nothing leaders began to get paranoid, thinking that the Catholics would bring in non-eligible voters to skew the elections in favor of democratic candidates. On August 6, 1855, violence erupted in Louisville, Kentucky, in the midst of a very controversial and hotly contested Kentucky election for governor. Fed, in large part, to anti-immigrant writings and anti-Catholic speeches given by Know-nothing leaders, Protestant mobs sparked what would be known as "bloody Monday". According to the *Louisville Daily Journal* by Monday morning the city was "...in possession of an armed mob, the base passions of which were infuriated to the highest pitch by the incendiary appeals of the newspaper organ and the popular leaders of the Know Nothing party."[254] The Know-nothings formed gangs to guard the polls, to make sure no cheating occurred, clearly this was voter intimidation at its best. As a result of voter intimidation, hundreds of voters refused to take part in the election. When a former congressman tried to intervene and disrupt the gangs guarding the polls he was beaten, then all hell broke loose. Protestant mobs attacked German and Irish neighborhoods, without mercy, setting many homes and churches on fire. At least 22 were killed and many more wounded in this street brawl, yet again another result of bigotry infecting the hearts of unassuming Americans.

Despite all the violence the Know-nothing party still remained a major threat in national politics, especially in the northern states. In 1856 the Know-nothings ran a ticket for president and vice-president, headed by former president, and southern sympathizer Millard

---

253 ibid
254 Bloody Work", *Louisville Daily Journal, August 7, 1855*

Fillmore and Andrew Donelson, Andrew Jackson's Nephew-in law. Although Fillmore was not much of a Know-nothing, as a matter of fact, he wrote nothing or spoke nothing regarding nativism or anti-Catholicism, the latter he especially didn't want to be tied to. Fillmore instead decided to accept the nomination for national unity in the face of growing regional hostilities regarding slavery, though he at least privately wrote of his dissatisfaction with immigrants' growing political power.

John C Fremont, the republican nominee, being the first republican presidential candidate, ran a campaign challenging slavery and condemning slave holders. Even Fremont, who himself was a Protestant, but had married a Catholic, was attacked as being a "papist", merely because of his association with a Catholic. The republican party and the Know-nothings fumed with each other, as both sides tried to wrangle the anti-slavery vote, though the republican party was the most organized of the two.

When it was all said and done, the democratic candidate, James Buchanan won a landslide victory over his challengers John C Fremont, who garnered 33% of the vote and the Know-nothing candidate Millard Fillmore, who captured 22% of the vote. Up to this time no third party had even come anywhere near this total that the Know-nothings were able to muster up. No doubt, some of the support the Know-nothings received were from Fillmore's popularity with some whigs who didn't cross over to the new republican party. Without the emergence of the Know-nothing party the general election would have been much closer than what it ended up to be, with a potential for an earlier start to the civil war. It is a bit disheartening that the Know-nothings were able to gain so much support, while brandishing anti-Catholic and anti-immigrant policies. In fact, the Know-nothings even won a state, Maryland, in the 1856 presidential election, winning with 55% of the vote of that state. To be fair, the republican party didn't run a ticket in the southern states, effectively meaning the election, in the South, was between the democratic ticket and the Know-nothing ticket, which explains why the Know-nothings gathered 22% of votes nationally. But even with this caveat, the Know-nothings almost squeaked out victories in Kentucky, Louisiana, Tennessee, and Florida, showing that prejudiced bigotry was more prevalent than realized.

After the 1856 elections, the Know-nothings declined rapidly. The party was losing anti-slavery votes to the more anti-slavery republican party, leaving anti-Catholic, nativism, as its only unique ideology. Lincoln, who by this time was becoming a major force in the republican party, further denounced Know-nothingism by stating "Our progress in degeneracy appears to me to be pretty rapid. As a nation, we began by declaring that "all men are created equal." We now practically read it "all men are created equal, except negroes." When the Know-Nothings get control, it will read "all men are created equals, except negroes and foreigners and Catholics." When it comes to that I should prefer emigrating to some country where they make no pretense of loving liberty—to Russia, for instance, where despotism can be taken pure, and without the base alloy of hypocrisy."[255] Such views were commonplace among many who began to become frustrated with what the Know-nothing party stood for. After the disastrous Dred Scott decision, the Know-nothing party fell to pieces, with its members either joining the democratic party or the republican party and Know-nothingism forever went down in history as a big sham, a party full of hate and prejudice. In 1854, 52 Know-nothings were elected to the House of Representatives, this

---

255 Browne, Francis Fisher (1914). *The Every-day Life of Abraham Lincoln: A Narrative and Descriptive Biography with Pen-pictures and Personal Recollections by Those Who Knew Him.*

declined sharply in 1856, however, when they only won 14 seats, by 1860, there was no such thing as a Know-nothing.

Just like how John C Fremont was heckled by being a supposed Catholic, which no doubt stole votes away from him, Catholic candidates running nationally faced the same treatment. Catholics running for national office were virtually unheard of until the 20th century, the risk of violence was too great for the candidates otherwise. The first major presidential candidate, who happened to be a Catholic, was Al Smith, a popular and highly effective governor of New York. The democratic party decided to name Al Smith their standard bearer, despite the deep resentment, including much of the South, against Catholics.

Later historians would name the reasons why Smith lost the election as the three p's, "Prohibition, Prejudice and Prosperity."[256] The first p, prohibition, was a major sticking point to many campaigns throughout the 1920s and 30s. Smith was against prohibition, as were many Americans, hence the reason why the democrats put an anti-prohibition statement in their party platform. Prohibition was supported, however, by the vast majority of Protestants, who still supported the republican party and their "traditional values", even when this meant severe economic inequality. The last p, prosperity, was in reference to the large economic boom that many large businesses were basking in, making huge sums of money, while paying their workers hardly anything to earn a living on. To the big business elite, this was certainly a booming economy, this could hardly be the mentality of the overwhelming population working paycheck to paycheck. Then, as well as now, when the stock market is doing well, everyone takes this to mean that the economy is booming, despite

---

[256] reprinted 1977, John A. Ryan, "Religion in the Election of 1928," *Current History*, December 1928; reprinted in Ryan, *Questions of the Day* (Ayer Publishing, 1977)

the fact that the accurate way to measure how well the economy is doing is by measuring the standard of living, which at this time was still painfully bad for many, especially farmers. The former president, Calvin Coolidge, nicknamed "Silent Cal", because of his hatred of speaking and doing much of anything, refused to allow relief to flow to the needy farmers in the middle of severe droughts, an effort that ruined farmers across the country. But Wall Street kept going strong and throwing money at propaganda stunts that the economy was great, which spelled doom for Smith, ironically little short of a year after the election the country would fly headfirst into the great depression.

The third p, prejudice, is quite obvious, there was no chance that a Catholic, at this point, would win. Historian Scott Farris notes that anti-Catholicism was the sole reason why Smith lost the election. And Bob Jones, a South Carolina minister, reckoned prohibition was a big deal but not as big as electing a Catholic, "I'll tell you, brother" he said "that the big issue we've got to face ain't the liquor question. I'd rather see a saloon on every corner of the South than see the foreigners elect Al Smith president."[257] Among the fears of many Protestants was that if elected Smith would ban freedom of worship, close Protestant churches, and end reading of the Bible, somehow forgetting that Smith was a Christian. These levels of fear mongering relates all the way back to when Jefferson ran for president in 1800. Jefferson, accused of being an atheist, and to some extent believed that Jesus didn't have God-like powers, was elected, causing many to hide their Bibles, believing that Jefferson would destroy them, which obviously wasn't true. But chaos would be chaos and people never really learn.

During the election of 1928, ministers actually wrote to each

---

257 Farris, Scott (2012). *Almost President: The Men Who Lost The Race But Changed The Nation*. Ottawa: Lyons Press

other trying to bring up petitions that would bar Catholics from serving public office. Anti-Catholicism was so bad that even southern states, which up until this time was solidly democratic, never voting for the party of Lincoln, began to switch sides and support the republicans, better than to elect a Catholic. In the end Smith lost handily, losing to republican candidate Herbert Hoover, 444 electoral votes to 87, with Smith only carrying a handful of states. Despite the overt anti-Catholicism of the election, Catholics came out in stronger numbers than ever to support the democrats, a coalition that would help send Franklin Roosevelt to the White House four years later.

Again nearly thirty years later, though with different results, John Kennedy ran for the democratic nomination as a Catholic. True, Kennedy was much more charming and debonair than Smith, however, the Catholic issue plagued him during the campaign, even though Catholicism, at the time, was the biggest Christian denomination in America. This time around fared much better for the Catholic nominee, as by this time there were so many Catholics in the country, eager to support their Catholic brethren, that the fact that Kennedy was a Catholic was an advantage, as Catholics came out in droves to vote for him. Kennedy was able to defend his Catholicism more elegantly that Smith did and was able to soothe the fears of those not ready to see a Catholic president, "I am not the Catholic candidate for president," he said. "I am the Democratic Party candidate for president who also happens to be a Catholic. I do not speak for my Church on public matters—and the Church does not speak for me."[258] Kennedy would later quip that if Catholics couldn't be trusted to run the government then a

---

258 Kennedy, John F. (June 18, 2002). "Address to the Greater Houston Ministerial Association". *American Rhetoric*

quarter of the population would forfeit running for any government office, simply because of their religion. He also made a very potent remark when he questioned why Americans were upset that he was running for president being a Catholic when nobody cared that he was a Catholic when he served in the Navy.[259] Apparently the country didn't care that he was a Catholic when his life was on the line in the middle of world war two.

Even with Kennedy's wit and charm, the Protestants had many reservations about him. As a matter of fact, Kennedy received less votes from Protestants than did the democratic nominee Adlai Stevenson, who lost badly to Dwight Eisenhower. Nobody knows for sure who really won the 1960 presidential election, with so much corruption, lying, and stealing that took place. Of course it helped that Kennedy's daddy was one of the wealthiest people in the country and literally was dirty enough to buy votes, nobody knows how many votes he bought. Some think that had Joe Kennedy not bribed the Illinois crime bosses, Illinois would have gone to Nixon and so with the presidency. However, historians can't say for a fact what exactly happened, and thus Kennedy became the first Catholic to win election for the president.

The second Catholic president of the United States is Joe Biden, another democrat. It's somewhat interesting that the Republican party hasn't had a Catholic presidential nominee, or a Jewish one, or a Muslim one, or anyone who wasn't a Protestant, maybe religion matters more than we think, at least for the republicans. It's a bit ironic as well that the least religious presidential candidate that the republicans have selected was Ronald Raegan, the hero of so many stalwart Christians. He was dubbed for his "traditional family values," while at the same time he was divorced, hardly talked to his

---

259 Reeves, Thomas. *A Question of Character: A Life of John F. Kennedy*

kids, and went to church only once or twice a year. Nevertheless, when Kennedy won the 1960 election that dramatically reduced the controversy over whether a Catholic could become president, and criticism since has been seldom heard.

A surprise to many people, as it isn't written about in many history books, is that the KKK was hostile to Catholics. Of course, when the KKK originated in 1868, its primary goal was to keep the blacks down, prevent them from having the rights that naturally belonged to them and intimidate blacks to vote for democrats. By the beginning of the 20th century, the Klan had shifted in some ways. While it still had the same vehemence against the black race, and in some ways kicked up the violence, including an increase in lynching, discrimination, and intimidation, the Klan also espoused anti-semitic and anti-Catholic beliefs. In a surprising twist, the Klan stated that they were "moral, law-abiding citizens dedicated to political and civil reform, civic improvement, and the defense of traditional American values," as though hatred and bigotry were the tenets of moral values and civic improvement.[260] Whereas the Klan was mainly centered in the South directly after the civil war, the newly formed Klan gained membership all across America, particularly in the Midwest, where Protestantism was strong, and conservative values won out.

The reasons why the Klan and other anti-Catholics targeted them was because of the supposed belief that Catholics didn't understand what it took to be an American and that they didn't understand how democracy works. In answering this charge the Catholics asserted their rights as Americans, and claimed that the Klan and nativists

---

260 Francis Paul Valenti, *The Portland Press, the Ku Klux Klan, and the Oregon Compulsory Education Bill: Editorial Treatment of Klan Themes in the Portland Press in 1922* (University of Washington, 1993)

were less patriotic than the Catholics, since they clearly didn't understand the concept of freedom of religion, a basic founding principle since the early days of the republic.[261]

With the rapid growth of the KKK, anti-Catholic rhetoric intensified, culminating into the burning of a Michigan church, set ablaze by the Klan, after it opened for just two weeks.[262] In 1921, an Alabama minister, E.R. Stephenson shot and killed Father James Coyle, after Coyle had performed the marriage ceremony of Stephenson's daughter, who converted to Catholicism. Stephenson acquired the legal help, with the help of the Klan, of the influential Hugo Black. Black, who would later be named to the Supreme Court, was a known leader of the KKK and held dozens of rallies and gave hundreds of speeches in which he lambasted Catholics and decried the growth of Catholicism in the country. Ironically, Black would serve as one of the most liberal justices to have ever served on the court, yet all of his exposure with the Klan helped influence some of his anit-semitic and anti-Catholic decisions.

Early on it became apparent that the trial was not fair. The Klan paid for the trial on Stephenson's behalf, and the judge, Judge Fort, was himself a Klansman and a close personal friend of Black. According to Geoffrey Watson, "The jury foreman was a senior Klansman. The majority of the jury were Klansmen", not exactly what you would consider a fair and just trial. Stephenson pleaded not guilty by reason of insanity, how often have we heard this one, even as Stephenson's own daughter had testified against him. I personally believe that it would take one extremely bad dude in order for his own daughter to testify against him with the same ferocity

---

261 Dumenil, Lynn. "The Tribal Twenties: 'Assimilated' Catholics' Response to Anti-Catholicism in the 1920s," *Journal of American Ethnic History*
262 Shannon, William V. (1989) [1963]. *The American Irish: a political and social portrait.*

that Stephenson's daughter Ruth had when she claimed that her dad had been plotting this for a long, long time. Ruth stated that she often heard her dad make threats about Coyle and that her father was prone to fits of violence.[263]

Black, for his part, took to berating witnesses by insinuating that they were Catholics, shouting "You're a Catholic aren't you?" Not exactly what anyone from Alabama wanted to hear. Black even recited the Klan's prayer before the court as a means to justify his client.[264] Not surprising, Stephenson got off with nothing, was acquitted and released, and died thirty years later, free.

After Franklin Roosevelt ushered into the white house, the Catholics came out in big numbers to support the democrats, and many Protestants began to accept Catholics due to their effort in world war two. Some democrats, however, like former vice president under Roosevelt, Henry Wallace, believed that Catholics were secretly engaged in a conspiracy to control the democratic party. When Wallace lost his presidential bid in 1948, he directly blamed the Catholic church as the conspirators against him. He even opposed NATO, believing it was the Catholics that had created world war two to begin with.[265] For some reason, although historians don't know for sure, the famed Eleanor Roosevelt had some misgivings about the Catholic church, griping about how funds shouldn't be used to fund parochial schools, though it is much more likely that Eleanor had misgivings about Catholics due to her husband's constant affairs with Catholic ladies, obviously not every Catholic should be blamed due to the president's misdeeds.[266]

---

263 <u>Stephenson is Bound Over to Grand Jury after Preliminary</u>", *The Miami News*
264 ibid
265 Culver and Hyde, *American Dreamer*
266 Elliot Roosevelt and James Brough (1973) *An Untold Story*, New York: Dell

As noted, after Kennedy won election, and even during the Raegan revolution, which saw Catholics join Protestants in the Christian right movement, anti-Catholicism weakened to the point where it never has become an issue any longer. That doesn't mean that religion doesn't have negative connotations to it. As is the case with the Jewish population, the climb upwards to equality hasn't been an easy one by any stretch. Even today we still see an ugly anti-semitic tilt. In an age when most people believe that freedom of religion is one of the main components of what makes America a special place to live, Jews are still being persecuted throughout the land.

From the moment that Jewish people started arriving in the colony of New Amsterdam, later New York, governor Peter Stuyvesant petitioned to have them expelled from the colony, a move that would fail, however, due to the Jews' financial leverage. He did succeed, however, in denying the Jews freedom to worship in their own synagogues, in the hopes that they would accept Christianity. When they didn't bow down and do what the Dutch had insisted on, and in the process managing to build some synagogues, Judaism was allowed, in bits and pieces. Fast forward to the civil war, and anti-semitism was on full display. This time at the hands of celebrated civil war hero and future president Ulysses Grant. While at the time serving as general during the civil war, Grant issued General order number 11, expelling Jews under his control, "The Jews, as a class violating every regulation of trade established by the Treasury Department and also department orders, are hereby expelled ... within twenty-four hours from the receipt of this order." The order was, thankfully, rescinded by Abraham Linclon, but not before the order went into effect in numerous cities and towns.[267]

Between 1880 and 1920 Jews flooded the United States, just

---

267 Chanes, Jerome A. (2004). *Antisemitism: a reference handbook*.

like the Irish did before them, and similar to the Irish the Jews were distrusted in their new home. During the latter half of the 19th century, some Jewish families, note the word some, started banking businesses, making the lie that Jews controlled the banking industries. Prominent populist leader Mary Elizabeth Lease, would blame the Jews among others for the depression hitting the farmers, a tactic that if used enough would tick off large groups of people and create vicious mobs, like those seen against the Catholics. Another so-called conspiracy was that the Jews were at the center of the struggle to make gold the standard of US currency, drawing the ire from silverites in the democratic and populist parties who wanted silver to be used to cause inflation therefore reducing the massive debts that farmers had accumulated. All of this gave the impression that the Jews were at the center of a wealthy conspiracy to keep working people down, a theory very close to the Nazi blame game that would come in a few decades.[268]

Between 1881 and 1914, Jews arrived in America in increasing numbers. Most of the Jewish folks coming over to the States were those trying to escape deep poverty and religious persecution back home. Somehow, many Jews in America began to flourish and create businesses that grew rapidly, quickly becoming the envy of most Americans, which might have had something to do with the hatred. Not surprisingly, for whatever reason people tend to view those who are doing well to have rigged the system and have some sort of imaginary power within Congress and most importantly the banks. The political and economical rise of the Jews drove white Christians crazy.

---

268 Albanese, Catherine L. (1981). *America, religions and religion*. Wadsworth Pub. Co. By the 1890s antisemitic feeling had crystallized around the suspicion that the Jews were responsible for an international conspiracy to base the economy on the single gold standard.

In the beginning years of the 20th century Jews were discriminated against in a whole plethora of areas, including employment, housing, clubs and organizations, and even teaching positions at universities and colleges. In some states and regions Jews were barred from certain hotels and restaurants, a similar feature to black discrimination.[269]

Things got from bad to worse when in 1913 Leo Frank was brutally lynched, again by a bigoted mob. It all began when a thirteen year old girl, Mary Phagan, was heading down to the pencil factory to gather her pay of a whole $1.20 from working a long, tiring twelve hour shift, nobody seems to mind that a thirteen year old was working a twelve hour shift at a pencil factory, but people sure got riled up about the rest of the story.[270]

Leo Frank was the man that paid her, and was, unfortunately for him and the girl, the last one to supposedly see her alive. Her body was found later that night in the cellar of the factory, all bloody, bruised, and broken. Soon reports about the young girl's brutal death sent shockwaves throughout the community and the people wanted action and justice, as fast as possible, for all they knew a murderer was on the loose. At once, all eyes turned toward Leo Frank. And why not Leo Frank? He was first and foremost the last person to see her, he was a Northerner by birth and didn't belong to Atlanta, the scene of the crime, and above all others he was a Jew, and Jews couldn't be trusted, everyone knew that. No one really seemed to care that there wasn't any definitive proof as to who committed the murder. There were notes, however, that police quickly determined were murder notes, in it it reads "he said he wood love me land

---

269 The Jews in America The Atlantic
270 "The Lynching of Leo Frank - the Temple." n.d. Www.the-Temple.org. https://www.the-temple.org/leo-frank.

down play like the night witch did it but that long tall black negro did boy his slef."[271] This letter was confusing to the prosecutors, who had no idea what this note could have meant, though it was speculated that the phrase the "night witch" meant the night guard.

In any case this couldn't have possibly led to the prosecution of Leo Frank, a man who wasn't in charge of the night shift and had no plausible reasons for committing such a grievous crime. First, Frank was a supervisor, while not the most prestigious job in the world, it did pay somewhat generously and was viewed with envy by fellow factory workers. What makes it that much worse was that Phagan was picking up her last check, the factory had decided to move on without her labor, because they lacked the necessary materials. Maliciously attacking Phagan seems like something a supervisor would not do, especially when the innocent girl was let go. Another reason why it couldn't have possibly been Frank was because the murder scene was so hastily conducted. If Frank was trying to conceal a murder scene, it's most likely that he wouldn't have just dropped the body in the basement, especially when he openly acknowledged that he had seen her shortly before her death.

The police, nevertheless, convicted Frank, due to his nervousness throughout the interview process, surely if you were being interrogated for a murder you did not commit you'd be nervous too. The police didn't care, they needed a suspect or they'd face public outcry, and they found one in the name of Leo Frank. The public, now turned into a mob because of the vicious, anti-semitic, newspaper attacks against Frank, went everyday to the courthouse to cheer on the leading prosecutors and were ecstatic as soon as the verdict was

---

271 Golden, Harry. A Little Girl is Dead. World Publishing Company, 1965. Retrieved June 25, 2011. (published in Great Britain as The Lynching of Leo Frank) Henig, Gerald. "'He Did Not Have a Fair Trial': California Progressives React to the Leo Frank Case"

read, convicting Frank of an execution. Frank's lawyers desperately sought an appeal, going so high as reaching the governor of Georgia. Meanwhile Georgia's anti-semitic newspapers were selling at record high rates and anti-semitism swept through the city of Atlanta all the way throughout the South.[272]

The governor of Georgia, John Marshall Slayton, personally thrusted himself in the case, in order to make a satisfactory decision regarding Frank. He personally visited the pencil factory, read over 10,000 pages in documentation, and came to the conclusion that Frank's conviction rested on highly superficial evidence. He thus commuted Frank's sentence to life in prison, which didn't put the mob at ease. There's not a huge difference between an execution, at the hands of the government, and life in prison, either way the public would never deal with the supposed convict again. This didn't matter to the public, who had been following the trial, mostly through deeply anti-semitic newspapers, that had often gone on rants about Jews. The mob wanted justice, and justice to them meant that someone had to die. As a result the mob in Atlanta stormed the governor's mansion, leaving Slayton no other choice but to call out the National Guard to quell the violence. The mob scared Slayton so much that by the time he left office, which happened to be a few days later, he fled as fast as he could, leaving Georgia not to return again until nearly ten years later when things had begun to die down.[273]

As we have learned with vicious mobs, they don't easily turn away and resort back to ordinary civilian life, they want destruction and chaos, and most likely won't leave until they get what they want. In this case what they wanted was Leo Frank. The mob, after having been routed by the National Guard, had turned its attention to the

---

272 ibid
273 ibid

prison where Leo Frank was quietly resting. Apparently the prison guards didn't do a whole lot to stop the mayhem, as the mob easily barged through the prison and dragged Frank back to Phagan's home town, a move most likely to assure that Frank would have to deal with those who were most pissed off.

On August 17 1915, on an otherwise beautiful day, Frank was lynched by a mob, who consisted of some pretty prominent members, including among them the son of a US senator and various members of the KKK, hellbent on killing a Jew. The mob didn't care about the courts, they didn't care about the evidence, they didn't even care that their handpicked governor had looked into the case and found the trial dubious. The mob mercilessly killed a now proven innocent man before looking into the details. You would think that before someone, or in this case a mob, would kill someone, with parents and brothers and sisters, that they would at least have the decency to look into matters and not receive all of their information from blatantly biased and hate-filled reports.[274]

It is now proven that Jim Conley had committed the murder. Jim Conley was the factory janitor, who had apparently intimidated witnesses from speaking the truth. Shortly after the lynching, the anti-defamation league was created with an intense focus on combating anti-semtism in the United States. Once, Jews regularly served in the nation's public offices. However, it took decades for Jews to be elected to public office after the lynching, mainly because of all the anti-semtic language and beliefs now spiraling the country.[275]

During world war one things didn't look much better for the Jewish population either. Anti-semites were running amok, smearing Jews as "enemies of the people" and upgrading them for allegedly being "war profiteers." When the anti-semitism spread like wildfire

---

274 ibid
275 ibid

in all ranks of American life including the military, where an Army recruiting manual stated "The foreign born, and especially Jews, are more apt to malinger than the native-born," this caused president Wilson to condemn the rhetoric.[276] It didn't help that Jews had little place to hide. Deeply resented among Christians as being Jesus deniers, Jews were easily identifiable with their surnames and unique accents.

After world war one, anti-semitism kicked up a whole gear. Quotas restricted Jews from reaching higher institutes of learning, though they may well be more qualified than anyone else. Very famously, Harvard, after seeing Jews as 22% of the total student body, determined that they had a "Jewish problem."[277] Other medical schools, such as Cornell, Columbia, Pennsylvania, and Yale had quotas in place. In 1935, Yale only admitted five Jews of the more than 500 students who applied. Dean of students "Dean Milton Winternitz infamously remarked, "Never admit more than five Jews, and take no blacks at all" ain't that sweet.[278] Jews were totally excluded from other universities like Stanford, which later apologized for its misdeeds. Around this time, the great Henry Ford, whom capitalists love to brag over his invention of the modern assembly line factory system, created a newspaper, *The Dearborn*, where he mercilessly berated Jews and spread anti-semitic propaganda. He even went so far as to praise Adolph Hitler's autobiography *Mein Kampf,* in which Hitler describes Jews as the "parasite."[279] More alarming, in

---

276 Hang the Jew, Hang the Jew". *Anti-Defamation League*
277 Leonard Dinnerstein, Antisemitism in America (New York, NY: Oxford Univ. Press, 1995).
278 Gerard N. Burrow (2008). *A History of Yale's School of Medicine: Passing Torches to Others*. Yale University Press.
279 GALE. n.d. "History of Antisemitism in America | Gale." Www.gale.com. https://www.gale.com/primary-sources/political-extremism-and-radicalism/collections/history-of-anti-semitism.

his book, which Ford praised, Hitler alluded to the extermination of the Jewish race which "must necessarily be a bloody process." Was Ford advocating for the extermination of the Jews as well? And where exactly did Americans learn this type of hate? After all the Jews hadn't done anything worth hating for. Ford believed that the Jews were the ones interested in starting the wars, since they were most likely the ones to gain from starting wars, "International financiers are behind all war. They are what is called the international Jew: German Jews, French Jews, English Jews, American Jews. I believe that in all those countries except our own the Jewish financier is supreme ... here the Jew is a threat," a bit of irony here, especially when considering the next war was started not because of Jews, but instead because of the hatred of Jews.[280] Certainly Ford didn't help matters when he stated in 1915 "I know who caused the war: German-Jewish bankers," a comment that may very well have given extra support to Hitler and his evil plans.[281]

Most of the white Christians' disdain for Jews was based in the belief that Jews were plotting to overtake Christians as the most numerous and powerful religious group in America. Of course, it didn't help that many of America's most inspirational ministers, preachers, and priests, like Father Charles Coughlin had been openly preaching about the dangers of Judaism and Jews in general. For some reason, maybe just to add some sort of conspiracy other than outright bigotry, a rumor circulated that the Jews were actually in kahoots with the communists, America's sworn enemy. Father Coughlin did much to perpetuate these rumors, as he may have very much believed them. He would go off on tangents on public radio against the Jews. Coughlin was even dismayed at the Roosevelt

---

280 *The Dearborn Independent*
281 Watts, Steven,*The People's Tycoon: Henry Ford and the American Century*, Vintage, 2006

administration, mostly for winning the support of a number of Jews and even including them in his administration, a detestable act according to Coughlin, and some demagogues went further and called Roosevelt's widely successful New Deal the "Jew Deal." And when the Nazis began violating Jewish rights and spreading violence Coughlin did little to calm the anti-semitic fears among Americans by condoning the violence and even blaming the Jews for it as "the Lenins and Trotskys,...atheistic Jews and Gentiles" had murdered more than 20 million Christians and had stolen "40 billion [dollars]...of Christian property."[282] Apparently this helped him sleep at night.

Public polls of Jews in America were drastically low. Almost 60% of Americans held a low opinion of Jews, considering them "greedy", and "dishonest", among other things.[283] It's not hard to imagine why the polls showed this level of distrust among the Jews with all of the very loud "leaders" making vicious attacks to serve their own personal or political advantage. Surprisingly, the poll found over 40% of Americans believed that Jews had too much political power in the US, and in 1945, astonishingly, that figure rose to almost 60%, this coming right after the horrors of the holocaust, and images of all the jewelry and clothing that were found at the camps as well as images of crematoriums that were widely circulated all across the world. I ask again where is the sympathy?

I already have mentioned that the KKK had risen during the 1920s, the lynching of Leo Frank was a major escalator to their rise. Even US immigration laws passed in the 1920s had a strong

---

282 "Father Coughlin Blames Jews for Nazi Violence." n.d. History Unfolded: US Newspapers and the Holocaust. https://newspapers.ushmm.org/events/father-coughlin-blames-jews-for-nazi-violence.

283 Jaher, Frederic Cople (2002). *The Jews and the Nation: Revolution, Emancipation, State Formation, and the Liberal Paradigm in America and France.* Princeton University Press

anti-semitic tilt to it, as it placed quotas on Eastern European countries, who had a large population of Jewish citizens. With the rise of Nazis in Germany and Neo-Nazis in America, who now had large audiences over the radio waves, physical attacks against Jews rose dramatically, as many radio stations publicly advocated for such attacks. Americans who came to admire Hitler, (surprising, but yes there were Hitler supporters in America, just like how there are Putin supporters here), even painted swastikas on Jewish owned businesses, like they were cool to terrorize a whole race of Americans. (By the time that Americans were doing this Hitler's motives were widely known, and Nazi suppression was cautiously being watched throughout the world.) It's even more concerning that Americans were doing these atrocious acts, while Nazi Germany was literally running over Europe. The hate was real.

With all of the repressive acts that the Nazis were perpetuating, American public opinion was still against Jews, that throughout the 1930s laws were still in place to limit Jewish immigration, even as millions of Jewish lives were at risk, and the Nazis were busy building concentration camps to keep the "undesirables" out of Germany, yet Americans were still showing little sympathy for Jews. Many historians have even speculated that Franklin Roosevelt had indeed known since 1941 that Jews were being exterminated in the concentration camps, yet he purposely decided not to bomb the railroads leading to the camps. Just think how many lives would have been saved had he just done this one simple act and destroyed the rail lines.

One of the calamities that really irks me is the fact that there are people who actually believe that the holocaust never happened, that it was all drummed up by the Jews and their sympathizers. How can anybody have these views? Haven't they seen the images of the starving people, who are literally skin and bones? Haven't they seen the camps and the images of the gassing chambers? Haven't they been schooled enough to know the truth? Apparently not. These modern day anti-semites believe in a few different theories: that the Nazis just deported the Jews and didn't exterminate them, that Nazis never exterminated Jews by use of the gas chamber, ect., that the actual number of Jews killed in the concentration camps is significantly lower than the 6 million figure, and that the entire holocaust was a hoax. Again, this is flat out crazy. And newsflash, even if one Jew had died during the war that is still one Jew too many, and the allegation or conspiracy that the number 6 million is too high is just flat out ridiculous. Interestingly enough holocaust denial is outlawed in 18 countries, many of them important and close allies with the United States, the United States is not one of the countries to have it banned. In fact, there were many of them, proudly wearing anti-semitic regalia at the January 6th insurrection, apparently anti-semites like to fit in at conservative rallies, especially ones where Donald Trump is speaking.

Just as disturbing was the Unite the Right rally in Charlottesville, Virginia, in 2017. By the time of this publication some of us will have totally forgotten the events that lead to the Unite the Right movement, others will never forget. Prior to this event, progressives around the country had been rightly clamoring for removal of certain statues that were fundamentally un-American or brought out the worst of America. These included racist memorials, shrines, and of course the Confederate flag, though loved as a symbol of the Dukes of Hazzard, was still a sign of racism and depression for many African Americans. Many statues celebrating the works of confederate generals were removed in numerous cities, and the

Robert E Lee statue in Charlottesville was the next target. Firstly, it makes every sense to remove this statue of a man who, while a good general, fought against his better judgment and the United States. We don't have statues celebrating Henry Clinton or General Cornwallis, why should we have one of Robert E Lee? Some will say it's part of heritage or history, if that's the case it belongs in a museum, not in city parks where little kids wonder why men who fought against our country are still being celebrated.

Needless to say, when the right-wingers, egged on by disgraced, twice impeached, Donald Trump, found out that Lee may be next on the chopping block, they got together and formed a protest of sorts. All sorts of people were there that day, some curious bystanders, journalists, and the like, but many who took part in the Unite the Right rally were the worst among us. They were white-nationalists, those who believe that the white race is fundamentally superior to that of any other. Alabama US senator Tommy Tuberville tends to think that not all white nationalists are bad, that's a curious position, but shows that many republicans still don't want to upset their white-nationalist base. Others were Neo-Nazis, the new form of Nazism.

In what was truly an extraordinary spectacle, the rally consisted of these bigots who shouted to the top of their lungs "Jews will not replace us!" Where did they learn this hatred and why do they share these beliefs? A Hitler sympathizer and member of the Neo-Nazis, ran his vehicle into a crowd of counter-protesters, those who had the courage to stand up against this nonsense, and killed Heather Heyer and injured numerous others. All throughout the rally, violence erupted when the counter-protesters were attacked by the white-nationalists. In the Unite the Right Rally many could be seen wearing Trump's signature MAGA hat, others could be seen wearing anti-semitic clothing, like those who are holocaust deniers.[284] It was difficult to see anybody that was not white in the Unite the Right rally.

Donald Trump did nothing. He watched it all unfold on tv, probably with glee, these were his supporters, these are the ones who propelled him to victory. You can imagine the confusion in his heart when his advisors told him he better go out and condemn the rally. Yet, Trump had a very difficult time with this. Instead, he chose to say that there were many good people on both sides. Really? Many good people on both sides? Excuse me but I never believed that white-nationalists, and Neo-Nazis were good people. Moreover, if you're a good person then how can you harbor so much hatred in your heart? Those concepts don't make sense to me. But Trump did Trump, he didn't want to alienate his main political base, so he didn't directly condemn the racists that day, or any other day for that matter. This, supposedly, was the reason why Joe Biden decided to throw his hat in the ring. He, like so many other Americans with decency and common sense, couldn't believe the things that were happening in this country. I still can't believe that little under 60 years after the civil rights movement, where so much has been advanced and children are taught in classrooms that are colorblind that this would happen, that there would be so many people joining arm and arm together to support racists ideologies. Something's wrong America. If this is the way of the future then we are in trouble. If this is the way of the future then we haven't learned anything from the past and prejudices will never die.

---

284 Sganga, Nicole. 2021. "What to Know about the Civil Trial over Charlottesville's Deadly 'Unite the Right' Rally." Www.cbsnews.com. November 19, 2021. https://www.cbsnews.com/news/charlottesville-unite-the-right-rally-trial-what-to-know/.

To be fair, there are plenty of groups targeting the Jewish population, still to this day. They come from both the left and the right. Some radical Islam groups are targeting the Jews, all because they have land in the Middle East. Now, I don't think that it's fair that the Jews are taking over Palestinian land, without at least a neutral third party, but this is no reason for violence and bloodshed. Most of the resentment, of this sort, comes from other Middle Eastern countries. I still don't know what the problem is here in America, why so many people still have resentments against the Jews. Even growing up in the 2010s and going to school, I heard lots of Jew jokes all the time. Many jokes were, in my opinion, horrifying, especially the ones that had to do with the concentration camps. Of course, there are always evil people in the world, but to my astonishment many other kids would laugh at these jokes, which I always took to mean that they held no respect for the millions of Jews that were killed in the camps, that they had no respect for the families that were separated, that they held no human decency and compassion. What kind of world are we living in? I even heard of anti-semitic writings being found in school classrooms, to the likes of "Hitler was a great guy." Really? I always try to put myself in other people's shoes. I know sometimes that that's hard, but when we do these things and imagine ourselves in the middle of the concentration camps and when we imagine our family being separated from us, not knowing if they are safe or in harm's way, then we can sympathize and empathize with everyone.

10   HATRED OF MEXICANS

Right now those who are being targeted, like the Irish Catholics and Jews before them, are the Hispanics and the Muslims. If you ever realized, America tends to move from one extreme to another. First, when the Puritans came they excluded those whose religion was different from theirs. Then all the anger was against the Irish Catholics coming in, then Eastern Europeans in the late 1800s early 1900s, then Jews. All of the resentment was because these groups were coming into America at scorching high numbers at one point. Now most of our immigrants are Hispanic, coming from Mexico, Guatemala, Honduras, ect. Since the main entryway is not over oceans and on boats, but instead across the border and by foot, this has heated up the political motivations of some who are anxiously using this as political gold.

Mexico achieved independence not very long after the United States, achieving freedom from Spanish rule in 1821. The United States had long been interested in its own affairs, long being an isolationist country before it became a political term. George Washington had urged in his farewell address that the United States should remain free from foreign entanglements, these would only hurt the developing nation and set it back from progress. Washington was very astute to make this point. Had America got into every minor disagreement and controversy the country would quickly be run over by bigger, more powerful countries, like the British or French. Nobody really thought that Spain was a threat.

Once a main superpower who had chartered discovering missions to the Americas and built settlements, Spain was rapidly becoming a declining power, not able to keep supplying her colonies and being too weak militarily to stop independence movements. Thus, when Mexico wanted to achieve independence from Spanish rule, the Americans remained quiet. They didn't want to tick off a foreign country, who they conducted much trade with, when they knew that Mexico inevitably would be an independent nation. And so when Mexico won independence nobody was really shocked.

Trouble began brewing by the 1830s however, over what to do with the territory of Texas. Texas had been part of Mexico, but had fought for its own freedom and independence from them. Mexico didn't want to say goodbye to Texas, it was a huge landmass that was great for agriculture and ranching. Texas all along had wanted to become part of the United States and was eager to join the union, the problem was, not everybody wanted them to join the States. Martin Van Buren wasn't sure what to do with the Texas problem because it would sow dissension and chaos in the country, who had meticulously set up a country of equal slave and free states. Even though Mexico had abolished slavery by then, and technically Texas too had abolished slavery, even though this wasn't heavily enforced, the citizens of the States knew that if Texas were admitted it would become a slave state.

Through all the fighting that ensued, including the legendary battle of the Alamo, Mexico was finally determined to leave Texas alone. Texas still had strong predilections of joining the Union, as a matter of fact, it almost dominated the 1844 presidential election, with the democratic nominee, James Polk supporting Texas annexation and the whig nominee, Henry Clay, wishy washy at best on the subject.

As you probably know Texas became part of the Union, becoming official at the end of 1845, therefore becoming the Lone Star State.

Most of the citizens of Texas were indeed Americans anyway, moving to Texas for better land and for the sole purpose of expansion. Some citizens, however, were Mexican by origin, therefore, the States had actively annexed land with Hispanic settlers. After the Mexican-American war, a war that was fought to expand American interests at the expense of Mexico, the Utah, New Mexico, and California territories now became part of the United States, again with a decent population of Hispanics living in the state. The United States guaranteed that Hispanics living in these territories would be granted full US citizenship and have all the rights that come with it. That did little to stop the lynchings.

What most people don't realize is that lynchings were quite common, especially in the South-West region. It is believed that between 1848 and 1928 at least 597 Mexican-Americans were lynched, many of these lynchings occurred in areas where no formal judical systems had been set up, therefore no justice was hashed out.[285] Reasons as to why Mexican-Americans would be targeted included stealing, murder, witchcraft, and even speaking Mexican.

In Downieville, California, a legend by the name of Josefa Segovia was lynched by, again, a vicious mob. Downieville became a bursting little town after the gold rush of 1848-49 sprang upon California. Most of the residents who resided there were young men, destined to be rich and strike back home with literal gold in their pockets. These were not business men, not the proper and gentlemanly men, these were men who were rough, violent, and scary. You could imagine what would happen if an innocent woman strode before them. WIth all of that pent up testosterone something bad was bound to happen, and oftentimes did, with all of the brothels and prostitutes

---

[285] Carrigan, William D. and Clive Web. "The lynching of persons of Mexican origin or descent in the United States, 1848 to 1928" Archived September 3, 2014, at the Wayback Machine *The Journal of Social History* 37:2

that would visit the men. Through it all there were, of course, a few women living in the town, most of them living there long before the gold miners had invaded their town. Josefa was one of them.

During the fourth of July celebrations in the summer of 1851, Downieville became a place of parading, singing, and drinking. Most of the people in Downieville passed the time by getting violently drunk. An Australian miner, known as Cannon, was one of the drunkards that night. As men often do when in a drunken stupor, Cannon wandered onto the premises of Joesfa's home, where she lived with a man named Jose, who was likely to be her husband. Cannon broke into the house and "created a riot and disturbance," I'm not really sure what exactly that entails, but you can try to figure it out.[286]

Later the next day, Cannon went to the local doctor, most likely to take care of his horrific hangover, asking for medicine. Jose, not surprisingly, was maddened at the state of his kicked-in door. Knowing that Cannon was at the doctor's, Jose decided to confront him and probably ask Cannon to pay for the damages. Soon a shouting match followed, in which Cannon was heard to say slurs against the Mexican-American couple. When Cannon decided to go back to the house, in the hopes of continuing the fight Josefa stabbed him in the heart. Cannon died.

The Steamer Pacific Star reporter, the same one that described Josefa as pretty, "so far as the style of swarthy Mexican beauty is so considered," said she "presented more the appearance of one who would confer kindness than one who thirsted for blood."[287] Clearly Josefa didn't look the part of a killer, but exactly the opposite, as

---

[286] Mejia, Brittny. 2019. "She Was Hanged in California 168 Years Ago — for Murder or for Being Mexican?" *Los Angeles Times*, December 6, 2019. https://www.latimes.com/california/story/2019-12-05/downieville-california-mexican-woman-hanging.

[287] ibid

someone who exhibited kindness. The jury nonetheless convicted her of murder and sentenced her to hang. Jose was ordered to leave town within 24 hours, a task which he dutifully took up, probably because the town wasn't safe for him, or any other Mexican anymore.

Why she was accused and convicted so quickly, without anyone looking into the facts that her house was broken into twice, by a drunkard, who was most likely looking for a fight, rests on a theory that foreigners were not wanted in that town. In most goldmines, crime was rampant. Stealing, murder, adultery, ect. were all commonplace. An easy way to shift the blame from the anglo-saxons whites, who were the cause of all the violence, was to just blame the foreigners. Think about it, if a whole group of people accuse others of the reasons why things are bad, particularly those in a minority, they have power over them, they can group up and target them, while in the meantime keep stealing, committing murders, and committing sexual crimes. Joesfa, therefore, was an easy target. She was Mexican by heritage and not like the others of the gold-mining town. It didn't matter that she was defending herself from violence, she killed a white man, that meant the gallows.

What we do know is that the trial against Josefa was deeply unfair. The whole trial took about an hour, with nobody willing to defend her, mostly because of fear from the local drunken crowds. Even more abhorrent, most of the jurors were Cannon's best friends, hardly a fair way to conduct a trial, but this is how it was in gold-mining towns, Josefa just found herself in a deeply unmerciful setting.[288] Even a local doctor, who theoretically should have good standing within

---

[288] "On This Day in 1851 – Josefa 'Juanita' Segovia, Rough Justice or Legal Lynching? - Crimescribe." 2020. Crimescribe.com. July 4, 2020. https://crimescribe.com/2020/07/05/on-this-day-in-1851-josefa-juanita-segovia-rough-justice-or-legal-lynching/comment-page-1/.

the community was ostracized for speaking up on Josefa's behalf, pointing out that Josefa, in all likelihood was pregnant and should not stand trial. The doctor was forced out of court for speaking up in Josefa's defense and eventually had to leave Downieville. The "mob" even gave worse treatment to a Nevada lawyer by the name of Mr. Thayer. Mr. Thayer had been protesting the unfair trial by asserting that the court should at least gather information to see if a murder had been committed, as far as he was concerned it looked like this was purely self-defense. Mr. Thayer was thrown out of court for these views and severely beaten by members of the community. The local community was already dead set on sealing up Josefa's fate, determining her guilty even before a trial had commenced.[289]

And so it was. Josefa's last words were "Adios Senores." ("Goodbye, Sirs."), and that was it.[290] She was dead within minutes. It's hard to imagine that the situation would have been the same if this was a white woman who had stabbed an intruder hellbent on committing violence. In all likelihood the white woman would have been sympathized, crowds would have come out and supported her against the evils of testosterone-pumping men. And even if the locals would have accused her of murder she most likely would have gone to prison for a few years instead of being publicly executed, most other civilized cities would have found it abhorrent for the town to kill a white woman for self-defense. Yes, it seems likely that the reason why justice was hashed out so ruthlessly, without fairness or even common sense, was because Josefa was of Mexican heritage. She wasn't the typical Anglo-Saxon, she was different, she couldn't be trusted. Her values were different, her culture was different, even her religion was different. It all created the perfect storm, and prejudice ruled the day.

---

289 ibid
290 ibid

Texas, by far, had the most violence in the Southwest. Texans would do some of the most horrific things imaginable to Mexicans, such as; whipping, lynching, burning, branding, ect. And they would target folks with Mexican heritage for all sorts of silly reasons that don't make sense today, among them: competing for jobs against the white man, speaking too loud, and loving a white woman.[291] If doing these things was enough to solicit cruel and unusual punishments, then we would all be guilty of these things and be punished. It almost seems that the white Anglo-Saxons in the region were reaching to punish the Mexicans, therefore anything that they did was fair game for punishment.

One particular area that hasn't changed much over the years is the unfounded obsession that immigrants will take good paying American jobs. This claim is just flat out ridiculous and falls flat on its face when we look at the facts. In fact, the immigrants who come to America do exactly the opposite. According to Brookings senior fellow, Vanda Felbab-Brown, the issue has been blown out of proportion to meet a politician's personal political success, or in another word, those who seek to undermine immigrants' economic impact on America are demagogues. "The impact of immigrant labor on the wages of native-born workers is low... However, undocumented workers often work the unpleasant, back-breaking jobs that native-born workers are not willing to do."[292] Ain't that a slap in the face to all of those anti-immigration zealots. In most cases the immigrants are helping our economy, taking the jobs that nobody really wants. The immigrants, who are overwhelmingly Hispanic,

---

291 Alfredo, Mirandé (2020). *Gringo Injustice : Insider Perspectives on Police, Gangs, and Law.* Taylor & Francis Group
292 Hoban, Brennan. 2017. "Do Immigrants 'Steal' Jobs from American Workers?" Brookings. August 24, 2017. https://www.brookings.edu/articles/do-immigrants-steal-jobs-from-american-workers/.

take these jobs because they have no other choice, they just want to make a living in the land of opportunities. Felbab-Brown describes some of these jobs to be gutting fish, or, as in the case with the overwhelming number of immigrants, working farm fields. She argues, instead of centering immigration policy on mass deportation, we should really be focusing about how to provide citizenship for those that are filling in the unwanted jobs from American markets. This makes sense, especially today, when so many employers are looking for employees in this "workers market." And, bonus, if immigrants, whether legal or illegal, are working for low-wage jobs that Americans don't want, that means that American citizens can be focused on finding better paying jobs, therefore making the economic status of Americans that much better.

Yet, somehow, the statistics and policy recommendations from highly skilled professionals, who are experts in their fields, don't get the recognition that they should. Instead, what wins the day are soundbites, used by petty politicians looking out only for themselves, that fundamentally raise the tension and hatred against immigrants for doing things that they don't actually do. In 2015, then-candidate Donald Trump, became a master of insulting people and stooping down to a very low level to insult a whole race. Speaking about Mexicans, "They're taking our jobs. They're taking our manufacturing jobs. They're taking our money. They're killing us."[293] Ain't that sweet.

What makes this even more troubling is that this hatred or flat out ignorance surrounding the Hispanic immigrants isn't just afflicting the older folks, it's even afflicting our youth. The day after Trump won the presidency, even though losing to Hillary Clinton by three million popular votes, children at Royal Oak middle school

---

293 Ibid

in Detroit began loudly chanting in the cafeteria "build that wall, build that wall." Really? Do sixth and seventh graders really know what's going on politically in the world or do they just hear soundbites and get amused? Do they have an opinion of their own yet, or do they just echo what their parents are saying at home? And have sixth and seventh graders actually looked into our immigration crisis and the truth behind it, or are they just echoing the words of the president to be, as if he's our country's new role model? I remember when people thought that Ruth Bader Ginsberg or Barack Obama were our nation's role models, and for good reason, they both were unabashedly destroying barriers that defined women and blacks for so long, they were deeply inspirational and kids dreamed of becoming like them. Now, to at least many kids in the country, kids who hear what Trump and his republican friends have to say about immigrants and Mexicans in general, calling them rapists, criminals, thugs, drug dealers, have found a new hero. That's what's terrifying.

Can you imagine the psychological effects that Hispanic children at Royal Oak middle school went through during this sad tirade? I can only imagine the hollow feeling deep inside that these poor kids had when they heard the chants of their peers, seemingly calling them out as undesirable and not worthy enough to be in the US. One of their classmates who just happens to be Hispanic, was dumbfounded with terror when she witnessed the event unfolding. "It was so hard to look and just watch and not being able to do anything because I was afraid" she said, "I was so scared."[294] And that makes sense. Imagine, for instance, that a politician began running a campaign, with a serious, cult-like following, with all

---

294 CNN, By Kelly Wallace and Sandee LaMotte. 2016. "The Collateral Damage after Students' 'Build a Wall' Chant Goes Viral." CNN Digital. December 28, 2016. https://www.cnn.com/2016/12/28/health/build-a-wall-viral-video-collateral-damage-middle-school/index.html.

sorts of slogans and soundbites calling out your race and making provisions directly attacking those like you as part of their platform. You probably wouldn't be too comfortable.

She went on to give media interviews describing her experiences within her school, which happens to be overwhelmingly white majority. "I've had people make jokes about me and my culture," she said. "They make jokes about Mexicans. They make jokes about blacks. And it's disheartening, and it hurts me physically."[295] Soon afterwards classmates began treating her differently because she had the courage to call out how despicable her classmates were acting, she was even avoided at school for doing the right thing. She hit the ball right on the head when she mentioned that if the kids were chanting "Trump, Trump, Trump" it would have been a completely different thing, they are just showing support for their candidate. However, when you start breaking down someone else's culture and heritage it is not just disrespectful but insanely rude. It makes me wonder, where is the discipline within this school?

It would be one thing if people from all backgrounds and political ideology call out crap for what it is. That's not what's happening today. So-called decent and good people still support Trump and politicians like him even though he has such a despicable record on immigration. I once met a young man, who wasn't able to vote yet, thankfully, and conversed with him on a number of subjects. Among the questions I asked this young man was who his favorite president is? He responded by saying Obama, and I asked him why. He didn't really know. Then he said he liked Trump, again I asked him why. His response was what I think a typical Trump supporter would say: "Merica". Hmm.

---

295 ibid

"Can you explain, what did Trump do that was so great in your view?'

"He built the wall."

"Why is that so important?"

"To keep the Mexicans out."

"What's the problem with Mexicans?"

"I don't know."

And there you have it. I don't really know exactly how to process this conversation. What comes to mind is that this individual doesn't know a whole lot about politics, history, or current events, at all. The fact that he could only name two presidents, who happen to have been the last former presidents tells you all you need to know about the research that this young man put in to know his facts. But what's interesting is that he supported Trump first for "Merica", which I think means the false narrative that Trump actually put America first and that nobody else seems to care about America except Trump, which is totally laughable, especially with the danger we all went through having the most erratic, unfit man to be president in our country's history. His second reason for liking Trump was that he built a wall to keep Mexicans out. This is interesting in a number of ways.

First, the facts actually show that in the four years of Trump's presidency, only about 16 miles of fencing actually went up where there wasn't fencing before. That's a heck of a lot of progress isn't it? To be fair, to Trump and his allies, many miles of wall were built, but mostly to provide more fencing to areas that already had them, or to create new fencing where the old fencing was. Now, do you remember on the campaign trail, Trump received standing ovations and shouts of glee from diluted audience members for stating that he would make Mexico pay for the wall? This might sound quite harsh, but who in their right mind actually believed this garbage? Those that did believe that Trump was magically going to make Mexico pay for that wall must've been smoking dope. Under what circumstances would Mexico ever be bullied into building a wall for America because one man, who happens to love to hear himself speak, tells Mexico they have to do this. This is insane. It makes just as much sense to have myself announce to the world that I'm going to make the city of Fresno build me a brand new mansion overlooking the water because they fined me for speeding. But hey people believed it. They drank Trump's kool-aid, and they're still doing it. They just heard Trump brag over and over and over again about how nobody builds better than he can, and that he can hash out deals better than anyone. Apparently this is enough to qualify anybody to make outrageous statements that couldn't be further from the truth.

To the surprise of nobody, who actually thought it through, Mexico didn't pay for the wall, you know who did? We did. The American taxpayers. I don't know about you but I don't want my money to be going into some half-ass scheme that I don't believe in. From 2017-2020 the wall cost the American taxpayers over 15 billion dollars.[296] Think about that. 15 billion dollars for a medieval wall. Most other countries would invest that kind of money in an advanced detection system so that they can catch people who come in right as they do it, or invest more in our border patrol police. Instead we spent 15 billion dollars on a wall that, as Trump supporters showed when they jumped the fences at the Capitol on January 6th, can be easily hopped over, dug out beneath, or simply walked around, as the wall would need hundreds of more miles to go

---

296 Isacson, Adam. 2020. "400 Miles of Harm: There Is Nothing to Celebrate about Border Wall Construction." WOLA. October 29, 2020. https://www.wola.org/analysis/400-miles-of-harm-nothing-to-celebrate-about-border-wall-construction/.

before it actually became a barrier. According to Wola, an advocacy group in America focused on human rights, 70% of that money was never appropriated from congress. That means that Trump took the money from other areas that desperately needed the funding, in a very dictatorial way, bypassing the people's representatives. Not to mention that Trump gave the okay to waive environmental protocols to build his precious wall, as well as waiving laws that protected historical sites and Native American lands.[297] When old Donny-boy wants something, he gets it, even if it means breaking standard protocols and laws that were passed long ago for future generations. Worse, Trump seemed to have put the fencing where not a whole lot of people would see it, putting the fencing "where illegal border crossings have been relatively low in recent years."[298] Hmm. That's a kick in the giblets.

When we see what the environmental effects of pushing ahead on this wall it really brings into perspective that everything we do has consequences. The wall "construction, enabled by multiple waivers of the Endangered Species Act, is cutting off migratory corridors for jaguars, ocelots, black bears, bighorn sheep, coati, mountain lions, javelina, raccoons, hooded skunks, mule deer, and smaller species. It has destroyed numerous decades-old saguaro cacti on national parkland. It is harming fragile, scarce freshwater sources like the Quitobaquito oasis in Arizona's Organ Pipe National Monument—home to unique species of turtle and fish and being drained, via nearby wells, to mix cement for wall foundations—and the San Pedro River in southeast Arizona, one of the largest undammed rivers remaining in the southwest United States. Walls will trap debris during monsoon desert rains, risking flooding that

---

297 ibid
298 ibid

could even uproot the barrier itself. Meanwhile, dynamiting and similar demolition are ongoing in the nearby Guadalupe Canyon region, forever gouging scars into stunning, rugged landscape that was already impenetrable to border crossers. In Texas, wall construction threatens to torpedo a 40-year effort to consolidate a Lower Rio Grande Valley Wildlife Refuge."[299] So we see that a corrupt politician, who gets his support from those who hate Mexicans and Hispanics, in a process of building the wall, which would give him a huge political victory over the democrats and anybody else that disagrees with him, is destroying the environment for countless numbers of animals within the ecosystem.

It often isn't talked about when we think about the risks involved with crossing the border as well. We often don't see the people who cross the border, we only get statistics from news outlets or see videos of "caravans" crossing the border, looked at like animals. However, each and every single person who chooses to make that trip is oftentimes traveling hundreds, in some cases, thousands of miles to reach the States. Some of my colleagues and friends, who happen to have different opinions than I do regarding immigration policy, will say that these immigrants shouldn't be coming in, they're not Americans and America is only meant for American citizens. I tell them, the simple answer is you're wrong. In most cases these people who are risking their lives to come to this country have a belief that this land is the land of opportunities and believe in the American dream. They think that this land is so good and this country so great to literally leave everything they know, in some cases leaving their families behind, to risk it all, to travel thousands of miles just for the opportunity of becoming an American. To me it doesn't get a whole lot more American than that. How many current Americans

---

299 ibid

would risk their lives and do the same? Just because we are born in America does not mean we are better than anybody else. It doesn't mean that everybody else is inferior. And, for Heaven's sake, we have to stop thinking that we are entitled because of where we were born, and at the same time denying those rights to those who deserve it just as much, or even more than most Americans today. I say to all who refuse to allow immigrants to come in and experience our country that they must hate this country if they think it isn't good enough for others. If Americans truly loved their country they would want to share it with others so that others can brag and be proud with them.

It needs to be said that when illegal immigrants choose to risk it all and cross the border they risk many challenges, the most threatening is dehydration. Because of the extra barriers that are erected to "keep the Mexicans out" immigrants are now dying at higher numbers due to dehydration. Think about the habitat, all the deserts and heat around the region, that makes a deadly perfect storm. Well over 7,000 migrants have died of dehydration just in this century.[300] Not a whole lot of people seem to look at these people with sympathy. Aren't these people? Don't they have families? Instead they are looked at by many who just view them as "illegals" and criminals who got what they deserved. This is flat out wrong. The world deserves better. Two women, one pregnant, just recently, as in 2020, died trying to cross the border. We don't hear about it, but we do hear Trump and his allies make ever more soundbites against them.

Why do so many people agree with Donald Trump about the "Hispanic problem" and immigration? The answer is quite simple and quite sad at the same time. It's because there is a strong growing

---

300 ibid

number of white nationalists that are gaining political power within the United States and who found their champion in Donald Trump. Their concern… waning white power. Yep, you read that right. There is a growing number of Americans who actually think that Hispanics, or blacks, or Asians, ect, will be more powerful and numerous in the near future than the white race. This is ridiculous, but the reason why immigrants receive so much flack. They just want to extend white dominance. They, for obvious reasons, clung to Trump, and why not? He consistently showed that he was the most racist nominee that we have seen for quite some time. He consistently cried out that he was going to "make America great again," and then go on and on about how he was going to "build a great, big, beautiful wall." This implies that immigrants, especially the Hispanic immigrants are what is not making America a great country, as if their presence is destroying the greatness of America. How laughable.

Why have we normalized politicians and other individuals to constantly use the deportation card? There is no denying it that we do have an immigration problem but it really depends on what end of the spectrum you look at it. I think we have an immigration problem based on how horribly we treat immigrants, in some cases locking them in cages like animals, others think we have an immigrant problem because too many people are coming in. Either way you look at it, we have an immigration problem. Instead of trying to fix the problem and come up with viable, common-sense, solutions, politicians have made it a habit for decades now to threaten to deport immigrants, who just happen to have families, friends, and jobs in America. Why have we allowed ourselves to get to this point? And haven't you noticed that recently this rhetoric has been used against Mexicans, Hispanics, and Muslims as opposed to traditionally white countries?

After Americans began to get used to the influx of those that were different, like the Irish Catholics, Eastern Europeans, and Jews, Americans started to shift their attention and focus to those who were closer home. Maybe people didn't like the Hispanics coming into the country, maybe they tolerated them. Or, more harshly, as we have seen, they killed, seriously wounded, or harassed them. But when did we start seriously thinking about deporting individuals because they were different? The answer, quite frankly, is much earlier than most Americans realize. Massachusetts, in 1794, six years after the Constitution was ratified, passed a law that allowed them to deport poor Irish immigrants. The law, while not only targeted the Irish as a group, targeted specifically the poor. Based on old English law that regulated the movement of the poor and paupers, early American colonists held a deep antipathy for the poor, seeing them as nothing much better than dirty beggars who don't work for a living. Massachusetts law would place these unfortunate poor Irish immigrants "any place beyond [the] sea, where he belongs."[301] In other words it didn't matter where they would deport the poor to, just as long as they were far from Massachusetts as possible.

Four years later, in 1798, the Alien and Sedition Acts, passed by a Federalist government that looked suspiciously on immigrants for political reasons, allowed the president to deport any foreigner that he thinks is a national security threat. Could you imagine if this law was not graciously repealed? Donny-boy Trump would have a field day deporting anybody who disagrees with him. What a lovely

---

301 "The Irish Were the First Targets of Deportation." n.d. Irish Echo Newspaper. Accessed May 18, 2024. https://www.irishecho.com/2017/4/the-irish-were-the-first-targets-of-deportation#:~:text=Massachusetts%20law%20provided%20that%20any.

scenario for republicans, nothing like bowing down to the beast. Thank God that law was repealed as fast as possible by Thomas Jefferson's republican party.

To understand the dynamics of the law we must look at why the federalist passed the alien and sedition acts. There is some similarity as to what is happening now compared to what happened then. Back in the 1790s when the country was young and impressionable, there were two major political parties that we already talked of, the Federalist and the Republicans. These parties hated each other. The Federalists were the rich man's party, the party that looked down on democracy and those that were different from their proto-typical voter base, white-male Protestants. Republicans, on the other hand, were open to the idea of democracy, received much support from the lower class system, and welcomed immigrants with open arms since immigrants overwhelmingly supported the republicans.

When the federalists were in power, they grew anxious to keep hold of that power. Seeing the rising influx of immigrants swarming the country in great numbers they felt as if their own power was waning. They had to do something and something fast. So they got together to devise one of the most horrific and deplorable laws known to the United States, certainly one that will always go down in infamy, the Alien and Sedition Acts. Among other things these laws increased the amount of time that immigrants had to wait to become US citizens from 5 to 14 years, which played out huge for stopping immigrants' growing political power and that of the republicans. Another part of the law, more well known, was the law that allowed the president, at this time a federalist, John Adams, to deport foreigners, basically at will. In addition the law allowed the government to imprison editors for malicious publishing, allowing the president to imprison just about anybody that disagreed with him. The law especially went after republican newspaper editors, most of whom were foreigners. In fact, many prominent editors were arrested and served time for their crime of expressing the freedom of the press.

In a shocking twist, the only aspect of the Alien and Sedition laws that are still in place is the section that allows for the deportation of foreigners who might be a security threat, though this is only expressly permitted in times of warfare. For instance, if America ever got involved into a conflict with Mexico, many Mexican immigrants would be terrorized and may very likely be suspects for deportation, even if they have lived in America for over twenty years.

The laws were a colossal disaster for both the country and the Federalist power, which never held a national majority ever again. This level of urgency on the part of the federalists and the desperation to combat immigrant power caused them to make a massive mistake in calculating the effects of taking on one particular sector of individuals. Modern republicans today should take this as a lesson. Instead of attacking immigrants to make a political point and to combat immigrant power, who now are overwhelmingly democratic, republicans should work with democrats to prevent unlawful entry but to work for a humane immigration policy as well, instead of focusing all of their attention to a medieval wall and deportation strategies. But this, as you know, is not the case. Republicans still overwhelmingly throw fire at immigrants, especially in republican primaries where the leading candidates are the ones most vocal about deporting those who are desperate to become American citizens.

11 DEPORTATIONS

One often overlooked tidbit of history is the Bisbee deportations. The Phelps Dodge Corporation was a large mining company that owned operations In the Southwestern reaches of America, primarily in Arizona and New Mexico. The company specialized in copper mining, among other things, and employed many poor, working-class, and Mexican-Americans. The pay for the workers in the mill was meager, especially for the amount of dangers that lurked with any work in mining. The discrimination was pampent in the mines, with Mexican-Americans and other minorities earning significantly less than white male workers.

Routine strikes were common in the mines, so much so that the miners joined part of the IWW, the International Workers of the World, one of the most powerful unions in the United States. With the continuance of the first world war and America's involvement into that effort caused a dramatic need in copper, forcing the miners to increase their production. You would think that with the new demand for copper the mining company would focus on hiring more workers to help with the extraction. Not the case. The company and its overseers forced the miners to work longer hours, running a 24/7 operation, without giving the miners any increase in pay. What an outrage.[302]

---

302 "Remembering the Bisbee Deportation, the Most Infamous Event in Arizona Labor History." 2021. 12news.com. 2021. https://www.12news.com/article/news/local/arizona/remembering-bisbee-deportation-labor-day-infamous-event-arizona-history/75-96935cc9-c741-4139-9df2-02a4e7be5234.

As was mentioned, working in these mines was frighteningly dangerous. Accidents were common and miners were asked to clean their wounds themselves, then get back to work. This included anything from minor cuts and bruises to broken bones and infections. Workers had to use the first aid kit to treat themselves, but what happens if the first aid kit was far from them, as what frequently happened? So the IWW organized more than 5,000 workers to strike in several different cities in Arizona. The strikers had some very minimum demands for their employers: two men to work on machines, two men to work together in all areas, to discontinue all blasting during shaft work, the abolition of all bonus and contract work, to abolish the sliding scale, all men under ground a minimum flat rate of $6.00 per shift and top men $5.50 per shift, and no discrimination to be shown against members of any organization.[303] This to me sounds like they had a few goals that were fundamental human rights concerns. To increase their wages, which they deserved, to outlaw discrimination based on race and ethnicity, and to improve working conditions to make it safer. What's wrong with that?

As usual the company didn't like that. For some reason, but most likely just because of the enormous amount of power that the mining company had, the local sheriff was under their wings. The sheriff made a statement that he had acquired a posse of some 1,200 men and called for more to arrest the "strange men" who were simply asking for their human rights. "I, therefore, call upon all loyal Americans to aid me in peaceably arresting these disturbers of our national and local peace," Wheeler, the sheriff said. "I am determined if resistance is made, it shall be quickly and effectively overcome."[304] The posse eventually grew to 1,500 men thanks to

---

303 ibid
304 ibid

the sheriffs pleading, and quickly subdued the striking miners, rounding up 1,200 of them. They weren't put into jails. Instead they were deported into neighboring New Mexico. Why New Mexico? The vast desert. The authorities went through the effort to show the strikers they had no power, the power belonged to the mining company, not the workers.

Fred Watson was one of the miners that was deported with the group. He recalls that the train that he was loaded upon had no food and water and the train car was covered in sheep dung. What a lovely ride. How humane and just. The strikers were then placed right smack dab in the middle of the desert without anything but the clothes on their back, without food and water in the scorching heat.[305] When the president, at the time Woodrow Wilson heard of the deportations he set up a committee to make a report of the incident. Though the report came back with some harsh words for the deporters, even going so far as to ask for the sheriff to be arrested, no convictions were brought to suit and the sheriff and the posse got off scott free.

This event marks the first time a major deportation took place, most of the deportees in the Bisbee case were, not coincidentally, of Hispanic heritage. What's interesting about this deportation was that the deportees were not moved to a different country but a different state. Clearly, especially with no criminal investigations or convictions against the sheriff and the posse that forcibly deported these striking miners, this event gave positive reinforcement to those in charge that they could remove "undesirables" from within their states or even within the country on scales that we've never seen before. Indeed, shortly after this the federal government deported thousands in the Palmer Raids.

---

305 ibid

The Palmer raids were carried out by the attorney general under Woodrow Wilson, Alexander Mitchell Palmer. Palmer didn't trust immigrants, many of whom he considered radicals who were anarchists and were the ones causing trouble throughout the country as the nation was trying to conduct a great worldwide war. The anarchists were accused of bombing federal buildings during this period, and Palmer believed he found the perfect targets. Of course, it didn't help that at the same time these investigations into immigrant groups were going on Russia was in the midst of a civil war that would see the communists take over the country. Fear of a communist takeover here in America conducted by immigrants was the new hysteria and Palmer was the man to crash it down and burn it. And again, it didn't help that Palmer himself was the target of one such anarchist bomb attack, with the bomb destroying his home.

Palmer was a deeply ambitious man, not content only to serve as attorney general, he wanted to go all the way to the top, that of course means the presidency. As a bid to gain political momentum for the presidential contest, Palmer went all in on attacking the immigrants radicals. He wrote letters and articles describing the dangers that leftist immigrants posed in the United States. Thanks to Congress, Palmer had a lot of tools to work with. Among them was the newly passed Espionage Act of 1917 which the *First Amendment Encyclopedia* describes as prohibiting "obtaining information, recording pictures, or copying descriptions of any information relating to the national defense with intent or reason to believe that the information may be used for the injury of the United States or to the advantage of any foreign nation."[306] The act also made it a crime for anyone to obstruct the enlistment process or to cause someone

---

306 Asp, David. 2023. "Espionage Act of 1917 (1917)." The Free Speech Center. December 15, 2023. https://firstamendment.mtsu.edu/article/espionage-act-of-1917/.

to be disloyal to the United States and its military. Under this law 74 newspapers had been denied mailing privileges as they were determined to be too "lefist".

The Espionage Act of 1917 targeted socialists in particular. Most socialists in America at the time wanted the United States not to get involved in overseas conflicts with European powers. It was the same old philosophy that even Geroge Washington had advocated in his Farewell Address, to remain free from foreign entanglements. Yet, when socialist Charles Schenck was distributing flyers opposing US entry into world war one he was arrested under the Espionage Act. The case went all the way to the Supreme Court, where the court ruled in favor of the Espionage Act, therefore making the act constitutional, even though it was in clear violation of the first amendment and the right of free speech and free press.

The Sedition Act of 1918 further diminished the role of freedom of speech, at least in wartime. Under the law, it was illegal to "incite disloyalty within the military, use in speech or written form any language that was disloyal to the government, the Constitution, the military, or the flag; advocate strikes on labor production; promote principles that were in violation of the act; or support countries opposed to us in war."[307] To me, some of these laws make sense. We should never incite disloyalty within the US military, nor should we support US enemies in wartime. This makes about as much sense as supporting the Taliban or terrorist groups today. However, one should never be arrested and imprisoned for thinking that going to war is a bad thing. This happened to socialist leader Eugene Debs. Debs ran for president five times, once even in prison after being arrested under the Sedition Act. Under US law at the time, the US

---

307 Boyd, Christina. 2009. "Sedition Act of 1918 (1918)." The Free Speech Center. January 1, 2009. https://firstamendment.mtsu.edu/article/sedition-act-of-1918/.

forced enlistment upon young American men into a war thousands of miles away. Debs gave a speech opposing the forceful enlistment of our young men, for that speech he was arrested and imprisoned, though president Warren G Harding would pardon him three years later. More than a thousand were arrested and imprisoned due to this law, most of them were socialists, whose only crime was to oppose our young men getting killed and maimed in a European conflict.

Based on the ammunition of these new laws passed by congress, Palmer was in a position to strike fear into the hearts of those radical immigrants. His agents raided the headquarters of communist, socialist, and anarchist leaders. More frighteningly he even had labor union headquarters raided. Think of that. Labor unions. The biggest reason why so many people were able to jump out from poverty and into the middle class with an opportunity to achieve the American dream, and now even they were being raided, with the belief that they were the radical ones. That they were the ones that were crazy. They just supported workers rights. Basic workers rights. And now they were under attack.

To be fair, the United States at the time had a pretty good amount of socialists and even communists in the country. The reasons are simple. The United States, thanks to progressives, finally were starting to care about its workers. The day, which in some cases would end up being 12 or even 16 hours, was shortened to 8 hour shifts. Child labor laws were put up to guard against the exploitation of poor children. And, laws were passed to provide worker compensation in some of the most dangerous fields. The history of these laws are very interesting and I would do a disservice to this book if I didn't mention a brief history of these three laws that came to fruition after much determination on the part of normal workers.

In the United States, the history of the 8-hour workday is quite interesting and yet confusing at the same time. Beginning just three years after the inception of the US constitution, Philadelphia carpenters were the first workers to demand a shorter work day. What did they demand all the way back in 1791? A ten hour work day. That's all. Their phrase was from six to six with two hour long meals in between.[308] This precipitated the first strike in America which was carried out by Irish coal-throwers demanding a ten hour day. Nearly 20,000 workers took to the streets for justice. For too long these workers, who mostly were in the occupation of trades, were forced to work from sun-up to sun-down. This isn't a major problem in the winter months when the sun shines for maybe around eight to ten hours. It is a big deal, however, during the summer months when the sun could be shining for fifteen to sixteen hours. Could you imagine working for sixteen hours in a row? No wonder why they were striking. I have a feeling you would do so too.

Some of the strikes were unsuccessful, however, some worked. In 1835 the striking workers not only succeeded at receiving a ten hour workday but they also got a pretty nice pay increase. Look at that for determination. Strikes can work. This applied to only a few occupations. Those like the Boston ship carpenters had to wait until 1842 to see an eight hour workday. Others desperate pleas fell on deaf ears. Why did the workers need to strike to get what they wanted? Don't you think that business owners and employers would understand the needs and concerns of their employees? In some instances yes. In others, not even close. In fact, these strikers, and strikers in general, as we will find out, were always looked at by those in power as a nuisance to society. Why couldn't they just man up, work, and keep their mouth shut? Can't they see that they are

---

308 Philip S. Foner, *History of the Labor Movement in the United States, Vol. 1, From Colonial Times to the Founding of The American Federation of Labor*, International Publishers, 1975, pages 116–118

being ridiculous? Excuse me, but the only thing ridiculous is when an employer doesn't have the guts to stand side by side with their workers. This means to offer them quality pay and decent hours. The fact that anybody needs to strike means that the workers' initial desperate appeals fell on deaf ears and nobody on top listened. This is why they had to miss multiple days, in some cases months, to strike. To prove a point. Their work was needed. Now pay them adequate wages and give them decent hours.

Those occupations that still did not have an eight hour day were obviously desirous to receive an eight hour workday. So much so that the clamor over an eight hour day was all the talk in Chicago of 1864. Workers were so much in favor of it that it became a law in the Illinois state legislature, though it was deeply ineffective with lots of loopholes sprinkled everywhere within it. Note to all the lawmakers, and to interested citizens, nobody wants a law crazy with loopholes, this does nothing to help matters and is just a big waste of time. Just like our tax laws and all the loopholes within it to give the wealthiest 0.01% big savings.

Anyway, because Illinois lawmakers were unwilling to put on their big-boy pants and stand up to some of the wealthiest companies and people, probably because of the massive campaign contributions that the wealthy dole out to their favorite politicians, Illinois workers were still on their own, having to continue working through mind-boggling conditions. In Chicago a citywide strike actually shut down the economy for a week before it finally fell through, a situation that could have easily been avoided had the legislature just listened to the people and did its job.

In August of 1866 the National Labor Union, the largest labor organization at the time, passed a provision calling for an eight hour workday, "the first and great necessity of the present to free labor of this country from capitalist slavery, is the passing of a law by which eight hours shall be the normal working day in all States of the American Union. We are resolved to put forth all our strength until this glorious result is achieved."[309] The movement began gaining national attention, to the point where congress passed a law in 1868 which lowered federal workers to an eight hour work day, notice the word federal, this didn't cover everybody. President Andrew Johnson, who throughout his political career had been a favorite among the poor and working class, surprisingly vetoed the law, though it was overridden by congress a few days later. Though federal working men finally had a major breakthrough with the eight hour workday, they still suffered, this time because their wages were cut some 20% of what they were making before, thus taking the joy out from under them.[310]

After numerous strikes, many of which turned violent, including the Haymarket Square riot, and many others involving unions, an eight hour workday still proved elusive. However, the United Mine Workers won an eight hour workday in 1898 and the AFL, the American Federation of Labor set May 1st of 1890 as the day when workers should work an eight hour day, if not then there would be more strikes and potentially more violence. As the years went on the eight hour workday actually picked up serious political momentum. Teddy Roosevelt, in the 1912 presidential election, running for the progressive Bull-Moose party, advocated for an eight hour workday in his party's platform, the first presidential candidate to openly endorse such a move. Of course we idolize Teddy for numerous reasons, among which was his serious determination to conserve the environment, believing that when the environment is healthy we are healthy too, but he was also super influential when it came

---

309 "United States v. Martin, 94 U.S. 400 (1876)." n.d. Justia Law. Accessed May 18, 2024. https://supreme.justia.com/cases/federal/us/94/400/.
310 Richard F. Selcer (2006). *Civil War America, 1850 To 1875*

to progressive causes, many of which supported worker's rights. We have to tip our caps to Teddy here as being ahead of the time and having the guts to take on major wealthy corporations and businesses and to make his bed with the American people. And, of course, when Teddy Roosevelt spoke people listened. Teddy Roosevelt didn't win the election that year, despite breaking records for a third party candidate, but the eventual winner Woodrow Wilson, a fellow progressive, would support proposals equally satisfying for working-class individuals.

I have long said, and still believe, that when workers spend much time at work, let's say they work a twelve or even a ten hour shift, their productivity slows down as they begin to be more groggy as the day goes on. Let's face it, most people feel most energized when they first arrive at work. They grab their Starbucks coffee and they're ready to go. At noon they might still be up and running, feeling good and ready to tackle what comes next. But by the time that three or four comes around most everybody is starting to feel worn out and tired, ready to go home and be with their family, or cats. This is true for people working in any field, whether that be teaching, healthcare, law enforcement, construction, and postal workers. It somewhat astounds me that most nurses can work a twelve hour shift. I get that this might actually be a wanted commodity for many nurses, given the fact that they only need to work around three to four days and get three or four days off per week. The problem with this is nurse burn-out. So many nurses feel strained by the time their work is done that they literally dread coming into work the next day, especially when they work in high stress, high emotional jobs like that. Added on top of that, if I were a patient undergoing an IV infusion, I would want someone who is fresh and energized to be working on me, as compared to a nurse that has been there for eleven hours and just wants to go home because they're so tired.

It's not just healthcare. Many employers have actually found that when their workers work longer hours, production goes down, this is especially true in manufacturing. When the Ford motor company decided to shorten its workers' hours and roughly double their pay to $5 a day, rival companies hated the move. This meant that rival companies would have to do the same or eventually see their workers leave for better conditions. In many ways the Ford motor company did what companies should be doing today. Think about it, if employers are having a hard time filling in jobs there are a few things they can do to increase applications, provide good salaries and employee benefits. When Ford motor company did this they were ahead of the game, and to the consternation of its rivals, the move actually increased productivity and had a huge influx in profits, which nearly doubled within two years.[311] That should be a lesson for everyone. When a company treats its workers like actual human beings, giving them satisfying wages and good employee hours and benefits, production skyrockets as well as profit margins. This is no coincidence. Happy workers mean greater morale, which in turn produces more money. This is a pretty simple formula. Afterwards, Ford's major rivals all followed suit and offered their workers a higher salary and an eight hour day to boot.

Woodrow Wilson would go on to ask congress to pass a law that barred companies from forcing its workers to work more than eight hours a day. This new action was officially called the Adamson Act, named after Georgia representative William Adamson, which did exactly that. This law was designed to protect railroad workers, who

---

311 Ford Motor Company "Henry Ford's $5-a-Day Revolution" Archived 6 May 2011 at the Wayback Machine, *Ford*, 5 January 1914

were forced to work long hours for no additional pay, a 20th century form of exploitation. Not only did this law set the maximum amount of hours at eight, but also called for overtime pay, therefore if a railroad company still wanted its workers working more than eight hours a day they would be required to pay for overtime, not just simply work for free, as had been the case prior. In a surprising move, especially given the Supreme Court's reluctance to support anything that might help working people, forcing lawmakers to create a constitutional amendment to include income taxes to make sure that the wealthy pay their fair share, in this case allowed the eight hour workday to be upheld, therefore we didn't have to create an amendment to our constitution to provide basic working rights.

The Adamson Act only benefited railroad workers, not the vast majority of workers that were consistently working more than they should have. In 1937, thanks to the Fair Labor Standards Act, a part of the New Deal legislation that FDR had magically pushed through, a maximum forty hour work week was established with overtime pay. Finally we arrived at an eight hour day or forty hour week with the government to back us up. Of course, employees can still work longer but will be paid extra for their services in the form of overtime pay.

What is wrong with allowing workers to work eight hours instead of ten or twelve hours a day? Nothing. It's crazy to think now but when all of these striking laborers were making a big stink over these unfair working situations they were regarded as "lunatics," "crazies," and last but not least "radicals". Radicals? For what? Demanding fair hours and fair wages to go along with it. Yeah that's crazy right there. Instead, the real radicals here were the ones that forced their workers to continue working under unfair practices. Forcing them to strike and even firing them for having principles and morals and wanting to see their families for a few extra hours each day. Wow, they're loonies aren't they? Most of the striking workers were considered dangerous for the economy, even though they were being exploited. Many of the workers joined labor organizations and other groups, some political like the socialists and the communists. This caused some federal employees and politicians, in other words those in high places with lots of money, to look negatively upon the striking workers, many of whom just happened to be foreigners. They charged that all workers were socialists and needed to be watched, spied on, and looked out for. These workers were about to upset the entire economy, at least for the wealthy few with all the power.

Not so long after the government began becoming serious about an eight hour workday they also got serious about eliminating child labor laws. Actually, throughout the history of America, dating all the way back to the 1600s, children were a key component of the economy. They were used to complete all sorts of jobs consisting mostly of working on the farm and completing household chores. As soon as children, of mostly poor or middle income families, were around two or three years old, or old enough to walk, they were responsible for helping the family with laborious tasks. These are different from simply helping clean the dishes and house, though they certainly did these things as well. These tasks, before the industrial revolution and the age of factories and machines, were simply to help the household earn extra money.

As a matter of fact, the idea for children to work came from the American ancestors, the English. They believed that idle children, those that were not brought up working and learning the value of work ethic, would instead resort to a life of crime and poverty.[312]

---

312 Elizabeth L. Otey, *The beginnings of child labor legislation in certain states* (Washington, DC: Government Printing Office, 1910),

For this reason, cash strapped families would eagerly submit their children to apprenticeships, therefore the family can earn a little extra cash, though not great, and most apprentice masters would supply the children with food and housing, all of this the family would otherwise have to pay if their children were still in the house. If you were born in an impoverished family or even a middle class family there is little doubt you would be shipped off to learn a trade somewhere far away. You would think that apprentice masters would be known as exploiters by forcing these kids to work and paying them very minimal wages, if at all, yet they were actually considered heroes. Taking these kids and teaching them how to earn a living was considered by many to be charitable.[313] Many historians will even rave about how important apprenticeships have been throughout the course of our history. Indeed, without apprenticeships our history would look very remarkably different. Some of our most famous American founders were apprenticed. George Washington started out as an apprentice working as a surveyor of land, a role in which he would later go on and make much money, paving the way for him to become a leader of our country and the continental army, while creating the wonderful tourist destination of Mount Vernon. Benjamin Franklin was also apprenticed in a printshop, where he learned the trade of writing, creating all sorts of wonderful prints such as the farmer's almanac, among many other things. Without Franklin's background in the apprenticeship his legendary wit may have been never known and our history forever altered. Likewise, the legendary Paul Revere was apprenticed in the trade of becoming a silversmith, a trade that he perfected throughout his life, causing him to become a well-known, highly trusted, neighbor in the Massachusetts community.

---

313 ibid

However, there is a stark difference between apprenticeships and what would become the norm in the 19th and 20th centuries. Apprenticeships were a major plus for many families and children, considering it as another form of schooling, where children could meet with and interact with highly successful tradesmen, doctors, and lawyers, to create a path for themselves in that particular trade. However, what apprenticeships did end up doing was creating a culture in which it was socially acceptable to send children off to work, even if they were just eight or nine years old.

Once the industrial revolution took hold and more factories were being sprouted up to create an abundance of goods, factory employers and supervisors needed to find workers to fill these factory positions. Many of these positions went unfilled, nobody wanted to work in those dismal conditions, where the work was extremely dangerous, and the pay was so low that it wasn't even close to worth it. Even when the economy went into downward spirals and adults were increasingly searching for jobs in the factories, employers would hire children over adults. The reason? Children were far easier to exploit, easier to manipulate, easier to pay substantially less than adults. This created numerous problems. Adult workers were being thrown out of their jobs for cheaper labor, children. And what about the factory owners? They were making huge bucks. They didn't care that they were paying their children workers starvation wages, they were making money and that's all that mattered to them. Not surprisingly, the wealth inequality skyrocketed thanks to the greedy owners of these factories. In the 1890s the top 4,000 families owned more than the bottom 11.6 million families combined, (many of the wealthiest families were owners of such factories.) While this number seems astronomical it is nothing to the wealth inequality that we see today (we will talk about this more in further chapters), though it is still alarming that the same people who were literally paying children starvation wages, where the same ones who were flaunting their wealth, creating the phrase the "gilded age."[314]

The gilded age was a different time, people actually wanted to show the world how much wealth they had. Accordingly a Mrs. Stuyvesant Fish once threw an expensive dinner party to celebrate her dog who later arrived wearing a $15,000 collar with diamonds embroidered on it.[315] By contrast in 1890 11 million of the nation's 12 million families earned less than $1,200 a year.[316] That's about $40,000 today. Some may think this number isn't too shabby, remember this is how much a FAMILY earns per year, not individuals. The fact that 92% of American families made less than this is appalling. Even worse, the average family income was roughly $380 per year. That's roughly $12,700 per year for a family today. Most families at the time had anywhere from five to eight kids to take care of as well. Meanwhile Mrs. Fish was spending lavishly on her dog, buying her a collar that cost more than an entire year's income for most families. That's appalling. But the motto of the gilded age, at least for those wealthy capitalist, was "if you could make money dishonorably then do it, and honorably if you must then do it." This is the definition of socialism for the rich. What an upside down world.

The wealthy industrialists had many different groups of people to exploit, which is why they made so much money. They could exploit newly arrived immigrants that were desperate to make some money, and they could exploit, as we already mentioned, children,

---

314 Rothman, Lily. 2018. "How American Inequality in the Gilded Age Compares to Today." Time. February 5, 2018. https://time.com/5122375/american-inequality-gilded-age/.
315 PBS. 2019. "The Gilded Age | American Experience | PBS." Pbs.org. 2019. https://www.pbs.org/wgbh/americanexperience/features/carnegie-gilded/.
316 ibid

which made it a win-win for the likes of Andrew Carnegie, Nelson Rockefeller, and JP Morgan and co. Because the urban poor were so impoverished, many of them turned to political groups, such as Boss Tweed's political machine for some very much needed financial relief. The system pretty much worked like this; political organizations would reach out to the poor and vulnerable to offer them financial rewards for their political support. That's it. Political machines were literally buying votes, which led to, as you may have guessed it, a huge problem with corruption infiltrating the government. This corruption would come back later to hit America hard, and it can be traced all the way back to unchecked capitalism and the greed of the industrialists.

During the industrial revolution it became expected that children, who grew up in impoverished families, would be forced to work to provide an extra few cents for the family. Every cent they earned would go to the family, not the child, not for their savings or for their schooling. Children, at this time, mostly worked in mines, where they were exposed to hazardous chemicals and breathing in unhealthy amounts of coal which led to respiratory issues later in life. They also worked in factories, the textile industries, canaries, agriculture, newspaper boys, shoe shiners, peddlers, and messengers.[317]

It goes without saying that children were often injured or even killed in some of these very dangerous jobs, such as working in mills or factories. Most of the injuries came from unguarded machinery, or lax regulations at the factory which literally allowed hundreds of children to be operating some of the most dangerous equipment without any supervision whatsoever. Michael Ward, a doctor who specialized in children's health recorded that "When I was a surgeon

---

317 Museum of Tolerance. n.d. "Child Labor during the Industrial Revolution Museum of Tolerance." *Museum of Tolerance*. https://www.museumoftolerance.com/assets/documents/children-who-labor-handout-2.pdf.

in the infirmary, accidents were very often admitted to the infirmary, through the children's hands and arms having being caught in the machinery; in many instances the muscles, and the skin is stripped down to the bone, and in some instances a finger or two might be lost. Last summer I visited Lever Street School. The number of children at that time in the school, who were employed in factories, was 106. The number of children who had received injuries from the machinery amounted to very nearly one half. There were forty-seven injured in this way."[318]

Other more gruesome observations have been made regarding incidents in the textile factories. One such observer in a textile factory was haunted by one particular scene, though he saw many like it throughout his experience at the factory. He tells the story of "a girl named Mary Richards, who was thought remarkably handsome when she left the workhouse, and, who was not quite ten years of age, attended a drawing frame, below which, and about a foot from the floor, was a horizontal shaft, by which the frames above were turned. It happened one evening, when her apron was caught by the shaft. In an instant the poor girl was drawn by an irresistible force and dashed on the floor. She uttered the most heart-rending shrieks! Blincoe ran towards her, an agonized and helpless beholder of a scene of horror. He saw her whirled round and round with the shaft - he heard the bones of her arms, legs, thighs, etc. successively snap asunder, crushed, seemingly, to atoms, as the machinery whirled her round, and drew tighter and tighter her body within the works, her blood was scattered over the frame and streamed upon the floor, her head appeared dashed to pieces - at last, her mangled body was jammed in so fast, between the shafts and the floor, that the water

---

318 Simkin, John. 1997. "Child Factory Accidents." Spartacus Educational. September 1997. https://spartacus-educational.com/IRaccidents.htm.

being low and the wheels off the gear, it stopped the main shaft. When she was extricated, every bone was found broken - her head dreadfully crushed. She was carried off quite lifeless."[319]

Though the story is quite gruesome and hard to hear, this incident didn't prove to be a major shockwave throughout the factories. Indeed, the very next day the workers were right back to the factory to continue another hard day's labor, again many of the workers, kids. In the factories it wasn't uncommon for children to have broken bones and ripped off skin. It was part of normal everyday life in the factories. And if a child, or any employee of the factory, were to happen to miss a few weeks or months recovering from a broken limb, well they could just kiss their jobs good-bye. Once they lost their jobs it was nearly impossible for them to gain further employment, especially with the influx of child labor.

Another reason why factory employers preferred the children as opposed to adults, was because children were much easier to subdue into obedience. Indeed, it was routine for factory overseers to stand outside of the factory doors and whip children who happened to be just a minute or two late. Children would be susceptible to this kind of violence, whereas an adult would most likely have fought back. In the factories, the owners wanted the children primarily to work the machines because the machines were quite prone to clog up and when this happened the overseers would force the children to unclog the machines, reaching in and pulling fabric out of a moving, live, machine with their little hands, thus putting them directly into the line of fire. Yet, at this time in history it was perfectly acceptable and the owners could laugh their way to the bank paying these unfortunate children literally starvation wages. Indeed children were oftentimes paid quite substantially less than their

---

[319] ibid

adult counterparts, some even earning 20% less, even though their wages were already quite low. Most children were only paid about $0.50-$0.60 cents a day. Not an hour. A full day, consisting of ten to twelve hour shifts would net them roughly fifty cents a day.[320] That's about twelve dollars in today's money. Talk about exploitation. Talk about the greed of the patriotic "capitalists." It is very true that the wealthy literally were living high off the hog, making extraordinary amounts of profit off of the backs of children, who were working just so that their family can survive in some sort of twisted, flipped upside down world. While wives of these tycoons could afford to buy diamond studded collars for their dogs, many other families had to send their children to factories where they may be mutilated and, in extreme cases, killed, just to earn an extra fifty cents. Meanwhile that extra fifty cents could mean all the difference for that family. That could keep them eating, allowing them to purchase bread to prevent them from starving.

I'm not quite sure why some people hold the likes of these greedy tycoons as heroes or "great men" who rose from rags to riches and were the epitome of the American dream. These people do not represent the American dream at all. How can you call someone who is okay exploiting children as living the American dream? They should go down in history with the likes of all the other crooks and thugs who wronged humanity. I'm talking about the likes of the factory owners, overseers, and supervisors. I'm talking about the Carnergies, Rockefellers, and Morgans. It is true that some of these individuals gave a lot of money to charity, but in my view they should have never had this level of wealth by exploiting their workers.

---

320 Beck, Elias. 2016. "Child Labor in the Industrial Revolution." History Crunch. History Crunch. October 5, 2016. https://www.historycrunch.com/child-labor-in-the-industrial-revolution.html#/.

In the mines, children faced even grimmer situations. In the coal mines, children were often used in great supply due to their ability to crawl through tunnels that were either too low or too narrow for bigger adults. Thus, the employers liked to keep the children around, again for exploitation purposes. Children who worked in the coal mines often worked from sunup to sundown, roughly ten to twelve hours daily with very few breaks. Naturally when children had to work as early as 4 AM, they would tend to doze off during the middle of their shifts, creating very dangerous situations within the mines. Children being run over after falling into the paths of the giant coal carts were quite common, as were multiple fatalities whenever a gas explosion went off.

Needless to say that when anyone works in a coal mine the potential for longer term illnesses are quite common and come with the stresses of the job. For instance, most young children who spent a year or two working in the coal mines developed lung cancer at a very early age and death before the age of 25 years old for these unfortunate children was the norm.[321] Yet again, the children were forced into this, it was the only way they could survive, and, for that matter, help their families survive.

One thing that's quite distressing that not a lot of Americans know is that child labor is still prevalent in many developing countries. According to the International Labor Organization, over 215 million children are put to work each and every day, more than half of them work in extremely dangerous fields, such as mines, factories, and other highly undesirable jobs. In the Democratic Republic of Congo, many children are working in artisanal mines,

---

321 "Child Labor | History of Western Civilization II." n.d. Courses.lumenlearning.com. https://courses.lumenlearning.com/suny-hccc-worldhistory2/chapter/child-labor/#:~:text=four%20were%20employed.-.

roughly consisting of nearly 40% of the mining workforce.[322] In polls conducted, where researchers have reached out to the kids working in these mines, about 19% of them have said that they have witnessed children dying in the mines. Nearly 90% have said that they have had severe pain from their labors, and nearly 70% have experienced severe and persistent coughing, an early sign of lung disease. Some girls have even experienced genital diseases after becoming exposed to toxins while being forced to wade waist-deep in highly acidic water.[323] This clearly is a travesty, and only a brief mention of the many other cases in which children are getting the raw end of the stick, having to work off poverty in some of the worst ways imaginable. Yet, as the children are risking their lives in the mines, or fields, or factories, there are a few who are holding lavish dinner parties in their snobby mansions with their expensive cars and extravagant yachts. How can we let this happen? Again, the wealthy control everything. They have the power in the Democratic Republic of Congo, and in wealthy countries like the United States.

In these countries, where children are still forced to work, they do not have safety regulations that help to ensure that children will not be seriously injured or even killed. They are still ruled by oligarchs, who control the government with their vast amounts of wealth, all at the expense of the vast majority who continuously struggle with poverty. For decades upon decades the United States did not have these safety regulations, they were forced into it by the workers, who were standing up for their human rights.

---

[322] World Vision Staff. 2016. "Child Labor: Children Reveal Horror of Working in Mines | World Vision." World Vision. December 22, 2016. https://www.worldvision.org/child-protection-news-stories/child-labor-children-reveal-horror-working-mines.
[323] ibid

The first ever attempt to regulate the conditions of child labor, in terms of legislation, did nothing to eliminate the practice of child labor, only to make it safer for children to continue to work. This piece of legislation, which was passed all the way back in 1802, was called the Health and Morals of Apprentices Act 1802, it only merely stated that factories must be kept clean to prevent diseases and what not. Throughout the coming decades more laws were passed to regulate child labor laws. The Factory Act of 1844 banned women and young adults, ie. children, from working more than twelve hours a day, while those 9-13 years old were banned from working more than 9 hours a day.[324] While child labor was still common, at least the government was doing something to try to stop the madness.

You want to know the worst part of this? These laws were passed by Great Britain. Where was America at the time? Still deeply entrenched with child labor. Indeed, while Great Britain was passing laws that severely curtailed the amount of hours that young people could work, the United States was still just getting started with the influx of child labor. Many factories and employers were openly encouraging children to work for their factories, while also forcing them to work twelve to fourteen hour shifts. Indeed, the first major piece of child labor legislation passed in America was in the early 1900s, even though multiple state governments tried to stop the madness long before the federal government lifted a finger.

At first, the primary issue with child labor in America wasn't the fact that children were working as low as six years of age, that they were being exposed to dangerous and deadly working conditions, and that children in the workforce were deflating the wages of adults, the problem came with education. America, in its earliest

---

324 "Child Labor | History of Western Civilization II." n.d. Courses.lumenlearning.com. https://courses.lumenlearning.com/suny-hccc-worldhistory2/chapter/child-labor/#:~:text=four%20were%20employed.-.

years, was still heavily Puritan with puritanical spirit, regardless of what denomination Americans were a part of. Part of this spirit was the belief that children should have a strong work ethic and have a deep abiding faith in the Almighty, a faith that they could only develop if they could read the Bible, which meant that children had to read. When children worked in the factories, fields, and mines, they were neglected the opportunity of schooling. Clearly, if they were to develop a strong faith they needed to be educated. Which is why a movement to at least regulate child labor originated in the states. Of course, not everybody in this period was religious, but even for the more secularist Americans, the very thought of democracy could not flourish unless each individual within that democracy was properly educated, meaning that they could make intelligent decisions about their country. This paved the way for the movement to grow, covering all religious denominations and lack thereof.[325]

Connecticut became the first state to mention child labor in 1813 when they passed a law that required children working in factories to be taught the basics; reading, writing, and basic math. Believe it or not, some parents were actually upset with laws like Connecticut's. They viewed any law, whether good or bad, on the part of education to be infringing on parents' rights to raise their kids the way they think is best. Does this remind you of anything? During COVID school boards did a phenomenal job keeping kids safe right in the thicket of the pandemic, enacting policies like safe distancing, disinfecting all surfaces routinely, and even shutting school districts down. Now obviously shutting the schools down was harmful for the children both socially and academically, but we should still be thankful for the school boards for making these

---

[325] Walter I. Trattner, *Crusade for the children: a history of the National Child Labor Committee and child labor reform in America* (Chicago: Quadrangle Books, 1970)

decisions. I personally would rather have my child be a year behind academically than to have either my child or a member of my family get seriously sick or even die because a school decided to stay open in the midst of the pandemic. That's irresponsible. So many parents intimated school board members for making children wear masks. Why? Because masks were infringing on "personal rights", in other words, people can choose whether or not to wear a mask. That's flat out selfish. During the pandemic you wore a mask to protect other people, don't be so selfish.

Just like during COVID, Americans in the early 1800s didn't like state governments mandating what their children needed to learn. This is crazy. What's so bad about the law? At least children were mandated to have an education. WIthout these laws in effect children would work in factories and not have the basic skills required to be an asset to the US economy and succeed on their own. The fact that parents would object to this is mind-blowing. Yet, despite the pushback from some angry parents, many more states adopted policies similar to that of Connecticut's, thus at least laying the groundwork for the beginning of a conversation about child labor.

In 1842 Massachusetts passed a law outlawing children under the age of twelve from working more than ten hours a day, which Connecticut followed suit, though their law raised it to fourteen years of age.[326] By the middle of the 1840s, most New England states had laws on the books regulating the practice of child labor, though none of them were particularly effective, or even worthwhile. Some laws actually provided strong loopholes, giving parents the right to consent for children as young as five or six to work within the factories, something that impoverished families did so commonly, forced by their economic insecurity. Other laws explicitly

---

326 ibid

gave factory owners huge giveaways that seemed quite suspicious. These laws allowed children to work more than ten or twelve hours if this work was on a voluntary basis. Well, who in their right mind would want to work a fourteen hour day with the last two to four hours being for free? The answer, quite simply, is nobody. So why was this a problem? Factory owners could routinely use this law to their advantage to push children workers to work longer days for free. If a child refused, they could simply be beaten or fired and replaced with the next young poor child whose family was desperate enough to send off to the factory. It's little things like this that make me wonder who the laws are supposed to protect. Helpless children, who should be in schools, or greedy industrialists who want to build their third mansion? Obviously, to the congressmen making this law they listened to the greedy industrialists, they at least could give them campaign contributions and bribes, poor children from impoverished families could give them nothing but a headache.

Like anything, the more heavily prominent something becomes, the more likely it is to gather the interest of the American public. In this case, during the 1870s when child labor was on the rise, and gruesome stories from the children who worked at the sites were told, more lawmakers were forced to give it some attention. In 1872, the Prohibition party, who mostly stood for the prohibition of alcoholic beverages, was the first party to advocate for the abolition of child labor.[327] This view, however, was not shared with the general populace, and the Prohibition party was a very weak organization that had no chance to garner any real support for any

---

327 Schuman,Michael. n.d. "History of Child Labor in the United States—Part 2: The Reform Movement : Monthly Labor Review: U.S. Bureau of Labor Statistics." Bureau of Labor Statistics. Accessed May 19, 2024. https://www.bls.gov/opub/mlr/2017/article/history-of-child-labor-in-the-united-states-part-2-the-reform-movement.htm#_edn28.

substantial issue. It goes without saying that if any of the two major political parties, that being either the democratic or republican parties, stood up and denounced child labor, and had the guts to take on the wealthy industrialists, child labor would have ended much sooner, and many children's lives could have been saved. Of course, both major parties then, like now, are still tied at the hip with special interest groups that use their money to influence the process of lawmaking.

Two years later, in 1874, twenty children were killed, many of them were girls with the youngest among them just five years old in a Granite Mill in Massachusetts, one of the states with some of the most regulations on child labor. The mill erupted on fire and the doors were locked, preventing them from an accessible escape route. These young girls were burned alive, suffocated from the smoke, or were killed in an attempt to jump to safety.[328] Could you imagine being in their shoes? Could you imagine your five year old going through this?

As sad as this situation was, it finally started to get people riled up about the conditions in these factories and mills, though not at first. Initially the main newspaper headlines were focused purely on the fire and not so much as to why there were so many children in the factories in the first place. In all honesty, the fire accident made people more concerned about making factories more fire-proof, or at least better fire mitigating systems. Some citizens were thoroughly disgusted with the idea of children being subjected to this kind of work, as in the words of one such Massachusetts man "take the children out of the factories."[329]

---

328 ibid
329 Marjorie E. Wood, "Emancipating the child laborer: children, freedom, and the moral boundaries of the market in the United States, 1853–1938"

In the years 1885-1889 ten states set the minimum age to work, while another six states passed laws further diminishing the amount of hours children could work. Yet still, the federal government had no official law on the books regarding child labor. And despite the increase of certain state laws, regulating the use of child labor, in the 1890s more children actually worked in the factories and continued to rise. In the year 1890, almost twenty percent of children between the ages of 10-15 were employed, that's one out of every five![330] Again, just like in the reconstruction period, it was the South that was primarily dragging its feet on the issue of child labor. Most of the child labor regulations were passed in northern states. For decades reformers had held on to hopes that the South would become advanced enough to take children out of the factories, but decade after decade they were disappointed. By the early 1900s reformers had had enough. They would end child labor once and for all. It didn't matter if the country was ready for it. It didn't matter if the South's economy was still relying on it. It was inhumane and not American. Child labor had to go.

The first celebrated proponent of child labor laws was a minister named Edgar Gardener Murphy. Murphy was a staunch white supremacist, while at the same time deplored the lynching that were commonplace, especially in the South. Why does this matter? I just think it's interesting that the first real proponent of regulation and legislation against child labor was also somebody who harbored really evil thoughts against those that were black. Murphy was born and raised within a household and state that looked upon blacks as being inferior, hence Murphy learning hatred and racism at a young age. He would later go on to win the admiration of Booker T Washington for his views on racial reform and in opposing the

---

330 Trattner, *Crusade for the children*

Alabama constitutional convention of 1901, that would disenfranchise blacks, codify segregation, and set up literacy tests to vote.[331] This proves that just because you are born in a racist family or grew up in a state where discrimination and other draconian laws are acceptable and celebrated, that doesn't mean that you can't branch out from that and stand up for what's right, like what Murphy did with child labor.

Murphy was disgusted, as he should be, by how many children were working in the factories and mills in his home state of Alabama. About one out of every four textile workers, in Alabama, were children. To Murphy this was a national crisis, not just an Alabaman crisis. He soon founded the National Child Labor Committee (NCLC) in 1904, an organization dedicated to promoting "the rights, awareness, dignity, well-being and education of children and youth as they relate to work and working."[332] The organization quickly became the leaders of the movement to ban child labor through legislation.

The NCLC was not alone in invoking the evils of child labor. Mary Harris "Mother" Jones took up the cause and supported the strike of some 10,000 striking children in Kensington Pennsylvania. She used public shows, in some cases bringing in children who had been seriously wounded working in the factories, with their fingers and hands all torn to pieces and mashed up, due to the gruesome working conditions of the mills and factories when preaching to the crowds for the wow factor. She even took some of the children and marched them to President Theodore Roosevelt's house, in New York, to prove a point and get some executive support for this

---

331 "Murphy, Edgar Gardner." n.d. Encyclopedia of Alabama. https://encyclopediaofalabama.org/article/edgar-gardner-murphy/.
332 About NCLC". Out Reach Science. January 2015.

heart-wrenching issue. Good old TR sympathized with the children but felt hand tied, "the children had the President's heartfelt sympathy", said secretary B.F. Barnes, "but under the Constitution, Congress had no power to act. . . . The states alone have the power to deal with this subject."[333] Pretty timid response for TR. I thought he was the mighty trust buster? I thought he had gonads? Apparently not when it came to protecting kids.

In the meantime, North Carolina was getting serious about reducing the amount of hours that children would work, though the law still would have allowed children to be extraordinarily exploited, it still was met with fierce pushback from the Cotton mill lobbyists. The Cotton Manufacturers' Association claimed that if the bill was passed all of the cotton mills would close. Have you heard that one before? Of course, the industry lobbyists had all the money and influence that they single handedly caused the bill to fail, not even one member of the state legislature chose to support, although initially the law had the backing from many citizens and seemed a shoe-in to be passed.[334]

Outlandishly the factory lobbyists in congress blamed the NCLC for "stirring up" agitation over the issue of child labor. Of course, to them the radicals were the ones who were trying to gut child labor and to move on in a progressive way, to send children off to schools and not factories, and to raise the wages of the men and women who worked in these fields. The lobbyists worked hard to

---

333 Juliet Haines Mofford, *Child labor in America* (Carlisle, MA: Discovery Enterprises, 1997)
334 Schuman,Michael. n.d. "History of Child Labor in the United States—Part 2: The Reform Movement : Monthly Labor Review: U.S. Bureau of Labor Statistics." Bureau of Labor Statistics. Accessed May 19, 2024. https://www.bls.gov/opub/mlr/2017/article/history-of-child-labor-in-the-united-states-part-2-the-reform-movement.htm#_edn45.

push the narrative that the Northern NCLC was trying to slay the southern way of life, as if the southern way of life was child labor and depressing wages.[335]

While the interest groups were busy trying to suppress the increase of hostility for child labor, national labor organizations were firmly on board with regulating the practice, including the powerful American Federation of Labor or the AFL. The AFL saw it like it was, with the increase of children in the factories, mills, and mines, that meant that wages for adult workers would be suppressed, as they would have to compete with cheaper labor. More so thinking of the children, the union knew that if children were working in these factories, often working more than ten hours a day, there would be little schooling to be had, with this children would grow into adulthood without the necessary skills to advance themselves and have a brighter future. It was an early cycle of poverty that had to break. Meanwhile, the powerful elite industrialists now had two enemies, the NCLC and the unions to contend with, both of which they tried mercilessly attacking in the press, accusing them of being "socialists", "communists" and "agitators".

Finally in the year of 1906, almost a full century since children had been working in the factories, a bill was brought to national attention in the halls of congress. Senator Albert Beveridge was the congressman to introduce the measure and the gist of the bill would be to prohibit interstate commerce of any goods that had been produced with the hands of children under the age of 14. This brilliant tactic would have driven a wedge right into the heart of the factories who relied on child labor because it was easy and cost effective, now this law would severely curtail the industry if they continued to use child labor to produce its products. "We cannot permit any man

---

335 Sallee, *The whiteness of child labor reform*,

or corporation" explained Beveridge, "to stunt the bodies, minds, and souls of American children. We cannot thus wreck the future of the American Republic."[336] He seemed particularly upset with the South, a region he grew up in, for supporting the institution so thoroughly, calling it the greatest stain in the south. He also hit the nail right on the head when he mentioned that congress must pass a nationwide law as opposed to each state individually trying to pass laws and regulations. Some states would, undoubtedly, allow the practice to continue, and "even if in one or a dozen states good child labor laws were still executed, the business man in the good state would be at a disadvantage to the business man in the bad state."[337]

Though this law would have done wonders and effectively put an end to child labor in America as we know it, the bill still didn't gain a whole lot of traction. Industry special interest groups put the pressure on congressmen to vote against the bill, and, again, president Theodore Roosevelt virtually killed the bill with his open opposition to it. No doubt these special interest groups ruled, and still rule Washington to this day. They made threats to congressmen and even the president to get the bill to die a lonely and decisive death.

Like all things, however, just because congressmen and presidents are timid, that does not mean the American people are. Public momentum was growing, now with virtually all Americans, large labor unions, and reform organizations clamoring for an end to child labor, the factories knew their time was short, yet that didn't stop them from lashing out. "This labor union plot against the advancement and the happiness of the American boy" said one manufacturing lobbyist, it "is also a ploy against industrial expansion

---

336 Trattner, *Crusade for the children*, p. 87
337 Albert J. Beveridge, "Child labor and the nation," in National Child Labor Committee, *Child labor and the republic* (New York: American Academy of Political and Social Science, 1907), p. 118.

DEPORTATIONS   291

and prosperity of the country."³³⁸ I mean come on, who believes this crap? Apparently our representatives, that's who. Even worse, "I say it is a tragic thing to contemplate," said one incredibly wealthy individual. "If the Federal Government closes the doors of the factories and you send that little child back, empty handed; that brave little boy that was looking forward to get money for his mother for something to eat."³³⁹ I don't want to beat this thing to death but, again, most children were forced into working by their families where they literally earned starvation wages. Instead if children left the workforce employers would have to pay adult workers more, and that's what all of this was about. It wasn't to help the poor little kids that the industrialists were saying these things, it was to fatten their already fat pockets and trick the American public into letting the corporations continue their exploitation. Believe me folks, this happens all the time in America today and I'm sick of it.

Finally in 1912 real progress was made. Despite incoming newly elected president Woodrow Wilson's initial opposition to signing any federal law regulating child labor, believing it to be unconstitutional, he soon found it to be politically important to show the country that the democratic party was on the side of the people. A law surfaced soon afterward that would ban children working in certain facilities such as mines, factories, and canneries and would eliminate interstate trading with products that were made by children, something very similar to Beveridge's law some six years earlier. Although most of the congress was on board with this new law, giving it a huge majority of support 233-43, the special interests groups were still an obstacle that hadn't yet been defeated. Due to lobbyist objections, the bill was never brought forward to the Senate, an oddity,

---

338 Chaim M. Rosenberg, *Child labor in America: a history* (Jefferson, NC: McFarland & Company Inc., 2013), p. 183
339 Zelizer, *Pricing the priceless child*, p. 95

especially when considering the level of support that the bill had. Nevertheless, the bill was reintroduced in the next session of congress in 1916, this time called the Keating-Owen Act, which essentially was the exact same bill. As always there were some objections to the bill brought about by the factory owners and special interest groups, namely, that children would be deprived of the opportunity to learn vital skills necessary to succeed in life. Of course, these groups considered succeeding to mean making little more than a dollar a day. Some other examples of fear mongering tactics that these groups used was that it would hurt widows who were reliant on their children working to give them money, a flat out absurd objection.[340] Firstly, if the factory owners were actually concerned about the plight of the widowed then they certainly wouldn't be exploiting their children, paying them a fraction of what they would be for other adult workers. In fact, it almost seems like a double whammy, not only are the factory owners paying orphan children diddly, but they are also depriving them of any opportunity to advance in life, as well as to be there emotionally for their widowed parents. That argument is just flatly a slap in the face to the many widows out there, some widowed because of the horrid working conditions of the mill.

Despite the attempts of the greedy few, even asserting that any child labor regulations would violate state constitutional rights, the bill still passed, this time with an even greater margin of 343-46, proving that the American people were more than ready to move on and stand up for workers' rights. After considerable debate in the senate, the bill passed 52-12, after Wilson encouraged southern democrats to back the bill. 10 of the 12 senators to vote no were southerners. The other two senators to vote no were from

---

340 ibid

Pennsylvania, which had more children working the mills than all of the southern states combined.[341] Nevertheless, president Wilson was eager to sign the bill into law, that way he could explain to voters all the amazing things he had accomplished over the last four years. It's sad but true, had Wilson not been up for reelection that year he would likely have vetoed the law and children would again be allowed to work in some of the most miserable factories known to man.

The law was very effective at helping children avoid the toils of factory life, gutting factories of some 150,000 children. There you have it. That was the end of child labor in America right? Well, not quite. Shortly after the bill was passed and signed into law, the United States supreme court, by now notorious for being the court of the privileged few and not the working many, decided to throw a wrench into the plans of the reformers, and for that matter, every other sane human being in America. In 1918, the supreme court voted to overturn the Kaeting-Owen law, by doing this factories were again free to exploit children, lucky factories.

I just want to take the time to reflect on all of the horrendous decisions that the supreme court has decided that really made our country look bad in the eyes of the world. Here are just a few; overturning civil rights laws in 1883 so that white supremacists could keep on terrorizing blacks, the Plessy vs. Ferguson ruling that separate can in fact be equal, upholding the internment of Japanese Americans during world war two, upholding the forced sterilization of those with intellectual disabilities "for the protection and health of the state," and of course the Dred Scott decision.[342]

---

341 Trattner, *Crusade for the children*, p. 131
342 Sullivan, Casey. 2015. "13 Worst Supreme Court Decisions of All Time." FindLaw. October 14, 2015. https://www.findlaw.com/legalblogs/supreme-court/13-worst-supreme-court-decisions-of-all-time/.

It seems like the supreme court is ruling on the side of the people right? Absolutely not. I don't know why the supreme court rules in favor of the wealthy few, the privileged, the racists, demagogues, and bigots, instead of the vast majority of Americans. In this ruling, the supreme court sided with factory, mill, and mining special interests, ruling that children can still be exploited without any penalties under the law. Who do you think the court was listening to? Wealthy factory owners, or the children?

Congress, by this point firmly on the side of the people, decided that it had to act, or intervene, or do something to stop this madness. They decided to create a ten percent tax on businesses that would still use child labor. Again, the supreme court sided with the special interests and struck down this law, even though Congress has every right to tax certain businesses especially when conducting commerce. Lawmakers were flabbergasted, they tried everything under the books to eliminate child labor, including a constitutional amendment, though this had to be abandoned due to a lack of support for the amendment process. The amendment process likely takes years or even decades to go through all of the hoops, too long for many reformers to wait. Even Franklin Roosevelt tried to eliminate child labor through executive order, though this as well was stricken down by the nation's highest court. The supreme court once again royally screwed the Americans over, and clearly didn't care much for our children either.

By this time child labor in the United States was drastically reduced, though in some states factories were still encouraged to participate in the whole sickening practice. And while the supreme court was still showing the world that it only listened to greedy industrialists and not the desperate cries of American children, FDR was caught in a battle over the courts. What he wanted was a court that represented the interests of all Americans, instead of the wealthy few. For far too long the court had been way too conservative. Instead, when Roosevelt insisted on an idea to add justices to the supreme court that would look ideologically like the American people, he was heckled on both sides of the partisan line, with opponents calling it brazen attempts to pack the court. Had FDR been able to "pack the courts" child labor would have ended sooner, and a vast array of New Deal programs that would have energized the economy in the midst of the great depression would have been upheld.

Sooner or later, old conservative judges washed away from the scene and FDR had the golden opportunity to appoint judges of his liking, and so he did. Shortly after FDR got his court majority congress passed a child labor law in part of its Fair Labor Standards Act, or FLSA, this time the child labor law was upheld by the court. According to the *US bureau of statistics,* the FLSA included child labor provisions modeled on the Keating–Owen Act, established the first federal minimum wage ($0.25 per hour), limited the workweek to 44 hours, and created the Department of Labor's Wage and Hour Division (WHD) to enforce the law.[343] The law and the increase of family wages, thanks largely in part to FDR's New Deal programs, with the goal specifically to employ more adult workers in government programs that paid well, did much to decrease the amount of children working in the factories and the mills.

Can you imagine all of the children that could have spent their days in schools and spending time with their families and friends instead of working in depressing factories had the supreme court

---

[343] The Department of Labor Children's Bureau was initially given responsibility for the child labor provisions in cooperation with the Wage and Hour Division (WHD). Today the WHD is responsible for enforcing these provisions. The Children's Bureau currently is part of the Department of Health and Human Services and focuses on issues related to child welfare.

stepped up and listened to the American people? It is true that the supreme court has the responsibility to judge the laws and determine the constitutionality of laws passed by congress, but upon reflection, it seems that the supreme court was behind the ball on numerous occasions that seriously set America back and caused our great land of liberty to be a laughing stock all over the world. Haven't you ever noticed that most, if not all, of the disastrous decisions made by the supreme court in American history was decided by conservative majority courts? When the liberals took control of the court during the tenure of FDR they quickly upheld laws passed by congress to eliminate child labor. Why did it take so long? Why didn't the conservative court do the right thing? And more, if the liberals on the supreme court thought that it was constitutional to eliminate child labor, and has been so for almost a century now, without being overturned by the preceding conservative courts, why had the previous conservatives courts used that as an excuse? Perhaps, maybe, they received donations from wealthy factory owners? Just like Clarence Thomas and Samuel Alito think it's okay to accept donations from incredibly wealthy people and then continue to issue rulings, some in which these same wealthy donors were included in the cases. If you think that's fair then you're a lunatic.

When the first reformers of child labor started to speak out against the atrocities being thrown at our children, wealthy elitists called them crazy, "disturbers of the peace" and worse things. In a word, those who simply wanted children treated like children, instead of animals, were considered radicals and left-wingers, some even called them communists. Quite frankly, the only thing radical about this were the wealthy industrialists that kept deceiving the people into believing their lies for their own money-packing interests. These people should be ashamed of themselves for doing this to innocent children, instead some of these same people are heralded by conservatives for living the American dream. If living the American dream means exploiting children to become rich, then these same conservatives should be praising oligarchs in Congo and Saudi Arabia.

It took guts for all of the brave men, women, and children who stood up against the atrocities of child labor. These people should be the heroes, not factory owners, and the likes of Carnegie, Rockefeller, and Morgan. We should have never had to toil and struggle to pass laws protecting our children like we had in the 1800s and early 1900s. While most other countries had long banned or put severe restrictions on child labor well before the United States lifted a finger, these same industrialized countries were laughing at the American people. Why didn't they have the guts to do what was right? And again, the factory interest groups were so far deceiving the American people that they actually called the reformers radical, although we were one of the last industrialized nations to regulate child labor. Pretty sad America. Pretty sad.

The last action, which we will mention here, in which the unions were a central part of, was the beautiful thing now known as workers' compensation. This is a brief overview, not nearly as detailed as the child labor issue, yet it needs to be talked about because before the introduction of workers' compensation laws. Employees were subject to heinous injuries, not paid for the medical bills by their employers, and, in some cases, even fired for missing work due to an injury that occurred at work. That's why the issue is important, and it doesn't take someone with little understanding to realize that when employers had to cover the injury costs they would lose money, hence the factories and mills were adamantly opposed to the workers' compensation bills.

Dating all the way back to the Law of Ur, which is sometime around 2,050 B.C., yes before Christ, workers were compensated directly due to injuries sustained while at work. According to the National Library of Medicine, The code of Hammurabi from 1750 B.C. provided a similar set of rewards for specific injuries and their implied permanent impairments. Ancient Greek, Roman, Arab, and Chinese law provided sets of compensation schedules, with precise payments for the loss of a body part. For example, under ancient Arab law, loss of a joint of the thumb was worth one-half the value of a finger. The loss of a penis was compensated by the amount of length lost, and the value an ear was based on its surface area."[344] While some of this is very specific, at least they had codes protecting workers from even the most disturbing accidents. Workers, in these ancient times, could at least count on the law being on their side and rest assured knowing that they had some form of work insurance just in case something might happen the next day that would fundamentally alter their lives.

These systems shortly disappeared after the rise of feudal rule, in which peasants were given land and opportunities at the direction of the king, who was mostly ambitious for his own money and reputation, not the interests of his commoners. The form of workers' compensation that we are more familiar with today was the result of Otto Von Bismarch.

It is no small wonder that by the time Otto Bismarch became the ruler of Germany the country was going through a very serious socialist phase. Did this mean that the country was a socialist republic like the Soviet Union would later become? No. In actuality the country was going through the motions that most countries

---

344 Geerts A, Kornblith B, Urmson J. Compensation for Bodily Harm. Brussels: Fernand Nathan; 1977. pp. 7–211. [Google Scholar]

do at least every once in a while, and that movement sparked great interest in worker rights and quality of life.

Otto Bismarch certainly didn't give two cares in the world about the plight of workers, but he had been pressured for years by the far left wing of the political establishment to provide some form of protection for workers. In fact, like most dictators, Bismarck was so annoyed with these leftists that he outlawed the Social Democratic Party, beginning a series of political oppression.[345] Bismarch was no fool however, he perfectly knew that if he were to keep his power by means of crushing down every opposition group that that would look quite shady to the Prussian people. In order to maintain the Prussians' loyalty to him, he enacted policies that the everyday Prussian was longing for.

Bismarck's first dip into worker protection was the Employers' Liability law of 1871, this law provided some protection for workers working in certain dangerous fields, for example, the railroads, factories, mines, ect. This law, while important for standing up for the average worker and providing protection against dangerous accidents that may occur while on the job, was still largely ineffective due to the limited scope of protection and the few jobs that qualified for it. The real gem was the Workers' Accident Insurance in 1884. In effect it helped to cover any accident that a worker of Prussia may incur while on the job, a pretty satisfactory addition for the Prussian people. This law was the first modern workers compensation law passed in the world, think about that. This happened not all that long ago, yet long before America was willing to offer the same benefits to its own workers. The reason for the law being passed in

---

[345] Guyton, G P. 1999. "A Brief History of Workers' Compensation." *The Iowa Orthopaedic Journal* 19: 106–10. https://www.ncbi.nlm.nih.gov/pmc/articles/PMC1888620/#R3.

the first place? The socialists in Prussia. The Prussian people put up a pressure campaign and Bismarch relented, knowing the importance of winning their support.

The law was followed a few years later with better laws that provided stipends for workers when their jobs produced long-term illnesses. Think about how important these laws were to the Prussian people. Now, when the Prussians went working in the mines, if they developed lung cancer or other diseases and needed off of work they could do so and be compensated for all the work lost and medical bills that kept piling up. In the past, if an employee came down with lung disease and missed a few weeks of work they were likely fired and quickly replaced.

While the rest of the world saw a dictatorship move ahead with advancing workers rights, they were also determined to do something, knowing that their time was coming when the public would cry out for help. If a brutal dictator can stand up for the needs of their commoners, then why couldn't democracies, who directly elected their representatives, do the same? Great Britain tried to follow in the footsteps of the Prussians, yet they only accomplished the Employer's Liability Act, which didn't do a whole lot at protecting these poor workers. Worse, the law held a provision that the employer had to be found of willingly neglecting workplace safety and the employer had to agree that the employee was hurt on the job. Do you actually think that any employer would willingly agree to pay for their employee's injuries? In some cases I bet there were some pretty honest employers who actually cared about the health and well-being of their workers. In most cases, however, employers would never agree to such things, think about all the money they would lose if they allowed their employees to collect compensation, that would be tragic for them, they would lose a little bit of their salary and there's no way they would allow that to happen. Needless to say, not many compensation claims went through, it was tough for workers to even file such claims, they could be fired just like that by an angry boss who doesn't want to deal with insubordinate workers. Even worse still, Great Britain still had the "right to die" contracts, which essentially denied the workers a chance to sue employers for their injuries. Most workers would be forced to sign such contracts as a condition for taking the job, leaving them with no other choice, either sign an unfair contract or not have a job. If they then got their hand crushed by a machine and had to miss work to receive medical care they had no right to sue their employer at all, meaning that the British compensation law didn't even apply to them because they were forced to sign the "right to die" contract.[346]

After years of worker protests and pleas, the British parliament finally did something, thus The Workers' Compensation Act was proposed in Parliament in 1893. Notice the key word here is proposed. Just because a law is proposed doesn't mean that it becomes law. The Act was actually modeled on the Prussian version of the workers' compensation bill and was meant to cover all workers just like that one. However, as soon as the bill was proposed the special interest groups did its thing and tried to bring the bill down. This effort was spearheaded by the manufacturing interests of Great Britain, in other words, the greedy elite industrialists who owned the manufacturing plants and didn't want to pay another nickel for their workers, even though they were already paying them a pitifully low wage. These manufacturing lobbyists even went so far as to try to get parliament to keep the "right to work" contracts in the law, therefore employers could totally circumvent the new law, rendering it totally useless and just for show. Do you think these special interests

---

346 Hadler NM. The disabling backache, an international perspective. *Spine.* 1995

groups were on the side of the people or the incredibly wealthy few industrialists? To even push for "right to die" contracts is stunningly obvious that these groups only look out for the wealthy that have money and influence, their goal was to try to buy power. It took roughly five years, because of the special interest groups, to get the law finally passed, thankfully, in 1897.[347]

Now that Great Britain, arguably America's closest twin, had passed a law protecting workers, pressure was now mounting across the Atlantic to do the same. I hate to have to mention the fact that again, on a very critical issue that ordinary everyday people want, the United States of America was behind the eight ball again and waited for other countries to do something great. They would, again, have to follow.

In the United States reformers had been organizing for decades, emerging around the late 1800s with the Populist party, which did extremely well in more rural states where big money wasn't influencing politics, and then really picking up steam with the entrance of the muck-rakers. The muck-rakers were highly educated investigative journalists who often shone a light on the plight of the common man while also highlighting everyday problems such as racism, and women suffrage. The muck-rakers received their name from Teddy Roosevelt, who had called them out for raking up the muck of society. Roosevelt was concerned over how the muck-rakers conducted their journalism, they focused too much on the bad and not enough on the good. According to the Theodore Roosevelt Center, TR had supported change that the muck-rakers were suggesting, but with caution.

"plea is not for immunity to but for the most unsparing exposure of the politician who betrays his trust, of the big business man who

---

347 ibid

makes or spends his fortune in illegitimate or corrupt ways. There should be a resolute effort to hunt every such man out of the position he has disgraced….It is because I feel that there should be no rest in the endless war against the forces of evil that I ask that the war be conducted with sanity as well as with resolution." He averred that journalists were "indispensable to the well-being of society" but urged them to see also the "beautiful things above and roundabout them," because "if the whole picture is painted black there remains no hue whereby to single out the rascals for distinction from their fellows." Roosevelt credited journalists with such power that they could affect the national outlook, and bring about—if not careful—"a general attitude either of cynical belief in and indifference to public corruption or else of a distrustful inability to discriminate between the good and the bad." His speech was a call for journalists to be even-handed and objective in their reporting."[348]

Muck-rakers didn't like the name that was attributed to them by the president. Instead of being a kind and enlightening name, it suggested that they were the bottom of society by raking up the muck. Some notable muck-rakers included Ray Stannard Baker, Louis Brandeis, Frances Kellor, Edwin Markham, Frank Norris, Jacob Riis, Upton Sinclair, Lincoln Steffans, Ida Tarbell, and Ida B. Wells.[349] Upton Sinclair is famous for his work in *The Jungle,* a book that portrayed an immigrant family and their struggles to survive in a every man for himself world. Initially the immigrant family comes to America to seek out a better life for them and their loved ones but quickly realize that the economy is rigged by big boss millionaires that exploit not only them but millions of people just like

---

348 "TR Center - Muckraker." 2019. Theodorerooseveltcenter.org. 2019. https://www.theodorerooseveltcenter.org/Learn-About-TR/TR-Encyclopedia/Culture%20and%20Society/Muckraker.
349 ibid

them. Sinclair himself was a journalist, who had spent much time investigating the conditions of meat-packing plants, the industry that Jurgis, the Lithuanian immigrant in *The Jungle* would end up working in. Sinclair had meant for the book to showcase how immigrants were being exploited throughout our country, instead he had showcased to the world the gross conditions of the meat-packing industry, which he had seen first-hand as an investigative journalist.

One of Sinclair's most famous lines in the book illustrated to many that change needed to come, "(The fertilizer workers') particular trouble was that they fell into the vats; and when they were fished out, there was never enough of them to be worth exhibiting, - sometimes they would be overlooked for days, till all but the bones of them had gone out to the world as Durham's Pure Leaf Lard!"[350] Yes, though extreme, these things would occasionally happen and the people in the late 1800s and early 1900s would definitely eat meat that contained plenty of things that we, today, would not consider edible meat. Nonetheless, people around the country were appalled by the book, mostly because of the unsanitary conditions of the meat-packing plants, not necessarily because of the plight of this poor immigrant family. In fact, that part nearly unanimously got overlooked, Upton Sinclair famously wrote that "he aimed to hit them in the heart, instead he hit them in their stomachs."

Sinclair's efforts did not go for naught, however. His work single handedly led to the creation of the Food and Drug Act of 1906 and the Meat Inspection Act of the same year. Together, these two new laws would work to inspect that meat served to the public was clean and safe to eat, that food being served under certain labels

---

350 Guyton, G P. 1999. "A Brief History of Workers' Compensation." *The Iowa Orthopaedic Journal* 19: 106–10. https://www.ncbi.nlm.nih.gov/pmc/articles/PMC1888620/#R3.

were indeed those things. An example of this would be if a company is selling a pound of beef, the ingredients would have to contain a hundred percent beef, not mice and other critters that happened to fall in the vaults.

Reformers, like Sinclaire, were able to gain momentum, thanks to the increase of organized labor. Pressure mounted, at least somewhat, in congress for a nationwide movement to help ordinary workers. In 1906 and 1908 Congress passed the Employers' Liability Acts, which, essentially, gave some protection to railroad workers who were injured on the job, although the workers had to prove that the employers' negligence is what caused the injury, again an almost impossible task. Because the task to prove that an employer deliberately broke safety rules or broke the law was so difficult hardly any claims were made and the law, though important as a stepping stone, was largely ineffective. As a consequence the people wanted more, more protection and less coddling of the industries.

States, for the most part, didn't have much faith in the federal government to do anything worthwhile, at least in regards to workers' rights. Many states grew increasingly impatient with congress' slow rolling process and tried to create worker compensation laws themselves. New York, Maryland, Massachusetts, and Montana had tried in the late 1800s and early 1900s to pass workers compensation laws, laws that would cover virtually all employees from workplace incidents. All of these efforts failed, however, when these laws couldn't muster up the strength to overcome all of that special interest power that was on the side of the companies.[351]

---

351 Guyton, G P. 1999. "A Brief History of Workers' Compensation." *The Iowa Orthopaedic Journal* 19: 106–10. https://www.ncbi.nlm.nih.gov/pmc/articles/PMC1888620/#R3.

In a kind of screwed up way of thinking, most congressmen thought that the issue should be resolved in the states. I never quite understood this at all. For example, if New York were to pass a worker compensation law protecting them against dangerous working conditions, meanwhile Mississippi decides it doesn't need a law like that, why wouldn't workers swarm to New York and states like it to provide some sort of insurance? Secondly, what kind of legal drama would ensue if a company provides services to different regions of the country and conducts interstate business? If the company is based in New York but the accident happens in Mississippi then what would happen? Would the employee get his due compensation? Or would the courts do as they always do and support the rich and powerful at the expense of the common laborer? It seems that most congressmen weren't thinking about this dilemma as they just simply delegated it off to the states, another example of congressmen not wanting to work. Thankfully, due to the efforts of president Taft, interstate workers were covered from accidents due to a law passed in 1909, but that still left out the vast majority of workers still.[352]

The first workers compensation law passed in the United States happened to come from one of the most progressive states in the union, at least at the time, Wisconsin. Before this piece of monumental legislation the only thing that injured workers could do was to sue their employers in a civil suit or "file a tort." This was simply just hoping and praying for the best case scenario up against extremely long odds, it would prove extremely difficult to prove that the employer was negligent. Even though the odds were tilted totally in the employers' favor, the juries in Wisconsin repeatedly sided with the employee, shocking the establishment to its knees

---

352 Haller JS. Industrial accidents-worker compensation laws and the medical response. Western J of Med. 1988

and worrying them about the potential influx in torts, which in the long run could do much more damage to any company that simply paying for workers compensation and bypassing the courts. Thus, by this time, in Wisconsin, not only were major labor unions supporting workers' compensation, but employers were too, as long as it would reduce torts.[353]

When Wisconsin passed its workers' compensation law, it essentially eliminated the no-fault system, meaning that workers would no longer need to prove that employers' purposely showed negligence in regards to worker safety. This provision allowed for more courteous and harmonious relationships between the employer and employee. Now, they didn't have to settle matters in courts. The law provided these essential provisions:
- certain wage loss benefits,
- the cost of medical treatment,
- certain disability payments and
- payments for vocational rehabilitation retraining.[354]

The law fundamentally helped both employers and employees so that neither was left behind, that's the kind of leadership and common-sense energy that we need today. The law was quickly followed by nine other states who followed Wisconsin's lead in the same year. By the time that Mississippi passed a workers' compensation law in 1948 every state in the union had passed some form of comprehensive workers' compensation reform. One might wonder why Mississippi took so long to pass the much needed reform, but the answer lies in the conservative traditions of that state. Since its founding Mississippi has always been one of the most conservative

---

353 "Brief History." n.d. Dwd.wisconsin.gov. https://dwd.wisconsin.gov/wc/brief-history.htm#:~:text=In%201911%2C%20Wisconsin%20adopted%20a.
354 ibid

states in the union, we caught glimpses of this in regards to slavery, Jim Crow laws, and the common disregard for its workers. In all reality the biggest reason why Mississippi passed the workers' compensation reform was because of pressure, every state had passed it except for Mississippi, making it the odd one out. The pressure from conservative special interests groups had taken its toll, and continues to take its toll on Mississippi and southern states alike.

Part of the reason for all of the haggling was the belief that this would lead to socialized medicine. How many times have we heard this one before? Every time the government tries to protect individuals and help them with the risks of everyday life, conservatives, often prodded by the workings of the special interests, try to fear-monger the public into believing that something was unusual about the people who were trying to help people. They were not all of the sudden liberals or intellectuals, they were instead radicals, socialists, communists. And for what? Supporting common sense reforms? It is the nature of this book to point out that the struggle for some of the very things that we take for granted today was more difficult than many people realize. That these "radicals" actually provided for some of the most precious aspects of life that we have today. Imagine life without workers' compensation. Would you ever feel totally safe at work, knowing that if something would happen, God forbid, you could be financially ruined? Imagine life with child labor. Would you feel comfortable sending your kids off to work in some of the most dangerous fields, earning meager wages? Or would you feel comfortable working with children, who are threatening your own paychecks? And imagine what life would be like if our employers forced us to work twelve to fourteen hour shifts, working the same job for more than sixty hours a week. Would you ever be able to care for your family like you do now? Would you feel like you couldn't give any attention to you or your loved ones because you're so exhausted from the expanded labor?

Yet for all of these things, that we take for granted today, the wealthy elite, those who controlled the fountains of government, derailed the brave men and women who fought these machines as radicals, disturbers of the peace, and cooks. They labeled the labor unions, and those who sympathized with these common sense laws and regulations as being socialists, communists, or worse. They saw these men and women as a threat to our country, as ushering in a change that the United States couldn't make. That leaves us, in a very turn-about fashion, to pick up where we left off- the Palmer raids.

So, as we discussed, the Palmer raids had been targeting certain groups, who were deemed dangerous to the community, for the simple reason of trying to stand up for ordinary people and workers. The targets were labor unions, socialists, and communists. The situation was not improved when the socialists took over Russia in the Russian civil war of 1918. That event led many Americans to turn on those who were "red," or had communistic sympathies. All of the sudden they didn't trust their neighbors, friends, and even family members. This was known as the first "red scare".

It all started when some shipyard workers went on strike demanding better wages for their families. The movement received widespread support among the local and national labor unions who sympathized with their cause. The strike caused more than 60,000 local workers to strike, which terrified the city, mostly because the economy would take a massive hit. Newspaper editors decried the labor unions to stop, many took this to mean that the labor unions were being buoyed by foreign influence, especially from socialist countries, one newspaper editor in denouncing the strike went as far as to say "This is America – not Russia."[355] Isn't it interesting that these newspapers blamed the workers for being upset over their shriveling wages? By comparing these workers to those in Russia, the newspapers were trying to paint these ordinary workers as being socialists. And for what? Just for demanding an increase in wages, from their previous starvation wage. And isn't it curious that hardly any newspapers looked at these striking workers for what they actually were. That being average Americans that just wanted the best for their families, while working for bosses and industrialists who were making bank, making God knows how many times more than what their average worker made. By the way, the website *History* even describes the industrialists in no certain good terms, proving that it's not just my words, the website writes, "These men used union busting, fraud, intimidation, violence and their extensive political connections to gain an advantage over any competitors."[356] And who do you think the newspaper editors and politicians would listen to when deciding what to publish or what type of governance they should proceed with? It certainly wasn't the poor who could barely gather enough money to buy a loaf of bread for their families, let alone contribute to a cause, political or otherwise. Of course, these powerful men, at the time men at least, listened to other powerful men with money. The industrialists could buy politicians, have you ever heard of a political machine? In essence, this is what it was. These industrialists could make huge contributions to politicians

---

355 Murray, Robert K., *Red Scare: A Study in National Hysteria, 1919–1920* (Minneapolis: University of Minnesota Press, 1955)
356 editors, history.com. 2018. "Gilded Age." HISTORY. A&E Television Networks. February 13, 2018. https://www.history.com/topics/19th-century/gilded-age.

to do their own bidding, without having to disclose the money, in a dark-money type atmosphere.

One of the most worker friendly presidential candidates of all time was William Jennings Bryan. He ran on the democratic ticket numerous times, but in 1896 he thoroughly denounced the banks and the power they controlled over the lives of everyday Americans. He argued that the banks could virtually do anything they wanted because they owned politicians, they owned Capitol Hill, and they owned the presidency. They could manifest something and make it happen because of all the scared politicians that didn't want to cross these wealthy magnets. Bryan didn't give a damn about pissing off people with money and power. He stood up to the banks and do you know what he got out of it? JP Morgan, one of the wealthiest people in American history went on a spending spree against him. He and John Rockefellor spent so much against him and toward the republican candidate William McKinley, no one knows exactly how much due to the laws that shielded this information, that the election was totally swung to the republicans. In other words, Bryan had the people's support, but not the money. Meanwhile, McKinley had the industrialists' support and big business spent big money for him. Even though he didn't receive a lot of support from working people, money speaks, attack ads were rolled out against Bryan and Bryan simply couldn't keep up. Morgan and company called Brian "deranged" and "crazy". These are tough words, especially considering that he was idolized by so many and captured the hearts of the working class. So, apparently, the ones that stand up for the little guys are crazy, at least to the wealthy elitists.

And so money controlled everything, people were afraid to cross big money, and as a result, populist movements were often looked at with disregard and disrespect. They looked at the striking Seattle workers as crazy men with crazy designs. The Seattle mayor even dispersed 3,000 police officers and federal troops to get the workers back to work. The time has come", he said, "for the people in Seattle to show their Americanism ... The anarchists in this community shall not rule its affairs."[357] The national press was even more severe with their pushback, calling the striking workers "Marxists" (it's never a good thing to be called a marxist, conservatives for over a century now have been using this term to denounce liberal critics.) The term Marxism comes from Karl Marx, who created his own form of economic theory that approved for the collective ownership of property to be given to the masses. In theory this plan was uniquely utopian, no longer would any classes define where you stood in society, yet the plan would ultimately come to fail. Asking for collective ownership of all property and most jobs essentially paying the same, the system collapsed hard as we've seen with some other communist countries, who derive their economic policies based on the ideas of Karl Marx.

Clearly, the striking workers were not marxists, believing that a doctor should be paid the same as a mine worker, but they did believe that the jobs that they performed were important, that they should be paid more for their services, and that employers couldn't trample on their God-given rights. That didn't stop the political attacks being leveled at these workers, however. Another paper called them out as "a revolutionary movement aimed at existing government." And that it was only a stepping stone "from Petrograd to Seattle," in another comparison between the Russians and the strikers.[358] I'm going to sound like a broken record here but I ask again, why were the strikers being targeted as being "marxists" and trying to form

---

357 ibid
358 ibid

a revolutionary movement? For just simply bettering their wages? Correct me if I'm wrong here, but I'm almost certain that there is nobody in this country that wouldn't want to be paid more for the work they do. According to the dissenters, who consisted of newspaper editors, politicians, and wealthy industrialists, all of us are "marxists" and all of us are engaged in some sort of revolutionary plot to overtake our government. So much for us being patriotic. Apparently being patriotic is the definition of being railroaded by your employer. How delightful.

Unfortunately, the big-money interests usually get what they want. By being able to completely control the news markets and advertising they virtually crushed the strikers' movement. All of the sudden, ordinary Americans were becoming afraid that their country would turn to Marxism and would be another Russia being controlled by the reds, this was based off of all the fear-mongering that the press and other powerful influencers were trying to manipulate to the public. As a result, the Seattle strikers shut down their movement and went back to work after losing the support of the majority of the people. It can be easily understood that these workers felt ostracized from the community and feared that their jobs would be given to strike-breakers, who didn't really care about their basic rights.

Even though the strike formally ended due to the collaboration of the labor unions involved, Seattle mayor Ole Hanson wasn't shy to take all of the credit for ending the strike himself. He was lavishly praised in the press and he became an overnight celebrity, apparently the big money bosses were so pleased with him they made his name a huge publicity statement, encouraging others, who are in a position of power, to quit the fight for workers' rights and to instead be a strike-breaker. Because of his ongoing fame, Hanson resigned from his mayor post less than six months later, obviously onto bigger and better things. He would later go around on tours of the United States, giving lectures about the "dangers of Bolshevism", another term to describe communists. The lectures proved to be quite lucrative as he earned about $38,000, no small sum in those days, in about six months (that equates to around $550,000 today), all of this just because he decided to attack workers. [359]

A few months later, still in the year 1919, the AFL decided to grant charters to police unions to join the group. With the increase of police organizations joining unions to promote their causes, the Boston police decided now was their time to go on strike and advocate for wage increases and better working conditions, not an unreasonable request.[360] This wasn't so easy though, police commissioner Edwin Upton Curtis, intervened and asserted that police departments have no right to form or enter into any unions. To play devil's advocate, it probably wasn't the smartest decision for the police department to go on strike, especially in a bigger city like that of Boston. It makes sense then that the people of Boston were extremely alarmed and most likely wouldn't be on the side of the workers who were supposed to keep them safe. For good cause, they considered these striking workers to be derelicting their duty, and it came with consequences as the streets were incredibly dangerous for a few nights as lawlessness ruled the day and much damage was done to the city because there simply wasn't a police presence to discourage law and order. On the other hand, what were these police officers supposed to do? Did they have an extremely important

---

359 Foner, 77n; Noggle, 102–03; Ole Hanson, *Americanism versus Bolshevism* (Garden City, New York, 1920),

360 Hagedorn, Ann, *Savage Peace: Hope and Fear in America, 1919* (NY: Simon & Schuster, 2007)

job? Yes they did, but at the same time we can't use that argument against them. If they were being paid poorly for keeping the streets safe, and their working conditions were brutal then what choice did they have? The commissioner already told them that they had zero right to join a union that would advance these goals, so how would they be heard? How would they get their point across? They did the only thing they could think of at the time, even though it certainly was not a popular move.

The strikers, who happened to be police officers who were charged with keeping them safe and had done so to this point, were called "deserters," and "agents of Lenin," Lenin being the leader of the bolshevik movement in Russia.[361] President Woodrow Wilson, who had ushered in many of the reforms that the working masses had praised him for, called it "a crime against civilization."[362] People in high positions everywhere in the United States were calling out the police officers, decrying their efforts to "sovietize" the country. One senator, Henry Cabot Lodge, showed anger against all labor unions, believing them to be a tool used by the Soviets to destroy the country. Pretty crazy thoughts huh? Especially considering that today, over a century later from Lodge's remarks, labor unions are still fighting for basic rights and better conditions for their workers, not in trying to "communize" the country. Nevertheless, the paranoia was there. The Ohio State Journal posted "When a policeman strikes, he should be debarred not only from resuming his office, but from citizenship as well. He has committed the unpardonable sin; he has

---

361 Murray, Robert K., *Red Scare: A Study in National Hysteria, 1919–1920* (Minneapolis: University of Minnesota Press, 1955),
362 Pietrusza, David, *1920: The Year of Six Presidents*

forfeited all his rights."³⁶³ So now police officers don't have a right to want better working conditions and a modest salary increase?

The labor unions were beginning to understand that the American people were not with them, instead they were constantly being fed what the special interests wanted to portray. As a result, the labor unions urged the police officers to go back to work, and accept the low wages. There was only one problem with that, however. The police commissioner was unwavering to take them back, and so all of the striking police officers now found themselves out of work, just simply because they were protesting meager wages. Massachusetts governor Calvin Coolidge made a name for himself by opposing Samuel Gompers, the head of the AFL, and by refusing to heed to the demands of the police officers, even though he realistically could have done the right thing and proposed a wage increase for the workers. Instead, he stood against the workers and did the bidding of the wealthy elitists who wanted to destroy the unions because unions made employers pay a couple extra nickels, and they couldn't have that could they? And how exactly was Calvin Coolidge rewarded? Well, he was named the vice-presidential candidate for the republicans a year later, eventually winning and becoming president himself when Warren Harding died, possibly because Harding was poisoned (most likely by Harding's wife. Harding's own wife, Florence, refused to have an autopsy report, which was a little suspicious.) It really makes you wonder, though, why Coolidge would be rewarded for trying to break up union power. Obviously, the republican party was moving further away from the American people and further into the grips of the business elite.

So Labor unions were, and still to this day, got a really bad rap,

---

363 Murray, Robert K., *Red Scare: A Study in National Hysteria, 1919–1920* (Minneapolis: University of Minnesota Press, 1955),

but the labor unions just fought for rights, basic, human rights. And there were times that the labor unions and the workers didn't particularly see eye to eye on certain matters. In most cases, the labor unions were the ones who were urging moderation to the incensed workers, asking them to not get their movement in trouble by risking something that would hurt their chances. For instance, the AFL didn't advocate for the steel workers to go on strike in the year 1919, instead openly advising them to not strike. The steel workers didn't listen, though. 98% of the steel workers decided to go on strike. This is kind of a big deal, it's hard to get more than two people to agree on something, in politics it's hard to get 50% of people to believe in something, let alone 98%. Steel workers in some of the most heavily populated cities went on strike, damaging the steel economy and scaring the bejeebers out of their wealthy industrialist bosses.[364]

Steel mill owners tried desperately to turn the tide of the ongoing debate, pouring lots of money and other resources to try to defeat the effort in the press, sometimes by doing some very shady things. They even went so far as to undermine the AFL committee co-chairman, William Foster, by calling him all sorts of things, none of them good, and all seeming to suggest that Foster and the rest of the AFL leadership were all a bunch of radicals, even though the AFL had urged the steel workers to caution. One might think, why did so many steel workers go on strike? How bad must've the conditions been in order for 98% of workers to go on strike to plead their case and miss work?

In an early effort to use the race card, many steel owners tried to push the narrative that most of the striking workers were immigrants,

---

364 Brody, David, *Steelworkers in America: The Nonunion Era* (NY: Harper Torchbooks, 1969),

not pure blooded Americans. This idea didn't help the fact that immigrants had been looked at for years as those most likely to disrupt order and to cause chaos, even if the claims were fundamentally untrue. It was the case then, as it is now, to throw the most vulnerable populations under the bus to find easy scapegoats for what's wrong with society. In this case wealthy business owners were accusing the immigrants for starting all the raucous with the strikes and the labor unions, it never occurred to them that a simple fix was just to pay them a living wage (immigrants in particular were more likely to strike because they often were easily manipulated into low wages by their employers.) Though totally racist and bigoted, these steel owners, using immigrants as the catalyst for everything wrong, were very shrewd. They knew that many Americans were deeply distrustful of immigrants and were more likely to look down upon everything that immigrant culture brought to the table, such as drinking, and even different foods. Indeed, many Americans were prone to believe that immigrants were the cause for all vice and many openly called for the deportation of those immigrants. By blaming the immigrants in this way, the steel owners were able to successfully pitch the idea that only the radical immigrants were the ones "disturbing the peace" and needed to be put in their rightful place. They somehow forgot that many of the striking workers were not immigrants, but "pure-blooded" Americans who took to the streets because of their poverty. That's not how the public perceived it, however, and were quick to ridicule the strikers in all the worst ways.

Steel companies had little remorse for exploiting their now-currently striking workers, as they brought in tens of thousands of strike breakers, somehow finding a new class of people to exploit while at the same time fattening their own wallets. The strike breakers that came in to fill the role of the striking steel workers were overwhelmingly African Americans or Mexican Americans, the same groups who at the time were having a mighty difficult time finding employment, mainly due to discrimination and racism, that they felt determined to get a job which they openly knew they were being exploited with. All the strike-breakers made matters worse though, strikers would wait and attack the strike-breakers, viewing them as pushovers who were taking advantage of their current plight. It wasn't uncommon for huge clashes to ensue. It got so bad that the local authorities got involved after they had long ago proven to openly back the wealthy business owners. Police would raid the strikers and send many of them off to prison, where they were held, oftentimes without any reasonable reasoning.[365]

Crazily enough, even congress got involved, though not for good reasons, as usual. The senate decided that they had better investigate this problem, shortly after they came up with the brilliant idea that these strikers were actually plotting the overthrow of the government. How did they reach these conclusions? I really can't say. Apparently, like the fear-mongering that we had seen in the last few strikes, the wealthy steel owners were so good at manipulating the media and other prominent, powerful individuals that many people saw anybody that was striking as a potential government overthrower. Ain't that something? So, remember, if you are ever displeased with your job for whatever reason, whether that be insufficient wages or deplorable working conditions, other Americans, at least at the time, believed that you were working maliciously against the government, plotting its downfall. How ridiculous! Even US senator Kenneth McKellar proposed to set up a penal colony in the Philippines to deport all of those convicted of this horrible crime, that is to join

---

365 Rayback, 287; Brody, 244–253; Dubofsky and Dulles, 220

a union and strike for better conditions.[366] Think of that, a penal colony! You know who gets stuck at penal colonies? The worst of the worst of criminals. Criminals that are branded as being so horrible and odious that they can't even be housed in a prison in the US, instead they would have to survive all by themselves, excluded from all of civilization. Now that's a pretty high price to pay for wanting a better salary.

By early 1920 most of the strikers had given up and had returned to work, dejected and beaten. Most had been turned away because the strike-breakers had stolen their positions, and thus thousands were left out of work. The bottom line, we have talked about these strikes to death. The reasoning for going through all of these strikes was to show that the public discontent was there and had remained there for many different professions and regions of the countries. All across the country, workers were standing up for their rights and for better wages. What's wrong with that? I'd be concerned if they didn't, considering how little they were being paid. But what was the widespread public reaction? That these workers were radicals, that they were being unreasonable, and that they were trying "communism" or worse. By this time there was a huge conspiracy that common laborers, labor unions, and reformers were trying to overthrow the government and instead place a communist agenda on all of the nation. It didn't matter much that none of the three really wanted a communist government and that there was virtually zero evidence to support these charges, most Americans were terrified by the accusations, accusations that were created by the business owners, wealthy elitists, and other sources of wealth and influence. These labor unions, common laborers, and reformers were the same people

---

366 "Bill Provides Penal Colony in Philippines for Anarchists". *The New York Times*. October 25, 1919.

and groups that helped to end twelve and fourteen hour workdays, ended child labor, and advocated for workers' compensation. All of these things are some of the most important rights that we have as common American workers, but then they were considered radicals, and targeted as such.

Here's where talks of deportations pick up again. Mitchell Palmer, the attorney general, was hellbent on ending the "radicals" reign and wanted results to back him up. His answer? Figure out who they can deport. At least then they can say they had "solved" the issue. As a result they targeted who they could, that being "aliens" or immigrants who were deemed too dangerous for the public safety. In a desperate move, Palmer even turned to the notorious J Edgar Hoover, then just a young lad, to help document information against some radical immigrants, priming them for deportations. It wasn't all Palmer's fault, the senate kept its pressure up by demanding that Palmer do something, even questioning him as to why he didn't deport anybody yet.[367] Isn't that nice.

In what would get much much worse, at the end of 1919 and beginning of 1920, the government began a roundup of suspected radicals, all of them for no other crime than being members of organizations that the government didn't like, such as the young socialists club. The authorities, without a legal warrant, set up wiretaps within some supposed radicals' work or homes. Sometimes they put wiretaps in some areas that nobody would have suspected, therefore gaining evidence against leftists.

When it was all said and done, some 550 people were arrested and deported for their alleged involvement in some shady movements,

---

367 Coben, Stanley, *A. Mitchell Palmer: Politician* (NY: Columbia University Press, 1963)

movements like supporting basic human rights.[368] The actual number of those that were deported should have been much greater had it not been for Labor secretary Louis Post, who actually believed that in order for somebody to be arrested, let alone deported, there needed to be sufficient evidence that they had actively engaged in an attempt to overthrow the government or prove some sort of harm to the public, something that the vast majority of those arrested did not have. But the deportations just kept coming, even respected legal scholars cried foul at what they were witnessing. This was a clear violation of the Constitution and the rule of law, but that didn't matter to Palmer and most of the rest of Congress, as they were being fed by the wealthy industrialists, and again they only listened to the wealthy powerful few.

In this environment, where the government was demanding to see a chorus of deportations, they were naturally upset that only a little more than 550 aliens had been deported. They expected way more, there were certainly more than 550 radical leftists out there, they couldn't have gotten all of them already. Suspecting that Post was behind the massive slowdown in deportations, the congress threatened to impeach and censure Post.[369] Think about that for a second. The congress, the so-called beacon of liberty, threatened to impeach a cabinet secretary because he wouldn't allow for more people to be deported, without evidence, and reason. HMMMM.

Some of the captured leftists were deported, while others were sent to concentration camps while the charges were pending. Yes, you read that correctly, concentration camps. This was long before the Japanese internment camps that we've heard so much about, and no, the leftists were never compensated for the incredible wrongness

---

368 Dominick Candeloro, "Louis F. Post and the Red Scare of 1920". *Prologue: The Journal of the National Archives*
369 ibid

of this act by the government. They lost everything, families, all money, possessions, ect.

Not all of the leftists who were attacked were even foreigners, or the poor and helpless. Some of them were high ranking officials who had even been elected by the people. In 1920, in the grand state of New York, the citizens had elected five socialist members to their state assembly. This is no different than the people of Maine choosing to elect a Libertarian or Green party candidate. New York's assembly leader, a republican named Thaddeus Sweet wasn't too kind to his colleagues who were his equals in every regard. The party was "a membership organization" he hollered, "admitting within its ranks aliens, enemy aliens, and minors."[370] He somehow suggested that these assemblymen and their "red" party's platform was against all the values of Americans and New York, forgetting the fact that it was New York voters who elected them in the first place by exercising their own right to vote, and the people happened to vote for the socialist candidates. This drove the establishment nuts. They were terrified at what the socialists, with all of their support from the people, could do. Think about it. What would these businesses do if all of the sudden they had to be held accountable for their actions? If they had to stop paying their workers starvation wages while they themselves sat on thrones of gold and diamonds? If they had to be regulated to stop the lies and corruption constantly spewing from those at the top? This clearly was too much for most in the establishment, who were constantly being fed by the wealthy and those on top, and they felt threatened by this new party's power and strength.

---

370 Waldman, Louis, *Albany, The Crisis in Government: The History of the Suspension, Trial and Expulsion from the New York State Legislature in 1920 of the Five Socialist Assemblymen by their Political Opponents* (NY: Boni and Liveright, 1920)

As a result, politicians, mostly republicans, attacked these socialist assemblymen with all of their strength, mostly by spreading lies and propaganda. This propaganda of course made the socialists seem like the enemies of the people, instead of having the people look at the truth of the situation and the rampant increase of wealth inequality that was now getting even more out of hand. They fundamentally scripted the propaganda to make the socialists look as if they were Soviets in nature and supported the overthrow of democratic, capitalist governments for that of socialism, though there is zero evidence of any of this. Instead, the assembly committee, tasked with discussing if the assembly could expel the socialist members, voted 7-6 that the body had "the right of the Assembly to exclude members is fundamental, inherent, and exclusive."[371] The assembly then had a full vote on the measure to remove the socialists from the body by an overwhelming vote of 140-6. If you hadn't guessed, all five socialists voted against the measure with help from one lone democrat, with all other democrats siding with the republicans out of fear that they would look soft on communism.

Immediately after the vote speaker Sweet was congratulated with letters, postcards, calls, ect. Most of these came from the individuals that they were able to brainwash through an intense propaganda campaign. He racked up lots of financial support from those in very powerful positions, as well as receiving political endorsements from the establishment. Two of the expelled assemblymen issued a statement, essentially decrying the effort as unlawful and wrong on it's face, "the constitution has been lynched."

In a sensational twist, in September of 1920, all five socialists were

---

371 Confessore, Nicholas. 2009. "When the Assembly Expelled Socialists for Disloyalty." City Room. October 21, 2009. https://archive.nytimes.com/cityroom.blogs.nytimes.com/2009/10/21/when-the-assembly-expelled-socialists-for-disloyalty/.

re-elected to their former positions, reinforcing that this is, indeed, what the people of New York wanted and voted for. Yet again, the socialists were attacked within the assembly. Spearheaded by the republicans and leader Sweet, three of the five socialists were expelled again, this time the vote was closer however, 90-45. Why were these three socialists expelled? Your guess is as good as mine. The three who were expelled were August Claessens and Louis Waldman of Manhattan, and Charles Solomon of Brooklyn. Apparently there was something about them, maybe a certain history that led to the immediate expulsion of these three. The other two socialists, Samuel Orr and Samuel A. DeWitt of the Bronx successfully heeded off votes to expel them. Nonetheless, they decided to resign from their seats as an effective protest and sign of solidarity with their expelled socialist friends. In researching these pieces I am incredibly outraged that members of a government can simply expel any member for really any reason, even though the people had voted for that candidate. In this case, the people of New York had voted for these socialists in back to back elections. They wanted these candidates, but just because they were different and had different political beliefs than the political establishment they were kicked out. To me this is fundamentally wrong. The US constitution and most state constitutions allow for members to be kicked out of any body for disorderly behaviors. So apparently, at least in New York in the 1920s, this meant that anybody who had dissenting political opinions could be canned, despite overwhelming public support? That's crazy. And totally unfair for democracy and justice.

Incredibly, never giving in to increasing pressure, Orr and Solonon decided to win their seats back again less than a month later. They both won, and a new socialist member was added to the assembly as well, Henry Jager of Brooklyn. By now, there was a new governor, who had the keen awareness that attacking these socialists were doing more harm than good for the republican party, and so the party had stopped relentlessly attacking the socialists, allowing them to remain for the remainder of the session. It also helped that Sweet was no longer the assembly leader.

Interestingly enough, the first, so-called, red-flag laws had nothing to do with weapons or fire-arms of any sort. The red-flag laws of the early 1920s were laws passed by only a few states initially, Kansas, Rhode Island, and Massachessetts, and then exploded beyond all means to 24 states in a matter of a year. What exactly were the red-flag laws? It really depended on the state and the scenario. All had to deal with socialism and all were about the fear of rising threats to the pre-established establishment. Some states had laws on the books that prevented individuals of said state from making certain phrases or statements that might indicate a belief in an extremist movement, perceptively against the government of the United States, with the socialists in mind, even conceding the fact that the socialists weren't ever advocating for an overthrow of the United States government. Essentially, if you talked like a socialist you were a socialist. Other states, in a show of desperation, banned certain colors like black and red, the colors associated with socialism.[372] Some may have conceded that outlawing colors was a bit too far, but to the politicians, whose career and power were potentially at risk if socialism prevailed over their own policy positions, saw it as just the beginning of what must necessarily happen if the radicals don't die down.

So when did this craziness officially start to die down? Like all

---

[372] Franklin, F.G. "Anti-Syndicalist Legislation," *American Political Science Review*, v. 14 (1920), 291–8

prejudiced thinking, the end would eventually come by essentially falling on its own sword, or death to self. After Palmer and Hoover unleashed venom and went after suspected radicals, by interrogating them and rummaging through their records and possessions like a band of wolverines, they came to the conclusion that these radicals had to be up to something more cynical. This something was the complete overthrow of the United States government as the newspapers and politicians had been clamoring about all along. The suspected date was for sometime in May in the year 1920. Why so specific? Palmer had thought that they had gathered enough intelligence to successfully indicate that the radicals were planning an attack and when it would occur. But this evidence was gathered much in the same way that intelligence officials had claimed that Iraq had weapons of mass destruction, in a word, hastily, and with political considerations to go along with it. It almost seemed that had, in fact, the "radicals" went along with the plan that the government conjured up, the public officials would be happy and vindicated. They would be heralded on shoulders and shown as heroes throughout the land.

But it didn't quite turn out this way. Palmer and Hoover went all in on the crusade, Hoover by warning the American people to be aware of potential catastrophes like political assassinations, bombings, and other attacks, Palmer by insisting he had a list of individuals who were potentially suspects of the plot. I included the part about how Palmer created a so-called list of socialists because we would see another demagogue go even more insane with his list of individuals connected with the socialists almost four decades later, Eugene McCarrthy, in the second red-scare of the century. I don't know what it is about lists, but they never turn out to be anything good for the American people.

What Palmer was trying to do was, by creating a list with suspected domestic terrorists, connect Europeans involved with the radicals, suspecting that the radicals were being fed information and ideas by Eastern European powers who wanted the United States to take a leftist turn. Local police forces around the country began preparing for the worst, asking its officers to stay on alert for up to thirty hours at a time. Yet, with all of the alarm and warnings, the month came and went. Nothing happened. Absolutely no activity on the part of the imaginary radicals.

In an embarrassing twist of fate, the government was now in the uncomfortable position of having to tell the American people that the lie they had created was indeed a lie, and issue an apology to the American people that their machinations did not work. Immediately as the month came and passed, Americans, regardless of what their political affiliation was, made a mockery out of Palmer and the government at large. Everybody is laughing at Mitchell Palmer's May Day "revolution" cried the *Boston American,* "The joke is certainly on A. Mitchell Palmer, but the matter is not wholly a joke. The spectacle of a Cabinet officer going around surrounded with armed guards because he is afraid of his own hand-made bogey is a sorry one, even though it appeals to the humor of Americans. Of course, the terrible "revolution" did not come off. Nobody with a grain of sense supposed that it would. Yet, in spite of universal laughter, the people are seriously disgusted with these official Red scares. They cost the taxpayers thousands of dollars spent in assembling soldiers and policemen and in paying wages and expenses to Mr. Palmer's agents."[373] What a pity.

The context of public opinion, at the time, was one of a people

---

[373] Ackerman, Kenneth D., *Young J. Edgar: Hoover, the Red Scare, and the Assault on Civil Liberties* (NY: Carroll & Graf, 2007)

thoroughly disappointed and tired of the political drama unfolding. More and more Americans came to the opinion that individuals can choose to support any political group or party of their choosing, as long as that political party or organization does not threaten the United States government or spread a hateful message. The socialists certainly were not trying to undercut the government, instead it focused on what many today would call common sense reforms. Many of the positions advocated for by the socialist party were being seen on a nationwide scale already, like the end of a fourteen hour workday, the end of child labor, and for the protection of workers. Clearly, these individuals were not trying to overthrow the US government, but it did expect that government to stand with the American people and enact common sense reforms. Now the American people were beginning to see that.

Of course, with many things that are wrong in history, particularly American history, (people think they are right at the time) it took until after the atrocity was committed before they began to wake up and realize that what they did was wrong. It took after the fact for Americans to pressure the government to end all future raiding, which it did. It took after the fact for arrested so-called radicals to be released. And it took after the fact that the government called Palmer's raids illegal, the deportations illegal, and the hastily constructed "justice" illegal. It shouldn't have taken that long, that's the problem. Palmer was disgraced after all the mayhem, his dreams of winning the democratic nomination for president all but dashed. Hoover, on the other hand, was just beginning his reign of domestic terror, he would build a long and lasting career as the head of the FBI. He loved to do illegal activity at the FBI, such as wire-tapping some of the most influential and best Americans like Martin Luther King Jr. He even has a building named after him in Washington

DC, the J Edgar Hoover FBI headquarters. I'm not sure why he's still celebrated today when looking purely at the history of some of his bright ideas.

It's also interesting when we look at the history of Labor day. Labor day is a great time of year to celebrate the history of labor and to, graciously, have a day off and spend time with family and friends on a beautiful May day. However, labor day has a somewhat controversial story, America had tried to resist it as much as possible, "The ruling class did not want to have a very active labor force connected internationally," said Peter Linebaugh, author of *The Incomplete, True, Authentic, and Wonderful History of May Day*. "The principle of national patriotism was used against the principle of working-class unity or trade union unity."[374] Many politicians and other business owners in powerful positions, see Labor day as a way to perpetuate the beliefs of Karl Marx and that of communism. Yet, Americans today would be appalled to see the holiday destroyed. A holiday that was bent on remembering the workers of the past who paved the way for us to work with better protections, more rights, and better pay.

The history of labor, more adequately the struggle of labor rights, led to the rise of whole-hearted opposition from the wealthy industrialists. They caused a stink and began fear-mongering the American people into believing lies and other grossly untrue beliefs regarding labor. The politicians, and other men in high position, had always listened to these wealthy elitists. They had money. And they gave that money to the politicians, if not directly, then through campaign financing. Of course, these politicians will listen to them. Which explains why progress has been, and continues to be, so slow in

---

374 Bowman, Emma. 2022. "What Is May Day? For the Most Part, the Opposite of Capitalism." *NPR*, April 30, 2022, sec. History. https://www.npr.org/2022/04/30/1095729592/what-is-may-day-history.

America. We are, more often than not, the last industrialized nation to move forward with progressive reforms. This is true with labor, which eventually led to the first ever mass deportation movement.

In a full swing, now we are back to talking about deportations, though deportations, for the most part, in the 20th century, besides the red scares, were mostly based on ethnicity. Most people don't realize that during the Great Depression, even with a democrat in the White House, FDR, almost 2 million Mexicans were deported back to Mexico. The belief being that the US economy was sliding, people were hurting, they didn't need more "outsiders" coming in and taking American jobs. What people don't often realize is that most of the Mexicans that were deported were actually American citizens. Some estimates show that nearly 60% of the Mexicans deported were American citizens.[375] Why were they targeted? Because they were an easy target. They looked different from traditional Americans. Using this logic though could mean that any US citizen could be deported because they come from a certain ethnic group. Most of the Mexican-Americans that were deported were children, who were believed to have crossed the border illegally, yet were US citizens, having been born in the United States. And again, people don't realize but many of the deportees were rounded up by governmental force. Could you imagine being rounded up in the middle of the night and thrown out of your own house into some distant land?

Things didn't get much better for the Hispanic community throughout the years. In fact, in 1952 Congress passed a law called the Immigration and Nationality Act of 1952, which essentially outlined how the US preferred certain immigrants that were highly skilled and talented while shunning those who were poor and

---

375 Gratton, Brian; Merchant, Emily (December 2013). "Immigration, Repatriation, and Deportation: The Mexican-Origin Population in the United States, 1920-1950" (PDF). Vol. 47, no. 4. The International migration review. pp. 944–975

meager. Obviously lawmakers didn't seem to care a whole lot about the Statue of Liberty which is ascribed these words: Give me your tired, your poor, Your huddled masses yearning to breathe free, The wretched refuse of your teeming shore. Clearly, this is just a joke, or America is extremely hypocritical. We were supposed to be the land in which everybody was welcome, even the poor, the sick, the lame, the tired, ect. But when push comes to shove, where is the compassion? Where is the humility? Where is the love? Nowhere to be seen, it seems. The law, in 1952, even arrested or heavily fined those Americans who were trying to shelter illegal immigrants. Could you imagine being sent off to jail just for helping another human being, providing them food, water, shelter, or clothing? How unjust and inhumane.

You would think that as time goes by things would get better, right? Wrong. Even as recent as president Barack Obama, who protected children of illegal immigrants from deportation through what is now known as the dreamers, deported almost three million illegal immigrants.[376] Where exactly do they go? Nobody seems to know for sure. Oftentimes they get sent to some of the most dangerous, and squalid places imaginable, where there is widespread crime and human trafficking, because they have nowhere else to send them. It's also important to note that many republicans want to gut the protection for the dreamers, even though for many of the children this is the only land they have ever known and they call this place home. Now the republican party cares more about separating children from their families than they do about compassionately dealing with the immigration crisis.

Trump, who somehow gets much support from Christians, even though he pleasured in grabbing women by the pussy and paid off

---

376 "Obama Has Deported More People Than Any Other President". *ABC News*

porn stars right before the election, created the zero-tolerance policy. That policy was exactly as it sounded, zero-tolerance for compassion and human understanding. Under Trump, more than 5,000 children were separated from their families. Can you imagine the terror that these children went through, the trauma, and suffering? That is unthinkable and shame on Trump and his republican allies for making any child co through that traumatic experience. Thankfully, the Biden administration has some dignity and human respect to end the disastrous policy and focus on reuniting children with their families, however, there are still some 1,000 children who are still not reunited with their parents. This is probably because nobody knows where their parents are. The separation policies quite literally sent deportees wherever it was convenient for the government, making it almost impossible to know where these childrens' parents are today. And yet, millions upon millions of Americans support Trump and this policy and continue to vote for him, despite the fact that he single handedly separated children from their families. Isn't that a Christian act? Shame.

One thing that's quite sad, though not surprising, is that the enforcement of immigration laws are different, not depending merely on political ideologies, but on economic progress as well. For instance, immigration police seem to be very lax in areas where illegal immigrants are needed for cheap labor, like in agriculture, where big farms need many laborers to produce their huge profits. This is especially prevalent in the strawberry business. Of course, without these illegal immigrants the economy would be vastly different, declining in most agricultural towns. We can't have that now, right? Well, that's why nobody seems to care as much about cracking down on the illegals when they might lose money right. But they do care when they believe they have to take care of them.

That's ludicrous. Illegal immigrants are afraid to come out and ask for any assistance from the government. This is easy to understand. If they do step up to receive help from the government they would need to come out with their illegal status and risk deportation. Because of this, illegal immigrants often go without crucial visits to doctors, which, of course, means that they have lower life expectancies because they don't receive the care they need out of fear. And illegal immigrants don't have social security numbers, so they don't get the good paying jobs that Americans are scared of losing, and don't receive any entitlement program benefits either. But, a whole political party decided that the winning strategy is to go after the most vulnerable.

Mexican-Americans have always been ostracized from the general public, maybe because most uneducated Americans deem all Mexican-Americans as illegals, and if they support Trump, they believe they are rapists, drug dealers, and thugs. But somehow, Trump just picked up on an already vulnerable group. I've already detailed how Mexicans have always been treated differently than traditional white, Protestant, Americans, but this is even shown in our more recent history. Dating back to world war two, which wasn't that long ago, some 500,000 Hispanic Americans served in the arm forces. That's a pretty sizable number, and they should be celebrated and praised for their service right? No. When most of these Mexican soldiers arrived back home they were denied basic medical care that was due to them. Even some Mexican-Americans who were killed in combat were denied funeral services because they were Mexican-American, as is the case with Felix Longoria.

During this period there was a nasty rumor going around. Due to the rise of attacks on police officers there needed to be a scapegoat, and that scapegoat turned out to be, who else, the Hispanics. That's an easy people to blame, right? The fact is that white people were most likely the culprits of the police attacks. But nonetheless, with all of the rumors something was bound to happen, most white people were pissed at Mexicans, regardless of who they were or where they lived. It didn't help that the newspapers and other media programs were depicting Mexican-Americans as dirty filthy criminals, and the worst part, foreigners who couldn't be trusted. To most uneducated Americans, who didn't know what really was going on but received all of their knowledge based on popular sentiments of the day, Mexicans had to be punished. This resulted in the Zoot Suit Riots.

We have evidence, from our not so distant past, that when popular sentiment is spread against a certain group hate arises from it. Just like when Donald Trump began calling COVID-19 the "China-virus", which was his way of shifting the blame onto somebody else other than him, loyal Trumpies began a hate filled barrage against Asian people, didn't matter that most of them were not of Chinese descent. The bottom line is if you looked Chinese you were Chinese, at least to these sick people who think it's okay to hurt others because of what their "idol" says. Because of Trump, there were instances where Asian-Americans were attacked while waiting for the bus and left for dead, the elderly were attacked and, in the most severe cases, people were killed. And for what? For being of Asian descent during the midst of a public health emergency that the Trump administration botched. According to post-pandemic surveys, one out of every six Asian-Americans have experienced a hate crime personally. Perhaps more staggering is the amount of Americans who think that Asain-Americans were responsible for COVID-19, roughly one in five.[377] That's insane! Asian-Americans did more to

---

377 Lee, Jennifer. 2022. "Confronting the Invisibility of Anti-Asian Racism." Brookings. May 18, 2022. https://www.brookings.edu/articles/confronting-the-invisibility-of-anti-asian-racism/.

stop the spread of COVID than most white Americans did. They wore masks way more than white Americans did, were more likely to safely distance themselves, and were much more likely to receive the COVID vaccines compared to whites. Many republicans should be blamed for the COVID deaths, since they were way more unlikely to practice social distancing, get vaccines, with some believing it to be the mark of the devil, and for causing such a stink by wearing a COVID face mask. I got a newsflash, wearing a mask, though it may not be the most enjoyable thing to do, was a patriotic thing to do. You wear masks not to protect just yourself from the virus but to protect those who are most vulnerable. That should never have been a topic of debate. But many republicans fought back against wearing masks, saying that it was their right to either wear or not wear a mask. How selfish! Asian-Americans were way more likely to combat the spread of COVID than any other group, and yet they were unfairly targeted thanks to the scape-goat card.

Well, the same-ish type of thing happened in the 1940s with the Zoot Suit riots, just without all of that pandemic stuff. Many Hispanics were thrown out by this time, with many deportees being American citizens to help free up the economic landscape for traditional Americans. Some areas, as we mentioned, kept a Hispanic population purely so that they could work in some of the most dangerous and disgusting fields that normal everyday Americans wouldn't be caught dead doing. This obviously allowed employers to exploit their Hispanic workers, paying them starvation wages, while expecting them to work twelve hour days, this is especially true when their workers were illegals. This led to massive poverty among the Hispanic population. With Hispanic children being left out of the economic picture, this led to delinquency. All this painted a nasty picture for the Hispanic community.

Many Americans began to resent the Hispanics, public opinion was against them. Attacks against the Hispanic community became more commonplace, many attacks being without warrant and completely unfair. Before long, massive riots took place pinning Mexican-Americans against white Americans in a form of race protest that we don't often talk about today. The big, and worst, of the riots took place on June 9th, 1943, when some 5,000 American servicemen went berserk and started attacking Hispanics, nevermind that they were doing absolutely nothing wrong, the fact is that they looked like Hispanics and as far as they were concerned that was a crime.

When news of the rioting came to the White House, first lady Eleanor Roosevlet wrote in an op-ed "The question goes deeper than just suits. It is a racial protest. I have been worried for a long time about the Mexican racial situation. It is a problem with roots going a long way back, and we do not always face these problems as we should."[378] What a brave woman, standing up in the face of evil to declare that we don't address racism the way that we should as a country. Do you know what the response to her op-ed was by the public? Not so good. The very next day, another newspaper called out Roosevelt for her op-ed. They were extremely disappointed that the first lady would not stand up for the white Americans and somehow tied her to the communists, saying that she most likely had communist ties. For the record, I don't know what communism has to do with overt racism but it seems that for most conservatives the easy thing to do about anything they disagree with is to call it communistic and move on without having a rational conversation of the problems of the country. It seemed nobody wanted to have any conversation as to why Hispanics were targeted in this way, and

---

378 "Los Angeles Zoot Suit Riots". *Los Angeles Almanac*. Archived from the original on August 1, 2010.

more shockingly why so many Americans joined the band-wagon and quite literally beat up fellow Americans. This was only 80 years ago. Apparently to the white Americans at the time they still felt that this was theirs and only their land, they wouldn't be happy sharing this land with those who have a different religion, customs, or food.

It wasn't just in terms of violence that Mexicans were discriminated against, but in virtually all the ways that blacks were discriminated against too. In many counties, Mexican-Americans were not allowed to serve on juries, unfairly tipping the judicial system against the Hispanic population. Businesses didn't let Hispanics use their facilities or apply for employment. And in most Southern states, Hispanics were forced to live far away from whites, having separate neighborhoods, mostly because of real estate companies' discriminatory rules and guidelines.

In the 1970s most immigrants were coming into the US through the Southern border, even though there was fencing, theoretically up to keep them out, that didn't stop the influx of migrants that wanted a better life for themselves and their families. Anti-Hispanic hate had been brewing for centuries in the US and had still not completely subsided. Many Americans were still galled at the fact that anybody can just come in and live in the United States, what a travesty. Many red-necked country folk hated this fact and were determined to do something about it. If the government wasn't going to act tough and deny these people the chance to get in, they would do it themselves. And in fact, many took it upon themselves to be a kind of immigration posse gang. Though totally illegal in every sense of the definition, these gangs had a plan in mind to capture immigrants and teach them a lesson, hopefully then they can tell their friends that they are not welcome here, just like how blacks aren't welcome there either.

Manuel García Loya, Eleazar Ruelas Zavala, and Bernabe Herrera, all men between the ages of 18 and 25, were just three of many that made the daring attempt to travel hundreds of miles to the promised land.[379] Just as they crossed the Mexican-American border, where they ended up in southern Arizona, their path took them onto the pasture owned by the Hanigans, the kind of people that wanted to create an immigration posse group. This was highly unfortunate for these migrants. Earlier in the book we briefly mentioned the brave white families that took runaway slaves in their homes on the underground railroad, well this situation is the exact opposite. There is no compassion in this story, and Hanigans were not the kind of people who were there to show love to their fellow man. Instead, the Hanigans saw this as their opportunity to get even.

Thomas and Patrick Hanigan had spotted these unfortunate migrants, in their typical hillbilly pickup truck. They suddenly approached the now terrified migrants demanding an explanation as to why they were in the US and more importantly why they dared trespass on their land. Obviously not pleased with their answer, or maybe because they just didn't speak Spanish, the Hanigan brothers decided to take matters into their own hands. They bound up the migrants, tying their feet and hands together and then forced them into their hillbilly pickup truck. They did what a typical criminal would do, they drove them out into the middle of nowhere, where their screams could not be heard for miles and miles. Now that the Hanigans had them right where they wanted them, they proceeded to beat them almost to the point of unconsciousness. If that weren't terrifying enough, the Hanigans also amused themselves playing

---

[379] Cadava, Geraldo. n.d. "From Hanigan to SB 1070: How Arizona Got to Where It Is Today." History News Network. Accessed May 19, 2024. https://historynewsnetwork.org/article/130543.

around with the men's genitals, pulling out a knife and slowly moving to cut them off. Before they left the migrants to die in the middle of an abandoned field they also took all of their possessions.[380]

Amazingly, the migrants survived the ordeal and ran their way back to Mexico, the only place that would accept migrants in need of hospitalization. The doctors were flabbergasted as to what they saw, to some of them this was the most gruesome beating that they ever had to treat. They immediately called for the Mexican police who called the Mexican consulate in Douglas, Arizona, the place of the crime.[381]

When the Hanigans were accused of the crime and for torturing the migrants, the neighbors in Douglas, Arizona came to the Hanigans defense. This was an issue of protecting private property they argued, as if somehow asserting that if someone steps foot on your property you have every right to torture and even kill those on your property. Watch out next time you ever wander onto private property, according to the folks in Douglas, Arizona you could be tortured for doing so. What a lovely country ain't it?

Nonetheless, justice has to prevail right? Well, at least the Hanigans were arrested and tried in a court of law. The problem? There was an all white jury from a town with deep prejudice against the Hispanic community. Believe it or not, the all white jury acquitted the Hanigans of the crime, meaning that they got off scot-free, in yet another case of the justice system failing to mete out justice. They insisted that illegal immigrants had no rights and since they had no rights they had no rights to violate. Nevermind declaration of independence with the phrase that all men are created equal..

---

380 ibid
381 ibid

with inalienable rights. Apparently these rights didn't apply to those that were not Americans, or more appropriately white Americans.

When the jury reached its verdict, the Mexican consul in Douglas, Arizona, lamented that the ruling "opened the hunting season for every illegal alien who comes into the United States," as now more and more immigrant haters, like the Hanigans, would be encouraged to go after this vulnerable community.[382] In an ironic change of fate, after the Hanigan brothers were acquitted numerous times before a court of law, Thomas Hanigan, one of the bros, was caught transporting 574 pounds of marijuana. Hanigans' neighbors must've felt pretty stupid for defending the Hanigans and their attempts to stop southern border crossing. Part of this awkwardness felt on the part of Douglas' residents was in the fact that they had defended the Hanigans precisely because they believed that it was the illegals that were bringing in illegal drugs and thus had to be stopped, while at the same time the very people they were defending were caught up in the illegal drug trade business. How laughable!

History News Network describes how the border in Arizona soon became a hotbed of violence, even after Thomas Hanigan was caught with illegal drugs. "Threats of violence against Mexicans—if not actual violence—characterized the Arizona border region of the 1970s, as they do today. Men and women wielded guns and vowed to use them to defend themselves and their property. The KKK seized the moment to bring their campaigns of exclusion to the Arizona border. In the wake of the Hanigan incident, David Duke sent Klan members to patrol the border and hunt for undocumented Mexicans. Such actions during the late 1970s were precursors to the vigilante organizations operating in Arizona today."[383] Yes, even

---

382 ibid
383 Ibid

the infamous David Duke was involved. This is the same guy, by the way, that endorsed Donald Trump because of Trump's embrace of white nationalism (Trump never downplayed or rejected the endorsement of the former Klan leader. In fact, during the white supremacist rally in Charlottesville, Duke had nothing but good to say about the president, "we are going to take our country back. We are going to fulfill the promise of Donald Trump. That's what we believe in, that's why we voted for Donald Trump. Because he said he's going to take our country back.")[384] Apparently Duke didn't just have a thing for blacks, it extended to Hispanics as well.

At the time that this was all going down, Congress was in the efforts to push massive immigration reform, something that can't seem to be done in today's dysfunctional Congress. In 1972, Congress had attempted to pass reforms that would have sanctioned employers from knowingly hiring illegal immigrants. However, many progressive voices were appalled by such a law, seeing it as though fundamentally not wrong, it would still subconsciously discriminate against Hispanic Americans who are looking for employment. Interestingly enough, it took more than a decade later for this to actually become law, with the Immigration Reform and Control Act passed in 1986. Under this law, employers were sanctioned if they hired illegal immigrants, though this still didn't affect employers much, as it was barely ever enforced and when it was big-money lawyers helped get them out of it. The law also beefed up enforcement at the southern border, putting more border agents in the most frequented crossing spots. This was the last time that Congress passed any comprehensive immigration overhaul.[385]

There are a few funny things regarding this immigration reform.

---

384 Dickerson John, *The Hardest Job in the World: The American Presidency*, Random House, 2020
385 ibid

Though the law explicitly stated that any employer who knowingly hires an illegal immigrant would be fined, that didn't stop our 45th president from hiring illegals to help build his Trump hotels. The *Washington Post* described how Trump had not only hired illegal aliens to work in some of the most menial tasks, getting paid extremely meager wages while Trump was more than on his way to becoming a billionaire, but still was hiring illegal aliens when he was president, all while winning fame and watching his political star rise by calling out immigrants and their "invasion."[386] It looks like the president was able to have a win-win scenario, that is pushing to pay his illegal workers less and winning over the souls of staunch conservatives at the same time.

It's also noteworthy that even with the dramatic rise in border patrol agents that were sent to the southern border to "protect" private property and stop the "invasion" that didn't stop illegal immigration at all. In fact, even after the government started to spend billions upon billions of dollars protecting the southern border, illegal crossing just kept continuing to rise. Experts say this is most likely due to the employers that are consciously hiring illegal immigrants, those like Trump who are giving them reasons to come into the country and avoid capture. (To be fair, I am whole-heartedly for immigration. I make the point because it is the actions of people like Donald Trump that are causing illegal immigration to keep growing, not what conservatives keep asserting that we need to build bigger, more beautiful walls.)

Conservatives, who are now reading this, may wince a bit when they hear the next anti-immigrant proposal. It actually came from the very liberal, progressive, migrant-loving state of California.

---

386 Levin, Bess. 2019. "Report: Trump Happily Employing Undocumented Workers While ICE Rounds Them Up." Vanity Fair. Vanity Fair. August 9, 2019. https://www.vanityfair.com/news/2019/08/trump-organization-undocumented-workers.

To be fair, California wasn't always so liberal, they elected Tricky Dick Nixon to Congress many times for Pete's sake. Regardless of this, many people would be surprised to learn that California, who is now harboring illegal immigrants from some of the inhumane policies of more conservative states, passed proposition 187, and it wasn't even close.

Passed in 1994, which wasn't all that long ago folks, proposition 187 was an initiative that firmly discriminated against illegal immigrants. According to the Library of Congress, the proposition "restricted undocumented immigrants from the state's public services, including access to public education and healthcare. In addition, the proposition directed teachers and healthcare professionals to report any individuals suspected of being undocumented to the Immigration and Naturalization Services (INS) or the California Attorney General."[387] That's a lot to take in huh? To make matters worse, the guidelines on how to tell if someone was an undocumented immigrant was spotty at best, leading many people to falsely accuse and discriminate against Hispanic Americans.

As always, this kind of legislation was mainly the cause of an economic downturn, which led Californian's to find someone to blame, and they found illegal immigrants. "Proposition 187 was approved during a turbulent period of economic recession in California," states the Library of Congress, "urging many citizens to view undocumented immigrants as scapegoats. Upon the proposition's passage, Governor Pete Wilson advocated for the referendum's immediate implementation, ordering healthcare facilities and school districts

---

[387] Thurber, Dani. n.d. "Research Guides: A Latinx Resource Guide: Civil Rights Cases and Events in the United States: 1994: California's Proposition 187." Guides.loc.gov. https://guides.loc.gov/latinx-civil-rights/california-proposition-187#:~:text=In%201994%2C%20California%20voters%20flocked.

to deny services to undocumented individuals.[388] So not only were undocumented immigrants denied a proper health care system, unless in emergency situations, but they were denied education. What do you think happens to youth when denied a good and satisfactory education? They turn to violence, they turn to gangs, they turn to drugs. What was California thinking? And by denying human beings access to health care many people were left suffering with nowhere to go and nobody to help them. People unnecessarily died. A few years later, thank God, a judge overturned the proposition declaring it unconstitutional. In 2004, California lawmakers tried again with a similar proposition, this time it was wisely turned down by the voters.

As recently as 2010, Arizona lawmakers did the unthinkable. They passed a law much more inhumane and unjust. The law was called "Support our Law Enforcement and Safe Neighborhoods Act," a nice little name for a new law, a name that would signal nothing seriously wrong. But something was seriously wrong. The law REQUIRED police officers to determine someone's immigrant status whenever there is reasonable suspicion that they may be illegal. The law was also called the "show me your papers" law, based upon the fact that every Hispanic in Arizona had to walk around with their citizen paperwork just because they were of Hispanic descent. The law unfairly targeted those who looked Hispanic. And if you were caught by the police without citizenship papers that would be a misdemeanor. Cesar Escalante, a professor of agriculture and applied economics at the University of Georgia, acknowledged that "SB 1070" the name of the law "had significant mental health

---

388 Ibid

repercussions on Hispanic adolescents, including Hispanic adolescents who are legal residents."[389]

Escalante had conducted research that showed that after the law, Latino adolescents were 5% more likely to consider suicides than Latinos in any other state. They proved also less likely to perform physical activities and had a higher chance of extended sadness.[390] A young girl from Arizona, who is now a dreamer, and whose name I will not mention here, recalls the staggering levels of fear she experienced growing up in Arizona. "I remember just looking at my mother and sister any time they'd walk out the door and feeling this sense of anxiety and a drop in my stomach, really wondering if that would be the last time I'd see them," she said. "From this young age, and as a result of this law, I was faced with the very real threat of family separation — it honestly became my biggest fear."[391] Her worst fear became her reality really fast, as in the case with many others just like her, "I came home from school and found out my sister had been stopped by a police officer and she was going to be deported. I felt helpless, I was angry, I was disillusioned, I was wondering why nobody was fighting back." Now she fights back with other activists working through grassroots means to bring humanity and justice to the forefront of what America stands for. Today she is fighting for immigration reform that is compassionate and sustainable.

This young lady's experience is the experience that most all undocumented immigrants face every day. Can you imagine the fear of knowing that at any given point your family can be ripped from you? It's appalling especially when immigration laws are made and

---

389 Reznick, Alisa. n.d. "'Show Me Your Papers': A Decade after SB 1070." News.azpm.org. https://news.azpm.org/p/news-splash/2020/7/30/177558-show-me-your-papers-a-decade-after-sb-1070/.
390 Ibid
391 Ibid

carried out by people that have no idea of what these immigrants deal with on a day to day basis. Of course, it's easy to make draconian laws against a certain type of people who live in constant fear when you yourself never have to experience the fear. Of course it's easy to support deportations when nobody is aware of the families that are separated, the fear burning in the hearts of those being attacked. That's the problem with immigration policy today. So many Americans are so eager to support candidates who propose some of the most draconian immigration policies, like the zero-tolerance policy. Why do they support these laws? Because they have never had to experience them, that's why. If they did have to experience them I guarantee you they would have a different opinion on the matter.

Today, states like never before are taking matters into their own hands to help defeat immigrants. Texas and Florida proudly boast about shipping off migrants to some other cities and states that are a little more welcoming, typically democratic states. It's interesting that nobody seems to care about how much Florida is spending to fly migrants to California, what a huge waste in state revenue that they could be using in other areas like education and housing. It's very depressing when republicans use the immigration card to chastise democrats. The simple reason is that democrats, with few exceptions, want to welcome all sorts of people into the nations. That's what America has always been about, a melting pot where everybody has a chance to achieve the American dream. The republicans care about making big statements about curbing illegal immigrants, building walls, and deporting hundreds and thousands of migrants at a crack. In republican politics this seems to be the biggest talking point.

Die-hard conservative governor of Florida Ron Desantis likes to make remarks about how bad the immigration crisis is under president Joe Biden. After Desantis signed one of the most harsh anti-immigration laws in American history he didn't hide behind closed doors but seemed to embrace the fact that he was becoming a villain right in front of so many eyes. "The Biden Border Crisis has wreaked havoc across the United States and has put Americans in danger," he wailed. "In Florida, we will not stand idly by while the federal government abandons its lawful duties to protect our country. The legislation I signed today gives Florida the most ambitious anti-illegal immigration laws in the country, fighting back against reckless federal government policies and ensuring the Florida taxpayers are not footing the bill for illegal immigration."[392] No longer would Floridians have to be on the hook for paying for illegal immigrants' health care, instead they are perfectly content to let the migrants die without it.

Yes, republicans like to blame democrats for all of the undocumented immigrants in the country. Yet, when we look at the statistics of the Trump administration, an administration that rose to prominence with its determination to deport immigrants and "build a wall," a "big, beautiful wall," in Trump's words, the number of crossing did not go down but went up. Even after Trump was bragging about how much wall he was putting up, migrants still came in, swelling into the US. In president Obama's last full year in office, 2016, there were roughly 106,000 migrants who successfully crossed the border and got away from border patrol. That's a high number right? In 2020, under Trump's watch, and in the midst of a global pandemic, the number of migrants who crossed the

---

392 "Governor Ron DeSantis Signs Strongest Anti-Illegal Immigration Legislation in the Country to Combat Biden's Border Crisis." 2023. Flgov.com. May 10, 2023. https://www.flgov.com/2023/05/10/governor-ron-desantis-signs-strongest-anti-illegal-immigration-legislation-in-the-country-to-combat-bidens-border-crisis/.

border and got away sky-rocketed to 156,000.[393] Clearly, all of the wall building and other derisive measures have proven itself not to work. If the wall was succeeding why would migrants getting away from border patrol agents actually be rising? If Trump was the cure for immigration, then why were there more migrants crossing the border under his administration than Obama's? Clearly, Trump was not the answer either. Sorry republicans.

But the frustrating part is that even with these statistics that tell us that the border policies under Trump aren't working at stopping illegal immigration, we still have a considerable amount of conservatives that still believe he is the magical force that will end it. What evidence do you have? What statistics are you looking at? Obviously these people are getting all of their information from Fox news. It's always easy to blame the administration at the time for an uptick in illegal immigration, which is exactly what the republicans are doing now, but it's hard to blame your hero. This puts republicans in a hard place. Trump had his opportunity and nothing changed, you know besides the fact that we spent billions of dollars that could have gone to cancer research on a wall that doesn't do anything.

One particularly heavily used piece of rhetoric by the republicans is that immigrants are bringing in drugs, particularly fentanyl. The sad reality, whether we would like to believe it or not, is that the vast majority of drugs sent over the border into the US are smuggled there by US citizens, not illegal immigrants. Here again we see an uncomfortable fact and the need to find someone, other than ourselves, to blame. Why not blame the Mexicans? Why not just blame all immigrants? That would be easy enough wouldn't it?

As Kylie Murdock states, "In February 2023, a 37-year-old woman

---

3932022. Cato.org. 2022. https://www.cato.org/blog/trumps-border-policies-let-more-immigrants-sneak.

was caught smuggling $1 million worth of fentanyl and meth across the US-Mexico border into California in the fuel tank of her 2016 pickup truck. She wasn't an undocumented immigrant trying to sneak across the border. She was a US citizen entering through the Andrade Port of Entry. And this is the rule, not the exception."[394] It is safe to say, though terribly depressing, that more people are dying each year due to fentanyl related overdoses. That's why the issue is so urgent, and why we drastically need to do something to prevent these types of things from happening. I am convinced, however, that blaming a certain group of people doesn't help the situation in the least, it only scapegoats and allows the problem to keep perpetuating.

But instead of trying to find a healthy, wholesome, solution to the problem republicans are blaming the increase in fentanyl deaths on the democrats "open border" policies. I take issue with this mostly because there is zero evidence of any democratic proposal that would open the border. In fact, many proposals that the democrats offered and republicans shut down would have increased the technological capabilities of defending the border, and preventing smugglers from entering the states. Sometimes republicans forget that there are other, more effective, ways to prevent border crossings other than a medieval wall that doesn't work.

WOLA, Advocacy for Human Rights in Latin Americas, got it exactly right. "The vast majority of heroin, fentanyl, methamphetamine, and cocaine", they reported, "that crosses the U.S.-Mexico border does so at ports of entry."[395] There you have it folks, the vast

---

[394] "The Truth about Fentanyl Trafficking – Third Way." n.d. Www.thirdway.org. https://www.thirdway.org/memo/the-truth-about-fentanyl-trafficking.
[395] wola. 2016. "Eight Reasonable Border Security Proposals (That Are Not a Wall)." WOLA. 2016. https://www.wola.org/analysis/eight-border-security-proposals/.

majority of illegal drugs pass through at ports of entry, not through rugged, distant terrain where most illegal immigrants cross. And what most democrats are advocating are those sensors to crack down on illegal smuggling. "Federal law enforcement agencies need the best possible visibility of what is crossing the border. There have been promising trials showing that low-cost sensor and communications equipment —integrated fixed towers, remote video surveillance systems, tethered aerostats, dismounted radars, and others—can do this. Aging, low-resolution cameras on the line could also be upgraded."[396] This sounds like really complicated stuff, but really it's not. Essentially these technologies, without spying on US citizens, monitor and track those that enter the country illegally. Think about it, if an illegal immigrant crosses the wall, how is the government going to track them? With the sensors the migrants could be detected as well as help border patrol agents catch any smuggling happening outside of the ports of entry.

Perhaps the republicans like to label the democrats as having an open-border policy, no doubt that it's good politics for them, but also because the democrats have a platform that is fundamentally more compassionate towards migrants. Whereas republicans like to make big shows to their constituents about removing and deporting migrants, often brandishing them as enemies, the democrats have taken a humane approach. As soon as president Biden was elected, in a landslide election against Trump, he immediately declared that the federal government would not rest until each family that was separated under Trump was reunited. Or perhaps it's because democrats want to protect the millions of dreamers who were born, or spent most of their lives growing up in America, from deportation that the republicans label them as having an open border. It's sad

---

396 Ibid

that anyone, regardless of who it is, would use such a touchy subject for their own political advancement as the republicans have.

It's certainly easy for the republicans to make attacks on Biden and the democrats for the drugs crossing the border. They already set up the framework deriding the democrats for being soft on immigration, now, kick them hard with the lie that immigrants bring in illegal drugs, this way democrats look like they're being soft on drugs. The Biden administration has proposed many changes to our immigration system, such as beefing up rules and regulations to curb illegal crossings by providing more consequences for illegal crossings. The Biden administration has also been very tough in its capturing of illegal drugs. Murdock explains that when the Biden administration seizes fentanyl and other drugs that should be praised as stopping potential overdoses, not used as a political talking point.

Experts have continually gathered more and more data on this issue within the last few years. They have come to the conclusion that, as we mentioned, drugs are coming into America with the use of tractor-trailers, or passenger cars owned by US citizens who are aiding and abetting the cartels, while no fentanyl has been seized from migrants who cross not at a port of entry. This signifies a different issue at stake. It's not the migrants, it's the enforcement of our own citizens that's the problem. CBS news reported "People just don't believe that others would be so brazen as to bring drugs through a legal crossing point where they know there's a potential for them to be checked. They just think logically, it makes more sense to try to sneak [them] in," said David Bier, associate director of immigration studies at the Cato Institute. "It's actually a lot easier for Border Patrol to spot a human crossing a border than it is for an inspector to spot drugs within a tractor-trailer full of goods."[397] This is quoted from an expert, this is not just me talking here. So, for politicians who are upset, as they should be, with the drugs that are pouring into our border instead of blaming an innocent group of people who just want a better home for them and their families, why don't you attack the source at the root? Why don't you crack down more against smuggling in ports of entry?

Some politicians like to act tough against China, and so they demand China to stop sending in drugs like fentanyl and other damaging drugs. While it's true China does send over harmful drugs to the US, it is pale in comparison to the amount crossing the southern border. Why don't politicians acknowledge this fact and go after our own citizens who are caught up in these illegal acts? The answer is quite sad. It's not good politically to go after our own citizens, it's much more attractive to go after those who aren't entitled to our rights and customs, like the migrants. President Biden has committed more time trying to attack the illegal flow of drugs, capturing more than any other administration, than by building a wall, and because of this he is being attacked by the republicans.

Here are the stone hard facts about fentanyl, keep in mind republicans like to blame migrants for the crime and democrats for being sympathetic to them. 1,322 of the 1,533 charged fentanyl trafficking offenders were US citizens, that's a whooping 86%. Just 0.02% of illegal migrants have been caught with illegal drugs. "More than 96% of fentanyl seizures along the border since the start of fiscal year 2023 have been at legal US ports of entry." And while republicans like to blame Biden and the democrats for the

---

[397] Sganga, Nicole, and Camilo Montoya-Galvez. 2023. "Fentanyl Seizures Rise at U.S.-Mexico Border — Here's Why." CBS News. February 3, 2023. https://www.cbsnews.com/news/fentanyl-seizures-rise-u-s-mexico-border-heres-why/.

increase in fentanyl related deaths, these deaths have been going on for decades, in republican and democratic administration alike. "Fentanyl deaths have been increasing since 2014, with significant increases during the Trump Administration. From 2016 to 2020, fentanyl deaths in the US increased by 191%, compared to a 25% increase from 2020 to 2021."[398]

These are not statistics that I made up, these are the hard facts that tell quite a different story than what most republicans want to tell you. Murdoch points to the efforts that Biden has made to go after the actual smugglers. These attempts include: launching operation blue lotus, which is a "coordinated operation among Customs and Border Protection (CBP), Immigration and Customs Enforcement (ICE), Homeland Security Investigations, and federal, state, tribal, and local law enforcement to target the smuggling of fentanyl. In just its first week, Operation Blue Lotus seized over 900 pounds of fentanyl and made 18 arrests." Installing scanners that will help to determine if vehicles crossing the border have illegal drugs. Increasing the budget for border patrol agents so that they can focus on finding the smugglers. And last but not least, working with businesses to help find illegal drugs and report them to the government.[399] How can anybody say the democrats are snoozing and allowing people to die. All of this at the same time republicans want to drastically slash the budget of all things except tax-breaks for the rich and funding for the wall. Using these statistics how can you make an argument that building a wall will help to limit the amount of drugs consistently crossing the border. In fact, statistics show it does nothing to hinder drug trafficking. Let's spend our money in effective ways, not just politically advantageous ways.

---

398 "The Truth about Fentanyl Trafficking – Third Way." n.d. Www.thirdway.org. https://www.thirdway.org/memo/the-truth-about-fentanyl-trafficking.
399 ibid

DEPORTATIONS   355

Texas, that great Lone Star State, has been in the midst of a controversy for quite some time now. Just like their cousin Florida, Texas republicans have been trying to tell their constituents that they are tough on illegal immigrants (even copying Florida's idea of flying migrants to California.)

On top of this, Texas has taken an actively hostile approach in its dealings with migrants. Nothing says you are not welcomed here more than some sort of physical barrier. Not satisfied enough with Trump's progress on the wall, Texan authorities decided that more needed to be done, particularly when it came to protecting Texas from the water entrances like the big, beautiful, historic, Rio Grande. (Side-note, more than 90% of the illegal drugs carried in through US ports of entry make their way to Arizona and California, not Texas, making the combating illegal drug argument Texan autorites make mute.) Texas governor Greg Abbot, decided to kick things up a notch, show fellow Texans that he's serious about combating migrants, and stick it to the liberals and their "open border policies." This culminated into Abbot erecting not a wall but a system of buoys to prevent migrants from coming over.

Apart from it looking incredibly odd and out of place, the buoys have sparked a lot of criticism since its adoption. Obviously, nobody within Abbot's administration, including him, had the mental capacity to understand that the buoys formed a huge safety risk. Therefore when news came out describing the floating dead bodies of migrants pushed up against the buoys a shock rang out in the rest of the states.

"This horrifying news is so sadly predictable," cried Laiken Jordahl, Southwest conservation advocate with the Center for Biological Diversity, told the Border Report. "We've warned that people and wildlife would die from the day Gov. Abbott deployed these lethal traps in the river. "Each day the floating wall and concertina wire are allowed to stay up, more migrants will be injured or killed and more wildlife will suffer. Gov. Abbott is turning this beautiful river — the lifeblood of South Texas — into a death trap for people and wildlife. He must be stopped."[400] Yet, the Texas republicans and conservative voters did nothing to stop the madness, even when they were warned by experts and wildlife officials that this was irresponsible behavior. All the republicans wanted to do was to stop the migrants, to them it didn't matter if they would be killed, if the ecosystem would be forced to go through severe change, and if it was against the law. When warned about the cost of life that the buoys could inflict, governor Abbot did nothing but keep touting the barrier.

Have you ever seen pictures of these buoys? These are not small, easy to crawl over buoys. These buoys are massive. It wouldn't take much for migrants crossing the buoys to run out of strength and struggle to tread water, eventually drowning. Can you imagine it storming, and struggling already, just to be hit with a massive buoy preventing you from safety? Where is the compassion there? Where is the human understanding? Aren't migrants fellow human beings like you and me? Instead, Texas is hitting them with buoys. Again, what does the Statue of Liberty say? Give us your poor, your huddled masses. What is so American about putting up buoys to keep people out? That certainly is not an American ideal.

The Mexican authorities were the first to spot "the body of a lifeless person stuck in the southern part of the buoys that were placed in the Rio Grande."[401] A few hours later, Mexican officials spotted another lifeless body about three miles upriver. Where were the US authorities? The only ones that had anything to say were

---

400 "'Death Trap' Marine Barrier Draws Criticisms after Body Found in Texas Buoys." 2023. BorderReport. August 3, 2023. https://www.borderreport.com/immigration/death-trap-marine-barrier-draws-criticisms-after-body-found-in-texas-buoys/.
401 Ibid

the Mexican authorities who had found the bodies. From the very beginning Mexico was fundamentally opposed to these barriers for more reasons than one, it doesn't take a rocket scientist to figure out that this is a bad idea. "We reiterate the position of the Government of Mexico that the placement of wire buoys by Texas authorities is a violation of our sovereignty. We express our concern about the impact on the human rights and personal safety of migrants," Mexico's Foreign Ministry said in a statement.[402]

When challenged to defend the barriers, Abbot couldn't say anything. Instead, he let others speak for him, namely his spokesperson Andrew Mahaleris. Mahaleris didn't really answer the charges competently. Instead, he did what typical republicans do when they are attacked, they blame someone else. Which is exactly what Mahaleries did. He regretted the loss of life, but went on to explain that the incidents had to do with "the reckless open border policies of President Biden and (Mexican) President López Obrador."[403] That's a typical republican right there. And yet, the barriers remain. More people will be hurt or killed with every day that the barrier is up. There's got to be a better way of doing things than that.

In a very roundabout way, this chapter mentions the cold hard reality of the United States. That being that there has always been a scapegoat and always somebody to blame. I could go on and on to talk more at greater length about the different ways that America tried to suppress immigration, whether that be the Irish, Catholics, Jews, Italians, Eastern Europeans, Asains, ect. My point here is to point out that at every time in American history there has always been at least one group of people that were considered inferior or less than. Lies were made about different groups of people to

---

402 Ibid
403 ibid

keep them out. For the Irish it was that they would bring not just papist influence but all sorts of vices like alcohol and gambling, even though this was being practiced all over the US, especially in the wild West. For Jews, it was that they were corrupt and you couldn't trust them. Today, reckless, inhumane politicians are calling Hispanic immigrants drug dealers, rapists, and thugs. They are calling Muslims "extremists" who want to hurt the country. These fears have always been blown way overboard and we look at these opinions decades or even generations later and we are startled to learn that our ancestors could be so naive as to think the way that they did. Someday, our kids and grandkids are going to say "I can't believe that they built a wall to keep people out who just wanted a better life. Our great-grandkids are going to say "I can't believe that our ancestors were so racist as to deny migrants from Middle Eastern countries from enjoying our beautiful country. Let's not make that mistake.

Today, conservatives love to say that anybody who supports dreamers and comprehensive immigration reform are radicals. They often deride liberals as wanting "open borders" and drugs to flow in like never before. None of these things are true, yet they gain traction at the polls for perpetuating the lie. The Know-nothings considered it radical to allow the Catholics in. The anti-semites thought it radical to keep Jews excluded. When will we learn?

I will leave this chapter with a personal story of mine. I live in a rural town, where everybody knows everybody. I have met one young lady who fled from a gang-infested country in Central America. She, like most other illegal immigrants, have overstayed their visas. If they return home, they will never have the opportunity to come here again. So, immigrants have to make the tough decision as to what to do. She came to America because she witnessed a gang fight that led to an innocent bystander's death. Being moral and honest she reported the killing to the country's authorities. Because of the brave and heroic part on her behalf she was now public enemy number one for the gang.

Left with no other option she came to the US where her brother was staying, her brother serving for the US army. Now that her visa has run out she now has to wait some 16 years until she can fully become an American citizen. Think about that. 16 years. That's 16 years that she will be contributing to our economy. She lives in constant fear, day to day and hour by hour that she will suddenly be deported. This means she has to be very careful picking a job, mostly choosing jobs that pay very low wages because she doesn't have a social security number. This means that she has very limited options for housing, staying with people who sympathize with her cause This means that she is reluctant to receive medical care and other necessities in life. If she was deported and sent back to Belize her life would be at serious risk, yet she still lives in constant fear right here in the US because of republicans desire to "get tough on migrants."

Some people just can't see the irony in it. Some of the people that she has grown very close to, and those same people love her to death, somehow can't come to the realization that they can help her. The vast majority of people in her life that adore her as a person and root for her to succeed and receive citizenship are the same people who are ardent Trump supporters. They don't see the irony in the fact that they support a candidate, from a party, that has decided to wage war against undocumented immigrants. They support a president who was elected on the false promise of building a wall to keep them out. How can people who are so compassionate for this young lady, offer her words of encouragement, and then turn around and vote for something totally opposing everything that they have just said to this young lady? The hypocrisy.

The sad realization is that most people don't fully understand what they are doing. Most people don't fully understand that the candidate they support or the political party that they align with could be doing things that are inhumane and unjust. What does this mean? I hate to say it, but the vast majority of Americans are either ill-informed or totally uneducated when they make decisions on who to vote for. This is unfair in so many ways. This is unfair for the politicians running. This is unfair for the country. This is unfair for me, who actually does research before making any decisions on who to vote for. And lastly, this is unfair for you. So many people are carried away with nice sounding sound bites. So many people will only vote for candidates who are must watch tv, you never know what's going to happen. Lastly, it's easy to vote for a candidate when all you hear is the slogan, "Make America Great Again" or hear policies that will never happen but they sound good like Mexico is going to pay for the wall or we are cracking down on China. It's harder to see how these policies will directly affect ordinary people, even those we don't see everyday. All of these things we have to consider before we make a decision. How is getting tough on migrants going to affect people? What will throwing a barrier of buoys in the Rio Grande going to do to people? Will it help people or hurt people? Will it save people or will it kill them? The same can be said about climate change. Will the Willow project help the environment or hurt it? What's more important to me, money or the future of our environment?

12 WOMEN

It was a radical idea to allow women to have the right to vote. No way, men in the 19th century thought, would women ever be competent enough to understand the art of politics. It was way too sophisticated of a business for them. Instead, women should just keep to their domestic business, cleaning the house and watching the kids. This is what they're good at. It's all they know.

Of course, if someone were to believe these things today they would be brandished as a male chauvinist pig. They would be so short-sighted and self interested that they probably won't end up with a lady as a wife at all. It would be crazy to think of a United States where women didn't have the opportunity to vote for their future. And yet, in the 18th, 19th, and even early 20th centuries it was considered a radical idea for women to vote, or participate at all in the political realm. Again, this is just another example of how an idea that was considered radical at the time is scoffed at today.

Abigail Adams once quipped to husband John Adams:

"I long to hear that you have declared an independency -- and by the way in the new Code of Laws which I suppose it will be necessary for you to make I desire you would Remember the Ladies, and be more generous and favourable to them than your ancestors. Do not put such unlimited power into the hands of the Husbands. Remember all Men would be tyrants if they could. If perticuliar care and attention is not paid to the Laidies we are determined to foment a Rebelion, and will not hold ourselves bound by any Laws in which we have no voice, or Representation."[404]

---

404 Abigail Adams to John Adams, March 31, 1776, Braintree Massachusetts

In her own elegant way, Abigail Adams reminds her husband, John, that the men creating the laws in the new republic "would be tyrants if they could." Knowing that they were the ones making the laws, and thus the ability to trample on the rights of the ladies, Abigail cautioned her husband to remember the rights of the ladies, otherwise the ladies would have to stir up a little trouble of their own and raise a little hell against the unfair laws that the men had made.

It is ultimately a sad reality that neither John Adams, nor any other prominent man of the period, did much to ensure that the ladies were remembered and that their rights would be guaranteed to be upheld. As a matter of fact, nothing is mentioned in the Declaration of Independence or the Constitution regarding ladies, more importantly their rights to property and to vote. Instead, all of the men left it up to the states to do as they please in regards to the ladies.

New Jersey seemed to be way ahead of its time, at least for a short amount of time. The New Jersey constitution granted all adult men and women the right to vote, as long as they owned a specified amount of property. Even though it was much harder for women to accumulate property than it was for men to be able to do so, there were a considerable number of women who were eligible to vote and they did. Women with enough property enjoyed the right to vote until 1807 when men crafted laws to ban women from voting. In all actuality, women who occupied the right to vote often did so in hotly contested races. Thus, not surprisingly, both major political parties at the time easily scapegoated women, whom they believed were just pawns of their husbands and would vote whichever way their husbands would. This, they considered, was no different than if children could vote. Since children clearly don't know enough about politics they would just vote the wishes of their parents. It was the same reasoning for excluding women from a chance to vote.[405] Making matters worse, there was no chance in hell that any woman would be elected to public office during this time, making it less likely that the ladies would actually receive any representation in Congress or elsewhere.

Women couldn't even own property or control it in most states until the middle of the 19th century. Up to that time, women were literally at the mercy of their husbands and were wholly dependent on them. Because of these laws if a woman's husband died, the widow would most likely live a life of poverty and struggle to get by, as long as she was not born of wealthier families. Some states though, graciously, passed laws to protect widows and allow them to own the property of their deceased husbands. It is because of the conditions of the widows that more and more states began to pass more favorable property laws, however, to many it came too late to help.

In the political climate of the antebellum period of the US only white men could vote, in some states still poor white men were knocked out of the process of voting. Just like Abigail Adams predicted so long ago, women would start to raise a little hell. In the UK Mary Wollstonecraft wrote a book entitled *A Vindication of the Rights of Women* where she wrote that women were equal to men and that they should be treated with equal dignity, respect, and education.[406] If they received equal education as men then

---

405 "Women's Suffrage in New Jersey 1776-1807: A Political Weapon." n.d. Www.law.georgetown.edu. Accessed May 19, 2024. https://www.law.georgetown.edu/gender-journal/in-print/volume-xxi-issue-3-spring-2020/womens-suffrage-in-new-jersey-1776-1807-a-political-weapon/#:~:text=It%20argues%20that%20both%20parties.

406 Wollstonecraft, Mary. 2021. "A Vindication of the Rights of Women by Mary Wollstonecraft: Summary & Analysis - Video & Lesson Transcript | Study.com." Study.com. 2021. https://study.com/academy/lesson/a-vindication-of-the-rights-of-women-by-mary-wollstonecraft-summary-analysis.html#:~:text=Lesson%20Summary-.

they can be the type of citizen that Jefferson long wished, one that stays up to date on intellectual capabilities so that they can become valued members of society. Obviously, because most poor families couldn't send their children to school and most colleges were open only to men, women were routinely shut out of education, thereby denying them a chance to move up in society and challenge men for good paying jobs.

She wasn't the only woman who started to push back from an oppressive political atmosphere. Sarah Grimke published *The Equality of the Sexes and the Condition of Women.* She argued that God had made the sexes equal and that they deserved to be treated with equality. Of course, it was a nice sign that more women were able to publish their own works and throughout the 1830s and 40s more Americans began reading novels as a form of pastime. Even humble farmers would come in from the fields and take pleasure in their reading materials, which were increasingly being written by women. Women authors gained increasing attention from women readers who enjoyed reading about stories like them. Even though the writing profession wasn't a high paying one by any means, some of their works were widely published, as was *The Equality of the Sexes and the Condition of Women.* With more feminist writings infiltrating the growing reading public, public sentiment began to grow, ever more slowly to increase women's rights and suffrage, though initially this was only gaining steam mainly from women. The men who controlled the government didn't share womens' enthusiasm.

In fact, when the federal government authorized the trail of tears, where hundreds of thousands of first Americans were forcibly removed from their homes, women increasingly petitioned the government to end the horrific oppression. When their petitions were read in Congress it was regarded with contempt by the lawmakers.

Senator Thomas Hart Benton even laughed at the ladies who were going through the trouble of petitioning lawmakers urging them to stay out of politics if they knew what was good for them.[407]

Initially women became immobilized during the anti-slavery crusades of the 1830s and 40s, overcoming fierce pushback from some quarters of abolitionists. In fact, some abolitionists broke off from the American anti-slavery society of William Lloyd Garrison because he directly accepted the need to work for abolitionism and feminism at the same time. Thus, the abolition movement splintered into rivaling groups that potentially stunted its growth. Regardless, women played an increasingly active part in politics for the first time thanks to the abolition movement. Frederick Douglass once remarked that future studies of history will show the huge contribution of women in the abolition movement, and should thus be remembered for their exploits in authorship, publishing, and in the underground railroad.

Some of the most adamant critics of women empowerment came from southern white men and religious leaders who condemned not just abolition but the idea that women could participate in politics or a national movement. When the Grimke sisters went on a speaking tour, lashing out against the peculiar institution of slavery, it was widely made fun of and the ministers of the Congregational Church sent out a statement brandishing them for their actions. Nevertheless, Angelina became the first woman to speak before a state assembly, doing so in 1838 in Massachusetts, again speaking out against slavery.[408] After this event it wasn't so uncommon to see women speakers and lecturers go on tours. The North was more receptive, though not by much. Nearly all female speakers had their

---

407 Saunt, Claudio. 2020. *UNWORTHY REPUBLIC : The Dispossession of Native Americans and the Road to Indian Territory*. S.L.: W W Norton.
408 Flexner, Eleanor (1959). *Century of Struggle*. Cambridge, MA: Belknap Press of Harvard University Press

fair share of hecklers and troublemakers loudly disapproving of this new spectacle. When women held routine meetings discussing their efforts to increase their rights and suffrage, men infiltrated these meetings and broke them up. Susan B Anthony, a women's rights crusader who is heralded today, got it right when she said, "No advanced step taken by women has been so bitterly contested as that of speaking in public. For nothing which they have attempted, not even to secure the suffrage, have they been so abused, condemned and antagonized."[409]

Even though women made a name for themselves in public by doing what traditionally belonged to men and men only, women continued to persist. Women were a major part of the temperance movement, where concern for excessive drinking was growing largely because drunken husbands would come home and abuse the wife and children. Women's voices rang loud and eventually, though almost a century later, we got the 18th amendment, banning alcohol consumption, thanks to the influence and power of the ladies' temperance societies.

Even though women nudged their way into mainstream issues, to the dismay of white men, their voting rights were a different story. The United States followed the example of Great Britain with their system of coventure that they had established in the middle ages. This meant that women had virtually no legal existence of their own. When women married a man they became one according to the law and women held almost no legal existence of their own. This made it difficult for women suffrage groups to gain any sizable traction. A woman who filed for divorce in 1862 because her husband horsewhipped her was denied, the reasoning, "The law gives

---

409 Susan B. Anthony, "Fifty Years of Work for Woman," *Independent*, 52 (February 15, 1900), pp. 414–17. Quoted in Sherr, Lynn (1995), *Failure is Impossible: Susan B. Anthony in Her Own Words*, p.134. New York: Random House

the husband power to use such a degree of force necessary to make the wife behave and know her place."[410] Given this gross injustice women were hamstrung from enjoying basic mobility and freedoms, even to escape an abusive husband. This might explain why women spent more time battling male drunkenness than they did pursuing the right to vote, at least initially.

Over time states began to loosen laws designed to prevent women from receiving an equal share of rights and property, though most of the effort was made on behalf of rich dads who wanted their daughters to have the rights to the property that the parents owned to be given to their daughters and not their husbands. This opened the gates a little for some concerted action on the front of women's suffrage.

In 1848, Elizabeth Cady Stanton Lucretia Mott invited a group of abolitionists activists to Seneca Falls, New York. The group consisted mostly of women but did contain a few men in their ranks. They were assembled primarily not to discuss further efforts at abolitionism but to discuss womens' rights. Nearly 300 men and women attended this meeting where most agreed "American women were autonomous individuals who deserved their own political identities."[411] Indeed they made use of the Declaration of Independence as inspiration, though tweaking the famous opening passages just slightly, "We hold these truths to be self-evident," proclaimed the Declaration of Sentiments which were produced by the delegates attending, "that all men *and women* are created equal, that they are endowed by their creator with certain inalienable rights, that among these are life, liberty, and the pursuit of

---

410 Victoria E. Bynum (1992). *Unruly Women: The Politics of Social and Sexual Control in the Old South.* University of North Carolina Press,
411History.com Editors. 2024. "Women's Suffrage." HISTORY. A&E Television Networks. February 20, 2024. https://www.history.com/topics/womens-history/the-fight-for-womens-suffrage.

happiness."[412] (Actually, the Declaration of Sentiments followed the example of the Declaration of Independence almost to a tee, especially when they used the same format to list their grievances as Thomas Jefferson did against British tyranny.) This was a nice way of saying that women were legally entitled to the same rights that white men had enjoyed among them the right to vote. Somehow, strangely, when Elizabeth Cady Stanton proposed an amendment that granted women the right to vote even her husband thought that this was a foolish idea, as well as some pretty radical, feminist, women. (The measure passed after abolitionist Frederick Douglass signaled his support for women suffrage. This, of course, didn't really mean anything unless Congress would amend the Constitution or the states voluntarily would change their voting laws, though this gave women hope and was the first sign that a national movement was beginning to bring women their rights.)

Shortly after the Seneca Falls Convention many of the same speakers hosted a convention in Rochester, New York. This made history because this was the first time in which a womens' rights convention was actually chaired by a woman, something that was considered incredibly radical at the time.[413]

During the 1850s the womens' rights movement picked up steam, with women speakers addressing the country in greater volume than ever before and likeminded feminists joining the ranks together and collaborating, like Susan B Anthony and Elizabeth Cady Stanton who met in 1851 and proved to be quite the pair. Together over the decades these two would form a partnership that truly complimented each other in more ways than one. Anthony was the lead organizer, while Stanton was the philosophical one, the one that would write

---

412 Ibid
413 McMillen, Sally Gregory (2008). Seneca Falls and the Origins of the Women's Rights Movement. New York: Oxford University Press

speeches and articles for the cause. It wasn't uncommon for Anthony to read speeches written by Stanton at public events. Anthony and Stanton, while fighting for the suffrage all the same, gave preference to immediate rights for women. Even Anthony, who would long be remembered for her efforts at trying to secure women suffrage once remarked, "I wasn't ready to vote, didn't want to vote, but I did want equal pay for equal work," a view shared by most working and middle class women at the time.[414]

Though the womens' rights movement was making some serious headway, it began to lose steam due to the growing agitations swarming the country in the 1850s and 60s. With so many problems, most of which the slavery issue, plaguing the country it was hard for these feminists to gain enough traction during this time. Perhaps more than anything, most feminists were also strong anti-slavery advocates. During the ongoing struggle over slavery these ladies devoted most of their time in advocating for the emancipation of slaves and for a humane and justifiable reconstruction policy. For the time being, at least until the slavery strife was over, womens' rights would have to take the backseat.

Together, Stanton and Anthony teamed up to form the Womens' Loyal National League, the first womens' political organization. The group collected almost 400,000 signatures in a petition to advocate for the abolition of slavery, which was far and away the largest petition known at that time.[415] All throughout the civil war, the feminist organizations worked hard for political viability while also fighting for equal rights, blacks and whites, and men and women alike. However, after the civil war ended the Womens' rights conference was up and running again, which brought the movement back into

---

414 National Woman Suffrage Association, *Report of the International Council of Women, Volume 1*, 1888
415 Venet, Wendy Hamand (1991). Neither Ballots nor Bullets: Women Abolitionists and the Civil War. Charlottesville, VA: University Press of Virginia

the heat of things, especially when the Congress and nation ratified the 13th, 14th, and 15th amendments expanding rights for certain groups, just not women. With Congress and the nation in general expanding rights for newly freed blacks, the women, naturally, thought that they would be next. Unfortunately, they would have to wait a long time as the new voting rights for newly freed blacks, and long-free blacks, would have the right to vote, just not women.

With many abolitionists, like Douglass publicly supporting the womens' cause and advocating for universal suffrage, some of their republican allies were hesitant to increase the suffrage. They preferred to wait until it was proven that black men would be able to vote without intimidation and suppression. They figured it made more sense to attack one issue at a time, women suffrage would just have to wait until black men would be able to vote with ease, maybe after that women would have the right to vote just like them. (Some women actually publicly tried to discourage the 15th amendment from passing. The 15th amendment is what gave black citizens the right to vote. Women believed that this was an insult after all of their advocacy and conventions.)[416]

Womens' rights groups initially supported the republican party in overwhelming numbers because of that party's human rights efforts, yet, after the passage of the 15th amendment the tide began to change. Many women switched sides and supported the rivaling democratic party, who were adamantly opposed to the 15th amendment. Anthony and Stanton actually wrote a letter to the 1868 Democratic National Convention in which they lambasted the republican party. "While the dominant party has with one hand lifted up two million black men and crowned them with the honor

---

[416]History.com Editors. 2024. "Women's Suffrage." HISTORY. A&E Television Networks. February 20, 2024. https://www.history.com/topics/womens-history/the-fight-for-womens-suffrage.

and dignity of citizenship, with the other it has dethroned fifteen million white women—their own mothers and sisters, their own wives and daughters—and cast them under the heel of the lowest orders of manhood."[417] This may seem like desperation on the part of these organizations to abandon a party that was more in line with their way of thinking, however, it must be remembered that these women had been fighting so long for this cause that they felt their time could not wait any longer and thus were willing to throw their support to the political party that would support their wishes. (In the election of 1872, most abolitionists and womens' rights groups would support the rivalring group the Liberal Republicans because of the corruption of the Grant administration. These groups, however, forget that Grant himself fought strongly for black rights and discouraged the growth of the notorious KKK, which was steadily growing in the southland.)

Shockingly, in 1872, Susan B Anthony was arrested for violating the Enforcement Act of 1870, which was mostly to cut the influence of the KKK, all because she cast a vote for president. To be fair, it was a crime for a woman to vote at the time, this was election fraud. The judge instructed the jury to nail her guilty and he passed on her a $100 fine, quite a hefty sum at that time, especially for a woman to pay, as women were chronically paid less than men were even back then. Anthony responded, "I shall never pay a dollar of your unjust penalty," what pushback from this spunky lady, and, she never did pay that fine.[418] Anthony was never officially pardoned for her crime until 2020, long after she died.

Shortly thereafter, in 1878, a personal friend of Susan B Anthony

---

417 Stanton, Anthony, Gage, Harper (1881–1922), Vol. 2,
418 Ann D. Gordon. "The Trial of Susan B. Anthony: A Short Narrative". Federal Judicial Center. Retrieved August 21, 2014.

who happened to be a United States senator from California, Aaron Sargent, introduced the first amendment for womens' suffrage. The amendment would finally pass forty years later with the exact same wording, though this didn't mean that the fight was an easy one.[419]

In some states/ territories women did enjoy the right to vote. This consisted only of far-western states who desperately needed women to travel to those areas, there was an over-abundance of men and only very scarcely any women. With inclusive voting laws, these states hoped that this would woo women to make the trek westward in what would otherwise be a pretty rough and mediocre life as a western housewife. Among the earliest territories that allowed women to vote were Wyoming in 1869 and Utah in 1870. Utah holds the distinction of letting women vote first because they held earlier elections. One party that I find particularly intriguing was the Populist party of the 1880s and 90s. This party endorsed the idea of women suffrage, among other progressive reforms that would have made the United States a much better country. Nonetheless, the Populist party was never able to muster a significant amount of national support, though they did receive many votes from westerners who were disenchanted with the political system of Washington and the two main, leading, parties. It was largely due to the Populist party that Colorado allowed women the right to vote in 1893 and Idaho in 1896.[420] The suffrage movement got another boost when the Grange, a political party popular in Mid-western states that received huge support from farmers, endorsed universal suffrage. Even the American Federation of Labor (AFL) endorsed women's suffrage in 1890.

---

[419] Flexner, Eleanor (1959). Century of Struggle. Cambridge, MA: Belknap Press of Harvard University Press
[420] DuBois, Ellen Carol. (2020). Suffrage: Women's Long Battle for the Vote. New York City: Simon & Schuster.

You would think that with all of these groups endorsing and publicly supporting women's suffrage it was only a matter of time until women could vote and receive many other rights. This, unfortunately, is superficial thinking here in the United States. Of course, again, there will always be people morally opposed to change. This was true with emancipation, the civil rights movement, and it was true with giving women an equal say. In 1887, a proposed amendment to give women the right to vote was defeated in the senate, all those rich white men didn't seem to care very much to see their wives be able to vote. Curious huh? Even at the state level, eight states rejected statewide amendments that would give women the vote shortly after labor organizations and third parties ushered in their support.[421]

Some opposition was hard to fathom. In 1895, Massachusetts held a referendum approving of womens' suffrage in municipality races if it passed. In a surprising turn in an otherwise very liberal state, the measure failed miserably, only achieving a little over 30% of the vote when even women were allowed to vote in the referendum. This was a big set-back to the womens' cause.[422] Some other older religions, such as the Catholics were opposed to womens' suffrage believing that the man was the paternalistic leader of the family and thus voting belonged to him and him only, or else the family wouldn't be dominated by men anymore. Southerners were also opposed to womens' suffrage, though obviously this was not a universal opinion, because of their commitment to child labor and exploiting poor workers who had to work for miserably poor wages.

---

421 Dann, Norman Kingsford (2021). *Passionate Energies. The Gerrit and Ann Smith Family of Peterboro, New York[,] Through a Century of Reform*. Hamilton, New York: Log Cabin Books.

422 Massachusetts Women's Suffrage for Local Elections Advisory Question (1895)". *Ballotpedia*. Retrieved October 2, 2023

They believed that if women voted they would be overwhelmingly opposed to these issues because of their morality. It is an absurd reality that women were denied the right to vote because they were perceived as being moral and may vote in a moral-minded way. If that doesn't tell you something is wrong with the system I don't know what would. And, for those politicians who were worried about being thrown out of office because of their immorality, if women were allowed to vote, it made sense that they would vigorously oppose this measure tooth and nail. Newspapers too turned out against womens' rights. Some of them, like the *New York Times* argued that if women could vote then they would want to become soldiers, mechanics, and the likes, virtually they would want to do all the things that men, and only men, to them at least, could do that is of course, "if the men are not firm and wise enough and, it may as well be said, masculine enough to prevent them."[423] The question would be how much would insecure men fight against women?

Believe it or not, there were quite a few women who disagreed with the whole womens' rights thing. They were actually against their own interests, just like younger people today who care about the environment yet vote for republican candidates who say "drill baby drill." Most of these groups who devoted themselves to suppressing the womens' rights movement claimed that women suffragists were like socialists and that if women were allowed to vote then socialism would gain traction in the country. If women could vote they "would reduce the special protections and routes of influence available to women, destroy the family, and increase the number

---

[423] The Uprising of the Women," *New York Times* May 5, 1912, quoted in Sandra Adickes, "Sisters, not demons: The influence of British suffragists on the American Suffrage Movement," *Women's History Review* (2002)

of socialist-leaning voters."[424] What utter nonsense. Why is every bit of progress challenged by those who think that every change is a resort to socialism? It should also be noted that at this time there wasn't any major country on earth who even tried to dabble in socialism. If they didn't know what would happen, given no exact evidence to point to, why were they so opposed to it? Nevertheless, they equated womens' suffrage to socialism.

Most upper class women consisted of those most opposed. This was due to the fact that most upper class ladies had close connections to politicians, mainly through their rich husbands. In this way they already had political influence way above that of most poor white men and certainly middle class and poor women. Why would these women give up their power to give to others who have been historically marginalized? It is a dog-eat-dog world out there, especially in the United States where capitalism is king, that women would not band together and support each other to provide for their universal rights. Back then, as I believe it is now, women, and men, only cared about their own immediate benefits and advantages. It should go without saying that the population that was most adamantly opposed to women suffrage where those with conservative views, this aligned closer to the republicans and the democrats in the South.

By this time, dejected but still not utterly defeated, women, led by Stanton and Anthony, changed gears a little. In previous arguments women argued that they should have the right to vote because they are the same as men and deserve the same rights entitled to them. By the early 1900s these advocates instead decided that they needed to display their differences. Indeed, since women were different from men, had different skills, opinions, and temperaments, they

---

[424] Blee, Kathleen M. (1999). "Antifeminism". In Mankiller, Wilma P.; et al. (eds.). *The Reader's Companion to U.S. Women's History*. Houghton Mifflin Harcourt

too deserve to have a say in their own futures. They can use their domesticity to improve the moral conscience of the nation and thus vote for moral, reform-minded, politicians.[425] It was a genius strategy on their part since they were able to garner the support from many competing interests that were able to justify their sympathies with the womens' movement. Among the contrasts of interest were the supporters of the temperance movement, who believed that if women could vote they would support anti-alcoholic lawmakers (even though this also hurt them among German and Irish immigrants who would never support prohibitionist candidates) and middle class racist whites who believed that if women were able to vote they would uphold white supremacy, believing that minorities were destroying America's moral compass.

By the time any amendment giving women the right to vote would have to be passed by 3/4ths of the states, no small task with virtually the entire south strongly opposed to giving women the right to vote. (It didn't help that southerners didn't want to see black women going to polls anytime soon.) They would need some help from the southern states if the womens' suffrage movement was to succeed nevertheless.

It no doubt helped that other countries were beginning to expand their suffrage to all inhabitants regardless of gender. New Zealand was the first country to allow women to vote in 1893. Australia followed suit in 1903. In all, twenty countries preceded the United States in granting women the right to vote. Among them: Finland in 1906, Norway in 1907, Denmark and Iceland in 1915, Canada and the Netherlands in 1917, Austria, Canada,

---

425 History.com Editors. 2024. "Women's Suffrage." HISTORY. A&E Television Networks. February 20, 2024. https://www.history.com/topics/womens-history/the-fight-for-womens-suffrage.

Estonia, Georgia, Germany, Hungary, Ireland, Kyrgyzstan, Latvia, Lithuania, Poland, Russian Federation, United Kingdom in 1918, and Belarus, Belgium, Luxembourg, Netherlands, New Zealand, Sweden, Ukraine in 1919.[426] Again the United States was behind the ball despite generations of efforts on behalf of womens' rights groups. This may have been the reason why other US states like California and Washington expanded suffrage in 1911 and 1910 respectively, joining more western states to expand the right to vote. Pretty soon state after state (with the exception of the southern states) allowed women to vote, if not nationally then on a statewide, or municipality level. With an increase of women voters, congressmen from those districts and states began to support the national womens' suffrage movement, or else they would have been roundly defeated at the polls by these women and their sympathizers.

National interest was steadily growing and before long, in 1916 both major political parties, democrats as well as republicans, endorsed womens' suffrage in their national platforms, finding it much more convenient to support this issue rather than oppose it. The reality of the situation though was one that was much more different than a clear-cut solution as some state rights men strongly believed it should be left to a state by state basis, with each state doing what it wished. The problem with this, however, is that southern women would be totally locked out of the right to vote by their power hungry husbands and fathers.

Meanwhile, a revolutionary by the name of Alice Paul, a Quaker woman from New Jersey, took the womens' movement to a whole new level. The quiet organizing wasn't working. It was tried for generations with little nationwide results to back it up. Instead, what was needed was a more militant approach. Through Paul,

---

426 "Women's Suffrage." 2019. Ipu.org. 2019. http://archive.ipu.org/wmn-e/suffrage.htm.

the womens' movement would resort to hunger strikes and White House pickets urging president Woodrow Wilson to let women vote. This new form of advocacy was meant to get the wider public to see and feel the womens' rights movement, not just hear about them. This strategy proved really effective at getting out the word and sparking conversations. Yet, with all the militancy of the suffrage movement it wasn't until the United States entered into World War 1 when women were thrusted into the national scene picking up jobs in the factories and mills that the men had left to go to war. The women who joined the workforce was one of the main reasons why the American economy didn't implode with so many of the men leaving their jobs for war. More respect was given to the women who heroically stepped up and did their duty to help America's war effort.[427] All of the sudden people started to think "if women can do this then certainly they could and should vote."

President Wilson came to the defense of women and their cause by stating to the senate, "We have made partners of the women in this war; shall we admit them only to a partnership of suffering and sacrifice and toil and not to a partnership of privilege and right?"[428] At this point it was only a matter of time before women held their cherished right that they've been fighting for for so long. Some representatives actually lost their seats in Massachusetts and Delaware because of their opposition to suffrage, clearly showing that public opinion favored the suffrage movement and that suppression wouldn't be acceptable to the American public.

---

427 History.com Editors. 2024. "Women's Suffrage." HISTORY. A&E Television Networks. February 20, 2024. https://www.history.com/topics/womens-history/the-fight-for-womens-suffrage.
428 *The Public Papers of Woodrow Wilson: War and peace*, Baker and Dodd (eds.), p. 265, quoted in Flexner (1959)

The actual amendment granting women suffrage went through some ups and downs nonetheless. As was already mentioned some members of Congress had been advocating for womens' suffrage for years and years and even offered bills and amendments to this point. However, up to this point they were all roundly defeated, not even close. In 1915, the House of Representatives brought forward a suffrage bill, though this was defeated 204-170, with Southerners voting almost to a man against the proposal, all the progressives voted for it 6-0.[429] As a result, before Wilson listed his support for the womens' movement he had to be very careful so as not to alienate the southern democrats who offered him the greatest support. After New York passed a resolution supporting womens' suffrage, he offered his unequivocal support to the measure.

Another bill was introduced in 1918, this time it passed the House, though it needed to do so with a 2/3rds majority, which it did with one vote. It then was ushered into the United States senate, where Wilson again made an appeal to pass the measure. Unfortunately, the senate couldn't muster a 2/3rd majority to pass the proposal, falling two votes short 53-31. In 1919 it was tried again, this time the senate failed to ratify the amendment by one vote 54-30.[430] Still, after all the haggling and fighting, women still couldn't vote and by such an agonizingly close vote. The public, shocked, didn't know just what to do. Both major political parties were stunned. They had both advocated for womens' suffrage, in their own unique way, and felt that they had betrayed their constituents who were counting on them to do what was right.

So, president Wilson, unsatisfied and desperately wanting the amendment passed for the presidential election of 1920, called for

---

[429] "On passage of H. J. Res. 1, proposing to the state legislatures a woman's suffrage amendment to the constitution. (P.1483)".
[430] "S653037 Y=55, N=29 JONES, N.M. TO PASS H.J. RES. 200".

a special session of Congress to hash this out. There was only one thing on mind; the suffrage movement. Again, the House took up the proposal, passing it 304-89, a total blow-out. One wonders if some of the congressmen just voted for the proposal because of pressure or just because they were tired of the issue at this point. All eyes then turned to the senate, they had to come through this time, if they didn't then women would have to wait until another presidential election was decided, again without their consent, approval, or say. The senate this time did its job passing the proposal 56-25.[431] Again, most of the opposition came from conservative senators, most of them southerners.

Now, finally, at last, it was up to the states to pass the amendment. Wisconsin, along with Michigan, and Illinois holds the grand distinction of being the first states to pass the amendment just days after it was passed by Congress. Kansas and New York followed suit not very long after.[432] Texas, of all states, became the first southern state to pass the amendment against significant opposition from anti-suffragists. With Texas' support, the overall amendment looked like it was on its way to an easy passage. I mean if Texas could pass the amendment then any state could pass the amendment, even states in the deep south. However, a little less than a month later, the Georgia legislature became the first state to vote against the ratification of the 19th amendment. Alabama, a few months later, became the second state to vote against ratification. Now the amendment started to look a little gloomy again. South Carolina followed the likes of her sister states, Alabama and Georgia, in rejecting the

---

431 "TO PASS HJR 1. -- Senate Vote #13 -- Jun 1, 1919." n.d. GovTrack.us. https://www.govtrack.us/congress/votes/66-1/s13.
432 "State-By-State Race to Ratification of the 19th Amendment - Women's History (U.S. National Park Service)." 2021. Www.nps.gov. March 15, 2021. https://www.nps.gov/subjects/womenshistory/womens-suffrage-timeline.htm.

measure. The Old Dominion, Virginia, and Maryland didn't pass the measure either, causing many reformers to sweat a little.

However, even in the face of the losses in Alabama, Georgia, and South Carolina, Virginia, and Maryland the womens' suffrage movement still received a great reception in most other states, just not in the south. It was supported overwhelmingly in the north, midwest, west, and south-west and it was rejected overwhelmingly in the south. Eventually, enough states passed the amendment to the point where it was one state shy of becoming the law of the land. The problem was the last vote didn't come easy. The next three states to vote rejected the amendment, though this might not have been surprising, Mississippi, Delaware, and Louisiana. It is hard to believe that after so much struggle and movement regarding this issue that so many men, and not-so-smart women, would be against finally giving women the right to vote, especially after so many other industrialized countries had voted to give their ladies this right. Again, America was behind the game on this issue as well.

All it took was one more state to pass the proposal, but the next state to vote was Tennessee, a border southern state. "After a long series of victories," said the National Park Service, "the defeats in Delaware and Louisiana brought final ratification perilously close to failure. Tennessee was meeting in special session to consider the amendment and (suffragists) and Antis marshalled their forces at the capitol in Nashville, staying at the nearby Hermitage Hotel... yellow roses worn by the Suffs, red for the Antis. The Senate had voted to ratify, so it was up to the House. The vote was on August 18, and it looked like there were enough red roses on the House floor for the amendment to go down. One member wearing a red rose in his lapel, Harry Burn, thought of the letter in his pocket from his mother, Pheobe (nicknamed "Febb"), who had written,

"Dear Son... Hurray and vote for suffrage and don't keep them in doubt... Don't forget to be a good boy..." Harry cast the tie-breaking vote for the amendment. With this, Tennessee became the 36th state and the amendment had passed the threshold for ratification by three-fourths of the states. It was on its way to Washington to be certified as the 19th Amendment to the U.S. Constitution."[433]

It is very true that the whole outcome of the 19th amendment and giving women the right to vote came down to one individual from Tennessee who happened to remember his mother right before he voted. Thank God he had a good mother. What a happy ending right? Well, it still wasn't quite over. After the Tennessee legislature voted to pass the suffrage amendment, anti-suffragists still believed that they had a chance to squash the amendment. They called for another vote to reconsider the measure, though this effort failed on its face when no legislature wanted to change his vote, thus ratification was finally won and women would have the right to vote in the 1920 presidential election. Finally, it was all over and women all over the US, in the north as well as in the south could breathe a sigh of relief.

(As a side note, Maryland didn't pass the amendment until 1941, Virginia in 1952, Alabama in 1953, Florida and South Carolina in 1969, Georgia in 1973 after being proposed in 1970, Louisiana in 1970, North Carolina in 1971, and Mississpipi being the last state to ratify in 1984, some 64 years after women had shown their competence in political affairs and voted accordingly. Alaska and Hawaii did not vote, being admitted in 1959, long after the amendment had been ratified. Of course, for the states that ratified the amendment after the amendment had already been passed was

---

433 Ibid

just a symbolic gesture, yet, it still is sad that these states waited so long to pass this common sense, human rights, measure.)

As soon as the amendment became law, some 26 million American women were now eligible to vote. Believe it or not, many men had feared that if women were allowed to vote then they would form some sort of womens bloc in the political process. This scared the bejeebers out of party loyalists who still wanted their parties to triumph in the elections. This prompted some common sensical proposals such as womens' maternity care and the establishment of the Women bureau within the US department of labor to placate the women.[434] Right or wrong, women would, and still are, tend to be more concerned about issues that directly affect them such as the gender pay gap and adequate educational opportunities. Because women had the right to vote this prompted politicians to actually care, or seem to care about women's issues. If it had not been for the 19th amendment women would still be left completely out of the political spectrum and their rights could be easily trampled on. This should have been an issue that gained nationwide approval and support and even here we saw politicians and groups in power try to brand these reformers who simply advocated for the right to vote in a democracy as radicals, and worse, socialists. How wrong were they?

In the first presidential election that women across the nation were allowed to vote, in 1920, they came out overwhelmingly for republican presidential candidate Warren Harding, who trounced his opponent, democrat James Cox. Part of this reason could be because they viewed the republican party to be the party more devoted to womens' rights and moral issues, as it undoubtedly was.

---

434 Baker, Jean H. (2009). *Women and the U.S. Constitution, 1776–1920.* New Essays in American Constitutional History. Washington, D.C.: American Historical Association

The democratic party was still, largely because of the conservative southern democrats, the party less likely to support women's causes and moral issues, despite the fact that in many cases northern democrats were much more liberal on these issues than most republicans. It is slightly ironic that women, whom conservatives were worried would be more likely to support socialistic and progressive candidates, would overwhelmingly support Harding and other republicans in the future, who proved to be much more conservative than their democratic opponents on the national stage.

Catholic women initially were hesitant to vote and didn't register on a large scale basis until Catholic issues came to greater light when the first Catholic presidential candidate was on the electoral slate. In this case Catholic women registered and voted for Catholic Al Smith against Herbert Hoover in 1928, even though he lost by a lop-sided margin.[435] Black women, even though theoretically could vote due to the amendment, were still largely left out of the voting process because of the Jim Crow laws in the south that prevented most blacks, men as well as women from being able to exercise their right to vote.

And so it was that women were finally able to get the suffrage which they had so long desired. And even though they were able to select their own candidates it didn't necessarily mean that women were electing women to represent them. Mostly, women got to choose which man they wanted to vote for, lacking any sizable women candidates. Women weren't often elected because of a myriad of reasons. Chief among them was the fact that many men simply didn't trust women, believing that they would abandon conservative principles

---

435 Allan J. Lichtman, *Prejudice and the Old Politics: The Presidential Election of 1928* (1979)

and adopt radical reforms. Also, women just simply weren't in a strong position to run for office, many of them having either no professional job, or a very low paying one, which in most circumstances would mean that they don't have a whole lot of influence to sustain a competitive run.

Even though women couldn't vote in the 18th and 19th century, they could still run for office, in a weird twist. Even so, women didn't run for office often. The first woman to run for president was Victoria Woodhull, a woman with a decent amount of influence, being very close to Cornelius Vanderbilt. She ran on the Equal Rights Party ticket in 1872. As far as we know, Woodhull received an incredibly dismal result in the election. She received zero electoral votes and a horrible share in the popular vote, even though the exact number is unknown. (She reportedly did receive at least one vote from a Texas man who claimed he voted for her because he didn't like Grant.)[436] She attempted to run for president two different times with the same results. Men certainly weren't ready for a woman to become president, or become a Congresswoman, or mayor, or any other political post.

In 1884 Belva Lockwood became the first woman admitted to practice law before the highest court in the land, the Supreme Court. She ran for president in 1884 on the Equal Rights Party ticket. According to *Notable American Women,* she received about 4,100 votes," a still pitiable amount.[437] The shocking thing with the vote, however, especially considering that women could not vote and most newspapers were bitterly opposed to Lockwood, she still accumulated more than 4,000 votes from men. There was support

---

436 Victoria Woodhull, the Spirit to Run the White House". *www.victoria-woodhull.com*. Retrieved November 6, 2019

437 Edwin Louis Dey, "Before Shirley Chisholm", *The Washington Post*, June 26, 1984

somewhere for Lockwood, most likely from former abolitionists or other "radical" voters.

Things were starting to look up for women who wanted to see fellow women gain control of the reins of government, though it started on a local level, when Susanna Slater was elected mayor of Argonia, Kansas in 1887. She was the first woman elected to such a high office.[438] Her situation was incredibly interesting. On one hand it is hard to believe that she was elected to the post given that the country had not elected a single woman to lead a governmental post let alone one that was a mere 27 years old. However, some could consider the reason why she was elected was because both her father was the first mayor of the city and her husband was a city clerk. Initially, her nomination on the ballot was intended to embarrass women because the men nominated her sure that she would lose. Incredibly, she didn't even know that she was on the ballot until after the votes had been cast.[439] Surprisingly, some political groups came around and threw their support for her at the last minute and it was enough to help her win the seat. Although she only served for roughly about a year, her elevation to this seat was huge for women all across the country. All of the sudden it seemed as if women could actually lead the government and lead it with efficiency and prudence. It wasn't so crazy anymore to see women starting to get elected at other local levels.

Another huge milestone for women was when Laura Eisenhuth became the superintendent of public education in North Dakota in 1892, the first woman to hold that office and the first women elected on a statewide basis throughout the nation. (Of course, it

---

438 Center For American Women And Politics. 2022. "Milestones for Women in American Politics." Cawp.rutgers.edu. 2022. https://cawp.rutgers.edu/facts/milestones-women-american-politics.
439 Weatherford, Doris. *Women in American Politics: History and Milestones*. SAGE Publications, 2012

helped that North Dakota was one of the most liberal states, at least to women, at the time.) Then two years later three women were elected to the Colorado House of Representatives, Clara Cressingham (R), Carrie C. Holly (R), and Frances Klock, another republican.[440]

Martha Hughes Cannon became the first woman state senator in Utah in 1896, thus women had broken the state office bar. Women had to wait a little later until they had a representative in the federal government but nonetheless had a champion in Jeannette Rankin who became the first woman ever to be elected to the US Congress. Rankin, who was a leading suffragist in New York prior to her election, won her seat largely because of her grassroots organizing that she had honed with her suffragist organization skills.

When United States entry into world war one was being debated and voted upon by Congress Rankin was one of only around 50 Congresspeople to vote against a resolution of war. Rankin, tried to stress her patriotism despite the no vote, "I wish to stand for my country," she said, "but I cannot vote for war."[441] She felt that it was her duty, being the first female congressperson, to vote no to war and strive for peace everytime that she could. She stood up for her values and genuinely believed that America had no reason for being drawn into a war of this great of a magnitude. Nevertheless, Rankin was harassed by the papers, despite the fact that 49 other male representatives voted against the measure too. Apparently it was super easy to undercut and attack a vulnerable woman in Congress and these editors didn't hold back.

In actuality, Rankin's no vote for war made men even more hesitant to give women the right of suffrage. Men, especially younger men, yearned for war and desperately urged the United States to

---

440 Ibid
441 Shirley, Gayle C. (1995). More than Petticoats: Remarkable Montana Women (1st ed.). Helena, Mont.: Falcon Press.

enter the conflict. Not doing so would be a dishonor to American values and interests and would make us look cowardly and timid, not the vision that most American men wanted other countries to view them. Thus, women, like Rankin, were no good in politics, they are too soft and can't be trusted to promote American values.

Even though Rankin got quite a bit of heat from naysayers for her no vote on war, she went on to chart out quite a progressive record for herself, such as advocating for worker welfare initiatives and the development of an eight-hour workday. The Montana legislature in 1918 decided to change the terms of Rankin's House seat from being one of two at-large districts into a western district which was overwhelmingly democratic, which spelled trouble for Rankin who was a republican. She decided to run for a US senate seat, had she won she would have also been the first woman senator, however, she finished a distant third in that race, faring very badly in the general election. Rankin would serve in the US House again, but this time in the 1940s. (She was the only lawmaker who voted against the United States entry into both world wars.)

All of these women had served the nation in different ways before they had even constitutionally gained the right to vote. Now that Congress had passed, and the states had ratified, the 19th amendment, for the first time on a national basis women could vote for other women to represent them.

In an interesting case, Rebecca Latimer Felton became the first woman to serve in the US senate in 1922, albeit for one day, as she was a political appointee. She was a successful suffragist, which gathered her quite a bit of fame in the womens' movement. The sad truth, however, is that she was horribly racist, believed in the idea of segregation, and had even advocated for the lynching of blacks.[442] Not that sweet of a story for the first woman to serve in the senate.

---

442 Ibid

In 1927, Nellie Tayloe Ross, a democrat from Wyoming became the first woman governor in the nation. She was elected after her husband, who had just been the governor, died and left an opening. Ross served for two years and was not reelected to the post, but she was considered to be the 1928 vice-president on the democratic ticket, gaining 31 votes, but eventually losing to Joseph Robinson, who had more nationwide appeal. [443] Since then we have had 48 women governors follow Ross's shoes, 29 democrats and 19 republicans. 34 of these women were elected in their own right, 3 replaced their husbands, and the remaining 11 became governors by right of constitutional succession.[444] 2022 made records with twelve women either holding office or being elected to the governorship. It is still a male dominated field, with 38 men to just 12 women holding governor chairs, however, women are making inroads and have proven very successful at what they do.

The United States senate seemed a tougher nut to crack for women. This would have made sense since the senate was more the chamber that tended to be more privileged and aristocratical. In fact, it was made by the Founders to be a check on the more democratic, closer to the people, House of Representatives. However, in 1932 a woman was elected in her own right breaking this barrier. Her name was Hattie Wyatt Caraway who, despite the fact that she had been appointed to fill the position when her husband died in office in 1931, surprised the democratic party, and the voters, by insisting that she would seek the nomination herself. (She was the first woman senator that decided to run for election herself.) Characteristically of the woman herself, she knew that she had to run saying, "The time

---

443 Ibid
444 "History of Women Governors." n.d. Cawp.rutgers.edu. https://cawp.rutgers.edu/facts/levels-office/statewide-elective-executive/history-women-governors#:~:text=Of%20the%2049%20women%20governors.

has passed when a woman should be placed in a position and kept there only while someone else is being groomed for the job."[445] My wife would say "what a badass." Indeed, Caraway wouldn't back down even from the stiffest competition. Really, Caraway didn't have a whole lot of support, other than the famous "Kingfish" himself, Huey Long, who went on a whole stumping campaign on her behalf. One of the reasons why Long went out of his way to support Caraway was because the two had very similar ideologies, both being populist southerners who despised the wealthy few and sought aid to the distressed and impoverished. Caraway trounced her primary challengers, accumulating more than twice the amount of her closest opponent in the democratic primary. (As she was from Arkansas, a safely democratic state like all the southern states who would never vote for the party of Lincoln, the democratic primary is the only real election that mattered, thus Caraway, in effect, won the prize.) Not a bad showing for the first woman senator who attempted to run on her own with just a year of senatorial experience in the deep south which had fought so vehemently against womens' suffrage.

Caraway then went on and ran again in 1938, this time going against a representative named John Little McClellan. The only main reason that this election was memorable was because of McClellan's slogan, "Arkansas Needs Another Man in the Senate," a very clear shot at women, and in particular, at least to him and his fellow chauvinists, women politicians, who he believed couldn't govern effectively.[446] Despite the heated attacks against Caraway, she did overcome this challenge, though narrowly, becoming the first woman senator reelected.

---

445 CARAWAY, Hattie Wyatt | US House of Representatives: History, Art & Archives". *history.house.gov*. Archived from the original on February 15, 2019
446 Hattie Caraway, the First Woman Elected to the U.S. Senate, Faced a Familiar Struggle With Gender Politics". *Smithsonian Magazine*. Archived from the original on January 8, 2020

It appears that Caraway really enjoyed her time in the senate, as she attempted to run for her seat again when her term came up in 1944. This time, however, she didn't win the democratic primary. She didn't finish 2nd either, or third, but fourth in the primary. It rarely, if ever, happens that a sitting United States senator finished a distant 4th in their party's primary election. A huge reason that Caraway lost was because her constituency, who may have felt ill at ease elected a woman senator to represent them. Another reason why she may have lost was because of the popularity of William Fulbright, the popular US representative, who went on to win the election, though this doesn't explain why she finished fourth in the primary.

Throughout her work in the senate, Caraway found herself on the same side ideologically with all of the New Deal's positions, aligning closely with FDR, and thus being the typical progressive democrat. At least in most ways she was progressive, however, she never completely forgot her stomping ground and joined the efforts to filibuster an anti-lynching bill. Think about it, who in their right mind would oppose a bill that prohibited Americans from lynching one another? It's one of the biggest blots on Caraway's record, maybe the only one, but apparently she was okay with whites mercilessly committing violence on any blacks they wanted. Not something that you would expect from the first woman to be elected to the senate.

Later in her senate career Caraway supported the equal rights amendment, which was a proposed amendment that would have provided equal rights to every American regardless of sex. The amendment failed, but we will talk about it more later in this chapter. She also supported the famous G.I. Bill, for which she was heavily criticized at the time. The G.I. Bill consisted of many things that assisted veterans coming home from World War two, including providing them with free or heavily reduced college tuition. However, when she supported the bill she drew the ire of folks who perceived her and the bill to be "socialist."[447] This perhaps is another reason why she lost her third run for the senate. Prior to Caraway, women who became senators were mostly appointed there because their husbands died in office, or were appointed for a very short period of time, lastling mostly for less than a year. Caraway, however, defied the notion that women can't become senators of their own and successfully ran for the senate seat numerous times. Her decision not to back down to men in authority provided hope for so many women and girls all around the country to follow their dreams and be a source of light for a country that desperately needed it.

All together, there have been 60 women who have served in the United States senate, most women after the 1940s got elected in their own right. 44 of these 60 women served after 1991.[448] The 118th Congress (2023-2025) broke records for the amount of women in the senate. There are currently 25 women senators for the 118th Congress, 15 are democrats and 9 are republican (one is an independent.)[449] It's kind of shocking that we have had 60 women senators in our whole history as a nation, yet, nearly half of them are currently serving. It took a long time to get where we are but we still have plenty of work to do because women still only represent 25% of the senate, a steep underrepresentation of the nation as a whole.

On the cabinet level of the presidency, Francis Perkins made history as Franklin Roosevelt's secretary of labor. She was the first

---

447 Ibid
448 Leppert, Rebecca, and Drew DeSilver. 2023. "118th Congress Has a Record Number of Women." Pew Research Center. January 3, 2023. https://www.pewresearch.org/short-reads/2023/01/03/118th-congress-has-a-record-number-of-women/.
449 "U.S. Senate: Women Senators." n.d. Www.senate.gov. https://www.senate.gov/senators/ListofWomenSenators.htm.

woman to serve in a cabinet post, and she was one of the most outstanding secretaries of labor that the nation has ever had. Nominated in 1933, Perkins was one of the driving forces of the great New Deal legislation. Perkins, despite her later progressive values, grew up in a fundamentally conservative household. Only when Perkins went to school did she see poverty, and the experience changed her life, and her political ideologies forever. When she asked her parents about poverty, they responded that people experience poverty because of laziness or alcohol, the usual answers then as it is now.[450]

Not long after this excursion into the more poverty stricken parts of town Perkins witnessed women and children toiling away in factories and mills. From these experiences Perkins came away with many things that forever altered her life's course. "From the time I was in college," she said, "I was horrified at the work that many women and children had to do in factories. There were absolutely no effective laws that regulated the number of hours they were permitted to work. There were no provisions which guarded their health nor adequately looked after their compensation in case of injury. Those things seemed very wrong. I was young and was inspired with the idea of reforming, or at least doing what I could, to help change those abuses."[451] And it was that her long career began in a bid to destroy the abuses of the "machine" and protect workers and consumers at large. Her and her fellow students helped start the National Consumers League, an organization that educates workers about a variety of topics and fights for their interests, as well as, of course, fighting for the rights and protections of consumers who may buy ineffective or unsanitary products.

Soon after graduating Perkins became a teacher near Chicago

---

[450] Frances Perkins Center. 2023. "Her Life." Frances Perkins Center. 2023. https://francesperkinscenter.org/learn/her-life/.
[451] Ibid

where she spent her free time working in settlement houses for the urban poor. Working with those who were impoverished led her to have a sort of spiritual change, she eventually changed her name to the name we know her by today and even changed her religious affiliation. She said later in life, "I had to do something about unnecessary hazards to life, unnecessary poverty. It was sort of up to me. This feeling … sprang out of a period of great philosophical confusion which overtakes all young people."[452] And so, she was off to change the world, not caring at all about the limitations of being a woman. She famously remarked, "Being a woman has only bothered me in climbing trees."[453] What a badass.

Throughout Perkins' career prior to becoming the secretary of labor she advocated hard for shorter work days and better working conditions. During the Hoover administration she challenged the president who deceivingly declared that unemployment was declining and that the Depression was soon on the way to recovery. Obviously, this statement by Hoover was not true and when Perkins called him out for the comment and gained nationwide attention and publicity.

When Franklin Roosevelt cruised into the White House it was an incredibly shrewd move to appoint Perkins to be secretary of labor. Not only was she the first woman to be appointed and confirmed to the cabinet but she also was a trailblazer advocating for workers' rights. It was one of his greatest political appointments of all time. When she was confirmed, she felt it her duty as an American to drop her private life to help the masses, "I came to Washington to work for God, FDR, and the millions of forgotten, plain common workingmen" she would later remark.[454]

---

452 Ibid
453 Ibid
454 Ibid

Incredibly, Perkins would serve for the entirety of Roosevelt's presidency, 12 years. Through her time as secretary she helped put through many of Roosevelt's New Deal policies and helped shore up initiatives to help the middle class. After she left the cabinet level shortly after FDR passed away, Perkins still served the public in Truman's administration, just not at the cabinet level, proving that she truly cared about the overall success of the nation and middle class Americans. It is an understatement to say that Perkins truly believed she was the best fit for the jobs that she commanded. Indeed, nobody could do it better and she was a god-send to so many middle class Americans and she knew it.

So far, there have been a total of 66 women who have served in a cabinet position, some of them serving in multiple roles. 43 of these ladies were nominated by democratic presidents and 23 women were nominated by republicans presidents. (Other notables for cabinet women: the first black woman appointed was Patricia Roberts Harris who was appointed by Carter (D), the first Latina woman appointed was Aida Alveraz who was appointed by Clinton (D), the first Asian woman appointed was Elaine Chao, the wife of republican senate leader Mitch McConnel who was appointed by George Bush, and the first Native American woman appointed was Deb Haaland who was appointed by Biden (D) almost 75 years after Perkins.[455]) President Joe Biden has appointed the most women in his cabinet totalling 13 women, or more than ⅕th of the total number of women who have ever served in the cabinet. Truly, president Biden's cabinet looks like America, he at least diversified his cabinet. Never before had women had this kind of representation here in the United States before.

---

455 "WOMEN APPOINTED to PRESIDENTIAL CABINETS." 2021. https://cawp.rutgers.edu/sites/default/files/resources/womenapptdtoprescabinets.pdf.

Women having served all in pretty much all positions in government left one glaring hole yet to be filled; any representation on the presidential level. In 1952, the democrats almost nominated a woman to be the running mate of Adlai Stevenson, their presidential nominee. As a matter of fact, two women were in consideration, India Edwards and Sarah Hughes. Unfortunately, for the ladies, both of these women withdrew in order to support Estes Kefauver, who they wanted to be supported unanimously. Women did get a vice presidential nomination, however, in the end when the progressive party ran Charlotta Spears Bass, the first woman ever to be a vice presidential nominee. The problem with it was that the progressive party was a lackluster party in the 1950s and both Bass and the progressive party went down to disastrous defeat and didn't receive a whole lot of attention.

Sarah Palin's nomination as the vice presidential candidate for the republicans in 2008 under John McCain shocked the political world. In all reality, Palin was a surprising pick not because she was a woman but because she simply had very little experience and actually proved to be more of a problem to the republicans with some of her thoughtless rhetoric.

In 2020 it was basically all but assured that Biden would pick a woman VP, especially when Biden promised voters that if he received the nomination he would select a woman candidate. He decided to choose Kamala Harris, who was the first of many things including first female vice president when she and Biden won the election, creditably, and the first African-American and Asian American vice president. Look at all the firsts. We are living in history.

(I don't have to say this but of course Hillary Clinton was the first woman to be nominated by an official party. She lost to Donald

Trump despite getting almost 3 million more votes than he did, it's just another example of the electoral college being unfair to the American people who actually elected Clinton instead of Trump. It makes no sense that a few thousand people in Michigan, Wisconsin, and Pennsylvania means more than nearly 3 million. She should have been the first woman elected president, but alas we have to wait. It will happen eventually, just how soon nobody can say. It seems, though, much more likely that the first woman president will come from the democratic party, probably pretty soon.)

Not to leave out the Supreme Court, Sandra Day O'Connor was the first woman who was appointed to the Supreme Court. Appointed by Ronald Raegan, O'Connor became a fixture on the Supreme Court and was known for her impartiality and intelligence. Incredibly, throughout the entire history of the Supreme Court only six women have served out of 115 justices total. Four of the six are currently serving on the court, making it the most gender diverse branch in the federal government currently.[456]

Other notable achievements for ladies include Minnie Buckingham Harper who became the first black woman to be elected to a state legislative body in 1928 in West Virginia. It took roughly an extra 30 years for a black woman to be elected than it did for a white one, clearly showing the double barriers of being a woman and being black at the same time. (Two years later, the first Latina women were elected to the state legislature of New Mexico, Fedelina Lucero Gallegos and Porfirria Hidalgo Saiz.)[457] Shirley Christolm became

---

456 "Women on the Supreme Court." n.d. RepresentWomen. https://www.representwomen.org/women_supreme_court#:~:text=The%20United%20States%20Supreme%20Court.
457 Center For American Women And Politics. 2022. "Milestones for Women in American Politics." Cawp.rutgers.edu. 2022. https://cawp.rutgers.edu/facts/milestones-women-american-politics.

the first black US representative from New York in 1968, a few years later she became the first black woman to run for president.

In comparison to other countries the United States falls far behind other countries in terms of diversity in representation. In Rwanda, 49 of the 80 seats in the lower chamber are filled with women, making up 61% and leading the world in female representation. Next is Cuba with 53%, Bolivia 53%, Mexico 48%, and Sweden 47%.[458] As of today, the United States is tied for 76th place in terms of female representation with 23.6% in the House of Representatives women and 25% in the senate. That falls to the likes of Afghanistan, China, and Somalia.[459] Again, not very good company to be in.

In 1960, Sirimavo Bandaranaike became the first female head of state in the world when she became the prime minister of Sri Lanka. As of 2019, 59 countries have elected a woman head of state, the United States still has not had one. (Some countries similar to the US that have elected a female head of state include the UK in 1979, Norway in 1981, Ireland in 1990, France in 1991, Canada in 1993, Switzerland in 1999, Finland in 2001, Germany in 2005, South Korea in 2006, and Australia in 2010, just to name a few.)[460] It's clear that the United States is yet again falling far behind other countries. Some countries have even elected multiple female prime ministers and presidents including Switzerland with five and Finland with four.[461] There are reasons why women have not been elected

---

458 Inter-Parliamentary Union. 2019. "Women in Parliaments: World Classification." Ipu.org. February 1, 2019. http://archive.ipu.org/wmn-e/classif.htm.
459 Ibid
460 "All the Countries That Had a Woman Leader before the U.S." 2016. Cnn.com. CNN. 2016. https://www.cnn.com/interactive/2016/06/politics/women-world-leaders/.
461 Buchholz, Katharina. 2023. "Infographic: Which Countries Have Been Female-Led?" Statista Infographics. January 19, 2023. https://www.statista.com/chart/3994/which-countries-have-had-a-female-leader/.

more often in the United States whether that be in Congress, to the presidency, or the state and local government. It's not radical to believe that women can be effective leaders on the national stage, it's radical to think otherwise, and yet so many conservative men and women still believe that government is a man's job. That's got to change if we want to have a more robust, problem-solving democracy. Maybe if there were more women representing America there would be less gun violence, paid family leave, higher minimum wages, and benefits in programs that affect women and children, especially an increase in funding for childcare centers which are being squeezed out in this economy.

Even worse, the United States has not even passed the Equal Rights Amendment yet. The ERA was basically a measure that provided equal rights for all genders. The text of the amendment says this "Equality of rights under the law shall not be denied or abridged by the United States or by any state on account of sex. The Congress shall have the power to enforce, by appropriate legislation, the provisions of this article."[462] That doesn't sound too controversial does it? And yet, the fight over the amendment is just another story of fear-mongering that conservatives used to push people who are not like them down.

The ERA was drafted in 1923 by two women suffragists, Alice Paul and Crystal Eastman. They believed that the 19th amendment was an important step, but just because women had the right to vote this doesn't mean that they wouldn't be treated as second-rate citizens.

---

462 Alex Cohen, and Wilfred U. Codrington III. 2019. "The Equal Rights Amendment Explained | Brennan Center for Justice." Www.brennancenter.org. October 9, 2019. https://www.brennancenter.org/our-work/research-reports/equal-rights-amendment-explained?utm_medium=PANTHEON_STRIPPED&utm_source=PANTHEON_STRIPPED.

The amendment would guarantee that nobody could discriminate against women just solely because of their gender.

Lawmakers introduced the measure in 1923 in Congress, but it didn't gain any serious traction until the 1970s.[463] Of course, a reason why it languished in Congress could be attributed to the fact that men dominated congress. Throughout the 1920s-1970 only ten women served in the senate, the picture wasn't much rosier in the House either. Thus women really didn't have a whole lot of lawmakers fighting for them.

Finally in the 1970s more women were elected to Congress and because of their efforts they pushed a vote on the ERA through Congress. Because the ERA shouldn't really be controversial the amendment passed both houses of Congress and went to the states for ratification. The kicker, Congress passed the amendment with a seven year deadline, meaning that the amendment had to be ratified by enough states within seven years or else it would be declared dead.

The amendment passed many state legislatures very quickly, 30 states passed the amendment in the first year.[464] However, just like most good things, people came against it. The conservatives teamed up with the religious right coalition to stop the amendment dead in its tracks. I have no idea why so-called religious people would oppose an amendment to stop discrimination. That is a very un-Christian and non-religious thing to do. Nevertheless, the pressure that they extolled on state legislatures halted the amendment dead in its tracks.

As was mentioned, most states had passed the amendment well before the seven year timeline. Of the states that did not ratify on time many were in the deep south. Among them: Illinois, Virginia, Nevada, Arizona, Utah, Oklahoma, Arkansas, Missouri, Louisiana, Mississippi, Alabama, Georgia, Florida, South Carolina, and North

---

463 Ibid
464 Ibid

Carolina. With all of these states not ratifying the amendment it did not become law and enshrined in the Constitution. Indiana, Illinois, and Nevada passed the amendment since and in 2020, after Virginia's legislature turned democratic, Virginia passed the amendment putting the amendment at the required 38 state threshold. The problem is that the seven year time limit is well passed and would need to be voted on all over again and numerous states have revoked their passage of the amendment. Nebraska, Tennessee, Idaho, Kentucky, and South Dakota have all revoked the passage of the amendment, meaning that they no longer agree with the amendment. Surprisingly, North Dakota revoked the amendment in 2021! I have no idea why they would go through the motions to revoke an amendment geared at guaranteeing equality. Instead of figuring out budget issues or trying to help the future citizens of North Dakota, lawmakers there want to deprive their citizens of equality. This is madness!

Still to this day, the United States is viewed very negatively to foreign nations who laugh at how we treat minorities and those who are different. Failing to pass the ERA is proof enough of the fact that the United States is not serious about equality, they are still being lied to by conservatives who think that it's too radical for women and LGBTQ individuals to have equal rights. Somehow this idea that all people should be treated with respect and have equal rights, that not one group is superior or somehow better, is still a radical thought as it always has been.

Part 2

THE PRESENT

13   WEALTH INEQUALITY

The topic that roused up enough dissatisfaction to warrant me writing this book has to do with the issue of poverty. I will be quite frank, we have an issue with poverty in this country and all over the world. The cold hard facts are simply hard to swallow. Every single night we have countless individuals who are sleeping in the streets, millions of children who are malnourished, and roughly half of all Americans are living paycheck to paycheck. I will get into the specifics a little later in this chapter. All of this at the same time we are seeing in this country the most egregious levels of wealth and income inequality that we have ever seen in the history of our great land. We are increasingly becoming more of an oligarchic country than a thriving democracy. So few of us actually have any power at all, with most of the power being shifted to those at the top. Where there is money there is power and where there is power there is money. It's a sad reality that leaves so many out of the political process, and it's an equally sad reality because this is the primary reason why we are still seeing massive levels of poverty in this country and are not taking the adequate steps to address it.

And what about the poverty all over the world? The United States is one of the wealthiest countries in the world. Yet, we still see massive poverty here. It is much worse in other underdeveloped countries, like many in the African and Southeast Asia regions. Do we as wealthier people have any responsibility to end this kind of income inequality and address poverty worldwide? Or is it not our problem? Of course, different people will tell you different things, but I argue that we do have a moral obligation to end worldwide poverty once and for all. Many naysayers will tell us that it can't be done, that what we are trying to accomplish is a utopia that will never happen here in this earthly world, but I am here to tell you that we have the resources in this world to guarantee that nobody is hungry and no one without a shelter.

What do I mean when I say that we are dealing with massive wealth inequality that we have never seen before? I mean to say that so much money is concentrated in so few hands and this is leading to worldwide problems. In no way, shape, or form am I proposing that the rich should lose all of their money. Indeed, if they work hard to get what they have it's good for them. But what I am saying is that it is completely unfair and inhuman to award so few people with so much while at the same time we see so many with so little.

I once was in a class one day when the professor, who works with poverty and energy issues told me something that I will never forget. He put up two pictures side by side. One picture was a ginormous man with an equally large beer belly that was literally hanging well over his shorts. The other picture showed a group of children huddled into the corner of their hut. All of them were so skinny you could see their rib cages. My professor then quipped a line that is seared into my memory. He said, "Here in America people are dying because they eat too much, while at the same time in other countries people are dying because they eat too little." This made me think, where are our priorities? Inequality doesn't just mean money after all. It also includes what we need to get by. We need food to survive. Some people have so much food that they eat so much that they literally die because of it. Others can't even find the necessary food to stay alive. This is what I'm talking about when I mention inequality. And here is where the chapter will start off.

One key question arises when we talk about the growing wealth and income inequality and that is whether or not we believe that something can be done about the growing inequality. Should we just have a laissez faire type of economy, where the government just lets capitalism run its course, have companies become monopolies, and see individuals make billions of dollars a year? Or should we see a regulated capitalism, where there are safeguards to businesses and the amount of money that CEOs can make? I believe, quite honestly, that we need to have a government that does provide these safeguards and I will show you why later in this chapter.

For those that believe in a laissez faire type of economy they see all this meddling and intervention by the state or federal governments as being a nuisance. However, those that support a laissez faire type of government would also at the same time be supportive of monopolies, which control complete sectors of our economy, shutting out all competition. (Currently, we see monopolies in numerous fields. Perhaps the biggest monopoly today is the beef industry.) But even in the times where we see the most laissez faire approach to politics and government, we still as a nation where we are totally opposed to monopolies for hurting ordinary, hard working people. So, we already don't have a laissez faire approach, in regards to how we treat monopolies, and I would say it's a safe bet to assume that most people are opposed to monopolies, we have a regulated capitalist economy just on that fact alone. But we could do much more to spread the income to reach all of us and not just the top few.

According to the United States Census Bureau, almost 12% of Americans live in poverty, or roughly 38 million people.[465] That's a lot of poverty. And contrary to popular opinion, the vast majority

---

[465] Bureau, US Census. 2023. "Income, Poverty and Health Insurance Coverage in the United States: 2022." Census.gov. September 12, 2023. https://www.census.gov/newsroom/press-releases/2023/income-poverty-health-insurance-coverage.html#:~:text=The%20official%20poverty%20rate%20in.

of poverty in the country happens to be in the southern portion of the US and mostly rural areas. The data to this metric is completely telling. In 2022 the state with the highest poverty is New Mexico, with 18% of its total population reaching poverty levels. New Mexico is mostly a purple state, with a heavily diverse population. The second highest is Mississippi with 18%, followed by Louisiana 17%, Arkansas 16%, Oklahoma 16%, Kentucky 16%, West Virginia 16%, Alabama 15%, Texas 14%, South Carolina 13%, Florida 13%, and Georgia 13%.[466] Well besides this being a rather large list, do you see anything that catches your eye? These states are overwhelmingly in the south. Why is it that we have so much poverty in the south? There could be a number of reasons for the massive poverty. One could be the messy reconstruction era and the Jim Crow laws that followed. These laws held back blacks and other minorities from making decent wages and discriminating against them having an equal opportunity to make a living. Another reason is that most of the states in the south are controlled by republicans. Why does this matter? Because republicans hate raising the minimum wage. In most of these states the minimum wage is still $7.25, well below living standards. And most of these states, led by conservatives, have a very low safety net with very little benefits, low unemployment insurance, and high costs for health care. (Most of these states have not expanded medicaid for their citizens during the Affordable Care Act, in a purely partisan move.) Coincidence or no? You can decide for yourself. I think that the politics of the region prove a key reason why we see such huge poverty rates in the south.

The level of poverty affects our children as well. Roughly one in five children are now living in poverty. This means that they are missing out on everyday necessities because they were born in a

---

466 "U.S. Poverty Rate by State 2018 | Statista." 2018. Statista. Statista. 2018. https://www.statista.com/statistics/233093/us-poverty-rate-by-state/.

poverty stricken household, where they are much more likely to be malnourished and undereducated. At the other end of the spectrum, seniors, those over the age of 65, have a poverty rate of 15%.[467] We are letting down our grandmas and grandpas every day that we just ignore the facts. Native Americans are disproportionately the most likely group to end up in poverty with 26% of Native Americans falling below the poverty threshold. Next, is black Americans, where 21% are struggling in poverty. Hispanics is at 17%, and whites and Asian Americans are at 10%.[468] Why do we have such startling differences in these demographics? Clearly, this is a pattern and not merely a coincidence.

I often discuss with people who have different political views than I do about the impact of poverty. To some people, who happen to be republican or conservative by nature, they think that poverty is a choice. People wind up in poverty because that is how they choose to live. They think they will get handouts from the government and live for free while the rest of us work hard for a living. If they just decided to be smart with their money they wouldn't be in this problem. The overall assumption from these people is that those who struggle with poverty choose to be because they don't care about money or they don't know how to use it properly. I get this especially from people who have saved up a lot of money or are used to budgeting. They might say that those who struggle with poverty should save a little every month to get out of poverty.

The problem with these arguments is that nobody actively chooses to live in poverty. That is absurd. If someone had a chance to have a really nice house or to live in a shack, most people would choose to live in a decent house with their family. Secondly, these arguments are mostly from those who have had it relatively easy in life. They

---

467 Poverty USA. 2022. "The Population of Poverty USA." Povertyusa.org. Poverty USA. 2022. https://www.povertyusa.org/facts.
468 Ibid

don't understand the reality that most people in poverty are faced with everyday. So, let's play a hypothetical. Let's assume that we have a husband and a wife with two kids. We have a family of four here. To be in poverty status with a family of four you make barely less than $26,000. That's a pitiable sum. Economists always say that you should never spend more than 30% of your income on housing. So, for a family of four that makes $26,000 that amounts to about $7,800 in living expenses, even given government assistance.

So, that family has $18,200 left to spend on other necessities. What about childcare? Childcare today for one child is more expensive than it is for a full year's tuition in college. This is an incredibly shocking amount that leaves many people struggling to find childcare or even attempting to stay at home instead of work. If they spend roughly $10,000 with government assistance on childcare they have $8,200 left to spend. Groceries, again with government assistance roughly equates to around $5,100 for a family of four. This means we have $3,100 left to spend on everything else. This includes healthcare, transportation, clothes, internet, ect. This means that this family of four hardly has any money to put away for college or any investments that would get them out of poverty. Honestly, the number one way someone can get out of poverty is to achieve higher levels of education. I call it the poverty circle. If you don't have enough money to go to college you don't get a degree. If you don't get a degree you don't get a good paying job. If you don't get a good paying job you end up in the same position, poverty. This is the poverty loophole that people continuously get stuck in. The sad reality is if you're born into poverty you are 90% likely to die in poverty. That my friends is not a coincidence, that is a pattern that our country has been complacent about. We can do better and we must, but how? For one thing we need to come up with better solutions to help make sure that everyone receives an equal opportunity to succeed in life. Success shouldn't just be based on what your situation is like when you were born. In this way we are letting down so many people, including a huge amount of minorities, who have been pushed down for centuries. Think about the positive economic impacts that can be made in our country if we set about to reduce the poverty rates in this country.

Let's contrast these heart-wrenching statistics with some that are on the opposite pole. Based on the statistics of 2022 the richest person in the US, indeed the world, is Elon Musk, the CEO and co-founder of Tesla. Musk's total net worth is $251 billion. You read that right, $251 billion. Now I'm all for entrepreneurs and innovation, but I don't believe that anyone, even if they made a cure for cancer, should be able to own $251 billion. He had owned seven houses, before selling them in 2021, at the same time when millions of Americans are having the most difficult time affording a small house on a crime ridden street. Jeff Bezos, former CEO of Amazon owns $150 billion. One has to ponder, what do these people do with all of that money? Can you imagine the expensive houses, the gold trimmed china, and the fancy yachts?

The bottom 50% of Americans, including roughly 200 million Americans combined wealth is a little more than $250 billion.[469] This means that Elon Musk has just enough to own more wealth than 200 million Americans combined. Here are some more alarming statistics. The top 10 percent of households by wealth, hold on average $7 million, as a group they make about 70% of the total household wealth.[470] In contrast, the bottom 50% of households by wealth

---

469 Inequality.org. 2018. "Wealth Inequality in the United States." Inequality.org. 2018. https://inequality.org/facts/wealth-inequality/.
470 Kent, Ana, and Lowell Ricketts. 2023. "The State of U.S. Wealth Inequality." Www.stlouisfed.org. October 18, 2023. https://www.stlouisfed.org/institute-for-economic-equity/the-state-of-us-wealth-inequality.

have around $51,000, a very respectable net worth at that. But, as a group they only hold 2.5% of the total household wealth. Black families owned about 24 cents for every $1 of white family wealth, on average. That's the same proportion that a Hispanic household makes as well, in proportion to what a white family makes.[471] The top 1% take home 54% of the total wealth in a given year. And on a level with other countries that have similar levels of wealth inequality according to indexing, the United States falls in the same category as Iran, Turkey, Ghana, Kenya, and Ecuador.[472] Notice none of these countries has strong, thriving democracies. Notice how all of these countries could be considered underdeveloped. This is shocking. Not even Russia with all of its oligarchs falls to the same level as the United States. All of Europe and other advanced economies all over the world have significantly lower levels of wealth inequality than the United States, especially Norway and Finland. What gives? Why do we have such horrible levels of inequality?

As a country we have been very reluctant to "tax the rich." When we do so, some conservatives cry foul because we are a capitalist society and any taxing of the rich can be considered socialist, even if that means taxing them just a few extra cents. This is one of the prime reasons why our wealth and income gaps have grown so fierce the past few years.

We should all be alarmed at the rise of wealth and income inequality for a number of reasons. Not only is it affecting the amount of money that middle class and poor people take home everyday, but it also negatively affects the economy. A recent article from Renewing

---

471 Ibid

472 Siripurapu, Anshu. 2022. "The U.S. Inequality Debate." Council on Foreign Relations. Council on Foreign Relations. April 20, 2022. https://www.cfr.org/backgrounder/us-inequality-debate.

America hits the nail right on the head. It says "Inequality is a drag on economic growth and fosters political dysfunction, experts say. Concentrated income and wealth reduces the level of demand in the economy because rich households tend to spend less of their income than poorer ones." And what happens when poorer households don't have the money to buy? Economist Joseph Stiglitz mentions that "When those at the bottom of the income distribution are at great risk of not living up to their potential, the economy pays a price not only with weaker demand today, but also with lower growth in the future."[473] Moral of the story here is that when the income is concentrated in just a few hands these rich individuals will likely hold onto it, as they don't actively need to buy, or they end up buying from specialized industries such as yachts and other luxury goods. When middle class and poor households buy they buy the items that they need, which provides a positive economic step in the economy as a whole. So when somebody says "I don't care how much money Jeff Bezos has" tell them the truth of what that does to the economy.

We should also be concerned because wealthy people have a huge influence on the political process. They certainly have the means to be able to spend huge sums of money on political campaigns. Who's voice matters more to the ears of our politicians: mine, when I spend $20 on a campaign because that's all that I have, or the Koch brothers who spend hundreds of millions of dollars on campaign contributions. The sad reality is the majority of our politicians would listen to the Koch brothers a hell of a lot more than me just because my $20 isn't going to totally fund their campaign. We are

---

473 Siripurapu, Anshu. 2022. "The U.S. Inequality Debate." Council on Foreign Relations. Council on Foreign Relations. April 20, 2022. https://www.cfr.org/backgrounder/us-inequality-debate.

at an uneven playing field in more ways than one. Perhaps this is why we have one of the most lopsided tax systems in the world. Our politicians are spending more time hobnobbing with wealthy elitists, while not taking the time to get to know the struggles of the American people. We are at a further disadvantage in today's day and age when it costs so much to run a political campaign. Due to the need to reign in more money candidates are much more likely to accept enormous sums of money from the richest Americans to help fund their campaign. I wrote about this in a previous chapter, but it makes it increasingly likely that the people who run for office are of the upper classes and can afford to run. The average worker, mailman, nurse, teacher, ect can very rarely find the resources it takes to run a campaign, which also gives the wealthy even more advantages.

Throughout American history we have seen shifts of income and wealth inequality happen at profound rates. For example, in a previous chapter we mentioned how the robber barons in the gilded age were making ungodly amounts, while the rest of the United States was struggling to get by, even forcing their children to work in factories to help put food on the table. Now, times were different back then. The standard of living was exceptionally brutal for the vast majority of Americans, but we still saw economic inequality even in these times. However, these levels of wealth inequality slowed down some after the turn of the 20th century and the progressive reformers who helped usher in so much change. Indeed, these reformers needed to persuade congressmen to pass the 16th amendment which allowed governments to pass taxes based on someone's income, as opposed to the flat taxes that republicans still want to pass today. In fact, it was the conservatives back then that caused such a frenzy over the income tax to begin with, it was initially proposed in 1909 and had the support of even a republican president. But, conservatives delayed and delayed until they couldn't delay any more and the 16th amendment was ratified in 1913. This new form of progressive taxation certainly did much to help lower the amounts of income inequality as those that were better off had higher tax rates to pay for basic governmental expenditures.

Here is a brief history on taxation. The passage of the 16th amendment wasn't actually the first time the government passed an income tax. The first time this was done was during the administration of Abraham Lincoln, in the midst of the civil war. The tax records show that in 1862 if you made more than $300, you would pay a 3% tax. If you made more than $10,000 you were taxed 5%. That's equivalent to earning about $305,000 today that you would be taxed to this amount.[474] That's a pretty wide jump, but the 5% tax didn't really affect that many people because there weren't that many people who made that kind of money back then. This was purely just to pay off the war though, it was never intended to last more than a few years, and by the year 1867 the income tax essentially did not exist anymore.

Fast forward to the year 1913, when the 16th amendment was ratified and we see some modest taxation rates. The highest rate was 7% for incomes over $500,000. These rates tended to stay the same throughout the world war one year. Income and wealth inequality was much lower mostly because of the war production, putting people to work in decent paying jobs. Also, business owners and executives made more than their workers but not usually more than 50 times

---

[474] "$10,000 in 1862 → 2024 | Inflation Calculator." n.d. Www.in2013dollars.com. Accessed May 19, 2024. https://www.in2013dollars.com/us/inflation/1862?amount=10000.

more. Then after the great war the United States experienced what was to be known as the roaring twenties, when production was high and the overall feeling was one of economic success. Yet, the term that we use today to define the 1920s wasn't all sunshine and happy for the vast majority. In fact, the 1920s is when the United States saw some of the worst income and wealth inequality. During this time economists considered an income of $2,500 to be just enough to cover basic needs, however nearly 60% of Americans fell below this threshold. Worse, nearly 40% made less than $1,500.[475] So much for the roaring twenties huh? I guess it just gets that phase because of how well the richest of the rich were doing.

It was even so much worse for minorities who suffered the hardest. Mexican Americans frequently noted how they didn't have access to a toilet and most nights didn't have meat or fresh vegetables to eat. Native Americans didn't see economic bounties either, "A 1928 report on the condition of Native Americans found that half owned less than $500 and that 71 percent lived on less than $200 a year."[476] Not exactly what you would call thriving by any means.

During the 1920s there was a huge shift of where the wealth was going. While the bottom 93% of Americans saw their take home incomes actually decline, the top one percent saw their share in the overall economy climb from 12% to 19%, and the richest top five percent of Americans saw their share climb from 24% to 35%.[477] This spelled doom for the economy as the rich tend to use their disposable income on the richest luxuries and save large sums of their money there was a downsprial in demand in almost every

---

[475] "Digital History." 2021. Www.digitalhistory.uh.edu. 2021. https://www.digitalhistory.uh.edu/disp_textbook.cfm?smtid=2&psid=3432#:~:text=During%20the%201920s%2C%20there%20was.
[476] Ibid
[477] Ibid

sector. Soon, because the vast majority of Americans couldn't use any disposable income on goods, factories and businesses started to close and massive layoffs and unemployment was the result.

In the midst of the so-called economic boom, the federal government had a pretty extensive income tax bracket. So, hang in there with me as we go through this. In 1927, there were 23 separate tax brackets, that's a lot of tax brackets. Today we have seven tax brackets. The fact that they had 23 different tax brackets all the way back in 1927 means that they cared that the income taxes were targeting those that could afford to pay more. Now, keep in mind that back then the amount of revenue needed to fund the government and any other additional resources was incredibly smaller than what is needed today. Back then those that made less than $4,000 paid a 3% tax rate, that was the smallest rate. The largest rate was for those who made over $100,000 where they paid a rate of 25%. This was when, in the 1920s, the government actually reduced taxes because the great war no longer threatened the world.

These rates show something quite interesting. The top bracket, where people made more than $100,000 was only taxed about 25%, and there were certainly a lot of people who made more than that. John Rockefeller had a net worth of about $1.2 billion, or what would be the equivalent of $21 billion today. George Baker had a net worth of $150 million. Edward Harkness had a net worth of $125 million, and so on and so on.[478] Do you think that the tax rates were fair back then? I don't think so. It's impossible to know how much Rockefeller made each year, but on average he made

---

478 Peterson-Withorn, Chase. n.d. "From Rockefeller to Ford, See Forbes' 1918 Ranking of the Richest People in America." Forbes. Accessed May 19, 2024. https://www.forbes.com/sites/chasewithorn/2017/09/19/the-first-forbes-list-see-who-the-richest-americans-were-in-1918/?sh=1d50f0e4c0d2.

roughly $25 million each year, this is in terms of 1927 currency. Do you think it's fair for somebody making $100,000 a year to pay the same amount of taxes as somebody making $25 million a year? If you do, I profoundly disagree. This is how in the 1920s the income and wealth inequality exploded. Manufacturing was hitting record profits and the overwhelming amount of money was going into the pockets of the business owners and top executives, not in the pockets of the workers who helped earn that money. And to make it worse, the government took the side of the wealthy robber barons with its tax code that left the likes of Rockefeller laughing all the way to the bank.

With income inequality becoming more and more divisive the economy completely collapsed and we got what is now known as the Great Depression. It's equally sad that the Great Depression didn't hit the wealthy hard at all, as a matter of fact they were hardly hit. The Depression mostly hit farmers, who were struggling with crops and the Dust Bowl, and the working class who were now shoved off into unemployment and Hoover shacks. That's the way recessions and depressions work. They hit the poor and working class really hard while leaving the wealthy elite hardly nicked.

Following the Great Depression, we got a totally new, effective, leader in FDR who went to work for the working people and is generally regarded as a traitor to his class because he grew up in wealth. He quickly put people to work in government programs such as the Civilian Conservation Corp, which brought jobs to many young people working on public works projects. He also signed Glass Steagall, which was designed to prevent massive recessions like the one they were just getting out of from happening again. (The republicans pressured Bill Clinton to repeal Glass Steagall in 1999. Less than nine years later we had another massive recession.) The reason Glass Steagall matters is that it prevents wealthy investors and banks from making risky investments that could potentially derail the economy when they fail.

FDR also oversaw the implementation of a drastically new income tax system. Because of the Great Depression and the massive wealth inequality that precipitated that with a few holding all the concentration of wealth while the rest of America was living in poverty, the vast majority wanted to implement much higher tax rates on the enormously wealthy. Indeed, these Americans saw that the government could tax the wealthy their fair share and then put people to work in decent paying jobs, or create programs that would reduce poverty by creating a social safety net.

In 1933, FDR's first year as president there were a whopping 55 tax brackets. If you made less than $4,000 you paid an 8% tax rate. In a drastic increase, if you made $100,000 your tax rate would be 56%, that would be the equivalent of about $2.5 million today. Finally, if you made more than a million dollars your tax rate would be 63%, $1 million was worth $23 million back in 1933. As you can see the tax rates were staggering compared to what they are now, but the wealth and income inequality took a nosedive. Finally, people were making better wages and the economy was straightening out and becoming stronger because people had more buying power.

This kind of fair taxation allowed Roosevelt and his fellow democrats to create social security, a law that provides some reassurance for the elderly to be able to retire in confidence. It is very true that prior to this law many people still worked well into their 70s and 80s just to get by. This provided them a little protection and a sigh of relief. Bonus, it also provides relief for those who just lost their job providing unemployment insurance, which was particularly beneficial to the people at the time of the Depression. Wilbur Cohen, former secretary of Health, Education, and Welfare noted "If any piece of social legislation can be called historic or revolutionary, in breaking with the past and in terms of long run impact, it is the Social Security Act."[479]

Huey Long, governor of Louisiana, received the idea of social security from one of his political rivals. However, Long saw how popular the measure was with ordinary Americans and was the first to officially put the position in his national platform. (Long would be assassinated in 1935 after showing signs of challenging Roosevelt for the democratic nomination.) Nevertheless, social security certainly, like all good things, had its opponents. Conservatives worried that social security would shrink the workforce, citing that it would allow people to sit out on the sidelines longer without a job because they would have this safety net. This never proved true, however, as social security allowed older folks to finally retire, which opened up new positions which were quickly taken by younger generations.

Conservatives also reverted back to what they typically do, call everything socialist. Senator Thomas Gore of Oklahoma, in a hearing with secretary of Labor Frances Perkins, asked "Isn't this socialism?" She said that it was not, but he continued, "Isn't this a teeny-weeny bit of socialism."[480] Indeed, any proposal that even hinted at helping the working class is always branded as being somewhat socialist. It's crazy looking back now at how popular social security has become to hear that all the way back then conservatives believed this to be socialist. Indeed, if any politician would be foolish enough to try to take down social security they certainly would hear from their constituents. (This has not stopped some republicans, including

---

479 Social Security Administration. n.d. "Social Security History." Www.ssa.gov. https://www.ssa.gov/history/50ed.html#:~:text=Roosevelt%20signed%20the%20Social%20Security.
480 Altman, Nancy J. (August 14, 2009), "President Barack Obama could learn from Franklin D. Roosevelt", *Los Angeles Times*

Florida senator Rick Scott from endorsing plans for social security to gradually sunset. Others call social security a ponzi scheme like republican senator Ron Johnson) When the Social Security Act passed only a few congressmen voted against it, the majority being conservative republicans of course.

Other attempts by FDR to get people working again and provide everyone with a decent safety net in case someone loses a job or gets hurt were met with loads of success. These include the Works Progress Administration (WPA), the Civil Works Administration (CWA), the Farm Security Administration (FSA), and the National Industrial Recovery Act (NIRA) just to name a few. Unfortunately, some of these measures were ruled unconstitutional by a majority conservative court, where the majority of the justices were nominated by republican presidents. Of course, these justices were tied to big-money interests enough to block some of FDR's brilliant programs. It's all too funny that today, scholars and economists alike herald the Roosevelt administration for lowering the wealth gap, putting people back to work, and improving the economy while he did it. The republicans, now as then, label the New Deal as the raw deal and consider a socialist takeover of the government. Perhaps they feel this way because the rich and greedy corporations finally had to pay their fair share.

The wealth distribution further escalated when in 1935 Congress passed and FDR signed a new tax law that raised rates even more for those at the top of the income ladder. In 1936, taxes for the poor and middle class stayed the same, but now those who earned more than $1 million paid a tax rate of 77%. The highest bracket was for those who earned $5 million and they were taxed 79%.[481] This means that for an individual who makes $5 million, they still get to

---

[481] "Historical Federal Individual Income Tax Rates & Brackets, 1862-2021." 2021. Tax Foundation. August 24, 2021. https://taxfoundation.org/data/all/federal/historical-income-tax-rates-brackets/.

take home $1,050,000, while at the same time helping the poverty stricken keep food on the table. And don't feel sorry for these people, if their net income was still $1 million this would equate to earning $23 million in 2023. This certainly isn't any excuse for a pity party.

The majority of economists, both right and left leaning will tell you that these policies helped the United States get out of the Great Depression and put more money in the hands of the working people. All of the sudden they had exposable income gains and could spend these on all sorts of goods, which, in turn, created more businesses and manufacturing plants, which created more jobs, which caused the economy to make a massive swing upwards. It was a win-win. Even the incredibly wealthy were better off. Yes, they had to spend more in taxes, but their businesses and investments were thriving in this period of economic growth.

Taxes remained this high all the way through the 1930s and even went higher during the midst of World War Two. Obviously, because America was battling on two different fronts, money was quite literally flying out of the hands of the government. So, extra revenue needed to be accumulated. Believing that the rich could help deliver us lots of money fast, more tax laws were passed that created shocking tax rates for the extremely rich. Now, I mind you that taxes at this period were higher for every single bracket, even those desperately poor, however, the government did tax the wealthy an exorbitant amount, and quite frankly, if it didn't we very well could have lost the war. Taxes on the highest bracket in 1942 was for those who made an income anywhere greater than $200,000, the tax rate was 94%. The wealthy at this time did not bother with the high income taxes, they thought of it as their duty to the country. The country needed them and they were going to help fund the war, and they did it with courage and optimism. After the war taxes trickled down a hair, but the incredibly wealthy were still asked to pay their fair share, with the top tax bracket consistently paying a tax rate of 91% or 92% until 1964.[482] And throughout all of this time we had democratic presidents and republican presidents that all kept the income taxes the same. Nobody would accuse General, and president, Eisenhower of being a socialist with these tax rates. But again, the economy was surging, the vast majority of Americans were employed with good paying jobs and the income inequality was virtually never discussed.

In fact, in 1964, due to tax cuts that were proposed by JFK and carried out by Lydon Johnson, the richest Americans were taxed at a rate of 77% and down to 70% the very next year. All of this when the United States was at war in Vietnam. These tax rates held steady until 1982, when president Raegan, riding the wave of ultra conservatism by riding on the backs of the Christian conservative crusade, drastically lowered taxes with the belief that this would spur economic growth in a period of inflation and high oil prices that had more to do with OPEC nations than it did with the US's taxing policies. Do you remember how many tax brackets we had in the 1930s and 40s? Some 55 brackets. Now, in the year 1987, thanks to Raegan's massive tax cuts we had a massive reduction in the number of tax brackets, going all the way down to 5.

Believe it or not the tax cuts actually taxed the poor more, as the tax rate for the lowest bracket was 14% just the year before, now the lowest tax group had a tax rate of 15%. What an injustice! When you make a tax cut, shouldn't that tax cut be universal so that it helps everybody, not just the ultra rich? Of course, this was all by design, the poor and working classes were overwhelmingly democratic while the richer folk tended to be staunch republicans.

---

482 Ibid

So, in a way Raegan was just rewarding his rich followers who helped elevate him to his office. Nevertheless, the tax rate for middle income folks, who made more than $28,000 was 28%, most working class people fell in this category. The highest bracket was for those who made more than $90,000, who paid a tax rate of 38%. That's it. That's the new tax brackets. In the past, there were brackets that progressively taxed those that had extraordinary wealth. Now, that tax system is broken, and we got Raegan's tax cuts instead. Essentially what this did is created a system for the ultra-rich to pay as little in taxes as possible. Hardly fair at all for the working class who labor long and hard for what they earn.

The whole idea of this economic philosophy is something called trickle-down economics. Trickle-down economics essentially means that when the wealthy have an ungodly amount of money then eventually they will spend it in the economy and maybe create some jobs. So, in the long-term it was believed that this money would trickle down from the immensely rich to reach the middle class and then the working class eventually. The problem is this idea never works. It was attempted in the 1920s when the republicans controlled the government and had very small tax rates for the incredibly wealthy at a time of economic boom, with the belief that the rich would give back to the poor. Well, that never happened and what we got instead is the Great Depression. Indeed, "The money was all appropriated for the top in the hopes that it would trickle down to the needy. Mr. Hoover was an engineer," wrote humorist Will Rogers, "he knew that water trickles down. Put it uphill and let it go and it will reach the driest little spot. But he didn't know that money trickled up. Give it to the people at the bottom and the people at the top will have it before night, anyhow. But it will at least have passed through the poor fellows' hands."[483] Lawmakers should have been paying attention to this fact, instead all they were paying attention to was the money fattening their own wallets.

Conservative and liberal economists agree that the economic philosophy of trickle down is all a sham, created by the wealthy to hold onto their vast sums of wealth and put a stranglehold on the working class. In fact, major reforms reducing taxes on the rich lead to higher income inequality," announced Julian Lindberg and David Hope of the London School of Economics and Political Science. "In contrast, such reforms (such as progressive taxation on the wealthy) do not have any significant effect on economic growth and unemployment."[484] There you have it folks, these are esteemed economists who denounce trickle down economics as increasing the wealth disparity in the country and leading to worsening economic strains of middle class Americans. Worse, they say that when we tax the wealthy their fair share we don't see any corresponding loss of jobs or decrease in economic stability, a direct contrast to what Reagan and hard-right republicans were preaching to the public when they shoved these tax cuts down our throats.

In 1980, the year that Raegan was elected president, CEOs did quite well. They held prestigious and grueling jobs and got paid significantly more, though not a gut-wrenching amount more. In that year CEOs made about 26 times more than their workers. Meaning if the average worker made $15,000 a year, then the CEO would make $390,000, that's the equivalent of about $1.5 million today. So, you can see that CEOs were doing fabulously well, but they weren't

---

[483] Srikanth, Anagha. 2020. "Huge New Study Shows Trickle-down Economics Makes Inequality Worse, Researchers Say." *The Hill*. https://thehill.com/changing-america/respect/poverty/530731-huge-new-study-shows-trickle-down-economics-makes-inequality/.

[484] Ibid

destroying the economy with the astounding wealth inequality that we would see. By the end of Raegan's presidency, thanks to his tax cuts, deregulations, and cut back in welfare programs, CEOs made 44 times what their average worker made.[485] That's a lot of growing inequality in only a few measly years.

Economist John Komlos cites "Reaganomics" with its tax cuts "which he says favored the rich by increasing their wealth and political clout. In tax year 1985, for example, he said the top 1 percent gained a $350,000 windfall," while leaving the middle class virtually forgotten about without any tax relief.[486] Even George H.W. Bush called out Reaganomics for what it was, calling it "voodoo economics." You know it means something when a very conservative oil guy like George H.W. Bush thinks that this kind of economic plan is dangerous.

When it was all said and done the republicans, and some democrats, under Raegan destroyed the middle class, and made life unbearable for the poor. Unfortunately, his economic plan is still being used in the US and countless republicans believe Raegan to be their hero. This is a sticky situation. We have proof that trickle down economics doesn't work. We have proof that trickle down economics hurts everybody but the richest few. And we have proof that trickle down economics only increases the wealth inequality and income disparities. This only leads to economic ruin as we have seen during the roaring 20s which led to the Great Depression. Reagan supporters will claim that the economy rebounded during

---

485 Bivens, Josh, and Jori Kandra. 2022. "CEO Pay Has Skyrocketed 1,460% since 1978: CEOs Were Paid 399 Times as Much as a Typical Worker in 2021." Economic Policy Institute. Economic Policy Institute. October 4, 2022. https://www.epi.org/publication/ceo-pay-in-2021/.
486 Hartsoe, Steve. 2019. "The Road to Trump Began with Reaganomics & the Loss of the Middle Class, Economist Says." Today.duke.edu. January 29, 2019. https://today.duke.edu/2019/01/road-trump-began-reaganomics-loss-middle-class-economist-says.

this period, however, a key reason is because oil prices went down due to the OPEC countries finally releasing more oil and reducing prices. This is the primary reason why republicans seem to think that trickle down economics is the most amazing thing since sliced bread.

Ever since Raegan's tax cuts the top bracket has never been over 39.6%, which is where it stood when Trump was elected into office. In the meantime, we had presidents who have slightly raised and drastically lowered the tax rate for those at the top. Believe it or not, George H.W.Bush actually raised taxes after promising "read my lips no new taxes" because the government was desperately short of funds and Bush needed to do something. Instead of completely gutting social programs that ordinary Americans rely on every day he took the high road and raised taxes on the fabulously wealthy, though only slightly. Bill Clinton raised taxes on the top bracket to reach 39.6% only to have the rate reduced to 35% when George Bush became president. Barack Obama then increased taxes to the level of president Clinton, and then all hell broke loose with Trump, who just like George W Bush before him wanted to pander to his wealthy campaign contributors and pass an even bigger tax cut for the super wealthy.

One thing is quite interesting in the taxing process, that seems to go back and forth like a ping-pong. With the exception of George H.W. Bush every republican president has sought to lower taxes on the well-off, while the democrats want the wealthy to pay their fair share and have raised taxes, though only slightly. When Trump was elected, with a republican majority in both houses of Congress, he promised to lower the tax rate for the uppermost brackets. On paper, the tax cut doesn't look horrendous. However, in reality it was another story. The key component here is that the super rich would get at least a 2% reduction on taxes. This bracket would now fall for those who make $600,000 or more and they would have to pay 37% in taxes. Meanwhile, the poor and middle class hardly saw anything to gain from these huge tax cuts. Imagine somebody like Lebron James, an exceptional athlete, though he makes nearly $48 million each year. First off it would take the average American to work for 800 years to make what Lebron James makes in 1 year. That's outrageous. That means that cops, teachers, firefighters, and the like who serve our communities so well and sacrifice so much would have to work 800 years to make what somebody playing a sport that kids have to pay to play in school for a living. That to me is insane. But, anyways, take James' salary of $48 million. If he is taxed at a rate of 37% he still gets to take home $30,250,000. Compare that to a teacher who makes $55,000 a year and is taxed at 22%, they take home $43,000. Lebron James still makes roughly 710 times more than that teacher. Does he deserve it 710 times more? Does that sound like a fair tax code to you? So much for progressive taxation.

Let's dig in a little bit more though. At a re-election rally in Montana, Trump claimed that "Republicans passed the biggest tax cuts in American history, the biggest in American history. Everybody in this room is better for them. Everybody is better for them."[487] Obviously he knew how to fool these people, who gave him a rousing applause after the lie of a line. Not only did the disastrous tax cuts increase the federal deficit by almost $800 billion but it also leaves out the middle class and poor, who might see temporary relief but will lead to disaster in the long run.

Republicans love to lambast the democrats for "running up the deficit" with social programs that include social security, medicaid,

---

[487]"The Middle Class Needs a Tax Cut: Trump Didn't Give It to Them." n.d. Brookings. https://www.brookings.edu/articles/the-middle-class-needs-a-tax-cut-trump-didnt-give-it-to-them/.

WIC, food stamps, and safety net programs that people rely on. However, it's incredibly ironic that these same republicans, who are so called "budget hawks" would run up the deficit so much, and have the gall to talk about cutting government programs like social security and medicare to provide more tax breaks for the rich and powerful. According to the "Congressional Budget Office (CBO), extending the Trump tax cuts would add $3.5 trillion to the deficit through 2033."[488] That's a pretty big deficit because we gave the wealthy an extensive tax cut, one that they don't need. Just think what we could do with $3.5 trillion instead. Maybe we could actually reduce homelessness in our country, or ensure that every kid has a decent education. Instead the republicans wanted to give Lebron James another $5 million in tax cuts.(I have nothing against Lebron James by the way, I'm only using him as an example.) And they decided to do this when the richest Americans have seen the highest rise in income. According to the Brookings Institute "Incomes of the top 20 percent rose by 97 percent from 1979-2014—over twice as much as middle-class incomes."[489] So, the republicans bright idea was to lower taxes dramatically for those at the top at the same time that actual middle class earnings have remained stagnant since 1979, or roughly since Raegan and his tax cuts took effect.

By the year 2027, these tax cuts will hit the poor especially hard. The percent change after tax has the poorest Americans losing 1% of their income, while the middle class lose 0.3%. The highest earning income will gain 0.4%, the top 5% of incomes will get a positive change of 1%, and the top 0.1% of incomes will get an increase of

---

488 "Extending Trump Tax Cuts Would Add $3.5 Trillion to the Deficit, according to CBO | U.S. Senate Committee on the Budget." 2023. Www.budget.senate.gov. May 16, 2023. https://www.budget.senate.gov/chairman/newsroom/press/extending-trump-tax-cuts-would-add-35-trillion-to-the-deficit-according-to-cbo.
489 "The Middle Class Needs a Tax Cut: Trump Didn't Give It to Them." n.d. Brookings. https://www.brookings.edu/articles/the-middle-class-needs-a-tax-cut-trump-didnt-give-it-to-them/.

1.4% to their incomes.[490] On paper that might not seem like a lot, but it does significantly matter. The poor, who already struggle to scrape up what they can now will be worse off and Elon Musk will be made richer.

Take a two-person family that makes $35,000 a year. They will lose about $350 dollars every year due to the new tax structure. A middle class family will lose roughly $400 a year. While Lebron James' income will roughly be worth $4 million more per year. That's insane.

Income taxes were not the only categories that saw a massive cut. Corporate taxes took a huge tumble as well, as it was at 35% and was dropped to 21% in the belief that this would spur economic growth and create jobs. However, economists both liberal and conservative say that these tax cuts have not spurred the kind of economic surge that was predicted and sighted more companies taking their new revenue from the tax cuts not by investing in new areas or creating jobs but by providing kickbacks to their investors, who are overwhelmingly of the richer classes.

According to Oxfam International, we need to abandon the idea of trickle down economics and develop a progressive form of taxation. "Billionaires have seen extraordinary increases in their wealth. During the pandemic and cost-of-living crisis years since 2020, $26 trillion (63 percent) of all new wealth was captured by the richest 1 percent, while $16 trillion (37 percent) went to the rest of the world put together. A billionaire gained roughly $1.7 million for every $1 of new global wealth earned by a person in the bottom 90 percent. Billionaire fortunes have increased by $2.7 billion a day. This comes on top of a decade of historic gains —the number and

---

490 Ibid

wealth of billionaires having doubled over the last ten years."[491] And yet, we pass more tax cuts for the wealthy, it doesn't make sense. (It should also be noted that during the period of Trump's tax cuts, not a single democrat supported them. They were all passed thanks to the support of republicans.)

The Center on Budgets and Policy Priorities has this to say about Trump's tax cuts, "Like the Bush tax cuts, the tax cuts enacted in 2017 under President Trump benefited high-income households far more than households with low and moderate incomes. The 2017 tax law will boost the after-tax incomes of households in the top 1 percent by 2.9 percent in 2025, roughly three times the 0.9 percent gain for households in the bottom 60 percent, TPC estimates. The tax cuts that year will average $54,220 for the top 1 percent — and $220,310 for the top one-tenth of 1 percent. The 2017 tax law also widens racial disparities in after-tax income."[492] On average the top 1/10th of 1% receives a $220,310 tax break thanks to Trump. What do you think they're going to do with that money? Buy another house? Of course, the tax breaks also significantly hurt the racial income gap as well, but that's for a later time. I have written extensively about a lot of numbers and calculations, please pardon me for this. My point here is simply to show you that we can make all of these assertions and allegations like the "Trump tax cuts will hurt working class Americans." But, I wanted to show you as well

---

[491] Oxfam. 2023. "Richest 1% Bag Nearly Twice as Much Wealth as the Rest of the World Put Together over the Past Two Years." Oxfam International. January 16, 2023. https://www.oxfam.org/en/press-releases/richest-1-bag-nearly-twice-much-wealth-rest-world-put-together-over-past-two-years#:~:text=The%20report%20shows%20that%20while.

[492] After Decades of Costly, Regressive, and Ineffective Tax Cuts, a New Course Is Needed: Testimony of Samantha Jacoby, Senior Tax Legal Analyst, Center on Budget and Policy Priorities, Before the Senate Committee on the Budget, May 17th, 2023

the calculations that prove this point. And here is where I will leave all of these numbers and taxing policies.

I will only say that these tax cuts have proven disastrous for the wealth and income inequality that we see today. The inequality is only getting worse and worse with every passing year. Today, CEOs make well over 400 times more than their average worker. And these numbers seem to suggest the highest jumps when there is a relaxation in our taxing policies. Do CEOs work 400 more or harder than the average worker? No, I think not. But the problem is we are letting them walk away with all of this money and this is doing a detriment to our overall economy. Imagine if the Walton family, who owns Walmart and is worth about $240 billion, gave each of their workers $20 an hour. That's not unreasonable and they would certainly have enough money themselves to live on. Instead, our laws make it very clear to CEOs and business owners that they can take all that they want at the expense of their workers. Is that what capitalism is about? I think at this time the rich don't need a tax break, they are already doing phenomenally well. We should instead be focusing on those who actually need the help. But, whenever democrats propose for the rich to pay their fair share in taxes to help shoulder the burden the republicans cry out that they are "socialist", that they "want the government to take over our lives", and that they "support the biggest tax increase in American history." All of which are meant to scare the typical voter into voting with the republicans, all of these are lies.

The cold hard fact is that ever since the Great Depression, leading up to the time of Raegan, we have had a progressive tax structure. The rich were taxed according to what they could pay and we had general economic prosperity. We had a low level of wealth inequality.

And we had the middle class actually increasing in wages. Today, because of the massive tax cuts, we have more inequality. We have more poverty. And the middle class has been stuck in a conscious state of mediocrity.

Today, for the first time since the Great Depression we are seeing more people living paycheck to paycheck. We are seeing more people struggling to keep the lights on at home. We are seeing more people having a hard time putting food on the table for their families. We are seeing an increase in homelessness. And we are seeing levels of depression and economic instability at very high levels. In America we are the richest nation on earth. However, one who is visiting this great country might believe that we are an oligarchy at the same levels of Saudi Arabia and Yemen. We need to make sure that everybody in this country has what they need to survive. Enough is enough with pandering to the rich and powerful. It is time for our politicians to have the guts to take on these wealthy special interests, who by the way also spend millions of dollars in campaign contributions to the republican party. More than anything it is time that the American electorate get smart and elect candidates that stand up for the working and middle classes, not the top one percent.

Economists cite numerous reasons why we are seeing the level of wealth inequality like we are currently seeing, besides the obvious unfair taxing practices. One of the reasons, experts say, is the decline of unions all throughout America. In a report issued by the US Department of Treasury officials concluded that "Unions can improve the well-being of middle-class workers in ways that directly combat these negative trends (income inequality). Pro-union policy can make a real difference to middle-class households by raising their incomes, improving their work environments, and boosting their job satisfaction."[493] That's interesting. Essentially what they are saying is that unions increase worker wages. Actually, union members, on average, make around 25% more than their non-union counterparts.[494] Then, if that's the case, why the hell don't we see more unions? The cold hard truth is that unions have always been under attack by right-wing, conservative groups who liken unions to socialism. Do you see any trends here? You should by now. Everything that conservatives historically have disagreed with they call socialist to scare the voters. Again from the Treasury Department "Union membership peaked in the 1950s at one-third of the workforce. At that time, despite pervasive racial and gender discrimination, overall income inequality was close to its lowest level since its peak before the Great Depression, and was continuing to fall. Over the subsequent decades, union membership steadily declined, while income inequality began to steadily rise after a trough in the 1970s. In 2022, union membership plateaued at 10 percent" where it currently sits.[495]

We have seen in recent days efforts made by republican controlled states all over the country to strike unions down once and for all. One of the laws that has been proposed over and over again is the so-called right to work laws. A right to work law is actually the last thing that workers need, despite the name. The law is designed particularly to weaken unions by weakening union membership. The

---

493 Feiveson, Laura. 2023. "Labor Unions and the U.S. Economy." U.S. Department of the Treasury. October 26, 2023. https://home.treasury.gov/news/featured-stories/labor-unions-and-the-us-economy#:~:text=Unions%20can%20improve%20the%20well.

494 Siripurapu, Anshu. 2022. "The U.S. Inequality Debate." Council on Foreign Relations. Council on Foreign Relations. April 20, 2022. https://www.cfr.org/backgrounder/us-inequality-debate.

495 Ibid

law grants workers to enter into a job without paying union dues if that employer is unionized. This means that to those workers who just don't give a damn, they don't automatically pay union dues, which deprives the union of members and desperately needed funds in order to negotiate better wages and working conditions. It's truly in every workers' benefit to pay union dues and have a union that's fighting for them. The law places a horrible handicap on those who diligently pay their union dues, as when the union negotiates better wages for the workers even those who haven't paid a damn nickel will get the benefits. The case here is who would pay union dues if they know somebody else is paying for them? That's completely unfair and it drains the unions' power.

A notorious right to work law that is often mentioned is the disastrous Wisconsin law. Wisconsin republicans rode the wave of the tea-partiers, who gained prominence largely because they lied about Barack Obama's healthcare plan. As a result, the republicans gained majorities in the Wisconsin senate, assembly, and governorship in the form of Scott Walker. Besides doing a lot of really crummy, and potentially unconstitutional things like gerrymandering Wisconins's districts so badly that they are now the most gerrymandered state, they also set about as quickly as possible to pass the right to work law. They ended up doing just this after flying the law through both houses, even after the democrats fled Wisconsin to prevent the senate from having a quorum. By refusing to listen to experts and have public debate, the republicans quite literally shoved the legislation down Wisconsinites' throats. This prompted weeks-long protests in the Wisconsin state capitol from liberals, union members, and average workers alike, who knew that this law would be catastrophic for the working population. Shouts of "hey hey, ho ho, Scott Walker has got to go" could be heard in every direction in Wisconsin. After all the fiasco, Walker was put up in a recall election, the first ever recall election for a Wisconsin governor, as ordinary workers left and right signed the petition to give Walker the boot for turning his back on them.

All this time Walker received heavy support from millionaires and billionaires, the same people who would benefit tremendously from this action. In his 2010 and recall election the Koch brothers spent hundreds of millions of dollars through third-party organizations to hide their influence to help Walker win.[496] The whole truth of the slimy, rushed, effort to destroy Wisconsin's unions was caught on tape in one of the most politically embarrassing moments of all time.

Walker was so excited when he received what he thought was a phone call from David Koch, one of the brothers that funded all of his campaigns. But, in reality it turned out to be a blogger impersonator pretending to be Koch. The conversation ended up being longer than 20 minutes. Though the comments that Walker made were not career ending by any means, it still brought political turmoil as Walker mentioned that he almost sent out some "distubers" to trouble the protesters. Walker also made news with his comments "for layoff notices and the various strategies" he considered to "punish Democratic lawmakers who have fled the state in protest of his budget proposal.[497] So, we have here instigating trouble and punishing political opponents from a state governor. Isn't that just wonderful.

---

[496] "The Koch Brothers and Scott Walker Go Way Back." n.d. NBC News. https://www.nbcnews.com/meet-the-press/kochs-scott-walker-unknown-future-storied-past-n345806.
[497] Madison, Lucy. 2011. "Wis. Gov. Scott Walker Pranked by Journalist Posing as David Koch - CBS News." Www.cbsnews.com. February 23, 2011. https://www.cbsnews.com/news/wis-gov-scott-walker-pranked-by-journalist-posing-as-david-koch/.

Besides a governor being totally embarrassed by a social media personality, the right to work law proved to be even worse, but not for the governor who received tons of money from his wealthy friends, but for Wisconsinites all across the board. Frank Manzo IV, an economist, noted that the right to work law that Wisconsin passed actually hurt the overall economy, as it does in any and all right to work states. In fact, "Those 'right-to-work' states see slower economic growth, lower wages, higher consumer debt levels, worse health outcomes and lower levels of civic participation."[498] The lower levels of civic participation can be due to the overall hopelessness in the political process from working class individuals. They see bickering and fighting by both parties resulting in worsening conditions for them. It's a lose-lose situation.

The right to work law hurt working class Wisconsinites and the economy as a whole. Democrats across Wisconsin labored hard, but to no avail, to block the bill and then repeal the bill once it passed the republican legislature. When, in 2018, Tony Evers, a democrat, defeated Scott Walker in the governor's match, the Wisconsin Manufacturers and Commerce, a right-wing business group, and other conservatives groups fought hard to prevent governor Evers from repealing the law, something Evers pledged to do. Conservatives call any attempt at repealing the right to work law as an "attack on worker freedom."[499] They conveniently ignore the fact that the right to work laws are literally destroying the middle and working class.

It should also be mentioned, just as a quick note, that the Wisconsin republicans did much more to harm the working community besides destroying the unions. They also repealed Wisconsin's

---

498 "Workers Lost Ground on Wages in Wake of Wisconsin's Anti-Labor Laws." n.d. PBS Wisconsin. https://pbswisconsin.org/news-item/workers-lost-ground-on-wages-in-wake-of-wisconsins-anti-labor-laws/.
499 ibid

prevailing wage law that since the 1930s had required a wage floor for workers on state-funded capital projects.[500] Instead of having a formula, which favored workers, when determining worker wages, the republicans were intent on letting economic factors play a role in how construction workers were paid. However, since the repeal of the law, construction workers' salaries have declined 5.5% in Wisconsin. Over that same course of time, construction company executives' salaries rose by $111 million, and that's just in Wisconsin.[501] There is no hiding it. After republican meddling the richer got much richer while the working class suffered. That's what happens when you pass these laws that make no sense and don't help the average person at all.

In all, 27 states currently have a right to work law on the books. All of the states that have a right to work law in effect are either republican dominated or are significant swing states, such as Wisconsin and Virginia. Do you remember earlier when we looked at the states with the highest poverty levels? We noticed that the states with the highest poverty levels happened to be in the South. Well, every southern state, going all the way up to West Virginia, has a right to work law. This might help explain why this region is still bogged down with incessant poverty. The unions in the region are virtually non-existent, which means that the average worker in these states is getting the raw end of the deal. On a national stage republican lawmakers have really taken a liking to the right to work laws. According to the Guardian "Nearly all Republican lawmakers in Congress oppose proposals that would make it easier to unionize. One hundred and eleven Republican House members and 21 senators are co-sponsoring a bill that would weaken unions

---

500 Ibid
501 ibid

by letting workers in all 50 states opt out of paying any fees to the unions that represent them."[502]

The statistics are overwhelming. Economists largely point out that the period with the greatest economic prosperity for middle class Americans and the least levels of wealth inequality was the mid 1950s when the richest were fairly taxed, with the highest income bracket taxed 91%, and the highest level of unionized workers. Ever since, republicans have been attacking these crucial economic stabilizers. We have seen more income inequality and the middle class has been left behind. In the early 1980s more than 20% of workers belonged to a strong union. That was before Raegan ushered in a new republican dream bent on crushing unions, which he did by threatening to fire striking workers. Now, sadly, only about 6% of workers belong to unions.[503] Economists point out that even if workers don't belong to unions, they still see economic impacts of unions because unions help raise the wages of entire sectors. So, even if you're not in a union you should still support them because you could benefit from having them around fighting for better wages, benefits, and workplace safety measures. The decline in unions has also hit minority Americans particularly hard as they are much more likely to unionize than other demographics.

Thankfully, president Biden has understood that unions built the middle class and helped usher in economic prosperity for millions. President Biden was the first American president to actually join

---

502 Greenhouse, Steven. 2022. "Republicans Want Working-Class Voters — without Actually Supporting Workers." The Guardian. October 25, 2022. https://www.theguardian.com/us-news/2022/oct/25/republicans-working-class-voter-unions-worker-protections-organize.
503 Siripurapu, Anshu. 2022. "The U.S. Inequality Debate." Council on Foreign Relations. Council on Foreign Relations. April 20, 2022. https://www.cfr.org/backgrounder/us-inequality-debate.

strikers out on the picket line. That's a major symbolic step signaling that Biden has got the backs of American workers, something conspicuously missing in the Trump years. And the numbers suggest that president Biden is not the only one who is supporting the unions. Roughly 72% of the American electorate support the writers strike in Hollywood, which signifies that unions gather support from all across the country. Even better, roughly 75% of Americans supported the union's strike against the three leading auto manufacturers that were raking in huge profits while offering their employees low wages. In fact, accounting for inflation, automobile workers' wages have actually gone down 30% in the last 50 years. All told, 61% of Americans think unions help the economy rather than hurt it. And unions across the board see support from 67% of the electorate.[504] That's pretty good news for union advocates. But, why do we still see union membership dwindling? Mostly because republicans have announced and waged a full on war with the unions. And with Joe Biden supposedly "the most pro-union president" why is there still a disconnect? Part of it stems from Barack Obama and Bill Clinton who, while democrats, still walked a tight line and pandered to the likes of conservatives. Even though Joe Biden is much more progressive than either of these two former presidents, the public wants to see more action taken to preserve and protect the unions.

The Nation reports "Labor law reforms that would make it easier to organize, collectively bargain, and win contracts are stalled in Congress (especially since the House is now in Republican hands), (and) corporations such as Starbucks and Amazon continue to block mass movements for unionization" often with the support

---

[504] Nichols, John. 2023. "Most Pro-Labor President in History? Joe Biden's Not There Yet." Www.thenation.com. September 4, 2023. https://www.thenation.com/article/politics/labor-president-joe-biden/.

of conservatives who back these companies in the midst of labor fights.[505] As a matter of fact, when Bernie Sanders chaired a committee regarding how Starbucks suppressed the organization of labor unions republicans on the committee often decried the hearing calling it a sham and that Starbucks is well justified in their attempts to block unions. And to all of the Starbucks and Apple workers, poor and middle class Americans, and college grads who attempt to join a union, these republicans label them as "woke, leftwing and obsolete."[506]

As of September 2023 there has been a mounting campaign to boycott Starbucks over their union-busting tactics.

The Pro-Act, which was designed to make it easier for workers to join unions was passed in the House thanks to democratic support, but received 205 negative votes, all from republicans. Even sadder, the senate had no chance of passing the act because the senate still operates with a draconian rule that essentially requires a supermajority vote of 60 out of 100 for any significant bill to pass instead of a simple majority. If passed the law would negate all of the right to work laws in the 27 states. Obviously, you don't need me to tell you how much the republicans fought against this bill. Right from the beginning Virginia Foxx, a big-wig republican described democrats as being in "the pocket of Big Labor," forgetting the fact that republicans are in the pockets of big business. And instead of looking at all the benefits of unions and what they do for the economy, Foxx went even further, "Unions are hitting the panic button and praying that Democrats can gin up a PR campaign to cover up the

---

505 Ibid
506 Greenhouse, Steven. 2022. "Republicans Want Working-Class Voters — without Actually Supporting Workers." The Guardian. October 25, 2022. https://www.theguardian.com/us-news/2022/oct/25/republicans-working-class-voter-unions-worker-protections-organize.

declining numbers and lack of interest in union membership."[507] Obviously, they will only tell what they want to while leaving out critically important information.

Things under Trump weren't very peachy for unions either. Trump never walked the picket lines or showed any kind of support for organized labor in the slightest. Yet, he tries to make pitches to labor unions that he is their candidate and that they should support him. He never once uttered a kind word about a union or supported them in any of their fights for fair wages. Instead, Trump has been the architect of several pieces of legislation that hurt the working class like the massive tax cuts that went to his wealthy friends. It's incredibly telling when Shawn Fain, the UAW president put Trump in his place when he said that a second Trump term would be a "disaster" for workers.[508] And AFL-CIO president Liz Shuler had this to say about Trump:

"The idea that Donald Trump has ever, or will ever, care about working people is demonstrably false. For his entire time as president, he actively sought to roll back worker protections, wages and the right to join a union at every level. UAW members are on the picket line fighting for fair wages and against the very corporate greed that Donald Trump represents. Working people see through his transparent efforts to reinvent history. We are not buying the lies that Donald Trump is selling. We will continue to support and organize for the causes and candidates that represent our values."[509]

The AFL-CIO has listed a number of grievances under the Trump

---

507 Ibid
508 Goldman, David. 2023. "UAW President Has Some Harsh Words for Trump | CNN Politics." CNN. September 19, 2023. https://www.cnn.com/2023/09/19/politics/fain-trump-detroit/index.html#:~:text=In%20a%20letter%20sent%20to.
509 "Donald Trump's Catastrophic and Devastating Anti-Labor Track Record | AFL-CIO." 2023. Aflcio.org. September 27, 2023. https://aflcio.org/press/releases/donald-trumps-catastrophic-and-devastating-anti-labor-track-record.

administration like waging "an assault on the economic rights of federal workers, repeatedly undermining their voice on the job." Stacking "the National Labor Relations Board with union-busting corporate lawyers, denying working people our right to organize through a fair process." Defending a "right to work in a brief to the U.S. Supreme Court in the case of Janus v. AFSCME Council 31." And "Trying to rip off tipped workers by implementing a proposal that would probably result in servers doing more nontipped work and at a lower pay rate than previously required."[510] And that's just to name a few of the anti-worker positions of the Trump administration. How then can he have the guts to ask working people for their vote? That's ludicrous and he knows it.

Thankfully, we need not despair as president Biden has shown that he has the leadership to support unions and the working people. "The infrastructure bill, one of the major achievements of his (Biden's) presidency so far, includes robust pro-labor language and requirements, as do many other pieces of legislation. The president has issued important executive orders, including one mandating project labor agreements on major federal construction projects. And appointments aimed at cleaning up the mess that former president Donald Trump made of the National Labor Relations Board, which have made it easier for unions to overcome employer intimidation and illegal firings during organizing drives and struggles to secure first contracts."[511] Obviously, there are many things to be proud of in the Biden administration including its efforts to increase union power and membership. To the contrary republicans still have a grip on the electorate and they constantly push for union-busting and anti-union measures to deprive the people of an equal chance to make

---

510 Ibid
511 Ibid

a good salary. Remember even republican president Eisenhower said this during his years in office "Only a handful of unreconstructed reactionaries harbor the ugly thought of breaking unions. Only a fool would try to deprive working men and women of the right to join the union of their choice."[512] Perhaps republicans should listen to these words of wisdom from an American hero. Clearly, Eisenhower understood, times were much better during his administration, before his party blew everything up. He understood that unions help build the middle class and provide more wealth in the pockets of the masses.

Another obvious and self explanatory way to increase wages is to pass a minimum wage increase. Today the federal minimum wage is $7.25. That's pitiful. The last minimum wage increase was all the way back in 2009. That's 15 years ago. That's equally pitiful. If we were to raise the minimum wage to keep pace with inflation from 2009 the new minimum wage would at least be $11. That's still pitiful but a lot better than $7.25.

History of the first minimum wage can be traced to Melbourne, Australia in 1896, to deal with the inadequate pay that women were plagued with working in the sweat-shops while their employers were making bank. During this time minimum wage laws were gaining steam in all of Europe and the United States. By 1923, 15 US states and the District of Columbia passed a minimum wage law. However, these laws were ruled unconstitutional by a business friendly, conservative, supreme court. So, in the meantime, throughout the 1920s and most of the 1930s poor laborers were being exploited by employers who took advantage of high unemployment to offer their workers substandard wages. It took until 1937, when Franklin Roosevelt finally put enough liberal justices

---

512 Ibid

in the court for the United States to pass a federal minimum wage law that wasn't overturned by the courts. Ever since then, workers had some sort of protection against greedy business owners and the like. The highest that the minimum wage has ever been, in terms of purchasing power, was in 1968, when the federal government raised the minimum wage to $1.60, the equivalent of $15 today. (It should be noted that this was accomplished by a democratic president and congress.)

This, however, does not mean that the minimum wage hasn't been challenged in some states and even federally by some republican lawmakers. Currently, all of the Southern states with the exception of Arkansas, Florida, Virginia, and Missouri have a minimum wage of $7.25. This includes states with incredibly high poverty rates like Mississippi, Alabama, Louisiana, Kentucky, Tennessee, Texas, South Carolina, and Oklahoma, just to name a few. Curiously, the states with the lowest levels of poverty have some of the highest minimum wage laws. Vermont has a minimum wage of $13.18. Massachusetts has a minimum wage of $15. Washington has a minimum wage of $15.74. Connecticut has a minimum wage of $15. Does anybody put two and two together to realize these trends? The fact is that most of the states with the highest poverty still have the lowest minimum wages, while the lowest poverty states have the highest minimum wages. That's a coinkydink.

When president Biden was inaugurated, one of the first things on his agenda was to raise the minimum wage to $15 an hour. And why not? Workers haven't seen any significant increase in wages in over 40 years and the vast majority of Americans support raising the minimum wage to at least $15 an hour, according to polls.[513]

---

513 McGahey, Richard. n.d. "Republicans in Washington Block Biden's Vital Minimum Wage Increase." Forbes. Accessed May 21, 2024. https://www.forbes.com/sites/richardmcgahey/2021/02/27/republicans-in-washington-block-bidens-vital-minimum-wage-increase/?sh=ed45b58f72c9.

However, this dream was not to be as in order for it to pass the senate would have to overcome that pesky filibuster, where they need to have at least 60 votes. With having 50 republican senators at the time this was proven to be an impossible task. Every single senate republican voted against the proposal as well as a handful of senate democrats, who are either incredibly old or are really conservative, including the thorn in Biden's side Joe Manchin. With the majority of Americans supporting a minimum wage increase, why have these senators not listened to the will of the people in continuing to block any increase? Again, many of these lawmakers receive huge contributions from big time businesses and companies. These businesses pressure our lawmakers into suppressing the wages of ordinary workers so that they don't have to spend an extra red cent in the pockets of their workers.

Around the time that this debate was being hashed out as to whether to raise the minimum wage to $15 an hour, a report suggested by the Congressional Budget Office (CBO) "analyzed the macroeconomic impact of the standard minimum wage reaching $15 per hour in 2027. The data reported 10.9 million workers would be directly affected, while an additional 9.2 million workers would potentially be affected. The total directly or potentially affected workers by 2032 would surpass 23 million."[514] That's a lot of people positively affected. And, I would also like to point out that when more people have more money that means that they will need less support from the government and be less reliant on poverty programs, i.e. welfare. Republicans often rant about how we need to get less people reliant on the government and become

---

514 Maverick, J.B. 2024. "What Are the Pros and Cons of Raising the Minimum Wage?" Investopedia. January 5, 2024. https://www.investopedia.com/articles/markets-economy/090516/what-are-pros-and-cons-raising-minimum-wage.asp.

more independent, well there's isn't a better way to do that than raise the minimum wage, which they are adamantly opposed to doing.

According to Cap 20 a $15 an hour minimum wage would have led "to an annual wage increase as large as $8,000 for some of the lowest-wage workers. A $15 minimum wage would also help reduce stubborn gender, racial, and ethnic wage gaps for women, Black, and Latino workers, who are overrepresented among those earning less than $15 per hour. Most notably, if a $15 minimum wage had been in place in 2021, Black women would have experienced the largest reduction in their pay gap on record."[515] What a great way to reduce wealth and income inequality while at the same time closing racial disparities in income. Cap 20 also mentions that one in four workers make less than $15 an hour. That, my friends, is pitiful. Think of all the people that are being left out on receiving a pay raise. The CBO predicts that raising the minimum wage would boost 1.3 million people out of poverty. How's that for tackling poverty?

Researchers have also come to the conclusion that an increase of $1 in the minimum wage could have saved approximately 27,000 from 1990 to 2015 from suicides, while an increase in $2 could have prevented 57,000 deaths.[516] These deaths could have been prevented especially from low-income communities and those without a college education, as this demographic tends to struggle more with day to day expenses. Research also suggests that raising the minimum wage would significantly reduce crime, especially in the south. Come on, this is a win-win solution.

Let's look at hypotheticals. If a worker in Mississippi made $7.25

---

515 Khattar, Rose, Sara Estep, and Lily Roberts. 2023. "Raising the Minimum Wage Would Be an Investment in Growing the Middle Class." Center for American Progress. July 20, 2023. https://www.americanprogress.org/article/raising-the-minimum-wage-would-be-an-investment-in-growing-the-middle-class/.
516 Dangor, Graison (January 8, 2020). "Raising the Minimum Wage by $1 May Prevent Thousands of Suicides, Study Shows". *NPR.org*

an hour, the current minimum wage there, and worked full time they would make roughly $15,080 a year, well below the poverty line. Think about all the government programs that they would be forced to be on to pay their bills and survive. That's insane. Most likely, these individuals would have to work 60-70 hours per week just to get by, something that no American should have to do. At a time when the Scandinavian countries are experimenting with a 32 hour workweek, should we have workers in the wealthiest country on earth working 70 hours? That's disgraceful.

If we raised the minimum wage to $15 an hour, that same worker would make about $31,500. Still not the greatest but it does provide some breathing room for them and their families. Even more progressives are fighting to push for a minimum wage of $17 an hour. This would produce a salary of about $35,360 per year. Under these conditions workers would not be forced to rely on the government for help.

One of the big cries from conservatives is that raising the minimum wage will increase inflation, thereby hurting everyone else. This is a completely bogus assumption. I think that if the Walton family had to take a couple bucks out of their massive fortune to pay their workers $15 an hour they could do so without raising the prices of their products. And if these same corporations and businesses have enough money to pay their CEOs millions, in some cases, billions of dollars every single year, then they can afford to pay their workers a decent salary while at the same time keeping prices low. We should never use this line of reasoning to deny raising the minimum wage, if we do we are just falling into the trap that these greedy CEOs and corporate executives are placing out hoping that we bite. If that's the case where inflation truly rises then we have an issue with capitalism. We would have an issue because these executives are raising prices just so that they can earn more money while fleecing the rest of the population.

Clearly, one of the biggest ways that we can reduce poverty in this country is to raise the minimum wage. When we do this, those with lower incomes will finally be able to boast a better salary and provide for their families, which, in turn, creates jobs and expands the economy. Why wouldn't we do this? A key reason is republican blockage of anything that has to do with the minimum wage. They blocked president Biden from increasing the minimum wage, though he successfully signed an executive order raising the minimum wage for government workers, and zero republicans have signaled any support whatsoever. Also, to all of the workers in Alabama, Mississippi, Louisiana, and other die-hard conservative southern states, if you don't elect some democrats to office then you will continue to see massive poverty, crime, and inequalities. Don't expect anything to change under republican leadership within your states. And here in America? Don't expect anything to change anytime soon if we keep electing republicans, who hobnob with greedy capitalists, not the everyday worker.

It's not a radical idea. Here are just a few countries with higher minimum wages than the US: Luxembourg, Netherlands, Belgium, UK, France, Japan, South Korea, New Zealand, Australia, New Caledonia, Denmark, Finland, Iceland, Italy, Norway, Singapore, Sweden, Switzerland and Canada.[517] Remember, these are just a few. There are many more, but do you notice a trend? All of these countries are developed countries. All of these countries have a lot of wealth. And all of these countries have significantly lower rates of wealth inequality.

---

517 Velocity Global. 2023. "Minimum Wage by Country in 2023: A Guide for Global Employers." Velocity Global. June 2, 2023. https://velocityglobal.com/resources/blog/minimum-wage-by-country/.

Poverty is so wide-spread in this country, even though we supposedly are the wealthiest country in the world, that we see chronic homelessness everywhere we go. In this country currently there are nearly 600,000 people sleeping on the streets in our country.[518] This is more than the entire population of Wyoming. What gives? Why are there so many homeless people on our streets? Believe it not, most of them are not migrants, these are US citizens that have been left behind by us.

I have had the pleasure of volunteering in numerous homeless shelters. It's not the prettiest or nicest place to stay. If anybody is truly ignorant enough to believe that the homeless choose to be homeless I encourage them to visit a homeless shelter, or better yet, stay in one for the night. In many shelters there are twenty to thirty cots in one room, or the same amount of beckbeds, making it nearly impossible to sleep and be energized for the next day. And, most shelters have rules, like the only way homeless people can stay at the shelter is if they have an active plan in place to get out, many of them need to have a job or have one lined up. Honestly, homeless shelters aren't fun, they are a necessity, that's why people go to them in the winter and that's why they are needed. Some municipalities and cities are actively scrambling to come up with a solution for the homeless problem. This even looks like coming up with a homeless style complex full of little mini homes, such as is being contemplated in California and other states with a high number of homeless individuals. That takes a lot of money to create these units of housing for the homeless. Imagine the amount of taxpayer dollars that are used to help pay for these projects. The numbers are staggering. Yet,

---

518 USAFacts Team. 2023. "How Many Homeless People Are in the US? What Does the Data Miss?" USAFacts. March 16, 2023. https://usafacts.org/articles/how-many-homeless-people-are-in-the-us-what-does-the-data-miss/.

when we ask the top one percent to pay a little bit more so that we can do something about this problem, republicans cry foul. Think of all the money this would save. Yet, alas, here we are.

Let's take a deeper look at some statistics. Pacific Islanders are the demographic most likely to become homeless, with some 121 homeless per 10,000. This is followed by blacks, 48 out of 10,000, and then Native Americans 44 out of 10,000. Whites and Asians are the least likely to experience homelessness. Minorities aren't the only demographic that experience homelessness at extreme rates. Veterans experience homelessness at a much higher level than the overall population. There are roughly 33,500 homeless veterans today.[519] If politicians cared enough about our homeless veterans they would do something about it. It is disgraceful that anybody who puts on a military uniform to defend this country should have to go through so many trials and hardships. We should take care of them, not leave them out on the streets. And why are there so many veterans who are homeless? Just like the vast majority of those who are homeless they have either fallen on hard times or are dealing with a severe substance abuse problem. You would think that our lawmakers would make it easier for our veterans to receive the healthcare that they need, but that's not currently happening, obviously we wouldn't have this homeless crisis to begin with.

The key finding within these studies is that the majority of the homeless population are within areas that lack affordable housing. Washington D.C for example has one of the highest homeless rates because housing that is somewhat affordable is just non-existent for those who are experiencing homelessness. Don't get me wrong, there are homeless people in every state, but at least this situation

---

519 Ibid

can be manageable. First, we can have a progressive tax code that levels the wealth inequality that we are seeing, but even easier we can invest in affordable housing so that we are not squeezing out a whole group of people who otherwise wouldn't be able to live anywhere. Another important project that we can accomplish, using extra revenues from a progressive form of taxation, we can invest in mental health services for all of our towns and cities so that our people's needs are met. As I've said before the majority of those in the homeless shelters struggle with addiction or other forms of mental health issues, which might explain why so many veterans are homeless (PTSD, depression, among other things.) When we invest in our community to make sure that everyone is getting the services they need, we can finally be on the upward trajectory to reduce mental health all across the country, which will then reduce the homeless population.

    The cruel reality is that mental health care can be incredibly hard to find, and it's even worse for people living in poverty. I once sought out a therapist for my own struggles with mental health, namely depression. My health insurance wouldn't cover the expenses for me seeking out mental health care, meaning that every week when I visited my therapist I would have to pay $100 out of my own pocket. Well, I'm not made out of money, so I decided I couldn't see him anymore. This is the reality with many all across the country, especially those who struggle to make ends meet. Many who live in poverty don't have access to good healthcare coverage, or none at all, which means that if they struggle with mental health all of the expenses from their treatment comes from their own pocket, something that poverty-stricken people cannot even begin to ponder. All of their income is going towards food, housing, childcare, they certainly don't have the money to care for themselves. This is why we need to make sure that healthcare insurance covers mental health and make sure that everybody has access to healthcare, not just the rich and powerful, which is why I support a healthcare for all solution to the nation's healthcare issues. This lack of healthcare undoubtedly leads more and more people to homelessness. It's not a radical idea if it helps get people off the streets. We should all be on board with this. Not only does a reduction in homelessness cause people to feel more safe in communities but it also raises property values, it's truly a win-win scenario.

When we think about poverty, a lot of us fail to realize that poverty affects us in so many different ways. One crucial area is the area of health. We just talked about how people with poverty often experience mental health issues and this can lead to homelessness, but what about other forms of health? Do people with poverty have better health than those that are fabulously wealthy? The answer is that people living in poverty often experience much worse health outcomes than those living luxurious lives, which can shock some people because we might view rich people as eating all the amazing food that they want, with their creme brulees and caviar, however, the rich often have greater access to healthier food options, something those living in poverty lack.

On average the richest American men live 15 years longer than the poorest men (87-72 years) and the richest American women live roughly 10 years longer than the poorest women (88-78 years).[520] The life expectancy for impoverished individuals is the lowest in Nevada, Indiana, Ohio, and Michigan, especially in Detroit where the poorest men live 6 years less than the poorest men in New York

---

520 "The Equality of Opportunity Project." n.d. Www.equality-of-Opportunity.org. http://www.equality-of-opportunity.org/health/#:~:text=Income%20in%20the%20United%20States.

City. Some of these statistics could have to do with racist policies and practices that the city or town enacted as well, such as poor water quality in Michigan, like in Flint, which is a predominantly black city. Studies have shown that the poor tend to live longer in bigger cities where there is a lot of government spending such as New York City and San Francisco, while areas that lack funding are the hardest hit.

The Brookings Institute got it exactly right when they said "There's nothing particularly mysterious about the life expectancy gap. People in ill health, who are at risk of dying relatively young, face limits on the kind and amount of work they can do. By contrast, the rich can afford to live in better and safer neighborhoods, can eat more nutritious diets and can obtain access to first-rate healthcare. People who have higher incomes, moreover, tend to have more schooling, which means they may also have better information about the benefits of exercise and good diet."[521] Because the wealthy have access to better areas and can afford to buy healthy foods such as fruits, vegetables, and dairy they can live much more healthy and balanced lives compared to those with limited incomes who can only buy what they can afford. Often these individuals buy junk food because it is cheaper and this doesn't give them the nutritional balanced diet they deserve. This makes their health worse as they have a higher likelihood of diabetes, cardiac issues, and various cancers eating processed foods as opposed to fresh foods. It is entirely true that at the same time we see rising income inequality we are seeing rising life expectancy inequality as well. In the last ten years the richest

---

521 Reeves, Richard V., and Simran Kalkat. 2016. "The Growing Life-Expectancy Gap between Rich and Poor." Brookings. February 22, 2016. https://www.brookings.edu/articles/the-growing-life-expectancy-gap-between-rich-and-poor/.

Americans have actually increased their life expectancy three years, while the poorest Americans have seen no gain whatsoever.

This also affects social security in more ways than you would think. If lawmakers don't figure out something to increase funding for social security or somehow keep it solvent it could run out of money by 2037. Democrats want to raise taxes on the wealthy to help offset the costs of social security. Many people don't realize that there is a cap on the amount of taxes that the wealthy have to pay on social security. Right now somebody earning $160,000 a year pays the exact same amount in social security taxes as somebody who makes $1 billion. Do you think that's fair? Just think if we taxed progressively on this issue. Not only would we be able to fund social security for generations to come, but we also would be able to lower the age to receive social security benefits. Republicans want to do the opposite. Instead of making the wealthy pay their fair share in taxes, they want to cut benefits and raise the minimum age to receive any benefits to 67, or even 70, years old. That is ridiculous and absurd to even fathom. Here we have poverty stricken Americans, who have been paying into the social security fund their whole lives only getting to receive the benefits for 5 years, on average, if this happens. Meanwhile, the incredibly wealthy, who already have lots of money and a sizable nest egg most likely don't care, they still get benefits on average for 20 more years before they die. You have to ask yourself, whose side do you think the republicans are on? Certainly not on the side of those with limited incomes. These republicans have got to get their priorities straight.

What's even more shocking is how many countries have a higher life expectancy than the 72 years that men experiencing poverty have. All told, 126 countries have a higher life expectancy than poor folks have in this country. Beating the US in this category are all the developed countries of the world, including the EU. Some other countries are just quite shocking: China, Argentina, Colombia, Lebanon, Jordan, Vietnam, Belize, Russia, North Korea, Honduras, El Salvador, Libya, Venezuela, Syria, Iraq, and India.[522] All of these countries have a higher life expectancy than those in poverty in America. I don't care what you say, that's embarrassing. We can and should do better.

We have an even more serious problem with the amount of food waste that Americans throw out every single year. Feeding America has claimed that currently 44 million Americans face hunger. Yet, each year Americans throw away 119 billion pounds of food, this equates to about 130 billion meals and $408 billion in wasted food.[523] The study included key reasons why the number is so high. Chief among them is that families throw away tons of uneaten food each year, with each member throwing away roughly 325 pounds of food each year.[524] Shockingly, another big reason why so much food is thrown away or not used is because farmers tend to leave their crops just sitting in the fields, not gathered, because of low crop prices or, believe it or not, too many of those crops on the market. That's insane. We should at least do something with these crops like pay the farmers to ship them to poverty stricken countries so that they have something to eat. Do you see the irony here? In this country

---

[522] Worldometer. 2023. "Life Expectancy by Country and in the World (2023)." Worldometers.info. 2023. https://www.worldometers.info/demographics/life-expectancy/.

[523] Feeding America. 2023. "Food Waste in America | Feeding America." Www.feedingamerica.org. 2023. https://www.feedingamerica.org/our-work/reduce-food-waste#:~:text=How%20much%20food%20waste%20is.

[524] Recycle Track Systems. n.d. "Food Waste in America in 2020: Statistics & Facts | RTS." Recycle Track Systems. https://www.rts.com/resources/guides/food-waste-america/#:~:text=That.

we throw food away because we have too much of it. While in other countries people are dying every day because they don't have enough of it. We can do something and should. Lastly, much food is thrown away because it's not meeting suppliers' standards with color and size.[525] That's ridiculous. This means that big industries will turn down perfectly good food just because it may look a little unappealing for consumers. You can see here that this is all about money, nothing else. They will only accept crops that give them the most return in profits. All of this together results in about 40% of the food raised and grown here in America to be wasted. (This is also completely unfair for animals who give their lives to be our food source, when much of it ends up being wasted.)

I've seen a grotesque amount of waste in my own life. Before I settled down with my current career I used to work at a hospital washing dishes. I was appalled at how much food I had to throw away. On any given night I probably threw away at least 75 chicken meals. That is such a huge waste, and I'm not saying we shouldn't feed our patients, but we need to be smart about our food.

So, what can we do about it? Well, for starters it begins and ends with us. We need to eat the food we buy or donate it to organizations or people who will eat that food and need it. We also shouldn't throw away food just because it's a couple days past its expiration date. This is just a warning that the food needs to be eaten soon, it doesn't mean the food will go bad on that day in particular. Another thing that we can do is pressure companies to put an end to the deliberate wasting of food that happens every single day just so that they can earn an extra couple of bucks. Moreover, the government needs to create a composting program that allows individuals to get

---

525 Feeding America. 2023. "Food Waste in America | Feeding America." Www.feedingamerica.org. 2023. https://www.feedingamerica.org/our-work/reduce-food-waste#:~:text=How%20much%20food%20waste%20is.

rid of food waste that can still be used by our environment in other ways. The government should also support farmers who produce a crop to be able to export it to needy countries who don't have as many resources as we do. Not only would this provide an adequate income for the farmers but it would improve the image of the US throughout the world as we would be leaders in humanitarian aid. We also need to make sure that everyone in this country has enough to eat. So many poor Americans are resorting to poor diets where they lack the nutrients they need to maintain a healthy diet, and many are resorting to unhealthy foods as the cheaper alternative. This means that we need to increase the amount that needy families get when it comes to food stamps. Currently, republicans want to reduce the amount that low-income people receive in the form of food stamps, they also want to eliminate or drastically cut food programs in school that give children a free breakfast, lunch, and in some cases dinner.

This idea is not radical. Sweden, Brazil, Finland, Estonia, some parts of the UK, and even Rwanda provide free lunch for their students. India has been serving up free lunch for their students since 1995 and it only costs the government about $2.8 billion a year to do this.[526] Now, in America this figure may be a little more expensive, but still this is a minor expenditure for the government to make. In contrast, the US spends approximately $900 billion on the defense budget every year. That's roughly 400 times more than what it would cost to give every kid a meal. I think that we can do that. That will reduce childhood hunger, which improves educational outcomes and provides a pathway out of poverty for these children.

Think about what would happen if we didn't give sports stars,

---

[526]"Which Countries Are Already Serving up School Food for All? | Sustain." n.d. Www.sustainweb.org. https://www.sustainweb.org/blogs/mar23-countries-have-universal-free-school-meals/.

celebrities, and music icons millions upon millions of dollars just for doing a job that many of us would pay to do. Just think about how many meals that $48 million would buy. An incredible amount, and yet this is just one year's worth of salary for Lebron James. And, right now Joe Burrow, Cincinnati Bengals quarterback, is the highest paid NFL player making $55 million a year. This is about $3.25 million per game. Given this, it would take a teacher about 56 years to make what Joe Burrow makes in three hours, this is assuming that all of the teacher's salary will go towards that $3.25 million, not on other expenses like food, housing, education, childcare, ect. Think about how much $55 million would help poverty stricken families, how many meals this would buy for hungry families. This is embarrassing and so many other important things can be done with this money. I'm sure that Joe Burrow is a decent guy, but I don't think he deserves to get paid 1100 times more than me just for playing football. That's ridiculous.

Finally, in this country we have horrific wealth gaps when it comes to race. On average, in 2020, whites made a median income of $80,000. (I use median because the mean can grossly overestimate how much a demographic makes because of people like Zuckerburg and Musk whose salaries would inflate the numbers. Using the median gives us a true sense of the statistics.) Hispanics averaged $58,000 a year, and blacks averaged $48,000 a year.[527] That means that in any given year, blacks make about $30,000 less than whites per person. That's alarming.

According to the Brookings Institute, an average white family

---

527 Peter G. Peterson Foundation. 2022. "Income and Wealth in the United States: An Overview of the Latest Data." Www.pgpf. org. November 9, 2022. https://www.pgpf.org/blog/2023/02/income-and-wealth-in-the-united-states-an-overview-of-recent-data.

has approximately $171,000 in net worth, this also accounts for debt, while the average black family has about $17,000 in net worth, roughly ten times less. I still hear people today talk about why we even talk about inequality or equity in terms of race anymore because now things are equal. These statistics prove that they couldn't be more wrong. How can we say that things are equal today if we still see these kinds of disparities?

The reason why we still see these levels of inequality is because of past racist policies and procedures that still haunt the black community today. Dating all the way back to the days of Jim Crow and the black codes were the racists that totally kept the blacks from achieving any prosperity and closed all areas of opportunity to them. In fact, right after slavery many southern laws were created to keep the newly free blacks into a condition similar to slavery, without any opportunity to own any of their own land. Without this opportunity it is virtually impossible to accumulate any real wealth. Even some staples of FDR's New Deal kept the blacks from achieving greatness, with limited access to the GI bill, Social Security, and Fair Labor Standards Act. Fast forward to not so long ago where redlining and other racist policies denied black communities from receiving much credit to own their own homes or businesses. These have all contributed, in their own ways, to the level of racial inequalities that we see today. This might explain why so many minority groups have a higher likelihood of experiencing homelessness, hunger, and poverty in general. It is the dream of every American to eventually, perhaps, own their own home, or at least have enough wealth to live comfortably. Sadly, this is not the case in America today when we see so much poverty and so little ways to get out of the poverty trap. We don't see that today when half of all Americans are living paycheck to paycheck. As I've already mentioned earlier in the chapter, three individuals hold more wealth than half of all Americans, that, my friends, needs to change in order for us to take on poverty and wealth and income inequality.

Lastly, I want to close this chapter by looking at the poverty of other countries. Yes, we should look after ourselves first before we help anybody else, meaning we should help impoverished families here in America before looking abroad. But, I just want to point out that we have enough wealth and materials and food for every single person in the world if only we tried to reach everyone and had equitable policies. Economists look at a key demographic when concluding studies. They often look at those who are in extreme poverty, where they make less than $2.15 a day. 8.4% of the world's population fit that category before the pandemic. Now, it is 9.3% of the population.[528] Think about this for a second. That is almost one out of every ten people who are living below $2.15 a day. How could they afford anything? We often complain here, and some of those complaints are genuine problems, but have any of us here tried to live on $2.15 a day? Probably not. We have hunger here in America, just imagine what it's like in some of the most impoverished regions of the world. This is most felt in Africa where some estimates show that roughly 38% of all Africans fall below the extreme poverty line.

The reason why I mention this is because I think it's sick that somebody like Elon Musk can literally make upwards of $25 billion a year, while there are so many people literally starving in the world. I think it's sick that Elon Musk makes roughly $600 a second.[529] It would take someone living in extreme poverty to work a whole year

---

528 "Overview." n.d. World Bank. https://www.worldbank.org/en/topic/poverty/overview#:~:text=The%20global%20extreme%20poverty%20rate.
529 Muroki, Denis. 2023. "This Is How Much Elon Musk Makes Every Year, Day, Hour, and Second." History-Computer. April 12, 2023. https://history-computer.com/how-much-elon-musk-makes/.

to make the money that Elon Musk makes in one second. Think about that? How can anybody say that the way our economic systems are running is just fine and dandy?

Tonight roughly 830 million people will go to bed extremely famished. Elon Musk's wealth alone could feed all of these people many times over. Just one man can literally feed the world with all of his wealth. Thanks to COVID and the Ukrainian war things are a lot worse. Almost ⅕th of the entire population now face food insecurity because of the conflicts in Ukraine and Israel. We need to think about our roles more in defining how we will help. Will we just sit by and do nothing while almost ⅕th of the world's population is starving? Will we just keep giving huge rewards to the richest of the rich because they control the world?

Nothing that I proposed is radical. Cutting food waste certainly isn't radical. Eliminating poverty here in the US and abroad shouldn't be radical. Lowering the wealth gap shouldn't be radical. Raising taxes on the wealthy certainly can't be defined as radical. If conservatives claim that it is, we have ample evidence how America was radical then when it taxed the richest few 70%, and during the 1950s 90%. How can we consider it radical when so many other countries have higher tax rates than the US and are currently doing much better in terms of economic power? The US has a total tax revenue of about 24.3% in GDP. Compared to other countries we are about right in the middle of the world in tax rates, even though we have some of the richest people on earth. Here are a few countries that have a higher tax rate than the US: France, Denmark, Belgium, Sweden, FInland, Luxembourg, Norway, Netherlands, Germany, Iceland, Poland, Spain, the UK, Canada, New Zealand, Japan, Israel, South Korea, and Switzerland, just to name a few. There are many more on that list.[530] And have you noticed anything here as well? These are all developed, industrialized nations, which means that the US falls at the bottom of the category when looking at advanced economies' tax rates. Indeed, the United States averages ten percent less in tax rates in terms of overall GDP than the entire rest of the world. Most of these other countries provide much greater social security benefits for its citizens, and all of them provide better goods and services than the US does.[531] In a way, the US loves giving tax breaks to the rich and powerful, who mostly dominate politics, and tell the rest of its population to do it themselves and don't expect much help.

It's not a radical idea to raise taxes to provide more benefits and services for middle class and working class Americans. If every other major country on earth is doing it, with great success, so can we. Oh, and by the way, these countries who do provide more of a social safety net for their citizens have lower stress rates than the US, greater life expectancies, and higher standard of living. It's time that we jump on board and do what these countries are doing. Who knows, it might actually make America great again.

President Joe Biden and his democratic allies have seen that the wealth inequality is only getting worse. That's why he's supported raising the tax rates for those who can afford to pay a little more. That's why he's called out republicans who want to strip away social security benefits for those that need it. That's why he's taken on monopolies, like the meat industry, who run up the prices of everyday necessities just because they have no competition and the American people have to spend what is dictated to them.

---

530 How do US taxes compare internationally. 2012. "How Do US Taxes Compare Internationally?" Tax Policy Center. 2012. https://www.taxpolicycenter.org/briefing-book/how-do-us-taxes-compare-internationally.
531 ibid

President Biden also supports raising taxes on what's known as the estate tax. An estate tax goes into effect when an "estate" or property is passed down from generation to generation. There is nothing wrong with a father giving his son his property and other belongings, known as an inheritance. However, if the government issues no tax on these items it is losing out on precious revenues that can fund programs that people need. If Donald Trump's dad left him with half a million dollars that is just fine and dandy. Trump is lucky to have a rich daddy. But isn't it just slightly unfair that he already has half a mill for doing absolutely nothing. It sort of reminds me of a hereditary king. The kingship is inherited by a very lucky son, or the daughter as the queen if there is no son. That son didn't do anything to earn that title, it was given to him because of his birthright status. That's exactly what happens when somebody with tons of money gives it to his children. Here in America he has every right to do that, but there should be taxes appropriately for this. Passing huge amounts of wealth from one generation to another is completely legal, but this adds to the wealth inequality that we see today, as the wealth remains concentrated in just a few hands, and often a few white hands. Republicans cry against the so-called "death tax" but if used appropriately it can be very effective and could help many people.

President Biden has also tried to establish a wealth tax that would mean that households with more than $100 million, so the top one percent, would have to pay 20% of their income. This is more effective than you would think because this includes money earned from investments and other capital gains like property gains, stock, bonds, ect, which is not technically considered income that can be taxed, as there are many different loopholes. Just ask Trump, he brags about never paying taxes because he's "smart," he knows how to cheat the system and screw over the American people.

Bottom line is that if these things are achieved we can reduce wealth inequality and increase the standard of living for all Americans, not just the richest few.

14 LGBTQ COMMUNITY

The same sad old story can be said of the LGBTQ community and states preventing this community from fully expressing themselves. The states are currently on a mission to destroy individuality.

There have been many efforts by the states and the nation throughout United States history that have aimed at suppressing the rights of the gay, lesbian, and trans community. Again, there have always been a group of people to blame or attack, in this case it't the LGBTQ community. Somewhere in the midst of the violence lies the theory that God somehow hates gays. That somehow God has caused violence and all sorts of other horrible things on the gay community. This is flatly absurd.

In all honesty, I myself am a Christian, have been for my entire life. When I was younger I held a deep phobia of gays, mostly because I grew up in a community where being gay just wasn't acceptable. Gays would be picked on, called "fagots," and avoided at all costs. It was just how it is in a small rural town. Nonetheless, as I grew up I started to realize the absurdity of treating human beings as less than just because the way they love somebody is different from what is the societal norm. I especially hate it when so-called Christians are against the LGBTQ community just because they love somebody in a different way.

For instance, I once went on a few dates with a Christian lady, who at the time I liked a lot. She told me that she doesn't believe that her dad will go to heaven because he is gay. She insisted, through all of my protestations, that her dad will go to hell, simply because her dad loved a man. I am no priest by any means, but I do believe a few certain things about Christianity and love. First, I, nor anybody else in this world has the right to judge whether or not a person will go to heaven or hell. If you are a Christian you should know that nowhere in the Bible does it mention how equally sinful people will judge the morality of others. That alone is the job of Jesus Christ. When we are putting ourselves in a position where we make decisions for Jesus then we are sinning because we are taking that power away from the Lord.

Secondly, I hate to say it, but we are all sinners. Every single one of us. I find it a little ironic that some of the most dire-hard Christians, who should know that they themselves are sinners, call out other people's sins so frequently. Jesus would tell you that before telling someone to get that piece of dirt from their eye to get the chunk of wood out of your own eye first.

I say all of these things about how Christians view homosexuality for a reason. The point is that most of the anti-LGBTQ rhetoric is from Christians, or other religious groups. We, I speak for myself as a Christian, are called to love. That doesn't mean we pick and choose. And loving to me is not forcing somebody to be who they are not, for homosexuals will never be truly happy that way. I also believe that if Christians want to showcase their faith, then they should be more inclusive to those that are different. Instead of telling congregants all of the horrible things they are doing wrong, they should teach about Jesus' unconditional love and grace. If I went to church and the pastor or priest went on a rampage about how sinful I was I certainly wouldn't want to go back. Christians need to be more supportive and loving. Isn't that what God would want? And isn't that what we are called to do as Christians? Not just to treat people the way we want to be treated, but also to evangelize the world?

I say this because I have heard and experienced stories that have broken my heart regarding how churches have wounded the hearts and souls of so many people, including so many kids. I once attended a church that had two pastors, the lead pastor and the youth pastor. At this church a young girl, in her teens, attended the service, eager to give her life to Jesus. The youth pastor may or may not have known that that young girl was dealing with some very severe depression and anxiety. And the youth pastor may or may not have known that that young girl was bisexual, afraid to admit that that was who she is and she couldn't help it. It's likely that the fact that she was bisexual gave her anxiety and depression. Not because she was upset that she was bisexual, that's who she was. It was mostly because of the way she was treated by the world, and the church because she was a homosexual.

That youth pastor, instead of praising God and his wonderful love and mercy, went on a rampage about the evils of homosexuality, how homosexuality was destroying the country and all of humanity with its wrong morals and influence. He went crazy with his descriptions of hell and how each and every single homosexual will experience the fires of hell. The young girl went home that night and proceeded to cut herself until she could finally feel again.

I have a slight newsflash for people. Heterosexuals sin as well, every time a heterosexual has sex before marriage, or engages in any sexual impurity before the vows, they are commiting a sin. This means that the vast majority of Christians have sinned just as much as homosexuals have. Yet these so-called Christians still like to destroy the lives of homosexuals.

One of my bosses, who I grew quite fond of for his genuine people skills among other things, was gay. On days where it was slow, not many people coming in or out, we would sit at the desk and talk about all sorts of different things. One day I asked him what his work experience looked like, why did he end up at a furniture store? He told me his life experiences and why he ended up working for Best Buy, Macy's, and a few other places. One of the places that he worked for was GameStop, he was the store manager, and a very successful one at that, consistently growing the store. I asked him why he left that place to work at a furniture store.

"Do you really want to know," he said.

"Yeah, I really want to know," I quipped back.

"They let me go because they found out I was gay."

His words cut into me like a knife. Here was this amazing guy, who had done great things for GameStop, being let go all because he liked men. That is absurd. He went on to tell me that the GameStop director was a very religious man and was uncomfortable having a gay running one of his stores. This was in the 2010s. Not very long ago. I immediately put myself into his shoes. What would it be like if I worked my butt off, did great, was making good money, and all the sudden fired because of the person that I loved? Nobody should have to experience those things, and the fact that he did is truly heartbreaking.

We can do so much better, and we will. But we have to realize that we have got to let past prejudices go. We got to do a much better job loving one another and truly putting ourselves into other people's shoes. How else are we going to make the changes we want to see?

Conservatives and other republican leaders, who have a seriously strong backing from religious folk, especially Evangelicals, tend to call LGBTQ supporters radicals, and crazy liberals who want to uproot everyday family values. I don't particularly think that upholding family values means demeaning human beings, discriminating against them, and provoking violence. As I write this book, many states are going through the motions to prevent homosexuals from truly being themselves, passing laws that would imprison doctors from performing hormone therapies and other procedures that trans individuals are advocating for. Some states are aggressively pushing back, prohibiting trans students from participating in sports and other events, a move that further isolates already depressed and anxious youths. Unfortunately, and this is the case in many other countries, not just the US, history has been very tough on homosexuals, all the way dating back to biblical times. To save some time, I will focus on only a few events, not the long drawn out history of anti-LGBTQ hate.

Since the founding of the very first settlement in the Western Hemisphere, anti-homosexual propaganda can be seen everywhere. In a famous engraving, dating all the way back to 1594, artist, Theodore de Bry, depicted a real event in which he drew the wide scale slaughter of indigenous Panamanians by the Europeans because the Pananmanians engaged in same-sex sexual intercourse. Because of the wide scale teachings of the Bible that called same-sex intercourse a sin, these Spaniards that committed this atrocity actually genuinely believed that they were in the right. They saw the Pananamians committing a sin, and as a response they would have to be punished. Instead of letting God do the punishing, the Spaniards believed that God had given them a right to punish. Nobody really knows, by the way, if the Pananamians had actually even learned anything about the Bible, how can it be a sin if they didn't know whether it was right or wrong? To the Spaniards this didn't matter, they were in the moral right and this meant a punishment only acceptable with death.

The drawing of this event is believed to be the first ever representation of homosexuality ever printed. When it was all said and done the Spanish killed roughly 50 Panamanians, by letting them get maliciously attacked by their vicious dogs. Not a very pretty way to go out. And for what? Again, loving in the wrong way. I want you to imagine for a second the absurdity of what took place in this event. An indigenous group, living in Central America for generations, living with their own customs, traditions, and beliefs, simply doing what they always had done, inviting Europeans into their lands and allowing them to live amongst them, only for the Europeans to disapprove of what the Indigenous people are doing and kill them. Could you imagine that? Being killed because a foreigner disapproves of what you have been doing for generations and is your custom? In a way it almost sounds a bit like modern day terrorism brought about by foreigners.

From this point until around the period of the creation of the American republic, not much was said about homosexuality, besides the pesky anti-sodomy laws. Sodomy directly translates to the act of anal sex between two males. It has been used since to roughly define all homosexuals, regardless of if they do anal sex or not. Many ancient colonial laws from the British regime discriminated against those who were homosexuals by passing anti-sodomy laws, forbidding the act, in some cases warranting death for these minor offenses. As a consequence not many people came out in those days. Why would you? If you did, you would likely be publicly humiliated through some sort of punishment.

It is widely acknowledged now, that there were at least a handful of men in Washington's army that were gay, though Washington never officially punished them. And in Virginia, at the same time, the law called for homosexuals to be given the death penalty, though Thomas Jefferson tried to come to the rescue. He proposed that instead of killing homosexuals they should just castrate them instead.[532] If you still think that's horrible it was at least better than

---

532 "Amendment VIII: Thomas Jefferson, A Bill for Proportioning Crimes and Punishments". Press-pubs.uchicago.edu.

the death penalty. It was no use anyway, the legislature never took up the bill meaning the death penalty was still in play, again giving reason why most men did not come out.

In the 19th and 20th centuries, states really buffed up their efforts to reduce homosexuality, and wanted to minimize as much as possible the act of having sex without the intention of procreation. To these Americans sex was simply to procreate and nothing more, hence it shouldn't be used for sinful purposes, including having sex with the same sex. It is interesting to note that all of the major laws that were passed that banned discrimination and other forms of hate, included protecting individuals because of race, ethnicity, gender, religion, ect, but nothing was said about sexual identity or homosexuals. These things had to be added in decades, in some cases centuries later.

In addition to the anti-gay laws, violence among the LGBTQ community has always been running rampant. This is still true today, as violence has been a very real thing in the lives of LGBTQ. Studies have shown that nearly 21%, and likely much higher, of LGBTQ have directly experienced violence due to the fact that they are part of that community.[533] What makes this so bad, besides the fact of the actual violence, is that many members are suffering from mental health disorders because of the increase of violence.

Despite popular opinion, anti-LGBTQ violence is on the rise, it's not getting better. In 2017, 16% of the hate crimes in the country targeted the LGBTQ community, this is in contrast to 1996 when

---

533 Flores, Andrew R., Rebecca L. Stotzer, Ilan H. Meyer, and Lynn L. Langton. 2022. "Hate Crimes against LGBT People: National Crime Victimization Survey, 2017-2019." Edited by Syed Ghulam Sarwar Shah. *PLOS ONE* 17 (12): e0279363. htttps://doi.org/10.1371/journal.pone.0279363.

it was 11%.[534] So, how can it be that in 1996 we had less incidences of hate related crimes to the LGBTQ community than we do now? After all, the Supreme Court has allowed same-sex marriages since 2015, and with every passing year more and more Americans believe that same-sex couples should be protected and have equal rights, at least that what the polling shows. One reason could be the increase in partisanship, the animosity towards people who are different and the hate that has arisen within the last few years among political dissidents. While it might be true that more people are tolerant of same-sex couples than ever before, a slight minority of Americans who disagree are doing so very loudly and very violently.

We are in a world of hurt when we have more violence now than when the infamous "don't ask don't tell" bill was in effect. In reality, the law barred the military from openly discriminating against homosexuals, while at the same time banning homosexuals from openly serving in the military. So, in essence officers could not ask a gay individual if they are gay, that way the officer would not engage in any sexually oriented discrimination against anyone serving in the armed forces. At the same time, a gay or lesbian serviceman/woman couldn't openly say they were homosexuals, if they did they would get the boot. It's ironic that the bill was passed to try to limit discrimination while at the same time discriminating against the LGBTQ community by not allowing them to serve. When president Obama repealed the law conservatives threw up their arms in disgust, apparently they would rather have LGBTQ service men and women serve behind closed doors or not serve at all. I have a newsflash, in today's day and age we need more men and women to step up and serve in our armed forces. Instead of

---

534 "Anti-LGBT Hate Crimes Are Rising — but We Really Don't Know How Much - Security.org." 2019. Security.org. 2019. https://www.security.org/resources/anti-lgbt-hate-crime-stats/.

making it harder to serve, lawmakers should make it easier to serve, that way we can keep our country safe. Preventing a large group of people from having the opportunity to serve is a disgrace to America.

In 1969, just a few months shy of the Stonewall riots in New York City, an incident took place that shook the core of the gay community. In a Dover hotel in Los Angeles, known for its gay atmosphere, where gay men would often strip naked publicly and hope to meet someone, police had a field day, raiding it looking for "faggots."[535] On one of the police's random raids they bumped into a male nurse, under the pseudonym of J. McCann, probably to protect his identity, checked into the hotel. While the police were raiding the hotel, officers Lemuel Chauncey and Richard Halligan alleged that McCann, whose real name was Howard Efland groped them, a highly unusual claim.[536] I really doubt that if the police were viciously attacking the hotel and forcing everybody out that anybody would come to the conclusion as to grope them. Anyway, the officers used this as a justification for what they then proceeded to do to Efland.

Not only did the officers arrest him, but they stripped him of his clothes, dragged him down flights of stairs by his feet and bulldozed him into the street surrounded by curious onlookers. Chauncey and Halligan both were big, brawny men, Efland, small, petite, and frail. Nevertheless, this didn't stop them from viciously beating Efland in front of bystanders. "The two police officers kicked him repeatedly, did knee drops onto his stomach, and savagely beat him," while

---

[535] Kohler, Will. 2023. "Gay History - March 9, 1969: The Tragic Death of Howard Efland by Police at the Dover Hotel." Back2Stonewall. March 9, 2023. http://www.back2stonewall.com/2023/03/lgbt-history-march-9-1969-police-beat-gay-man-death-los-angeles-hotel-raid.html.
[536] ibid

Efland could be heard screaming for mercy.[537] Nobody helped. But witnesses say that Efland died right there at the scene.

The police, in an effort to hide what really happened, claimed that Efland had died of a heart-attack, indeed, that's what they told his parents. It's interesting that they said nothing about how he was beaten out of consciousness. The coroner's report found no evidence of a heart attack, instead it found signs of excusable homicide. The report was not widely circulated and withheld from local newspapers. It took years afterwards for the true story to come out, and no accountability was taken on the part of the officers who needlessly took a life, all because Efland was gay. The police felt more and more like they could do no wrong. Which might have had something to do with the Stonewall raids a few months later, where the police raided the Stonewall Inn.

The Stonewall Inn was somewhat of a blue moon type of establishment, there weren't many establishments that welcomed gay people in the 1950s and 60s. In fact, during the 1950-60s, the FBI kept records of homosexuals. Everything from what their favorite restaurants were or even who their friends were was all carefully documented.[538] This spying technique on the part of the government spread fear throughout the gay community. Pretty soon, police organizations had enough info about where homosexuals gathered that they routinely raided gay bars and closed them for good. Customers were arrested and they were publicly humiliated in the papers.

It was common thinking of the time to perceive these homosexuals as different, not entirely like the blacks, where they were considered

---

537 ibid
538 Edsall, Nicholas (2003). *Toward Stonewall: Homosexuality and Society in the Modern Western World.* University of Virginia Press

as inhuman, but different mentally. There had to be something wrong with these people. They weren't made right.

In 1952, the American Psychiatric Association claimed that homosexuality was a mental disorder. I don't know why, but in this case, scientists needed to back up their claim with some sort of theory. The reason why people are homosexual had to do with childhood trauma of the other sex, the scientists theorized. Mostly, this had to do with a child-like fear of the opposite sex, this likely occurred through parental fights and disputes. To avoid these conflicts, individuals turned to homosexuality where they didn't need to deal with the other sex.[539] It was widely believed at this period that homosexuality was a mental issue, and it would remain so for decades and generations, some still think so today. However, in 1974, scientists removed homosexuality from the official manual of mental disorders.

It is conceivable then as to why many businesses were opposed to outwardly supporting gay rights causes. In many instances, gay bars were run by criminal organizations like the mafia. This is exactly what happened with the Stonewall Inn. In all reality, Stonewall was a crapfest. Many illegal activities took place there and police officers were routinely paid off to prevent them from crashing the fun. The gay community couldn't help it, however, this was the only bar in New York City that was accommodating to the gay community, even letting gays dance on the dancefloor.[540]

Troubling to the community was the fact that police raids still routinely took place, though these were often tipped off well beforehand, giving the owners enough time to prepare. However, one

---

[539] ibid

[540] Carter, David (2004). *Stonewall: The Riots that Sparked the Gay Revolution*. St. Martin's Press.

night the tip was waved off as being a "false alarm" the owners did nothing to prepare and the police raided the place.

I'm not going to get into exact details about the Stonewall Inn raids and riots, this has all been documented many times and many writings have been done regarding this. All that I want to mention is the obvious fact that wide-scale violence broke out between the Stonewall customers and the police that night and some nights after. The Stonewall riot led to dozens of arrests and a number of injuries, of both civilians and police officers.

This event really opened up the world to the struggles of the gay community. More and more celebrities stood up for the gay rights movement and the Gay Liberation Front and the Gay Activist Alliance began in earnest to fight for their rights. The problem here, as with every gay riot or police raid is the fact that gays explicitly were targeted. If heterosexuals were caught in a straight bar dancing there is no way in hell that the police would have raided the place arresting people at random.

The Stonewall riots was an awakening of gay pride and activism, though fortunately the Stonewall riots led to zero deaths and at worst involved skirmishes that didn't result in serious injuries. Of course, as we have seen throughout US history, when one group of people begin to assert their rights, whether that be blacks asserting equality, or Chicanos demanding fair treatment, there has always been a group of Americans who push to deny these rights, often through intimidation and violence. I want to point out, this is especially sad in the case of the gay community, as they were just fighting to be treated as normal people, not aliens and other crazy outsiders, they just wanted to feel normal. But that didn't stop some bigoted and prejudiced Americans from trampling all over them.

A few years after the Stonewall riots, in 1973, an arsonist set fire at the Upstairs Lounge, a local gathering spot for the LGBTQ community. When the flames finally petered out, 32 people had lost their lives, while another 15 were injured. At the time, this was the deadliest attack on the LGBTQ community. Many people have never even heard of the Upstairs fire, that's because the New Orleans community virtually did nothing to help the victims and their families grapple with what happened. The news only covered that there was a fire, nowhere was it mentioned that it was a direct attack on the gay community and the arsonist was never captured, to this day we still don't know who the bigoted individual was that decided to burn down the building with many innocent people inside. Worse, the authorities decided never to pursue likely suspects, most likely because they simply didn't care about finding justice for the gay community. It is all eerily similar to how justice was so hard to find for members of the black community. Justice, apparently, was used only when it was convenient for the whole majority, nevermind about minority rights.

There was little respect for the lives lost. "In a gross mishandling of victims' remains," *The Nation* describes, "four bodies were dumped into unmarked graves at the Resthaven Memorial Park cemetery. There would be no signage or plaque to mark where they were buried. To this day, the exact location of the bodies is unknown."[541] In fact, many in the gay community had very few options left to them. If they wanted to speak out they were at constant risk of being derided for their homosexuality. Johnny Townsend, who wrote "Let the foggots burn," apparently because that's what many of LGBTQ people heard in response to the fire, wrote "The way the city reacted

---

541 Sciallo, Andrew. 2023. "50 Years Later, the UpStairs Lounge Fire Is More Important to Remember than Ever." Www.thenation.com. June 22, 2023. https://www.thenation.com/article/society/upstairs-lounge-anniversary/.

after the fire was a hate crime in and of itself," he says. "Victims who survived couldn't tell anyone that were there [at the bar] or that their friends or lovers, who had died, for fear of being out."[542] In a way, there was no chance at seeking justice. It wasn't exactly a great time to announce that you are out. Most likely announcing that you were out of the closet would mean that your family and friends wouldn't have anything to do with you, that you would be shunned from the community and potentially the victim of violence.

It was clear that this violence wasn't going away. It was only intensifying. Yet, where was the justice? Where was the common human understanding? Instead when anybody stood up for gay rights they were heckled, beat up, called "faggot-lovers" or worse, called out for being gay themselves. It's no wonder with these attitudes and so much hate around them that it was hard for most people to stand up and do the right thing. With the increase of violence not one US president stood up to confront the hatred, and the vast majority of support groups were created by gay support groups, leaving most gay individuals with nowhere to turn except further into the gay community.

Obviously, because there were no direct consequences for assaulting the gay community, the attacks grew more targeted and more vicious. On June 21, 1977, Robert Hillsborough, and his roommate, Jerry Taylor, went out to a disco for a night of dancing. After leaving the dance floor headed for home, they decided to grab something to eat real quick before bed. They were doing absolutely nothing wrong, just two friends together having a meal. Yet, when they left the restaurant they were quickly confronted by a bigoted

---

542 ibid

gang, mostly consisting of young men, shouting anti-gay slurs in their direction.

To get away from the rowdy gang Hillsborough and Taylor ran as fast as they could to Hillsborough's car as the gang ran behind them, climbing onto the roof of the car and windshield to prevent an escape. That didn't deter Hillsborough, he stomped on the gas pedal and watched as the gang fell off the car, thinking that this scary nightmare was over. But, alas, it wasn't. The gang got into another vehicle, sped up, and followed the couple, though at a safe distance to prevent anyone from noticing.

When Hillsborough parked the car near the apartment and the couple got out to finally go to bed they were attacked again by the same gang bent on killing homos. Jerry Taylor was viciously beaten but managed to escape with his life. Hillsborough, on the other hand, had a different experience. Robert was brutally beaten and stabbed 15 times by a 19 year old named John Cardova. Cordova was so filled with rage at the sight of a gay man that as he was stabbing Hillsborough mercilessly he was heard screaming "faggot, faggot, faggot."[543]

When the neighbors heard all of the commotion and screaming they rushed outside to see the gruesome scene. When the gang saw the neighbors come out, threatening to call the cops, they fled, while the neighbors came to Hillsborough's rescue. It was all too late, however, as Hillsborough officially died at the hospital 45 minutes later. Unlike previous miscarriages of justice, the gang members were all arrested the following morning, wanted for the death of Hillsborough.

---

543 Kohler, Will. 2023. "Gay History - June 21, 1977: The Brutal Gay Hate Murder of Robert Hillsborough Rocks the Nation." Back2Stonewall. June 21, 2023. http://www.back2stonewall.com/2023/06/june21-brutal-murder-of-robert-hillsborough.html.

According to Back2Stonewall, Hillsborough's death struck a nerve within the gay community. "We live in a paranoid state," said Harvey Milk, who was preparing his run for the San Francisco Board of Supervisors, "and the death of Robert is only the culmination of a lot of violence that's been directed at us."[544] The pride celebration that took place a few days later hosted an astounding 300,000 people, a record for that event. Clearly the threat of violence was starting to make understanding Americans realize the dangers that the gay community faced everyday. People were finally getting on board to realize that rights are universal, you can't just pick and choose. Yet, San Francisco is a very liberal city. Most likely in many other cities, towns, and villages throughout the country that feeling would not be universal.

As it turned out violence just kept on brewing, even the famous Tennesee Williams, author of the well known *A Streetcar Named Desire*, was beaten up from a bigoted group that was anti-gay. Not even celebrities were safe! The list of gay individuals, bars, restaurants, and hotels that were attacked throughout the 70s, 80s, and 90s go on and on, seemingly without end. Apparently, even with the increase in pride awareness and celebrations the violence and hatred still flourished. Anti-gay laws were being passed, along with the "Don't ask don't tell" law. Republicans and conservatives rebranded themselves as the party for family values and tradition, frequently chastising LGBTQ individuals and anybody who sympathized with them. Worse, many conservatives labeled liberals and other gay advocates as doing the devil's work, by not calling out gays but by accepting them and their disgusting behavior. Of course, all of this together makes for a very hostile atmosphere. It's not hard for religious zealots, or bigots, who consistently listen to Fox News

---

544 ibid

and other conservative media outlets to grow indoctrinated with the beliefs that gays=sin, and if Americans allow gays to live and have rights within the country then God will punish us somehow.

The whole reason why I wrote this chapter stems from what I learned about Matthew Shepard. Shepherd was an energetic and optimistic young boy, schoolmates tended to grow really fond of him and he was well liked. He was fascinated with politics and went to school at the University of Wyoming for political science. Shepard was an Episcoplain and deeply religious, even serving as an altar boy during services.[545] He was very friendly and wanted everybody to be treated equally and fairly, indeed, he often found himself engaged in activities relating to equality.

In the evening hours of Oct. 6, 1998 Shepard went alone to the Fireside Lounge in Laramie, Wyoming, after a meeting of the campus LGBT student group and a stop at the Village Inn. According to the Wyoming Historical Society "At the Fireside, Shepard sat at the bar drinking from a bottle of imported beer. After somewhat more than an hour, he was approached by two men his own age: Aaron McKinney and Russell Henderson, high-school dropouts with roofing jobs. They had purchased a pitcher of beer with small change and eventually engaged Shepard in a conversation. Shortly after midnight, Shepard left the bar with McKinney and Henderson; police and prosecutors would assert that the two men lured Shepard, perhaps under the pretense of themselves being gay, but in fact with the intent of robbing him. In his police confession, McKinney repeatedly described Shepard as "a queer," "the gay," and "fag."[546]

---

545 Fortin, Jacey (October 11, 2018). "Matthew Shepard Will Be Interred at the Washington National Cathedral, 20 Years After His Death". *The New York Times*.
546 Marsden, Jason. 2014. "The Murder of Matthew Shepard | WyoHistory.org." Wyohistory.org. 2014. https://www.wyohistory.org/encyclopedia/murder-matthew-shepard.

The two drop-outs drove Shepard to a remote little village where very few people cross. The two teens robbed Shepard, but that was not all. Henderson used a clothesline to tie Shepard to a log fence and McKinney began punching and pistol whipping Shepard with a .357 caliber Magnum Smith and Wesson, with no mercy. An autopsy would report that Shepard received at least 19-21 strikes in the head, with the last strike permanently injuring his brain stem. "The only time I've ever seen those dramatic injuries were in high-speed traffic crashes," a disgusted Dave O'Malley, the lead investigator in the case speculated, "where there were just extremely violent compression fractures to the skull."[547] McKinney and Henderson left Shepard there, unconscious, to die.

There he remained for 18 whole hours when finally a kid riding on his bike spotted Shepard. Initially the boy was frightened, believing Shepard to be a scarecrow. Upon closer examination the boy realized that this was a live human being and rushed to the nearest household to get the authorities. "Reggie Fluty and emergency medical technicians responded. Fluty later reported that Shepard, who was 5 feet 2 inches tall and boyish in appearance, looked at first to be a child and that his face was caked in blood except where tears had left tracks along his cheeks" this according to the Wyoming Historical Society.[548]

The authorities, after realizing the gravity of Shepard's condition, immediately transported him to a hospital in Colorado, where he remained in a coma for four days, dying a slow painful death on the fifth day.

---

547 Sheerin, Jude. 2018. "Matthew Shepard: The Murder That Changed America." *BBC News*, October 26, 2018. https://www.bbc.com/news/world-us-canada-45968606.
548 Marsden, Jason. 2014. "The Murder of Matthew Shepard | WyoHistory.org." Wyohistory.org. 2014. https://www.wyohistory.org/encyclopedia/murder-matthew-shepard.

Unlike previous atrocities, the gruesome killing of Shepard provoked widespread anger and dismay. President Clinton sent his best wishes to Matthew's parents and denounced the attackers as "full of hatred or full of fear or both."[549] Politicians and celebrities far and wide were shocked at the event and gathered at a vigil for Shepard in Washington, in fact, thousands came.

Meanwhile, Henderson and McKinney had been caught after they came back to the city and got into another scuffle. Police recognized the gun in the backseat of McKinney's car and charged both Henderson and McKinney with the crime. And though there were many who grieved the horrific event, there were others who thought that the vicious murder was a good thing! Both Shepard's funeral and the court proceedings had to be heavily secured to guard against protesters. You might be thinking, who would protest a funeral? Believe it or not, there were some seriously demented folks who carried signs such as "God hates fags" in the wake of Shepard's killing. Don't believe me? Look it up. Fred Phelps, of the Westboro Baptist church can be seen holding signs with a picture of Shepard saying "Matt in hell", and "No special laws for fags." What kind of special laws do the LGTQ community receive? Especially in 1998? But that didn't stop him and other prejudiced, bigoted men and women from answering this sad event with more hatred and anger.

Wyoming, one of the most profoundly conservative states, who vote republican, no matter the circumstances, quickly became a danger zone for the gay community. Quite simply, gays just did not feel safe. And, shockingly, the defense team actually had the nerve to imply that Henderson and McKinney had attacked Shepard because

---

549 Sheerin, Jude. 2018. "Matthew Shepard: The Murder That Changed America." *BBC News*, October 26, 2018. https://www.bbc.com/news/world-us-canada-45968606.

he touched their leg. Obviously, this is hardly a reason to kill somebody, regardless of your sexual orientation, but the defense team was wise, they knew where they were, and they were in conservative Wyoming, a state that resisted most progressive actions. (Though thanks to the hard-line judge, both men are serving life in prison.)

After the court proceedings and sentencing, Shepard's parents set up the Matthew Shepard Foundation, which helped expand the horizon of hate crimes to include sexual orientation.[550] But Wyoming just kept doing its own thing. In the wake of Shepard's death, some Wyoming legislators thought that now would be a good time to bring about some common sense hate-crime bills. These bills would have extended the criminal intention of hate crimes to also include gay and lesbian intended crimes. But even this common sense bill didn't pass, ending in a 30-30 vote, never to be talked about again.[551] To this day Wyoming still does not have a criminal hate crime law, making it one of only five states to fit that description. In another 15 states, that do have a criminal hate crime law, conspicuously missing are protections for the LGBTQ community.[552] And you can probably guess where these states are located. The vast majority of these states are republican dominated. There's no way that LGBTQ rights will be adopted anytime soon. That leads us to the obvious question. How many Matthew Shepard's will it take for us to actually do something? This has nothing to do with religion, it has everything to do with human dignity and compassion.

---

550 ibid
551 Marsden, Jason. 2014. "The Murder of Matthew Shepard | WyoHistory.org." Wyohistory.org. 2014. https://www.wyohistory.org/encyclopedia/murder-matthew-shepard.
552 Sheerin, Jude. 2018. "Matthew Shepard: The Murder That Changed America." *BBC News*, October 26, 2018. https://www.bbc.com/news/world-us-canada-45968606.

Violence directed at the LGBTQ community is only growing throughout the years, it's not subsiding. We can blame that on a number of factors, among them the political firestorm and the emergence of the most politically divisive character in our country's history, Donald Trump. For many bigots, Donald Trump made hate and violence acceptable again. It wasn't something that needed to be hidden anymore but something that they could embrace. Obviously, I can't write a chapter on LGBTQ hate without mentioning the most deadly attack on the gay community in US history, that being the Orlando Nightclub shooting that left 49 innocent people dead and 53 more seriously wounded. Pulse nightclub, that Orlando nightclub, was targeted because it was a known gay nightclub.

The perpetrator of the attack was a New York man named Omar Mateen, who was once rumored to be gay himself, although these rumors turned out to be false. Mateen's father told investigators that Mateen had seen a gay couple kiss right in front of him and his family, a scene that visibly made Mateen angry.[553] This is presumed to have been the motivating factor of the attack. Just more reasons why we need to do something about automatic weapons.

Of course, none of this helps when there is so much animosity everywhere today. Sure, the gay community had a massive success with the Supreme Court decisions allowing for same-sex marriages, but so much more needs to be done. This is a moral issue and needs to be affected by the people that we elect, not through legislation alone but also with words. President Biden and most democrats do a great job of including everyone, regardless of who they are or what

---

553 Grimson, Matthew; Wyllie, David; Fieldstadt, Elisha (June 12, 2016). "Orlando Nightclub Shooting: Mass Casualties After Gunman Opens Fire in Gay Club". *NBC News*

gender orientation they may be. Sadly, this is not the case with most republicans who are pushing back like never before.

Currently, as I write this book, the ACLU is monitoring at least 496 anti-LGBTQ laws being passed by the state legislatures.[554] Not all of these bills will become law, as court challenges and governor vetoes might take out some of these, but the fact that so many bills are being debated and passed targeting the LGBTQ community is mind-blowing, especially as we are in the 2020s, things should be getting better, but obviously they are not. 15 laws have been passed banning gender affirming care for transgender youth, it doesn't even matter if the youths have parental consent, it is still banned. Isn't it ironic that the same party with the same lawmakers who cared so much about giving parents more rights during the COVID pandemic in schools now want to take away parental rights in regards to their own children's healthcare decisions?

Two laws explicitly targeted drag shows, even though this is just good old wholesome fun for the performers. And four state legislatures have banned certain school curriculums and books.[555] Some of these books, by the way, may just mention one itsy bitsy tiny little thing about someone or a character being gay and they are subjected to being banned. I am an educator and I happen to know that students connect better to the curriculum and tend to focus better when they feel accepted for who they are. Some very simple ways to help make sure everybody feels included within the school is by simply reading a diverse range of books. Books that have black girls and white boys. Books that have Muslim men and Christian

---

554 https://www.aclu.org/legislative-attacks-on-lgbtq-rights
555 Peele, Cullen. 2023. "Roundup of Anti-LGBTQ+ Legislation Advancing in States across the Country." Human Rights Campaign. May 23, 2023. https://www.hrc.org/press-releases/roundup-of-anti-lgbtq-legislation-advancing-in-states-across-the-country.

girls. Books that have gay boys and transgender penguins. There is no politicization here. In no way shape or form are children going to hear these books and then aspire to be gay, they are either gay or they're not, they don't pick and choose.

Among some of the most egregious laws passed by state legislatures within the last couple of years are these:

Arizona passed bill SB 1040 that "ban trans students and school personnel from using school restrooms that match their gender identity and allows people to sue schools if they share a restroom or similar school facility with a trans person."[556] Where are these folks supposed to go to the bathroom?

Louisiana passed a bill banning the use of gender affirming care, which is the process of interventions that help support an individual's choice of affirming care. Mostly related to switching genders.

Ohio passed two laws that are highly suspect. The first one they passed bans any trangender students from participating in school activities. These activities, doctors all agree, help reduce stress, anxiety, and depression levels. Taking these opportunities away from students will only make the mental health epidemic worse, not better. It seems that the states don't really care about our children after all, at least not Ohio, or any other state with those same laws. Another Ohio law would limit diversity, equity, and inclusion programs or training offered throughout the state, that includes workplace training that even deals with race, making this a race issue as well.

A Texas bill would criminalize drag shows. A drag show. I mean, come on people, might as well ban concerts and festivals while you're at it. This is a direct attempt to censure one group of people, who just happen to be different from the majority of Americans.

---

556 Ibid

Could you imagine being criminalized just for being who you are? What a disgrace!

Montana allows schools to expel students who are transgender.

Nebraska prohibits youth from receiving gender affirming healthcare.

Perhaps no state is quite like that of Florida. Florida's governor, the infamous Ron Desantis, boasts of all the "amazing" work that he has done as governor, like taking Florida back from the liberals who allowed equality. He has pushed an even more extreme stance on these social issues than Donald Trump, the twice impeached, and disgraced former president. Oh Ron, you just don't get it do you? You don't get that history never forgets and will come after you with strong vengeance.

Maybe his most shining hour, to him at least, was when he signed the good ole "Don't say gay law." The law reads like this: "Classroom instruction by school personnel or third parties on sexual orientation or gender identity may not occur in kindergarten through grade 3."[557] Okay, that might not be too horrible right? I mean how often does gender orientation come up anytime from kindergarten to third grade? But that's not the point, the point is that again the whole LGBTQ community is being targeted. It makes as much sense as to say nobody can talk about race, Martin Luther King Jr., or slavery before third grade. That is absurd.

Even during the press conference that he held before the signing, Desantis praised the law, criticizing the old morale booster saying that the phrase, "they can be whatever they want to be" was

---

557 Diaz, Jaclyn. 2022. "Florida's Governor Signs Controversial Law Opponents Dubbed 'Don't Say Gay.'" *National Public Radio*, March 28, 2022, sec. Efforts to restrict rights for LGBTQ youth. https://www.npr.org/2022/03/28/1089221657/dont-say-gay-florida-desantis.

"inappropriate" for children.[558] Apparently teachers can't tell their students that they can be anything that they want to be anymore, that's nice isn't it? What a wonderful world we live in.

One thing to note in all of these laws is that all of the laws have been passed and signed into law by republicans. This isn't just a crazy few individuals that want to take rights and equality away from people. This is a whole political party that has made attacking the LGBTQ community a central part of their platform. Creating laws that discriminate against the LGBTQ community and don't allow them to live as who they are is destroying the fabric of America and leading to so many problems, chief among them is mental health.

Republicans don't seem to care a whole lot about the mental health of the LGBTQ community. If they did they certainly wouldn't be attacking the community every chance that they can. They may disguise it as a religious issue or a family values issue, all of that is total baloney. What matters in America is equality and opportunity, not suppression and hatred. All of these things culminate into a sad reality that is facing the LGBTQ community and its struggles with mental health. It's a lot easier to fall into depression when you can't even be yourself and a whole political party is criminalizing you.

Across the board, members of the LGBTQ community have higher depression, anxiety, and suicidal ideation that non-LGBTQ individuals. A full 61% of LGBTQ indivduals between the ages of 18-29 have severe depression and anxiety, this is 16 points higher than non-LGBTQ individuals in the same age category.[559] It's even worse among LGBTQ youth. Almost 45% of LGBTQ youth had

---

558 ibid
559 Bureau, US Census. n.d. "Mental Health Struggles Higher among LGBT Adults than Non-LGBT Adults in All Age Groups." Census.gov. https://www.census.gov/library/stories/2022/12/lgbt-adults-report-anxiety-depression-at-all-ages.html#:~:text=Half%20of%20LGBT%20respondents%20ages..

seriously contemplated suicide in the last year. LGBTQ youth who had a sense of affirmation from family and peers were less than half as likely to contemplate suicide. LGBTQ youth who have found that schools are more accepting, call them by their preferred gender, have a wide range of reading materials, and talk about gender orientation in schools, are less likely to commit suicide than those whose schools are not accepting. These numbers all get worse when considering race as well.[560]

These are not my numbers. These are numbers that are highly visible through academic research and studies. It would be absolutely foolish if we didn't take these numbers into account. It takes all of us to make this better. How can we say that we are okay with more than half of LGBTQ individuals having depression and anxiety and not doing anything about it? How can we say that we want to make it worse? These laws that Florida and other republican led states are passing, that bar transgender youth from participating in sporting events, that ban certain books and curriculum about gender orientation from schools, and that demonize the LGBTQ community makes the matter worse not better. In effect, these republicans are doing the opposite of what we elect them for. They will be judged harshly by historians and 50 years down the line they will be judged with the ranks of George Wallace and David Duke.

For some reason, whenever activists get together to protest a law or action taken by the government, republicans usually like to label them as members of antifa or "hollywood." Quite frankly, most Americans have never heard about antifa, unless they watch Fox News constantly, and while the vast majority of Hollywood might be democratic, that is not always the case. For instance,

---

560 The Trevor Project. 2022. "2022 National Survey on LGBTQ Youth Mental Health." The Trevor Project. 2022. https://www.thetrevorproject.org/survey-2022/.

when LGBTQ groups and activists, many such activists consisted of concerned parents, protested the bill demonizing their sons and daughters, Desantis did the old usual republican quip. "I don't care what Hollywood says. I don't care what big corporations say. Here I stand. I am not backing down."[561] There you go Ron. I'm glad you're taking a stand on something. The only problem is, you're not taking a stand on the right issues. How about taking a stand against corporate greed? How about taking a stand on poverty and child hunger? How about taking a stand to fight depression and anxiety? Ron, you find yourself on the wrong side on all of these issues.

How would you feel if you were demonized because of who you are? How would you feel if you were prohibited from doing certain things, made to feel less than, and directly targeted? Why don't people get that this has the makings of Jim Crow all over again? Yet, this time it's directed at the gay community by the republicans, who all band together in an idolatry style of worship to their former president, who sows hatred and discord. It's time we fight for equal protection and equal rights. There's nothing fundamentally radical about that, yet that's not what conservatives keep pushing.

In the second Republican debate, which was a crap show, Vivek Ramswanswamy actually said that transgenderism is a mental health disorder. Really? Maybe it's comments like this that makes the LGBTQ community have such higher rates of depression and anxiety. Republicans don't seem to care.

23 states, every single one republican led, have passed bans on transgender students from participating in athletic programs. What

---

561 Diaz, Jaclyn. 2022. "Florida's Governor Signs Controversial Law Opponents Dubbed 'Don't Say Gay.'" *National Public Radio*, March 28, 2022, sec. Efforts to restrict rights for LGBTQ youth. https://www.npr.org/2022/03/28/1089221657/dont-say-gay-florida-desantis.

do you think that means for transgender students? The National Library of Medicine, not a partisan organization, has studied this issue for decades. In their published reports, the NLM says "Student-athletes are thought to be protected from mental health issues because of increased self-esteem, a sense of connectedness, and social support from their teammates. There is an established relationship between self-esteem and depression, indicating that self-esteem is associated with depression."[562] How can you dispute the facts? Athletic programs help children feel welcome and camaraderie with their teammates. Athletic programs help reduce the stress, anxiety, and depression levels of students. This in turn, lowers the suicide rates among youth, something that is trending upward at an alarming rate. And yet, republicans are prohibiting certain groups from participating in these events. How can they defend themselves in this? How can they prevent students from feeling welcomed and loved? How can they pass laws exacerbating the suicidal ideation of the LGBTQ community? Clearly, they don't care about the needs of the LGBTQ community.

Meanwhile the democrats are doing the exact opposite. President Joe Biden has tried to undo all the evils of the republican states, in regard to LGBTQ policies. Biden has directed the Department of Education to propose a rule making it illegal to ban transgender students from participating in sports. "Every student should be able to have the full experience of attending school in America, including participating in athletics, free from discrimination," said U.S. Secretary of Education Miguel Cardona. "Being on a sports

---

[562] Weber, Samantha R., Zachary K. Winkelmann, Eva V. Monsma, Shawn M. Arent, and Toni M. Torres-McGehee. 2023. "An Examination of Depression, Anxiety, and Self-Esteem in Collegiate Student-Athletes." *International Journal of Environmental Research and Public Health* 20 (2): 1211. https://doi.org/10.3390/ijerph20021211.

team is an important part of the school experience for students of all ages."[563]

However, as nice as the effort was, the proposal went nowhere because of the US supreme court. That court is so incredibly corrupt, with six conservatives on the court and only three liberals, that it doesn't accurately reflect the wishes of the American people. Some justices, like Clarence Thomas have even accepted HUGE donations from conservative donors, who asked him to join them on their million dollar yacht. Does that sound like America to you? Which side do you think Clarence Thomas is on, your's or his wealthy donor friends?

Anyways, this corrupt supreme court fails to stand up for LGBTQ rights, instead siding with states, who like to discriminate and spew hate. Clearly, anything that the democrats do, at least for now, doesn't really matter, it will just be turned upside down by the conservative supreme court.

It's also worth noting that the states that do not have transgender athletic bans are all democratic led. They are the states that offer support and understanding to the LGBTQ community. There's nothing radical here, it's just human compassion and love. Something clearly missing in republican states.

---

[563] Carrillo, Sequoia. 2023. "The Biden Administration Moves to Make Broad, Transgender Sports Bans Illegal." NPR. NPR. April 6, 2023. https://www.npr.org/2023/04/06/1168460726/biden-title-ix-transgender-sports-ban?ft=nprml&f=1085513404.

15 HEALTHCARE

One of the main reasons I decided to write this book is because of our healthcare crisis. I've seen firsthand how patients struggle to pay their bills and how long patients have to stay in hospitals to get the treatment that they need. I have seen it all because I worked at a hospital for nearly six years. Through that time I also witnessed the horrors of COVID and got to see first hand that this virus was no ordinary flu or cold, it was a monster that devastated people's lives. Maybe this is why I was frequently frustrated by Trump and other republicans who took the COVID pandemic so lightly. Honestly, I can say that I lost a lot of faith in people throughout the pandemic as people protested against wearing masks and didn't take any precautions to save people that were vulnerable. Yes, the healthcare system went through a scary time with COVID, but it faced a scary time before and is facing a scary time after the pandemic. I mean to suggest that our healthcare in this country is disastrous in the fact that many people can't or don't have access to the care that they need.

One of the ways in which republicans hammer against the democrats is their "radicalism" about healthcare. We have Obamacare as the law of the land today. That's a good healthcare policy, but in my view doesn't go far enough in addressing the needs that everyday Americans face. When other democrats, or independents offer a different healthcare proposal, mostly in the form of "Medicare for all," or some other program that is incredibly similar, republicans go off on them and label them as "socialists" and "crazy." In reality this idea isn't as crazy as people think, it's been attempted numerous times in America by republicans and democrats alike. And we need it now more than ever before. More people are deciding not to get the medical care they need because they can't afford it. We can do better in this country, it's about time we get this right.

It makes no sense that in the 21st century Americans still have to make the decision of whether to go to the hospital and get the care that they need or pay for their groceries. And it doesn't make sense that somebody with cancer should have to spend their last few hours arguing with their insurance company over what is covered and what is not. The sick should not be punished for being sick, they shouldn't have to spend tens of thousands of dollars just because they got cancer, or had a heart attack, or have diabetes. Is there anything fair in that?

Bernie Sanders certainly is not the first to advocate for a federal healthcare program that will guarantee healthcare as a human right not a privilege. This is the kind of system that we should be thriving towards and this is the type of program that will work for America. If it works for other countries it certainly can work for us. We should not leave anybody behind and, quite frankly, this is the moral thing to do.

When I think about where our country has been in terms of healthcare it almost makes me laugh. We have gone through quite a rough road to get to where we are today. The first thing that I think of is hygiene. It was very uncommon for everyday Americans, in the 18th and early 19th centuries, to take a bath more than once a year. The only people that would take a bath more than once a year were incredibly wealthy, while the rest of the population simply didn't have time or didn't care. Can you imagine the stink? And worse, can you imagine the health? Not surprisingly the health in this time period was very dismal. In fact, not accounting for all the unfortunate early deaths of children and babies, the life expectancy in the 1800s was around 65 years for men.[564] Shockingly this is only 7 years less than the life expectancy of poor men today, though I would venture to guess that hygiene is what did them in 200 years ago.

Even when Lewis and Clark went on their expedition through the woods they conversed with numerous physicians and experts about what they needed and needed to do to stay safe and healthy away from civilization. They ended up taking tons of different medicines and remedies for all sorts of things with them. In reality, not much at the time was scientifically proven. Most medicines doled out were just remedies believed to work by the doctors. In some cases, the medicines they used on patients actually made their symptoms much, much, worse. Think of our Founder George Washington, the poor guy was bled to death after the doctors stuffed him full of enemas and other atrocious things to make his sufferings much worse than they had to be. In fact, if they would have left him alone he probably would have survived.

Things didn't get much better as time went on. People routinely had to get drunk if they were to have a surgery, as there was no such thing as anesthesia back then. There apparently was no such thing as sterile equipment either. Doctors and scientists had no idea that their instruments were laced with bacteria and infection as they stuck them in people's bodies. Another president, James Garfield, was treated by doctors after he was shot in the back. The doctors proceeded to try to pry the bullet out of his torso with their filthy rotten hands. Not surprisingly, Garfield died because of an infection, he would have survived if the doctors just kept the bullet in his body, as he

---

564Basaraba, Sharon. 2012. "A Guide to Longevity throughout History, from the Prehistoric Onward." Verywell Health. Verywellhealth. September 18, 2012. https://www.verywellhealth.com/longevity-throughout-history-2224054.

was on the mend of recovery before the doctors intervened. Given these events we should all be thankful that we learned a thing or two about healthcare over the years. I feel better already.

In fact, even by the year 1908 there was no health insurance as of yet, and healthcare for the most part wasn't even regulated, meaning hospitals and doctors had a very broad interpretation of what they could do. Most doctors would be summoned to the homes of those who were sick or injured and the patient's would pay the bill out of pocket. Back in these times healthcare was much more affordable than what it is now, in fact, people were more concerned with missing out on work, and their subsequent paychecks, than they were about paying the medical bills.[565]

Insurance companies at the time just couldn't fathom the risks involved with insuring patients, as the AMA Journal of Ethics reports "Commercial insurance companies did not write health insurance policies in 1908; they saw no way to avoid the risks of adverse selection (those who were sick would seek coverage, and those who were healthy would not) and moral hazard (coverage would encourage the insured to seek unnecessary services), and they lacked the means to calculate risks accurately and set appropriate premiums. Within the next 10 years, many European nations would adopt some form of compulsory national health insurance, but similar proposals in the U.S. were rejected because of lack of interest and resistance from physicians and commercial insurers."[566]

At least initially, when health insurance companies first started dabbling in the field of protection they were out to help people to bear the costs of a workplace accident or sickness. However, every company starts out to make a profit, and these profits would soon

---

[565] Moseley, George. 2008. "The U.S. Health Care Non-System, 1908-2008." *AMA Journal of Ethics* 10 (5): 324–31. https://doi.org/10.1001/virtualmentor.2008.10.5.mhst1-0805.
[566] Ibid

get out of hand later down the road. But, back in the 1910s, insurance was reasonable due to the low costs of healthcare. And costs would remain low until the 1920s when reformers started to push for higher quality standards for hospitals and physicians. No doubt about it, these changes happened for the good, but obviously with an increase in technology and treatment methods came an increase in the cost of healthcare, and finally, hospitals were starting to sanitize their equipment to prevent wide-scale infections, this all led to healthcare getting a little bit pricey.

At first, doctors really resented having insurance companies around because these companies, doctors feared, would lower the prices that doctor's could get paid. So, some doctors banded together to create the insurance company Blue Shield. Slowly, but surely, these insurance companies started to get rich off of the backs of the American people. Not everyone needed care, they essentially were paying for what could potentially happen. In this case families paid more for healthcare than they otherwise would. Believe it or not, insurance companies were not seen as the bogeyman, instead they were seen as a sort of cure-all relief to protect working class people from injuries and illnesses that could easily put them in debt. Some state laws were even considered and passed to force people to have some sort of healthcare insurance. This idea was not that far out of right field because automobiles were starting to hit the road in increasing numbers and the government did the same thing with them, that is they forced car owners to have insurance. It wasn't until after the Russian revolution and the red scare that conservatives were able to muster up enough power to break these laws, citing them as "communistic."[567] Reformers lost their dream of compulsory health

---

567 Palmer, Karen. 2009. "A Brief History: Universal Health Care Efforts in the US." PNHP. 2009. https://pnhp.org/a-brief-history-universal-health-care-efforts-in-the-us/.

insurance, not because they wanted to fatten the pockets of the insurance companies but because they wanted everyone to get the healthcare that they needed and save lives, due to a hysteria. To be fair, these insurance companies did help ease the fear of Americans to go to the hospital if they get sick.

And why did the compulsory insurance plan fail? PNHP says it was due to the "opposition from doctors, labor, insurance companies, and businesses that contributed to the failure of Progressives to achieve compulsory national health insurance."[568] That is an awfully lot of special interests with a lot of power and money that opposed this plan. Insurance companies opposed the plan due to the fact that they would have to cover everyone, even those with pre-existing conditions who have a much higher likelihood of needing lots of treatment and care. It just goes to tell you that it was all about money. It was all about money then, and it still is today. But even here we have agitation brewing for a healthcare for all solutions to the healthcare problem.

During the Great Depression, FDR had wanted to pass a healthcare program to go along with his New Deal but the primary focus was to shift attention to social security and unemployment relief and unfortunately healthcare was left out of the loop for the entirety of that period. More than anything, Americans were just staying home when they got sick, they certainly couldn't afford to receive the care they needed during this period. As a matter of fact, FDR had wanted to include compulsory health care coverage in his social security program but top lawmakers gutted it from the program fearing that republicans wouldn't go along and pass the bill.

FDR even tried once again to get a universal healthcare plan. Named the Wagner Bill, after its sponsor Robert Wagner. The bill

---

568 Ibid

would have contained the same provisions that were gutted in earlier attempts. Unfortunately for the people, it was introduced in the midst of an election cycle that saw a rise in the conservative movement following the New Deal in 1938. With more liberal democrats being defeated, and conservatives joining Congress, the bill didn't really go anywhere and the American people still found themselves without universal care.

Again, we weren't quite done seeing an end to this effort, and in 1943, Wagner, again with the support of FDR and liberal democrats fought back with another bill. It became the famous Wagner-Murray-Dingell Bill. No surprise here, the bill called for a compulsory national health insurance program. According to the American Historical Association, "The bill provided that health insurance would be established by the creation of a national medical care and hospitalization fund, to which employers and employees would each contribute 1.5 percent of the first $3,000 of annual wages, making 3 percent in all...For every insured person and his family, the. medical care and hospitalization fund would pay for unlimited doctors' care including specialists, for hospitalization up to 30 days, X rays, and laboratory tests. Dental care, nursing, medicines and drugs would not be paid for."[569] Nothing too unusual here, just a hospitalization fund that would help ensure that every American got the care that they need. If they are paying for it, why not use it?

The bill received a lot of support from labor unions and the working class population, who viewed this as the greatest improvement since social security. However, the bill did have its fair share

---

569 American Historical Society, "Has a National Health Program Been Put Before Congress"https://www.historians.org/about-aha-and-membership/aha-history-and-archives/gi-roundtable-series/pamphlets/em-29-is-your-health-the-nations-business-(1946)/has-a-national-health-program-been-put-before-congress#:~:text=The%20First%20Wagner%2DMurray%2DDingell%20Bill&text=The%20bill%20provided%20that%20health,making%203%20percent%20in%20all

of naysayers, who said the typical when they disagree with a health care proposal, to call it "socialized medicine." In fact, "opposition groups said that the bill implied that sick people would have to depend on a doctor paid by the government to work only eight hours daily-emergency cases would have to wait until the doctor checked in. Patients would have to go to the doctor assigned to them by political bureaucrats, and doctors would become incompetent because methods and remedies would be fixed by bureaucratic superiors. Largely to oppose this bill, physicians and drug houses raised and spent over a quarter of a million dollars in giving out information of this nature."[570] It's clear that the organized opposition to this new plan was bent on destroying the bill to the point that they actively spread lies trying to defeat it. Like what normally happens, the public was quickly overwhelmed with all of this negativity surrounding the bill, even though much of this was completely untrue. In reality, many of the naysayers were ones who were subject to losing a little in wages if the bill passed. And, again, because of all the fear-mongering the bill was never passed in either house, though it received the support of many low-income Americans who stood to benefit most by the bill.

In 1945, FDR died after suffering poor health for years and finally having a stroke that did him in. As a result, Harry Truman became the next president of the US. He believed in a healthcare for all system, but instead of having a compulsory health insurance plan he actually favored a single payer universal health care plan. Where FDR had been more focused on providing care for the needy, Truman believed that the only functional way this would work is to provide universal health care for all classes of society, supporting the egalitarian method instead. The plan was practical as it would

---

[570] Ibid

include everybody and had proposals within it that were meant as a compromise to both sides, yet republican senator Robert Taft, son of president William H. Taft, had some pretty harsh words for the proposal, "I consider it socialism. It is to my mind the most socialist measure this Congress has ever had before it."[571] He even claimed that the proposal came right out of the Soviet Union's constitution. It didn't. But, this didn't stop him from lying to the American people about the proposal in an effort to kill it. Again, big special interests united together to prevent Truman from realizing his dream of universal coverage.

In 1946, the republicans took control of the Congress and essentially blocked everything that Truman had proposed. (Totally beside the topic of this chapter, republicans in 1947 passed, over Truman's veto, the Taft-Hartley Act that targeted unions by going after their power to strike, calling strikes illegal and decimating union membership.) Republicans in 1947 claimed that America would never have the "socialist dream" of nationalized healthcare and their big-money lobbyists were ripe with joy. This joy quickly subsided when Harry Truman was re-elected in 1948 after he barnstormed the entire country and spoke of the benefits of his health care proposals. Clearly, the American people were on-board with Truman's policies.

These special interest groups opposed to the nationwide healthcare plan thought that the day of reckoning was coming for them. The AMA in particular took out an additional $25 for its memberships in a bid to accumulate enough money to bring down the healthcare plan. "In 1945 they spent $1.5 million on lobbying efforts which

---

571 Palmer, Karen. 2009. "A Brief History: Universal Health Care Efforts in the US." PNHP. 2009. https://pnhp.org/a-brief-history-universal-health-care-efforts-in-the-us/.

at the time was the most expensive lobbying effort in American history."[572] They even went so far as to compare this healthcare proposal to that of Vladimir Lenin of the Soviet Union declaring that it was a "keystone" to Lenin's perfect state. These wealthy interests did a very good job of pinning the healthcare plan to socialists. At the time, there was wide-spread anti-communism. Not only were Americans deeply suspicious of communism abroad but they were equally, or even more, scared of communism at home. Richard Nixon rose to fame by falsely accusing his opponents of communism if they disagreed with him and took slightly more liberal positions on issues. He even went so far as to call Helen Gahagan Douglas, his opponent in the California gubernatorial campaign, "pink right down to her panties." These attacks believe it or not worked, as Nixon cruised his way to victory after victory by simply fear-mongering, a tactic that republicans would use over and over again throughout the century. Joe McCarthy would become infamous for calling out "supposed" communists in the US government. Most people were not communists, though some may have been a little more liberal than the times.

Nevertheless, because republicans successfully attacked the healthcare plan in the 1940s, comparing it to socialism and calling out all democrats who supported the proposal, while at the same time receiving contributions from their special interest friends, they were able to block the nationalized health care plan. So, instead of making sure that everybody had the health care that they needed, millions of Americans who couldn't afford coverage were left out in the dust. They either went massively in debt because they got sick or injured or they took the bullet and refrained from going to the hospital at all. Disappointed by the defeat, reformers looked for a

---

572 Ibid

more modest approach that would be the next best thing, that being healthcare coverage for the old and feeble. This would become known as Medicare.

The National Archives noted that "The 1950 census showed that the aged population in the United States had grown from 3 million in 1900 to 12 million in 1950. Two-thirds of older Americans had incomes of less than $1,000 annually, and only one in eight had health insurance. Between 1950 and 1963, the aged population grew from about 12 million to 17.5 million, or from 8.1 to 9.4 percent of the U.S. population. At the same time, the cost of hospital care was rising at a rate of about 6.7 percent a year, several times the annual increase in the cost of living, and health care costs were rapidly outpacing growth in the incomes of older Americans."[573]

Obviously there was a need to invest in a form of healthcare to offset these increasing costs that the nation's elderly were dealing with. At the time if you were an older American with a history of cancer or heart failure insurance companies could deny coverage and leave them with no way to afford their procedures and medication. In fact, Congress was forced to do something about this issue because of the increasing backlash regarding how ineffective and inhumane the healthcare system was becoming for the elderly. President Johnson signed the bill authorizing medicare in 1965 with Harry Truman in attendance in commemoration of his efforts to achieve universal coverage.

Of course there were critics of medicare as well. Mostly the same old fear-mongering was leveled by conservatives that saw this as a stepping stone to socialized medicine. Many conservatives were also opposed to the idea of giving the elderly universal health care,

---

[573] National Archives. 2021. "Medicare and Medicaid Act (1965)." National Archives. October 5, 2021. https://www.archives.gov/milestone-documents/medicare-and-medicaid-act.

as they feared that it would be too costly. They reasoned that the elderly have significant costs to health care, as opposed to younger, healthier individuals. With the increased costs of healthcare their reasoning was it would drive healthcare premiums through the roof. Nonetheless, this time their fear-mongering didn't succeed, as the vast majority of Americans saw through the bull crap and realized that this was necessary. Just imagine where we would be if we didn't have medicare. Today, medicare is one of the most prized programs that the government offers as assistance to those that desperately need health. Because of the recent republican tax cuts for wealthy people and companies some republicans have even stooped so low as to cut the benefits of medicare, against the will of the American people.

The same can be said of medicaid, resulting in medical coverage for those that had limited incomes and disabilities, passed and signed that same year. Medicaid called for the states to manage and fund the program, yet the federal government would take control of rules and policies. Again, insurance companies railed against these plans because they would lose their enormous revenues. Yet, more people than ever before were covered with healthcare that otherwise wouldn't be accessible for them. It is very clear that these programs, medicare and medicaid, were hugely popular with the people, who wouldn't be so forgiving if republicans cut the programs to give Elon Musk an additional $20 million in tax relief.

During the 1950s and 1960s there was much concern over a shortage of healthcare professionals. Indeed, some were even concerned that increasing accessibility for everyone to have healthcare would lead to long wait times because we just simply didn't have enough doctors available for everybody. So, the government, under the control of progressive-minded democrats, created a program under the Health Professions Educational Assistance Act of 1963.[574] The program created direct financial assistance to medical, dental, nursing, pharmacy, and other health professional schools and institutions to lower tuition rates and increase the programs that were available. This act single handedly helped create a surge in medical students, who all of the sudden could afford to spend twelve years in school to provide essential care to Americans.

In a similar way today, we hear a lot of rancor among conservatives who claim that if we have a medicare for all form of healthcare all of the sudden we would have extremely long waiting times because everyone would want to seek care. To me that's an incredibly stupid argument. How can you say that giving more people access to healthcare is a bad thing? Shouldn't that be what we strive for? For everybody to go to a healthcare clinic when they need to? For preventive care to guard against cancer or other maladies? Instead, many republicans say this would lead to unbearable wait times and resort to a healthcare scenario like Canada, where people wait for months to get the care they need. Well I've got something to tell them. We already have extremely long waiting times. We already have people waiting months to receive the care they need, so what's the difference? I once talked to an elderly lady who had issues with her kidney. She needed to wait four months before the next available appointment. So, why do we hear these grumblings? Because republicans want to sabotage a universal healthcare plan. If they really cared about the staffing shortages for our doctors, which are currently contributing to our long wait times, then they would pass a similar bill creating a program that would provide financial

---

574 Moseley, George. 2008. "The U.S. Health Care Non-System, 1908-2008." *AMA Journal of Ethics* 10 (5): 324–31. https://doi.org/10.1001/virtualmentor.2008.10.5.mhst1-0805..

assistance for healthcare professionals to make it more of an appealing career choice as one that was passed in 1963. I have an even better idea, free college tuition would most likely do the trick. Instead of medical students raking up hundreds of thousands of dollars in debt they could instead focus on obtaining their degree free of crippling debt. Maybe that would make it more desirable to become a doctor.

Anyways, getting back to previous efforts to increase healthcare coverage, we turn to a surprising source. That being Richard Nixon, who believed that everyone should have access to healthcare. In fact, the Commonwealth Fund has this to say about Nixon, "Perhaps because of a childhood plagued by health problems (two of Nixon's brothers died of tuberculosis, and he likely had a mild case himself), Nixon was deeply sympathetic to the health challenges facing Americans, and he came to believe in the necessity to cover everyone."[575] But, Nixon was a republican, meaning that this idea wasn't very popular among his own party colleagues. He decided the best way to achieve his means is to mandate healthcare coverage through employment and to increase governmental funding for the poor and elderly. If his plans were realized, everybody with a job would have immediate healthcare coverage, there would be a limit on what a family would have to spend on healthcare bills, and the "federal government would provide temporary subsidies to small and low-wage employers to offer employees affordable insurance."[576]

Nixon also wanted to eliminate medicaid but replace it with a program that would cap out of pocket expenses for those living in poverty, and eliminate premiums. Middle income folks could also buy into this kind of coverage. Essentially, this was very similar to

---

575 Seervai, Shanoor, and David Blumenthal. 2019. "Lessons on Universal Coverage from Richard Nixon." Commonwealthfund.org. commonwealthfund. May 23, 2019. https://www.commonwealthfund.org/blog/2017/lessons-universal-coverage-unexpected-advocate-richard-nixon.
576 ibid

the kind of healthcare plan that Hillary Clinton proposed in her 2016 presidential campaign.[577] Believe it or not, these proposals were pretty popular with both political parties. Unfortunately, the proposal fizzled because of Watergate, which essentially drowned out all other news.

Nonetheless, it is telling that one of the worst presidents in United States history, had the foresight enough to understand that more people needed quality coverage. Shortly after he resigned from office, the republicans turned their backs on his proposals. Gerald Ford, who succeeded Nixon to the presidency, initially focused his attention on healthcare but concluded, "We cannot realistically afford federally dictated national health insurance providing full coverage for all 215 million Americans."[578] Instead of putting their heads together to serve the people, they considered it much easier to just ignore the problem, while satisfying themselves that we couldn't afford healthcare coverage while at the same time spending massive amounts on military expeditions. And of course, hurting the healthcare for all effort, inflation would continue to get worse throughout the Ford year and lasting until the Raegan revolution.

When Jimmy Carter ran for president, he was adamant about having a universal form of healthcare. Leading the effort for universal coverage was Edward "Ted" Kennedy, who was passionate about this issue because of an experience he went through when his own son had a hospitalization scare. He devoted himself to making sure that everyone, rich and poor, had the opportunity that his son had, to receive adequate healthcare without being charged an arm and a leg. He was devoted to creating a single-payer system that would make the government the sole financial driver of healthcare

---

577 Ibid
578 "Presidents on Health Care | Miller Center." 2022. Millercenter.org. January 25, 2022. https://millercenter.org/health-care-policy/presidents-health-care.

coverage. Jimmy Carter supported this idea but quickly gave it up preferring to minimize the budget in response to the economic issues of the day. Carter understood that the democrats desperately wanted this but he didn't know how to proceed, "Everybody in the Democratic Party wanted a health care bill. The issue was what kind of a health care bill."[579] Wanting to please all sides, and believing that he couldn't possibly create a universal healthcare plan in one fell swoop, he determined to keep costs down and gradually cover all Americans. They would have "combined Medicare and Medicaid into one program. The government would have paid for the poor and the old, and we would have mandated employers—starting the way [Franklin] Roosevelt started the minimum wage—we'd mandate the big employers, who were already providing more than the mandate, to provide mandated coverage, and then gradually, over a period of time, cover everybody."[580]

This timid approach, though, did not satisfy Teddy Kennedy, who thought that this was a disaster that would inevitably lead to failure. This created a lasting breach between Kennedy and Carter, with the former running against the latter during the 1980 democratic presidential primary. Ultimately Carter defeated Kennedy in the primaries and lost to Ronald Raegan in the general election after Carter didn't do a whole lot to expand coverage after initially pledging to. As a result, his administration proved quite lackluster in many regards, healthcare among the top.

When Ronald Raegan was elected riding a storm of conservative sentiment throughout the country, mainly because the economy was tanking hard and the American people wanted something different, we got a real taste of what his administration would look like

---

579 Ibid
580 ibid

in his inaugural address, "In this present crisis, government is not the solution to our problem; government is the problem."[581] That pretty much sums up Raegan's plan on governing. So, even though healthcare for all was supported by many Americans, Raegan was content to do nothing on this subject. Raegan, the superhero to many conservatives today, led the government through the period when the elderly and the poor paid more for healthcare than at any other time up to this point, and instead found it more politically necessary to increase defense spending than to invest in the healthcare needs of the country.

Indeed, through subsequent administrations we have often heard of the healthcare crisis. Bill Clinton was devoted to tackling healthcare when he proposed a task force, headed by his wife, First-Lady Hillary Clinton, for the sole purpose of finding a nation-wide healthcare plan that would be affordable and efficient. In a speech, Clinton made a call for a healthcare plan very similar to that of what Richard Nixon proposed by mandating that employers provide healthcare coverage to their employees. But, this plan that was widely accepted from both parties in the 1970s drew sharp criticism from conservatives, libertarians, and health insurance companies.

Of course, you know that it has more to do with partisan squabbling than with common sense reasoning when lawmakers opposed the bill before the bill had even come out yet by organizing to defeat the measure. When Hillary Clinton testified in Congress about the merits of the plan and why Americans needed this coverage, republicans hammered her right from the beginning with questions that clearly indicated their enthusiasm for defeating the bill.

William Kristol, the leader of a policy organization for Congressional republicans said in a now notorious memo sent to

---

581 Ibid

republican lawmakers "The long-term political effects of a successful... health care bill will be even worse—much worse. ... It will revive the reputation of. ... Democrats as the generous protector of middle-class interests. And it will at the same time strike a punishing blow against Republican claims to defend the middle class by restraining the government."582 That says it all. Republicans were opposed to this bill for purely political reasons. They knew that if the plan had been passed it would help an overwhelming amount of Americans. Yet they feared that if a democratic administration had provided a major win for the American people the republican party would lose middle class voters forever. Let me ask you a question. Do you vote for somebody and spend taxes to support their income in Congress to do your will and help you and your neighbors, or do you elect them to play party politics at the detriment of you and your neighbors? If you chose the latter then you must be ecstatic over the republicans and their game here. They sacrificed helping the American people for their own political benefit, it doesn't get much lower than that in my estimation.

All of this and wide scale advertising against the proposal played into the hands of the bill's opponents. Of course, these big time special interests, like all of the healthcare insurance companies, had tons of money to spend trying to defeat the bill, meanwhile the American people couldn't compete with all of the money that these huge corporate titans were willing to spend. Unfortunately for Americans, the bill went down to defeat, a major blow for the Clinton administration. Now, to be fair, there were quite a few democrats who opposed the Clinton plan because they wanted to go further and advance to a single-payer healthcare system, but

---

582 Rick Perlstein, "Thinking Like a Conservative (Part Three): On Shutting Down Government Archived April 13, 2015, at the Wayback Machine", *The Nation,*

would have felt obliged to support a proposal that would benefit middle-class Americans than nothing at all.

When Hillary Clinton was no longer first lady and instead a senator from New York, with her eyes on the presidency herself, she came around to develop a more moderate approach to healthcare. She even went so far as to suggest that she learned a lot over the years and realized that she needs to cooperate with republicans to get a bill that would garner enough support from both parties to become law. That sounds pretty good on its face, of course you want to compromise as much as possible with the other side to achieve accomplishments. The only problem with this reasoning is that it was not practical at all. Republicans, with their big-money allies, have waged an all-out war against any national healthcare plan that may be conceived. Some even want to scale back medicare and medicaid. How can you cooperate with that? If you do cooperate with that then you would be giving the American people a significant blow to their healthcare coverage and drastically increase their expenditures.

In fact, it has been widely known that Hillary Clinton has received huge chunks of money from doctors, hospitals, drug companies, and insurance companies in campaign contributions, some of which spent huge sums of money in efforts to defeat her earlier program.[583] Maybe this has something to do with her sudden change in ideology. She has changed her stance on healthcare to align with all of the companies and associations that are giving her millions of dollars in contributions. That's what big-money does. And working with republicans, I mean come on, we should know better. From the republicans increasingly growing further to the right and accepting huge contributions from these special interests, we should know

---

583 Hernandez, Raymond and Pear, Robert. "Once an Enemy, Health Industry Warms to Clinton," Archived August 14, 2018, at the Wayback Machine *The New York Times*

that if we are to have a nationalized healthcare plan it would have to be passed by the democrats exclusively, which brings even more pressure to elect democrats at the national and even state levels.

This finally happened during the 2008 elections. The economy was pitiful, unemployment was high, and the great recession was making its impact all across the states. Obviously, there were many reasons for the recession but one of the big reasons was the subprime mortgage crisis that was fueled by widespread speculation that was growing in intensity since the Bush's and Clinton's deregulation of the financial industry. Given the state of the economy, it was pretty much common knowledge that the democrats were going to win big. Then candidate Barack Obama had campaigned on fixing the economy and providing a nationalized form of healthcare.

As expected, the 2008 election night was a big night for democrats. Obama carried 365 electoral votes compared to 173 for John McCain. Even better for democrats, they walloped the republicans in the House, winning 257 seats to 178. They also controlled the senate 57 seats to 41, with 2 independants. Thus the democrats saw an easy way to push for passage a healthcare plan that would extend coverage to all Americans. And they did, passing the Affordable Care Act, or "Obamacare" as the republicans derisively labeled it. In the senate the bill passed with every single democrat voting for it, while every single republican voted against it, in the House only one republican voted for it while every democrat voted for it. The law did many things, including dramatically expanding medicaid coverage, creating health insurance exchanges, mandating that everyone would have to obtain healthcare, just like car insurance, or be fined, and lastly and most importantly it banned insurance companies from refusing to insure those with pre-existing conditions.[584] Before the bill was passed a woman who had breast cancer would find it virtually impossible to find an insurance company that would insure them. As a result, many families with a loved one who had pre-existing conditions would find themselves deeply in debt trying to pay for the medical expenses or forgoing medical treatment in general to prevent their family's financial stability from crumbling. Needless to say many people died as a result. The law was clearly a big win for Americans and a big loss to insurance companies who now were forced to give up some of their profits to ensure that everybody has a quality insurance plan. This would explain why they were so opposed to this plan, as every important bill has its many opponents. This time again the republicans saw themselves on the same side as the insurance companies and big time lobbyists. Even Sarah Palin, the republican vice presidential candidate in 2008, described Obamacare as a great evil that would open the door to death panels. "The America I know and love," she cried out, "is not one in which my parents or my baby with Down Syndrome will have to stand in front of Obama's death panel so his bureaucrats can decide, based on a subjective judgment of their 'level of productivity in society."[585] Believe it or not, the overall idea was that Obama would force people who were sick to be euthanized. This, obviously, couldn't be more false, yet that didn't stop republicans from theorizing the worst, I even remember my grandmother,

---

584 KENTON, WILL . 2022. "Affordable Care Act (ACA): What It Is, Key Features, and Updates." Investopedia. September 23, 2022. https://www.investopedia.com/terms/a/affordable-care-act.asp#:~:text=The%20Patient%20Protection%20and%20Affordable%20Care%20Act%20(ACA)%20was%20passed.
585 Gonyea, Don. 2017. "From the Start, Obama Struggled with Fallout from a Kind of Fake News." NPR.org. January 10, 2017. https://www.npr.org/2017/01/10/509164679/from-the-start-obama-struggled-with-fallout-from-a-kind-of-fake-news.

who was a die-hard republican, telling me how Obama was going to euthanize her. Of course, it didn't help that conservative hero Rush Limbaugh praised Palin saying she's "dead right."[586]

Despite all the criticism, the law cut the number of Americans uninsured by half, and a study concluded that in just three years following the adoption of the ACA, 50,000 lives were saved that would have been lost without coverage. Another study concluded that roughly 43,000 lives would be lost annually if the ACA medicaid benefits were cut.[587] With these statistics it's hard to develop a strong opposition to the ACA. You have to ask yourselves a question, what's more important, saving lives or listening to the false attacks that republicans have been hurling at the ACA ever since its adoption.

Another important element to the ACA is its medicaid expansion provision. The ACA raised the threshold of income to receive medicaid coverage through the states in an effort to achieve universal healthcare, meaning more people would be eligible for medicaid coverage. States that chose to expand their coverage to reach a greater share of their population would have the prices covered by the federal government for the first three years. It was a win-win for states. They could now cover more of its people with healthcare than ever before and not have to pay a nickel for three years. It doesn't get much better than that. The problem is that many republican states saw this as a gimmick and decided to play political games instead of providing healthcare to their poorest citizens.

26 states and the District of Columbia right away agreed to the expansion, 10 other states quickly followed suit. Today, there

---

586 Ibid
587 Himmelstein, David; Woolhandler, Steffi (January 23, 2017). "Repealing the Affordable Care Act will kill more than 43,000 people annually". *The Washington Post*.

are still 10 states that have refused to expand medicaid so that those who make slightly higher than poverty wages can receive medicaid benefits. These states are: Wyoming, Nebraska, Texas, Mississippi, Tennessee, Alabama, Georgia, Florida, South Carolina, and Wisconsin. In the case of Wisconsin, when the ACA was passed and signed into law, thus doling out medicaid benefits, Wisconsin had a staunchly conservative governor, Scott Walker, and the worst gerry-mandered state in the nation heavily rigged for the republicans benefit. Thus to this day, Wisconsinites are still handicapped by the gerrymandered maps of 2010, even though a majority of Wisconsinites want medicaid expanded.

Have you noticed anything else with these states that have not expanded medicaid benefits? Two things jump out at me. One, all of these states are incredibly republican, meaning that under republican leadership there is no chance of expanding medicaid. And, two, most of these states, again, are in the deep-south, where the highest levels of poverty are. You would think that if so much of their population is living in poverty the state governments would try their damndest to help them, or at least give them the resources that every other state gives its citizens, but alas, it's no use. Republicans care more about playing petty games than ensuring that everybody within their jurisdiction has healthcare. That's pretty sad. It should be mentioned that a few heavily republican states have understood the complexities of healthcare and did the right thing to expand medicaid to reach the poorest community. These states include: Idaho, Utah, Montana, Missouri, Oklahoma, Arkansas, Louisiana, Kentucky, and West Virginia. At least the leaders of these states were able to leave politics behind and do the right thing.

A recent study found that mortality rates declined sharply for those states that decided to expand medicaid coverage. That same study found that in those states that did not expand coverage approximately 15,600 deaths occurred because of it through the years 2014-2017.[588] The states that have not expanded it can't argue that it would cost their state money, the federal government pledged to finance it, there is no excuse for this.

The ACA still to this day is highly controversial, mostly because of political considerations. Today, almost 65% of Americans have a favorable opinion of the ACA, while only 30% disapprove of the program, with the insurance companies still being the largest voice of dissent.[589] Yet this didn't stop Trump from attacking the ACA and almost dismantling the entire program just because it defined the Obama administration. The idea of "repeal and replace" has been at the top of republicans list for years ever since Obamacare was passed. They finally got the opportunity when Trump became president with a heavily controlled republican congress to do Trump's bidding.

In the summer of 2017, the republicans thought they had their brilliant chance to overturn Obamacare, with its pre-existing conditions and all. They certainly had a good opportunity to, they controlled all of the government. Yet, they had horrible leadership at the top. From the get-go the effort to "repeal and replace" Obamacare was bungled, confused, and truly humiliating for conservatives. Trump got a little ahead of himself on his first day in office when he signed an executive order to help "ease the burden of Obamacare as we transition from repeal and replace."[590] Most presidents use their

---

588 Miller, Sarah; Johnson, Norman; Wherry, Laura R. (January 30, 2021). "Medicaid and Mortality: New Evidence from Linked Survey and Administrative Data*". *The Quarterly Journal of Economics*
589 "Public View on ACA U.S. 2010-2021." n.d. Statista. https://www.statista.com/statistics/246901/opinion-on-the-health-reform-law-in-the-united-states/.
590 Luhby, Tami (January 9, 2017). "How Trump could use his executive power on Obamacare". *CNNMoney*

first day to help people get better outcomes, to help increase people's standard of living, and do something that would be memorable. Well, it was memorable all right. Trump instead of helping more people get healthcare resolved tried to kick millions of people off of their healthcare plans. This was a sign for all of us that a day of reckoning was coming.

In March, republicans in the House attempted to pass their own healthcare plan known as the American Health Care Act. The Commonwealth Fund states that the act "would repeal and replace the Affordable Care Act. The Congressional Budget Office indicates that the AHCA could increase the number of uninsured by 23 million by 2026."[591] Not only would it throw 23 million people off of their current healthcare coverage, thereby they would now be all on their own, some with daunting levels of medical debt because of it, but it would also:

"raise employment and economic activity at first, but lower them in the long run. It initially raises the federal deficit when taxes are repealed, leading to 864,000 more jobs in 2018. In later years, reductions in support for health insurance cause negative economic effects. By 2026, 924,000 jobs would be lost, gross state products would be $93 billion lower, and business output would be $148 billion less. About three-quarters of jobs lost (725,000) would be in the health care sector. States which expanded Medicaid would experience faster and deeper economic losses."[592]

Yes, it would be a total disaster on many fronts, even the economy would suffer because of this plan. Not surprisingly, this plan

---

[591] Leighton Ku, Erika Steinmetz, Erin Brantley, Nikhil Holla, and Brian K. Bruen, The American Health Care Act: Economic and Employment Consequences for States, June 2017, https://www.commonwealthfund.org/sites/default/files/documents/___media_files_publications_issue_brief_2017_jun_ku_economic_effects_ahca_ib.pdf

[592] Ibid

couldn't even garner enough support from House republicans to pass it, (with every democrat fundamentally opposed to the lackluster plan). At least initially. Months later, after much pressure from fellow colleagues and special interest groups, republican leaders were now able to strong-arm the rest of the party to fall in line with the plan. Consequently the law passed the House 217-213 and went on to the senate. The republican senate, on the other hand, found steep issues with the House plan and determined to create a healthcare policy of their own.

Finally, in June, the senate came out with the Better Care Reconciliation Act. The proposed law would, again, repeal and replace Obamacare, yet it proved to be only slightly better than the plan that the House republicans unveiled. This plan "would raise the number of uninsured by 22 million by 2026."[593] Studies have shown that the plan would:

"lead to significantly larger job losses and deeper reductions in states' economies by 2026. A brief spurt in employment would add 753,000 more jobs in 2018, but employment would then deteriorate sharply. By 2026, 1.45 million fewer jobs would exist, compared to levels under the current law. Every state except Hawaii would have fewer jobs and a weaker economy. Employment in health care would be especially hard hit with 919,000 fewer health jobs, but other employment sectors lose jobs too. Gross state products would be $162 billion lower in 2026. States that expanded Medicaid would be especially hard hit."[594]

Again, the effort would have left millions upon millions unemployed and hurt the economy immensely, yet the proposal kept moving along through the efforts of Trump and his cronies. It looked

---

593 Ibid
594 Ibid

as if the republicans were going to ram this law down the throats of the American people, I mean, they had the votes. All they needed was for all but two republicans to go along with the plan to pass it (Republicans had 53 seats to the democrats who had 47. A tie vote would have led to vice-president Mike Pence to cast his vote to break the tie, which would have passed the "repeal and replace" proposal.

All along the Better Care Reconciliation Act, and all efforts to "repeal and replace", were hastily conducted with very little research and thought. All along the only thing that mattered was seeking revenge on Obamacare and destroying it once and for all, even if they didn't have an adequate backup plan that would have covered those who would have lost insurance and those with pre-existing conditions. With republican senators Lisa Murkowski and Susan Collins voicing displeasure with the bill and voting against it all eyes turned towards senator John McCain, republican from Arizona. McCain had just returned to Washington after receiving a brain cancer diagnosis, which added to the drama of the room. Everybody in the senate chamber watched as John McCain walked into the chamber and gave the famous thumbs down sign indicating that he voted against the bill with the two other republican senators and all democrats, killing the bill as democrats could be heard, understandably relieved that millions of Americans had just kept their coverage, clapping and cheering in the background.

Trump, no doubt, was thoroughly ticked at the vote. According to reports, Trump had pressured McCain on the phone the night before the vote, urging him to vote for the bill because it wouldn't pass anyway.[595] This clearly was a lie. The votes showed that the result would be entirely dependent on the vote of John McCain.

---

595 Leigh Ann Caldwell, Frank Thorp V, Vaughn Hillyard, and Kasie Hunt. 2017. "Obamacare Repeal Fails: Three GOP Senators Rebel in 49-51 Vote." NBC News. NBC News. July 28, 2017. https://www.nbcnews.com/politics/congress/senate-gop-effort-repeal-obamacare-fails-n787311.

Trump knew this. He just wanted the bill passed in the worst way, even if that means lying to a man who was a prisoner of war in the Vietnam war and had just learned that he had incurable brain cancer. Very classy move indeed. Trump also tried to pressure Lisa Murkowski, republican senator from Alaska, who opposed all the republican versions of the bill, by threatening to remove federal funding from Alaska as a consequence for Murkowski's vote.[596] Either way, Trump's pressure campaign didn't work and republicans promised themselves this wasn't the last time they would challenge the popular Obamacare. They would defeat it one way or another. At least, that's what they told themselves before they went to sleep at night. They knew that Obamacare was increasingly becoming more and more popular and if they were to kill it they only had a little bit of time left.

But, it soon turned out that even republicans that voted for the "repeal and replace" of Obamacare hated the bill. Lindsey Graham had this to say about the republican bill, "The skinny bill as policy is a disaster. The skinny bill as a replacement for Obamacare is a fraud. The skinny bill is a vehicle to getting conference to find a replacement."[597] It was clear that this was just a pressure campaign to gut Obamacare to the point where republicans were worried that it wouldn't fix anything.

Trump still went on the offensive to try to destroy, to his ability, the important concepts of Obamacare. He essentially reduced all outreach and enrollment opportunities, leaving Americans in limbo regarding their healthcare plans. He promoted waivers that would decrease ACA enrollments while rolling back quality regulations, placing burdens on people and administration, who had to show

---

596 Ibid
597 Ibid

work requirements to receive care. And, last but not least, he cut insurance company subsidies making premiums for middle class Americans to rise 20%.[598] So much for reducing burdens. However, none of these moves negatively affected the outlook of Obamacare as it remains very favorable to the American people.

Today, most republicans have given up on their dream of repealing the ACA. You will find very few battlestate republicans actively campaigning to repeal Obamacare on their official campaign websites. It's almost as if they accepted the inevitable, that Obamacare is here to stay. In fact, some republicans are now praising the law, "I'm opposed to repealing the Affordable Care Act" stated Joe O'Dea, republican Senate hopeful from Colorado. He went even further saying that "the ACA's protection for individuals with pre-existing conditions was one of the most important reforms passed in a generation."[599] O'Dea is correct, the law will go down in history to the likes of Medicare and Medicaid, social security, and the TVA.

My goal in showing you the history of our nation's battle with healthcare was to show that ever since the early 1900s politicians from all sects of the country, from both major political parties have supported universal healthcare. Teddy Roosevelt believed in it. Woodrow Wilson believed in it. Franklin Roosevelt. Harry Truman. Dwight Eisenhower. JFK. Lyndon Johnson. Richard Nixon. Jimmy Carter. Bill Clinton. Why do we sit here and act like universal healthcare is some sort of novel idea? That it is radical and that it would harm our healthcare? To those that believe that this idea is radical and can never be done, I simply say that you have let too much Fox news

---

598 Thompson, Frank J. 2020. "Six Ways Trump Has Sabotaged the Affordable Care Act." Brookings. October 9, 2020. https://www.brookings.edu/articles/six-ways-trump-has-sabotaged-the-affordable-care-act/.
599 Kapur, Sahil. 2022. "Republicans Abandon Obamacare Repeal." NBC News. October 2, 2022. https://www.nbcnews.com/politics/congress/republicans-abandon-obamacare-repeal-rcna49538.

and right-wing extremism get into your head. You've clearly been listening to greedy insurance companies, who have been filling your head with all of this garbage. So, I will now turn to why we shouldn't just simply stop at Obamacare. Without question, Obamacare was a great step forward, but more work needs to be done. We need to guarantee healthcare as a human right, not just something that the rich and powerful can afford.

The COVID pandemic was awful in more ways than one. But, the pandemic increased the urgency for Americans to develop a single payer healthcare system that is robust and covers everyone. Studies have shown that over one-third of all COVID deaths were preventable if those patients had better health insurance. Essentially hundreds of thousands of people died during COVID because of lack of healthcare. That's madness. And because massive layoffs and furloughs were the result of the COVID pandemic almost 30 million Americans lost their healthcare coverage when they lost their jobs, showing the fact that a healthcare plan tied to employment can cause dramatic disturbances when or if Americans lose their jobs.[600] Even before the pandemic about 27 million Americans were without healthcare coverage at all, making it incredibly dangerous to be living their day to day lives, knowing that a hospital visit could severely put them into debt.

And what about insurance companies? They are making record profits because they get to dictate what kind of care you can get, where you can go, and when you can get certain procedures. It's a mess. Some conservatives rage against a healthcare for all option

---

600 Sanders, U. n.d. "OFFICE OF." https://www.sanders.senate.gov/wp-content/uploads/Medicare-for-All-2022-Exec-Summary-FINAL.pdf.

when right now movement for patients is already limited because of their insurance. That's no way to live.

And it's not like our healthcare is cheap. The US spends about $13,000 on healthcare per capita, which is way more than most other industrialized countries including the UK, which spends approximately $5,000 per capita. That is the gross rate with insurance, medicare, ect. The average American family spends almost $9,000 a year on healthcare, which is an outrageous amount, this includes insurance.[601] In fact, our healthcare expenses are roughly twice the size of all other developed nations, and our quality of care is not so great. It is unbelievable that these countries spend half as much on healthcare than we do when they guarantee healthcare to everyone as a right.

Even more insulting is that in all other industrialized nations on earth, they do guarantee healthcare to all of its citizens, except the United States. It makes sense then that those citizens of these countries don't find themselves with massive loads of medical debt. Do you know which country has a lot of medical debt? If you guessed the United States you would be correct. In the United States, roughly one out of ten, or 25 million Americans have some sort of medical debt. 11 million Americans owe debt greater than $2,000 and 3 million Americans owe debt greater than $10,000.[602] That is a nationwide embarrassment. Guess what, if you get cancer, if you have a heart attack, if you have a rare disease, if you

---

601 "The Real Cost of Health Care: Interactive Calculator Estimates Both Direct and Hidden Household Spending." 2019. The Henry J. Kaiser Family Foundation. February 21, 2019. https://www.kff.org/health-costs/press-release/interactive-calculator-estimates-both-direct-and-hidden-household-spending/.
602 "1 in 10 Adults Owe Medical Debt, with Millions Owing More than $10,000." n.d. KFF. https://www.kff.org/health-costs/press-release/1-in-10-adults-owe-medical-debt-with-millions-owing-more-than-10000/#:~:text=The%202020%20survey%20suggests%20Americans.

have diabetes, you shouldn't find yourself in massive debt. Nobody wants to get sick, nobody wants to have a brain aneurysm. Why then should they be forced to fall thousands of dollars in debt? It makes no sense. Nobody should have to decide whether to go to the hospital and get the kind of care they need or fall into unbearable debt. This is why so many more Americans die unnecessarily because they simply fear to go to the hospital and fall into so much debt. And the last thing that patients should be doing is arguing with the insurance company about what they will cover and not as they are literally on their deathbed, as Barack Obama's mother had to do when she suffered from cancer. The American people deserve better.

Medical debt, of course, is most likely to affect low-income folks at disproportionate amounts. 3 out of 4 Americans with medical debt currently make less than $40,000 a year. It is not their fault that they got sick. Even economically speaking, medical debt is horrendous for the overall economy as more than 60% of those experiencing medical debt have reported having to go without necessities like food, clothing, and basic household items, which is bad because they don't have what they need, but it also puts a drag on the economy when people have to hold their money and not spend in the national economy.[603] These studies of course have differed widely. As a matter of fact, other studies suggest that roughly 100 million Americans face medical debt or have difficulty paying off medical debt, making the study that I cited lowballing the numbers in these terms. As I've already stated, forcing millions of Americans to go into debt because of a health related cause is just flat out wrong

---

603 Lopes, Lunna, Audrey Kearney, Alex Montero, Liz Hamel, and Mollyann Brodie. 2022. "Health Care Debt in the U.S.: The Broad Consequences of Medical and Dental Bills - Main Findings." Kaiser Family Foundation. June 16, 2022. https://www.kff.org/report-section/kff-health-care-debt-survey-main-findings/.

and unfair. This leaves millions of Americans every year stressed out, knowing that they are just one disaster away from ending up in the red. That's a pretty picture.

Another disaster for the United States is how much we spend on prescription drugs. Of course, the price of drugs continues to rise to unprecedented levels within the last few decades. And why shouldn't they? The US currently has no laws on the book to prevent drug companies from running up their prices whenever they feel like it. Sometimes they charge $95 for one measly pill when it costs them only $0.25 to produce. That's totally unreasonable. According to the Peter. G. Peterson Foundation "The U.S. spends twice as much on prescription drugs as other comparatively wealthy nations, on average. In 2019, the latest year for which data are available, private insurers and government health programs spent $963 per capita on prescription drugs while comparable countries spent an average of $466."[604] That's not a good sign for Americans when they have to spend an arm and a leg for the same prescription drugs that are half as expensive in just about every other country on earth. Sweden, who has a great healthcare system, only spends roughly $270 per capita on prescription drugs. This does not mean that they get worse drugs. In fact, they get the same exact drugs, just potentially under a different name. It's because the Swedish government has regulations that block prescription drug makers from making outlandish profits when their own people desperately need these drugs to survive.

Do you remember the story of Martin Shkreli? Shkreli was an

---

604 Peter G. Peterson Foundation. 2022. "How Much Does the United States Spend on Prescription Drugs Compared to Other Countries?" Www.pgpf.org. November 7, 2022. https://www.pgpf.org/blog/2022/11/how-much-does-the-united-states-spend-on-prescription-drugs-compared-to-other-countries#:~:text=The%20 U.S.%20spends%20twice%20as.

entrepreneur in the pharmaceutical drug industry. He became the CEO of Turing Pharmaceuticals and his first thought was not how do I help people and make sure that people get affordable drugs that they desperately need to stay alive. Instead, his first reaction was "how do I get rich as fast as I can?" He very suddenly raised the price of the anti-parasitic drug Daraprim to $750 a pill, compared to what it was in 2015 at $13.50 a pill. I got news for you. Even $13 for a pill is outrageous, but $750? People literally died because they could not afford this drug. It disproportionately affected AIDS patients who needed the drug to stay alive. When asked about the 5,000% increase in prices, Shkreli said he should be thanked and that he didn't think it should be a crime. "Right now it's a free market" he squirmed "with each company to decide which price is proper… there's no doubt I'm a capitalist and I'm trying to create a big drug company." The FDA could do nothing, as there are no regulations that prohibits drug companies from price-gouging and ultimately making people decide between cutting these pills that saves their lives or cutting other necessary daily needs.

For hepatitis drugs for a year, the United States pays $31,000, other countries spend $23,000 comparatively. For anti-inflammatory, the US spends $4,500 compared to the rest of the world at $2,700.[605] I could go on and on and on and on with these statistics. But one statistic sticks out a lot and that is the cost of insulin. Yale School of Medicine says "Insulin is seven to 10 times more expensive in the U.S. compared with other countries around the world. The same vial of insulin that cost $21 in the U.S. in 1996

---

605 "How Do Prescription Drug Costs in the United States Compare to Other Countries?" n.d. Peterson-KFF Health System Tracker. Accessed May 23, 2024. https://www.healthsystemtracker.org/chart-collection/how-do-prescription-drug-costs-in-the-united-states-compare-to-other-countries/#Share%20of%20adults%20reporting%20that%20they%20took%20prescription%20medications%20on%20a%20regular%20or%20ongoing%20basis,%202016

now costs upward of $250. But it takes only an estimated $2 to $4 to produce a vial of insulin."[606] And talk about competition, which America is all about. There are only three big insulin manufactures: Eli Lilly, Sanofi, and Novo Nordisk. With only three large brand names maintaining a monopoly on the insulin business they can stage their own artificially high prices and force Americans to either pay or die. It sounds harsh but that's the reality.

The study conducted by Yale found that roughly one in four Americans ration their insulin to stretch the drug and pay less. Now there are all sorts of negative consequences with rationing insulin. Among these is the simple fact that everybody needs insulin to live. Without it we would die. So, for diabetics who are rationing their insulin because they can't afford it, they are drastically increasing the risk of dying or perpetuating already poor health and making the situation worse. Unfortunately, those who are most likely to die from a lack of insulin are younger people who decide to ration the drug because they can't afford the high prices every month.[607] People are literally dying because drug prices are so high. We have direct evidence of this, and yet we do nothing substantial to correct this abhorrence.

So, what we have with our current healthcare system is one that has high waiting periods, serious shortages in healthcare professionals, high prices for prescription drugs, in some cases ten times more than neighboring countries, high costs for healthcare, far surpassing that of every other industrialized nation on earth, and enormous

---

606 Lipska, Kasia. 2023. "The Price of Insulin: A Q&a with Kasia Lipska." Medicine.yale.edu. April 27, 2023. https://medicine.yale.edu/news-article/the-price-of-insulin-a-qanda-with-kasia-lipska/#:~:text=Insulin%20is%20seven%20to%210.
607 Ibid

insurance obstacles. What do we do with this? Working Americans already are taxed for medicaid and medicare coverage. Why don't we just finish the job, guarantee that everybody has universal coverage, and eliminate the need for insurance companies that have been making billions of dollars? It might seem kind of harsh to be targeting insurance companies but they are a significant problem in our healthcare system. Don't just take my word for it, look at the facts. In 2022, health insurance companies made serious bank. UnitedHealth Group made over $20 billion in profits, these are profits, after all of the expenses have been taken out. Cigna made slightly lower than $7 billion, Elevance Health made $6 billion, and CVS made about $4.2 billion.

Pennsylvania Capital Star argues that when insurance companies make this kind of money we should expect to see a thriving, robust healthcare system in the US today, but that's sadly not even close to reality as there are so many people uninsured and nearly 10% of our elderly population can't even afford rudimentary health insurance. That is appalling. These insurance companies "make money by not paying for health care. Their bottom line depends on refusing to pay for care and they are ruthless when it comes to protecting their profits. Anthem Blue Cross Blue Shield has been consistently underpaying reimbursements and inappropriately denying coverages. In 2021, 53% of Anthem's medical bills for the second quarter were unpaid, amounting to $2.5 billion."[608] That is precisely how insurance companies make so much money. They promise that their healthcare plan is the most affordable and the most far-reaching,

---

[608] Humble, Will, Pennsylvania Capital-Star August 10, and 2023. 2023. "Americans Suffer When Health Insurers Place Profits over People." Pennsylvania Capital-Star. August 10, 2023. https://www.penncapital-star.com/uncategorized/americans-suffer-when-health-insurers-place-profits-over-people/#:~:text=In%202022%2C%20 UnitedHealth%20Group%20made.

yet when push comes to shove and you actually need them they disappear entirely, leaving Americans to foot the bill themselves and falling farther behind in debt. Don't you think that there is a serious problem in the healthcare industry when there are literally 25 million Americans dealing with medical debt at the same time as their insurers are making billions of dollars in profits?

How many times have you been let down because of your insurance company? Another huge way that insurance companies make money is by requiring pre-authorization from your healthcare provider before going ahead with the surgery. The insurance companies are hoping that you abandon the needed surgery, which often happens when you need a pre-authorization because the wait times take so long. In fact, An American Medical Association survey found 94% of physicians surveyed said that prior authorizations lead to delays in receiving care and 80% said that prior authorizations can lead to treatment abandonment."[609] So, instead of getting your much needed treatment or procedure, your insurance company is playing God and controlling your life.

Our current healthcare system is owned and controlled by these insurance companies who have gotten fat off of the needs of the American people. These special interest agents exert much power and influence over our politicians. You've heard me say this before, but, they are literally buying our lawmakers to do their bidding, joining many other special interest groups in this category. In 2020 alone healthcare insurance groups spent a whopping $720 million just on lobbying lawmakers. Of course, this is the equivalent of a gumball to them, who make $20 billion a year. They certainly can afford it. Again I ask, who will lawmakers pay more attention to, the majority of Americans who struggle to get by, and thus have no real

---

609 Ibid

power to lobby, or these wealthy insurance companies who spend viciously to get lawmakers to create laws and programs favorable to these companies at the expense of the American patient?

I truly have nothing against all the great people who work in the insurance industry. However, I do think that it is sickening when these industries care more about their own profits than they do about the overall wellbeing of the people. That's got to end.

I also want to point out that maybe, just maybe, lawmakers aren't taking healthcare seriously because they get massive benefits from the government. According to the Heritage Foundation, "Members of Congress and other federal jobholders can choose from among dozens of alternative health plans each year, irrespective of their families' health condition. And when federal workers move to different jobs within the federal sector, they are able to keep the coverage of their chosen plan without any interruption of benefits. They can even keep their chosen plan when they retire. Few other Americans enjoy such healthcare security."[610] Of course, when our lawmakers have been in office for so long and have enjoyed great healthcare benefits that are paid for by American taxpayers they can easily forget about the plight that average Americans face in dealing with healthcare. Maybe, just maybe, they would be more sympathetic to the Americans deeply in medical debt. Maybe, just maybe, they wouldn't sit here and call any attempt to achieve universal healthcare radical.

In fact, it's radical not to have a universal system. Currently, we are the only industrialized nation without a nationwide universal

---

610 Ph.D, Robert E. Moffit. n.d. "Congress and the Taxpayers: A Double Standard on Health Care Reform?" The Heritage Foundation. https://www.heritage.org/health-care-reform/report/congress-and-the-taxpayers-double-standard-health-care-reform.

care program. 43 countries offer free or universal coverage to its citizens, believing that healthcare is a human right and not a privilege for the few and powerful. Among some of these countries are: Australia, Belgium, Brazil, Canada, Denmark, Finland, France, Germany, Greece, Ireland, Israel, Japan, Luxembourg, Netherlands, New Zealand, Norway, South Korea, Spain, Sweden, Switzerland, and the UK, just to name a few.[611] And apparently it's working wonderfully. In one report, the United States ranked 69th in the world in healthcare out of 104, falling with the likes of Algeria and Albania. Not surprisingly, on list after list the US falls well behind other advanced economies that have either a single-payer or other universal form of healthcare. Most studies consistently rank the highest performing countries on healthcare as Belgium, Switzerland, Finland, Norway, and Japan. If they can have a striving, compassionate healthcare system, so can we. It's a crime that other countries spend less on healthcare and prescription drugs but can still cover all of their citizens and do it for less. We can and should take lessons from them.

So, what needs to be done? As I've already discussed, it's not a radical idea that we develop a form of universal healthcare. Indeed, this is what we have been striving for for more than a century. From democrats as well as republicans, stopping now when 27 million Americans are uninsured is giving up on that dream and giving up on the rights of Americans. And it can't possibly be radical when every other major nation on earth guarantees healthcare to all of its

---

611 Wang, Catalina. n.d. "An Overview of Countries That Offer Free Healthcare." Www.skuad.io. https://www.skuad.io/blog/an-overview-of-countries-that-offer-free-healthcare#:~:text=visitors%20and%20foreigners.-.

people, we are the only ones missing out. And it's not a radical idea to have the government negotiate drug prices, every other country on earth has lower prices than we do.

When we adopt a healthcare for all system, studies have indicated that it would likely save American families nearly $5,000 a year. More studies have proven that it can dramatically improve health outcomes. A study conducted by Yale finds that if we had healthcare for all, about 70,000 lives each year would be saved.[612] That's a lot of people. That could be your mom, grandfather, sister, or son. Why wouldn't we be for this?

According to Public Citizen healthcare for all would:

1. Provide guaranteed health care to everyone;
2. Provide access to home and community-based care for all who need it;
3. Guarantee coverage for dental, vision and hearing services;
4. End medical debt and medical bankruptcies;
5. Reduce administrative waste by $500 billion per year;
6. End price gouging by pharmaceutical companies; and
7. Put an end to corporations profiting off the sick.[613]

People don't seem to realize it, but when we transition to a healthcare for all system, and by that I mean if you get sick you go to any doctor, clinic, or hospital you want to go to and the government will be there and pay the bill, there are so many other benefits. (Medicare for all is one way that we can achieve this kind of solution.) First, when the government takes care of the costs of

---

612 Public Citizen. 2020. "FACT CHECK: Medicare for All Would Save the U.S. Trillions; Public Option Would Leave Millions Uninsured, Not Garner Savings." Public Citizen. February 21, 2020. https://www.citizen.org/news/fact-check-medicare-for-all-would-save-the-u-s-trillions-public-option-would-leave-millions-uninsured-not-garner-savings/.
613 ibid

healthcare, employers won't need to provide healthcare coverage, which means that your employer can be released from this burden and give you a higher salary and benefits. One of the most absurd arguments I heard during the 2020 democratic primaries came from the Culinary Union. Now, don't get me wrong I am very favorable of unions, but the Culinary Union got it all wrong when they refused to endorse Bernie Sanders because of his medicare for all proposal. The Union argued that it spent too much time and effort battling to get good healthcare benefits, therefore they were opposed to medicare for all. What the Union fails to recognize is the fact that under a healthcare for all system their healthcare would be free, much better than having healthcare in the form of insurance that does not cover everything. They also fail to recognize that when their employer doesn't have to guarantee healthcare benefits that gives the unions more power to demand higher wages and retirement benefits. Why wouldn't they be supportive of this? This is good for workers all across the board. And it showed. The Culinary workers, despite being told not to by their union, voted in droves for Bernie Sanders and his medicare for all plan.

Not only can workers ensure more benefits across the board when their employers don't have to provide healthcare, but they will also have much less stress, not having to fear that if they lose their job they would also lose their healthcare. This pervasive fear keeps people in lower paying jobs just to have the benefits of healthcare and weakens economic mobility. Of course, another huge benefit is that it would promote entrepreneurs and small businesses as they won't be bogged down with making sure their employees have adequate healthcare. This will promote competition in the markets and reduce prices for the consumer, all the while supporting local communities.

We can see all of these amazing benefits if we commit ourselves to a universal healthcare system. Republicans and conservatives will hit back that this plan is too expensive, yet study after study has suggested the exact opposite, that in the long run we would actually spend less than we are currently. Yes, we would eliminate insurance companies, whose sole purpose is to make ungodly amounts of money on our healthcare, and this cost would be transported back to the government. The government, therefore, will have to increase taxes on the wealthy to help give everyone a right to healthcare. Currently, we are taxed separately for medicare and medicaid. Instead, if we developed a medicare for all system, there would be no need for medicaid and we could eliminate the taxes for this category, and bonus, republican led states who have not expanded medicaid yet would finally see their poorest individuals get the healthcare coverage that they deserve.

When republicans rail against how this plan would increase government in our healthcare system and lead to socialized medicine tell them the true facts. Tell them that this plan actually takes the government out of the picture, except of course when it's time to pay, then the government steps up and assumes its responsibility. It's a win-win for Americans as a whole and for the government. Wouldn't it be nice to finally be done talking about healthcare in national debates?

And, to close with my argument, in 2021 a study found that 69% of Americans believe that medicare for all should be adopted, including 87% of democrats, the majority of independents, and even half of republicans.[614] That's a striking amount. Democracy seems drowned out in this light. If so many Americans want medicare for

---

614 "Jayapal Introduces Medicare for All Act of 2021." 2021. Congresswoman Pramila Jayapal. March 17, 2021. https://jayapal.house.gov/2021/03/17/medicare-for-all/#:~:text=Medicare%20for%20All%20is%20supported.

all why isn't it the law of the land? Again, I'm going to sound like a broken record here, but, one reason is the fact that insurance companies spend almost a billion dollars a year lobbying lawmakers and spend wildly in campaign contributions. (In 2020, health insurers spent $128 million in campaign financing, most of this was given to republican candidates.)[615] You have to ask yourself, why do these insurance companies spend money on lobbying or campaign contributions? They certainly are not doing it for charitable concerns but instead are seeking to get something out of it.

Of course, democracies can't win in these circumstances. How can they? Lawmakers just want to keep on getting re-elected cycle after cycle and they will accept money wherever it comes from, almost like they're selling their souls. Some politicians, of course, do not accept money from special interests, but the vast majority do and it shows in the decisions that they make.

Given the circumstances, even though the vast majority of Americans are ready for medicare for all, nothing will change if we don't elect candidates who are supportive of this proposal, and this includes, as of now, only progressive democrats. Even president Joe Biden has not taken up the reins and had the courage enough to take on the insurance companies. Instead, he has tried to expand Obamacare, which is in itself better than nothing, yet, it is still leaving tens of millions of people behind.

Another common challenge I hear from conservatives is that medicare for all, and other single-payer healthcare systems really don't work and they use phony right-wing internet sources to back up their claims. I always refer to healthcare professionals when making healthcare decisions, because by and large they are the experts of

---

615 "Insurance | OpenSecrets." n.d. Www.opensecrets.org. https://www.opensecrets.org/industries/indus.php?ind=F09.

their field. Who should we listen to more in regards to healthcare, nurses, doctors, and health professionals, or right-wing politicians, who claim they know what the hell is going on? It doesn't take a rocket scientist to figure this one out. In study after study, experts have concluded that a medicare for all healthcare system is much more beneficial for patients than a for-profit healthcare industry. Not only will this improve competition among clinics, hospitals, and healthcare providers because patients will have more mobility and thus go to the best healthcare providers that work for them, but it will also increase patient satisfaction and prevent diseases and other negative health because it will incentivise patients to look after their preventative care. For women, this means that they can focus on getting a breast cancer screening early so that they have a greater chance of defeating cancer if they catch it quicker. This is common sense, and, unfortunately, patients don't get this option too often.

Medicare for all is also endorsed by over 60 organizations including, National Nurses United, American Medical Student Association, National Union of Healthcare Workers, and countless other working-class unions across the country who see the benefits that a medicare for all healthcare system would dole out to the people.[616] I don't know about you but I trust that the National Nurses Union, consisting of over 225,000 nurses dedicated to serving their patients and giving them the best possible care, knows what they are doing, and knows that we need universal healthcare coverage. I trust them a heck of a lot more than I trust in politicians, whether they

---

616 "NEWS: Sanders Introduces Medicare for All with 14 Colleagues in the Senate» Senator Bernie Sanders." n.d. Senator Bernie Sanders. https://www.sanders.senate.gov/press-releases/news-sanders-introduces-medicare-for-all-with-14-colleagues-in-the-senate/#:~:text=The%20Medicare%20for%20All%20of.

be democrats or republicans, when it comes to giving me the best possible care.

Right now, and it's an absurdity, but it's true, some hospitals, mainly those that are not for profit, are finding themselves deeply in debt because they have to care for everybody who walks through those doors, whether they have health insurance or not. This means that the hospitals have to foot the bill for long periods of time until it gets paid, and during this time everybody else's premiums are going up to help offset the costs. Not only that, but nurses and healthcare providers have come out strongly for medicare for all because they see firsthand the sufferings of their patients and the struggle to pay off all of their medical bills. It's heart-wrenching, which is why so many of them have literally gone out on the streets to advocate for the noble cause.

Authors of a medicare for all bill, which was signed by 14 US senators in 2022, list a number of reasons why it is increasingly making more sense to adopt a universal healthcare plan. They assert:

"About 44 percent of the adult population, some 112 million Americans, are struggling to pay for the medical care they need and over 70 million Americans are uninsured or under-insured because of high deductibles and premiums. In addition, life expectancy in the U.S. is much lower than most other industrialized countries and infant mortality rates are much higher."[617]

All of this can easily be corrected with a simple single payer system like medicare for all.

I worked the first few years of my professional life at a hospital in Wisconsin. There, I worked with a number of elderly ladies, some were well in their 80s and still working. I mustered up the courage

---

617 Ibid

one day to ask one of them why they are still working. Her name was Edith, and she has been working since she was 14. Edith told me that she has to work because she can't afford healthcare without it. I pondered this long and hard and came to realize that there must be many people like Edith in the country who are forced to work well into their retirement years just because they can't afford what should be known as a human right. I wondered, could this happen to me? Or my mother? If it could happen to Edith it could happen to anyone. We need a healthcare for all solution. It's not radical when we've been attempting it for over a century. It's not radical when every other major country on earth has implemented it, some a hundred years ago, and they are succeeding well beyond the wildest hopes of the United States. It's not radical when almost 70% of the American people support it. Let's cut the cost of our healthcare system. Let's eliminate the greed and recklessness of insurance companies. Let's negotiate the price of prescription drugs so that drug makers can't dictate who lives and who dies because their prices are so high. Let's guarantee everyone will get the equal opportunity to get the healthcare treatment that they need, not limit it to the wealthy and healthy. And finally, let's put people over profits and politics.

16 TUITION

Another great plan that has been conceived by progressive democrats, and again, championed by Bernie Sanders, Elizabeth Warren, Ed Markey, and co, is the idea that the United States should have universal tuition free colleges and universities. This plan would ensure that everyone, whether rich or poor, black or white, gay or straight, has the opportunity to achieve their dreams. In the year 2023 and beyond, no American should have to decide between supporting their families or going to college. As a consequence this chapter will be focused on the need to provide that universal tuition free college and for the need to improve our educational system.

A recent study found that on average, students spend over $10,500 yearly for in-state tuition, while out of state tuition is a staggering $27,560.[618] Anybody would be able to put it together that it undoubtedly costs more to go to school out of state, but I don't think anybody would be able to determine that it would be roughly $17,000 more. Think about if you or your children want to study a unique field like astrobiology in a small state that may not have it. That means in order to study their passion and dream they need to travel out of state and pay astronomical prices just to attend a few classes. That's not fair to middle class and poor Americans. Even $10,500 is a lot to spend per year on education. And this is coming from somebody who thinks that education is an incredibly

---

618 Knueven, Liz, and Ryan Wangman. 2020. "The Average College Tuition Keeps Rising, and It's Just the Start of College Costs." Business Insider. July 14, 2020. https://www.businessinsider.com/personal-finance/average-college-tuition.

important thing. I just don't want to see ordinary people get fleeced by these crazy prices.

In order for people to be able to pay for these out of control prices many of them, 70% of recent graduates, have to take out a student loan.[619] Let me state the obvious here: Student loans aren't free. It is not free money. Students have to pay off their loans, and these loans often accrue huge interest on them. This means that not only are students being left out, having to save and save and save until the have the resources to pay off their loan, but they also are hit in the face with even more money to pay off because of the big interest rates, which, by the way, can't be refinanced like that of a mortgage. Think about all the debt that Americans have to pay off. As of 2023, 30% of Americans still have student loans to pay off.[620] At this time Americans owe a staggering $1.77 trillion in student debt.[621] With each passing year, more and more people are falling into the vicious trap, with 54% of recent graduates finding themselves in school debt. The average debt per person is different per state. The DIstrict of Columbia leads the pack with the average student loan debt to be at $60,000, followed by Maryland, Georgia, Florida, Delaware, Alabama, and Virginia all with the average student loan debt to be over $47,000. Wyoming is last with its average student

---

[619] nair, madhu. 2019. "5 Essential Student Loan Facts Every Student Should Know." University of the People. April 7, 2019. https://www.uopeople.edu/blog/5-student-loan-facts-every-student-should-know/?utm_source=google&utm_medium=cpc&utm_campaign=ggl-display_pmax_us&utm_term=.

[620] Knueven, Liz, and Ryan Wangman. 2020. "The Average College Tuition Keeps Rising, and It's Just the Start of College Costs." Business Insider. July 14, 2020. https://www.businessinsider.com/personal-finance/average-college-tuition.

[621] Martinez-White, Dan Shepard Xiomara. 2023. "U.S. Student Loan Debt Statistics for 2023." LendingTree. August 10, 2023. https://www.lendingtree.com/student/student-loan-debt-statistics/#:~:text=Americans%20own%20%241.77%20trillion%20in.

loan debt to be at $30,000.[622] Think about how much this hampers the economy. If you live in the state of Georgia, think about how the average person with student loan debt has to pay $55,000. Think about all of the other ways your neighbor can spend that money. Maybe they could buy a house, a boat, a car, or simply go to restaurants more, buy things at stores, ect. All of these things would help the economy, as more spending generally produces a thriving economy. But, when your neighbor has to stop spending because they have to penny-pinch to make their loan payments on time, to the point where they never go out anymore, don't want to have kids, and can't afford to buy a house, this hurts the overall economy, which hurts your jobs, which hurts your paycheck.

In 1970, the average cost for a college education per year was around $755. Now, this is the equivalent of $5,000 today, but this is still under half of what college kids have to pay now.[623] How do we expect our kids to be able to study and pay off these skyrocketing prices? And for all of you out there who might say that when you went to college you had to pay it off, why should kids nowadays have to? The answer is quite simple, back then, you paid half of what college costs today for these young kids, of course we should help them out because they are our future and more and more kids can't afford to even go to college and are entering the workforce, making much less money at some fast food job or something of the sort.

Some kids, like the heirs of Donald Trump, Warren Buffet, and other incredibly wealthy parents can skate through college and not even have to worry about how much it costs. Everything is a game

---

622 Ibid
623 "Average Cost of College over Time: Yearly Tuition since 1970." n.d. Education Data Initiative. https://educationdata.org/average-cost-of-college-by-year#:~:text=College%20Costs%20in%20the%201970s&text=The%20average%20cost%20of%20tuition%20and%20fees%20

to them. They can party. They can slack off. They can sleep in late. And who cares? Their rich daddy will still pay the bills. That's not the case with the majority of Americans who have to pay off tuition themselves on their own hard work and dedication. This is another gigantic benefit for the wealthy and rich kids who descend from them. 20% of students who are not as privileged and need to work to pay off their schooling fail to graduate because they either can't afford it or their work is getting in the way of their success.[624] It also means that students who work while in school often take much longer to complete their degrees than those who don't have the same levels of responsibility. And, to all the naysayers that say that students should work because it gives them a sense of responsibility, the facts are that the vast majority of students while in college work at the same time, including 81% of part time students.[625] That leaves a burning question. To these students who need to work to pay off their schooling, is it worth it? I think about how expensive school is and how some degrees just don't pay well. Think about the field of education. Students who are enrolled in an education major to become a teacher have to pay off these high tuition rates, and at the end of the day, even when they have their degree they won't be paid well. I know dozens of teachers who are still paying off student loans. In fact, the day that president Joe Biden signaled that he would cut student loans of up to $20,000, many teachers celebrated and were beside themselves, just to have the republicans challenge and overturn it in court. You will also have students who work while in school having to decide what is more important,

---

624 Ecton, Walter, and Celeste Carruthers. 2023. "College Students Who Have Jobs Are Much Less Likely to Graduate than Their Privileged Peers, Shocking Study Finds." Fortune. January 11, 2023. https://fortune.com/2023/01/11/college-students-with-jobs-20-percent-less-likely-to-graduate-than-privileged-peers-study-side-hustle/.
625 Ibid

studying for an exam or coming into work for a 10 hour shift. No student should be forced to make these decisions and it's not fair that they have these burdens placed on their shoulders. No wonder why so many students struggle with mental health, they have so much pressure and stress.

This issue is personal for me in many ways. When I first graduated from high school and began my search for colleges or universities I had to settle with a college that didn't have the sort of degrees that I wanted just because they were cheaper and I couldn't afford to go to most four year universities. I am far from alone in this respect. Nearly 65% of students polled that college costs were a major factor for them determining where they go.[626] This means that most students are just resolved to go to the college that is most affordable regardless of if they have adequate degrees and programs. We are shopping for colleges, going with the cheapest one at the expense of the kind of quality we want to see in education.

One way that we can bring down tuition prices is by having local and state governments fund colleges and universities with adequate improvements. I don't mean here that Oklahoma should pay for all of Oklahoma's tuition rates, but each state can increase funding for their university systems. This looks like Oklahoma spending an extra funding package to help offset the costs of rising tuition. For example, the increase in funding can help make college improvements, pay for staff and upkeep, while keeping tuition rates lower. Currently, many university systems and colleges are raising prices

---

626 Lapovsky, Lucie. n.d. "Reducing College Tuition: An Idea Whose Time Has Come." Forbes. Accessed May 23, 2024. https://www.forbes.com/sites/lucielapovsky/2020/12/01/reducing-college-tuition-an-idea-whose-time-has-come/?sh=7f1792e94975.

because they have no alternative, they are not getting the necessary funding from state and local governments to keep the prices down.

A much simpler way we can solve the problem is by making schools and universities tuition free as this would provide uniformity throughout the country and again provide quality competition for colleges and universities with the highest performing schools having the highest number of applicants. Some people tell us that this is a radical idea that can't be done but let's look at the facts before we make any false judgments.

Many Americans fail to understand that in the early years of the American republic, many students lacked any education at all. Back in the 1700s and early 1800s children who didn't grow up in a rich household might have received no education at all and education was largely seen as something that only the richest families could afford for their children. The Puritans, largely in New England, were the first ones in America to really value education, mainly because they wanted everyone, including children to be able to read the precious Bible. They set up schoolhouses that served a wide variety of ages in a single room classroom. In the South, because of the often rural nature of living, schools were few and far between. Most children were educated at home or not at all. Privileged children had the benefit of working privately with tutors, as did a number of our nation's Founding Fathers. It largely remained this way for the entire 1700s.

After the American revolution, Thomas Jefferson was adamant about providing a form of universal public schooling. This was personal for Jefferson, as he was a deeply learned individual who believed that everybody should have access to reading, writing, and simple arithmetic. But Jefferson also believed that a functioning, thriving democracy can only work in countries where their people are well educated on the issues and thus can serve as valuable members in a society. He suggested that to provide universal public education tax dollars would have to be provided. In this effort he was flatly denied. Early Americans at this period were deeply suspicious of government and big-taxing policies, especially the South who were farther away from mainstream civilization.

However, as time dragged on and more people became more religious and intellectual, reformers banded together to get a national movement on public education. At long last, in 1840, a few public schools had begun to pop up here and there in the more affluent communities that could afford to tax their citizens to provide educational opportunities for their children.[627] The few public schools in the country were really a good step forward, but many hard-nosed reformers demanded more. They began calling for free, compulsory education for children all across the country, not just in rich neighborhoods but even in the places that were destitute.

Massachusetts became the first state to pass a compulsory public education law in 1852, with New York following behind them. Finally by 1918 every state had laws that set up public education as a requirement for children, with many mandating that they had to attend school until 14 years of age.[628] Of course, it gets a little muddy when we look at the differences between schools for boys, girls, blacks, Native Americans, ect. But that's for a different story. My point here is to show that even mandatory public education was disputed at various points in our history. Yet looking back it would be crazy to imagine a United States without a free public education system. If this were not the case many poor families would still have

---

627 Stephanie Watson. 2008. "How Public Schools Work." HowStuffWorks. February 13, 2008. https://people.howstuffworks.com/public-schools1.htm.
628 Ibid

a hard time educating their children just like poor Americans had trouble educating their youth in the colonial periods despite the fact that their children desperately wanted and deserved that education, especially since this was the only proven way to advance yourself in the world at the time. Hence, many of the poor children were forced to either work in factories and mills their whole lives or try to work out a living working on a farm. Whereas, wealthy children whose parents could afford a nice education would go on to become lawyers, doctors, esteemed military men, ect.

Around the same time that the United States saw an increase in free public education for children we also saw an increase in free public universities largely created on the same grounds as public education for children. In 1847, the Baruch College of New York was the first institution that provided levels of higher learning for free. They recognized that this would be a major opportunity for people of all income levels to achieve their dreams and strive to provide a better life for them and their families. Additionally, when the California university system was created in 1868 a serious debate raged whether or not the institution should be tuition free.[629] California at the time had a much lower population than many other states and this was thought to bring more movement to California and help its economy surge. The college board decided that the universities should be tuition free, which helped many poor and middle income teenagers get a quality education. The California university system remained tuition free until the legislature stopped

---

629 "The History of Tuition-Free Education in the U.S.A." 2017. University of the People. August 15, 2017. https://www.uopeople.edu/blog/the-history-of-tuition-free-education-in-the-u-s-a/#:~:text=In%20the%201860s%2C%20some%20of.

adequately funding the universities, in which case the universities had to start charging tuition rates again. This lasted nearly 100 years, however, as colleges in California still were tuition free until Ronald Raegan became the California governor and advocated for the legislature to gut the program. Obviously he did this because his political philosophy was that the government was the problem, though all the college kids that the government helped didn't think that was the case.

As a matter of fact, most colleges and universities in the 1800s were tuition free, giving minorities and poor kids a chance to succeed. At this time, "College education was considered a public good. Students who received such an education would put it to use in the betterment of society. Everyone benefited when people chose to go to college. And because it was considered a public good, society was willing to pay for it—either by offering college education free of charge or by providing tuition scholarships to individual students."[630] Do we not still think today that a college education is for the public good? What happens when people don't have a good education? Study after study proves that the higher degree you have the more money you make. That makes sense, but it will also lead to a reduction in poverty, a reduction in crime, and lead to a resilient economy with highly skilled workers so that we can compete with China and Europe with our workforce.

Even when prices began to rise at the end of the 19th century, college administrators still argued to keep the prices low for the students. Harvard president, Charles Eliot, insisted "I want to have the College open equally to men with much money, little money, or

---

[630] Adam, Thomas. 2017. "College Was Once Free and for the Public Good—What Happened?" YES! Magazine. July 20, 2017. https://www.yesmagazine.org/economy/2017/07/20/college-was-once-free-and-for-the-public-good-what-happened.

no money, provided they all have brains."[631] Again, the vast majority of Americans truly believed that when the masses are educated that leads to virtue and morality. The trend began to shift a little in the early 1900s when private colleges began attracting wealthy kids who wanted to be part of a sophisticated high class society and began joining these institutions in droves. The idea from these young rich kids was to have a great experience, not necessarily a great education, as these private schools lacked the necessary regulations to ensure that academic quality was met.

With the rise of private colleges, who were out to make massive profits from rich kids, most Americans didn't look favorably at college anymore, as it became more and more of an individual's own personal goal instead of becoming a common good.[632] Soon afterwards, people like John Rockefeller pressured colleges to start charging students for tuition, believing that that's how students developed responsibility and hard work. Somehow, Rockefeller forgot about how hard going to college and graduating is. To many, that is a full time job.

Nonetheless, with rich, influential people believing that colleges needed to pass the burden onto students, more colleges followed one another like sheep. All of this culminates into the current tuition based system that we have today.

So, how can republicans and other conservatives say that this is a radical idea? It's been done before in America with stunning success. Instead, these same people say that instead we should just focus on increasing scholarships and pell grants, like somehow this is going to fix the system. All told, only about one out of every eight students receive a scholarship. What about the other 7/8ths? Have

---

631 Ibid
632 Ibid

they been forgotten about? Even worse, for those students that are lucky enough to actually receive a scholarship about 97% of those scholarships are for less than $2,500.[633] That is a pitiful amount. That might cover a class or two, what about the 15 or 20 others? I mean come on. If they tell us that we need to increase scholarships then we would have to really increase scholarships to the point where this would cost the government a fortune, and republicans only increase funding for defense spending or tax breaks on the wealthy, and even then this would still leave out the vast majority of our students. So, clearly even though this is the only reasonable alternative to tuition free colleges and universities, republicans would still howl to the moon saying that it's too expensive and a radical idea. I mean come on let's get our priorities right.

Maybe republicans don't think that this idea is that important because so many republican lawmakers have so much money that they don't really realize the issues that the majority of their constituents are dealing with. Currently the average net worth for members of congress is over $1 million.[634] Given this fact, most of our lawmakers don't know what it's like to struggle to get through college, or struggle to put their son and daughters through college like the rest of us. Maybe if they did know what it's like they would actually stand up and fight for average people like you and me.

And nobody can assert that this is a radical idea when most other industrialized countries have had tuition free college for centuries.

---

633 Woodward, Matthew. 2023. "U.S. Scholarship Statistics: The Latest Data, Facts and Costs." Www.searchlogistics.com. February 6, 2023. https://www.searchlogistics.com/learn/statistics/scholarship-statistics/#:~:text=Approximately%201.58%20million%20scholarships%20are.

634 "Net Worth of United States Senators and Representatives - Ballotpedia." 2011. Ballotpedia. 2011. https://ballotpedia.org/Net_worth_of_United_States_Senators_and_Representatives.

Among the many countries that provide tuition free colleges to their students are: Argentina, Brazil, Denmark, Finland, France, Germany, Greece, Iceland, Luxembourg, Norway, Poland, Spain, and Sweden again, just to name a few.[635] I say that if these countries can provide free college for their students why can't we? It's absurd to say that we can't, when we've done it before and we are one of the only few industrialized nations not to provide these services for its citizens. Imagine all of the poor and middle class families that would finally be able to provide an education for their children. It's radical to not give our students tuition free college.

Talk about reducing the wealth gap that we are currently experiencing, nothing would close those gaps as much as providing universal college education. I've talked about this a lot in the previous chapter, but when people living in poverty can achieve a college education they have the ability to lift themselves out of their plight. I call it the poverty cycle. When someone is born in poverty they don't have the money to go to college and when they don't go to college then they don't graduate and when they don't graduate they end up having a low paying job, thus they stay in poverty. In 2021, only 12% of low income adults had earned a four year degree.[636] So the other 88% either went to a technical school, with the vast majority not going to college at all. That's our current system right there for you. Poor people again are left out.

Some people claim that if we give everyone the chance to achieve a higher level of education then everyone will be college educated, thus taking away the prestige of those who have already achieved

---

635 Carlton, Genevieve. 2022. "Countries with Free College." Www.accreditedschoolsonline.org. May 31, 2022. https://www.accreditedschoolsonline.org/resources/which-countries-offer-free-college/.

636 Drozdowski, Mark. 2023. "Should College Be Free? | BestColleges.com." Www.bestcolleges.com. Best Colleges. August 30, 2023. https://www.bestcolleges.com/news/analysis/should-college-be-free/#:~:text=The%20benefits%20of%20free%20college.

TUITION 553

this level. Well, that is an interesting idea, but this plan will actually place a greater level of prestige for those that achieve a higher education. Here's why. We only have a limited number of colleges and universities. With only a limited number of colleges, professors and faculty this means that if everyone went to college then the seams of the buildings would be bursting because they don't have the space for the increase in students. So, what does this mean? Essentially this will create a system where colleges and universities are accepting high performing students. This means that a college would only accept students that have a 3.0 GPA or higher, or create their own standards and requirements. No longer would colleges just accept those who can afford it, but they would accept the brightest and most talented. When colleges and universities are free it means that those born in a working class family that are high performing but not quite as lucky as to receive a scholarship have the opportunity to advance their lives. This also puts more responsibility on students in high school. Instead of slacking off and getting into trouble they will have to understand the significance of studying and getting good grades, as well as volunteering and having good community service. I think this is something that we can all get behind, especially since this places more pressure on families and parents who should encourage their children in education.

Of course, you don't need me to mention that those with higher levels of degrees get paid significantly more. Those with a bachelor's degree can receive twice as much as those with only a high school diploma. On average, those with a bachelor's can expect to make more than a million dollars more in their lifetime than those without a college degree.[637] That's an incredible award for those that take the

---

[637] Drozdowski, Mark. 2023. "Should College Be Free? | BestColleges.com." Www.bestcolleges.com. Best Colleges. August 30, 2023. https://www.bestcolleges.com/news/analysis/should-college-be-free/#:~:text=The%20benefits%20of%20free%20college.

time and energy to get a degree. Think about what that can do for the national economy. Not only will we have more advanced jobs to be able to compete with other nations but we will have more money to spend which helps the economy and builds good jobs.

Another benefit that often gets overlooked is the fact that when we make college tuition free it can slowly, over time, help reduce the growing federal deficit. Here's why. When more people receive a college degree and ultimately more people make more, then the government will be able to tax more and thus use the increase in revenues to curtail the deficit. Right now, the United States spends literally trillions of dollars a year on entitlements and welfare benefits. What kind of people need these benefits and help? Those that don't make enough money or those who haven't saved up enough. Well, again, when more people are educated and making more money this means that they will certainly be less likely to rely on these programs, thus reducing the overall amount that the US spends on these items.[638] I've always believed that nobody, in the richest country in the world, should need to rely on welfare or entitlement programs just to live.

Studies have also shown that college graduates are more likely to vote, to volunteer, to make philanthropic contributions, and even to donate blood.[639] (Of course, this is assuming that more colleges and universities spring up, and create a vast amount of new jobs to increase the overall student enrollment.) Overall, college graduates are much more likely to be politically engaged and community oriented, which could actually reduce crime. This would take care of the ignorance problem that is running rampant in our politics today. Too many people are so ignorant of political facts that they vote in a way that is directly opposing their own best interests, and they

---

638 Ibid
639 Ibid

don't even know it. As Thomas Jefferson said that a well-educated citizenry is essential to a thriving democratic republic, this is no more true than today when an overwhelming amount of republicans still think that the election was stolen and that an insurrection didn't happen contrary to all the evidence and experts who assert the exact opposite regardless of party affiliations.

In a previous chapter I talked of the need for a universal healthcare system where everybody, regardless of income, would have the opportunity to go to get the treatment that they need. Some republicans and conservatives think that we would have incredibly long wait times if this happened because everybody would go in and receive care. I got news for them, we already do have really long waiting times, and this is without nationalized healthcare. But, in order to reduce these long waiting times we need to create more doctors, nurses, and other healthcare professionals. The reason why we are struggling to recruit new doctors and healthcare professionals is quite obvious; we have one of the worst higher educational systems in the world in the fact that it costs so much and so few Americans can afford to go to college for 12 years. Many healthcare professionals have hundreds of thousands of dollars in school debt. That is outrageous. Who would want to become a doctor in America when it takes 15 years to pay off their school loans? I have a simple solution. Free tuition would help solve the issue. This would make it much easier for American students to fulfill their dreams of becoming a doctor, or a nurse, or a speech pathologist. But, republicans will keep on opposing tuition free schooling while at the same time crying about the massive waiting periods on healthcare. I have news for them: Get your priorities right. You have to do something, don't just sit on your hands, but try something different. This would take care of so many of our problems.

Overall, tuition free schooling would be a heaven sent for so many Americans throughout the country. You can't say it's radical when many other industrialized countries offer it and the United States has had an interesting history of tuition free schooling. Some people might say how do we pay for it? The answer is that undoubtedly this would be an expensive proposal. And, what happens if we enact medicare for all and tuition free schooling? This would lead to an ungodly amount of government spending, how would we pay for it all?

The truth of the situation is that this is going to cost some significant amount of cash. I would be lying if I said that this was going to be easy. However, I do believe that the wealthy are well off, well enough off that I think they can pay an extra couple of bucks to make sure that everybody has the opportunities to succeed in life. If we raised the taxes of those who earn more than $150,000 a year or married couples who earn more than $225,000 a year we could significantly increase the amount of revenues needed in our treasury. I would propose increasing the tax brackets to progressively increase until we reach the $20 million threshold, this would ensure that our taxing system is indeed progressive and fair. With the top bracket consisting of those who make more than $20 million a year, then we can tax the highest bracket 50%. I know you might be thinking that that is a high percentage but remember taxes were much higher until the 1980s, the rich I assure you will be okay. There is no doubt that they will still survive and do quite well. It may, however, put a damper on their plans to build a fifth house.

Again, you might say how are we going to do this? The republicans certainly would not be for this kind of tax plan and even some conservative democrats would say no to this proposal, how would this work? To be sure, there will be lots of great commotion regarding a tax policy like this. Republicans would call it the biggest tax hike in American history and special interests will spend hundreds of millions of dollars trying to fight against it. Yet, as Americans it is our duty to respond and be informed citizens. It is our duty to study and research candidates to make sure that we are voting for the right one despite all of the money that may be thrown in the election cycle.

Long story short, we need to elect some "radical" candidates to Congress and for the presidency so that we can accomplish these feats.

17 CLIMATE CHANGE

Climate change is the number one existential threat facing all of humanity. There are no ands, ifs, or buts. Many people believe that the end of all times will be because North Korea decides to go crazy and blow everybody up, or AI will take over the world. No. The number one reason why the world will end, at least if we maintain the current trends, will be because of climate change. This is a huge issue and the reason why I devoted a chapter in my book to climate change is because not enough people are taking this issue seriously. We hear about it a lot, but nobody seems to care. We just keep seeing China polluting the earth with their factories and we see Saudi Arabia pumping more oil and we think "what can we do about that?"

I hear so much nonsense from politicians who actually think that there is nothing we can do to slow climate change. They say China doesn't stop polluting, why should we? They say that climate change is a hoax created by the Chinese. They say that because of the state of our economy we just just continue fracking, and using fossil fuels to further develop the world. These people are flat-out wrong and crazy. Yet, every time a humanity-loving politician stands up and confronts the fossil fuel industry, these foolish people call them radicals. They call the Green New Deal radical. They even call the heroic Greta Thunberg a radical that was put up to it.

Nothing frustrates me more than when a friend tells me that the democrats are horrible because gas prices are up. Perhaps they forgot that gas prices are horrible everywhere because of one thing

COVID. Most people never lived through a pandemic like this. In fact, the last one even comparable was the Spanish Flu of 1918. Governments did what they thought was right to do, to save lives and protect their citizens. This means that they did shut-downs, or partial shut-downs to their economy, to protect people. This led to disturbances within the supply chain. Now, all of the sudden, people are sitting at home with nothing to do. So, what do they do? They buy things, they work on home improvements. Thus, the demand far outpaced the supply of products.

And, this was true with the oil markets. When governments started to shut-down and people didn't drive anywhere for fear of contracting the virus, oil rich countries severely cut down on the production of oil and gas. So, when people started traveling again like crazy, with the assumption that nothing was wrong, we didn't have enough gas to suit the needs of everybody. So, logically, when demand outpaces supply, prices go up, as they did with gas. This is not Trump's fault and this is not President Biden's fault. This is just how economics work. Actually, it's economics 101.

And yet, that doesn't stop people from saying "Oh my god, gas prices are so high." And all of those people, who really don't know anything about politics and economics, who put "I did that" stickers with a picture of Joe Biden near the gas pumps just don't know the facts regarding climate change. Any economist, or political scholar will tell you that presidents don't really have a whole lot of influence on the economy. Now, obviously certain actions that a president takes can impact the economy for the better or worse, but in large part this is only minuscule.

These perceptions that Biden and the democrats have caused high gas prices are just flat out wrong. The average gas price, per gallon, in 2023, was $3.80.⁶⁴⁰ As a matter of fact, in 2012, the price for gas was $3.90 per gallon. It is absolutely true that right now, prices are exactly where they should be, in accord to inflation. Yet, that doesn't stop all of the nay-sayers from ridiculing Biden and demanding more fracking and use of fossil fuels.

I shouldn't have to say this, it really goes without saying, but 99% of climate scientists say that climate change is occurring thanks to humans, primarily humans' use of fossil fuels. How can you disagree with climate scientists, who have spent their entire professional careers researching this issue? It's ludicrous. That's why the democrats and President Joe Biden are moving forward with positions geared toward reducing the advancement of climate change. Common sense tells you that this means going after fossil fuels, eradicating the use of fracking, which exploits mother nature's beauties for oil and gas and is very hazardous to the environment, and investing in new, alternative, sustainable energy sources. This includes the use of wind, geothermal, solar, biomass, among other things. This shouldn't be that hard. The future of our planet relies on this. Don't we want to see our children grow up and have children of their own in a clean, sustainable planet? And yet, it's so incredibly difficult. Why? Because of ignorance and greed.

You have to ask yourself, why would people be willing to burn more fossil fuels, and endorse pipeline projects that will only further destroy the planet? They only care about short-term profits. What, in the short-term, is going to get me better off? Clearly, the use of fossil fuels. But when we think this way, we totally drown out the voices of future generations, who will hate us for the selfish decisions that we make now.

---

640 AAA. 2022. "AAA Gas Prices." AAA Gas Prices. 2022. https://gasprices.aaa.com/.

So now, let's get to the facts. Across the world we are seeing catastrophic extreme weather events. Whether it be wildfires, earthquakes, hurricanes, droughts, flooding, you name it, we have been seeing more once-in-a-generation storms than ever before. It would take someone living under a rock to not acknowledge this. Just simply, we are seeing more horrible storms with devastating environmental and human impacts.

The election year of 2020 was a doozie. The Atlantic hurricane season produced 30 named storms, an extraordinary number. It seems as if every day during the summer we heard of another hurricane hitting the East coast. There were 13 hurricanes (second-highest on record), and six major hurricanes (tied for second-highest on record).[641] This is extraordinary because this is more than double the number during a normal year, and these hurricanes and storms don't show any signs of stopping. In 2021, there were 21 hurricanes that battered the East coast. And in 2023, at least 15 people were killed and more than $2.29 billion in property were destroyed.

Am I saying that fossil fuels created this mess? That is exactly what I'm saying. Now, to be fair, hurricanes happen. That is just the natural world of unpredictableness. However, fossil fuels, which 99% of climate scientists believe are the cause of climate change, are accelerating the rapid movement of weather related events, like hurricanes, among other things. So, in a way, when you use fossil fuels, whether that be driving 100,000 miles of filling up your gas tank, you are contributing to the destruction of the environment, through more weather related issues.

One of the biggest causes to climate change is global warming,

---

641 "The Top 10 Weather and Climate Events of a Record-Setting Year» Yale Climate Connections." 2020. Yale Climate Connections. December 21, 2020. https://yaleclimateconnections.org/2020/12/the-top-10-weather-and-climate-events-of-a-record-setting-year/.

and yes there is a difference. Think of a greenhouse. Greenhouses work because they trap the sunlight that warms the plants inside of the greenhouse, thus giving the plants life in colder climates, while simultaneously keeping the cold out. The same is happening to the earth's atmosphere. Fossil fuels, when burned, travel to the atmosphere where it essentially stays because of the gravitational pull. You might not think that is a bad thing, but it most certainly is. All of that gas surrounding earth's atmosphere from all of the years that we've been burning fossil fuels has continuously grown more and more into a bubbly mass. The problem? Heat from the sun can enter into earth's atmosphere but because of the greenhouse gas, from fossil fuels, it cannot escape thus making the earth hotter than it was designed to be.

With the climate generally getting hotter and hotter with every passing year this causes the oceans to heat up as well, which causes all sorts of problems with our biodiversity. When the oceans heat, it obviously begins to melt the polar ice caps, which in turn, causes sea levels to rise. By the end of the century scientists have warned that if we don't get our priorities straight the sea level can rise to around 12 inches.

Stephen Simpson, professor in marine biology and global change thinks differently. "That doesn't sound like much," he lectured, "but there are many large cities around the world, much built on reclaimed land, that are not more than 30cm above sea level. Millions and millions of people would be displaced."[642] Can you imagine what that would mean, not just for the world but for the US? Republicans already hate it when people come into their territory. Ironically, climate change will make the situation worse, and the

---

642 Tutton, Mark. 2019. "World's Oceans Absorbing 60% More Heat than We Thought, Study Says." CNN. January 12, 2019. https://www.cnn.com/2019/01/12/health/warm-ocean-effects-intl/index.html.

republicans don't do anything about it. In effect, the republicans are screwing themselves over. When New York and California fall into the oceans, all of those people are going to have to go somewhere. They probably will end up in Montana, West Virginia, and other republican strongholds.

According to Mark Tutton, "Rising sea levels are already causing more flooding in the US, and within the next 30 years, more than 300,000 US homes could be flooded every other week."[643] Doesn't that sound delightful? And more intense, long-lasting hurricanes can give their credit to a warming planet because when temperatures rise evaporation intensifies, which causes more extreme weather patterns.

For example, if an area is more prone to receive lots of rainfall, because of climate change that area will receive much more rainfall. And if an area is prone to dry conditions, that area will even become more dry as climate change persists, making death valley quite literal.

The greenhouse gasses we burn today will stay with us for generations. That's how the greenhouse gas effect works. Even if we shut down all of our fossil fuel companies and rely only on renewable energy, we will still see catastrophic problems with our climate. Thanks politicians! You really came through for us. What a disgrace that politicians care more about their wealthy fossil fuel executives than they do about the future of our planet. We deserve better.

Rising sea levels aren't the only worry, as Tutton points out, "Almost three-quarters of the world's coral reefs were affected by those heat waves and experts say warmer oceans mean these sorts of die-offs will become much more common."[644] Our oceanic biodiversity will be destroyed unless we do something. Because of warmer ocean temperatures, nutrients tend to become washed up on the

---

643 ibid
644 ibid

shore, which deprives fish of their food and causes a lack of oxygen in the oceans, which depletes the fish population.

FIsh populations and marine life aren't the only ones suffering from the tolls of human caused climate change. Human activity has already altered more than 70% of ice free land. That is staggering. Most of this is due to agriculture as humans need much more land to live on and also to feed the growing population. This causes many animal species to either try to adapt to new living situations or face extinction all together.

Already, climate change has made this situation so much worse. Local species have already faced extinctions as diseases are more likely to spread in warming climates, which in turn leads to more animals and plants going extinct, which in turn leads to more extinctions. The Paris Climate Accord, the first such convention of its kind in quite a long time, aimed at minimizing rising temperatures to at least no more than 1.5 degrees celsius. Since that time, I regret to inform you that we are on track to obliterate that goal and go much higher than that. Some scientists tell us that by the end of the century the earth will have warmed 3 to 4 degrees celsius if we do nothing.

To give you a little bit of perspective, 4% of current mammals will lose their habitat at an increase of 1.5 degrees celsius. At an increase of 2 degrees celsius 8% of mammals would lose their habitats. And at an increase of 3 degrees celsius, which we are well on our way of doing, 40% of mammals would lose their habitat.[645] It's not just the animals that are affected. We are affected too. Could you imagine the catastrophe of half of our animal species losing their population? We are talking about mass extinctions that the earth

---

[645] United Nations. 2022. "Biodiversity - Our Strongest Natural Defense against Climate Change." United Nations. 2022. https://www.un.org/en/climatechange/science/climate-issues/biodiversity#:~:text=On%20land%2C%20higher%20temperatures%20have.

has never seen before. We are talking about a severe decrease in food supply for our already impoverished regions. We are talking about, in all likelihood, the extinction of the human race.

We have also seen a prolific amount of wildfires, torching the United States and North American region. Do you remember the Canada wildfires? It's hard to forget. Those fires destroyed the atmosphere and made everyone stay inside because the air quality index was so miserable. If you or your pets were outside for any long extended periods of time, exposure to all the harmful chemicals would be devastating to the respiratory system. In 2020 and 2021, wildfires burned more than 10 million acres each year. And there's no sign that this will stop anytime soon. How many times do you turn on the news and see more news about devastating fires? It's embarrassing. Think about all the money that it takes to not only combat the fires, but also the amount of money it takes to rebuild an area after a fire. Why don't we do more at prevention instead of simply combating fires that have already set ablaze acre after acre?

Because of climate change the Western portion of the United States has experienced far drier and hotter conditions than any other time in history. This is all terrible news for wildfires. These conditions lead to monstrous wildfires that gain intensity and speed with every passing year. And the smoke from these fires are devastating. As mentioned, the Canadian fires' smoke caused 70 million Americans to be under an air quality warning. We shouldn't be forced to live like this. In 2020, fires in California alone burned more than 4 million acres, a size bigger than the state of Connecticut.[646]

---

646 "How Climate Change Is Fueling Extreme Weather." n.d. Earthjustice. Accessed May 23, 2024. https://earthjustice.org/feature/how-climate-change-is-fueling-extreme-weather?gclid=CjwKCAjw69moBhBgEiwAUFCx2MssZ27g_rLtg-KEwCvS-qr-FEXWq09OGrp-b0VFJujcjl65MDyiyehoCOAgQAvD_BwE.

Perhaps the saddest fact is that hundreds of thousands of people die every year to wildfires, and, on average, 33,000 people die each year due to wildfire pollution.[647] This is not counting the devastating toll on animals and the environment.

In the Brazilian Pantanal fires in 2020, new scientific research has indicated that more than 17 million animals perished in the fires.[648] And this is only the fires in Brazil, not counting all of the animals who were scorched to death in the entire world because of human-caused climate change. Not just that, but the vast majority, 85%, of wildfires are started by humans. That means that we are the problem, not just in starting the fires, but expanding them and making them a lot worse.

We all remember the first scene of Bambi, where adorable bunnies, possums, deer, and other wildlife creatures are running for their lives from a fire created by a man. Not only are the animals running for their lives, trying to avoid the harrowing and scorching death, but they are also at risk after the fire as their habitat is most likely destroyed. This leads those animals, who are lucky enough to survive the flames to find a new home, oftentimes in areas that are densely populated by humans, which isn't a good mix.

In fact, it gets worse, in the Australian wildfires in 2019-2020 an estimated 3 billion, you heard that right, 3 billion animals were killed.[649] This can have a deplorable effect on our ecosystem in

---

647 "Global Wildfire Deaths." n.d. Www.nfpa.org. https://www.nfpa.org/News-and-Research/Publications-and-media/NFPA-Journal/2021/Winter-2021/News-and-Analysis/Dispatches/International.
648 "New Study Confirms 17 Million Animals Killed Immediately by 2020 Wildfires in Brazilian Pantanal." n.d. Panthera. https://panthera.org/news-room/new-study-confirms-17-million-animals-killed-immediately-2020-wild-fires-brazilian-0#:~:text=Moreover%2C%20scientists%20estimate%20the%20death.
649 "Animals Are the Forgotten Victims of Wildfires." 2023. Green Matters. June 7, 2023. https://www.greenmatters.com/big-impact/what-happens-to-animals-in-wildfires.

general, as we lose whole populations of one species this leads to a cascading effect. For example, if three million deer lose their lives in wildfires in California, that severely reduces the amount of food out there for the wolf population which can cause further disturbances within the ecosystem. And all of this does not include the amphibians and reptiles that are killed with every wildfire.

With climate change still accelerating at a rapid pace, this increases the likelihood of droughts in the Western portion of the States as temperatures continue to rise. In fact, the American West is currently in the midst of a mega drought, a mega-drought that ranks among the worst that we have seen in at least 1,200 years.[650] Conversely, in the opposite region of the States, primarily on the East coast we are seeing increasing flooding potential. This is because with hotter temperatures, precipitation is much more intense in areas more likely to see precipitation. Flooding from the 2023 summer cost tens of millions of dollars, while some cities and towns are still trying to clean up. This, of course, doesn't help with our insurance premiums, as more than 12 million houses, which previously wasn't considered to be a flood risk now fall under that category, making affording a home much more expensive and the likelihood that these categories will continue to increase as climate change continues at its current pace.

Do you remember when Texas dealt with their disastrous snowstorm in January of 2021? What a mess that was. The storm caused much of Texas to fall off the power grid, leaving Texans with virtually no way of heating their homes. All of this while the Texas senator, Ted Cruz, who is an ardent supporter of fossil fuels left Texas with

---

650 "How Climate Change Is Fueling Extreme Weather." n.d. Earthjustice. https://earthjustice.org/feature/how-climate-change-is-fueling-extreme-weather?gclid=CjwKCAjw69moBhBgEiwAUFCx2MssZ27g_rLtg-KEwCvS-qrFEXWq09OGrp-b0VFJujc-jl65MDyiyehoCOAgQAvD_BwE.

his constituents literally freezing to death, to go to Cancun. Of course, he could afford that, he is one of the richest senators. He can go to Cancun anytime he likes. Meanwhile, over a hundred people died, and almost 300 billion dollars went towards damages. A snow storm in Texas, that's what I'm talking about when I mention extreme weather.

Again, these are universal facts written by climate scientists, experts who have been doing this their whole careers. These are not cherry-picked. How can you deny these facts? These experts have been sounding the alarm for a really long time, decades as a matter of fact. These scientists tell us that if we don't get our act together soon we will be facing irreversible damage to our environment and climate. In other words, if we don't get our act together now we're screwed. Our children will be screwed. And we will have nobody else to blame but ourselves. Don't say that nobody warned you.

When we keep pumping oil and gas and using fossil fuels this only accelerates climate change. Things will get a lot worse than what is happening now. And what do the republicans do? Worse than nothing actually. They continue to assert that the US needs to keep drilling. They are led by a twice impeached president who believes that climate change is a hoax created by the Chinese. How incredibly ignorant. And how incredibly ignorant for those that vote for him. Know your stuff people. Know your stuff.

None of what I'm telling you should be a surprise to you. I mean we all knew this when he was running. We knew that Trump would have a very pro-business administration. We knew that Trump would try to undo everything that President Obama had done in terms of protecting the environment. He campaigned on this, and still won, despite the fact of losing by more than three million votes. (The worst showing for any winning candidate, by a lot.) None of us then can plead ignorance when Trump did exactly what he said he would do, destroying any progress made on reducing the impacts of climate change.

The first thing Donny-boy did to destroy our future was his unilateral decision to pull us out of the Paris Climate Agreement. The Paris Climate Agreement was a set of legally binding resolutions passed at the Paris convention in 2015. You can't just say that a few countries showed up, a whopping 194 countries are participating in the Paris Climate Agreement. Obviously the world is starting to get a little bit more concerned over climate experts' warnings. Even oil rich countries like Saudi Arabia joined the agreement.

The agreement was nothing more than common sense initiatives that should have been passed decades ago. Nothing radical or new here. In fact, the UN's Climate Change website displays very moderate wording:

The Paris Agreement's central aim is to strengthen the global response to the threat of climate change by keeping a global temperature rise this century well below 2 degrees Celsius above pre-industrial levels and to pursue efforts to limit the temperature increase even further to 1.5 degrees Celsius. Additionally, the agreement aims to increase the ability of countries to deal with the impacts of climate change, and at making finance flows consistent with a low GHG emissions and climate-resilient pathway. To reach these ambitious goals, appropriate mobilization and provision of financial resources, a new technology framework and enhanced capacity-building is to be put in place, thus supporting action by developing countries and the most vulnerable countries, in line with their own national objectives. The Agreement also provides for an enhanced transparency framework for action and support.[651]

---

651 United Nations. 2015. "Key Aspects of the Paris Agreement." United Nations Climate Change. 2015. https://unfccc.int/most-requested/key-aspects-of-the-paris-agreement.

Essentially, the agreement makes certain that those participating will put forward their best efforts to mitigate climate change and prevent warming below two degrees celcius. It also means that we have got to pull our weight in regards to helping developing nations gather the financial strength to transform their energy system to renewable sources, which happen to be slightly more expensive and a burden for some developing countries. Nothing here is radical. This is all common sense stuff. Clearly it is if 194 countries agreed to this.

And yet, that was not enough for Donald Trump. The Paris Climate Agreement was something that Barack Obama took a lot of pride in, as he was a huge supporter of the summit. Trump was thoroughly set to destroy everything to do with Barack Obama, even if that means destroying the environment. But then again, Trump campaigned on this issue, he publicly supported boosting up the coal industry and was supported by many conservative republicans who just don't listen to science. In fact, in 2017, 22 republican senators sent Trump a letter, including Mitch McConnell, egging him on into leaving the agreement. These 22 senators have had a long history of climate change denialism. And to make matters worse these 22 had received more than $10 million in campaign contributions from the fossil fuel industry the past three election cycles.[652] Do you think they care about climate change? They make lots and lots of money off fossil fuel companies and they are old enough that the worst effects of climate change won't affect them. They don't care. They don't care about our children. They don't care about our environment. They only care about themselves and it shows.

At the same time, 40 democratic senators sent Trump a letter pleading with him not to leave the agreement, such a move would be

---

652 Tom McCarthy & Lauren Gambino, The Republicans who urged Trump to pull out of Paris deal are big oil darlings Archived June 1, 2017, at the Wayback Machine, *The Guardian*

devastating to the environment and to the credibility of the United States on the world stage. Of course, do you think that Trump would possibly listen to the democrats. Not a chance in hell. He agreed with the republicans, who had fattened their wallets thanks to the fossil fuel industry. This left the United States in an incredibly embarrassing situation being the only major country on earth left out of a world wide agreement. America first, Trump touted. According to the Brookings Institute "The United States stands alone among major emitters in the world in its efforts to repudiate the agreement."

In fact, when Trump decided to pull us out of the Climate Agreement, despite the overwhelming vast majority of Americans who wanted to stay, the US joined the ranks of countries like Syria and Nicaragua, who refused to agree to the agreement. That's a pretty sad day when we are compared to Syria and Nicaragua, two of the most corrupt countries on the face of the earth. Actually, shortly after the US pulled out of the agreement Syria and Nicaragua agreed to the Paris Agreement, leaving the US in lonely territory.

Environmentalists and scientists were dismayed at the news. David Suzuki, a Canadian activist remarked, "Trump just passed on the best deal the planet has ever seen."[653] While others claimed that the US would come to rue the day that it left the Paris agreement. Republicans on the other hand were exuberant. Mike Pence, the loyal VP, at least until the insurrection, praised Donald Trump's leadership, while concerning over how much the US would have to help other less fortunate countries, calling the agreement "a transfer of wealth from the most powerful economy in the world to other countries around the planet."[654] Where is humanitarianism? I thought

---

653 "Trump just passed on the best deal the planet has ever seen". *The Guardian*. June 2, 2017. Archived from the original on June 2, 2017
654 Sampathkumar, Mythili (June 2, 2017). "Vice President Mike Pence says climate change is just an issue for the left". *The Independent*. New York. Archived from the original on June 5, 2017

he was for charities? Apparently not. Pence was also dumbfounded as to why liberals would even care about climate change. He just doesn't get it.

Democrats severely criticized the move. Former president Bill Clinton bemoaned, "Walking away from the Paris treaty is a mistake. Climate change is real. We owe our children more. Protecting our future also creates more jobs."[655] As a matter of fact, as we will get to later, the Paris Agreement would have led to more jobs, not less. Though, of course, stripping the coal industry is a necessary step to achieve net zero global emissions, the republicans only care about the coal miners, not the rest of the country.

In a surprise statement, Trump claimed that he was elected to represent the people of Pittsburg, not Paris. Shortly after, the mayor of Pittsburg reminded Trump that 80% of Pittsburg voters voted for Hillary Clinton, not Donald Trump. More polls reveal that 70% of Americans supported staying in the agreement, while only 18% supported getting out of the agreement. Is this how democracies are supposed to function? Nevertheless, we were now out of the Paris Agreement. Sorry Pittsburg.

Because President Obama was forced to sign executive orders to put regulations to curb green gas emissions, purely because congress wouldn't lift a damn finger, that left the future of fighting climate change up in the air. Executive orders are not the same as congressional action. If congress passes a law and the president signs it, then that becomes the law of the land. However, executive orders can be overturned by any incoming president, which makes it totally precarious, especially with somebody like Trump waiting in the

---

655 "Paris climate agreement: world reacts as Trump pulls out of global accord". *The Guardian*. June 2, 2017. Archived from the original on June 1, 2017

wings. It is no surprise then when Trump attacked all of president Obama's executive orders fighting climate change.

In 2007 the US supreme court declared that greenhouse gasses are within the scope of the Clean Air Act, thus giving the president the authority to regulate greenhouse gasses through executive order if congress didn't act, which it didn't. President Obama saw the need to do something about the climate. He had listened to the experts and cared about our childrens' future. He initiated the Clean Power Plan, which, in effect, regulated the energy sector and placed rules that new coal powered plants cannot operate unless they had carbon capture technology. It was a rule purely aimed at reducing CO_2 emissions. That sounds pretty reasonable doesn't it? Apparently not, at least according to republicans who immediately railed against the president, believing that he didn't have authority to create the new regulations even though the supreme court gave him authority.

When Trump got in there he immediately waged war on the regulations. He gutted the Clean Power Plan and replaced it with a much weaker regulation that lowers CO_2 emissions by a measly 1%.[656] Way to go!

Another beautiful thing that President Obama initiated was the miles per gallon standard. Realizing, again by listening to the experts, that the vast majority of CO_2 emissions that the US produces each year has to do with transportation. Obviously, this is inevitable, people have to drive to work, get groceries, ect. However, he realized that we should still try to tackle this issue hard. By understanding that the US leads the world in innovation and creativity, Obama created regulations for the auto industry, mandating

---

656 "What Is the Trump Administration's Track Record on the Environment?" n.d. Brookings. https://www.brookings.edu/articles/what-is-the-trump-administrations-track-record-on-the-environment/#:~:text=Brookings%20counts%2074%20actions%20to.

that fuel economy standards would improve by 5% each year. For example, if a 2017 Ford Escape gets, on average, 25 miles per gallon, then a 2018 Ford Escape should get, on average, 26.25 miles per gallon. And it goes on like this every year. This holds the auto manufacturers accountable, but also allows them to be creative and find innovative ways to cut back on the fuel each car needs. We, as consumers, should really appreciate this. That means less stops to the gas station, and less money we'd be spending at the pump. It's a win-win for the economy and for the environment, as it would cut emissions substantially.

Unfortunately, Trump doesn't see it the same way. He was elected with the help of the fossil fuel industry. They gave substantially to his election, and re-election campaign. They voted for him in huge numbers. They essentially control the republican party, giving republican members in congress huge sums of money for campaign purposes. These republicans, and Donald Trump, know that if they cross the fossil fuel industry they will miss out on hundreds of millions of dollars each year in campaign money. In other words, again these crooked politicians only care about themselves. It's a huge shame.

Well, anyway, Trump gutted the miles per gallon standard. Why? Ask his fossil fuel friends. (Also, side note, his secretary of state, Rex Tillerson, was the CEO of Exxonmobil, one of the world's largest oil and gas companies.) Again, Trump put in place a severely weakened regulation that only called for auto-makers to increase the fuel economy by 1%. This means that a 2017 Ford Escape that on average gets 25 miles per gallon, then a 2018 Ford Escape would, on average, get 25.25 miles per gallon. Wow, big changes there huh? Virtually auto-makers don't have to do anything different to improve the fuel efficiency of their vehicles, while at the same time our vehicles are producing the same amount of climate change causing CO_2

emissions. Thanks Trump, you really came through for us. What a joke. (Also, as a side note, the new regulations signed by Trump prohibits California, and other liberal states, from creating their own energy proficiency standards. For years, California's fuel efficiency standards were much stronger, and better, than the United States.'

But that's not all. Trump also severely restricted the regulations on methane gas, a gas that is much more potent than CO_2. The rules prior limited venting and flaring of methane gas by fossil fuel companies on public lands. Now those rules are abolished, thanks to Trump. Worse yet, fossil fuel companies don't have to report now on how much methane gas is emitted through their drilling and fracking, leaving the public, and scientists completely unaware of just how bad the situation really is.

In 2016, Trump campaigned on reviving the coal industry, like it was somehow under attack. He has since cut back on coal regulations that would have forced fossil fuel companies to store coal ash, which contains mercury and arsenic among other things that cause water pollution. Now these companies can just burn coal and not have to worry about the burdensome task of capturing their ash. He promised that this simple little weakening of the regulations would help the coal industry get back on its feet, but this is to no avail. The coal industry has witnessed a 22% reduction under Donald Trump's watch.[657] This has nothing to do with the regulations, obviously, as he has severely reduced the regulations. This is due to the fact that oil and gas are increasingly becoming cheaper and many companies are switching to oil and gas. Sorry West Virginia, looks like the coal industry will be gone anyway, but I'm sure Trump is grateful for your support.

---

657 ibid

You know, nothing brings me closer to God than being outdoors and enjoying the wildlife. The beautiful mountains, hills, trees, and wildlife. Isn't that what life is really all about? I often find myself thoroughly relieved that we have national parks and forests, with land set aside for us to enjoy, hike, and have picnics with the family. One of the most beautiful and serene parts of the world is the National Wildlife Refuge. According to the Environmental and Energy Law Program, "The Arctic National Wildlife Refuge consists of more than 19 million acres of wilderness in northeastern Alaska. The refuge includes some of the most pristine, untouched lands and waters within the United States, with no roads, marked trails, or campgrounds. It provides important habitat for Porcupine caribou, denning polar bears, and other wildlife."[658] In short, it's just an incredibly beautiful piece of land, one that I recommend you visit and experience first hand.

In 1980 Congress passed a law that opened up this beautiful tract of land for oil and gas development, primarily due to the energy crisis facing the country at the time. It's interesting that we still haven't learned our lesson. Instead of being dependent on fluctuating oil and gas prices we could have been focusing on clean energy instead. We didn't then, and we still don't now, but look at how far ahead we could have been. Incredibly, no oil or gas lease sales were given until 2017, mostly because leaders realized the devastating environmental impacts this would have for generations. All that changed when Trump became president.

Shortly after Trump's inauguration, Congress passed the dreadful Tax cuts and Jobs Act. Among many horrible things that the law stood for, like drastically reducing the taxes for millionaires like

---

658 Just, Robin. 2019. "Arctic National Wildlife Refuge – Oil and Gas Development - Environmental & Energy Law Program." Harvard Law School. September 27, 2019. https://eelp.law.harvard.edu/2019/09/arctic-national-wildlife-refuge-oil-and-gas-development/.

Elon Musk and Donald Trump himself, the law also "authorized oil and gas exploration, leasing, development, and production on the Coastal Plain, and ordered the Secretary of the Interior to conduct at least two lease sales within 10 years."[659] Oddly enough, the leases were snuck into the bill to help provide revenue for the massive tax cuts. In other words, the environment would have to pay to give Elon Musk another 15 million dollars in tax breaks.

The first lease sales took place the day that Donald Trump left office, so even with the voters successfully ousting him, he is still doing much damage. Here are just a few reasons why drilling in the Arctic Wildlife Refuge is so devastating to the environment. According to Ellen Montgomery, director of Public Lands Campaign,

Drilling in the refuge would damage the habitat of "wolves, muskoxen, arctic foxes, wolverines, brown bears, golden eagles, tundra swans and snowy owls that call it home." It would also destroy the habitat of migratory birds who use this land as a breeding ground. Drilling would be catastrophic for the already declining number of polar bears, potentially eliminating up to a third of the polar bears within the region, as well as depleting the porcupines and the caribou herds.

When the rest of the world is moving forward with clean energy, it makes no sense to endanger our environments and animal species for the perpetuation of fossil fuel usage. The consequences of drilling could be irreversible as species die out and ecosystems are destroyed.

The vast majority of people do not want these lands to be drilled on. It makes no sense that a few wealthy fossil fuel entrepreneurs can totally grab the reins of government and push policies favorable to them down the throats of the American people.[660]

---

659 ibid
660 Montgomery, Ellen. 2021. "Drilling in the Arctic Is a Terrible Idea. Let's Stop before We Start." Environment America. January 11, 2021. https://environmentamerica.org/articles/drilling-in-the-arctic-is-a-terrible-idea-lets-stop-before-we-start/.

Clearly, the interests of the vast majority of Americans don't matter. All that matters is profits. Greed.

The Trump administration didn't just stop there. They also set about erecting fossil fuel infrastructure such as the Keystone XL pipeline and the Dakota Access Pipeline. Both of which are notorious, as republicans often boast of these projects and deride democrats for being radical by opposing them.

The Keystone XL pipeline was initially designed in 2008, by a Canadian company, which already sent oil to the US. It was designed to "transport the planet's dirtiest fossil fuel, tar sands oil, to market- and fast."[661] The pipeline had promised to send into the US billions of barrels of crude oil that was locked away in Canada's forests. The oil would be sent to refineries in Texas that would ship the oil overseas, not to American gasoline pumps. These are not my words alone. These are the words of experts, who happen to know the details of the Keystone XL pipeline. In many debates, republicans seem to think that the democrats have destroyed America, and gas prices are so high because Joe Biden shut down the pipeline. This flies in the face of what experts say. In no way was the pipeline created to resolve pressures faced by average Americans. It was strictly put in place so that oil could be exported, fattening the pockets of the fossil fuel barons like Rex Tillerson's, Exxon Mobil, Shell, and other fossil fuel companies. Again, these companies hold lots of weight and influence in the halls of Congress. They have lots of money to spend and they don't mind getting dirty by bribing candidates and sending them unlimited amounts of money for political favors. Why do so many Americans blame the shutting down of the Keystone

---

661 Lindwall, Courtney, and Melissa Denchak. 2022. "What Is the Keystone XL Pipeline?" Www.nrdc.org. March 15, 2022. https://www.nrdc.org/stories/what-keystone-xl-pipeline#whatis.

XL pipeline for increasing prices at the pump? Pure ignorance, plain and simple. The American people have become lazy, they don't like to research before sharing sentiments that aren't true. Think about that next time you blame Joe Biden for gas prices.

In America, we also already have many pipelines that run throughout our country. The reason that Keystone was so much different was the different materials being shipped. This isn't average oil, but slimy, slick, black substances that are derived from underneath Canada's forests, which means that obtaining this substance is incredibly difficult and environmentally devastating. Of course, it's the human condition of convenience that often causes the most issues. When gas prices rise, we as humans, get ticked and call for something to be done, which often results in oil and gas companies pumping more and more, with no regard for the environmental wellbeing, only on profits.

Thankfully, mostly due to the pressure that environmentalists were putting on him, President Obama, in 2015, decided, under the State department, to decline the construction of the northern section of the Keystone pipeline, which would have cut through Nebraska, the Dakotas, and Canada. (The Southern section runs through Texas and Oklahoma. It was already completed.) President Trump quickly decided to start the project up again, after heeding to the calls of the greedy fossil fuel companies. In fact, this did nothing to bring down prices at the pump, "Dirty energy lobbyists claimed developing tar sands would protect our national energy security and bring U.S. fuel prices down. But environmental reviews by both the Obama and Trump administrations concluded that the Keystone XL pipeline would not have lowered gasoline prices."[662] There you go, just another fact that republicans don't like to hear.

662 "What Is the Keystone XL Pipeline?" n.d. Www.nrdc.org. https://www.nrdc.org/stories/what-keystone-xl-pipeline#impact.

Some of the reasons why environmentalists pushed back so hard against the implementation of the Keystone pipeline is because the tar that runs through is much heavier, making it much more likely that the tar would leak through the pipes, damaging the environment. In fact, "one study found that between 2007 and 2010, pipelines moving tar sands oil in Midwestern states spilled three times more per mile than the U.S. national average for pipelines carrying conventional crude. Since it first went into operation in 2010, TC Energy's original Keystone Pipeline System has leaked more than a dozen times; one incident in North Dakota sent a 60-foot, 21,000-gallon geyser of tar sands oil spewing into the air."[663] That's a lot of pollution. And it's not like this stuff is great for the air and water. The EPA, again, using the experience of experts, have claimed that with the implementation of the pipeline greenhouse gas would increase dramatically. This form of tar oil emits 17% more carbon than normal oil. And with the pipeline running virtually across our whole country, every year the amount of greenhouse gas emitted would be the equivalent of more than 38 million vehicles on the road per year. That's a lot of needless greenhouse gas being burned every year just so that the fossil fuel companies can get more money in their wallets.

What often gets omitted from mention is the fact that a huge chunk of the pipeline goes through Native American lands. Many tribal lands are out there on the prairies of the Dakotas and Nebraska. Obviously, the Native tribes care much more for the protection of the environment than typical capitalists, who are just seeking to exploit it and make handsome sums of money. To the Natives, this is their home. This is where their ancestors lived and died and are still among them. In short, the environment is sacred to these tribes. I can't think of something more irreligious and more disheartening

---

663 Ibid

than a massive pipeline oozing oil on what we believe to be sacred. That is morally disgusting. Again, fossil fuel companies don't care. They don't care that it would trample all over the sacred grounds of Native tribes. They don't care that they are destroying the planet. They don't care that the overwhelming majority of Americans, and humanity in general, is in opposition to these projects. They only care about one thing. Big, juicy, money. They know they are destroying our planet, but they decide to care more about short term profits than the happiness of future generations. That's the biggest form of selfishness that there can be.

In fact, so many people stood up and demanded the president to destroy the pipeline and to stop drilling. This came from an unusual coalition including ranchers, religious leaders, environmentalists, young people, minorities, Native Americans, liberals, ect. Yet, in the face of all of this the fossil fuel companies felt undaunted. They knew they had money, and they weren't afraid to use it. They used hundreds of millions of dollars… to what? To give to charities? To give to the hungry? The thirsty? The homeless? NO. They spent hundreds of millions of dollars lobbying members of the US congress into doing the will of those companies, not the American people. Think of that. We elect representatives, with the absurd belief that they will actually represent us and our best wishes, and instead they take our votes and at the same time the money of the fossil fuel companies, who they feel obligated to represent more than the average voter. I for one can't compete, I admit. I don't have hundreds of millions of dollars to leverage my representative into doing what I want. We will never win this game if this is how it is. How can we compete with all of this wealth? We can't, and it shows.

Incredibly, in the two years that led up to the 2014 midterm elections, the fossil fuel companies spent a walloping $721 million dollars to court congressmen and women to do their bidding. And of course, the ones that received the prize were also the ones feverishly pushing for the completion of the pipeline.[664] In the same way, the fossil fuel companies decided to support Donald Trump whole-heartedly, giving him huge sums of money for his election purposes. It makes all the sense in the world, then, that he would fast-track the completion of the pipeline, even after President Obama had derailed it.

Moreover, the industry often makes remarks regarding how many jobs this will provide to hundreds of thousands of Americans. Not true. A State department report concluded that the pipeline would employ about 2,000 workers for only two years. So, not only is this a huge lie in terms of how many jobs this would create, but even the jobs it does create are only temporary at best. After the completion of the pipeline only 35 jobs would be permanent.[665] How is that for building a strong economy? What a crapshoot.

Thankfully, the American people got Trump out of there after four tumultuous years. President Biden, listened to the American people, and experts to make the determination that the pipeline needed to be cut off. Not only was the vast majority of Americans opposed to the Keystone, but most oil companies whittled down their usage of tar sand oil after the pandemic. On president Biden's first day in office he revoked the permit, thereby ringing the death knell of the pipeline once and for all. Thank you president Biden.

The Dakota Access pipeline is very similar to Keystone. Again, here we have a pipeline that the vast majority of Americans oppose, especially Native American groups, where the pipeline was infringing on their lands. President Obama put a halt into the construction of this project for more reviews to be conducted. However, Trump,

---

664 ibid
665 Ibid

who owned stock in the company, pushed for the construction to continue, despite widespread opposition. Thankfully, again, president Biden had the courage to stand up to these fossil fuel companies and put an end to this pipeline as well.

Trump also was hostile to air and water pollution regulations. He put more anti-regulation members on pollution committees and limited scientific research in the fields of pollution. Trump has been hellbent on removing regulations on fossil fuel companies. Why? Because these regulations make it a bit harder for fossil fuel companies to pollute, it also may cost fossil fuel companies a fraction of their profits to comply with these regulations, which is absurd. These companies have hundreds of millions of dollars that they can spend in campaign contributions but they raise hell whenever they have to comply with a regulation to preserve clean air and drinking water. Really? That is messed up.

So, what exactly can we do? It's not hard. All we have to do is listen to the experts, the environmental and climate scientists who have been warning us for a long, long time. They tell us that we have to transition away from the use of fossil fuels, develop clean energy; like solar, wind, geothermal, biomass, and create carbon capture technology. In all of these ways we will be doing exactly what the republicans have been pushing for for many years, being energy independent. That means we don't need to rely on Saudi Arabia to give us oil. We have our own energy supply that we can harness, like the sun, which isn't going away anytime soon, creating for us a sustainable form of energy. And once we perfect it, it will be cheaper and more efficient to use than fossil fuels. Sounds pretty good to me right? Why wouldn't we do these things? If we don't start advancing in clean energy technology we will fall behind China, Germany, and many other countries in development and innovation. Fossil fuels are a thing of the past. We should treat them this way.

Democrats, with the exception of a few who no longer can consider themselves democrats, support efforts to move away from fossil fuels and to invest in the future. Republicans have taken the opposite approach. They have been too busy making out with fossil fuel executives that they don't care to protect the environment. They keep pushing for more drilling and more pipelines and more fracking, instead of innovation and growth.

One example of what the democrats have tried to do is in the form of the Green New Deal, which derives its name from FDR's famous New Deal programs that helped millions upon millions of Americans get back on their feet after the Great Depression. Written by Ed Markey, a great progressive from the state of Massachusetts, and by Alexandria Ocasio Cortez, the up and coming star of the democratic party, the Green New Deal called on the federal government to wean itself from the usage of fossil fuels and instead invest in clean technology. The plan was to curb, significantly, greenhouse gas emissions, while at the same time guaranteeing good salaries for those who work in the clean energy industries.[666] There is nothing fundamentally radical here, and if you think so you clearly haven't been paying attention. Again, the bill just reiterates everything that scientists and experts have been telling us we need to do, ease off on fossil fuels and transition to a clean economy. What's so radical about that?

Variations of this proposal have been circulating for many years, so we can't act surprised that it's out there now. Think Tanks, columnists, and scientists have been flouting similar ideas for a long

---

[666] Friedman, Lisa. 2019. "What Is the Green New Deal? A Climate Proposal, Explained." *The New York Times*, February 21, 2019. https://www.nytimes.com/2019/02/21/climate/green-new-deal-questions-answers.html.

time. The movement just picked up the pace considerably ever since the election of Donald Trump and his anti-humanity policies. The resolution that was written was in response to the UN and federal scientists who have warned that if the world's temperatures continue to rise, we will see even worse catastrophes such as wildfires, droughts, and other natural disasters. This is from the UN, how can you call BS on that? The research shows that the US economy is likely to lose billions of dollars by the end of the century if nothing is done to confront climate change.[667]

The bill calls for the entire world to be net-zero by 2050, which means that the US must control carbon to a level where no additional carbon emissions are being accumulated in our atmosphere. In order for this to happen the US must take a leading role in this endeavor, as we are the second highest carbon-emitting country, and the highest carbon-emitting country per capita in the world, obviously our participation is a must. Many republicans claim that we should wait until China does something to confront climate change, but that's not what being a leader is about. A leader leads, not follows. And this bill would do that. The bill would also create good-paying jobs in the clean energy sector, guarantee that the government is taking actions to ensure clean air and drinking water, and declare that healthy food is a human right, not for just the privileged few. Often we see high poverty families have drastically higher obesity rates because unhealthy foods are cheaper, more affordable options. Worse, we often see higher poverty families have more health issues because they are near high pollutant sites and are eating food laced with chemicals and other risky ingredients. Nothing in the bill should give us pause. And yet, republicans still grill against it.

Republicans do exactly what you would expect them to do when

---

[667] Ibid

they disagree with something. They call it a socialist takeover. What exactly in this bill has to do with socialism or a takeover? Donald Trump claimed that the proposal would take away our airplane rights. I'm really confused by what he means there, but apparently he thinks that a transition to clean energy will take away our rights. Maybe he's also in favor of eliminating the TSA and security checks while he's at it, I mean those things take away my rights, right?

Tom Cotton, senator from Arkansas, who happens to be just a fire-eater from the extreme right flank of the party, beholden to special interests, said that the proposal would get rid of cars and have everybody ride light-speed rail "supposedly powered by unicorn tears."[668] Nowhere in the provisions is this mentioned. And, not to be outdone, republican senator from Wyoming John Barrasso warned that the ice cream, milkshakes, and cheeseburgers would be known only to history because under the Green New Deal "livestock will be banned."[669] (Just for the record, what we do to livestock and farm animals is totally horrendous as well, research what happens to chicken before they reach your plate.) Nevertheless, none of these outlandish allegations are even close to being mentioned in the provisions in the Green New Deal. So why do republicans say these things? It really has to do with psychology. Obviously, if I lived under a rock and only listened to Fox news, being constantly lied to, it would be easy to believe these lies if that's all that I hear. Of course, Fox news never mentions climate change or the impacts of global warming, so it's much easier for that part of the population, who only watch Fox news, to believe even the most God-forsaken horrible lies. Take the 2020 election for instance. The vast majority of people who get their news from a multitude of different media

---

668 Ibid
669 Ibid

outlets are much more likely to believe that the election was legitimate and Trump is just being a sore-losing baby. Conversely, those who only watch Fox news still have a conviction, to this day, that Trump won the election and that everybody else is brainwashed. Indeed, a co-worker once called me brainwashed for believing that Joe Biden rightfully won the election, even after I explained that experts from both parties agreed that there were no high levels of fraud and that Trump's claims are without merit.

The same thing is true with the climate crisis. If I hear that a proposal is being made by the political party that I strongly disagree with that would end ice cream as we know it I would be pissed and voice my opinions strongly against it. It works for the republicans. It is scientifically proven that the more that someone repeats a lie, the more likely people are to believe it as the truth. Again think of the election, all of Trump's lies have been repeated so often that more people are prone to believe it.

There is no evidence of any of these crazy allegations to the Green New Deal, if you think differently read the bill. I wonder why nobody holds people to accountability when they flat-out lie to the American people. Maybe it's because in today's day and age, and in the era of Trump, we just expect our politicians to lie. Yet, that shouldn't be the case. We deserve so much better. If republicans don't like the plan they shouldn't sit here, call it a socialist takeover running on unicorn tears that will outlaw hamburgers. Instead, they should be honest and tell the American people the truth of why they oppose it. The truth is that they are afraid to admit it. If they told the truth the American people would see that they only care about the profits of the fossil fuel industry, not the needs and wants of the American people.

Let's take a look at what happened when the democrats and Joe Biden were thrusted into power. Since president Biden has been in office, he has done a plethora of things to help save the planet. He committed to cut greenhouse gas emissions by at least 50% by 2030. That's a pretty lofty goal, clearly he understands the implications of climate change and how quickly we have got to move. He finalized this deal putting it under the Paris Agreement. Other countries have been eager to do the same or even to beat the target.

He proposed the Inflation Reduction Act of 2022, which yes had to do with inflation, but it was also the biggest allotment of resources to combat climate change ever passed in the US congress. The *World Resources Institute* praises Biden for this work. Among the many things that the law provides, the "Inflation Reduction Act establishes a comprehensive set of clean energy incentives, mostly through decade-long tax credits for everything from electric vehicles to direct air capture and sequestration of carbon dioxide."[670] Quite honestly, the tax credits provide consumers and businesses no excuse for developing clean energy initiatives and habits. Now, businesses who set up a system of carbon capture receive a tax credit. Now, consumers who buy an electric vehicle, which doesn't produce the devastating effects that a gas guzzling truck does, receive a tax credit. (If you're buying a new car it doesn't make sense not to get an electric one.) Now, businesses that store carbon, instead of emitting it, receive a tax credit. Just these provisions alone provide us with a much sturdier path towards reaching our goals. In fact, "Economic modeling indicates that the Inflation Reduction Act itself could reduce 2030 emissions by 1 billion tons, leaving a 0.5 billion ton gap to achieving the U.S. 2030 emissions target — a

---

670 Lashof, Dan. 2022. "Tracking Climate Action under the Biden Administration: Where Has Progress Been Made?" *Www.wri.org*, January. https://www.wri.org/insights/biden-administration-tracking-climate-action-progress.

gap that could be closed by complementary federal regulations and state and local action."[671]

He tackled super pollutants. Super pollutants are mostly hydrofluorocarbons (HFCs) and methane. And while these pollutants aren't emitted at the same frequency as CO2 they are much more potent and dangerous. It would be in vain to try to tackle climate change without tackling these super polluters. In the latter half of 2022, Biden proposed a Methane Action Plan, which is about 50 measures backed up by $20 billion to tackle methane emissions. Even better, the Biden administration has introduced an emissions fee on fossil fuel companies that emit methane. All of this while the EPA has also proposed stronger regulations to reduce methane emissions from oil and gas companies. "Biden also helped launch the Global Methane Pledge at the 2021 UN climate summit (COP26). As of January 2023, 150 countries have signed onto the pledge and committed to cut their total methane emissions by at least 30% by 2030."[672] How about that for progress?

He required that all new vehicles made after 2035 would be gas free. God knows we need that. But, republicans have attacked this proposal especially hard, blaming Biden for trying to destroy the auto industry, when in reality it would save the industry from foreign competitors. I always say it's better to be ahead of the game, as opposed to following everybody else. If we don't start investing in electric vehicles, then China and Vietnam will, and they will be kicking our butts globally because most other countries believe that climate change is an issue. And it gets even better. To incentivize consumers, who happen to be the worst when it comes to doing economically friendly things, Biden offered a serious tax credit to get people to buy an electric vehicle, some qualify for a $7,500 tax

---

671 Ibid
672 Ibid

credit, just for buying an environmentally friendly vehicle, as long as it's assembled here in the States, not China or Bangladesh.[673]

He has significantly improved the progress of carbon capture, using both natural (trees) and technological (chemical scrubbers) to do the job. Everyone should know that trees absorb a significant amount of carbon dioxide. Therefore, it makes perfect sense to plant more trees, not cut them down. If we have more trees that means that more carbon is being captured, less trees means less carbon is getting captured. It's not rocket science, but it's effective. The Biden administration has been very serious in their goal to plant millions of more trees throughout the country, if not more. Moreover, many other states are doing similar things. In Wisconsin, governor, Tony Evers, pledged "to protect and restore Wisconsin's forestland by conserving 125,000 acres and planting 75 million trees by 2030."[674] That's a big deal. And, oh yeah, Evers happens to be a democrat that gets absolutely zero support from the gerrymandered republican legislature. But, getting back to president Biden, "The Bipartisan Infrastructure Law," which Biden advocated for and signed, "includes significant investments in wildfire risk reduction and ecosystem restoration to protect and promote natural carbon removal." The law also provides tax credits for companies that take part in carbon sequestration activities, giving companies who care about the environment a huge head start and advantage.

He has reiterated his goal to reach 100% clean electricity by 2035. Being 100% clean means we are no longer relying on all of that gross, dingy fossil fuel usage. No longer will dirty oil be used as a primary energy source. Instead, president Biden has pledged to invest in new, up and coming, energy sources that are freely handed

---

673 Ibid
674 "Trillion Trees Pledge | | Wisconsin DNR." n.d. Dnr.wisconsin.gov. https://dnr.wisconsin.gov/topic/forests/trillionTreesPledge.

to us by God. All we have to do is use it. Use the sun. The wind. The water. On top of this they have also been active by creating tougher regulations regarding power plant emissions. All positives that will prevent the world greater harm. And quite frankly, something that should have been happening all along.

Last, but certainly not least, we have already talked about. He ended the horrible policies of the previous administration. President Biden shut down the horrible pipelines that weren't going to help us with the energy situation anyways and he brought us back into the Paris Climate Agreement, thank God. The World Resources Institute says it best"

"In addition to helping ensure completion of the Paris Rulebook during COP26 and agreeing at COP27 to establish a fund to help vulnerable countries deal with losses and damages from the impacts of climate change, the U.S. also helped launch the Global Methane Pledge, the First Movers Coalition on sustainable supply chains, and the Glasgow Leaders' Declaration on Forests and Land Use. And importantly, despite a challenging geopolitical relationship, formal bilateral climate discussions between the U.S. and China were reestablished during COP27, which can help the world's two largest greenhouse gas emitters find areas of common ground to confront the climate crisis."[675]

Finally the United States is showing some form of leadership capabilities again, something that was sorely lacking in the previous administration. Just getting back in the Paris Agreement is a big deal. It means to our allies, and the world at large, that one man alone can't unilaterally remove us from international compacts without some form of consequence from the American people. It shows the world that we do care about the environment and we are ready to

---

675 Ibid

lead again. We will show determination to help developing countries have the resources they need to transition from a fuel economy to a sustainable one. We will move forward with massive investments in solar and wind technologies. We will work with China to help mitigate the disastrous effects of climate change and make strong goals to take on the fossil fuel industry, both here and elsewhere, considering that we are the number one and two carbon polluters.

Now, are there ways that president Biden can improve on his climate agenda? Absolutely. We should never stop innovating and coming up with new solutions. But, president Biden is doing a terrific job transitioning us to a more sustainable path, and he should be commemorated for that, and re-elected just for this reason alone, in my humble opinion. And the decision is pretty simple. On one side of the coin, you have a party, the republicans, who don't even want to acknowledge that climate change is real. On this path there is devastation like we've never seen before. On the other side we see a president and a party, the democrats, who actually listen to the experts and are determined on doing what is right for our environment and future. Yes, it's pretty simple indeed.

I also want to point out that it seems rather strange to me that some of the most gorgeous places in the US today are some of the most conservative bastions in the country, supporting candidates that want further investments in fossil fuels. It makes no sense. Take, as an example, the Arctic Wildlife Refuge, which happens to reside in Alaska. Many state lawmakers and even Alaska's congressmen and senators have been over-eager to get federal oil leases so that companies can drill in the refuge. Well, why in the world would they do that? It's pretty simple. Money. Straight up money. You see, if more leases are allowed in the Wildlife Refuge that means that companies are investing in Alaska, which does a couple of things. It helps Alaska's workforce, creating more short-term jobs while helping Alaska's economy providing housing, recreation, and services. So, in effect, when Alaska's senator, Lisa Murkowski, begged Trump to allow leases in this protected area she was doing it just for the money.

In a similar way, West Virginia is home to some of the most beautiful, scenic trails and views in all of the country. Yet, West Virginia is one of the most conservative states in the union, voting for Trump and other die-hards by huge margins. The reason? Their economy is centered totally on coal. All together, almost 10% of West Virginians work in the coal mine.[676] Now, I will admit, this is a rather big number for such a small category, but this doesn't mean that the entire state should be under the influence of almighty coal. What about the other 90% of West Virgninians who have nothing to do with coal? And what about women? Only about 1.5% of women in West Virginia have a job involving coal. To put it simply, only a little more than 11,000 West Virginians work with coal. This means that there are more employees that would be affected if Arconic, a company based in the Philadelphia that creates aluminum sheets, went out of business, than if West Virginia gutted its coal mines and transitioned to clean energy, not even mentioning that more jobs would be created with the transition to clean energy. And, more striking, there are more than 1,800 businesses that have more employees than those currently employed in the West Virginia coal mines.[677] Yet, West Virginia's officials have held the rest of the country hostage when it comes to climate change.

Let's look a little closer. One of the reasons why West Virginia is

---

[676] "Experience in the Coal Mining Industry among West Virginia Residents West Virginia Social Survey Report." n.d. https://survey.wvu.edu/files/d/33d7657a-926e-4ea8-990d-795b457baeae/experience-in-coal-industry-accessible.pdf.
[677] "Companies Ranked by Number of Employees - Page 19." n.d. Companiesmarketcap.com. Accessed May 24, 2024. https://companiesmarketcap.com/largest-companies-by-number-of-employees/page/19/.

so red, politically speaking, was the use of the coal industry. I hate to say it but, West Virginians are having a hard time accepting that the US, as well as every other developed country, has to transition out of fossil fuels. Every other major country on earth realizes the implications of climate change. So, as democrats came to this realization they dramatically scaled up the production of clean energy technologies while placing regulations on the coal industry that is responsible for so much devastation. As the democrats moved in this position, West Virginians moved closer to the republican party, since that party is sleeping in bed with the fossil fuel interests. With West Virginia being one of the whitest states, this causes many minorities to move out. West Virginia is also overwhelmingly older than the rest of the nation, and much less likely to have a college education, with only 19% of residents holding a bachelor's degree.[678] (Those without college degrees are much more likely to support the republican party demographics show.) All of these things spell trouble for the democratic party, but so many still pin the blame on democrats insistence on transitioning to clean energy.

West Virginia senator, Joe Manchin, believe it or not, one of the few democrats in the entire state, has taken a vow to crush president Biden's efforts to confront climate change. Taking aim on the Inflation Reduction Act, commonly referred to the IRA, Manchin found a new enemy, pitching an "unrelenting fight against the Biden administration's efforts to implement the IRA as a radical climate agenda."[679] You might think that he just cares for the 10% of West

---

[678] "West Virginia: How the Bluest State Became the Reddest." n.d. NBC News. https://www.nbcnews.com/meet-the-press/ west-virginia-how-bluest-state-became-reddest-n697491.
[679] Luscombe, Richard, and Martin Pengelly. 2023. "Joe Manchin Vows 'Unrelenting Fight' against US Climate Law He Helped Pass." *The Guardian*, August 16, 2023, sec. US news. https://www.theguardian.com/us-news/2023/aug/16/ joe-manchin-inflation-reduction-act-climate-law-radical-agenda-joe-biden.

Virginians who work in the coal mines, but we must not forget that Manchin receives millions of dollars from his fossil fuel friends in campaign contributions and has extensive fossil fuel investments of his own, which he desperately wants to protect.[680] Maybe, just maybe that's why he's waged war against everything that president Biden tries to do. And maybe, just maybe, that's why he's seriously contemplating switching to the republican party, caring more for his money interests than the future of the planet. In fact, when Manchin was approached for his views following the deadly US wildfires in 2022, he responded in typical Manchin fashion, "Climate change is global climate" he stressed, "Most of the pollution today is coming from Asia."[681] Clearly, he doesn't understand that the US is the number two emitter. It's particularly bad because Manchin is the sole democrat destroying the hopes of hundreds of millions just in this country because of his reluctance to acknowledge climate change.

It's extremely ironic that from one of the most beautiful states, we get two senators (Shelly Moore Capito the other one), and two representatives all that want to destroy the beauty of the earth by supporting fossil fuels that warm the planet. Here is what will happen to West Virginia if she keeps electing these republicans and republican wannabees. More and more people will move into West Virginia because it is one of the more thinly populated areas of the country, due to the fact that oceans are rising and some parts of California and Florida are now underwater. With more extreme weather events increasing with the rate of climate change more and more people will flee hot spots, where extreme weather events are more likely to happen, this will further perpetuate the number of

---

680 Ibid
681 "The World Is on Fire, and Joe Manchin Still Doesn't Think the Issue Is Climate Change." n.d. The New Republic. Accessed May 24, 2024. https://newrepublic.com/post/173449/wildfire-joe-manchin-still-doesnt-think-issue-climate-change.

people moving into West Virginia, bringing in a lot more than what the West Virginians are used to and bringing in significant crime. Finally, West Virginia won't be immune from the weather disasters either, eventually her beauty will fade away as more people swarm there and the mountains will wither away to a shell of its former self.

But it's not just West Virginia and Alaska that really do harm. It is extremely ironic that the most beautiful states elect representatives that are hellbent on money, while at the same time not giving a crap about the state of their environment. This is true in Montana, the Dakotas, Oklahoma, and Texas, just to name a few. All of these states relentlessly vote republican at the ballot box, while the truth is that they are destroying their future when they do it.

So, what can we do? Oh much indeed. Firstly, you're probably not surprised to hear me say this, but, vote democratic. Most democrats support fighting climate change, transitioning to new clean energy sources, and being a leader on the global stage. Invest clean energy into your own life. Buy electric vehicles, which is much more economical thanks to president Biden's tax credits. It's also more affordable when in comparison to longer terms. It's more expensive to have a gas guzzling car when you have to spend $200 a month on gas, which is always dependent on supply chain issues. Drive less. It's pointless just to drive an hour to go shopping when in comparison to how many emissions that would produce. Recycle. Don't go to Starbucks and just throw away the plastic cup. Recycle it. Do your part. Invest in clean energy options of your own. There are plenty of ways to have a sustainable house, whether that's using solar panels on the roof or using geothermal technology. With every passing year solar panels are becoming more and more affordable. Right now taxpayers can even claim a 30% tax credit on the cost of implementing solar panels on your own house. That's a pretty good deal! Solar power will also make your monthly utility bills lower, as you don't need to rely on third-party utility companies to bamboozle you out of money. You can always leave the lights on too because of the solar batteries, which essentially means that power will never run out, regardless of what kind of weather we are having. Solar often can even increase the overall value of the home, I mean who wouldn't want a free power source attached to their house? Last but not least of course is the amazing benefits to the environment by going solar. There's no reason why the United States can't be leading the world in producing solar panels, especially if that's what the American people are craving. This needs us to do one simple thing....

Elect better representatives. It's not hard. We listen to candidates and we decide which one is better. We need to always research about candidates before we decide who to vote for. It's fair for the candidates, it's fair for yourselves, and it's fair for the community. As a rule of thumb, I never vote for a candidate who receives lots of money from fossil fuel interests. It's incredibly likely that they will do the will of the fossil fuel interest and not the American people's will. I usually always will vote for someone who is more aggressive in tackling the tough issue of climate change, not a mere moderate who wants to please the fossil fuel companies.

We should elect representatives who are serious about investing in clean energy: solar, wind, geothermal, biomass, hydropower, among other things. This means massive increases in our energy infrastructure. But guess what? When we do finally invest in clean energy, estimates show that the US would save about $20 billion a year in fossil fuel caused climate change disasters. Oh, and I forgot to mention, right now fossil fuel companies get massive subsidies.

That's right, the one special interest group that does more to harm the environment than any other is getting subsidies. The Oxford dictionary describes a subsidy as "a sum of money granted by the government or a public body to assist an industry or business so that the price of a commodity or service may remain low or competitive." And we do this for the big oil companies. That's crazy. It's not just the US who is at fault, although we are a big part of it. According to the International Energy Agency, fossil fuel handouts hit a total of over $1 trillion, yes you heard that right, 1 trillion dollars, while at the same time in 2022 big oil reigned in over $4 trillion in profits. I don't think they need any more subsidies. In the US, taxpayers are charged with giving over $20 billion in handouts to fossil fuel companies. What do we get out of it? Not much. Not even conservatives really know why. Conservative economist, Gib Metcalf, got it right when he suggested that "little if any benefit" talking about the subsidies "in the form of oil patch jobs, lower prices at the pump, or increased energy security for the country."[682] So, why do we keep giving the oil companies more? So that politicians give off the allusion that they are keeping prices low, when in reality these subsidies just fatten the wallets of the oil giants.

Perhaps the most egregious thing about these subsidies, besides my tax dollars being spent to pollute the environment, is the fact that instead of taxing pollution, the government is basically paying to pollute the environment. If we get away just purely from the hazards of climate change for a second, researchers at Harvard have concluded that just the air pollution alone from these oil companies

---

[682] "SEN. WHITEHOUSE on FOSSIL FUEL SUBSIDIES: 'WE ARE SUBSIDIZING the DANGER' | U.S. Senate Committee on the Budget." n.d. Www.budget.senate.gov. https://www.budget.senate.gov/chairman/newsroom/press/sen-whitehouse-on-fossil-fuel-subsidies-we-are-subsidizing-the-danger-#:~:text=You%20tally%20up%20the%20harms.

is responsible for the premature death of almost 9 million people annually. And yet, we subsidize them. That is absurd. And every republican can sit here all they want and blast president Biden's $1.2 trillion IRA, or the infrastructure act, or the COVID acts that wracked up the debt, but nobody seems to care about the money that would be spent on climate change disasters, with experts believing that the US would have to spend at a minimum at least $2 trillion by the end of the century just because of climate change issues.[683] That's money that our kids are going to have to pay for, and yet we subsidize fossil fuel companies. When you tally up all of the costs of subsidizing fossil fuel companies, this amounts to a whopping $650 billion a year, just in the US. That's almost more than the US spends on its military budget.

Other studies have concluded that throughout the globe, fossil fuel companies receive over $7 trillion annually from governments, an issue that's been inflated especially with the Ukraine war.[684] Everyone freaks out because the price of gas went up a couple of cents, which causes governmental leaders to give massive handouts to fossil fuel companies, who are currently breaking records for the profits they've made the last few years. Come on people, get smart.

I have a crazy idea. Some conservatives would even call this radical. Instead of spending almost $700 billion a year for the fossil fuel industry, let's instead use that money to subsidize clean energy. You might say, well we are already doing that. You'd be correct in that assumption, but we are not doing enough. We need to make it drastically easier for a family to buy an electric vehicle by increasing the amount of tax credits, to at least $10,000, to make it feasible

---

683 Ibid
684 Black, Simon, Ian Parry, and Nate Vernon. 2023. "Fossil Fuel Subsidies Surged to Record $7 Trillion." IMF. August 24, 2023. https://www.imf.org/en/Blogs/Articles/2023/08/24/fossil-fuel-subsidies-surged-to-record-7-trillion.

that the US will have a majority electric car force by the year 2030. We should make it much more affordable for homes to invest in solar and wind power by offering huge subsidies, such as 70% of the total cost. We should increase the US's manufacturing capabilities so that we are manufacturing clean energy technologies right here at home instead of China, by offering companies grants and other subsidies to get started. We need to push the recycling campaign so that our oceans and land aren't filled with single use plastics, which I will get to later in this chapter. Nobody can say that this is too expensive. Clearly, it's not. If we have almost a trillion dollars to give to the dirty polluters then we have the money to do this. And oh yeah, quit giving these massive subsidies to the polluters in the first place. That will go a long way in creating a more sustainable future for our planet.

We need to elect leaders who will electrify our country. Meaning that we need to have electric transportation, not just vehicles but transit, and other public transportation, like buses. If we do this, we will be golden as almost half of all carbon dioxide emissions are due to transportation, with trucks and other big vehicles doing the most harm. If we can eliminate the emissions from these big tanks, we will be doing the world a great service. President Biden has been doing this and then some, but we need to keep up the pressure and ensure that the leaders that follow will continue in his footsteps. And last, but not least, we need to work with our allies and foes alike to make sure that we are approaching the future with similar goals in mind. Whether that be setting new goals and standards, and, also very important, holding other countries accountable for not meeting agreed to standards. This takes all of us, not just the US or Europe. We all need to pitch in and do what's right for our kids and grandkids, it's not hard.

I deeply applaud Greta Thunberg for what she did. Standing up for a cause like she has is certainly not easy to do, especially on the world stage, taking on some of the most formidable and wealthy special interests in the world. But she felt a compelling reason for doing what she did. She knew it was now or never. We don't have time to wait, if we wait too long then the world as we know it will never be the same. Her story is equally interesting. She started getting involved in climate advocacy when she first persuaded her parents to adopt more of a green lifestyle at home. This is a small, but important, step. Everybody can do this. It isn't hard to start adopting a green oriented strategy within your homes. This is the first step, and this is just where Greta started.

At the young age of 15 she started to do something alarming. She started skipping school? Why in the world was she skipping school? She vowed that she would not return to school until after Sweden's election. She dutifully protested outside the parliament building where she called on voters to elect candidates that would take climate change seriously, not just dole out more subsidies for the fossil fuel companies. She did everything she could, after all she cared deeply about this and wasn't going to sit idly by and watch as the world continued in its dirty ways. She feverishly printed out fliers and distributed them to every passerby she could find until she ran out of them, then she would do it all over again the next day. This was her cause, and she was leading the fight.

She didn't just stop after the election either. She continued to protest until Sweden joined and met all of the standards in the Paris Climate Agreement. Obviously, Greta is a very brave and courageous young lady. But could you imagine doing this at 15 years of age? What were you doing when you were 15? Some of you might say getting drunk with friends, others would say doing homework.

Greta was quite literally changing the world. Obviously, her courage and audacity to stand up for just and right causes caused a massive amount of media attention. Pretty soon videos and pictures of Greta started to appear everywhere as she quickly became a worldwide hero and icon.

What Greta did was incredible. Yet, anyone can do it. It doesn't take a rocket scientist or a doctor to step up and do this. All it takes is a brave woman or man, boy or girl to stand up for a cause they believe in. Greta had one thing going for her. Her unending persistence in the face of adversity. Without question many people ridiculed and heckled Greta but she didn't back down. She only grew more resolved to fight for her cause with every attack being hurled at her. And as you may or may not know, many people followed Greta's lead. Young people throughout the world, in China, Portugal, Brazil, and the US started to protest to their governments to take climate change seriously and change the world. Does this work all the time? Not quite, at least not if we give up right away. The key is persistence. If Greta just quit school for a few days, protested, and then came right back to school right away without anything being done that certainly would have been an easy way out. She would've still received quite a bit of fame being a kid rockstar, but her overall message would have been for naught. Instead, she kept fighting until progress, and a movement was made.

Eventually she made it to the 2019 UN Climate Action Summit, arriving on a carbon-free yacht, where she lambasted the world's leaders for inaction and their seeming indifference for the catastrophes of climate change. You've heard me say this before, but most of the world leaders are grumpy old men, they don't care about climate change, they'll be dead before any of the devastating effects happen. They'll sell their souls just to get elected and then reelected. Greta called them out "how dare you?" Greta cried after detailing how world leaders are quickly falling behind their own goals at fighting climate change.[685] In all, she has won numerous awards including landing in the list of the 100 most influential people, and *Times* "person of the year."

But this doesn't mean that this was an easy ride for Greta. Greta has been arrested numerous times for voicing her beliefs. She has been constantly heckled by conservatives and doubters who think of her as "just a naive kid." She has been attacked by the fossil fuel companies who for whatever reason claim that she was put up to it by her parents to gain fame and fortune, something that Greta and the rest of the movement strongly deny. Even Trump got into the bullying. He routinely mocked Greta every chance he could. He knows that if Greta is successful then he would lose some funds from the industry. In one tweet Trump showed a video of Greta getting angry at the inaction of governmental leaders, which he made fun of. In a later tweet when he found out that Greta was nominated as person of the year by *Times,* instead of himself, he went on the attack against Greta, tweeting "So ridiculous. Greta must work on her Anger Management problem, then go to a good old fashioned movie with a friend! Chill Greta, Chill!"[686] What lovely words coming from the president of the United States, literally picking on a child. Apparently that's how he can feel better. Greta, showing quite a sense of humor, hit Trump where he's most vulnerable, after the 2020 election when he was very vocally challenging the legitimate election, tweeting "So ridiculous. Donald must work on his Anger Management problem, then go to a good old fashioned movie

---

685 "Video: 'How Dare You': Greta Thunberg at the United Nations". *The New York Times*. 23 September 2019.
686 Wamsley, Laurel (12 December 2019). "After Greta Thunberg Wins 'Time' Honor, Trump Suggests She 'Chill' And Watch A Movie"

with a friend! Chill Donald, Chill."[687] Even Trump's successor got into the fray when Biden, who then was a democratic presidential candidate took to twitter "What kind of president bullies a teenager? @realDonaldTrump, you could learn a few things from Greta on what it means to be a leader."[688]

When Trump's friend, Vladimir Putin, joined in the mix, believing that Greta is just being used and she doesn't understand that Africa uses oil because it doesn't have the money that Sweden does. In response Greta tweeted "Indigenous people are literally being murdered for trying to protect the forest from illegal deforestation. Over and over again. It is shameful that the world remains silent about this."[689] Clearly Greta was referring to the fact that these developing countries have been exploited time and again to fatten the pockets of the greedy fossil fuel titans, who keep perpetuating the lies being leveled against Greta. And clearly here, Greta was referring to how the forests, particularly the Amazon forests have been depleted due to the fat rewards of the exploiters.

As a reference, the deforestation of the Amazon is truly a disheartening occurrence. Almost five decades ago Brazilian authorities incentivized millions of people to colonize the rainforest, sporting increasing population and consumer demands as the reason. Of course, to these Brazilian leaders this means that more money will flow due to the depletion of the forests. With more colonization that means more factories and profits unimaginable. But what does this do for the environment? The huge dense Amazon rainforest

---

687 "Greta Thunberg mocks Trump over election fraud claims". Deutsche Welle. Archived from the original on 21 January 2021.
688 Stracqualursi, Veronica (13 December 2019). "Trump again mocks teen climate activist Greta Thunberg".
689 "Ativista Greta Thunberg muda descrição no Twitter para 'pirralha' após declaração de Bolsonaro" [Activist Greta Thunberg changes her Twitter's description to "brat" after Bolsonaro's declaration]. *G1* (in Portuguese). 10 December 2019

has helped keep the world much cooler thanks to the trees and plants absorbing much of the carbon that we go through each year. When we take these trees away not only do we cause environmental degradation and habitat loss, but we also directly speed up the rate of temperature increases. The primary reason why the forests are being depleted is to suit capitalistic demands revolving around the beef industry. With the forests out of the way this provides so much extra space for colonizers to create beef farms for exporting purposes. In other words, the deforestation of the Amazon has to do with money, greed, and selfish purposes. These leaders don't give a crap about the world, they only care about what will improve their interests, what will benefit them.

According to *Time,* former Brazilian president "Jair Bolsonaro, an unapologetic cheerleader for the exploitation of the Amazon, has the colonists' backs; he's sacked key environmental officials and slashed enforcement. His message: the Amazon is open for business. Since his inauguration in January, the rate of deforestation has soared by as much as 92%, according to satellite imaging."[690] Scientists believe that almost 17% of the forest has been gutted already, with the tipping point believed to be at 20%. And scientists have claimed that if the Amazon hits that 20% threshold, we could see temperatures rise by as much as 4 degrees celsius. Such a change could be catastrophic and would likely result in the Amazon being a barren wasteland instead of a luscious forest today. Ricardo Galvão, an official responsible for deforestation monitoring, who was fired for his data on deforestation by the Bolsonaro regime, believes that at this rate climate change will be virtually impossible to stop "If the

---

[690] Sandy, Matt. 2019. "The Amazon Rain Forest Is Nearly Gone. We Went to the Front Lines to See If It Could Be Saved." Time. TIME Magazine. 2019. https://time.com/amazon-rainforest-disappearing/.

Amazon is destroyed" he warned "it will be impossible to control global warming."[691] And what does Bolsonaro have to say about Greta Thunberg? He called her a "brat." Yes, he actually called Greta a brat because she stood up for the protection of the Amazon rainforest, when all he cares about is the protection of his wallet. Thankfully, Bolsonaro was defeated in his reelection campaign, though he received a lot of votes from conservatives in Brazil and received a lot of backing from the business elite. Not shocking.

    The moral of the story is that Greta Thunberg was just doing what she felt right to do. She was supporting a cause that she believed in. This is something that we all should do. If you care about the climate, do something about it. I care about the climate and that is one of the reasons why I am writing this book.

    We also need to curb the influence of single use plastics. This takes all of us. This isn't just on one person but it takes everyone. Pollution in general harms the environment in more ways than one. Pick up trash and recycle. I once saw a man, during a Fourth of July firework event, crowded in the downtown area, throwing away his empty beer bottle. The problem was that he threw it right into the bay of water below the bridge. I sat there astonished at what I had just witnessed. To believe that somebody could be so self-centered as to only care about what the most convenient way to throw out his beer bottle is, without taking into account how that bottle will harm the environment is shocking. The problem is, it's not just this one redneck guy that threw away his bottle in a bay of water. The problem is it happens much more frequently. This is where advocacy comes in. When we spread the word to recycle it should produce a movement dedicated to the carrying out of recycling. This provides

---

691 Ibid

a safer environment for us and for wildlife. For heaven's sake people, do your duty.

More urgently, we need to ban the use of single use plastics. Single use plastics are those plastic materials that are meant to be used only once and then quickly thrown away. There are a couple of points to this. On a smaller scale it is much more convenient to use single use plastics. We do directly see the harm most of the time. We just throw it away when we're done with it. This happens all over the place. I hate to say it but Starbucks is big on this. Two teenage girls will walk into Starbucks, get their drinks, and then throw out the plastic cup, just to do it all over again tomorrow. This isn't directly their fault, but they can improve. Next time you go into Starbucks buy a reusable cup and have them put your drink in that cup. This would save billions of plastic cups a year if everyone heeded to this practice. Think about the environment.

The other reason why single use plastics are so common is because they are cheap to use. Businesses will overwhelmingly use single use plastics if it is the cheapest option on the board, which it usually is. Often this leads customers to have little choice as to protecting the environment. One other way that we see this a lot is in the use of plastic bags at stores. Believe it or not, stores want you to use plastic bags when you are shopping. This is cheaper for the store, and they will try to cut costs at every turn. Instead, try to use paper bags as these are much easier to break down, or use reusable bags. They are much more common now than ever before. But we are not taking the necessary steps to achieve the results we would like to see. Each year Americans use over 5 trillion plastic bags. That's a pretty hefty number. And it's not that the whole world is to blame for this issue. On average, Americans use, per person, 365 plastic bags a year. Denmark uses, per person, 4 plastic bags per year.[692] Why is America so far behind? Because our leaders care more about the plastic interest than the interests of common Americans, that's clear.

Above all, we need to elect representatives who are serious about taking on single use plastics. Right now, companies are getting off easy, adhering to very few, if any, regulations that prevent them from using single use plastics. Generally, it's left up to the consumer if they want to buy single use plastics or not. Yet, the government should put standards in place that would bar manufacturers from creating single use plastics and instead regulate companies so that they create plastic products that are at least recyclable and can be reused again and again.

We should do this not because we want businesses to spend a drastic amount of money by restructuring the process, but we should do this for the environment. The dangers of single use plastics are startling. First, in order to make these plastics we burn a substantial amount of fossil fuels in the process, providing a double whammy on mother nature. Birds, and other small animals can often mistake plastics as pieces of food, thereby ingesting toxic materials in their body. Turtles, who often feed off of jellyfish find it almost impossible to distinguish between a jellyfish and a plastic bag. "About 34% of dead leatherback sea turtles have ingested plastics."[693] As a matter of fact, fish eat thousands of tons of plastic a year, and this only gets worse because this plastic will slowly but inevitably reach the top of the food chain, including us. It's crazy to think, but because of all the plastic in the environment now, humans eat, on average, the equivalent of a credit card in plastic each week.[694] You read

---

692 "10 Facts about Single-Use Plastic Bags." n.d. Www.biologicaldiversity.org. https://www.biologicaldiversity.org/programs/population_and_sustainability/sustainability/plastic_bag_facts.html#:~:text=
693 Ibid
694 Ibid

that right. Each week. This causes many health defects, like cancer, high blood pressure, among other things. Worse, scientists predict that by the year 2050 there will be more plastic in the oceans than fish. That's pretty scary when we think about how big and deep the oceans are. No doubt we are the cause.

What are global leaders doing about this issue? Not enough it seems. According to the Center for Biological Diversity "The fossil fuel industry plans to *increase plastic production* by 40% over the next decade. These oil giants are rapidly building petrochemical plants across the United States to turn fracked gas into plastic. This means more plastic in our oceans, more greenhouse gas emissions and more toxic air pollution, which exacerbates the climate crisis that often disproportionately affects communities of color."[695] So, instead of coming to the realization that this is a real problem for our future, a real problem for the oceans, and for habitat all over the world, fossil fuel giants still only care about their profit margins, not about the future of the ecosystem. That's pretty sad.

One fact that sticks with me, and is incredibly disturbing, is the fact that it takes roughly 1,000 years for one plastic bag to disintegrate. And even when it does finally disintegrate it doesn't do so peacefully, it transmits many tiny microplastics into the soil and atmosphere causing further pollution. Just think of that. One plastic bag does all that damage. And human species in a thousand years, assuming they are still around, will still be dealing with our irresponsibilities. And really there are no excuses, we have experts and scientists telling us what we are doing wrong and what we can do to improve. Yet, we still don't listen to them.

So, what can we do about it? Obviously, on an individual basis practice reusing bags when shopping or carrying supplies. If you don't have a reusable bag then opt for a paper bag. On a governmental

---

695 Ibid

basis, we should ban the use of plastic bags, which is what California did in 2014. There is nothing radical about this position, there will still be bags to be had, but bags that are much safer for the environment. As a government, we need to crack down on companies manufacturing single use plastics. Here's an idea, instead of giving fossil fuel companies those subsidies that we talked about, we can use that money as tax credits and subsidies for companies pledged to reducing their plastic footprints. That's a start. It shouldn't be this hard to pass this kind of legislation. Get a hold of your lawmakers and plead with them to do something about this madness. Elect leaders who are serious about lowering our plastic and carbon footprint.

Too often, when politicians or candidates, usually democrats, run on a platform of taking climate change and pollution seriously they are often heckled by conservatives for being too radical on the issue. Republicans chastised the Green New Deal, calling it built on "rainbow tears", when in reality all it would do was build stronger regulations against fossil fuel giants and transition to clean energy, something that the rest of the world is doing. Does that make it rainbow tears? Conservatives have been railing against president Biden and his efforts to increase electric vehicle production. I have a newsflash, European countries, who are much further ahead on the issue of climate change than we are, believe in electric vehicles. They are buying electric vehicles from China, not the US, because China has been investing in electric vehicles for years and years and is ahead of the game. There's no reason why Europe should be buying China's electric vehicles and not our own. But what were we doing when China recognized the potential for electric vehicles? We were providing subsidies to fossil fuel companies and Trump was deregulating the auto industry, making it easier to produce gas guzzling cars that will only benefit them for the short term. Our policy positions have been off for decades and now they are coming back to haunt us. Just think how well off our economy would be if we invested in clean energy much sooner, when scientists first warned us. We could be selling our electric vehicles all over the world, not being crushed by China. Way to go Trump and his fellow cult followers.

In fact, we have been warned for a long, long time about the dangers of climate change, so how can anybody say that these ideas are radical? All the way back to the beginning of the 20th century, we are talking as early as 1908, it was proven that CO_2 produces a greenhouse gas effect and can affect global temperatures, scientists had proved that we needed some CO_2 to stabilize the temperature, however, if we reduced CO_2 emissions by half we would fall into an ice age. Using this theory, from almost 120 years ago, anybody could come to the realization here that, based on scientists' predictions with more CO_2 temperatures go up, with less CO_2 temperatures go down. It doesn't take a rocket scientist to connect the dots. Therefore, this provided a warning that if we keep burning fossil fuels, which obviously produces CO_2 we would see a gradual rise in temperatures. Nobody at the time took this too seriously, I mean warning signs of climate change were few and far between. Nobody really knew the full consequences that burning fossil fuels would unleash.

Then, in 1938, Guy Callendar collected records from 147 weather stations across the world and made a startling observation; the world's temperature had increased by 0.3 degrees celsius. At the time, this slight increase was nothing to be too concerned about. So, again, nobody really paid close attention to Callendar's discoveries. Although Callandar at this early period drew a direct link to the burning of fossil fuels to be the reason for the increase in temperature.[696] But, why should leaders be concerned? After all, this was only a slight increase and the world was seeing massive economic booms thanks to the use of fossil fuels. This was a great discovery and people didn't want to let it go that easily. All this despite Callandar's clear warning.

Then in 1952, three scientists invented the first solar cell. According to UK Research and Innovation "The company (Bell Labs) wanted to extend its network of telephones in remote tropical regions. However, the standard batteries used at the time were unsuitable as they degraded too quickly in the hot, humid, conditions. (Daryl) Chapin (an engineer) was asked to look into other power sources and immediately thought solar power might work."[697] Solar cells were actually first developed more than a hundred years ago, though the first few models were too ineffective to be of much value. However, Bell labs was committed to creating a much more efficient solar cell for their business. Most solar cells in the market in the 1950s only converted about 0.5% of incoming light into electricity, but the trio of scientists working for Bell Labs was able to convert 6% of sunlight into electricity, a huge increase in efficiency in only a few years. Clearly, if other businesses and even the government paid more attention to Bell Labs and the scientific innovations they were making we would be in a different place. Had we cared more for solar energy then and invested in this new sustainable energy we could be maximizing the production as we speak. Clearly, this was an opportunity missed. And it's not like we didn't know what

---

696 UK Research and Innovation. 2021. "A Brief History of Climate Change Discoveries." Www.discover.ukri.org. UK Research and Innovation. October 21, 2021. https://www.discover.ukri.org/a-brief-history-of-climate-change-discoveries/index.html.
697 ibid

was going on. Further scientific discoveries left us with nobody to blame but ourselves.

In 1958, Charles David Keeling decided to look at the amounts of CO2 in the air and contrast that to CO2 levels in the water. Up to this time nobody had ever calculated or studied the amount of CO2 levels in the atmosphere, leaving much still unknown, of course, until Keeling arrived on the scene. Over the course of five years of study, Keeling came to the sad realization that CO2 levels were rising and they were rising fast.[698] Here, we should be able to put the pieces together. We have scientists that told us that an increase in CO2 meant an increase in global temperatures. We have scientists that told us that when we burn fossil fuels we emit CO2. And we have scientists who tell us that CO2 levels are rising. As a result, most people would be able to put two and two together and realize that when we burn fossil fuels the temperatures will increase and we should, way back in 1958, come to the realization that something needed to be done because Keeling proved that with every passing year CO2 emissions are only rising. Yet, we kept burning fossil fuels, and did virtually nothing to improve clean energy technology and innovation.

In 1967, another team of scientists created a model to see how the earth's climate has been changing. They came to a startling reality, "According to our estimate, a doubling of the CO2 content in the atmosphere has the effect of raising the temperature of the atmosphere (whose relative humidity is fixed) by about 2°C."[699] Wow, so way back then, in the 1960s we knew that if we doubled our carbon footprint we would see dramatic temperature increases.

---

698 Ibid
699 Ibid

That's incredibly sad, mostly because we were warned so many times, and yet here we are.

In the same year, another scientist, Dr. John Mercer, predicted that if we stay in our current path and see a continuation of global warming then the Antarctic ice sheets would collapse and cause massive devastation as sea levels would inevitably rise. Again, we were warned. But what did we do about it? Not a whole lot. In fact, some, mostly policy makers, thought that Dr. Mercer was way off when he warned that sea levels could rise by 5 meters. Yet, in 1995, a massive ice shelf collapsed and the same happened in 2002 and 2017. Now scientists are warning that the loss of ice is unstoppable because of the amount of greenhouse gas in the atmosphere.[700] Again, what would have happened if we had just heeded their warnings?

Fast forward all the way to 1985 and we see the new scientific discovery of lithium ion batteries. Founded by Japanese scientist Professor Akira Yoshino, the lightweight battery ushered in a revolutionary model for energy storage. These batteries have only improved over the course of the preceding decades and now can store vast amounts of energy that can completely erase the human need for fossil fuels. This idea of a lithium Ion battery was first proposed in the 1970s, that more than fifty years ago, we can't simply say that this idea of converting solar or wind energy and storing it in these batteries is a radical idea. We have been steadily working on it for fifty years.

Since the 1990s the UN, through its committees and the Intergovernmental Panel on climate change has been very vocal about their research. And that research shows that the earth is growing hotter and hotter every passing year. Since the mid-1990s, the UN and its members have heard year after year reports from

---

700 Ibid

scientists mentioning the catastrophic impacts of climate change. This led countries in the 1990s to set policy initiatives to cut carbon emissions and the usage of fossil fuels. This led to the creation of the Kyoto protocol, which includes 192 countries. The protocol asserted that global warming is, in fact, reality, and humans are the cause of it. In essence, the protocol established standards that industrialized nations were held to. Recognizing that industrial nations like the United States, the European Union, and China have been most responsible in global warming, the pact made sure that all industrialized countries would take certain steps to reduce the future growth of global warming and to curb emissions. This pact went into effect in 2004, after Russia and Canada ratified the protocol. The US signed the protocol in 1998, under democratic president Bill Clinton. I don't have many great things to say about Bill Clinton, but at least his administration understood the dire consequences of the escalating climate crisis. This meant nothing in effect though. In order for a treaty to become ratified the senate needs to pass it. This did not happen, unfortunately, because conservatives lambasted the treaty for going after industrialized nations only. Clearly, these conservatives missed the point that industrialized nations have spewed millions of tons of greenhouse gas more than the developing countries, who have relatively recently begun to use fossil fuels in their economy.

When George W Bush was elected he, not surprisingly, decided not to pressure congress into action on the Kyoto treaty. One might wonder why, but the answer is straightforward and simple. Not only did Bush receive huge backing from fossil fuel groups, but he himself was a massive oil tycoon, being the head of oil companies. To make matters worse, Bush's VP Dick Cheney was the chairman of an oil company named Haliburton, which got in all sorts of trouble in the Iraq war. Given these circumstances did you actually think that either of these two would give a damn about the climate crisis? Absolutely not. Not only did they dismiss the Kyoto treaty, but in the face of all the scientific evidence that fossil fuels are the reason for climate change they were too busy giving subsidies to fossil fuel companies and trying to open up the Arctic Wildlife Refuge for drilling.[701] This is all after Bush declared that the US was addicted to oil and had to do something about its gross addiction.

When Bush decided not to pursue the Kyoto treaty, he let down our allies all over the world who desperately wanted a binding treaty to fix the world's mess. The Tyndall Center for Climate Change research reported, "This policy reversal received a massive wave of criticism that was quickly picked up by the international media. Environmental groups blasted the White House, while Europeans and Japanese alike expressed deep concern and regret. ... Almost all world leaders (e.g. China, Japan, South Africa, Pacific Islands, etc.) expressed their disappointment at Bush's decision."[702] Clearly we were behind the game yet again, as all of our allies recognized the problem well before we did. As of now 191 countries have backed the agreement, the United States has not. Perhaps it has to do with the influence that these fossil fuel companies have in American politics.

It's also interesting that the countries who have had the littlest to do with climate change will be the hardest hit once climate change becomes too unmanageable. This does include those underdeveloped places like nearly all of Africa, Southeast Asia, and Latin and South

---

701 "Oil and the Bush Administration." n.d. Earth Island Journal. https://www.earthisland.org/journal/index.php/magazine/entry/oil_and_the_bush_administration/.
702 Dessai, S. (December 2001), *Tyndall Centre Working Paper 12: The climate regime from The Hague to Marrakech: Saving or sinking the Kyoto Protocol?*, Norwich, UK: Tyndall Centre, archived from the original on 31 October 2012

America. These countries are likely to be hit the hardest because the climate conditions they are currently facing are likely to be exacerbated by the increase in climate change. It makes sense then, that they would be trying to lead the fight to make sure that industrialized nations, who quite literally spew their emissions left and right, are cutting back on their fossil fuel usage. The Doha amendment that established a second commitment to the Kyoto protocol that would have cut global emissions has only been approved by underdeveloped countries. The developed countries who have gotten fat and rich off of fossil fuels have all yet to agree to this amendment.

I mention the Kyoto protocol here because this was another attempt by environmental scientists and other climate experts to get the world together to do something substantial to protect the environment from future harm. Unfortunately, the fossil fuel interests in all the advanced economies of the world and their political influence was too much to bear for even the responsible and intelligent lawmakers to overcome. Again, scientists and experts had wanted and the world did virtually nothing to quell these warnings. Even though the Kyoto protocol has been ratified by numerous other countries, the pact really fails because the United States has long held its opposition to it and without our help the treaty will fall flat on its face, with the US being the biggest economy in the world. It also failed because there has been no level of responsibility for all of those countries that signed the agreement. It means nothing if Germany signed and ratified the agreement only to keep pushing out greenhouse emissions. This is just paying lip-service, which is exactly what the agreement is to too many countries. When the people rise up and demand action, these countries can point to agreements like this to make the case that they are doing something, when in reality nothing will get done until we completely rid ourselves of the reliance and influence of fossil fuels.

In 1992 scientists came to the realization that higher levels of CO_2 in the ocean will make it harder for ocean creatures to build reefs. The prevalent belief throughout the world among scientists was that CO_2 was often absorbed by the oceans, which had been the case throughout history. Any excess CO_2 was absorbed through the oceans, the problem is now with the drastic amount of CO_2 emissions, the ocean is taking in more CO_2 than it should and it still is leaving much CO_2 to be thrusted up into our atmosphere. With oceans taking in more CO_2 emissions, they increasingly become more acidic. This prevents coral from getting its vital nutrients which they need to survive. With the coral reef dying off this drastically affects many other ocean creatures, especially those with a shell, including mollusks, clams, and oysters.[703] Scientists warned back in 1992 that these labels of oceanic acidification would only get worse with the continued burning of fossil fuels. Again, the world largely did nothing. Now we have seen the coral reefs a shell of what they once were due to the acidification in the oceans. Many species of fish have died off and many more are likely to come. This is all due to the irresponsibility of humans and the greed that drives them.

Throughout the 1990s wind power began to be realized, carbon was being captured underground as storage to protect the atmosphere, hybrid cars were invented to increase fuel efficiency and reduce greenhouse gas, and yet here we are in 2024, still mulling over if this is feasible or not. It's all a shame. We should have taken

---

[703] UK Research and Innovation. 2021. "A Brief History of Climate Change Discoveries." Www.discover.ukri.org. UK Research and Innovation. October 21, 2021. https://www.discover.ukri.org/a-brief-history-of-climate-change-discoveries/index.html.

the necessary steps long ago, but here we are still debating if we can satisfactorily use wind power, which is not 30 years old, and solar power, which is nearly 70 years old. We are still debating if we can build fuel efficient vehicles or electric vehicles today, even though they were doing this 30 years ago. Come on people. Keep the pressure on our representatives to invest in these technologies and accept the inevitable.

What's even more frustrating is that we had plenty of warnings about the cause of extreme weather. More than 20 years ago, in 2003, according to UK Research and Innovation "Professor Pete Stott, a scientist at the UK Met Office, published a paper in the scientific journal *Nature* showing that climate change had doubled the risk of the 2003 European heatwave that killed tens of thousands of people."[704] This claim is further backed up with scientific research and experimentation today, which proves that climate change is the catalyst for more devastating weather events. But this piece of information didn't cause our lawmakers here at home and those abroad to do anything significant to reduce greenhouse emissions. Are you spotting a trend in the warning signs?

As I've stated numerous times in this section, we were warned early and often by experts and scientists about the dangers of fossil fuels, and climate change and yet we were so slow to listen. The United States in particular has been extremely slow to do anything remotely close to establishing a sustainable future. The earliest policies that we enacted to preserve the planet happened under president Obama's two terms. However, many of his policies and proposals were quickly reversed by Trump, who received such staunch backing from fossil fuel interests, including huge campaign contributions. Indeed,

---

704 Ibid

most other developed countries have proposed far more audacious goals and timelines, well before the United States. In 2008, the UK established a law to reduce its greenhouse gas emissions by 80% in 2050, that's well earlier than the US started looking at that kind of a goal. The UK also became the first major country to commit itself to net-zero emissions by 2050, which was quickly followed by most other developed countries, except the United States, which was still in the administration of Trump. The United States finally committed itself to this goal under the leadership of President Biden.

Experts have already announced that the melting of the ice sheets is irreversible. If only we would have listened to the warnings we wouldn't be in this spot. There are so many greenhouse gas emissions in our atmosphere that our current levels of warming will never drop to what it once was, it will continue to be this hot. We will continue to see extreme weather events for the rest of our lives. Our goal now is to prevent it from getting much worse, which believe me, it can. Since 1990 we have seen the hottest years on record, with each passing year breaking the record of last year's. This means that even if we reduce greenhouse gas emissions to net zero today, we will still see temperatures hovering around where they are today, which spells trouble, especially considering how many people have died in the past few years due to weather and temperatures.

We have been warned for decades, nay, a century and we have done nothing to combat these warnings. Why do you think we don't do anything about it? The Fossil fuel lobby. That's why. In 2022, the oil and gas companies spent $125 million just on federal lobbying alone. If you are unfamiliar with lobbying, lobbying is "seeking to influence (a politician or public official) on an issue."[705] That tells you all you need to know. Every single year the industry is spending

---

705 Oxford Dictionary

all of this money to influence our politicians to do their bidding, this includes their efforts to drill into the Arctic Wildlife Refuge, to cut regulations, and to prevent the electrification of transportation. Instead of using this money to invest in the community, or to combat homelessness, or support our veterans, these companies not only are destroying our environment but are actively spending ungodly amounts to keep destroying our environment. Open Secrets, an organization committed to revealing the truth in government say it all, "Lobbying disclosures indicate the industry targeted a range of issues that will impact oil and gas companies as the global economy weans itself off fossil fuels, including rules governing methane emissions, oil and gas development on federal land and waters, and subsidies for carbon capture technology."[706] Maybe, this is why the United States is so far behind other advanced economies when it comes to dealing with climate change. This is embarrassing and all of our representatives should be ashamed.

Crazy enough, the $125 million the oil and gas industries spent on lobbying in 2022 was pale in comparison to the $285 million in lobbying the industry doled out in 2008, during the financial crisis. This is an alarming amount. And, it has been working, which is incredibly sad. The fossil fuel industry has been making record profits, "As Russia's invasion of Ukraine transformed the global fossil fuel supply chain, driving oil and gas prices to unprecedented levels, the industry's top lobbying spenders reported record annual profits. Chevron, ConocoPhillips, Exxon and Shell saw a combined $1 trillion in sales in 2022, 15% of which were profits. In June last year (2021), President Joe Biden singled out Exxon, which reported

---

706 Sayki, Inci, and Jimmy Cloutier. 2023. "Oil and Gas Industry Spent $124.4 Million on Federal Lobbying amid Record Profits in 2022." OpenSecrets News. February 22, 2023. https://www.opensecrets.org/news/2023/02/oil-and-gas-industry-spent-124-4-million-on-federal-lobbying-amid-record-profits-in-2022/.

a record $55 billion in profits, for making more money than God."[707] At least president Biden understands that this problem is insane. Instead of blaming president Biden for the high prices of gas, maybe people should be focusing more on the record profits of the fossil fuel industry. But somehow people don't seem to care too much about this fact, maybe it's because the fossil fuel industry is spending so much money to silence the voices in the discussion of this topic. They laugh a hearty chuckle when Americans are so ignorant as to blame president Biden for the increase in prices.

And where does this stand with the climate advocacy groups? According to Open Secrets, climate advocacy groups are outspent in lobbying by fossil fuel groups 27:1. So, for every dollar that advocacy groups spend in lobbying the fossil fuel complex spends $27. Who do you think our politicians will listen to more? These advocacy groups who are mustering up what they can, or these fossil fuel giants who are expending only what they don't need?[708] And these fossil fuel giants are targeting primarily one political group. That is the republican party, where the past 8 of 10 republican presidential candidates have been exorbitant millionaires or billionaires. These republicans have been good at a few things, cutting taxes for wealthy people like them, and by giving the fossil fuel giants everything they ever wanted. So, when fossil fuel companies need to reach out to somebody to pass some sort of gas or oil bill at the expense of the environment they know the drill, they go right up to the republicans and get whatever they want. What a lovely deal for them. What a horrible deal for the American people.

We can tell that the American people are left behind because we don't have the money to influence decisions. In 2023, the republican

---

707 ibid
708 Ibid

led House passed a bill that would have required the federal government to increase the development of fossil fuels on public lands. Thankfully president Biden threatened to veto the bill. On closer inspection, the measure was introduced by republican Cathy McMorris Rodgers, whose campaign raked in about $400,000 from the oil and gas industry just in the 2022 midterm election alone.[709] You call that fair? That should never be allowed to happen in the United States of America. Now you should understand that the real voice of the people doesn't hold as much weight in Congress as does the voice of the wealthy fossil fuel industry. One must wonder why we stooped so low in general. We should question why any representative should be receiving these kinds of funds from any special interest group. Clearly, if a representative is receiving hundreds of thousands of dollars in campaign contributions from the fossil fuel industry and only a few thousand from environmental advocates, which side do you think they will fight for? This is morally repugnant to everything that America stands for. We should do better.

And how much does the fossil fuel industry spend in campaign contributions? It is impossible for us to know exactly how much money is being spent on campaign contributions thanks to the dark money loophole, which allows corporations and industries to give to campaigns without officially disclosing this information. Thankfully, we do have some clarity on this issue. In 2022, the Koch brothers alone gave almost $28 million to republican led efforts. The next four are Occidental Petroleum at $8 million, Chevron at $7.6 million, American Petroleum Institute at $7.2 million, and Energy Transfer LP at $5.3 million. All of these companies have

---

709 Ibid

one thing in common. Every single red cent that they gave went to republican candidates.[710]

More to the point, Joe Manchin, the democratic senator of West Virginia, who single handedly has been the thorn in president Biden's side when it comes to climate change, has been the leading recipient of this fossil fuel money at almost $800,000. Maybe this is the reason why he decided not to support the IRA unless it provided for massive amounts of domestic oil drilling. Now it all makes sense.

Following the lone democrat to receive the funding from the fossil fuel complex is former House speaker Kevin McCarthy, who netted in almost $700,000. The rest that even deserve mention are all republican candidates.[711] This tells the story of our broken democracy. Anytime you have these billion dollar corporations spending what amounts to them as a gumball to influence candidates we have an issue. Candidates might say that this money does not influence their decision making but we have evidence to prove to the contrary. And, why would the Koch brothers, or Exxon Mobil donate to campaigns just for the fun of it? There is always an ulterior motive behind this. It's not because they want to give back to the community. Spending these ungodly amounts of money on a vicious campaign can hardly be called giving back to the community. And we have to look at why these companies are giving such large substantial sums to republican candidates. It is clear that they expect favors in return and they have gotten these favors. Maybe that's why republican senator Tom Cotton called the Green New Deal reliant upon "unicorn tears." Maybe that is why so many republican politicians heckle Greta Thunberg and fellow climate activists.

---

710 OpenSecrets. 2000. "Oil & Gas | OpenSecrets." Opensecrets.org. 2000. https://www.opensecrets.org/industries/indus.php?ind=E01.
711 ibid

These companies are also spending huge sums of money to change public perception. Among democrats and independents alike, who watch CNN, CBS, and NBC, the vast majority believe that addressing climate change should be a top priority. Among conservatives, who mainly watch Fox news, the vast majority think that we should spend more time focused on the economy even if that means harming the environment.[712] This is because Fox news does nothing to educate its viewers on the dangers of climate change, instead focusing more on conspiracy theories and right-wing politics. The experts are all concluding that if these viewers were given a diverse amount of programs and views they would be much more likely to think that climate change is an existential crisis.

Yet, 70% of all Americans believe that climate change should be taken seriously, and 80% of Americans think we need to invest more in renewable energy.[713] But that viewpoint is not the consensus with republican politicians, who only pander to the elite fossil fuel interests. The Brookings Institute remarks how far the United States are behind, and more appropriately how far behind the republicans are on this issue. The Brookings Institute had this to say:

"Many Republican legislators still reject the science of climate change, a position not held by other mainstream parties in democratic countries, but rising among far-right parties in Europe. Their positions have not kept up with their constituents, or even some business groups with which they are typically aligned. After the API made its announcement, Senator John Barrasso of Wyoming, the

---

712 Montanaro, Domenico. 2023. "Three-Quarters of Republicans Prioritize the Economy over Climate Change." NPR. August 3, 2023. https://www.npr.org/2023/08/03/1191678009/climate-change-republicans-economy-natural-disasters-biden-trump-poll.
713 Weisbrod, Katelyn. 2023. "Republican Leaders Want to Reinvent the Party's Climate Image. The Far Right Won't Let Them." Inside Climate News. February 21, 2023. https://insideclimatenews.org/news/21022023/republicans-far-right-climate-change/.

ranking Republican on the Senate Energy and Natural Resources Committee, issued a statement saying, "Proposals that impose a cost on carbon will hurt American families." In April, Representative Scott Perry of Pennsylvania announced at a hearing of a subcommittee of the House Foreign Affairs Committee that he planned to introduce a bill to withdraw the United States from the United Nations Framework Commission on Climate Change. He introduced his bill, which has no chance of passing, on Earth Day."[714]

Yes, the Brookings Institute got it right. We are falling behind and other European nations are laughing at us. Any plan that the democrats put to the table to address climate change is quickly excoriated by the republicans as "socialist." They never fully explain why doing exactly what every other major country on earth is doing is socialistic, they just use this card to scare the public into thinking this is a radical idea. Even more frightening is that the future of the republican party doesn't look much better. In the 2023 republican primary presidential debate, when the moderator asked "Raise your hand if you believe human behavior is causing climate change," no republican candidate raised their hand after looking sheepishly at one another to see if anybody would do it first. Clearly none of these candidates have the guts to take on the big political bosses in the republican party. They don't have the guts to stand up to the fossil fuel industry, so, they showed we would get more of the same if any of them are elected as president, something that the fossil fuel industry will support with hundreds of millions of dollars once again.

But, here again, we see Fox news denying climate change to its

---

[714] Gross, Samantha. 2021. "Republicans in Congress Are out of Step with the American Public on Climate." Brookings. May 10, 2021. https://www.brookings.edu/articles/republicans-in-congress-are-out-of-step-with-the-american-public-on-climate/.

viewers shortly after the debate when Laura Ingraham seemed to mock the question. "Record heat? Normal: It's hot, hot, hot all right, said Laura Ingraham on her Fox News show. After all, we're in the middle of a season called summer." (Fact check: More than 3,000 temperature records were shattered in the US for the month of July alone, something scientists say would be virtually impossible without human-caused climate change.[715] And in response to stronger, more ferocious hurricanes, Ron Desantis the republican governor and presidential wannabe responded in a very comforting way, "This is something that is a fact of life in the Sunshine State."[716] So, what essentially he is telling us is that we have to get used to these vicious hurricanes because it's a fact of life, when in reality scientists have concluded that hurricanes get much worse due to human caused climate change. The sad reality is that these conservatives are virtually married to the fossil fuel industry. If any of these candidates were to stand up and call out climate change for what it is, they would instantly lose hundreds of millions of dollars from the fossil fuel industry and galvanize other conservatives against them. In other words, it's a losing strategy for republicans to tell the truth about climate change, that's why none of them do it. It's also sad that, as of now, we have not seen one republican stand up on the side of the environment. They will just keep roping in all the oil and gas money and keep riding reelection wins in the most greedy self-serving way imaginable.

Yet, when climate activists and democrats push for a cleaner world they are constantly pushed back by these conservative groups. Republicans have called them "crazy", "naive", "radical",

---

715 Leber, Rebecca. 2023. "The First GOP Debate Reveals a Disturbing Level of Climate Change Denial." Vox. August 11, 2023. https://www.vox.com/climate/23815966/republicans-climate-change-denial-trees.
716 Ibid

and "socialist" just for trying to build a brighter world not just for our future generations of humanity but also for our wildlife and oceans. What's so radical about that? How can you call something radical when we have been warned about the impacts of this for so long, by experts mind you? How can you call somebody radical for proposing what every other major country on earth has done and done well? How can you call somebody radical when they are listening to the experts and scientists, who happen to know a thing or two about this? Or who should we listen to, experts and scientists, or fossil fuel companies and far right politicians who act like they know everything? The choice is ours. What are we going to do to build a brighter future? Do we heed the advice of scientists or do we keep elected republican officials who make more money from fossil fuel companies than they do representing us?

Thankfully, we have president Biden, who has dedicated his administration to helping to tackle climate change. While he has not, in my opinion, done a perfect job of fighting this complex issue, he has done more than any other president to get us on the right foot. Compared to what Trump did in office president Biden has been a heaven send, at least when it comes to our environment. Reelecting him and any democrat who believes in fighting climate change will do more for the environment than anything we can single-handedly do ourselves. I still will urge everyone to do their part. Listen to science. Stay up to speed on news and politics, and recycle, live life sustainably, and adopt clean energy measures in your own life.

CONCLUSION

Radicalism has looked different throughout the years, there's no doubt about that. However, there are certainly similarities between what is radical today and what was radical back then. Furthermore, most of what was conceived to be radical in our history isn't quite so radical anymore and often gets treated with shame and contempt among our people today. Let's not make the mistakes of the past.

In writing this book, there are so many examples that I can give as to our history that we would look at today and be ashamed that we even did that, or put up with it. To fight against these things, it was considered to be radical. Among the topics that I did not mention in my book is the dispossession of Native tribes and lands, the Japanese internments in WW2, and gun violence. Had I mentioned these this book would have been much longer than it already is. My point in writing the book is to show that when some people label an idea as being radical, really think to yourself if that's really what it is. Or, maybe it would be radical to just leave it alone.

The Commoner, a devoted truth-seeker and justice advocate, has committed their life to educating others. With a robust background in historical research and studies, they have spent many years in the classroom passionately teaching. The Commoner believes steadfastly in the importance of truth, especially when it pertains to the American public, viewing it as their duty to expose and discuss it. Their book, "Radical", draws from their wealth of knowledge and experience, appealing to history enthusiasts, political aficionados, and everyday people intrigued by current events and debates. The Commoner's work is a testament to their dedication to truth and justice.